FROM DAY TO DAY:

a calendar of notable birthdays and events

by
DAVID E. JOHNSON

The Scarecrow Press, Inc.
Metuchen, N.J., & London
1990

Rej
CT
105
J64
1990

British Library Cataloguing-in-Publication data available

Library of Congress Cataloging-in-Publication Data

Johnson, David E.
    From day to day : a calendar of notable birthdays and events /
by David E. Johnson.
       p.   cm.
    Includes index.
    ISBN 0-8108-2354-3
    1. Birthdays--Calendars. 2. Anniversaries--Calendars. I. Title.
CT105.J64 1990
394.2--dc20   90-43681

Tomorrow, and tomorrow, and tomorrow,
Creeps in this petty pace from day to day
To the last syllable of recorded time...

Macbeth

Contents

Preface

God created the earth. And the nights and the days. But people created dates. They did it by counting and naming the days and the months and counting the years. December 7, 1941, was a date-- "a date which will live in infamy," according to President Franklin D. Roosevelt. It was the seventh day of the twelfth month of the 1,941st year of the Christian Era. It was also a Sunday, the first day of the week, and the event which FDR referred to, the bombing of Pearl Harbor, began at 7:50 A.M. Hawaii time, or 1:50 P.M. Eastern Standard Time. Thus God gave us the light and the dark and the days, but we developed our own system of keeping and counting time, and, it must be said, of carrying out bombing raids.

A book of dates, such as this, logically could begin with a discussion of how our system of dates came into being and how time came to be measured. Why, for example, do we have seven days in a week and twelve months in a year? Why does a year consist of 365 or 366 days? Who divided a day into twenty-four hours instead of ten or a hundred, and who decided that sixty minutes constitute an hour? Where did the names of the days come from? Who named the months? Better still, who *misnamed* the months? December, the twelfth month, is named for *decem*, the Latin word for ten. The same inconsistencies apply to September, October and November, the ninth, tenth and eleventh months, which are named the seventh, eighth, and ninth months, respectively. How long have we had our system of counting time, and how did it get to us in its present form?

We will consider these questions first, by tracing the development of the calendar from the ancient Egyptians and Babylonians, through the

Greeks and Romans, to the present. We will then present chronologically the highlights in history of each day of the year, and consider which noteworthy events occurred and which famous persons were born on that day, beginning with January 1 and continuing through all 366 days to December 31. These accounts will be divided into twelve chapters, one devoted to each month. We will begin each chapter with a discussion of that month's history--how it got its name, its length, etc.--and what facts are pertinent to it, such as its flower and its birthstone. The list of notable birthdays and events of the month will then follow.

The daily lists of birthdays and events, of course, are alive, as much so as any living organism. Every month, and certainly every year, sees the emergence of new figures on the world's stage. New heads of state take office, new sports and entertainment figures burst upon the scene, and noteworthy events occur daily. But in compiling the list, we have to stop at some point. We also have to make choices about what to include and what to omit.

We have included all the notable birthdays we could put together, an ongoing task of most of the past decade, and we have gone to great lengths to assure their accuracy. Those omitted were either deemed less important--an obvious matter of opinion--or their dates of birth were unknown. Some like Socrates, Plato, Columbus, for example, are unknown to *everybody*, and some were unknown to us--Fred Lasswell (the cartoonist of *Snuffy Smith*) and Garry Trudeau (the creator of *Doonesbury*) come to mind--though we tried valiantly to get them. Others we were simply ignorant of--the persons as well as their birthdays--and we still are, so no examples can be cited.

Accuracy was, and is, a major problem. To compile 15,000 entries without making errors is, of course, impossible. Many of the errors are our own fault, and we willingly take the blame. These were compounded by compilation errors of overzealous researchers of the past. For example, the birthdays of Daniel Defoe, Peter Stuyvesant, and Henry Hudson don't seem to be known by the major encyclopedia compilers, but dates are alleged in other sources. Still other sources--trustworthy ones--give these same dates, except for the year, for other events associated with these men, such as the date of Defoe's death, of Stuyvesant's surrender of New Amsterdam to the British, and Hudson's discovery of Hudson Bay. Other errors seem deliberate, like the many varied accounts of birthdays of well-known movie stars, put out by studios or agents.

Another source of confusion is the change from the Julian Calendar to the Gregorian Calendar. This change was made by most of the Latin countries in 1582, but England and her colonies did not make the change until 1752. Russia did not make the change until 1918, and Greece waited until 1923. Thus Isaac Newton, born in England, thought his birthday was on Christmas Day, but he was born on the same day and year as others in the Latin countries who thought their birthday was January 4.

For years dates were listed as New Style or Old Style to at least identify the discrepancy, but most reputable references have adjusted to the new system. The problem lingers on, however, in many circles.

We have relied on most of the well-known encyclopedias for historical persons and events, and for the more contemporary ones, we have consulted current biographies, autobiographies, Hall of Fame lists, sports encyclopedias, movie biographical books, magazines, newspapers, radio, and television. We have done everything short of writing notable persons and asking for their birthdays. We were afraid of getting a response like one person got when he wired, "How old Cary Grant?" The great actor replied, "Old Cary Grant fine. How you?"

David E. Johnson
Division of Science and Mathematics
Birmingham-Southern College

The Calendar

Everybody at some time or other must have pondered the questions of how our present calendar came into being, how the months and days were named, who decided how many days make a week and how many make a month, how many hours in a day, how many minutes in an hour, and so forth. No one knows all the answers for certain, but we do know that our calendar, with slight modifications, had its origin with the great Roman leader Julius Caesar in the year 45 B.C. The *Julian* Calendar, which he put into effect at that time, over 2,000 years ago, is, with minor modifications, the same one we have today, an amazing fact and a monumental tribute to that remarkable general, historian and politician. The numbers of hours per day and days per week were determined by civilizations even more ancient than Rome, but the names of the days and months, as we know them today, were given to us by the Romans.

From the earliest times, people must have noticed that the seasons came regularly, the rivers flooded periodically, and the moon waxed and waned according to some schedule. It obviously must have occurred to them to count the number of sunrises to place an event, or to count the number of full moons to determine a time to sow and a time to reap, even in their earliest attempts at agriculture. They must have had words for *today*, *tomorrow*, and *yesterday* to describe the passing of the days. The rise of the priesthood must have dictated a need for placing religious festivals at periodic times, which must have been based on the seasons and hence on the sun. In short, it was imperative that the ancients try to reckon time by the positions of the moon and/or the sun.

1

The moon goes through a complete cycle in about 29½ days, a fact which undoubtedly led to the idea of a month. The sun, on the other hand, takes about 365¼ days to complete its cycle, which inevitably became the basis for a year. The lunations, or periods, of the moon are conveniently short and thus would be excellent time periods on which to base a calendar. But the seasons and therefore the times for planting and the times for harvesting depend on the sun's cycle, and unfortunately 29½ will not divide a whole number of times into 365¼. A *lunar* year of twelve months, or roughly 360 days, is too short to keep in step with the sun, and a year of 13 months is too long. In Caesar's time, for example, the planting season according to the calendar then in existence was eighty days earlier than it should have been, according to the sun. As we will see, Caesar solved the problem by basing the calendar on a *solar* year of 365 or 366 days with different lengths for the twelve months.

The earliest Roman calendar year, in the time of Romulus, the legendary first king of Rome, may have been one of only four months-- Martius, Aprilis, Maius and Junius or, as we know them, March, April, May and June. At any rate, these were the only months with names, and since they originally had thirty days each, it took three such "years" to approximate a solar year. The Romans had eight-day weeks, with the days unnamed, but simply lettered A, B, C, D, E, F, G and H. March, the first month of the year, thus began with day A, and it was the only month to do so. This may have been the way the early Romans kept track of New Year's Day.

About 738 B.C., Romulus, tradition has it, added six additional months to the original four. These new months had no names, but were simply numbered from five to ten as Quintilis (fifth), Sextilis (sixth), Septembris (seventh), Octobris (eighth), Novembris (ninth) and Decembris (tenth). The latter four are, of course, our September, October, November and December. At first Romulus gave 30 days to each of his ten months, but this resulted in a year of 300 days, which was not divisible by eight, and thus not a whole number of weeks. Four days were then added, one each to March, May, Quintilis and October, so that the new year had 304 days, and therefore precisely 38 weeks. The end of December marked the end of the year, which was followed by an uncounted winter gap, determined so that the new year beginning in March would correspond more or less with the seasons. Romulus and/or his religious leaders probably decided when March 1 had arrived.

Numa Pompilius, the second of the seven legendary kings of Rome (around 715 to 673 B.C.), is credited with creating the twelve-month calendar that survived more or less intact until Caesar's day. Numa added two months, Januarius and Februarius, our January and February, to the calendar of Romulus, creating a year of 354 days, just some eight hours short of a true lunar year (twelve lunations of the moon). His fifty additional days plus six days, one taken from each of the thirty-day months, were divided equally between the two new months. Thus March,

May, Quintilis and October had 31 days, January and February had 28, and the remaining months had 29. Since 354 days contained 44 eight-day weeks with two days left over, three consecutive days of December were labeled F days, so that the year would end with an H day and the new year would begin with an A day. Both March 1 and January 1 were A days, however, and an open question existed as to which was New Year's Day. Each day had its supporters, which seems incredible, until we realize that the clash of custom with religious and secular needs has led to wars over smaller things.

The *intercalary* days (days inserted between two days) were resented and immediately neglected, especially by the proponents of March 1 as New Year's Day. This prompted a later reformer, or perhaps Numa himself, to add a day to January, making a year of 355 days. A different kind of intercalation was then used. Five extra days were added between February 23 and 24, which were lettered but not numbered. This was the origin of the festivals of February 23, the *Terminalia*, and February 24, the *Regifugium*.

The Roman calendar now had 360 days, though five were uncounted; the year contained exactly 45 eight-day weeks and began with an A day, as desired, and March 1 regained its place as New Year's Day. Unfortunately, however, a lunar year is not a solar year, and the new calendar soon became incompatible with the seasons. During the period of the Roman Republic, still another intercalation was attempted to keep the lunar year in step with the sun. Instead of the five intercalary days, an intercalary month of 22 or 23 days was added in alternate years, after February 23, to the 355-day year of Numa. The new month was called *Mercedonius*, from a Latin word for wages, since its presence meant an extra month's pay. A cycle of four years was thus devised, with 355 days in the first year, 377 in the second, 355 again in the third, and 378 in the fourth. This produced an average length of 366¼ days per year, which was close to a solar year, but almost a day too long.

There were other changes made in the calendar during the days of the Republic which should be mentioned. Originally Numa seems to have placed his new months of January and February at the end of the year and retained March as the first month. The order appeared to be March, April, and so on, down to December, February and January. Thus during the periods when January was considered to be the first month, February was the last. In 452 B.C., however, the Decemvirs, a body of magistrates in ancient Rome, reversed the order of January and February, giving us our present ordering of the months. January seems to have become the first month, in the official political calendar at least, in 153 B.C. when the Roman consuls began to take office on January 1. March 1 continued to be New Year's Day, however, in the eyes of the religious leaders and the populace for a considerable time, probably up to the time of Caesar.

Even if the Roman priests had adhered strictly to the calendar of the Republic it still would have fallen out of step with the sun because the year contained too many days. But because of ignorance and neglect (probably deliberate) by the priests, the calendar, as the great historian Theodor Mommsen noted, "went on its own way tolerably unconcerned about moon and sun." As a consequence, by the middle of the first century B.C. the calendar was 80 days behind the sun. Drastic measures were called for, but history teaches us that politicians are treading on dangerous ground when they try to tamper with something as sacred as a nation's calendar. The ancient Egyptians, for example, had a 365-day calendar, and their astronomers knew that it needed an additional one-quarter day per year, but when the Egyptian king, Ptolemy III, tried in 239 B.C. to adjust the calendar he was met with such a storm of protest that he wisely gave up.

In 46 B.C. Julius Caesar entered the picture. He was in total control of both the Roman government and the Roman religion. He therefore had the power to adjust the calendar, and the world is fortunate that he also had the will to do so. Caesar's first step was to engage the services of Sosigenes, a learned Greek astronomer from Alexandria, Egypt. Together they introduced the reforms that are still the basis of our calendar.

Caesar first extended the year 46 B.C. to 445 days, bringing the old calendar into agreement with the sun. At the end of this "year of confusion," as the Romans called it, the new calendar went into effect, with January 1, 45 B.C., as the first day of the new year. Each year had 365 days, with every fourth year, a leap year, increased to 366 days by adding a day in February. Caesar also distributed the days among the months better than the old calendar did, giving 31 days each to January, March, May, Quintilis, September and November, and 30 to the remaining months, except for February, which had 29 (30 in leap years). It is not quite clear why Caesar short-changed February rather than one of the 31-day months, but some historians speculate that the Romans thought February was an unlucky month given over to the "infernal gods," and the shorter it was the better. Other authorities theorize that even numbers were considered unlucky, and thus the Romans felt there should be as many odd-numbered months as possible.

The Roman Senate honored Caesar in 44 B.C. by changing the name of Quintilis to Julius (July), and in 8 B.C. the emperor Augustus had Sextilis renamed Augustus (August). Probably because he wanted his month to have as many days as Caesar's, Augustus took still another day from February and added it to August. But this created three consecutive 31-day months (July, August and September), so he reduced September and November to 30 days each, and increased October and December to 31 days each. Despite the efforts of other emperors to rename months after themselves, this arrangement of Augustus has endured to the present day. We remember it by the adage, "Thirty days hath September, April, June and November. All the rest have 31 except February alone, which has 28, rain or shine, and in leap years 29."

The only other change made in the Roman calendar before the 16th century A.D. was made in A.D. 527 when Dionysius Exiguus, the abbot of Rome, moved New Year's from January 1 to March 25. Dionysius is also credited with fixing Christmas at December 25 and for originating the custom of dating events (B.C. and A.D.) from the birth of Christ. Before this time there were many *eras* used in counting the years. For example, the Roman Era, dated from the founding of the city of Rome, supposedly in 753 B.C., was widely used by Roman writers, who abbreviated it A.U.C., for *ab urbe condita* (the year of the founding of the city). Thus Caesar was assassinated in 709 A.U.C. (44 B.C.) and the Western Roman Empire fell in 1229 A.U.C. (A.D. 476).

The Christian Era is now the dominant dating system in the world, though many people may refer to it in different terms than A.D. and B.C., such as "The Common Era" (C.E.) and "Before the Common Era" (B.C.E.). It took some 200 years, however, for the new system to meet with universal approval. It was popularized by the great British scholar, the Venerable Bede, in the early 8th century, but the issue was not settled until the end of that century when Charlemagne, another strong leader like Caesar, adopted the system.

An interesting footnote to the Christian Era is that Dionysius picked the wrong year for the birth of Christ. According to the Gospel of St. Matthew, Herod the Great was alive when Christ was born, and it is an established fact that Herod died in 4 B.C., the year most historians accept as Christ's birth year. Other estimates are as early as 7 B.C. Another interesting fact of the Christian Era is that there is no year labeled zero. The year 1 B.C. is followed by the year A.D. 1.

It would seem that Caesar had solved the world's calendar problems once and for all with his Julian Calendar. It was, after all, too long by only 11 minutes and 14 seconds per year. This seemingly trivial error, however, resulted in a gain of one day every 128 years, which by the 16th century had added up to a total of 10 days. Easter, the first Sunday after the first full moon on or after the vernal equinox, taken as March 21, was therefore being celebrated further into the spring, and, of course, Christmas was pushed further into the winter. The Catholic Church dignitaries realized that something had to be done or these sacred holidays would eventually lose their traditional relation to the seasons.

In 1582, Pope Gregory XIII, after consultation with his advisors, decreed that October 5 of that year would be changed to October 15, thus shortening the year by the 10 days gained by the Julian Calendar. Then, to avoid the problem of Caesar's calendar, Gregory declared every fourth year to be a leap year, as before, except for centurial years (those ending in a double 0) not divisible by 400. That is, 1600 and 2000 would be leap years (divisible by 400), but 1700, 1800, 1900, 2100 and so on, would not be. Finally, Gregory's calendar restored January 1 as New Year's Day. The new *Gregorian* Calendar reduced the annual error to approximately 26 seconds, or one day every 3,323 years.

The Catholic countries adopted the Gregorian Calendar almost immediately, but because of the Protestant Reformation many other countries did not. England and her colonies, for example, waited until 1752 to adopt the new calendar and by then 11 days had to be dropped. George Washington, who was born on February 11, 1732, very sensibly switched his birthday to February 22. Russia adopted Gregory's "New Style" calendar in 1918 and Greece followed in 1923, the last European country to do so.

As we have noted, the Romans further divided the year into 8-day weeks, but they seemed to have reckoned the time of the month in an even more peculiar way. The first day of the month was the *calends* (or kalends), from which we get our word *calendar*, and the day at or near the middle of the month was the *ides*. The ides was the 15th day of the months of March, May, July and October, and the 13th day of the remaining months. Caesar, it may be recalled, was assassinated on the ides of March in 44 B.C. The ninth day before the ides, counting the ides as one day, was the *nones* (nine), which fell on the 7th day of March, May, July and October, and on the 5th of the other months. The Romans would count backward from these key days to place an event occurring on other days. For example, such and such happened on the 2nd day before the ides, or on the 4th day before nones, or on the 7th day before calends.

The seven-day week was first used by the Babylonians, perhaps because they regarded the number 7 as magical, but more likely because of the phases of the moon, 7 being approximately one-fourth of a lunar cycle. The days of the week were named for the planets, which in ancient times were conceived to be Saturn, Jupiter, Mars, Sol (the sun), Venus, Mercury and Luna (the moon). The earth was not counted, since it was believed to be stationary and the center of the universe, and the planets Pluto, Neptune and Uranus were, of course, unknown. The Roman Emperor Constantine introduced the 7-day week into the Roman calendar in the 3rd century A.D., using for the days the Latin names *Saturni dies* (Saturn's day), *Solis dies* (Sun's day), *Lunae dies* (Moon's day), *Martis dies* (Mars' day), *Mercurii dies* (Mercury's day), *Jovis dies* (Jove's, or Jupiter's, day) and *Veneris dies* (Venus's day). Our English equivalents of Saturday, Sunday and Monday are easily recognized as the first three of these, and the other four English weekday names were taken from Norse gods: Tuesday is *Tiw's day* (for Tiw, the god of war), Wednesday is *Woden's day* (for Woden, or Odin, the chief Norse god), Thursday is *Thor's day* (the god of lightning and thunder) and Friday is *Frigga's day* (Odin's wife and the chief Norse goddess). Today our week begins with Sunday and ends with Saturday, a custom inherited from the Hebrews, who considered Saturday (the *Sabbath*, or day of rest) to be the seventh day.

A *solar* day is the length of time it takes the earth to turn around once on its axis, but it is now thought of as a *day* of daylight and a *night* of darkness. The Sumerians, between 3,000 and 2,000 B.C., were the first to divide the days into parts, their day consisting of 12 *danna* (perhaps about two of our hours), each of 30 *ges*. It is to the Egyptians, however, that we owe our present system of 24-hour days, though the word *hour* was coined much later from a Greek word meaning "time of day." The Egyptians had 12 hours of day marked by the progress of the sun and 12 hours of night distinguished by the appearance of certain stars or constellations on the eastern horizon. The lengths of the hours varied with the lengths of the daylight periods, which varied with the seasons. Thus on the spring and autumn equinoxes (equal nights), around March 21 and September 23, the day and night hours were equal, but they differed on every other day. The differences were the greatest on the summer and winter solstices (the times when the sun is farthest from the equator, either north or south, and seems to "stand still"). These are usually the longest and the shortest days, respectively, occurring around June 21 and December 22.

Uniform hours came into general use soon after A.D. 1300 when the mechanical clock was invented. The first of these were large devices set in the towers of cathedrals, and the hours were announced by the ringing of bells. In fact, the word *clock* comes from the French *clocke*, an original word for "bell." As clocks became more accurate and their sizes scaled down considerably, due to the invention of the hairspring by the Dutch astronomer Christian Huygens in 1675, soldiers and sailors were able to carry them on their night watches. For this reason these portable clocks became known as *watches*, the name they have today.

Most scientific work today is done using the metric system, a beautiful measuring system handed down to us by the Greeks, which allows us to change from one unit to another by simply moving a decimal place (or multiplying by a power of ten). For example, one kilometer is 1000 meters. Our time measuring system, however, differs spectacularly from the orderly metric system, containing as it does multiples of 60 rather than of 10. We have, of course, 60 minutes (from a Latin word for "small") in an hour and 60 seconds (the *second* subdivision) in a minute (3600 in an hour). These numbers were handed down to us by the Babylonians, through the Greeks, who did not tamper with them, despite their zeal for the metric system. The Babylonians were good mathematicians and were fascinated with numbers. They particularly liked numbers like 6, which is divisible by 1, 2 and 3. They were enamored even more by 60, which is divisible by 1, 2, 3, 4, 5, 6, 10, 12, 15, 20 and 30; and 360 must have driven them out of their minds with ecstasy, since it has all the divisors of 60 plus 18, 24, 36, 40, 45, 60, 72, 90, 120 and 180. From the Babylonians we also get 360 degrees in a circle (each of which could have represented to them a day in the full circle of a solar year).

The planets move relative to the sun, but thousands of stars are fixed in the night sky and are visible from earth. They seem to move only because the motion of the earth gives us a different view of the sky from hour to hour and season to season. This panorama of stars that we see during the course of a year is called a *zodiac*, from a Greek word meaning "circle of animals." The name arose because the ancients, particularly the

Babylonians and later the Greeks, imagined patterns of stars to form animals in the sky. They divided the zodiac into 12 equal parts, or constellations, of 30 degrees each, called *signs of the zodiac*. Each sign is prominent in its turn in the night sky and then fades and disappears, becoming part of the day sky as the earth makes its yearly journey around the sun. The Latin names of the signs of the zodiac, which are still used today, are Aries (the Ram), Taurus (the Bull), Gemini (the Twins), Cancer (the Crab), Leo (the Lion), Virgo (the Virgin or Maiden), Libra (the Scales), Scorpio (the Scorpion), Sagittarius (the Archer), Capricorn or Capricornus (the Goat), Aquarius (the Water Bearer) and Pisces (the Fish).

Astrology is the study of the sun, moon, planets and stars in the belief that these heavenly bodies control the affairs of human beings and can be used to predict the future. Astrology probably had its origins with the Chaldeans, who occupied Babylonia in the 700s and 600s B.C. From the Chaldeans the knowledge of astrology was carried into Egypt and Greece whence it eventually reached Rome and the Arab world. It flourished in Europe in the Middle Ages and reached its peak in the 15th century, prior to the discoveries of Copernicus, Galileo and Kepler that the sun and not the earth was the center of the solar system.

Astrologers today, as in ancient times, cast *horoscopes*, which are diagrams showing the relative position of the planets and the signs of the zodiac. The sign in which the sun is located at the time of a person's birth is his or her *sign* of the zodiac (or more precisely, his or her sun sign). Thus you are a Leo if the sun was in Leo when you were born, and this is supposed to determine your character to a large extent. Astrologers are interested in the other planet signs, as well, such as moon signs, etc., to give them the complete picture, but for a less detailed, general interest the sun sign is the one usually considered. It is also the one given in the daily newspaper astrology columns.

1

January

January, the first month of the year, was added to the calendar around 700 B.C. by Numa Pompilius, the second of the legendary kings of Rome. At the same time he also added February to bring the number of months in the Roman calendar to our present total of twelve. January was originally the twelfth month, with February preceding it as the eleventh month and March following it as the first month of the new year. January first had 28 days and then 29 in the calendar of Numa, but Julius Caesar gave it 31 days in his Julian Calendar of 45 B.C., and this length has come down to us. In 452 B.C. the Decemvirs reversed the order of January and February, giving us the present ordering of the months.

March 1 was originally the Roman New Year's Day, but after the addition of January to the calendar there was a continuous battle between the adherents of March 1 and January 1 as to which day would begin the year. January 1 got a big boost in 153 B.C. when the new Roman consuls started the tradition of taking office on that day, and also Caesar made January the first month in his calendar. The issue, however, was not finally settled until 1582 when the Gregorian Calendar made January 1 the official New Year's Day.

January was taken from the Latin *Januarius* in honor of the Roman god Janus, who was always depicted as having two faces, one facing the past and one the future, an appropriate symbol for the beginning of the new year. Janus was also the god of gates and doors and held dominion over the beginnings of all human enterprises.

In addition to New Year's Day, January includes such holidays as *Epiphany*, the coming of the wise men (January 6); the birthday of Martin

9

Luther King Jr. (the nearest Monday to January 15); and in some southern states the birthday of Robert E. Lee (January 19). Also January 20 following each Presidential election is Inauguration Day, when the President of the United States takes the oath of office. January, in addition, is the birth month of U.S. Presidents Millard Fillmore, William McKinley, Franklin D. Roosevelt and Richard M. Nixon.

The birthstone for January is the garnet, and the snowdrop and the carnation are the special flowers for the month. Notable birthdays and events of January are as follows.

JANUARY 1 -- BIRTHDAYS

1449   **Lorenzo the Magnificent** -- The most famous member of the Medici family, who made Florence the most powerful and most beautiful city of his time

1467   **Sigismund I (the Old)** -- King of Poland, 1506-1548

1484   **Huldreich Zwingli** – The most important reformer in the Swiss Protestant Reformation

1618   **Bartolome Esteban Murillo** -- Spanish painter noted as the best interpreter of the gentle, optimistic side of Christianity, and known for works such as *The Immaculate Conception*

1735   **Paul Revere** -- American silversmith and Revolutionary War hero who made the famous midnight ride warning the patriots that the British were coming

1745   **Anthony Wayne** – American Revolutionary War general, known as "Mad Anthony" because of his reckless courage

1752   **Betsy Ross** -- American seamstress who some believe made the first U.S. flag that had stars and stripes

1767   **Maria Edgeworth** -- Anglo-Irish novelist

1819   **Philip Schaff** -- Swiss-born ecumenical leader and theologian

1819   **Arthur Hugh Clough** -- English poet

1854   **Sir James George Frazer** – Scottish anthropologist, noted for the famous book, *The Golden Bough* (1922), one of the great works of world literature

1856   **Tim Keefe** – Hall of Fame baseball pitcher with a record 19 consecutive victories in 1883

1863   **Baron Pierre de Coubertin** -- Frenchman who single-handedly revived the Olympic Games in 1896

1864   **Alfred Stieglitz** – American pioneer photographer and "father of modern photography," whose photographs are among the greatest ever produced

1879   **E.M. Forster** -- English novelist noted for works such as *Howards End* (1910) and *A Passage to India* (1924)

1879	**William Fox** -- Hungarian-born founder of Fox Film Corporation which later became 20th Century Fox
1884	**George W. Meyer** -- American composer noted for songs such as "For Me and My Gal," "In the Land of Beginning Again," and "There Are Such Things"
1889	**Charles Bickford** -- American stage, screen, and television actor and commanding character player in over 80 films
1895	**J. Edgar Hoover** -- First director of the FBI, who served from 1924 to 1972
1900	**Xavier Cugat** -- Spanish-born bandleader and "Rhumba King" of the Big Band Era of the 1930s and 1940s
1909	**Dana Andrews** -- American motion-picture and television actor with a 40-year career
1909	**Barry Goldwater** -- U.S. senator and presidential candidate in 1964
1911	**Hank Greenberg** -- Hall of Fame baseball player who hit 58 home runs in 1938
1913	**Eliot Janeway** -- American economist, author, lecturer, and columnist
1919	**J.D. Salinger** -- American novelist noted for *The Catcher in the Rye* (1951)
1919	**Carole Landis** -- American motion-picture actress
1924	**Earl Torgeson** -- Professional baseball player
1925	**Idi Amin** -- Dictator of Uganda in the 1970s
1927	**Doak Walker** -- Professional football player
1940	**Frank Langella** -- American motion-picture actor
1955	**Lamarr Hoyt** -- Professional baseball player

JANUARY 1 -- EVENTS

43 BC	Cicero delivered his "Fifth Philippic" (fifth of a series of speeches condemning Mark Antony) in the Roman Senate.
27 BC	Octavian became the first emperor of Rome, and took the name Caesar Augustus.
69 AD	Roman legions in Germany refused to renew the oath of allegiance to Emperor Galba.
1399	Tamerlane, the Mongol conqueror, left Delhi, India, after sacking it, massacring most of its inhabitants, and occupying it for a year.
1492	The Moors offered to surrender Granada to the Spanish. The actual surrender took place the next day, ending the Moorish hold in Europe.

1503   Columbus spent the day anchored off the site of present-day Coco Solo, Canal Zone, in Panama, on his fourth voyage to America. He never learned how close he was to the Pacific.

1651   Charles II was crowned King of the Scots at Scone. He was to become King of England in 1660 after the death of Oliver Cromwell.

1660   Samuel Pepys began his *Diary* with the words, "Blessed be God, at the end of the last year I was in very good health, without any sense of my old pain, but upon taking of cold."

1772   Thomas Jefferson married Martha Wayles Skelton.

1824   Haiti was proclaimed an independent country by General Jean Jacques Dessalines, the leader in the struggle against the French.

1824   James K. Polk married Sarah Childress.

1863   President Abraham Lincoln issued the Emancipation Proclamation, freeing the slaves.

1892   The Ellis Island Immigrant Station in New York Harbor was officially opened.

1901   The Commonwealth of Australia was established by the British Parliament.

1902   The first Rose Bowl football game was played, with Michigan beating Stanford, 49-0.

1913   The U.S. parcel post service began.

1916   The Rose Bowl game became an annual event with the game between Washington State and Brown in the new 101,385-seat stadium in Pasadena, California.

1931   The comic strip, *Joe Palooka*, by Ham Fisher, first began appearing, in the New York *Mirror*.

1935   The Orange Bowl game was played for the first time, with Bucknell defeating Miami, 26-0.

1935   The Sugar Bowl game was played for the first time, with Tulane beating Temple, 20-14.

1937   The Cotton Bowl game was played for the first time, with Texas Christian University beating Marquette, 16-8.

1954   The Tournament of Roses parade in Pasadena, California, became the first program to be televised in color on a nationwide network.

1959   Cuban dictator Fulgencio Batista resigned and fled to Dominica, as rebel leader Fidel Castro captured Santiago.

1963   "I have a dream," said Martin Luther King Jr. at the Lincoln Memorial in Washington, D.C., in a ceremony commemorating the centennial of the Emancipation Proclamation.

1975	Richard Nixon's aides, H.R. Haldeman, John Ehrlichman, and John Mitchell, were convicted in the Watergate cover-up trial.
1979	President Jimmy Carter opened United States diplomatic relations with the People's Republic of China.

JANUARY 2 -- BIRTHDAYS

1647	**Nathaniel Bacon** — American planter who led Bacon's Rebellion in Virginia in 1676 against the English colonial government
1727	**James Wolfe** -- British general and hero of the Battle of Quebec in 1759, which won Canada for the British Empire
1752	**Philip Freneau** -- Early American poet and journalist, known by many as the "Poet of the American Revolution"
1822	**Rudolf Clausius** -- German physicist who in 1850 formulated the second law of thermodynamics: "Heat cannot of itself pass from a colder to a hotter body"
1828	**Jeremiah E. Rankin** -- Composer of the hymn, "God Be with You till We Meet Again"
1857	**Frederick Burr Opper** -- American cartoonist and creator of *Happy Hooligan, Maud*, and *Alphonse and Gaston*
1863	**Lucia Zarate** — The world's lightest recorded adult, at 5.7 pounds when she was 17 years old
1865	**William Lyon Phelps** -- American author, educator, and literary critic who was influential in shaping American literary tastes of his time, and who taught the first American course in modern fiction
1870	**Ernst Heinrich Barlach** — German sculptor noted for works such as *The Reunion* (1930)
1885	**Marcel Andre** -- Distinguished character actor of the French stage and screen
1893	**Lillian Leitzel** -- German-born trapeze artist and "Queen of the Circus," who performed for both Barnum and Bailey and the Ringling Brothers
1894	**Arthur C. Nielsen** -- American tennis enthusiast and philanthropist who gave $3 million for building indoor courts
1895	**Count Folke Bernadotte** -- Swedish humanitarian and U.N. diplomat who was murdered in Jerusalem in 1948 while trying to bring about peace between the Arabs and the Jews
1896	**Lank Leonard** -- American comic strip artist and creator of *Mickey Finn*
1899	**Charles Howard** -- American painter
1904	**Sally Rand** -- American strip-tease artist and inventor of the fan dance

1920   **Isaac Asimov** -- American biochemist and novelist, noted for his
        worldwide bestsellers in science fiction

1922   **Renata Tebaldi** -- Italian operatic soprano and one of the great
        stars of her day

1925   **William J. Crowe** -- U.S. admiral and Chairman of the Joint
        Chiefs of Staff under Presidents Reagan and Bush

1927   **Gino Marchetti** -- Professional football player

1930   **Julius LaRosa** -- American singer and television entertainer

1936   **Roger Miller** -- American singer

1939   **Jim Bakker** -- American television evangelist defrocked in 1987
        because of a sex scandal involving a church secretary

1942   **Marvin Fleming** -- Professional football player

1947   **Calvin Hill** -- Professional football player

1949   **Mike Newlin** -- Professional basketball player

1963   **David Cone** -- Professional baseball player

JANUARY 2 -- EVENTS

1492   The last Moorist stronghold in Europe was wiped out as the
        forces of Ferdinand and Isabella of Spain occupied Granada.

1788   Georgia ratified the Constitution becoming the fourth state of
        the Union.

1842   The first U.S. wire suspension bridge was opened, spanning the
        Schuylkill River at Fairmont, near Philadelphia.

1900   U.S. Secretary of State John Hay announced the "Open-Door
        Policy" to facilitate trade with China.

1905   The Russians surrendered at Port Arthur in Manchuria in the
        last major military engagement of the Russo-Japanese War.

1921   Religious services were first broadcast over the radio, by Station
        KDKA of Pittsburgh.

1942   The Japanese occupied Manila in World War II.

1948   The American Federation of Musicians, under James C. Petrillo,
        started a recording strike.

1949   American comedian Jack Benny began his Sunday night radio
        program over CBS, after moving from NBC.

1959   The Russians launched the moon probe *Luna 1*, which missed
        the moon and became the first spacecraft to orbit the sun.

1968   South African surgeon Dr. Christiaan Barnard performed his,
        and the world's, second heart transplant. The patient in this case
        left the hospital and lived for more than a year.

| 1974 | President Nixon signed the bill requiring a 55 mph speed limit on all U.S. highways by March 2, 1974. |
| 1984 | W. Wilson Goode was sworn in as Philadelphia's first black mayor. |

JANUARY 3 – BIRTHDAYS

106 BC	**Marcus Tullius Cicero** -- Noted Roman statesman and orator, and the greatest of the ancient writers
1591	**Le Valentin** -- French painter
1698	**Pietro Metastasio** -- Italian poet and librettist
1793	**Lucretia Mott** -- American reformer, co-founder of the American Anti-Slavery Society (1833), and pioneer in the women's rights movement
1803	**Douglas Jerrold** -- English dramatist and journalist
1840	**Joseph Damien de Veuster** -- Belgian priest who gave his life to the care of lepers in Molokai, Hawaii
1840	**Henry Holt** -- American publisher who founded Henry Holt Company publishers in 1866
1879	**Grace Goodhue Coolidge** -- Wife of President Calvin Coolidge
1883	**Clement Attlee** -- British prime minister, 1945-1951, who succeeded Winston Churchill
1887	**August Macke** -- German painter
1892	**J.R.R. Tolkien** -- English fantasy writer and author of the monumental work, *The Lord of the Rings* (1954-1956)
1897	**Marion Davies** -- American stage and motion-picture actress, noted for her leading roles of the 1920s and for her 30-year affair with the famous journalist William Randolph Hearst
1898	**Zasu Pitts** -- American motion-picture and television actress, who appeared in over 100 silent and talking pictures in a 45-year career
1901	**Ngo Dinh Diem** -- First president of South Vietnam, 1955-1963
1905	**Ray Milland** -- Welsh-born motion-picture and television leading man and character actor in over 150 films in a 50-year career
1909	**Victor Borge** -- Danish comedian and pianist
1911	**Joseph Rauh** -- American lawyer and liberal political activist
1915	**Jack Levine** -- American painter noted for works such as *Gangster Funeral* (1953)
1916	**Betty Furness** -- American television performer and consumer advocate
1918	**Maxine Andrews** -- One of the singing Andrews Sisters, a highly popular harmony trio of the 1940s

1918   **Buddy Kaye** -- American author, saxophonist, and producer, noted for such lyrics as "Till the End of Time," "A-You're Adorable," and "Full Moon and Empty Arms"

1919   **Jesse White** -- American stage, screen, and television character actor with a career of over 40 years

1924   **Hank Stram** -- Professional football player, coach, and sportscaster

1926   **George Martin** -- Producer for the Beatles, 1962-1969

1930   **Carla Anderson Hills** -- Secretary of Housing and Urban Development under President Ford

1932   **D.X. Fenton** -- American author of children's stories

1932   **Dabney Coleman** -- American motion-picture and television actor

1936   **Betty Rollin** -- American journalist and author

1939   **Bobby Hull** -- One of the greatest goal scorers in National Hockey League history and its first player to score 50 or more goals in more than one season

1945   **Stephen Stills** -- American singer and guitarist with Crosby, Stills, Nash, and Young

1946   **John Paul Jones** -- British bassist with the Led Zeppelin musical group

1948   **David Lloyd** -- English tennis player

1950   **Victoria Principal** -- American actress noted for her role in the long-running television series *Dallas*

1956   **Mel Gibson** -- Australian motion-picture actor

JANUARY 3 -- EVENTS

1521   Pope Leo X excommunicated Martin Luther from the Roman Catholic Church.

1777   George Washington, in one of his most brilliant triumphs, defeated the British in the Battle of Princeton, N.J., in the Revolutionary War.

1841   Herman Melville boarded the whaler *Acushnet*, beginning his career of naval adventures that gave him the background for his novels, particularly his masterpiece *Moby-Dick*.

1847   The village of Yerba Buena in California officially changed its name to San Francisco.

1870   Construction of the Brooklyn Bridge began. It was the largest suspension bridge in the world when it was completed 13 years later.

1871   Henry W. Bradley of Binghamton, New York, received a patent for oleomargarine.

1882   Oscar Wilde, the famous Irish poet and wit, on docking at New York and being asked by customs if he had anything to declare, replied, "Nothing but my genius."

1920   Babe Ruth signed with the New York Yankees, having just been acquired from the Boston Red Sox.

1935   In a special plebiscite conducted by the League of Nations, the residents of the Saar Basin voted overwhelmingly for reunion with Germany.

1938   "The March of Dimes" campaign to fight infantile paralysis was organized.

1942   The Japanese began their siege of Bataan in World War II.

1959   Alaska was admitted to the Union as the 49th state.

1961   The United States severed diplomatic relations with Fidel Castro's Cuba.

JANUARY 4 -- BIRTHDAYS

1581   **James Ussher** – Anglo-Irish archbishop who claimed by his research that the world was created in 4,004 B.C.

1643   **Sir Isaac Newton** -- English giant of science, who discovered the law of gravity, invented the calculus, and discovered the secrets of light and color

1710   **Giovanni Battista Pergolesi** -- Italian composer noted for the comic opera *La Serva Padrona* (1733) and the religious work *Stabat Mater* (1729)

1784   **Francois Rude** -- French sculptor

1785   **Jakob Grimm** – German scholar who with his brother Wilhelm compiled the *German Dictionary* and wrote *Grimm's Fairy Tales* (1812, 1815)

1809   **Louis Braille** -- Inventor of the braille system of printing and writing for the blind (1829)

1813   **Sir Isaac Pitman** -- British schoolmaster who invented phonetic shorthand

1838   **Tom Thumb (Charles S. Stratton)** – Famous 40-inch, 70-pound midget with the P.T. Barnum show in the mid-19th century

1858   **Carter Glass** – American statesman and sponsor of the Federal Reserve Act of 1913

1859   **George Washington Carver** -- Noted black American scientist who revolutionized the agriculture of the South and made more than 300 products from the peanut

1877   Marsden Hartley -- American painter known as "the painter from Maine," and noted for works such as *Earth Warming, Mexico* (1932)

1878   Augustus John -- British painter known principally for his portraits of prominent people, such as David Lloyd George and George Bernard Shaw

1881   Wilhelm Lehmbruck -- German sculptor noted for works such as *Seated Youth* (1918)

1896   Everett McKinley Dirksen -- U.S. senator and Minority Leader, 1959-1969

1906   William Bendix -- American motion-picture and television actor

1907   Joe Marsala -- American composer, author, and conductor, noted for songs such as "Little Sir Echo"

1914   Jane Wyman -- American motion-picture and television superstar, who won the Academy Award in 1948 for *Johnny Belinda*

1920   William Colby -- Director of the CIA under Presidents Nixon and Ford

1925   Johnny Lujack -- Professional football superstar

1927   Barbara Rush -- American motion-picture and television actress, and leading lady of the 1950s and 1960s

1930   Sorrell Booke -- American stage, screen, and television actor

1930   Don Shula -- One of the most successful football coaches in the history of the National Football League

1932   Carlos Saura -- Spanish motion-picture director and one of the leading figures of the new Spanish cinema

1935   Floyd Patterson -- First boxer in history to hold the world heavyweight championship twice (1956-1959 and 1960-1962)

1937   Grace Bumbry -- American mezzo-soprano

1939   Dyan Cannon -- American stage, screen, and television actress

1941   Maureen Reagan -- Daughter of President Ronald Reagan and actress Jane Wyman

1951   Barbara Ann Cochran -- Professional skier

JANUARY 4 -- EVENTS

48 BC   Julius Caesar arrived in Greece in pursuit of his rival, Pompey, whom he later defeated at Pharsalus.

1076   Henry IV, King of Germany, convened the Synod of Worms, which declared Pope Gregory VII deposed.

1877   Cornelius Vanderbilt, the famous American financier, died at age 82, leaving an estate of $100 million, a prodigious sum for that time.

1885	The first successful U.S. appendectomy was performed by Dr. William West Grant in Davenport, Iowa. The patient was 22-year-old Mary Gartside.
1896	Utah was admitted to the Union as the 45th state.
1937	Italian troops landed in Spain to help Generalissimo Francisco Franco's rebels in the Spanish Civil War.
1948	Britain granted independence to Burma.
1960	Albert Camus, the noted French writer, was killed in a car accident near Sens, France, at age 46.
1965	T.S. Eliot, the famous American-born English poet, died in London at age 76.
1979	The Shah of Iran appointed Shahpour Bakhtiar prime minister, to appease his critics.

JANUARY 5 -- BIRTHDAYS

1548	**Francisco Suarez** -- Noted Spanish theologian and a founder of the philosophy of international law
1779	**Stephen Decatur** -- One of the most daring officers of the U.S. Navy during its early years, who is remembered for the famous toast, "Our country, right or wrong"
1779	**Zebulon Montgomery Pike** – American general and explorer, famous for his discovery in 1806 of Pikes Peak
1782	**Robert Morrison** -- First Protestant minister in China
1786	**Thomas Nuttall** -- Pioneer English botanist
1855	**King Camp Gillette** – Inventor and manufacturer of the safety razor and blade
1864	**Ban Johnson** -- Organizer and first president of baseball's American League
1871	**Frederick Shepherd Converse** – American romantic music composer
1875	**J. Stuart Blackton** -- English-born pioneer motion-picture director, screenwriter, and actor, who co-founded the Vitagraph Company in 1897
1876	**Konrad Adenauer** -- First chancellor of the West German Republic, 1949-1963
1877	**Henry Sloane Coffin** -- Noted American clergyman, author, and educator
1879	**Jack Norworth** – American composer, author, and actor, noted for songs such as "Shine On, Harvest Moon" and "Take Me Out to the Ball Game"

1887   **Courtney Hodges** -- American World War II general
1887   **Bernard Leach** -- English ceramist
1900   **Yves Tanguy** -- French-born surrealist artist noted for works such as *Fear*
1905   **Francis Henry** -- English-American composer, author, and guitarist, noted for songs such as "Little Girl," "Ain't It a Shame," and "Sugar Bun"
1906   **Dame Kathleen Kenyon** -- English archaeologist who excavated the ancient city of Jericho
1909   **Jean-Pierre Aumont** -- French actor and durable leading man of French, American, and international films with a 50-year career
1914   **Nicolas de Stael** -- French painter
1926   **Maria Schell** -- Austrian stage and motion-picture actress and sister of actor-director Maximilian Schell
1928   **Ali Bhutto** -- President of Pakistan, 1971-1977
1928   **Walter F. Mondale** -- U.S. vice president under President Carter, and presidential candidate in 1984
1931   **Alvin Ailey** -- American choreographer
1931   **Robert Duvall** -- American stage and motion-picture actor
1931   **Alfred Brendel** -- Austrian pianist
1932   **Chuck Noll** -- Professional football player and coach
1935   **Earl Battey** -- Professional baseball player
1938   **Juan Carlos I** -- King of Spain who was installed in 1975 following the death of dictator Francisco Franco
1941   **Charles McKinley** -- American tennis player
1946   **Diane Keaton** -- American stage and motion-picture actress
1947   **Eugene "Mercury" Morris** -- Professional football player
1948   **Charlie Hough** -- Professional baseball player
1951   **Don Gullet** -- Professional baseball player
1954   **Jim Gantner** -- Professional baseball player
1957   **Steve Fuller** -- Professional football player
1958   **Joe Cribbs** -- Professional football player

JANUARY 5 -- EVENTS

1066   Edward the Confessor, the last English king descended from Alfred the Great, died at age 64. The dispute over his successor led to the Norman conquest of England.
1477   The Swiss defeated the Burgundians and Charles the Bold at Nancy, France.

1776   New Hampshire became the first colony to form a government independent of Great Britain, adopting a temporary constitution.

1895   Captain Alfred Dreyfus, unjustly convicted of espionage, was stripped of his badges and buttons in Paris.

1914   Because of his great success with the Model T, Henry Ford raised his workers' pay from $2.40 to $5.00 per day and reduced the working day from 9 to 8 hours.

1919   The National Socialist Party, the forerunner of the Nazis, was founded in Germany.

1925   Mrs. Nellie Tayloe Ross, the first U.S. woman governor, was sworn in as governor of Wyoming.

1933   Calvin Coolidge died in Northampton, Massachusetts, at age 60.

1943   George Washington Carver, the great black American scientist, died at an approximate age of 84.

1948   Dr. Alfred C. Kinsey published his *Sexual Behavior in the Human Male*.

1949   President Harry Truman labeled his administration the "Fair Deal" in his State of the Union Address.

JANUARY 6 -- BIRTHDAYS

1367   **Richard II** – King of England, 1377-1399, and son of the great English warrior, Edward the Black Prince

1412   **Joan of Arc** -- French national heroine and beloved saint of the Roman Catholic Church, who led the French army to victory at the siege of Orleans in 1429

1425   **Henry IV (the Impotent)** -- King of Castile before the time of Ferdinand and Isabella

1580   **Captain John Smith** -- Leader of the English colonists who settled Jamestown, Va., in 1607 (His birthday is speculation, but he was baptized on January 9 when he was probably 3 days old)

1811   **Charles Sumner** – American statesman and noted abolitionist, and one of the founders of the Republican Party

1822   **Heinrich Schliemann** -- German archaeologist who became famous for discovering and excavating the ruins of ancient Troy

1828   **Ward Hill Lamon** -- American statesman and law partner of Abraham Lincoln

1832   **Gustave Dore** – French painter and sculptor, who illustrated a large number of literary masterpieces, such as Dante's *Divine Comedy*, Cervantes' *Don Quixote*, and Poe's *The Raven*

1838   **Max Bruch** -- German composer noted for works such as *Kol Nidrei* for cello and orchestra

1872   **Alexander Nikolaievitch Scriabin** – Russian composer and pianist, whose last six sonatas for piano (1908 to 1913) are considered masterworks

1878   **Dame Adeline Genee** -- Noted German-English ballet dancer

1878   **Carl Sandburg** -- American poet, biographer, and folk song collector, whose 6-volume *Abraham Lincoln* (1926, 1939) is considered by many to be the great biography of the 20th century

1879   **Joseph Medill Patterson** – Publisher of the Chicago *Tribune*, 1914-1925

1880   **Tom Mix** -- Legendary cowboy star of Hollywood silents and early talkies

1882   **Sam Rayburn** – U.S. congressman who served 49 consecutive years (1912-1961) and was Speaker of the House longer than any other person (nearly 17 years)

1883   **Khalil Gibran** – Lebanese writer and painter, noted for his great philosophical work, *The Prophet* (1923)

1910   **Wright Morris** -- American novelist

1911   **Joey Adams** -- American comedian

1913   **Loretta Young** -- American motion-picture and television actress, Hollywood leading lady of the 1930s and 1940s, and star of television in the 1950s

1914   **Danny Thomas** -- American motion-picture and television actor, singer, and comedian

1920   **Sun Myung Moon** – Korean evangelist and leader of the "Moonies"

1920   **Early Wynn** -- Hall of Fame baseball pitcher who won 300 career games

1920   **Jean Ipousteguy** -- French sculptor

1921   **Lou Harris** -- American public opinion pollster

1921   **Cary Middlecoff** -- Professional golfer

1924   **Earl Scruggs** -- American banjo player and songwriter with Flatt and Scruggs

1926   **Ralph Branca** -- Professional baseball pitcher who threw the famous home-run pitch to Bobby Thomson that gave the New York Giants the 1951 pennant over the Brooklyn Dodgers

1926   **Kid Gavilan** -- World welterweight boxing champion, 1951-1954

1929   **Vic Tayback** -- American actor noted for his role as Mel in the long-running TV series *Alice*

1931   **E.L. Doctorow** -- American novelist and editor, noted for works such as *The Book of Daniel* and *Ragtime*

1931   **Dickie Moore** -- Professional hockey player

1933	**Capucine (Germaine Lefebvre)** -- French motion-picture actress and model
1936	**Darlene Hard** -- Top-ranked U.S. tennis player in 1962
1944	**Bonnie Franklin** -- American television actress and star of the long-running show *One Day at a Time*
1946	**Harold Jackson** -- Professional football player
1946	**Syd Barrett** – Original guitarist with the Pink Floyd musical group
1957	**Nancy Lopez** -- Professional golfer and superstar

JANUARY 6 -- EVENTS

1266	Charles d'Anjou was crowned King of Naples and Sicily.
1540	King Henry VIII of England married his fourth wife, Anne of Cleves, despite his opinion that she had no looks and was "no better than a Flanders mare."
1759	George Washington married Martha Dandridge Custis in New Kent County, Virginia.
1872	Jim Fisk, famous American robber baron, was shot to death on the stairs of the Grand Central Hotel in New York by Edward S. Stokes, a rival for the favors of Fisk's mistress.
1898	Simon Lake, the developer of the method of submerging by negative buoyancy, used in today's submarines, became the first person to talk by telephone from under water.
1912	New Mexico was admitted to the Union as the 47th state.
1919	Theodore Roosevelt died at Oyster Bay, New York, at age 60.
1941	President Franklin D. Roosevelt called for a world with the Four Freedoms--of speech, of religion, from want, and from fear.

JANUARY 7 -- BIRTHDAYS

1718	**Israel Putnam** -- American pioneer and Revolutionary War general
1745	**Jacques Etienne Montgolfier** -- French balloonist who with his brother Joseph invented the first balloons to carry men into the air
1768	**Joseph Bonaparte** -- King of Naples, 1806, King of Spain, 1808, and brother of Napoleon Bonaparte
1800	**Millard Fillmore** -- 13th U.S. president
1830	**Albert Bierstadt** -- One of the greatest American romantic landscape painters

1844   **Saint Bernadette of Lourdes** -- Roman Catholic visionary to whom the Virgin Mary is said to have appeared 18 times in 1858 and told her to make known the healing powers of the springs of water in Lourdes

1845   **Louis III** -- King of Bavaria

1873   **Charles Peguy** -- French writer noted for works such as the poem, "Jeanne d'Arc" (1897)

1873   **Adolph Zukor** -- Hungarian-born pioneer filmmaker and co-founder and early president of Paramount Pictures

1890   **Maurice Evans McLoughlin** -- American Hall of Fame tennis player and National Champion in 1912 and 1913

1899   **Francis Poulenc** -- Member of "Les Six," a group of French composers in the 1920s that rejected romanticism and impressionism

1906   **Herbert Adolph Magidson** -- American composer and author, noted for songs such as "Enjoy Yourself," "Black-Eyed Susan Brown," "I'll Buy That Dream," "The Continental," and "Music, Maestro, Please"

1912   **Charles Addams** -- American cartoonist famous for his macabre humor and his amusing monsters in the *New Yorker* magazine

1913   **Johnny Mize** -- Hall of Fame baseball player who hit 51 home runs in 1947

1922   **Alvin Dark** -- Professional baseball player and manager

1922   **Vincent Gardenia** -- Italian-American stage, screen, and television actor

1929   **Terry Moore** -- American motion-picture actress

1930   **Eddie Le Baron** -- Professional football superstar

1930   **Douglas Kiker** -- American television news correspondent and host

1931   **Mack Mattingly** -- U.S. Senator

1934   **Reg Murphy** -- American journalist and editor

1938   **Lou Graham** -- Professional golfer

1943   **Leona Williams** -- American singer and songwriter

1945   **Alena Palmeova-West** -- Czechoslovakian tennis player

1948   **Kenny Loggins** -- American singer, songwriter, and recording artist

1950   **Ross Grimsley** -- Professional baseball player

JANUARY 7 -- EVENTS

1327   King Edward II of England was forced by Parliament to abdicate. He was murdered soon after.

1536   Catherine of Aragon, the first wife of King Henry VIII of England, died at age 50.

1610	Galileo, the great Italian scientist, discovered the four moons of Jupiter through his telescope. He named them the Medicean stars, after the Medici family.
1714	The first patent for a typewriter was given to English engineer Henry Mills.
1782	The Bank of North America, the first commercial bank in the United States, opened in Philadelphia.
1789	The first American presidential election was held, with George Washington an easy winner.
1830	Commercial railroad service was started in the United States by the Baltimore and Ohio Railroad Company.
1896	Fannie Farmer published her famous cookbook, *Boston Cooking School Cook Book,* one of the best sellers of all time.
1924	George Gershwin, the great American composer, completed the piano score of *Rhapsody in Blue.*
1927	The Harlem Globetrotters, the famous black basketball team, was founded by Abe Saperstein in Hinckley, Illinois.
1927	Transatlantic telephone service from New York to London began.
1929	The comic strip, *Buck Rogers,* by Phil Nowland and Dick Callins, first appeared.
1929	*Tarzan of the Apes*, created by Edgar Rice Burroughs and illustrated by Harold Foster, first appeared in newspapers.
1934	The comic strips, *Flash Gordon* and *Jungle Jim*, both by Alex Raymond, first appeared.
1942	The Japanese began their 3-month siege of Bataan in World War II.
1952	General Dwight D. Eisenhower announced that he would accept the Republican nomination for president if it were offered to him.
1953	President Harry Truman announced in his State of the Union Address that the United States had developed a hydrogen bomb.

JANUARY 8 -- BIRTHDAYS

1587	**Jan Pieterszoon Coen** – Chief founder of the Dutch East Indies
1638	**Elisabetta Sirani** -- Italian painter
1705	**Jacques Francois Blondel** -- French architect
1792	**Lowell Mason** -- American hymn writer, who wrote more than 1,650 religious compositions, one of the best known of which is "Nearer My God to Thee"
1821	**James Longstreet** -- Confederate general in the Civil War

1823   **Alfred Russel Wallace** -- British naturalist and explorer, noted for reaching independently the same explanation for evolution as Charles Darwin did

1824   **Wilkie Collins** -- English detective story writer noted for works such as *The Woman in White* (1860) and *The Moonstone* (1868), one of the world's greatest detective stories

1862   **Frank N. Doubleday** -- American publisher and founder of Doubleday and Company

1881   **William Thomas Piper** -- American airplane manufacturer

1883   **Patrick J. Hurley** -- American statesman and soldier, and secretary of war, 1929-1933

1885   **John Curtin** -- Prime minister of Australia during World War II

1891   **William Kiplinger** -- Founder of the *Kiplinger Letter*

1902   **Georgi Malenkov** -- Premier of Russia, 1953-1955, who succeeded Joseph Stalin

1904   **Peter Arno** -- American cartoonist who drew primarily for the *New Yorker* magazine

1911   **Butterfly McQueen** -- American theater and motion-picture actress, noted for her role of Prissy in *Gone with the Wind*

1912   **Jose Ferrer** --Puerto Rican-born stage and motion-picture actor and director

1915   **Walker Cooper** -- Professional baseball catcher, who with his brother, pitcher Mort Cooper, formed one of baseball's best-known brother batteries

1923   **Larry Storch** -- American actor and comedian

1924   **Ron Moody** -- English singer and stage, screen, and television actor

1928   **Sander Vanocur** -- American broadcast journalist

1930   **Doreen Wilbur** -- Professional archer

1930   **Soupy Sales** -- American comedian and television personality

1933   **Charles Osgood** -- American television news correspondent

1935   **Elvis Presley** -- "The King" of American rock and roll singers, and rock music's first multi-millionaire superstar

1937   **Shirley Bassey** -- English singer

1939   **Yvette Mimieux** -- American stage, screen, and television actress

1942   **Stephen W. Hawking** -- British theoretical physicist, considered by many to be the greatest since Albert Einstein, and author of *A Brief History of Time*

1946   **Robbie Krieger** --American guitarist with the Doors rock group

1947   **David Bowie** -- British rock singer and musician

1953   **Bruce Sutter** -- Professional baseball player

1957   **Dwight Clark** -- Professional football player

JANUARY 8 -- EVENTS

1198 Innocent III, the greatest of the medieval Roman Catholic popes, was elected.

1337 Giotto di Bondone, the Italian painter, died in Florence at age 70.

1642 Galileo, the great Italian astronomer and physicist, died in Florence at age 77.

1798 Amendment 11 to the Constitution was proclaimed, prohibiting any citizen of one state from suing another state.

1815 General Andrew Jackson defeated the British in the Battle of New Orleans in the War of 1812, two weeks after the peace treaty had been signed.

1835 President Andrew Jackson paid off the final installment of the national debt, the only president ever to do so.

1845 Felix Mendelssohn's "Hear My Prayer" was sung publicly for the first time, in London.

1918 Mississippi became the first state to ratify the Prohibition Amendment to the Constitution.

1918 President Woodrow Wilson announced his Fourteen Points as a basis for a post-World War I settlement.

1926 Ibn Saud was crowned King of Hejaz and Nejd, which he was to rename Saudi Arabia in 1932.

1959 Charles de Gaulle was inaugurated president of France's Fifth Republic.

1964 President Lyndon B. Johnson committed the U.S. to a "War on Poverty."

1976 Chou En-Lai, Chinese premier since 1949, died at age 78.

JANUARY 9 -- BIRTHDAYS

1554 **Gregory XV** -- Roman Catholic pope, 1621-1623

1590 **Simon Vouet** -- French painter

1658 **Nicolas Cousteau** -- French sculptor

1819 **William Powell Frith** -- English artist noted for paintings such as *Derby Day* (1858)

1856 **Lizette Woodworth Reese** -- American poet

1859 **Carrie Chapman Catt** -- American pioneer leader in the campaign for woman suffrage, and founder in 1920 of the National League of Women Voters, now the League of Women Voters

1870 **Joseph Baerman Strauss** -- Designer of the Golden Gate Bridge

1881 **Lascelles Abercrombie** -- British poet and critic

1890   **Karel Capek** — Czech writer, best known for his play, *R.U.R.*
        (Rossum's Universal Robots) (1921), in which he introduced the
        word *robot* to the language
1897   **Felisa Rincon de Gautier** -- Puerto Rican statesman
1898   **Dame Gracie Fields** -- English actress, singer, and comedienne,
        and the top box office draw in Britain in the 1930s
1900   **Richard Halliburton** — American adventurer, author, and lec-
        turer, noted for works such as *New Worlds to Conquer* (1929),
        and *The Orient* and *The Occident* (both in 1937)
1901   **Chic Young** -- American cartoonist and creator in 1930 of
        Blondie, one of the most popular comic strips of all time
1902   **Rudolf Bing** -- Manager of the Metropolitan Opera Association
        of New York City, 1950-1972
1904   **George Balanchine** — Russian-born American choreographer
        and founder of the New York City Ballet
1908   **Simone de Beauvoir** -- French philosopher and novelist, noted
        for works such as *The Second Sex* (1949)
1910   **Dick Henry Jurgens** — American composer, author, and orches-
        tra leader, noted for songs such as "Elmer's Tune" and "One
        Dozen Roses"
1913   **Richard M. Nixon** -- 37th U.S. president and the only president
        to resign the office
1914   **Gypsy Rose Lee** — American actress and writer, and burlesque
        queen of the 1930s, the best-known stripper of her day
1915   **Fernando Lamas** -- Argentine motion-picture actor and sporty
        Latin lover of Hollywood films of the 1950s
1915   **Henning Dahl Mikkelsen** -- American cartoonist
1922   **Sekou Toure** -- First president of the Republic of Guinea
1922   **Vic Mizzy** -- American composer and author, noted for songs
        such as "The Whole World Is Singing My Song," "Three Little
        Sisters," "My Dreams Are Getting Better All the Time," and
        "The Jones Boy"
1934   **Bart Starr** -- Professional football superstar
1935   **Bob Denver** — American actor noted for his role as Gilligan in
        the long-running television series, *Gilligan's Island*
1936   **Ralph Terry** -- Professional baseball player
1941   **Joan Baez** -- Noted American folk singer and guitarist
1941   **Susannah York** -- English stage, screen, and television actress
1944   **Jimmy Page** — British guitarist with the Led Zeppelin musical group
1950   **Bob Newhouse** -- Professional football player
1951   **Crystal Gayle** -- American country singer

1953   **Ivan De Jesus** -- Professional baseball player

JANUARY 9 -- EVENTS

1324   Marco Polo, the famous Venetian traveler, died in Venice at approximately 70 years of age.

1580   John Smith, the future captain of the English colony in Jamestown, Virginia, was baptized.

1788   Connecticut ratified the Constitution, becoming the 5th state of the Union.

1793   The first successful balloon flight in the U.S. originated in Philadelphia with George Washington, Thomas Jefferson, John Adams, Henry Clay, and Paul Revere in the audience.

1799   The world's first successful income tax was introduced, by English Prime Minister William Pitt to help finance the war between Britain and France.

1839   Louis Jacques Daguerre, the French inventor and painter, announced his perfection of the technique of making daguerreotypes, the first popular form of photography.

1861   Mississippi seceded from the Union, the second state, after South Carolina, to do so.

1873   Victoria Woodhull, the famous free love advocate, labeled the Reverend Henry Ward Beecher an adulterer in a speech in New York, repeating charges she had made earlier in print.

1942   The U.S. Joint Chiefs of Staff was created.

1945   Allied troops invaded the Philippine Island of Luzon in World War II, fulfilling General MacArthur's promise, "I shall return."

1960   Construction began on the Aswan High Dam in the Nile River in Egypt.

1970   The *Cosmos 318* space vehicle was launched by Russia.

1977   The Oakland Raiders beat the Minnesota Vikings, 32-14, in Super Bowl XI in Pasadena, California.

JANUARY 10 -- BIRTHDAYS

1480   **Margaret of Austria** -- Duchess of Savoy

1538   **Louis of Nassau** -- Leader of the Netherlands revolt in 1581 against Spain

1737   **Ethan Allen** — American patriot and soldier who led the Green Mountain Boys in the capture of Fort Ticonderoga from the British in the Revolutionary War

1760   Johann Zumsteeg -- German composer and conductor

1769   Michel Ney -- The most famous of Napoleon's generals

1834   Lord Acton (John E.E.D. Acton) -- British historian best remembered for his statement, "Power tends to corrupt and absolute power corrupts absolutely"

1843   Frank James -- Noted American Western outlaw of the late 1800s, and brother of the famous outlaw Jesse James

1850   John W. Root -- American architect noted for works such as Chicago's Rookery building (1886)

1862   Walter Travis -- Hall of Fame golfer

1883   Francis X. Bushman -- America's first screen idol, in the pre-1920s, whose acting career spanned 60 years

1887   Robinson Jeffers -- American poet noted for works such as "Tamar" (1924) and "Medea" (1946)

1889   John Held Jr. -- American illustrator and cartoonist noted for his *New Yorker* magazine cartoons and for the strip *Merely Margy*

1898   Arthur James Johnston -- American composer, conductor, and pianist, noted for songs such as "Cocktails for Two," "Troubled Waters," "One, Two, Button Your Shoe," and "Pennies from Heaven"

1904   Ray Bolger -- American dancer and actor, who played the scarecrow in *The Wizard of Oz*

1908   Paul Henreid -- Austrian-American stage and motion-picture actor and director

1910   Galina Ulanova -- Russian prima ballerina

1927   Gisele MacKenzie -- Canadian singer

1927   Johnnie Ray -- American singer, composer, and author, noted for songs such as "The Little White Cloud That Cried"

1931   Marlene Sanders -- American broadcast journalist

1938   Willie McCovey -- Hall of Fame baseball player who hit over 400 career home runs

1938   Frank Mahovlich -- Professional hockey player and superstar

1938   Sherrill Milnes -- American opera singer

1939   William Toomey -- American decathlon champion

1939   Sal Mineo -- American stage, screen, and television actor

1943   Jim Croce -- American rock singer and songwriter, noted for works such as "Bad, Bad Leroy Brown"

1944   Frank Sinatra Jr. -- American singer and son of the noted crooner

1945   Rod Stewart -- British rock singer and musician

1949   George Foreman -- World heavyweight boxing champion, 1973-1974

1953   **Pat Benatar** -- American singer
1959   **Dick Dotson** -- Professional baseball player

JANUARY 10 -- EVENTS

1356   Holy Roman Emperor Charles IV had the Reichstag of Nuremberg pass an act regulating imperial elections. This act became a part of the famous Golden Bull issued in December, 1356.
1645   Archbishop William Laud of the Church of England was beheaded for treason on orders of the Long Parliament.
1776   Thomas Paine published his famous pamphlet *Common Sense*, which played a principal role in leading the American colonies to revolt.
1861   Florida seceded from the Union, and later joined the Confederacy.
1870   The Standard Oil Company was incorporated by John D. Rockefeller.
1901   Oil was first discovered in Texas, near Beaumont.
1917   Buffalo Bill Cody, the great frontiersman of the American West, died at age 70.
1920   The League of Nations was established, with headquarters in Geneva, Switzerland.
1925   "Ma" Ferguson was sworn in as governor of Texas, the second woman governor in U.S. history, after Nellie Tayloe Ross of Wyoming (1925).
1929   The comic strip, *Little Annie Rooney*, by Brandon Walsh, first appeared.
1946   The first United Nations General Assembly met, in London.
1946   Man first made contact with the moon, as radar signals were bounced off the lunar surface.
1984   The United States and the Vatican established diplomatic relations after a break of 117 years.

JANUARY 11 -- BIRTHDAYS

1503   **Francesco Mazzuolli Parmigianino** -- Italian painter
1755   **Alexander Hamilton** – Brilliant American statesman and first secretary of the treasury
1807   **Ezra Cornell** -- American businessman, philanthropist, founder of Western Union Telegraph Company, and a guiding force in the establishment of Cornell University

1815   **Sir John MacDonald** – First prime minister of the Dominion of Canada, 1867-1873, and later in 1878-1891

1842   **William James** -- American philosopher and psychologist, author of the classic work, *The Principles of Psychology* (1890), and brother of the famous novelist Henry James

1859   **Lord George Curzon** -- British foreign secretary noted for the Curzon Line between Poland and Russia

1870   **Alice Rice** -- Author of *Mrs. Wiggs and the Cabbage Patch*

1872   **Wilfred Baddeley** – British tennis player and Wimbledon singles champion in 1891, 1892, and 1895

1873   **Dwight Whitney Morrow** -- American lawyer, diplomat, U.S. ambassador to Mexico, and father of poet Anne Morrow (Mrs. Charles A. Lindbergh)

1876   **Elmer Flick** -- Hall of Fame baseball player

1890   **Monte Blue** -- American motion-picture actor in over 200 films, beginning with *The Birth of a Nation* in 1915

1890   **Max Carey** -- Hall of Fame baseball player

1895   **Laurens Hammond** -- American inventor noted for the development of the electric organ

1897   **Bernard DeVoto** -- American writer, editor, and critic, who won the Pulitzer Prize in 1948 for *Across the Wide Missouri*

1899   **Eva Le Gallienne** – English actress, theatrical director, and producer

1903   **Alan Paton** --South African writer and author of *Cry, the Beloved Country* (1948)

1905   **Oveta Culp Hobby** -- First secretary of Health, Education, and Welfare (1953-1955)

1907   **Pierre Mendès-France** -- French premier of the Fourth Republic in the 1950s

1910   **Schoolboy Rowe** -- Professional baseball player

1911   **Zenko Suzuki** -- Post-World War II prime minister of Japan

1911   **Jumping Jack McCracken** -- Hall of Fame basketball player

1912   **Don "Red" Barry** – American motion-picture actor who was for many years one of the "Top Ten Money-Making Western Stars"

1915   **Veda Ann Borg** -- American motion-picture actress whose name has become a favorite quiz item among nostalgia buffs

1921   **Juanita Kreps** -- Secretary of Commerce under President Carter

1928   **David Wolper** – American film executive and founder of Wolper Productions

1929   **Rod Taylor** – Australian-born motion-picture and television actor

1934   **Gerald Rafshoon** -- American political media expert

1941   **Bobby Goldsboro** -- American singer and songwriter
1942   **George Mira** -- Professional football player
1946   **Naomi Judd** -- American country singer and partner with her daughter Wynonna in the mother and daughter Judd duo
1948   **Madeline Manning** -- Professional runner
1949   **Chris Ford** -- Professional basketball player
1951   **Brenda Kirk** -- South African tennis player
1952   **Ben Crenshaw** -- Professional golfer and superstar
1953   **Freddie Solomon** -- Professional football player
1954   **Gary Brokaw** -- Professional basketball player
1957   **Darryl Dawkins** -- Professional basketball player

JANUARY 11 -- EVENTS

1861   Alabama seceded from the Union and declared itself the Republic of Alabama, before later joining the Confederacy.
1878   Milk was delivered for the first time in glass bottles, by New York milkman Alexander Campbell.
1913   The *sedan*, a four-door automobile, was first introduced, at the National Automobile Show in New York, by the Hudson Car Company.
1915   Brewer Jacob Ruppert and engineer Tillinghast Houston purchased the New York Yankees franchise for $460,000, and began building it into baseball's greatest dynasty.
1923   France and Belgium occupied the Ruhr valley to force Germany to pay World War I reparations.
1928   Thomas Hardy, the great English novelist, died at Max Gate, near Dorchester, at age 87.
1935   American aviatrix Amelia Earhart left Honolulu for Oakland, California, to become the first woman to fly solo across the Pacific Ocean.
1942   The Japanese invaded the Netherlands East Indies in World War II.
1964   Surgeon General Luther L. Terry linked cigarette smoking to cancer.
1966   Alberto Giacometti, the noted Swiss sculptor, died at Chur, Switzerland, at age 64.
1970   The Kansas City Chiefs beat the Minnesota Vikings, 23-7, in Super Bowl IV in New Orleans.
1973   The Watergate break-in trial began in Washington, D.C.
1975   The Russians launched *Soyuz 17* with two cosmonauts aboard.

JANUARY 12 -- BIRTHDAYS

1588   **John Winthrop** -- Puritan governor of the Massachusetts Bay Colony, 1629-1630

1591   **Jusepe de Ribera** — Spanish artist nicknamed "Lo Spagnoletto" (Little Spaniard) in Italy where he spent most of his life, and noted for his paintings of Christian martyrs and saints

1628   **Charles Perrault** -- French poet and fairy-tale writer, best known for the famous collection, *Mother Goose Tales* (1697)

1729   **Edmund Burke** — Noted British statesman, orator, and writer, whose ideas became the philosophy of the British Conservative Party

1729   **Lazzaro Spallanzani** -- Italian experimental biologist, who was the first to show that the air carries microscopic life

1737   **John Hancock** — American patriot who was the first to sign the Declaration of Independence, writing his name boldly so "King George could read it without his spectacles"

1746   **Johann Heinrich Pestalozzi** -- Pioneer Swiss educator and great contributor to the development of educational practices and theory

1751   **Ferdinand IV** -- King of Naples

1810   **Ferdinand II** -- King of Sicily

1852   **Joseph Jacques Cesaire Joffre** — French World War I general and the first French soldier to be named Marshal of France

1853   **Curbastro Gregorio Ricci** -- Italian mathematician noted as the developer of tensor analysis

1854   **Albert Nelson Marquis** -- American publisher

1856   **John Singer Sargent** -- American painter best known for his portraits of fashionable people

1876   **Feozi Cakmak** -- Turkish marshal and statesman

1876   **Jack London** — American author noted for works such as *The Call of the Wild* (1903) and *The Sea Wolf* (1904)

1878   **Ferenc Molnar** -- Hungarian playwright and novelist, known for *Liliom* (1903) and *The Paul Street Boys* (1907)

1879   **Ray Harroun** — Winner of the first Indianapolis 500 automobile race (in 1911)

1884   **William Barr Friedlander** -- American composer noted for songs such as "Nikki" and "Araby"

1891   **Raeburn Van Buren** -- American comic strip writer and creator with Al Capp of *Abbie an' Slats* (1937)

1893   **Hermann Goering** -- German World War II air force commander and second to Adolf Hitler as a leader of Nazi Germany

1893   **Alfred Rosenberg** – Ideologist of the German Nazi movement

1895   **Bo McMillin** -- Hall of Fame football player

1899   **Fritz Crisler** -- Noted college football coach

1904   **Edgar Delange** – American composer noted for songs such as "Along the Navajo Trail," "A String of Pearls," and "All This and Heaven, Too"

1905   **Tex Ritter** -- American singer, cowboy actor, and "America's Most Beloved Cowboy" of the 1930s and 1940s

1910   **Luise Rainer** -- Austrian stage and motion-picture actress, who won two consecutive Academy Awards, for *The Great Ziegfield* (1936) and *The Good Earth* (1937)

1915   **Martin Agronsky** -- American broadcast journalist

1916   **Pieter Willem Botha** -- Prime minister of South Africa who succeeded Balthazar Johannes Vorster in 1978

1926   **Ray Price** -- American country music singer

1930   **James Farmer** -- American civil rights leader of the 1960s

1940   **Bob Hewitt** -- South African tennis player

1944   **Joe Frazier** – World heavyweight boxing champion, 1970-1973

1947   **Tom Dempsey** -- Professional football player who once kicked a 63-yard field goal

1949   **James W. Dietz** -- Professional rower

1950   **Patrice Dominguez** -- French tennis player

1950   **Randy Jones** -- Professional baseball player

1951   **Bill Madlock** -- Professional baseball player

1951   **Drew Pearson** -- Professional football superstar

1952   **Campy Russell** -- Professional basketball player

1953   **Terry Whitfield** -- Professional baseball player

1960   **Mike Marshall** -- Professional baseball player

1960   **Dominique Wilkins** -- Professional basketball player

JANUARY 12 -- EVENTS

532 AD The second Cathedral of Santa Sophia in Constantinople was destroyed by fire in the Nika insurrection.

1519   Holy Roman Emperor Maximilian I died at Augsburg, Germany, at age 60.

1687   Robert Cavalier, Sieur de La Salle, the distinguished French explorer, began his last exploration, on the coast of Texas.

1755   Moscow University was established by Czarina Elizabeth Petrovna.

1773	The first public museum in America was established, in Charleston, South Carolina.
1848	The Italian Revolution began in Sicily, the first of a number of 1848 European revolutions that ended the old political order.
1918	The Distinguished Service Medal was instituted by Congress.
1932	Mrs. Hattie Caraway of Arkansas became the first woman to be elected to the U.S. Senate.
1969	The New York Jets beat the Baltimore Colts, 16-7, in Super Bowl III in Miami. Jets quarterback Joe Namath "guaranteed" the victory before the game started.
1971	The long-running comedy, *All in the Family*, premiered on CBS television.
1975	The Pittsburgh Steelers beat the Minnesota Vikings, 16-6, in Super Bowl IX in New Orleans.
1976	The great English mystery writer Agatha Christie died at age 85.
1986	The space shuttle *Columbia* was launched with a crew of 7 including Bill Nelson, the first U.S. Representative to fly in space.

JANUARY 13 -- BIRTHDAYS

1381	**Saint Colette** -- Founder of the Coletine Poor Clares
1596	**Jan Josephszoon Van Goyen** -- Dutch painter who specialized in painting landscapes
1749	**Charles James Fox** -- Brilliant English statesman who supported the American colonies in their fight for independence
1804	**Gavarni** -- French caricaturist, lithographer, and illustrator (born Sulpice Guillaume Chevalier)
1808	**Salmon P. Chase** – U.S. statesman who was secretary of the treasury under President Lincoln and later Chief Justice of the Supreme Court
1834	**Horatio Alger** -- American author of more than 100 "rags-to-riches" books, such as *Ragged Dick* (1867) and *Tattered Tom* (1871)
1867	**Francis Everett Townsend** -- American physician who proposed the Townsend Plan, an old-age pension for all citizens over 60, in the 1930s
1882	**Domenico Savino** – Italian-born composer and conductor, noted for songs such as "Anchors Aweigh"
1884	**Sophie Tucker** -- American stage actress and "the last of the red hot mamas"
1885	**James V. Monaco** -- Italian-born composer and pianist, noted for songs such as "You Made Me Love You," "Six Lessons From Madam La Zonga," "I'm Making Believe," and "I Can't Begin to Tell You"

1886	**A.H. Ross** -- Inventor of the net and puck used in the National Hockey League

1886   **A.H. Ross** -- Inventor of the net and puck used in the National Hockey League

1890   **Elmer Davis** -- American news broadcaster and writer of the 1940s and 1950s

1903   **Kay Francis** -- American stage and motion-picture actress in over 60 films

1904   **Richard Addinsell** -- English composer best known for his *Warsaw Concerto*

1919   **Robert Stack** -- American motion-picture and television actor, who was "the first boy to kiss Deanna Durbin" in *First Love* (1939)

1925   **Gwen Verdon** -- American singer and actress, and top star of Broadway musicals in the 1950s

1931   **Charles Nelson Reilly** -- American actor and director

1933   **Tom Gola** -- Professional basketball player

1933   **Frank Gallo** -- American artist

1950   **Bob Forsch** -- Professional baseball player

1962   **Kevin Mitchell** -- Professional baseball player

JANUARY 13 -- EVENTS

1733   James Oglethorpe arrived at Charleston, South Carolina, with a charter to establish a colony in Georgia.

1864   Stephen Foster, the great American songwriter, died in New York at age 37 a few days after writing "Beautiful Dreamer."

1898   French novelist Emile Zola's famous headline "J'accuse" appeared in the French newspaper *L'Aurore*, charging that Alfred Dreyfus was unjustly convicted in the Dreyfus trial.

1930   The comic strip, *Mickey Mouse*, by Walt Disney, first appeared.

1941   James Joyce, the great Irish novelist, died in Zurich at age 58.

1947   The comic strip, *Steve Canyon*, by Milton Caniff, first appeared.

1953   The Russian government announced the arrest of nine Soviet physicians accused of plotting to kill leading Communist officials in the "Doctors' Plot."

1964   "I Want to Hold Your Hand," the first Beatles' record in America, was released by Capitol Records.

1974   The Miami Dolphins won their second straight Super Bowl, beating the Minnesota Vikings, 24-7, in Super Bowl VIII in New Orleans.

1978   U.S. Senator and former Vice President Hubert H. Humphrey died of cancer at age 66.

JANUARY 14 -- BIRTHDAYS

1131   **Waldemar I** -- King of Denmark, 1157-1182

1730   **William Whipple** -- American Revolutionary War general and New Hampshire signer of the Declaration of Independence

1741   **Benedict Arnold** -- American Revolutionary War general and the most infamous traitor in American history

1791   **Calvin Phillips** -- The shortest recorded adult male, at 26½ inches tall

1806   **Matthew Fontaine Maury** -- U.S. naval officer and scientist, whose wind and current charts of the oceans resulted in his being called the "Pathfinder of the Seas"

1836   **Henri Fantin-Latour** -- French painter and printmaker noted for his still lifes with flowers and for his portraits

1841   **Berthe Morisot** -- French painter

1847   **The Reverend Wilson Carlile** – Founder of the Church Army, a group of laymen in the Anglican Church concerned with social work as much as with the work of preaching

1850   **Pierre Loti** – French novelist noted for works such as *An Iceland Fisherman* (1886)

1863   **R.F. Outcault** -- American cartoonist and creator of *Buster Brown* and the first true comic strip, *At the Circus in Hogan's Alley*, featuring the Yellow Kid

1866   **Robert L. MacCameron** -- American painter

1874   **Thornton Waldo Burgess** – American author of children's books, best known for his stories about Peter Rabbit

1875   **Albert Schweitzer** -- Brilliant German philosopher, physician, musician, clergyman, missionary, and writer

1886   **Hugh Lofting** -- English-born writer and creator of Dr. Doolittle

1892   **Hal Roach** -- Pioneer American motion-picture producer and director whose career spanned over 50 years

1896   **John Dos Passos** – American novelist noted for works such as *Three Soldiers* (1921) and the trilogy, *U.S.A.* (1930, 1932, and 1936)

1901   **Bebe Daniels** -- American motion-picture actress who was one of the most popular stars of the silent era and also a leading lady of the talkies

1901   **Carlos Romulo** – Filipino diplomat and author, who served as president of the U.N. General Assembly in 1949

1909   **Joseph Losey** -- American motion-picture director with a career of over 40 years

1919   **Giulio Andreotti** -- Prime minister of Italy, 1972-1973

1919   **Andy Rooney** – American writer, producer, and television entertainer

1920   **George Herman** -- American broadcast journalist

1926   **Tom Tryon** – American motion-picture and television actor, screenwriter, and novelist

1938   **Jack Jones** -- American singer

1940   **Julian Bond** -- American state legislator (Georgia) and civil rights leader

1941   **Faye Dunaway** – American stage and motion-picture actress, and Academy Award winner in 1976 for *Network*

1947   **Gene Washington** -- Professional football player

1951   **Derrel Thomas** -- Professional baseball player

1952   **Terry Forster** -- Professional baseball player

JANUARY 14 -- EVENTS

1639   The Connecticut Colony adopted its first constitution, the "Fundamental Orders," which was the first written constitution in history.

1742   English astronomer Edmund Halley, for whom Halley's Comet was named, died at age 85.

1784   Congress ratified the peace treaty with Great Britain granting independence to the American Colonies.

1898   The great English author Lewis Carroll (Charles L. Dodgson) died 13 days before his 66th birthday.

1900   Giacomo Puccini's great opera *Tosca* had its world premiere at Rome's Teatro Costanzi.

1914   Henry Ford inaugurated his assembly line technique of manufacturing cars. With this new procedure, Ford workers were able to build a Model T in an hour and a half.

1943   President Franklin D. Roosevelt and Prime Minister Winston Churchill opened the Casablanca Conference in World War II.

1952   The *Today* show made its debut on NBC television stations, with Dave Garroway serving as host.

1954   The Nash and Hudson automobile companies merged to become American Motors.

1954   Joe DiMaggio, the great baseball player, and Marilyn Monroe, the star movie actress, were married in San Francisco's City Hall.

1957   Humphrey Bogart, the great motion-picture actor and screen legend, died in his sleep in Hollywood just short of his 58th birthday.

1964   In her first television appearance since the assassination of
        President Kennedy, former first lady Jacqueline Kennedy thanked
        the public for some 800,000 messages of sympathy.

1968   The Green Bay Packers beat the Oakland Raiders, 33-14, in
        Super Bowl II in Miami.

1973   The Miami Dolphins beat the Washington Redskins, 14-7, in
        Super Bowl VII in Los Angeles.

JANUARY 15 -- BIRTHDAYS

1622   **Moliere** -- French dramatist, born Jean Baptiste Poquelin, who
        was the greatest French writer of comedy

1654   **Paul Potter** -- Dutch painter and etcher

1675   **Duc de Saint-Simon** -- French memoirist and courtier (born
        Louis de Rouvroy)

1716   **Philip Livingston** -- A New York signer of the Declaration of
        Independence and member of the Continental Congress

1803   **Nathan Marcus Adler** -- Chief rabbi of the British Empire and
        founder of Jew's College and the United Synagogue

1809   **Pierre Joseph Proudhon** – French socialist, reformer, and writer,
        who believed in anarchism, a social order without government

1823   **Mathew B. Brady** -- Noted pioneer American photographer
        who became famous for his photographic record of the Civil War

1877   **Lewis Madison Terman** -- American psychologist, who devel-
        oped the Stanford-Binet Intelligence Tests

1891   **Ray Chapman** -- The only professional baseball player ever
        killed by being hit with a pitched ball, by Carl Mays in 1920

1891   **Osip Emilyevich Mandelstam** -- Russian poet

1892   **Hobey Baker** -- Hall of Fame hockey player

1899   **Goodman Ace** -- American comedian

1902   **Saud** -- Saudi Arabia's second king, 1953-1964, after his father
        Ibn Saud

1905   **Allie Wrubel** -- American composer and author, noted for songs
        such as "Zipa-Dee-Doo-Dah," "The Lady from Twenty-Nine
        Palms," "I'll Buy That Dream," and "Music, Maestro, Please"

1908   **Edward Teller** -- Hungarian-born American physicist and father
        of the hydrogen bomb

1909   **Gene Krupa** -- American drummer of the Big Band Era of the
        1930s and 1940s

1913   **Lloyd Bridges** -- American stage, screen, and television actor,
        with a career of over 40 years

1918   **Gamal Abdul Nasser** – Egyptian nationalist who led the revolt that overthrew King Faruk and established Egypt as a republic, and who served as prime minister and president, 1954-1970

1920   **Bob Davies** -- Professional basketball player

1926   **Rod MacLeish** -- American journalist and news commentator

1929   **Martin Luther King Jr.** -- The greatest of the American civil rights leaders of the 1950s and 1960s, who received the 1964 Nobel Peace Prize for his "nonviolent resistance" struggle for equal rights

1930   **Joe Grabowski** -- Professional basketball player

1933   **Ernest Gaines** -- American novelist noted for *The Autobiography of Miss Jane Pittman*

1934   **Walter Marks** -- American composer and author, noted for songs such as "I've Gotta Be Me," "Getting On," and "Must It Be Love?"

1937   **Margaret O'Brien** – Noted child star of Hollywood films of the 1940s, who won an Academy Award in 1944 as the "Outstanding Child Actress" of her day

1941   **Captain Beefheart (Don Van Vleit)** -- American rock singer

1943   **Mike Marshall** -- Professional baseball player

1949   **Bobby Grich** -- Professional baseball player

1949   **Howard Twitty** -- Professional golfer

1951   **Ernie Digregorio** -- Professional basketball player

1951   **Charo** -- Mexican actress and singer

1953   **Randy White** -- Professional football player

JANUARY 15 -- EVENTS

69 AD   Otho was proclaimed Emperor of Rome.

1559   Queen Elizabeth I of England was crowned in Westminster Abbey.

1701   Prussia was proclaimed a kingdom.

1759   The British Museum, the oldest of the great national museums, was opened to the public in Montague House in London, a site it still occupies.

1777   Vermont settlers declared their territory the independent republic of New Connecticut. The name was changed to Vermont the following July.

1842   The University of Notre Dame was founded by a group of French missionaries headed by the Reverend Edward F. Sorin.

1870   The donkey symbol of the Democratic Party first appeared, in a cartoon by Thomas Nast, depicting "a live Jackass kicking a dead lion."

1879   Gilbert and Sullivan's *HMS Pinafore* had its U.S. debut.

1890   The *Sleeping Beauty* ballet, by Peter Ilich Tchaikovsky, had its premiere at the Maryinski Theater in St. Petersburg.

1896   Mathew Brady, the great pioneer photographer of 21 United States presidents, died in poverty in New York at an approximate age of 73.

1919   Ignace Paderewski, the great pianist and statesman, became the first premier of the newly created state of Poland.

1929   The U.S. ratified the Kellogg-Briand Peace Pact, which condemned the use of war to solve international problems.

1943   The Pentagon, the world's largest office building, was completed, on the Virginia side of the Potomac River in Arlington.

1953   President Harry S Truman made his farewell address to the nation.

1967   Professional football's Super Bowl I was played in Los Angeles with the Green Bay Packers defeating the Kansas City Chiefs, 35-10.

1972   Margrethe II was proclaimed Queen of Denmark, as she became the first reigning queen in Denmark's history.

1978   The Dallas Cowboys beat the Denver Broncos, 27-10, in Super Bowl XII in New Orleans.

JANUARY 16 -- BIRTHDAYS

1409   **Rene I** -- King of Naples, Sicily, and Jerusalem

1749   **Vittorio Alfieri** — Italian dramatist and poet, noted for works such as *Filippo* (1775), *Saul* (1782), and *Oreste* (1786)

1752   **George Cabot** -- American Federalist Party leader

1757   **Samuel McIntire** -- American architect

1767   **Anders Gustav Ekeberg** -- Swedish chemist and discoverer in 1802 of the element tantalum

1815   **Henry W. Halleck** -- U.S. military scholar and Union general in the Civil War

1853   **Andre Michelin** -- French industrialist and co-founder with his brother Edouard of the Michelin Tire Company, noted for the world's first pneumatic automobile tires (1895)

1870   **Jimmy Collins** -- Hall of Fame baseball player

1874   **Robert William Service** -- Canadian poet and author of "The Shooting of Dan McGrew"

1878   **Harry Carey** -- American motion-picture actor in almost 400 films, called by the noted director John Ford the "bright star of the early Western sky"

1894	**Irving Mills** -- American composer, author, and singer, noted for songs such as "When My Sugar Walks Down the Street," "Sophisticated Lady," "Mood Indigo," and "Moon Glow"
1897	**Joseph Bodis** -- Hall of Fame bowler
1901	**Fulgencio Batista** -- Cuban dictator who was deposed by Fidel Castro in 1959
1907	**Alexander Knox** – Canadian actor and writer with a 40-year career
1909	**Ethel Merman** – American singer and actress with a career of over 50 years
1911	**Dizzy Dean** -- Hall of Fame baseball pitcher who won 30 games in 1934
1911	**Eduardo Frei** -- First Christian Democratic president of Chile
1928	**William Kennedy** -- American author noted for his Pulitzer Prize-winning novel *Ironweed* (1983)
1930	**Norman Podhoretz** -- American author and editor
1934	**Marilyn Horne** -- American operatic soprano
1935	**A.J. Foyt** -- American automobile racing driver and four times winner of the Indianapolis 500
1941	**Christine Janes** -- English tennis player
1942	**Barbara Lynn** -- American soul singer and guitarist
1946	**Ronnie Milsap** -- American country singer
1948	**Peter Kanderal** -- Australian tennis player
1948	**John Carpenter** -- American motion-picture director
1954	**Dave Stapleton** -- Professional baseball player
1957	**Steve Balboni** -- Professional baseball player
1960	**Sade (Adu)** -- Nigerian-English vocalist

JANUARY 16 -- EVENTS

1066	Harold II became the last Anglo-Saxon king of England.
1493	Columbus sailed from Samana Bay in present-day Haiti, starting his return trip on his first voyage to America.
1547	Ivan IV became the first Russian ruler to be crowned Czar (Caesar).
1556	Charles V, Holy Roman Emperor and King of Spain, abdicated rule of Spain.
1599	Edmund Spenser, the great English poet and author of *The Faerie Queene*, died in London at an approximate age of 47.
1778	France recognized the independence of the United States.

1794   Edward Gibbon, the great British historian, died in London at age 56.

1883   The U.S. Civil Service System was established.

1896   The University of Chicago defeated the University of Iowa, 15-12, in Iowa City, Iowa, in a basketball game that established the five-man basketball team.

1920   The 18th Amendment to the Constitution went into effect, prohibiting the sale of alcoholic beverages in the U.S.

1939   *Superman*, by Jerry Siegel and Joe Shuster, first appeared in newspapers.

1942   Carole Lombard, noted screen actress and wife of actor Clark Gable, was killed in a plane crash on Table Mountain, Nevada, near Las Vegas.

1964   The long-running musical *Hello, Dolly!* starring Carol Channing opened on Broadway.

1972   The Dallas Cowboys beat the Miami Dolphins, 24-3, in Super Bowl VI in New Orleans.

1979   Shah Mohammed Reza Pahlavi left Iran on "vacation," never to return.

JANUARY 17 -- BIRTHDAYS

1342   **Philip the Bold** -- Duke of Burgundy and youngest son of French king John II (the Good), who ruled France as regent for his nephew Charles VI (1380-1422)

1504   **Pius V** -- Roman Catholic pope, 1566-1572, who was made a saint in 1712

1600   **Pedro Calderon de la Barca** -- The successor of Lope de Vega as the leading Spanish playwright, and the author of works such as *Life Is a Dream* (1635)

1657   **Peeter van Bloemen** -- Flemish painter

1706   **Benjamin Franklin** -- American statesman, inventor, one of the most admired men of the Western world during his time, and one of the half-dozen greatest Americans of all time

1732   **Stanislaw Poniatowski** -- The last king of an independent Poland (1764)

1771   **Charles Brockden Brown** -- America's first important novelist, and the first American to make literature his major profession

1806   **James Madison Randolph** – Grandson of President Thomas Jefferson, and the first baby born in the White House

1820   **Anne Bronte** -- English novelist noted for *Agnes Grey* (1847) and *The Tenant of Wildfell Hall* (1848), and sister of novelists Emily and Charlotte Bronte

1834   **August Weismann** -- German biologist known chiefly for his theories of heredity and evolution

1863   **David Lloyd George** -- British prime minister during World War I

1871   **Earl Beatty David** -- First Sea Lord of England

1876   **Frank Hague** -- Jersey City mayor and political boss, noted for the remark, "I am the law in Jersey City"

1880   **Mack Sennett** -- American pioneer director, producer, and actor, who was the father of American slapstick motion pictures and the creator of the famous Keystone Kops

1884   **Noah Beery** -- American stage and motion-picture actor, brother of actor Wallace Beery, and father of actor Noah Beery Jr.

1886   **Ronald Firbank** -- English novelist

1886   **Glenn L. Martin** -- American pioneer airplane designer and manufacturer, whose Martin B-10 bomber was standard in the Army Air Force for many years

1899   **Al Capone** – American gangster who controlled the Chicago underworld in the 1920s

1899   **Robert Maynard Hutchins** – American educator and administrator who was noted for his unconventional theories about higher education

1899   **Nevil Shute** -- English novelist noted for works such as *Pied Piper* (1942) and *On the Beach* (1957)

1911   **Jackson Busher** -- Hall of Fame hockey player

1917   **Ulysses Simpson Kay** -- American composer

1922   **Nicholas Katzenbach** – U.S. attorney general under President Lyndon Johnson

1924   **Betty White** -- American comedienne and actress

1928   **Vidal Sassoon** -- English hairdresser and designer

1929   **Jacques Plante** -- Hall of Fame hockey player

1931   **James Earl Jones** -- American stage, screen, and television actor

1931   **Don Zimmer** -- Professional baseball player and manager

1933   **Sheree North** -- American stage, screen, and television actress

1934   **Shari Lewis** -- Noted American puppeteer

1942   **Muhammad Ali (Cassius Clay)** -- One of the greatest world heavyweight boxing champions, who held the title an unprecedented three times, in the 1960s and 1970s

1945   **Preston Pearson** -- Professional football player

1948   **Mick Taylor** -- British guitarist with the Rolling Stones, 1969-
        1974
1949   **Andy Kaufman** -- American comedian and actor
1952   **Darrell Porter** -- Professional baseball player
1953   **Mark Littell** -- Professional baseball player
1956   **Paul Young** -- British vocalist
1960   **Chili Davis** -- Professional baseball player

JANUARY 17 -- EVENTS

395 AD The Roman Empire was split into eastern and western parts
        upon the death of Emperor Theodosius I, whose will provided
        that his two sons would inherit the two parts.
1793   French King Louis XVI was condemned to death by the Na-
        tional Convention. He was guillotined four days later.
1794   Andrew Jackson and Rachel Donelson Robards were remarried
        in Nashville, Tennessee, after learning that their first marriage
        was invalid.
1893   Rutherford B. Hayes died in Fremont, Ohio, at age 70.
1917   The U.S. bought the Virgin Islands from Denmark for $25 million.
1925   "The business of America is business," proclaimed President
        Calvin Coolidge to a group of businessmen.
1929   Popeye the Sailor made his debut as a character in E.C. Segar's
        comic strip, *Thimble Theater*.
1945   Warsaw was liberated from the Nazis by Soviet and Polish
        soldiers in World War II.
1950   Eleven bandits robbed the Brink's headquarters in Boston of
        $2.5 million. They were apprehended nearly six years later, just
        a week before the statute of limitations expired.
1961   Patrice Lumumba, the first president of the Congo, was mur-
        dered by unknown assailants.
1961   In his farewell address, President Dwight D. Eisenhower warned
        the nation against the rise of the "military-industrial complex."
1971   The Baltimore Colts beat the Dallas Cowboys, 16-13, in Super
        Bowl V in Miami.

JANUARY 18 -- BIRTHDAYS

1689   **Montesquieu** -- Outstanding French political philosopher, whose
        major work, *The Spirit of the Laws* (1748), greatly influenced the
        writing of the U.S. Constitution

1754   **Vicente Martin y Soler** -- Spanish composer

1779   **Peter Mark Roget** -- British physician and scholar who invented the slide rule, but is best known as the compiler of Roget's *Thesaurus of English Words and Phrases* (1852)

1782   **Daniel Webster** -- The best-known American orator, and one of the ablest lawyers and statesmen of his time

1813   **Joseph Farwell Glidden** -- American farmer noted for the invention in 1873 of barbed wire

1841   **Emmanuel Chabrier** -- French composer noted for works such as *Espana* (1883) and the music for *The Reluctant King* (1887)

1854   **Thomas Augustine Watson** -- Alexander Graham Bell's assistant who first heard Bell's words, "Mr. Watson, come here. I want you," on his newly invented telephone in 1875

1863   **Konstantin Stanislavski** -- Well-known Russian stage director and actor, whose attempt to have the actor live the life of the character became known as the "Stanislavski method"

1867   **Ruben Dario** -- Nicaraguan poet and short-story writer, who was one of the most important poets in the Spanish language

1879   **Henri Honore Giraud** -- French World War II general selected by the Allies as French leader in North Africa

1882   **A.A. Milne** -- English writer noted for his Winnie-the-Pooh stories

1886   **Antoine Pevsner** -- Russian-born painter and sculptor noted for works such as *Construction in the Egg* (1948) and *Peace Column* (1954)

1887   **W. Franke Harling** -- English-born composer and conductor, noted for songs such as "Beyond the Blue Horizon"

1888   **Sir Thomas Octave Murdoch Sopwith** -- British aircraft designer and founder of the Sopwith Aviation Company, Ltd. (1912)

1892   **Oliver Hardy** -- Member with Stan Laurel of the Laurel and Hardy team, the most fabulously successful comedy duo the screen has ever known

1894   **Richard E. Berlin** -- American newspaper publisher and president of the Hearst Corporation

1896   **Art Kassel** -- American composer, author, and conductor, noted for songs such as "Don't Let Julia Foolya" and "You Never Say Yes, You Never Say No"

1904   **Cary Grant** -- American motion-picture actor and perennial favorite of movie audiences for more than three decades

1908   **Jacob Bronowski** -- Polish-American mathematician, author, and television host

1913   **Danny Kaye** -- American comedian, actor, and superstar in a career of more than 40 years

1922   **Constance Moore** -- American band vocalist, radio singer, and motion-picture actress

1925   **Sol Yurick** -- American novelist

1932   **Joe Schmidt** -- Professional football player and coach

1938   **Curt Flood** -- Professional baseball player whose lawsuit led to the modification of baseball's reserve clause and allowed players to negotiate new contracts periodically

1950   **Pat Sullivan** -- Professional football player

1954   **Scott McGregor** -- Professional baseball player

1957   **Tom Bailey** – British musician and singer with the Thompson Twins musical group

JANUARY 18 -- EVENTS

1486   King Henry VII of England married Elizabeth of York, uniting the Houses of Lancaster and York.

1535   Francisco Pizarro, the Spanish conquistador who conquered the Inca Indians, founded Lima, Peru.

1778   Captain James Cook, the great British naval explorer, discovered the Hawaiian Islands, which he named the Sandwich Islands, in honor of the Earl of Sandwich.

1862   John Tyler died at age 71.

1871   Wilhelm I of Prussia was crowned the first "kaiser" of the new united Germany.

1873   Edward Bulwer-Lytton, the noted English novelist, died at Torquay at age 69.

1911   Pilot Eugene Ely landed his plane on the USS *Pennsylvania*, in San Francisco harbor, for the first landing in history of an aircraft on a ship.

1912   English explorer Robert Scott reached the South Pole only to find that Norway's Roald Amundsen had arrived first.

1919   The Versailles Conference opened to draft a World War I peace treaty.

1936   Rudyard Kipling, the great English writer, died in London at age 70.

1943   The U.S. banned the sale of presliced bread for the duration of World War II to save on labor costs and equipment.

1976   The Pittsburgh Steelers beat the Dallas Cowboys, 21-17, in Super Bowl X. It was their second consecutive Super Bowl victory.

1980   The price of gold hit a record $845 per ounce.

JANUARY 19 -- BIRTHDAYS

1544　**Francis II** -- King of France, 1559-1560, during whose reign began the long and bitter rivalry between the noble houses of Guise and Bourbon

1736　**James Watt** — Scottish inventor who developed the steam engine and for whom the power unit, the watt, is named

1798　**Auguste Comte** — Noted French social thinker and philosopher, who founded the philosophy known as positivism

1807　**Robert E. Lee** -- Commander of the Confederate Army in the Civil War and one of the great generals in U.S. history

1809　**Edgar Allan Poe** -- One of America's greatest poets and short-story writers, noted for works such as the poems "The Raven" and "To Helen" and the short story "The Fall of the House of Usher"

1813　**Sir Henry Bessemer** -- British inventor and manufacturer, who developed the Bessemer process of converting pig iron to steel

1839　**Paul Cezanne** -- Noted French painter and leader of the post-impressionism school, whose style of composition changed the course of art

1866　**Harry Davenport** — American stage and screen actor who appeared in over 100 films

1887　**Alexander Woollcott** -- American journalist and tale-teller, known for his unusual personality and sharp tongue

1917　**John Raitt** -- American singer

1922　**Guy Madison** -- American motion-picture and television actor

1923　**Jean Stapleton** -- American actress who played Edith Bunker in the long-running television show, *All in the Family*

1926　**Fritz Weaver** -- American stage, screen, and television actor

1931　**Robert MacNeil** -- American broadcast journalist

1935　**Tippi Hedren** -- American motion-picture actress

1939　**Phil Everly** -- American singer and guitarist and one of the Everly Brothers

1943　**Princess Margriet Francisca** -- Daughter of Queen Juliana of the Netherlands

1943　**Janis Joplin** -- American blues singer, composer, and author, noted for songs such as "Mercedes Benz" and "Down on Me"

1946　**Tom Gorman** -- American tennis player

1946　**Dolly Parton** -- American singer, songwriter, and actress

1947　**Ann Woodruff Compton** -- American broadcast journalist

1948　**Terrence Hanratty** -- Professional football player

1950   **Jon Matlack** -- Professional baseball player

1953   **Desi Arnaz Jr.** -- American actor and singer, and son of entertainers Lucille Ball and Desi Arnaz

1957   **Ottis Anderson** -- Professional football player

JANUARY 19 -- EVENTS

1825   Ezra Daggett and his nephew Thomas Kensett received a patent for their process of storing food in cans.

1830   The famous Hayne-Webster debates began in the U.S. Senate on whether a state could nullify a federal law.

1853   Giuseppe Verdi's great opera *Il Trovatore* premiered in Rome.

1861   Georgia became the fifth southern state to secede from the Union.

1881   The Western Union Telegraph Company was created by a consolidation by financiers Jay Gould and William Vanderbilt of the Western Union Company with two smaller companies.

1929   Leon Trotsky, the ex-Bolshevist leader, left Moscow for exile to Alma-Ata in Kazakstan after his expulsion from the Politburo by Joseph Stalin.

1955   President Dwight D. Eisenhower held the first presidential press conference ever televised.

1966   Indira Gandhi was chosen prime minister of India, succeeding Lal Bahadur Shastri, who had died of a stroke.

1978   The last Volkswagen "Bug" was manufactured, as the Volkswagen Company changed over to the Volkswagen Rabbit. The move ended a production run since 1938 of over 19 million "Bugs."

JANUARY 20 -- BIRTHDAYS

1554   **Sebastian** -- King of Portugal, 1557-1578

1723   **John Goddard** -- Early American cabinetmaker noted for developing the block front on desks

1732   **Richard Henry Lee** -- American patriot and signer of the Declaration of Independence, who introduced the resolution declaring the American colonies independent on June 7, 1776

1775   **Andre Marie Ampere** — French physicist who discovered the laws of electromagnetism in the 1820s, and for whom the ampere, the unit of electric current, was named

1814   **David Wilmot** -- U.S. congressman who sponsored the Wilmot Proviso to prohibit slavery in new territories, and who helped found the Republican Party in 1854

1876   Josef Hofmann -- Polish-born American pianist and composer
1877   **Ruth St. Denis** -- Noted American dancer, dance teacher, and choreographer, with a 70-year career
1891   **Mischa Elman** -- Noted Russian-American concert violinist
1894   **Harold Gray** – American cartoonist and creator in 1924 of *Little Orphan Annie*
1894   **Walter Piston** -- American composer, noted for works such as the ballet, *The Incredible Flutist*
1896   **George Burns** -- Highly popular American comedian and actor in vaudeville, on radio, and in television and motion pictures
1897   **Mae Busch** – Australian-born American actress, who was a leading lady in silent films in the 1920s and a comic foil for Laurel and Hardy in the 1930s
1903   **Leon Ames** – American stage, screen, and television actor, who appeared in some 100 films
1904   **Alexandra Danilova** -- One of the great Russian ballerinas of the 1920s through the 1950s
1906   **Aristotle Onassis** – Greek shipowner and businessman, who was one of the wealthiest men of his time
1910   **Joy Adamson** -- Austrian-born naturalist, author, and artist
1912   **Walter Briggs** -- American baseball executive and longtime owner of the Detroit Tigers
1920   **Frederico Fellini** -- Italian motion-picture director, noted for films such as *La Strada* (1954) and *La Dolce Vita* (1960)
1920   **DeForrest Kelly** -- American actor noted for his role as the doctor in the long-running television series *Star Trek*
1922   **Ray Anthony** -- American bandleader of the Big Band Era
1926   **Patricia Neal** – American stage, screen, and television actress, who won the Academy Award for best actress in *Hud* (1963)
1930   **Edwin "Buzz" Aldrin Jr.** -- U.S. astronaut and the second man, after Neil Armstrong, to set foot on the moon
1934   **Camilo Pascual** -- Professional baseball player
1934   **Arte Johnson** -- American television actor and comedian
1937   **Bailey Howell** -- Professional basketball superstar with over 14,000 career points
1937   **Dorothy Provine** -- American motion-picture and television actress, dancer, and singer
1958   **Lorenzo Lamas** -- American actor and son of actors Fernando Lamas and Arlene Dahl

JANUARY 20 -- EVENTS

1265   The English Parliament met for the first time.

1479   Ferdinand, husband of Isabella and benefactor of Columbus, assumed the throne of Aragon at age 26.

1649   The treason trial of English King Charles I opened in Westminster Hall in London.

1788   The first Australian settlers, mostly convicts from England, arrived in New South Wales.

1801   President John Adams appointed John Marshall, "the great chief justice," to the Supreme Court.

1892   The first official basketball game was played, in Springfield, Massachusetts, by YMCA students of Dr. James Naismith, the game's inventor.

1936   King George V of England died at age 70 and was succeeded by his son Edward VIII. In 1987 it was revealed that his physician poisoned the mortally ill king to hasten his death.

1937   As a result of the 20th Amendment, President Franklin D. Roosevelt was inaugurated, and all future presidents will be inaugurated on this date, which was changed from March 4.

1941   President Franklin D. Roosevelt was inaugurated for an unprecedented third term.

1942   The Nazis held their notorious Wannsee conference in Berlin, at which they decided on their "final solution" of exterminating Europe's Jews.

1945   President Franklin D. Roosevelt was inaugurated for an unprecedented fourth term.

1954   The lowest temperature ever recorded in the lower 48 states, 70 below zero, occurred at Rogers Pass, Montana.

1961   John F. Kennedy, at his inaugural, said, "Ask not what your country can do for you; ask what you can do for your country."

1971   The first nationwide postal strike in British history began.

1977   Jimmy Carter was inaugurated as the 39th president, and set a precedent by walking down Pennsylvania Avenue from the Capitol to the White House.

1980   The Pittsburgh Steelers beat the Los Angeles Rams, 31-19, in Super Bowl XIV in Pasadena, California.

1981   The Iranians released the American hostages they had held for over a year only minutes after Ronald Reagan was sworn in as the 40th president.

JANUARY 21 -- BIRTHDAYS

1659   **Adriaen van der Werff** -- Dutch painter

1743   **John Fitch** -- American inventor and metal craftsman, who built and operated a mechanically successful steamboat 20 years before Robert Fulton built his *Clermont*

1813   **John C. Fremont** -- U.S. explorer and first Republican presidential candidate, in 1856

1821   **John C. Breckenridge** -- U.S. vice president under President Buchanan, and candidate for president in 1860

1824   **Thomas J. "Stonewall" Jackson** -- The South's greatest Civil War general, after Robert E. Lee

1829   **Oscar II** -- King of Sweden and Norway, 1872-1907, during whose reign the Norwegians gained their independence from Sweden (1905)

1854   **John Moses Browning** -- American inventor of pistols, rifles, and shotguns, noted especially for the Browning automatic rifle, or BAR

1855   **Ernest Chausson** -- French composer of the late 18th century

1871   **Bartley C. Costello** -- American lyricist noted for songs such as "El Rancho Grande"

1879   **Gilmour Dobie** -- Hall of Fame football player

1884   **Roger Baldwin** – Founder of the American Civil Liberties Union

1888   **Leadbelly (Huddie Ledbetter)** – Black American singer and guitarist who had an enormous influence on the folk music revival of the 1950s and 1960s

1892   **Robert Forsythe Irwin** -- Sponsor of Talking Books for the blind

1899   **Lew Fonseca** -- Professional baseball player

1900   **J. Carrol Naish** -- American motion-picture and television actor

1900   **John T. Scopes** -- American teacher who was the defendant in the famous Scopes trial, or "Monkey Trial," for teaching evolution

1905   **Christian Dior** -- Noted French fashion designer

1910   **Patsy Kelly** -- American dancer, actress, and highly talented comedienne, with a career of over 50 years

1919   **Jinx Falkenburg** -- American motion-picture actress

1922   **Paul Scofield** -- English stage and motion-picture actor who won the Academy Award in 1966 for *A Man for All Seasons*

1925   **Telly Savalas** -- American television and motion-picture actor, and star of the long-running television series *Kojak*

1925   **Benny Hill** -- British comedian and actor

1939   **Wolfman Jack** -- American radio and television personality

1940	Jack Nicklaus -- One of the greatest professional golfers of all time, and the first to win all four major golf titles at least twice
1941	Placido Domingo -- Noted Spanish operatic tenor
1941	Richie Havens -- American singer and guitarist
1942	Mac Davis -- American singer and songwriter
1952	Mike Krukow -- Professional baseball player
1955	Peter Fleming -- American tennis player
1956	Robby Benson -- American motion-picture and television actor

JANUARY 21 -- EVENTS

1793	French King Louis XVI was guillotined by the French revolutionaries.
1846	The London *Daily News* began publication.
1861	Jefferson Davis resigned from the U.S. Senate to join Mississippi in secession.
1908	The Sullivan Ordinance was enacted in New York City making it illegal for women to smoke in public. The punishment was a fine of $5 to $25 and up to 10 days' imprisonment.
1915	The first Kiwanis Club was founded, in Detroit.
1924	V.I. Lenin, Russian Communist leader and founder of the Soviet state, died of a brain hemorrhage at age 53.
1950	Alger Hiss was convicted of perjury, and subsequently sentenced to 5 years in prison.
1950	George Orwell, the noted British writer, died in London at age 46.
1954	The *Nautilus*, the world's first atomic-powered submarine, was launched at Groton, Connecticut.
1961	The American nuclear submarine *George Washington* completed a journey under the Arctic ice.
1979	The Pittsburgh Steelers defeated the Dallas Cowboys, 35-21, in Super Bowl XIII in Miami.

JANUARY 22 -- BIRTHDAYS

| 1440 | Ivan III (the Great) -- Grand Duke of Muscovy, who freed Russia in 1480 from its 240-year rule by the Tartars, and laid the basis for a unified Russia |
| 1561 | Francis Bacon -- Great English philosopher, statesman, and writer, noted for works such as *The Advancement of Learning* (1605) and *Novum Organum* (1620) |

1690	**Nicolas Lancret** -- French painter noted for works such as *The Dancer LaCamargo* (1730) and *The Pleasure Party* (1735)
1729	**Gottfried Ephraim Lessing** -- German dramatist and philosopher, often considered to be the father of modern German literature, and whose play, *Minna von Barnhelm* (1767), is one of the greatest German comedies
1788	**Lord Byron** -- The most colorful of the English romantic poets (born George Gordon Byron), noted for works such as "Childe Harold's Pilgrimage" (1812-1816) and *Don Juan*, left unfinished in 1824
1797	**John Harper** -- One of the four Harper brothers who founded the famous publishing house of Harper and Brothers
1802	**Richard Upjohn** -- American architect
1849	**August Strindberg** -- Swedish playwright and novelist, who was one of the key figures in the history of modern drama
1858	**Beatrice Webb** -- Noted British reformer and Fabian Socialist, who with her husband Sidney helped lead the British socialist movement in the late 1800s and early 1900s
1874	**Edward Stephen Harkness** -- American businessman and philanthropist who devoted his life to giving away the fortune his father made as a partner of John D. Rockefeller
1875	**D.W. Griffith** -- The single most important figure in the history of American films, and director of the 1915 classic, *The Birth of a Nation*
1879	**Francis Picabia** -- French artist
1890	**Fred M. Vinson** -- Chief Justice of the U.S. Supreme Court, 1946-1953
1897	**Rosa Melba Ponselle** -- American dramatic soprano, who was a leading star with the Metropolitan Opera in New York City in the 1920s and 1930s
1909	**U Thant** -- Burmese statesman and third United Nations secretary general
1909	**Ann Sothern** -- American stage, screen, and television actress with a career of over 40 years
1928	**Birch Bayh** -- U.S. senator in the 1960s and 1970s
1931	**Sam Cooke** -- American soul singer
1932	**Piper Laurie** -- American leading lady of Hollywood films of the 1950s and character actress of the 1970s and 1980s
1935	**Pierre S. Du Pont** -- Governor of Delaware
1937	**Joseph Wambaugh** -- American author
1940	**John Hurt** -- British-born motion-picture actor noted for the title role in *Elephant Man*

1955   **Lester Hayes** -- Professional football player
1957   **Mike Bossy** -- Professional hockey player
1959   **Linda Blair** -- American motion-picture actress

JANUARY 22 -- EVENTS

1789   The first American novel, *The Power of Sympathy*, by Sarah Wentworth Morton ("Philenia"), was published in Boston.
1840   The first British colonists landed in New Zealand.
1881   Cleopatra's Needle, an ancient Egyptian obelisk, was erected in New York's Central Park.
1901   Queen Victoria of England died at age 81, ending a reign of nearly 64 years, the longest of any British monarch.
1905   "Bloody Sunday" occurred in St. Petersburg, on which Czar Nicholas II of Russia bloodily suppressed an assault on the Winter Palace.
1907   Richard Strauss's opera *Salome* made its debut at the Metropolitan Opera in New York, shocking the audience with its "Dance of the Seven Veils."
1917   President Wilson asked for an end to World War I, saying that there must be "peace without victory."
1944   Allied troops landed near Anzio, Italy, 33 miles south of Rome, in World War II.
1972   Denmark, Great Britain, Ireland, and Norway signed the Treaty of Brussels, agreeing to join the European Common Market.
1973   Lyndon B. Johnson died of a heart attack in Johnson City, Texas, at age 64.
1973   The U.S. Supreme Court legalized abortions for women during the first three months of pregnancy in the landmark *Roe v. Wade* decision.

JANUARY 23 -- BIRTHDAYS

1598   **Francois Mansart** -- French architect
1730   **Joseph Hewes** -- Member of the Continental Congress, North Carolina signer of the Declaration of Independence, and executive head of the U.S. Navy who appointed John Paul Jones a navy officer
1762   **Christian August Vulpius** -- German historical novelist and brother-in-law of the great German writer Johann Wolfgang von Goethe

1783	Stendahl (Marie Henri Beyle) – One of the leading 19th-century French novelists, noted for works such as *The Red and the Black* (1831), one of the great books of world literature
1832	Edouard Manet – French artist who revolutionized painting in the mid-1800s by using subject matter for visual effect rather than for telling a story
1840	Ernst Abbe – German physicist who with Carl Zeiss developed the Zeiss works into the world's leading manufacturer of optical goods
1862	David Hilbert – German mathematician noted for his classic work, *Foundations of Geometry* (1902)
1869	Herbert David Croly – American political philosopher and founder in 1914 of the *New Republic* magazine
1878	Edwin Plimpton Adams – American physicist and author of *The Quantum Theory*
1884	George McManus – American cartoonist and creator of *Bringing Up Father* and the characters Maggie and Jiggs
1887	Percy Wenrich – American composer and pianist, noted for songs such as "Put on Your Old Gray Bonnet," "Silver Bell," "Moonlight Bay," and "When You Wore a Tulip and I Wore a Big Red Rose"
1898	Sergei Mikhailovitch Eisenstein – Latvian-born motion-picture director and one of the giant creative talents and theorists of the screen
1898	Randolph Scott – American motion-picture actor, who was a strong and silent Western star, and the ideal of two generations of filmgoers
1906	Bob Steele – American motion-picture and television actor and cowboy star of the 1930s
1907	Dan Duryea – American motion-picture and television actor in over 60 films
1915	Potter Stewart – U.S. Supreme Court justice, 1958-1981, who on his appointment was the second youngest justice in 105 years
1919	Ernie Kovacs – American actor and zany, creative comic of television and motion pictures
1924	Frank R. Lautenberg – U.S. senator
1928	Jeanne Moreau – French stage and motion-picture actress and director
1932	George Aliceson Tipton – American composer noted for scores for films and TV, such as *Phantom of the Paradise*, *Soap*, and *Benson*
1947	Kurt Bevacqua – Professional baseball player
1953	Pat Haden – Professional football player

1957   **Princess Caroline** -- Daughter of Prince Rainier and Princess
          Grace of Monaco
1963   **Akeem Olajuwan** -- Professional basketball player

JANUARY 23 -- EVENTS

27 BC   Augustus Caesar (Octavian) founded the Roman Empire that
          would last until A.D. 476.
1294   Boniface VIII was elected Roman Catholic pope.
1516   Ferdinand of Aragon, husband of Queen Isabella and sponsor of
          Columbus, died at age 63 and was succeeded by his grandson
          Charles I.
1789   Georgetown University was founded in the colonial village of
          Georgetown, which later became a part of Washington, D.C.
1845   Congress established election day in the United States as the
          first Tuesday after the first Monday in November.
1849   Elizabeth Blackwell graduated from the Geneva (New York)
          College of Medicine to become America's first woman physician.
1893   Phillips Brooks, American clergyman who composed "O Little
          Town of Bethlehem," died at age 57.
1943   The British Eighth Army under General Bernard L. Montgom-
          ery took Tripoli from Rommel's Afrika Corps in World War II.
1948   General Dwight D. Eisenhower refused to run in 1948 for
          president.
1950   The Israeli parliament proclaimed Jerusalem the capital of Israel.
1960   Dr. Jacques Picard and Lieutenant Donald Walsh touched the
          ocean bottom at 35,820 feet in the Pacific's Mariana Trench in
          the U.S. Navy bathysphere *Trieste*
1968   The U.S. reconnaissance ship *Pueblo* was seized by the
          North Koreans.
1973   President Nixon announced that an accord had been reached to
          end the Vietnam War.

JANUARY 24 -- BIRTHDAYS

76 AD   **Hadrian** -- Roman Emperor, A.D. 117-138, who was one of the
          "five good emperors"
1544   **Gillis van Coninxloo** -- Flemish painter
1664   **Sir John Vanbrugh** — English playwright and architect who
          satirized the manners of his day in works such as *The Relapse*
          (1696) and *The Provoked Wife* (1697), and who designed Blen-
          heim Palace

1670	**William Congreve** – English dramatist who wrote in his play, *The Mourning Bride* (1697), the famous line, "Music has charms to soothe a savage breast"
1679	**Christian Freiherr von Wolff** -- German philosopher and mathematician
1705	**Farinelli (Carlo Broschi)** -- Noted Italian castrato soprano
1712	**Frederick II (the Great)** -- King of Prussia, 1740-1786, and one of the great Prussian heroes of the 18th century
1732	**Pierre Augustin C. de Beaumarchais** – French dramatist noted for his comedies, *The Barber of Seville* (1775) and *The Marriage of Figaro* (1781)
1746	**Gustavus III** -- King of Sweden, 1771-1792
1818	**John Mason Neale** -- English hymn writer and prolific translator of such hymns as "O Come, O Come, Immanuel"
1860	**Bernard Henry Kroger** -- American businessman who in 1883 founded the Kroger chain of grocery stores
1862	**Edith Wharton** -- Noted American novelist and author of such works as *Ethan Frome* (1911) and *The Age of Innocence* (1920)
1870	**William G. Morgan** -- American YMCA physical director who in 1895 invented volleyball
1888	**Henry King** -- American motion-picture director with a 50-year career, who directed such films as *Twelve O'Clock High* (1949) and *Tender Is the Night* (1962)
1899	**Hoyt Vandenberg** -- U.S. World War II general and Air Force chief of staff, 1948-1953
1915	**Mark Goodson** -- American television producer
1917	**Ernest Borgnine** -- American motion-picture and television actor, who won the Academy Award in 1955 for his role in *Marty*
1918	**Oral Roberts** -- Noted American evangelist
1922	**Ava Gardner** -- American motion-picture actress and Hollywood's "love goddess" in the 1940s and 1950s
1925	**Maria Tallchief** -- American ballerina of North American Indian descent, and one of the first American ballerinas to gain international fame
1926	**Alfredo Poveda Burbano** -- Head of Ecuador's ruling junta
1927	**Paula Hawkins** -- U.S. senator
1928	**Desmond Morris** -- British zoologist and author, noted for *The Naked Ape* (1967)
1930	**Ernest Sheldon Lieberman** -- American composer, author, and singer, noted for songs such as "The Windows of Your Mind," "The Best Is Yet to Come," and "Baby the Rain Must Fall"

1936   **Doug Kershaw** -- American country violinist

1941   **Neil Diamond** -- American singer and composer, noted for works such as "Song Sung Blue," "Jonathan Livingston Seagull," and "September Morn"

1943   **Sharon Tate** -- American motion-picture actress

1949   **John Belushi** -- American motion-picture and television actor and comedian

1958   **Atlee Hammaker** -- Professional baseball player

1961   **Nastassja Kinski** -- German-born motion-picture actress

1968   **Mary Lou Retton** -- American gymnast and darling of the 1984 Olympics

JANUARY 24 -- EVENTS

41 AD   Rome's insane emperor Caligula was murdered by a tribune of the guard after he had insulted the army and threatened to kill the members of the Roman Senate.

1556   The greatest loss of life in history from an earthquake occurred in Shensi, China, when 830,000 people were killed.

1848   A gold nugget was discovered by James Wilson Marshall at Sutter's Mill in California, leading to the Gold Rush of 1849.

1894   Lobster thermidor was first served, in Paris.

1908   The first Boy Scout troop was organized, by Sir Robert Baden-Powell in England.

1916   The U.S. Supreme Court ruled that the federal income tax was constitutional.

1922   Eskimo Pie was patented by Christian K. Nelson, of Onawa, Iowa.

1924   The Russian city of Petrograd was renamed Leningrad in honor of the revolutionary leader, Vladimir I. Lenin, who had died three days earlier.

1935   Canned beer went on sale for the first time, in Richmond, Virginia.

1943   The Casablanca Conference in World War II concluded, with President Roosevelt's call for "unconditional surrender" of the Axis powers.

1945   Russian soldiers crossed the Oder River into German soil for the first time in World War II.

1965   Sir Winston Churchill, Britain's great World War II leader, died at age 90 of a stroke suffered on January 15.

JANUARY 25 -- BIRTHDAYS

1540   **Edmund Campion** -- English Jesuit who was hanged in 1581 on orders of Queen Elizabeth for his attacks on the Anglican Church and for allegedly conspiring to dethrone her

1585   **Hendrick van Avercamp** -- Dutch painter

1627   **Robert Boyle** -- Irish chemist and physicist who formulated Boyle's law of gases

1708   **Pompeo Batoni** -- Italian painter

1736   **Joseph Louis Lagrange** -- Noted French mathematician and author of the famous work, *Analytical Mechanics* (1788)

1743   **Friedrich Heinrich Jacobi** -- German philosopher

1759   **Robert Burns** -- The national poet of Scotland, noted for works such as "To a Louse," "Auld Lang Syne," and "Comin' Thro' the Rye"

1814   **Francis Harrison Pierpont** -- Governor during the Civil War of the "Restored Government of Virginia," the western part that remained loyal to the U.S., which under his guidance became West Virginia in 1863

1825   **George Edward Pickett** -- Confederate general whose charge (Pickett's Charge) in the Battle of Gettysburg ranks as one of the great events in American history

1860   **Charles Curtis** -- U.S. vice president under President Hoover

1874   **W. Somerset Maugham** -- One of the most popular British authors of the 1900s, noted for works such as *Of Human Bondage* (1915) and *Cakes and Ale* (1930)

1874   **Hewlett Johnson** -- English religious leader known by his enemies as the "Red Dean of Canterbury"

1881   **Emil Ludwig** -- German-born author who wrote famous biographies of Bismarck, Napoleon, Lincoln, Beethoven, and Goethe

1882   **Virginia Woolf** -- British novelist and critic, noted for works such as *Mrs. Dalloway* (1925) and *Between the Acts* (1941)

1886   **Wilhelm Furtwangler** -- Noted German conductor with the Berlin Philharmonic Orchestra and the New York Philharmonic Symphony

1896   **Harry Link** -- American composer and publisher, noted for songs such as "These Foolish Things"

1899   **Paul-Henri Spaak** -- European statesman, leader of the Socialist Party in Belgium, and secretary-general of NATO, 1957-1961

1906   **Mildred Dunnock** -- American stage, screen, and television actress

1919   **Edwin Newman** -- American television journalist and author

1924   **Lou Groza** -- Professional football superstar who scored 1,608 points in a 21-year career

1933   **Corazon Aquino** -- President of the Philippines, who succeeded Ferdinand Marcos in 1986

1935   **Dean Jones** -- American stage, screen, and television actor and singer

1937   **Don Maynard** -- Professional football player

1943   **Jack Snow** -- Professional football player

1944   **Leigh Taylor-Young** -- American motion-picture actress

1952   **Alfred Jenkins** -- Professional football player

JANUARY 25 -- EVENTS

1533   King Henry VIII of England secretly married Anne Boleyn, his mistress of the past six years.

1579   The Union of Utrecht was formed, which later became the Dutch Republic or the Netherlands.

1787   Shays' Rebellion occurred in which Daniel Shays, a Massachusetts farmer, led 1200 men in an attack on the Federal arsenal in Springfield, Massachusetts.

1858   Felix Mendelssohn's famous "Wedding March" was played in a wedding for the first time--the wedding of Queen Victoria's daughter.

1871   William McKinley married Ida Saxton.

1890   "Nellie Bly" (reporter Elizabeth Cochrane) returned to New Jersey, completing a 72-day trip around the world, beating the record of the hero of *Around the World in Eighty Days*.

1915   Transcontinental telephone service began as Alexander Graham Bell in New York again spoke the famous words, "Watson, come here, I want you," to Thomas Watson in San Francisco.

1934   John Dillinger, Public Enemy Number One on the FBI's list, was captured in Tucson, Arizona. He later escaped in March but was killed in July.

1956   The atomic submarine USS *Swordfish* was launched.

1959   American Airlines made the first scheduled transcontinental flight of a Boeing 707, opening the jet age in U.S. commercial aviation.

1961   President Kennedy held the first live presidential press conference on television.

1964   *Echo 2*, the U.S. communications satellite, was launched in the first joint Russian-U.S. experiment.

1971   Idi Amin seized power in Uganda, ousting President Apollo Milton Obote.

1981   The Oakland Raiders beat the Philadelphia Eagles, 27-10, in Super Bowl XV in the Superdome in New Orleans.

JANUARY 26 -- BIRTHDAYS

1582   **Giovanni Lanfranco** -- Italian painter

1714   **Jean Baptiste Pigalle** -- Court sculptor to King Louis XV of France

1831   **Mary Mapes Dodge** -- American author noted for the famous children's book, *Hans Brinker, or, The Silver Skates* (1865)

1832   **Rufus H. Gilbert** -- Noted elevated railroad builder

1852   **Pierre Paul F.C.S. de Brazza** -- Founder of the French Congo

1877   **Kees van Dongen** -- French painter

1880   **Douglas MacArthur** -- One of the leading American generals of World War II, and commander of all American Army forces in the Pacific

1884   **Roy Chapman Andrews** -- Famous American explorer and leader of expeditions for the American Museum of Natural History, and a leading authority on whales

1905   **Maria von Trapp** -- Austrian musician and matriarch of the singing von Trapp family who inspired the famous motion picture, *The Sound of Music*

1905   **Al Goodhart** -- American composer and pianist, noted for songs such as "Auf Wiedersehen, My Dear" and "I Apologize"

1912   **Howard W. Cannon** -- U.S. Senator, 1968-1981

1912   **Alfred Sheinwold** -- American bridge expert, columnist, and author

1913   **Jimmy Van Heusen** -- American popular composer noted for songs such as "Moonlight Becomes You," "Swinging on a Star," "High Hopes," and "Personality"

1918   **Nicolae Ceausescu** -- Romanian head of state

1923   **Sid Wayne** -- American composer and author, noted for songs such as "I'm Gonna Knock on Your Door," "Two Different Worlds," and "It's Impossible"

1923   **Anne Jeffreys** -- American motion-picture and television actress

1925   **Joan Leslie** -- American stage and screen actress and dress designer

1925   **Paul Newman** -- American stage and motion-picture actor, director, producer, and superstar

1926   **Moira Shearer** -- Scottish ballerina and motion-picture actress

1928   **Roger Vadim** -- French motion-picture director noted for such works as the sensational *And God Created Woman* (1956), starring his then wife Brigitte Bardot

1928   **Eartha Kitt** -- American stage and screen actress and singer
1929   **Jules Feiffer** -- American cartoonist and author
1935   **Bob Uecker** -- Professional baseball player who used his unheralded career to become a television personality
1944   **Angela Davis** -- American black militant philosophy professor
1950   **Jack Youngblood** -- Professional football player
1952   **Tom Henderson** -- Professional basketball player
1961   **Wayne Gretzky** -- Professional hockey superstar known as "The Great Gretzky"
1963   **Andrew Ridgeley** -- British guitarist with the Wham! musical group

JANUARY 26 -- EVENTS

1699   The Peace of Karlowitz (Hungary) marked the eclipse of the Ottoman Empire, as the Turks were forced to give up nearly all of Hungary and the Turkish part of the Ukraine.

1788   Sydney, Australia, was founded by Captain Arthur Phillip and a cargo of convicts from England.

1802   Congress authorized a national library, the forerunner of the Library of Congress.

1808   William Bligh, the captain of the *Bounty* during the famous mutiny in 1789, was arrested for tyranny in his capacity as governor of New South Wales, Australia.

1837   Michigan was admitted to the Union as the 26th state.

1861   Louisiana seceded from the Union.

1905   The 3,106-carat Cullinan diamond, the largest ever discovered, was found in the Premier mine of South Africa by Captain M.F. Wells.

1917   The U.S. Army Tank Corps was created.

1942   The first American Expeditionary Force of World War II arrived in Northern Ireland.

1945   Larry MacPhail and Dan Topping bought the New York Yankees baseball team for $3 million.

1950   India became a republic, as the new constitution went into effect.

1962   The U.S. lunar probe, *Ranger 3*, was launched.

1971   Charles Manson and three of his followers were convicted for the first-degree murder of actress Sharon Tate.

1980   Frank Sinatra sang before 175,000 people at the Maracana Stadium in Rio de Janeiro, the largest crowd ever assembled for one performer.

JANUARY 27 -- BIRTHDAYS

1571 **Abbas I (the Great)** -- Shah of Persia, 1588-1629, and the greatest of the Safavid kings

1756 **Wolfgang Amadeus Mozart** -- One of the world's three or four greatest composers, who wrote over 600 works, including 41 symphonies and *Don Giovanni*, perhaps the world's greatest opera

1775 **Friedrich Wilhelm J. von Schelling** -- German philosopher whose works are considered to be a major link between Immanuel Kant and G.W.F. Hegel

1805 **Samuel Palmer** -- British artist

1814 **Eugene Emmanuel Viollet-le-Duc** -- French architect, restorer, and writer, who in the 1840s directed the restoration of Notre Dame Cathedral in Paris

1823 **Edouard Lalo** -- French composer noted for works such as the violin concerto, *Symphonie Espagnole* (1873)

1832 **Lewis Carroll (Charles L. Dodgson)** -- English author of the famous story, *Alice's Adventures in Wonderland* (1865), and its continuation, *Through the Looking Glass and What Alice Found There* (1871)

1850 **Samuel Gompers** -- U.S. labor leader and principal organizer of the American Federation of Labor

1859 **Kaiser Wilhelm II** -- World War I leader and last emperor of Germany, 1888-1918, whose reign marked the end of the great Hohenzollern dynasty that had ruled Prussia since 1701

1872 **Learned Hand** -- Judge of the U.S. Court of Appeals, 1924-1951, and one of the most able judges in American history

1885 **Jerome Kern** -- Famous American composer noted for songs such as "Smoke Gets in Your Eyes," "Ol' Man River," "All the Things You Are," and "Why Do I Love You?"

1895 **George Gard Desylvia** -- American composer noted for songs such as "April Showers," "Somebody Loves Me," "If You Knew Susie," "Button Up Your Overcoat," and "Sonny Boy"

1895 **Harry Ruby** -- American composer, author, and pianist, noted for songs such as "Who's Sorry Now?" "I Wanna Be Loved by You," "A Kiss to Build a Dream On," and "Three Little Words"

1900 **Hyman G. Rickover** -- American admiral and father of the nuclear-powered submarine

1908 **William Randolph Hearst Jr.** -- American newspaper publisher and son of the founder of the Hearst chain

1918 **Skitch Henderson** -- English-American bandleader

1921 **Donna Reed** -- American motion-picture and television actress

1936   **Troy Donahue** -- American motion-picture and television actor
1940   **Bob Wynn** -- Professional golfer
1945   **Nick Mason** -- British drummer of the Pink Floyd rock group
1947   **John Lowenstein** -- Professional baseball player
1948   **Mikhail Baryshnikov** -- Noted Russian-born ballet dancer
1952   **Brian Gottfried** -- American tennis player

JANUARY 27 -- EVENTS

1302   The great Italian writer Dante Alighieri was expelled from Florence forever by the Guelphs, one of the two contending political factions in the city.

1521   The Diet of Worms was opened to hear the charges against Martin Luther.

1689   Peter, the future great czar of Russia, was forced into a marriage at age 17 with the beautiful but stupid Eudoxia Lopukhina.

1851   John James Audubon, the great American naturalist, died in New York City at age 65.

1854   The Canadian Great Western Railway began operations.

1870   Kappa Alpha Theta, the first Greek-letter sorority, was founded at Indiana University, now De Pauw University.

1880   Thomas A. Edison patented his incandescent lamp.

1888   The National Geographic Society was founded in Washington, D.C.

1943   The U.S. Eighth Air Force staged the first all-American air raid on Germany in World War II, bombing Wilhelmshaven in broad daylight.

1944   The Russians broke the German siege of Leningrad in World War II.

1967   In the first U.S. space disaster, three American astronauts, Virgil Grissom, Edward White, and Roger Chaffee, were killed in an Apollo launching-pad fire.

1973   A cease-fire accord was signed in Paris by the United States and North Vietnam, ending the Vietnam War.

JANUARY 28 -- BIRTHDAYS

1457   **Henry VII** -- First English king of the House of Tudor, 1485-1509, who came to the throne as a result of his killing Richard III at Bosworth Field, which ended the Wars of the Roses

1582   **John Barclay** -- Scottish satirist and Latin poet

1611   **Johann Hevelius** -- German astronomer

1706   **John Baskerville** -- English printer and inventor of the Baskerville printing type, whose first book from his press, an edition of Virgil in 1757, amazed readers by its elegance

1784   **George Hamilton-Gordon** -- British prime minister of the Victorian Age

1825   **Benedetto Cairoli** -- Italian statesman who served three times as premier of Italy

1841   **Sir Henry Morton Stanley** -- Noted British explorer of the African continent, who, upon finding the British explorer David Livingstone, greeted him with the famous line: "Dr. Livingstone, I presume?"

1847   **George Wright** -- Hall of Fame baseball player who was the first batter in National League history, leading off the opening game on April 22, 1876

1858   **Eugene Dubois** -- Dutch anatomist and anthropologist, who in 1891-1892 discovered the fossilized bones of Java Man, believed to have walked erect on the earth a million years ago

1873   **Colette** -- One of the outstanding French writers of the 20th century (born Sidonie-Gabrielle Colette), noted for works such as *The Vagabond* (1910) and *Gigi* (1945)

1884   **Jean Piccard** -- Swiss chemist, pioneer in stratospheric balloon exploration, and twin brother of physicist Auguste Piccard

1884   **Auguste Piccard** -- Swiss physicist, pioneer in the use of the bathyscaph for underwater research, and twin brother of chemist Jean Piccard

1887   **Arthur Rubinstein** -- Polish-born American concert pianist and one of the greatest keyboard virtuosos of the 20th century

1892   **Ernst Lubitsch** -- Noted German-American motion-picture director of such classics as *Ninotchka* (1939) and *To Be or Not to Be* (1942)

1903   **Samuel Manuel Lerner** -- Romanian-born composer, author, and publisher, noted for songs such as "Popeye the Sailor Man" and "Is It True What They Say About Dixie?"

1911   **Lee Metcalf** -- U.S. senator, 1958-1978

1912   **Jackson Pollock** -- American painter and exponent of Abstract Expressionism, noted for works such as *One* (1950)

1913   **Judith Allen** -- American stage and motion-picture actress and leading lady of the 1930s

1915   **Kermit Goell** -- American lyricist noted for songs such as "Near You," "Ever True Evermore," and "Huggin' and Chalkin'"

1918   Bob Hilliard – American lyricist noted for songs such as "Mention My Name in Sheboygan," "Civilization," "Be My Life's Companion," and "Dear Hearts and Gentle People"

1929   Claes Oldenburg -- American sculptor

1932   Parry O'Brien -- The greatest shot-putter in history

1933   Susan Sontag -- American author

1936   Alan Alda -- American stage, screen, and television actor, son of actor Robert Alda, and star of the long-running television comedy, *M*A*S*H*

1943   Susan Howard -- American television actress

1944   Marthe Keller -- Swiss stage, screen, and television actress

1950   Barbi Benton -- American motion-picture and television actress

1959   Dave Sharp -- Welsh guitarist with the Alarm musical group

JANUARY 28 -- EVENTS

814 AD The great Holy Roman Emperor Charlemagne died of pleurisy in Aachen at age 72.

1547   King Henry VIII of England died at age 55 of syphilis and cirrhosis of the liver.

1596   Sir Francis Drake, the great English seaman, died of the plague near Nombre de Dios in the West Indies, and was buried at sea by his crew.

1807   The first gas-lit street was illuminated in Pall Mall, London.

1871   Paris surrendered to the Germans, ending the fighting in the Franco-Prussian War.

1878   The *Yale News*, the first daily college newspaper, began publication in New Haven, Connecticut.

1902   The Carnegie Institution was established in Washington, D.C.

1915   Congress created the U.S. Coast Guard, by combining the Revenue Cutter Service and the Lifesaving Service.

1916   Louis D. Brandeis was appointed as the first Jewish justice to the Supreme Court.

1938   President Franklin D. Roosevelt asked Congress to permit the building of a two-ocean U.S. Navy.

1939   William Butler Yeats, the noted Irish poet, died at Roquebrunne, France, at age 73.

1958   Roy Campanella, the great Los Angeles Dodger catcher, was seriously injured in an automobile accident in New York, ending his baseball career.

1973   Hostilities officially ended in the Vietnam War.

1986   The U.S. space shuttle *Challenger* exploded at Cape Canaveral, 73 seconds after lift-off, killing all seven crew members.

JANUARY 29 -- BIRTHDAYS

1688   **Emanuel Swedenborg** -- Swedish scientist, philosopher, and theologian, whose followers founded the Church of the New Jerusalem based on his biblical interpretations

1737   **Thomas Paine** -- American Revolutionary War patriot, whose writings, such as the famous pamphlet *Common Sense* (1776), encouraged the Continental Army during the darkest days of the war

1749   **William Sharp** -- English printmaker

1756   **Henry "Light-Horse Harry" Lee** -- American Revolutionary War officer and father of Civil War general Robert E. Lee

1782   **Daniel Auber** -- French composer

1843   **William McKinley** -- 25th U.S. president

1860   **Anton Chekhov** -- Russian playwright noted for works such as *The Seagull* (1896) and *The Cherry Orchard* (1904)

1862   **Frederick Delius** -- English composer noted for works such as "Over the Hills and Far Away" (1895) and "Appalachia" (1902)

1866   **Romain Rolland** -- Nobel Prize-winning French novelist best known for his ten-volume novel, *Jean-Christophe* (1904-1912)

1874   **John D. Rockefeller Jr.** -- American financier, only son of the founder of the Standard Oil Company, and builder of Rockefeller Center in New York City and restorer of Williamsburg, Virginia

1878   **Barney Oldfield** -- Famous American automobile racer who was the first to drive an automobile a mile a minute (1903) and whose name became synonymous with speeders

1880   **W.C. Fields** -- American actor and comedian who played swindling characters whose beliefs were "Never give a sucker an even break" and "Anyone who hates children and dogs can't be all bad"

1884   **John Schommer** -- Hall of Fame basketball player

1892   **Richard Norris Williams** -- American Hall of Fame tennis player and National Champion in 1914 and 1916

1900   **Dynamite Sonnenberg** -- "King of Wrestlers," who introduced the flying tackle

1901   **Allen B. Du Mont** -- American engineer who perfected the cathode-ray tube and who founded the Du Mont Television company

1912   **"Professor" Irwin Corey** -- American comedian

1916   **Victor Mature** -- American motion-picture actor and leading man of the 1940s and 1950s

1918   John Forsythe -- American stage, screen, and television actor
1918   Bill Rigney -- Professional baseball player and manager
1923   Paddy Chayefsky -- American playwright and screenwriter who won Academy Awards for the scripts of *Marty* (1955), *The Hospital* (1971), and *Network* (1976)
1933   Ron Towson -- Member of the 5th Dimension singing group
1939   Germaine Greer -- Australian-born feminist and author, noted for works such as *The Female Eunuch*
1942   Claudine Longet -- Motion-picture actress
1942   Katharine Ross -- American motion-picture and television actress
1945   Donna Maria Caponi -- Professional golfer
1945   Tom Selleck -- American television actor, noted for the long-running series *Magnum, P.I.*
1952   Tommy Ramone -- American musician with the Ramones musical group
1953   Oprah Winfrey -- American actress and television hostess
1954   Tony Galbreath -- Professional football player
1955   Jonathan Smith -- English tennis player
1960   Steve Sax -- Professional baseball player
1960   Greg Louganis -- U.S. Olympic diving champion, 1984 and 1988
1964   Roddy Frame -- British musician and singer with the Aztec Camera musical group

JANUARY 29 -- EVENTS

1327   Edward III was crowned King of England.
1819   Singapore was founded by English colonial officer Thomas S. Raffles of the East India Company.
1820   George III, King of England during the American Revolution, died insane at Windsor Castle.
1845   Edgar Allan Poe's famous poem, "The Raven," was first published, in the New York *Evening Mirror*.
1850   Henry Clay introduced his omnibus bill in the U.S. Senate, which was later passed as the famous series of Acts known as the Compromise of 1850.
1861   Kansas was admitted to the Union as the 34th state.
1886   The first successful gasoline-driven car, the Motorwagen, was patented by Karl Benz, a German engineer.
1900   Baseball's American League was organized in Philadelphia by Ban Johnson.

1936   The first five players were elected to the Baseball Hall of Fame. They were Ty Cobb, Walter Johnson, Christy Mathewson, Babe Ruth, and Honus Wagner.

1956   H.L. Mencken, the noted American writer and critic, died in Baltimore at age 75.

1963   Robert Frost, the noted American poet, died in Boston at age 88.

1968   Adolph Rupp became the winningest basketball coach in history as the University of Kentucky beat the University of Mississippi for his 772nd victory.

JANUARY 30 -- BIRTHDAYS

1628   **George Villiers** -- English politician, writer, and second Duke of Buckingham

1687   **Balthasar Neumann** -- German architect

1720   **Bernardo Bellotto** -- Italian painter

1775   **Walter Savage Landor** — English poet, essayist, and novelist, whose best-known work is *Imaginary Conversations* (1824-1848)

1866   **Gelett Burgess** -- American writer and illustrator, noted for "I Never Saw a Purple Cow"

1882   **Franklin D. Roosevelt** — 32nd U.S. president, and the only president to be elected to a third and a fourth term

1894   **Boris III** -- King of Bulgaria, 1918-1943

1911   **Roy Eldridge** -- American trumpeter and musician

1912   **Barbara Tuchman** -- American novelist and biographer, noted for works such as *The Guns of August*

1914   **David Wayne** -- American stage, screen, and television actor

1914   **John Ireland** -- American stage and motion-picture actor

1923   **Walt Dropo** -- Professional baseball player

1923   **Dick Martin** -- American comedian and co-star of television's long-running Rowan and Martin's *Laugh In*

1925   **Dorothy Malone** — American motion-picture and television actress

1927   **Olof Palme** -- Prime minister of Sweden, 1969-1976 and 1982-1986, who was murdered in a Stockholm street in 1986, the first major Swedish official to be assassinated since King Gustavus III in 1792

1928   **Harold Prince** -- Noted Broadway producer-director

1931   **Gene Hackman** -- American stage, screen, and television actor, who won the Academy Award for *The French Connection* (1971)

1933   **Louis Rukeyser** -- American television commentator and stock market analyst

1934   **Tammy Grimes** -- American stage and motion-picture actress
1937   **Vanessa Redgrave** -- British stage, screen, and television actress, and daughter of actor Michael Redgrave
1937   **Boris Spassky** -- Russian world champion chess player
1943   **Martin Balin** – American singer with the Jefferson Airplane musical group
1943   **Dave Johnson** -- Professional baseball player and manager
1955   **Nolan Cromwell** -- Professional football player
1955   **Mychal Thompson** -- Professional basketball player

JANUARY 30 -- EVENTS

1649   King Charles I of England was beheaded at Whitehall for treason.
1730   Czar Peter II of Russia died of smallpox on his wedding day.
1815   The U.S. Congress authorized the purchase of Thomas Jefferson's library as the nucleus of the new Library of Congress, the original having been burned by the British in 1814.
1835   The first assassination attempt on a U.S. president occurred as an insane gunman, Richard Lawrence, tried unsuccessfully to fire two pistols at Andrew Jackson. Neither went off.
1917   The first jazz record, "The Darktown Strutters' Ball," was cut, by "The Original Dixieland Jazz Band" in New York.
1933   German President Paul von Hindenburg named Adolf Hitler chancellor.
1933   The long-running radio program, *The Lone Ranger*, was aired for the first time.
1937   German chancellor Adolf Hitler publicly repudiated the Versailles Peace Treaty.
1940   The first U.S. Social Security checks went out, totalling $75,844.
1948   Mahatma Gandhi, India's great spiritual and political leader, was assassinated by a Hindu fanatic in New Delhi.
1948   Orville Wright, the great American aviation pioneer, died in Dayton, Ohio, at age 76.
1965   The state funeral of Sir Winston Churchill was held in London.

JANUARY 31 -- BIRTHDAYS

1624   **Arnold Geulincx** -- Dutch metaphysician and logician
1734   **Robert Morris** -- Pennsylvania signer of the Declaration of Independence and "financier of the American Revolution"

1735   J. Hector Grevecoeur -- French-American essayist

1752   Gouverneur Morris -- American statesman and diplomat, member of the Continental Congress, and one of the key figures in the Constitutional Convention in 1787

1769   Andre Jacques Garnerin -- The first man to drop from a balloon in a parachute, over the Parc Monceau in Paris on October 22, 1797

1797   Franz Schubert -- Great Austrian composer whose *Symphony in C Major* and *Unfinished Symphony (Symphony No. 8 in B minor)* are two of the immortal works of music

1806   Fletcher Harper -- One of the four Harper brothers who founded the famous publishing house of Harper and Brothers

1830   James G. Blaine -- Influential 19th-century American political leader and U.S. presidential candidate in 1884

1831   Rudolph Wurlitzer -- American bank clerk who founded the Wurlitzer organ company in 1856

1848   Nathan Straus -- American merchant and philanthropist, who did more for New York City's welfare in the first quarter of the 20th century than any other person

1860   James Gibbons Huneker -- American critic and author

1875   Zane Grey -- American novelist who wrote over 60 popular books about the American West, such as *Riders of the Purple Sage* (1912)

1881   Alfred Harcourt -- American publisher and founder in 1919 of Harcourt, Brace, Inc.

1885   Anna Pavlova -- Russian ballerina and most famous dancer of her generation, best known for the three minute solo, "The Dying Swan," that often moved audiences to tears

1892   Eddie Cantor -- American stage and screen comic actor and singer

1894   Isham Jones -- American composer, conductor, and pianist, noted for songs such as "On the Alamo," "It Had to Be You," and "I'll See You in My Dreams"

1902   Edward Beverly Mann -- American writer of Western novels

1902   Leo Corday -- American composer noted for songs such as "There's No Tomorrow" and "See the USA in Your Chevrolet"

1903   Tallulah Bankhead -- One of the American theater's most brilliant and legendary actresses, and daughter of U.S. Representative William B. Bankhead

1905   John O'Hara -- American novelist and short-story writer, noted for works such as *Appointment in Samarra, Butterfield 8,* and *Ten North Frederick*

1913   Don Hutson -- Professional football superstar and member of the great Hutson-to-Isbel passing combination

1914   **Jersey Joe Walcott** -- World heavyweight champion, 1951-1952

1915   **Bobby Hackett** -- American trumpeter

1915   **Garry Moore** -- Noted American television personality of the 1950s and 1960s

1915   **Thomas Merton** -- American poet and religious writer, noted for *The Seven Storey Mountain* (1948)

1916   **Frank Parker** -- American Hall of Fame tennis player who ranked in the top ten seventeen consecutive years (1933-1949)

1919   **Jackie Robinson** -- The first black major league baseball player (1947) and Hall of Famer

1920   **Stewart Udall** -- Secretary of the Interior under President Kennedy

1921   **John Agar** -- American motion-picture actor, better known as the first husband of the famous child actress Shirley Temple

1921   **Mario Lanza** -- American singer and motion-picture actor

1923   **Carol Channing** -- American comic actress, entertainer, and singer of stage, screen, and television

1923   **Joanne Dru** -- American model and motion-picture actress, and sister of TV host Peter Marshall

1923   **Norman Mailer** -- American novelist, noted for works such as *The Naked and the Dead* (1948) and *The Armies of the Night* (1968)

1925   **Charles E. Silberman** -- American author

1925   **Benjamin Hooks** -- American civil rights leader and executive director of the NAACP

1929   **Jean Simmons** -- English-born motion-picture and television actress

1931   **Ernie Banks** -- Hall of Fame baseball player with 512 career home runs

1934   **James Franciscus** -- American television and motion-picture actor

1937   **Suzanne Pleshette** -- American stage, screen, and television actress

1938   **Beatrix** -- Queen of the Netherlands

1940   **Jessica Walter** -- American stage, screen, and television actress

1941   **Richard Gephardt** -- U.S. Congressman

1943   **James Watt** -- Secretary of the Interior under President Reagan

1944   **Szabolcs Baranyi** -- Hungarian tennis player

1947   **Nolan Ryan** -- Professional baseball pitcher who struck out 19 men in one game, 383 in one season, both records, and has the most career strikeouts in the history of baseball

1951   **Phil Collins** -- Record producer and lead singer and drummer with the rock group Genesis

1953   **Roosevelt Leaks** -- Professional football player

1953   **Louie Wright** -- Professional football player
1955   **Virginia Ruzici** -- Romanian tennis player
1956   **Johnny Rotten (John Lydon)** -- Singer with the Sex Pistols musical group
1957   **Shirley Babashoff** -- Professional swimmer

JANUARY 31 -- EVENTS

1606   Guy Fawkes, the ringleader in the Gunpowder Plot against the English Parliament, was hanged in London.
1865   Jefferson Davis, President of the Confederacy, appointed General Robert E. Lee commander-in-chief of all Confederate armies.
1917   Germany served notice that it would begin a policy of unrestricted submarine warfare in World War I.
1934   President Franklin D. Roosevelt fixed the price of the U.S. dollar in terms of gold at $35 per ounce.
1945   U.S. Army Private Eddie Slovick was shot for desertion by a firing squad. He was posthumously pardoned nearly 40 years later.
1949   NBC broadcast *These Are My Children*, the first daytime soap opera on television.
1950   President Harry S Truman announced the order to develop the hydrogen bomb.
1958   The first U.S. satellite, *Explorer 1*, was launched, leading to the discovery of the Van Allen radiation belt.
1971   U.S. spacecraft *Apollo 14* was launched with the third crew of astronauts (Alan Shepard, Edgar Mitchell, and Stuart Roosa) to land on the moon.

2

February

February, the second month of the year, got its name from *Februarius*, which is derived from the Latin verb *februare*, meaning "to purify." The Romans celebrated a "Feast of Purification" during the month at which the people repented of their wrongdoing and offered sacrifices to the gods.

February, along with January, was added to the Roman calendar by Numa Pompilius, the second king of Rome, around 700 B.C., at which time it had 28 days. Its length was increased to 29 days in Caesar's Julian Calendar of 45 B.C., and reduced back to 28 days when Emperor Augustus made his adjustments in 8 B.C. This is, of course, its present length, except in leap years when it has 29 days. February originally preceded January in the early calendar, but in 452 B.C. the Decemvirs interchanged the two months. Thus when January became the first month, February became the second.

Special days of February include Groundhog Day (February 2), when legend has it that six weeks of winter weather will follow if the ground hog sees its shadow; Abraham Lincoln's Birthday (February 12); Valentine's Day (February 14); Susan B. Anthony's Birthday (February 15); George Washington's Birthday (February 22), which is a legal holiday celebrated on the third Monday of February; and, of course, every four years, February 29 is Leap Year Day. Presidents William Henry Harrison and Ronald Reagan were also born in February.

The birthstone for February is the amethyst, and its special flowers are the violet and the primrose. Notable birthdays and events of February follow.

FEBRUARY 1 -- BIRTHDAYS

1552 **Sir Edward Coke** -- Brilliant English courtroom lawyer who in 1594 was selected over Sir Francis Bacon as Queen Elizabeth's attorney general

1787 **Richard Whately** -- English archbishop and social reformer

1801 **Thomas Cole** -- Early American painter who was a leader of the Hudson River school, the first American group of landscape painters, and who was noted for works such as *The Voyage of Life*

1828 **Meyer Guggenheim** -- American industrialist and philanthropist who founded the Guggenheim fortune in mining and smelting

1859 **Victor Herbert** – American conductor, composer, and "prince of operetta," noted for works such as *Babes in Toyland* (1903) and *Naughty Marietta* (1910)

1869 **Frederick Allen "Kerry" Mills** – American composer, author, and violinist, noted for songs such as "Meet Me in St. Louis" and "Red Wing"

1874 **Hugo von Hofmannsthal** -- Austrian poet and dramatist best known for writing the words for the operas of the German composer Richard Strauss

1882 **Louis S. Saint Laurent** – Prime Minister of Canada, 1948-1957

1887 **Harry Scherman** – Co-founder with Maxwell Byron Sackheim in 1926 of the Book-of-the-Month Club

1887 **Charles Bernard Nordhoff** -- American novelist and traveler, noted with James Norman Hall for *Mutiny on the Bounty*, *Pitcairn's Island*, and *Men Against the Sea*

1891 **James P. Johnson** -- American composer and pianist, noted for songs such as "If I Could Be with You One Hour Tonight" and "Runnin' Wild"

1894 **Herman Hupfeld** -- American composer, author, and singer, noted for songs such as "As Time Goes By"

1895 **John Ford** -- The first motion-picture director to win Academy Awards for four movies (*The Informer*, *The Grapes of Wrath*, *How Green Was My Valley*, and *The Quiet Man*)

1896 **Anastasio Somoza Garcia** -- Dictator of Nicaragua, 1936-1956

1900 **Stephen Potter** -- English author noted for works such as *Gamesmanship* and *One-upmanship*

1901 **Clark Gable** – "The King" of Hollywood in the 1930s and 1940s, who won the 1934 Academy Award for *It Happened One Night*, and whose most famous role was Rhett Butler in *Gone with the Wind*

1902 **Langston Hughes** -- American poet and short-story writer, noted for works such as *The Weary Blues* (1926) and *The Best of Simple* (1961)

1904	**S.J. Perelman** -- American writer known for his humorous satires, many of which are collected in *The Most of S.J. Perelman* (1958)
1905	**Emilio Gino Segre** -- Italian physicist who shared the 1959 Nobel Prize with Owen Chamberlain for co-discovering the antiproton
1906	**Hildegarde (Loretta Sell)** -- American singer and actress
1907	**John Canaday** -- Noted American art critic
1908	**Albie Booth** -- Noted football player and coach at Yale, known as "Little Boy Blue"
1924	**Pierre Rinfret** -- American economist
1926	**Stuart Whitman** -- American stage, screen, and television actor
1937	**Don Everly** -- American singer and guitarist, and one of the Everly Brothers singers
1937	**Garrett Morris** -- American actor and comedian
1938	**Sherman Hemsley** -- American television actor noted for his starring role in the long-running show, *The Jeffersons*
1940	**Herve Filion** -- The most successful harness racing driver in North America
1944	**Dick Snyder** -- Professional basketball player
1944	**Paul Blair** -- Professional baseball player
1947	**Karen Krantzche** -- Australian tennis player
1948	**Debbie Austin** -- Professional golfer
1948	**Rick James** -- American soul singer
1965	**Princess Stephanie** -- Princess of Monaco and daughter of Prince Rainier and Princess Grace
1968	**Lisa Marie Presley** -- Daughter of Elvis Presley

FEBRUARY 1 -- EVENTS

1328	King Charles IV (the Fair) of France died at age 33, ending the line of Capetian kings descended from Hugh Capet, that began in A.D. 987.
1691	Roman Catholic pope Alexander VIII died after a two-year reign.
1790	The United States Supreme Court held its first session.
1814	English poet Lord Byron's poem "The Corsair" was first published.
1861	Texas seceded from the Union.
1862	Julia Ward Howe's great poem, "The Battle Hymn of the Republic," was published for the first time, in the *Atlantic Monthly*.
1884	The first *Oxford English Dictionary* was published by James A.H. Murray, who had largely compiled it single-handedly.
1896	*La Boheme*, Giacomo Puccini's great opera, premiered in Turin, Italy.

1898	The Travelers Insurance Company of Hartford, Connecticut, issued the first automobile insurance policy, to Dr. Truman Martin of Buffalo, New York, for $11.25.
1917	Germany began unrestricted submarine warfare in World War I.
1920	The Royal Canadian Mounted Police was formed as a merger of the Northwest Mounted Police and the Dominion Police.
1933	Adolf Hitler ordered the Reichstag dissolved as one of his first acts upon assuming control of Germany.
1949	RCA Records issued the world's first 45 rpm single.
1951	The United Nations General Assembly condemned China as an aggressor in Korea.
1956	Autherine Lucy became the first black student admitted to the University of Alabama.
1958	The United Arab Republic (a union of Egypt and Syria) was proclaimed by Egyptian president Gamal Abdel Nasser and Syrian president Shukri Al-Kuwatli.
1960	Four black students staged the first "sit-in" protest, at a lunch counter in Greensboro, North Carolina, which had previously refused to serve them.
1979	Ayatollah Ruhollah Khomeini returned to Iran after 15 years in exile.

FEBRUARY 2 -- BIRTHDAYS

1208	**James I (the Conqueror)** -- King of Aragon
1522	**Lodovico Ferrari** -- Italian mathematician who first solved the general quartic equation
1602	**Michelangelo Cerquozzi** -- Italian painter
1650	**Nell Gwyn** -- One of England's first actresses, and mistress of King Charles II
1745	**Hannah More** -- English writer
1803	**Albert Sidney Johnston** -- Confederate general in the Civil War who was killed in the Battle of Shiloh
1852	**Abdulhak Hamid (Tarhan)** -- One of the greatest Turkish romantic writers
1854	**Stephen H. Horgan** – Inventor of the halftone method of printing pictures
1859	**Havelock Ellis** – British author and psychologist, noted for his seven-volume work, *Studies in the Psychology of Sex* (1897-1928)
1875	**Fritz Kreisler** -- Austrian-born virtuoso violinist and composer, who ranks as one of the best-loved violinists of all time
1882	**James Joyce** -- Irish novelist noted for the two great works, *Ulysses* (1922) and *Finnegans Wake* (1939)

1882   Geoffrey O'Hara – Canadian-born composer and author, noted
        for songs such as "K-K-K-Katy"
1884   S.Z. "Cuddles" Sakall -- Hungarian-born stage and motion-
        picture actor with a 40-year career
1891   Frank Foyston -- Hall of Fame hockey player
1895   George Halas – Pioneer of professional football, who organ-
        ized, owned, and coached the Chicago Bears
1900   Carroll Righter -- American astrologer and newspaper columnist
1901   Jascha Heifetz -- Russian-American violin virtuoso
1901   Louis Kahn -- American architect
1905   Ayn Rand – American writer, novelist, and exponent of objectiv-
        ism, known for works such as *The Fountainhead* and *Atlas Shrugged*
1906   Gale Gordon -- American motion-picture and television actor
1909   Frank Albertson -- American motion-picture actor
1911   Jussi Bjoerling -- Swedish operatic and concert tenor of the
        1930s and 1940s
1912   Burton Lane -- American composer and author, noted for songs
        such as "On a Clear Day You Can See Forever," "Feudin' and
        Fightin'," "How Are Things in Glocca Morra?" and "Everything
        I Have Is Yours"
1915   Abba Eban -- Israeli foreign minister and ambassador to the U.N.
1919   Ann Fogarty -- American fashion designer
1923   James Dickey -- American poet and novelist, noted for works
        such as *Madness, Buckhead and Mercy* (1970)
1923   Bonita Granville – American stage and motion-picture actress
        and leading lady of the 1940s
1923   Red Schoendienst -- Professional baseball player and manager
1926   Valerie Giscard d'Estaing -- President of France in the 1970s
1927   Stan Getz -- American saxophonist
1927   Herbert E. Kaplow -- American broadcast journalist
1937   Don Buford -- Professional baseball player
1937   Tommy Smothers -- One of the two Smothers Brothers, Ameri-
        can comedians
1940   Helga Hoesl -- West German tennis player
1942   Bo Hopkins -- American motion-picture actor
1942   Graham Nash -- American actor and guitarist with the Crosby,
        Sills, and Nash group
1947   Farrah Fawcett -- American model and motion-picture and
        television actress
1954   John Tudor -- Professional baseball player
1955   Ed Simonini -- Professional football player

FEBRUARY 2 -- EVENTS

506 AD The *Brevarium*, a code of laws for the subjects of Alaric II, King of the Goths, was drafted at Toulouse.

1440 Frederick III was crowned Holy Roman Emperor.

1585 Hamnet and Judith, twins of William Shakespeare and Anne Hathaway, were baptized.

1653 New Amsterdam (now New York City) was incorporated.

1709 Alexander Selkirk, a Scotsman whose experiences on a lonely island inspired Daniel Defoe's story of Robinson Crusoe, was rescued from his island by English Captain Woodes Rogers.

1831 Gregory XVI was elected Roman Catholic pope.

1848 The Treaty of Guadalupe Hidalgo ended the Mexican War and gave all the Mexican land north of the Rio Grande to the United States.

1876 Baseball's National League was founded under the name National League of Professional Base Ball Clubs.

1893 The first motion-picture close-up was filmed at the Edison studio in West Orange, N.J., when cameraman William Dickson photographed comedian Fred Ott sneezing.

1922 James Joyce's great novel *Ulysses* was published in Paris.

1943 The last German troops surrendered in the Stalingrad pocket, completing the Russian victory in World War II. Only 90,000 Germans were left of the original 350,000-man army.

1953 President Dwight D. Eisenhower announced that the Seventh Fleet would no longer block Chinese Nationalist raids from Formosa against the Chinese mainland.

1957 Actress Elizabeth Taylor married movie producer Mike Todd three days after she divorced actor Michael Wilding.

FEBRUARY 3 -- BIRTHDAYS

1795 **Antonio Jose de Sucre** -- South American general who liberated Ecuador and Bolivia from Spain and served as the first president of Bolivia

1807 **Joseph E. Johnston** -- Confederate general in the Civil War

1809 **Felix Mendelssohn** -- German composer, pianist, and conductor, noted for five symphonies and for such other works as the oratorio *Elijah* (1846)

1811 **Horace Greeley** -- Prominent American journalist, founder of The New York *Tribune*, and 1872 presidential candidate, who popularized the phrase, "Go west, young man"

1821   Elizabeth Blackwell – First woman physician in the United States

1826   **Walter Bagehot** -- English economist, political analyst, sociologist, and author

1842   **Sidney Lanier** -- One of the greatest American poets, in the view of some critics, noted for works such as "Sunrise," "The Marshes of Glynn," and "Song of the Chattahoochee"

1853   **Hudson Maxim** -- American inventor of smokeless gunpowder, a self-propelled torpedo, and Maximite, an explosive more powerful than dynamite

1859   **Hugo Junkers** -- German aircraft designer

1865   **David Lawrence Pierson** -- Originator of Constitution Day (September 17th)

1874   **Gertrude Stein** -- Influential American author, noted for works such as *Three Lives* (1908) and *The Autobiography of Alice B. Toklas* (1933)

1883   **Marie Wagner** -- American Hall of Fame tennis player

1887   **Georg Trakl** -- Austrian poet

1889   **Carl Theodor Dreyer** -- Danish motion-picture director noted for works such as *Day of Wrath* (1943)

1890   **Larry MacPhail** -- Noted baseball executive who introduced night games in 1935

1894   **Norman Rockwell** -- Noted American artist especially known for over 300 *Saturday Evening Post* cover paintings between 1916 and 1963

1895   **Nick A. Kenny** -- American lyricist, noted for songs such as "There's a Gold Mine in the Sky," "Love Letters in the Sand," and "Leanin' on the Old Top Rail"

1898   **Alvar Aalto** – Finnish architect, city planner, and furniture designer

1899   **Red De Bernardi** -- Hall of Fame basketball player

1907   **James A. Michener** -- American novelist, noted for works such as *Tales of the South Pacific* (1949), *Sayonara* (1954), *Hawaii* (1960), and *The Source* (1965)

1912   **Jacques Soustelle** -- French anthropologist and politician

1918   **Joey Bishop** -- American comedian, motion-picture actor, and television personality

1918   **Stanley Earl Cowan** -- American composer noted for songs such as "Do I Worry"

1926   **Shelley Berman** -- American comedian

1931   **Peggy Ann Garner** -- American stage, screen, and television actress, and noted child star of the 1940s

1933   **Paul Sarbanes** -- U.S. senator

1938   **Emile Griffith** -- World welterweight (1961) and middleweight (1966-1967) boxing champion

1940	**Fran Tarkenton** -- Professional football superstar and television personality
1941	**Carol Mann** -- Professional golfer
1945	**Bob Griese** -- Professional football superstar
1947	**Dave Davies** -- British guitarist with the Kinks musical group
1949	**Bake McBride** -- Professional baseball player
1950	**Morgan Fairchild** -- American motion-picture and television actress
1951	**Eddie Dibbs** -- American tennis player
1952	**Ben Malone** -- Professional football player
1952	**Fred Lynn** -- Professional baseball player
1953	**Keith Hancock** -- Australian tennis player
1956	**John Jefferson** -- Professional football player
1957	**Tony Butler** -- Irish bassist with the Big Country musical group

FEBRUARY 3 -- EVENTS

590 AD	Gregory I (the Great) was elected Roman Catholic pope.
1468	Johannes Gutenberg, the famous pioneer printer of the Gutenberg Bible, died at approximately 73 years of age.
1889	The notorious American Western outlaw, Belle Starr, was shot and killed by an unknown assailant.
1898	The National Biscuit Company was incorporated by a consolidation of four baking companies.
1917	The United States broke diplomatic relations with Germany because of the German announcement of unrestricted submarine warfare.
1924	Woodrow Wilson died in Washington, D.C., at age 67.
1930	President Herbert Hoover appointed Charles Evans Hughes chief justice of the Supreme Court.
1945	U.S. troops entered Manila in World War II.
1959	Buddy Holly, influential American rock star, was killed in a plane crash near Mason City, Iowa, at age 22.

FEBRUARY 4 -- BIRTHDAYS

| 1688 | **Pierre Carlet de Marivaux** -- French playwright, novelist, and essayist, best known for his comedies, such as *The Game of Love and Chance* (1730) |
| 1693 | **George Lillo** -- English playwright noted for *The London Merchant* (1731), which became a model for dramatists in 18th-century Europe |

1802   **Mark Hopkins** -- Famous American college teacher and president of Williams College, 1836-1872

1864   **Louis Michel Eilshemius** -- American landscape painter

1865   **Abe Isoo** – One of the founders of the Japanese socialist movement

1869   **William "Big Bill" Haywood** -- American labor organizer and early leader of the Industrial Workers of the World (IWW)

1871   **Friedrich Ebert** -- First president of the German Weimar Republic, established after the defeat of Germany in World War I

1873   **George Bennard** -- American composer noted for "The Old Rugged Cross"

1881   **Fernand Leger** -- French painter noted for such works as *Three Women* (1921)

1881   **Kliment Yefremovich Voroshilov** -- Russian World War II general

1889   **Walter Catlett** -- American stage and motion-picture actor

1897   **Ludwig Erhard** -- West German statesman and chancellor, 1963-1966

1902   **Charles A. Lindbergh** – American aviator who in 1927 made the first nonstop solo flight across the Atlantic Ocean

1904   **MacKinlay Kantor** -- American novelist, noted for *Long Remember* (1934) and *Andersonville* (1955)

1905   **Eddie Foy Jr.** -- American stage and motion-picture actor, and son of the celebrated vaudeville star Eddie Foy

1906   **Dietrich Bonhoeffer** -- Noted Protestant theologian executed by the Nazis

1911   **Byron Nelson** -- Professional golfer and one of the game's immortals

1913   **Rosa Lee Parks** – Alabama black woman whose refusal to move to the back of the bus precipitated the civil rights movement in Alabama in the 1960s led by Martin Luther King Jr.

1915   **Ray Evans** -- American songwriter who with Jay Livingston wrote popular songs such as "Buttons and Bows," "Mona Lisa," "Golden Earrings," and the TV theme for *Bonanza*

1917   **Yahya Khan** -- President of Pakistan, 1969-1971

1918   **Ida Lupino** – American motion-picture and television actress, director, and screenwriter

1921   **Betty Friedan** -- Prominent American feminist, author, and journalist

1923   **Conrad Bain** -- American television and motion-picture actor

1929   **Neil Johnston** -- Professional basketball superstar with over 10,000 career points

1938   **Donald Riegle** -- U.S. senator

1943   **La Rue Florence** -- Member of the 5th Dimension singing group

1943	**Cheryl Miller** -- American motion-picture and television actress
1945	**David Brenner** -- American actor and comedian
1947	**J. Danforth Quayle** -- U.S. vice president under President Bush
1948	**Alice Cooper** -- American rock and roll singer
1948	**Ron Jessie** -- Professional football player
1959	**Lawrence Taylor** -- Professional football player

FEBRUARY 4 -- EVENTS

1789	The first U.S. Electoral College unanimously elected George Washington as the first president, and it also elected John Adams as the first vice president.
1801	John Marshall, "the great chief justice," began his term on the U.S. Supreme Court.
1861	The Confederate States of America was formed in Montgomery, Alabama.
1881	Thomas Carlyle, the great Scottish essayist and historian, died at age 85.
1894	Adolphe Sax, the inventor of the saxophone, died in poverty. There were no saxophones at his funeral.
1899	The Philippine Rebellion against the United States began, led by Philippine patriot Aguinaldo. The revolt was put down in March, when Aguinaldo was captured.
1915	Germany declared the waters around Britain to be a war zone, with the intention of attacking any ships it found there in World War I.
1926	John Giola of New York City danced the Charleston for 22 hours and 30 minutes, a record.
1941	The United Service Organizations (USO) was founded.
1945	The World War II Yalta Conference began, with Franklin D. Roosevelt, Winston Churchill, and Joseph Stalin attending.
1957	The comic strip, *Miss Peach*, by Mell Lazarus, first appeared.
1964	The 24th Amendment was proclaimed, banning poll taxes in the United States.
1971	Rolls-Royce, Ltd., the famous English automobile company, declared bankruptcy.
1974	Patricia Hearst, granddaughter of William Randolph Hearst, was kidnapped by a group called the Symbionese Liberation Army.

FEBRUARY 5 -- BIRTHDAYS

| 1534 | **Giovanni Bardi** -- Florentine musician, writer, and scientist |

1626   **Marquise Marie de Sevigne** — French noblewoman, noted for the famous letters she wrote in the mid-1600s, in which she belittled such things as coffee, Racine's poetry, and the use of condoms as a contraceptive

1723   **John Witherspoon** -- Member of the Continental Congress and a signer of the Declaration of Independence

1725   **James Otis** -- One of the most forceful leaders and orators in the American colonies' struggle for independence from Great Britain

1788   **Sir Robert Peel** -- Famous British statesman and prime minister, who founded the London police force and the British Conservative Party

1808   **Carl Spitzweg** -- German painter

1837   **Dwight L. Moody** -- American evangelist, who founded the Moody Bible Institute and the Moody Press in Chicago

1838   **Abram Joseph Ryan** -- Southern American poet known as the "Poet of the Confederacy"

1840   **John Boyd Dunlop** -- Scottish veterinarian who developed and manufactured the first pneumatic (air-filled) tire

1840   **Sir Hiram Stevens Maxim** -- American-born inventor of the Maxim machine gun, and brother of inventors Hudson and Hiram Percy Maxim

1848   **Belle Starr** -- Notorious American horse thief and outlaw of the 1870s and 1880s

1848   **Joris Karl Huysmans** -- French-born Dutch novelist, noted for works such as *Marthe* (1876) and *Against Nature* (1884)

1871   **Maxine Elliott** -- American stage actress

1878   **Andre Gustave Citroen** -- French manufacturer of the famous Citroen automobile

1894   **Ange Lorenzo** -- American composer, conductor, and pianist, noted for such songs as "Sleepy Time Gal"

1898   **Ralph Emerson McGill** -- American journalist and longtime editor of the Atlanta *Constitution*

1900   **Adlai E. Stevenson** — U.S. Democratic presidential candidate in 1952 and 1956 against General Dwight D. Eisenhower in both years

1903   **Joan Payson** — First owner of the New York Mets baseball team

1906   **John Carradine** -- American stage, screen, and television actor, who appeared in more than 170 motion pictures in a career of over 50 years

1907   **Norton Simon** -- American industrialist

1915   **Robert Hofstadter** — American physicist who shared the 1951 Nobel Prize in physics

1918   **Tim Holt** -- American Western motion-picture actor and son of actor Jack Holt

1919	**Andreas Papandreou** -- Greek statesman
1919	**Red Buttons** -- American stage, screen, and television comedian and actor
1922	**Bernard Kalb** -- American television newsman and U.S. State Department spokesman under President Reagan
1926	**Arthur Sulzberger** -- Publisher of the New York *Times*
1934	**Hank Aaron** – Most prolific home run hitter in professional baseball, with a career total of 755
1937	**Lionel Tiger** -- American anthropologist and author
1937	**Stuart Damon** -- American television actor
1938	**John Guare** -- American playwright
1942	**Roger Staubach** -- Professional football superstar
1943	**Eddie Belmonte** -- American jockey
1943	**Craig Morton** -- Professional football player
1945	**Bob Marley** -- Jamaican reggae singer of the 1970s
1950	**Jan Hordijk** -- Dutch tennis player
1951	**Elizabeth Swados** -- American composer, writer, and director

FEBRUARY 5 -- EVENTS

46 BC	Marcus Cato, the Roman philosopher, committed suicide by stabbing himself, on learning of the victory of his enemy, Julius Caesar, over Pompey at Thapsus.
1631	Roger Williams, future founder of Rhode Island, arrived in Boston from England.
1826	Millard Fillmore married his former teacher, Abigail Powers.
1861	Coleman Sellers, a Philadelphia inventor, patented his *kinematoscope*, a motion picture device.
1881	Phoenix, Arizona, was incorporated.
1887	Italian composer Giuseppe Verdi's greatest tragic opera, *Otello*, was first performed, at Milan's La Scala.
1929	The comic strip, *They'll Do It Everytime*, by Jimmy Hatlo, first appeared.
1937	President Franklin D. Roosevelt proposed that up to 6 additional Supreme Court justices be appointed, prompting his critics to charge him with trying to "pack" the Court.
1945	The U.S. Third Army under General George S. Patton broke through the Germans' Siegfried Line in World War II.
1951	Sylvia Green Wilks, the daughter of Hetty Green, the miserly "Witch of Wall Street," died, leaving an estate of over $90 million.

1971   U.S. astronauts Alan Shepard and Edgar Mitchell landed on the
        moon while astronaut Stuart Roosa remained in the command
        module of the *Apollo 14* mission.

FEBRUARY 6 -- BIRTHDAYS

1665   **Queen Anne** -- Queen of England, 1702-1714, first queen of the
        joint kingdom of Great Britain and Ireland, 1707-1714, and the
        last monarch of the House of Stuart

1756   **Aaron Burr** -- U.S. vice president, 1801-1805, whose promising
        career ended disastrously when he killed Alexander Hamilton in
        a duel in 1804

1802   **Sir Charles Wheatstone** -- English physicist and inventor best
        known for his work on electrical measuring devices, the best
        example of which is the Wheatstone bridge

1807   **Hiram Sibley** -- American financier who with Ezra Cornell in
        1856 organized the Western Union Company

1833   **J.E.B. "Jeb" Stuart** -- Confederate Civil War general who distin-
        guished himself in the first Battle of Bull Run and in the Wilder-
        ness Campaign

1838   **Sir Henry Irving** -- One of the greatest stage actors and most
        successful theater managers of the 19th century

1888   **Haven Gillespie** -- American composer noted for songs such as
        "That Lucky Old Sun" and "Santa Claus Is Coming to Town"

1895   **Babe Ruth** -- The greatest slugger in baseball history, whose
        records of 714 career home runs and 60 single-season home runs
        stood for nearly 40 years

1899   **Ramon Novarro** -- Romantic idol of Hollywood silent films of
        the 1920s

1902   **Louis Nizer** -- Prominent English-born lawyer and author, noted
        for his autobiography, *My Life in Court*

1902   **Leon T. Rene** -- American composer and author, noted for
        songs such as "When the Swallows Come Back to Capistrano"

1903   **Claudio Arrau** -- Chilean pianist and teacher noted for his many
        concerts and recordings

1908   **Amintore Fanfani** -- Three-time premier of Italy, 1954, 1958-
        1959, and 1960-1963

1911   **Ronald Reagan** -- American actor and 40th U.S. president

1912   **Eva Braun** -- Mistress of Adolf Hitler who reportedly married
        him in 1945, the day before they both committed suicide

1920   **Zsa Zsa Gabor** -- Hungarian-born stage, screen, and television
        actress, and sister of actress Eva Gabor

1920   **William Jovanovich** -- American publisher and one of the founders of Harcourt Brace Jovanovich

1927   **Smokey Burgess** -- Professional baseball player noted in his later
years as a highly effective pinch hitter

1927   **Hugh Haynie** -- American editorial cartoonist

1931   **Rip Torn** -- American stage, screen, and television actor

1931   **Mamie Van Doren** – American stage and motion-picture actress

1932   **Francois Truffaut** -- French motion-picture director

1939   **Mike Farrell** -- American motion-picture and television actor
noted for his role in the long-running TV series *M*A*S*H*

1940   **Tom Brokaw** -- American television host and newscaster

1941   **Fabian (Forte)** – American teeny-bopper idol, singer, and actor

1941   **Gigi Perreau** -- American child star of Hollywood films of the
1940s and early 1950s

1945   **Donald Cockroft** -- Professional football player

1947   **Charles Hickcox** -- Professional swimmer

1947   **Rik Massengale** -- Professional golfer

1949   **Manuel Orantes** -- Spanish tennis player

1949   **Richie Zisk** -- Professional baseball player

1950   **Natalie Cole** -- American singer and daughter of the noted
singer, Nat King Cole

1968   **Molly Ringwald** -- American motion-picture actress

FEBRUARY 6 -- EVENTS

1685   King Charles II of England, the first of the restored Stuart line,
died at age 54.

1778   France signed an alliance with the United States to help fight the
British in the Revolutionary War.

1788   Massachusetts ratified the U.S. Constitution, becoming the
sixth state.

1843   "The Virginia Minstrels," the first minstrel show produced in
America, was staged in New York City.

1862   General U.S. Grant's Union troops captured Fort Henry in
Tennessee in the Civil War.

1899   The U.S. Senate ratified the Treaty of Paris, formally ending the
Spanish-American War.

1911   The Rolls-Royce mascot, "The Spirit of Ecstasy," was cast for
the first time.

1933   The 20th Amendment to the U.S. Constitution was proclaimed,
moving the date of the president's inauguration from March 4 to
January 20.

1943   General Dwight D. Eisenhower was appointed commander-in-chief of all the Allied forces in North Africa.

1952   King George VI of England died of lung cancer at age 56, and was succeeded by his daughter, Elizabeth II.

1959   The U.S. first successfully test-fired the Titan intercontinental ballistic missile from Cape Canaveral.

FEBRUARY 7 -- BIRTHDAYS

1477   **Sir Thomas More** -- Great English author, statesman, and scholar, known for the famous book *Utopia* (1516)

1741   **Henry Fuseli** -- Anglo-Swiss painter noted for works such as *The Nightmare* (1781)

1804   **John Deere** — American manufacturer and inventor who invented the first steel plow and became the most famous plow-maker in the world

1812   **Charles Dickens** -- England's greatest novelist and one of the most popular writers of all time

1817   **Frederick Douglass** -- American slave who escaped and became a noted author and speaker and the leading spokesman of American Negroes in the 1800s

1834   **Dmitri Ivanovich Mendeleev** -- Noted Russian chemist who devised the periodic table of the elements

1867   **Laura Ingalls Wilder** -- American author of pioneer stories for children, such as *Little House on the Prairie* (1935)

1870   **Alfred Adler** -- Austrian psychiatrist who introduced the term *inferiority feeling*

1883   **Eubie Blake** -- American pianist and "grand old man of ragtime," who wrote "I'm Just Wild About Harry," and was active to age 100

1885   **Sinclair Lewis** -- One of America's greatest novelists, noted for works such as *Main Street* (1920), *Babbitt* (1922), and *Arrowsmith* (1925)

1911   **Josef Mengele** — Nazi physician and Auschwitz "Angel of Death," who performed ghastly experiments on Jewish prisoners and was accused of murdering 400,000 people in World War II

1918   **Ruth Sager** -- Noted American geneticist

1920   **Eddie Bracken** -- American stage, screen, and television actor

1923   **Keefe Brasselle** -- American motion-picture actor, television producer, and author

1932   **Alfred M. Worden** -- U.S. astronaut and pilot of the command module of *Apollo 15*

1932   **Gay Talese** -- American author and journalist
1950   **Marilyn Cochran** -- Professional skier
1950   **Burt Hooton** -- Professional baseball player
1953   **Robert Brazile** -- Professional football player
1954   **Dan Quisenberry** -- Professional baseball player and one of the greatest relief pitchers of all time
1957   **Carney Lansford** -- Professional baseball player
1960   **Steve Bronski** -- British singer and songwriter with the Bronski Beat musical group

FEBRUARY 7 -- EVENTS

1613   Michael Romanov was elected czar of Russia, becoming the first of the Romanov czars.
1827   The first ballet group formed in the United States performed the ballet *The Deserter* at the Bowery Theater in New York City.
1878   Pope Pius IX died at age 85, ending a term of 32 years as pope, the longest reign in papal history.
1901   Queen Wilhelmina of the Netherlands married Henry, Duke of Mecklenburg-Schwerin.
1904   A fire began in Baltimore that lasted for 30 hours and destroyed some 1,500 buildings.
1936   A special flag for the office of vice president was created on executive order of President Franklin D. Roosevelt.
1940   Walt Disney's motion picture *Pinocchio* had its world premiere.
1948   General Dwight D. Eisenhower resigned as army chief of staff and was succeeded by General Omar Bradley.
1950   The United States recognized South Vietnam.
1964   The Beatles arrived in America for the first time, and were greeted by 10,000 fans at New York's Kennedy Airport.
1971   Women in Switzerland were given the right to vote.
1974   The island of Grenada was given its independence from Great Britain.

FEBRUARY 8 -- BIRTHDAYS

1577   **Robert Burton** -- English scholar and poet
1580   **William Herbert** -- Earl of Pembroke
1591   **Guercino (Giovanni F. Barbieri)** -- Italian painter
1612   **Samuel Butler** -- English satirist, who in his famous poem, "Hudibras," popularized such proverbs as "Spare the rod and spoil the child"

1819   John Ruskin -- English writer on art, literature, and social issues, who was probably the most influential critic of Victorian England

1820   **William Tecumseh Sherman** -- U.S. Civil War general, famous for his "March to the Sea" in Georgia in 1865

1828   **Jules Verne** -- French novelist and pioneer science fiction writer, noted for works such as *Twenty Thousand Leagues Under the Sea* (1870) and *Around the World in Eighty Days* (1873)

1866   **John Henry Whitley** -- Noted Speaker of the English House of Commons

1868   **Lionel Walter Rothschild** -- English zoologist, member of the House of Commons, and founder of the Rothschild Natural History Museum

1880   **Franz Marc** -- German painter

1886   **Charlie Ruggles** -- American stage and motion-picture actor who appeared in some 100 films

1888   **Dame Edith Evans** -- English stage, screen, and television actress

1894   **King Vidor** -- Famous American motion-picture director, noted for films such as *Duel in the Sun* (1947) and *Solomon and Sheba* (1959)

1911   **Elizabeth Bishop** -- American poet who won the 1956 Pulitzer Prize for her book *North and South: A Cold Spring*

1914   **Bill Finger** -- American comic book writer, who with Bob Kane created *Batman*

1919   **Buddy Morrow** -- American trombonist

1920   **Lana Turner** -- American stage, screen, and television actress, and glittering star of the 1940s

1921   **Hoot Evers** -- Professional baseball player

1921   **Willard Marshall** -- Professional baseball player

1925   **Jack Lemmon** -- American stage, screen, and television actor who won Academy Awards for his work in *Mister Roberts* (1955) and *Save the Tiger* (1973)

1931   **James Dean** -- American motion-picture actor and object of posthumous adulation unequaled since Valentino

1932   **John Williams** -- American composer and successor to Arthur Fiedler as conductor of the Boston Pops Orchestra

1937   **Clete Boyer** -- Professional baseball player

1940   **Ted Koppel** -- American television broadcast journalist

1941   **Nick Nolte** -- American motion-picture and television actor

1942   **Robert Klein** -- American comedian

1949   **Brooke Adams** -- American stage, screen, and television actress

1956   **Marques Johnson** -- Professional basketball player

1968   **Gary Coleman** -- American television actor

FEBRUARY 8 -- EVENTS

1587   Mary, Queen of Scots was beheaded at Fotheringay Castle on orders of England's Queen Elizabeth I.

1693   The College of William and Mary, the second oldest in the United States to Harvard, was chartered by King William III and Queen Mary II of England.

1800   A ceremony was held at the Church of the Invalides in Paris to mourn the death of George Washington, which had occurred some two months earlier.

1837   For the only time in its history, the U.S. Senate chose the vice president, selecting Richard Mentor Johnson after none of the candidates received a majority of electoral votes.

1861   The Confederate States of America was founded when seven states that had seceded agreed to a constitution in Montgomery, Alabama.

1904   The Japanese attacked and decimated the Russian fleet at Port Arthur in a surprise assault that started the Russo-Japanese War.

1910   The Boy Scouts of America was incorporated in the District of Columbia by U.S. businessman William D. Boyce and others.

1915   The great D.W. Griffith movie, *The Birth of a Nation*, premiered at Clune's Auditorium in Los Angeles, marking the beginning of modern moviemaking.

1918   *The Stars and Stripes*, the American Expeditionary Force's official newspaper, was published for the first time.

1924   The first execution by gas chamber took place at the Nevada State Prison in Carson City, Nevada, when Chinese-American Gee Jon was executed for murder.

1932   Jack Dempsey, the great heavyweight boxer, defeated two opponents, Buck Everett and Jack Roper, in exhibition bouts in Milwaukee.

1940   The Nazis shot every tenth person in two villages near Warsaw in reprisal for the deaths of two German soldiers in World War II.

1943   Allied troops took Guadalcanal in the Solomon Islands from the Japanese in World War II.

1952   Elizabeth II was proclaimed Queen of England.

1955   Georgi Malenkov, Joseph Stalin's successor, in a surprise move, resigned, to be succeeded as Soviet premier by Nikolai Bulganin.

1974   The U.S. *Skylab* mission ended after a record-breaking 84 days in space.

FEBRUARY 9 -- BIRTHDAYS

1700   **Daniel Bernoulli** -- Noted Swiss mathematician and member of the famous family of mathematicians that included his father John and his uncle Jacob Bernoulli

1773   **William Henry Harrison** -- 9th U.S. president and grandfather of the 23rd president, Benjamin Harrison

1789   **Franz Gabelsberger** -- Inventor of the calculating machine

1814   **Samuel J. Tilden** -- U.S. presidential candidate in 1876 who probably had the election stolen from him

1826   **John Alexander Logan** – Union Civil War general who helped organize the Grand Army of the Republic, and who was credited with naming May 30, 1868, as the first Memorial Day

1863   **Anthony Hope** -- English author noted for *The Prisoner of Zenda*

1866   **George Ade** -- American humorist and playwright, noted for works such as *Fables in Slang* and *County Chairman*

1874   **Amy Lowell** -- American poet and critic, best known for "Sword Blades and Poppy Seeds" (1914) and the biography *John Keats* (1925)

1885   **Alban Berg** -- Austrian composer noted for works such as the opera *Wozzeck* (1925) and *Three Orchestral Pieces* (1914)

1891   **Ronald Colman** -- English stage and motion-picture actor and leading man in both silents and talkies

1899   **Brian Donlevy** – Irish-born stage and motion-picture actor in nearly 100 films

1902   **Fred Harman** -- American cartoonist and creator of *Red Ryder* (1938)

1902   **Chester Lauck** -- American actor who portrayed Lum Edwards in the radio show, *Lum and Abner*, of the 1930s and 1940s

1907   **Dit Clapper** -- Hall of Fame hockey player

1908   **Seymour "Sy" Miller** -- American composer, author, and pianist, noted for songs such as "Let There Be Peace on Earth (And Let It Begin with Me)"

1909   **Heather Angel** -- English stage, screen, and television actress

1909   **Carmen Miranda** -- Portuguese-born singer, dancer, and actress of the 1930s and 1940s, billed as the "Brazilian Bombshell"

1909   **Dean Rusk** -- U.S. secretary of state under Presidents Kennedy and Johnson

1914   **Ernest Tubb** -- One of America's leading country music singers of the 1940-1980 era

1914   **Bill Veeck** -- Noted American baseball executive

1922   **Kathryn Grayson** -- American singer and actress of the 1940s and early 1950s

1925	**Vic Wertz** -- Professional baseball player
1928	**Roger Mudd** -- American television newscaster and commentator
1939	**Barry Mann** -- American songwriter
1942	**Francois Jauffret** -- French tennis player
1942	**Carole King** -- American songwriter and singer
1945	**Mia Farrow** -- American stage, screen, and television actress, and daughter of director John Farrow and actress Maureen O'Sullivan
1952	**Danny White** -- Professional football player

FEBRUARY 9 -- EVENTS

1119	Calixtus II was crowned Roman Catholic pope.
1825	The House of Representatives elected John Quincy Adams president, after the 1824 election in which Andrew Jackson led the popular voting but did not get an electoral majority.
1861	Jefferson Davis was elected president of the Confederacy.
1870	The United States Weather Service was established.
1881	Fyodor Dostoevsky, the great Russian novelist, died in St. Petersburg at age 59.
1893	*Falstaff*, the last opera of the great Italian composer, Giuseppe Verdi, had its world premiere at Milan's La Scala.
1895	The Minnesota State School of Agriculture defeated Hamline College, 9-3, in the world's first college basketball game.
1942	The French luxury liner *Normandie*, while being refitted as a transport ship, burned and capsized in New York Harbor.
1943	U.S. troops under Major General Alexander Patch finally won the World War II Battle of Guadalcanal, begun the previous August.
1950	U.S. Senator Joseph McCarthy started a 4-year "witch-hunt" by charging in a Wheeling, West Virginia, speech that the State Department was riddled with Communists.
1964	The Beatles made their American television debut on the *Ed Sullivan Show*.
1969	The first Boeing 747, the world's largest airplane, began its first flight, from Paine Field in Seattle, Washington.
1971	California's San Fernando Valley was rocked by an earthquake that measured 6.5 on the Richter scale.
1984	Soviet premier Yuri Andropov died, only 15 months after he had succeeded Leonid Brezhnev.

FEBRUARY 10 -- BIRTHDAYS

1499	**Thomas Platter** -- Swiss writer and humanist

1775   **Charles Lamb** -- Noted British essayist and critic of the romantic movement of the early 1800s, who used the pen name "Elia" for many of his essays

1846   **Ira Remsen** -- American chemist and founder in 1879 of the *American Chemical Journal*, the first American journal in the field of science

1858   **Walt McDougall** -- American comic strip and political cartoonist, whose front-page work, *The Royal Feast of Belshazzar Blaine and the Money Kings,* may have cost James Blaine the 1884 election

1868   **William Allen White** -- American journalist and editor, known in the early 1900s as the "Sage of Emporia"

1890   **Boris Pasternak** -- Russian writer noted for the novel *Doctor Zhivago* (1957)

1892   **Alan Hale** -- American actor and director who appeared in over 100 films

1893   **Jimmy Durante** -- American comedian, songwriter, and entertainer, nicknamed "Schnozzola" for his long, bulbous nose

1893   **William "Big Bill" Tilden** — American tennis player who dominated the game in the decade of the 1920s, and who is considered by many to be the greatest player of all time

1894   **Harold Macmillan** -- British prime minister, 1957-1963

1894   **Herb Pennock** -- Hall of Fame baseball pitcher who worked in 617 games in a 22-year career

1898   **Dame Judith Anderson** -- One of the finest actresses on the 20th-century English-speaking stage

1898   **Bertolt Brecht** — German playwright noted for works such as *The Three Penny Opera* (1928) and *The Caucasian Chalk Circle* (1944-1945)

1904   **John Farrow** -- American motion-picture director who shared in the Academy Award for the screenplay of *Around the World in 80 Days* (1956)

1905   **Walter Brown** -- American basketball executive who organized the Boston Celtics basketball team

1907   **Lon Chaney Jr.** — American motion-picture actor in some 150 films, who like his famous father specialized in monster and villain roles

1913   **Merriam Smith** -- American author and journalist

1914   **Larry Adler** -- American musician

1915   **Allie Reynolds** -- Professional baseball pitcher who pitched two no-hit games in 1951

1920   **Alex Comfort** -- American gerontologist and author of *The Joy of Sex* (1972)

1927   **Leontyne Price** -- American opera singer and one of the most celebrated sopranos of her time

1930   **Robert Wagner** – American motion-picture and television actor
1939   **Roberta Flack** -- American soul singer
1946   **Dick Anderson** -- Professional football player
1950   **Mark Spitz** -- American swimming superstar who won seven gold medals in the 1972 Olympics
1963   **Lenny Dykstra** -- Professional baseball player

FEBRUARY 10 -- EVENTS

1755   Montesquieu (Charles de Secondat), the great French philosopher, died in Paris at age 66.
1763   The Treaty of Paris ended the French and Indian War and gave the French empire in India and North America to the British.
1837   Alexander Pushkin, Russia's most celebrated poet, was killed at age 37 in a duel defending his wife's honor.
1840   Queen Victoria of England married Prince Albert of Saxe-Coburg-Gotha.
1863   Tom Thumb, the star midget of P.T. Barnum's circus, married Lavinia Warren, "the smallest woman alive."
1899   Herbert Hoover married Lou Henry.
1904   Japan formally declared war on Russia two days after hostilities had begun in the Russo-Japanese War.
1933   Singing telegrams were introduced in New York by the Postal Telegraph Company.
1942   The first "golden record" was presented by RCA Victor to bandleader Glenn Miller for his recording of "Chattanooga Choo Choo."
1942   The last civilian automobiles rolled off the assembly lines in Detroit as the U.S. geared up for war production.
1949   Arthur Miller's famous play, *Death of a Salesman*, made its debut, at New York's Morosco Theater.
1957   The comic strip, *On Stage*, by Leonard Starr, first appeared.
1971   *Apollo 14* splashed down from its moon voyage.

FEBRUARY 11 -- BIRTHDAYS

1466   **Elizabeth of York** -- Daughter of King Edward IV of England and wife of Henry VII, whose marriage to her united the houses of Lancaster and York
1535   **Gregory XIV** -- Roman Catholic pope, 1590-1591
1657   **Bernard de Fontenelle** -- French man of letters, scientist, and philosopher, noted for works such as *Dialogues des Morts* (1683)

1760   **Richard Allen** — American slave who bought his freedom and founded the African Methodist Church (1816), the first black denomination in the United States

1821   **Auguste Mariette** -- French Egyptologist

1839   **J. Willard Gibbs** -- One of the greatest American theoretical physicists, thought by some to be the father of modern physical chemistry

1847   **Thomas A. Edison** -- Probably the greatest inventor in history, whose 1,100 inventions include the electric light, the phonograph, and the motion-picture projector

1863   **John "Honey Fitz" Fitzgerald** -- American businessman and politician, and grandfather of President John F. Kennedy

1881   **Carlo Carra** -- Noted 20th-century Italian painter

1889   **John Mills** — American singer and member of the Mills Brothers group

1900   **Tommy Hitchcock Jr.** -- The greatest polo player of all time

1904   **Sir Keith Jacka Holyoake** -- Governor General of New Zealand

1907   **William Levitt** — American industrialist who brought mass production methods to the housing industry, and became the biggest builder of houses in the U.S. in the 1940s and 1950s

1908   **Sir Vivian Ernest Fuchs** -- British geologist and Antarctic expert, who commanded the British Commonwealth Trans-Antarctic Expedition in 1957 and 1958, the first to cross Antarctica

1909   **Max Baer** -- World heavyweight boxing champion, 1934-1935

1909   **Joseph Mankiewicz** — American director, producer, and screenwriter, who won Academy Awards for *A Letter to Three Wives* (1949) and *All About Eve* (1950)

1912   **Rudolf Firkusny** -- Czechoslovakian pianist

1920   **Farouk I** -- King of Egypt, 1936-1952

1921   **Lloyd Bentsen** -- U.S. senator and Democratic candidate for vice president in 1988

1924   **Budge Patty** -- American tennis superstar

1925   **Virginia E. Johnson** — American psychologist noted for human sexuality studies with Dr. William H. Masters

1925   **Kim Stanley** -- American stage and motion-picture actress

1926   **Eva Gabor** -- Hungarian-born stage, screen, and television actress, and sister of actress Zsa Zsa Gabor

1926   **Leslie Nielsen** -- American stage, screen, and television actor

1934   **Mary Quant** -- English fashion designer

1934   **Tina Louise** -- American stage, screen, and television actress

1936   **Burt Reynolds** -- American motion-picture and television actor, and virile leading man of the 1960s, 1970s, and 1980s

1949   **Ben Ogilvie** -- Professional baseball player

FEBRUARY 11 -- EVENTS

1650   Rene Descartes, the great French mathematician and philosopher, died in Sweden at age 53.

1752   The Pennsylvania Hospital, the first incorporated hospital in the U.S., opened in Philadelphia.

1812   The word *gerrymander* came into the language to describe the political redistricting done by Massachusetts governor Elbridge Gerry.

1858   French schoolgirl Bernadette Soubirous had her first vision of Our Lady of Lourdes in the French town of Lourdes near the foothills of the Pyrenees.

1861   President-elect Abraham Lincoln and his wife left Springfield, Illinois, for Washington, D.C.

1929   Vatican City became a sovereign state with the signing of the Treaty of the Lateran.

1943   General Dwight D. Eisenhower was made a full general in the U.S. Army.

1945   The World War II Yalta Conference concluded with a statement by Roosevelt, Churchill, and Stalin of their intentions to occupy Germany and form the United Nations.

1965   President Lyndon B. Johnson announced U.S. policy to help South Vietnam.

1979   Moslem revolutionaries took over the government of Iran, with Mehdi Bazargan selected as prime minister by Ayatollah Khomeini.

1983   The space shuttle *Challenger* returned to earth after an eight-day mission, featuring the first untethered spacewalk by astronauts.

FEBRUARY 12 -- BIRTHDAYS

1567   **Thomas Campion** -- Elizabethan English composer, poet, and physician, noted for his four *Books of Airs*

1606   **John Winthrop Jr.** -- Colonial governor and later governor of Connecticut, and son of the Puritan governor of the Massachusetts Bay Colony

1663   **Cotton Mather** -- Noted American Puritan scholar and minister, and son of the Puritan minister Increase Mather

1746   **Thaddeus Kosciusko** -- Polish patriot who fought for freedom in America and in Poland, known for this reason as the "Hero of Two Worlds"

1768   Francis II -- Austrian ruler who became the last monarch to hold
        the title of Holy Roman Emperor

1775   **Louisa Catherine Johnson** – Wife of President John Quincy Adams

1791   **Peter Cooper** – American inventor and philanthropist who in
        1830 built the "Tom Thumb," the first commercial American
        steam locomotive, and in 1859 founded the Cooper Union

1809   **Charles Darwin** -- English naturalist noted for the theory
        of evolution

1809   **Abraham Lincoln** – 16th U.S. president, considered by most
        historians to be the greatest of all the presidents

1813   **James Dwight Dana** – American geologist, mineralogist, zoolo-
        gist, and author

1828   **George Meredith** -- English poet and novelist, noted for works
        such as *The Ordeal of Richard Feverel* (1859) and *Diana of the
        Crossways* (1885)

1878   **Joseph Edgar Howard** -- American composer and actor noted
        for songs such as "I Wonder Who's Kissing Her Now" (with
        Will Hough)

1880   **John L. Lewis** -- American labor leader who formed the Com-
        mittee for Industrial Organization (CIO), and who was presi-
        dent of the United Mine Workers from 1919 to 1960

1884   **Max Beckmann** -- German painter

1884   **Alice Roosevelt Longworth** -- Daughter of President Theodore
        Roosevelt

1893   **Omar N. Bradley** -- U.S. World War II general whose Twelfth
        Army Group of about 1,000,000 men was the largest fighting
        force ever amassed in battle under the American flag

1898   **Roy Harris** -- American composer whose best-known works are
        his *Symphony No. 3* and *An American Overture*

1903   **Chick Hafey** -- Hall of Fame baseball player

1904   **Ted Mack** -- Host of the *Original Amateur Hour* on radio and
        television

1911   **Silvestre Antonio Guzman Fernandez** – President of the
        Dominican Republic

1912   **Tex Beneke** – American singer and bandleader who took over
        the Glenn Miller band after Miller was killed in World War II

1915   **Lorne Greene** -- Canadian stage, screen, and television actor,
        who played Ben Cartwright in the long-running television series
        Bonanza

1916   **Joseph L. Alioto** -- Mayor of San Francisco in the 1970s

1917   **Dom DiMaggio** -- Professional baseball player and brother of
        baseball great Joe DiMaggio

1919   **Eddie Robinson** -- College football coach at Grambling State University with over 340 career victories, a record in both college and professional football

1919   **Forrest Tucker** – American motion-picture and television actor

1923   **Franco Zeffirelli** -- Italian motion-picture director noted for films such as *Romeo and Juliet* (1968)

1926   **Joe Garagiola** – Professional baseball player and television sportscaster

1930   **Arlen Specter** -- U.S. senator

1932   **Princess Astrid** -- Princess of Norway

1934   **Bill Russell** – Professional basketball superstar, and one of the greatest defensive centers in basketball history

1935   **Ray Manzarek** -- Keyboard player with the Doors rock group

1938   **Judy Blume** -- American writer and author of juvenile fiction

1938   **Johnny Rutherford** -- Noted American racing car driver

1945   **Maud Adams** -- American actress and model

1951   **Kjell Johansson** -- Swedish tennis player

1955   **Chet Lemon** -- Professional baseball player

1959   **Larry Nance** -- Professional basketball player

FEBRUARY 12 -- EVENTS

1541   Santiago, Chile, was founded by Spanish explorer Pedro de Valdivia.

1554   Lady Jane Grey, pretender to the throne of England after the death of Edward VI, was beheaded along with her husband on a charge of high treason.

1733   James Oglethorpe founded Savannah, as Georgia's first colonial settlement.

1736   Maria Theresa, the great queen of Austria, married Francis Stephen, Duke of Lorraine.

1793   The Fugitive Slave Act was passed by the U.S. Congress, allowing owners to recover their runaway slaves merely by presenting proof of ownership before a magistrate.

1804   Immanuel Kant, the great German philosopher, died in Konigsberg, East Prussia, at age 79.

1818   Chile gained its independence from Spain.

1878   Frederick Thayer patented the baseball catcher's mask.

1909   The National Association for the Advancement of Colored People (NAACP), America's oldest civil rights organization, was founded in New York City.

1912   The Chinese Republic was formed by Sun Yat-sen.

1915   The cornerstone for the Lincoln Memorial was laid in Washington, D.C.

1917   The comic strip, *The Gumps*, by Sidney Smith, first appeared.

1924   George Gershwin's *Rhapsody in Blue* was first performed, with Gershwin himself at the piano, at Aeolian Hall in New York.

1938   Adolf Hitler demanded concessions of Austrian Premier Kurt von Schuschnigg, who had no alternative but to give in. A month later Hitler took over Austria anyway.

1971   J.C. Penney, the noted American merchant, died at age 95.

FEBRUARY 13 -- BIRTHDAYS

1457   **Mary of Burgundy** -- Wife of Maximilian I of Austria and daughter of Charles the Bold of Burgundy

1674   **Prosper Jolyot Crebillon** -- French playwright noted for works such as *Idomeneus* (1705) and *Electra* (1717)

1682   **Giovanni Battista Piazzetta** -- Venetian painter and illustrator

1728   **John Hunter** -- English surgeon and anatomist, noted as the founder of experimental surgery

1754   **Charles Maurice de Talleyrand** – French statesman noted for his diplomatic achievements under Napoleon and at the Congress of Vienna

1755   **Philibert Louis Debucourt** -- French painter

1805   **Peter Gustav Lejeune Dirichlet** -- Noted German mathematician

1849   **Lord Randolph Churchill** -- English politician and father of Sir Winston Churchill

1873   **Feodor Ivanovich Chaliapin** – Russian opera singer and the leading interpreter of his time of bass roles in Russian and Italian opera

1877   **Sidney Smith** -- American comic strip writer and creator in 1917 of *The Gumps*

1885   **Bess Wallace** -- Wife of President Harry S Truman

1888   **Georgios Papandreou** -- Three-time prime minister of Greece

1892   **Grant Wood** -- American artist noted for the famous painting, *American Gothic* (1930)

1903   **Georges Simenon** -- French reporter, writer, and creator of Inspector Maigret

1908   **Lennie Hayton** -- American jazz composer and conductor

1910   **William Bradford Shockley** – American physicist and co-developer of the transistor

1915   **Lyle Bettger** -- American stage, screen, and television actor

1918   **Patty Berg** -- One of the greatest women golfers in history

1919	"**Tennessee" Ernie Ford** -- American humorist and singer
1920	**Eileen Farrell** -- American opera singer and "supersoprano"
1924	**Jean-Jacques Servan-Schreiber** -- French journalist, politician, and author
1933	**Kim Novak** -- American motion-picture actress and number one box-office attraction in the 1950s
1933	**Emanuel Ungaro** -- French fashion designer
1934	**George Segal** -- American stage, screen, and television actor
1938	**Oliver Reed** -- English motion-picture actor and leading man of British and international films
1941	**Bo Svenson** -- American actor
1942	**Carol Lynley** -- American motion-picture and television actress
1944	**Sal Bando** -- Professional baseball player
1944	**Peter Tork** -- American singer and member of the Monkees musical group
1944	**Stockard Channing** -- American motion-picture actress
1951	**David Naughton** -- American motion-picture and television actor

FEBRUARY 13 -- EVENTS

1542	England's King Henry VIII had his fifth wife, Catherine Howard, beheaded on charges of adultery.
1571	Benvenuto Cellini, the great Italian sculptor and writer, died in Florence at age 70.
1635	The Boston Public Latin School, the oldest public school in America, was opened.
1689	William and Mary were formally proclaimed King and Queen regnant of England.
1728	Cotton Mather, the famous American theologian and preacher, died in Boston at age 65.
1741	*The American Magazine*, the first magazine in America, was published in Philadelphia by Andrew Bradford, three days before Benjamin Franklin published *The General Magazine*.
1883	Richard Wagner, the great German composer, died in Bayreuth at age 69.
1914	The American Society of Composers, Authors, and Publishers (ASCAP) was organized in New York City by composer Victor Herbert and others.
1937	The comic strip, *Prince Valiant*, by Harold Foster, first appeared.
1945	The Russians took Budapest from the Germans in World War II after 49 days of fighting.
1960	France exploded its first atom bomb in the Sahara Desert.

FEBRUARY 14 -- BIRTHDAYS

1404   **Leon Battista Alberti** -- Italian Renaissance architect, painter, and author, who designed the Rucellai Palace and the church of Santa Maria Novella in Florence

1602   **Francesco Cavalli** -- Italian opera composer noted for works such as *Giasone* (1649) and *Calisto* (1651)

1766   **Thomas Robert Malthus** -- English economist noted for his famous "Malthusian theory" that the population will eventually outrun the food supply

1768   **Ivan Krylov** -- Russian fable writer

1824   **Winfield Scott Hancock** -- Union Civil War general and candidate for U.S. president in 1880

1838   **Edwin Ginn** -- Founder in 1866 of Ginn & Company publishers

1856   **Frank Harris** -- Journalist and author, noted for the erotic book, *My Life and Loves* (1923)

1859   **George Washington Gale Ferris** -- U.S. engineer who designed the world's first Ferris wheel, a structure 250 feet tall with 36 passenger cars at the Columbian Exposition in Chicago in 1893

1865   **Carl Thomas Anderson** -- American cartoonist and creator in 1932 of the comic strip *Henry*

1882   **George Jean Nathan** -- American author, editor, and drama critic

1894   **Jack Benny** -- American actor, comedian, and superstar, with a durable and influential career in American comedy that spanned over 60 years

1905   **Thelma Ritter** -- American motion-picture performer who was an excellent character actress of the 1950s and 1960s

1907   **Johnny Longden** -- Noted American jockey with over 6,000 winners

1913   **Mel Allen** -- American sportscaster and author, noted especially for his broadcasts of the New York Yankees' baseball games in their great pennant-winning years

1913   **Woody Hayes** -- Winningest football coach in Big Ten history, with 14 conference titles and 3 national champions at Ohio State

1913   **James R. Hoffa** -- American labor leader and president of the Teamsters Union in the late 1950s and 1960s

1913   **James A. Pike** -- American clergyman, Episcopal bishop, and outspoken advocate of social justice

1915   **Irving Gordon** -- American composer noted for songs such as "Unforgettable" and "Mister and Mississippi"

1921   **Hugh Downs** -- American television personality

1923   **Cesare Siepi** -- Italian basso

1931   **Bernie "Boom Boom" Geoffrion** -- Professional hockey player

1932   **Vic Morrow** -- American television and motion-picture actor
1934   **Florence Henderson** -- American television actress
1935   **Mickey Wright** -- One of the top professional women golfers
1937   **Magic Sam Maghett** -- American musician and the "last great original Chicago blues man"
1941   **Paul Tsongas** -- U.S. senator
1944   **Carl Bernstein** -- American columnist and author, and one of the principal figures in exposing the Watergate scandals
1946   **Gregory Hines** -- American motion-picture actor and dancer
1950   **Philip Dent** -- Australian tennis player

FEBRUARY 14 -- EVENTS

44 BC   Julius Caesar was made dictator of Rome for life.
269 AD   The Roman priest Saint Valentine was beheaded in Rome on Palatine Hill.
1130   Innocent II was elected Roman Catholic pope.
1400   Ex-King Richard II of England died in prison. It is very likely that he was murdered.
1779   Captain James Cook, the famous British navigator, was killed by the natives at Owhyhee, Hawaii.
1849   James K. Polk became the first U.S. president to be photographed while in office when he posed for the noted photographer Mathew Brady in New York City.
1859   Oregon was admitted to the Union as the 33rd state.
1864   Union general William Tecumseh Sherman captured Meridian, Mississippi, in the Civil War.
1876   Elisha Gray filed for a patent on his telephone a few hours after Alexander Graham Bell had filed for his. The Supreme Court eventually ruled Bell was the rightful inventor.
1884   A double tragedy struck Theodore Roosevelt as his wife Alice died in childbirth and his mother died of typhoid fever.
1895   Oscar Wilde's masterpiece, *The Importance of Being Earnest*, premiered in London's St. James Theatre.
1903   The Department of Commerce and Labor was established by Congress at the request of President Theodore Roosevelt.
1912   Arizona was admitted to the Union as the 48th state.
1918   The motion picture *Tarzan of the Apes* was released for the first time.
1929   The "St. Valentine's Day Massacre" occurred in Chicago as 7 members of the "Bugs" Moran Gang were murdered in a garage. Police suspected the Al Capone gang did the killing.

1949   Chaim Weizmann was elected first president of Israel.

1966   Wilt Chamberlain set a National Basketball Association scoring record of 20,884 points after only seven years of play.

FEBRUARY 15 -- BIRTHDAYS

1368   **Sigismund** -- King of Hungary and Bohemia and Holy Roman Emperor, 1433-1437

1564   **Galileo (Galilei)** -- Italian astronomer, mathematician, and one of the greatest scientists of all time, who discovered the law of falling bodies and first observed the 4 bright satellites of Jupiter

1571   **Michael Praetorius** -- German composer of church music, noted for *Syntagma Musicum* (1615-1620) and two books of hymns

1705   **Charles Andre Van Loo** -- French Rococo painter

1710   **Louis XV** -- King of France, 1715-1774, noted for his mistresses, Madame de Pompadour and Madame Du Barry, and for his cynical remark, "After me the deluge!"

1726   **Abraham Clark** -- New Jersey signer of the Declaration of Independence and member of the Continental Congress, the Congress of the Confederation and the U.S. Congress

1748   **Jeremy Bentham** -- English economist and philosopher who founded the philosophy that became known as Utilitarianism

1797   **Henry Englehard Steinway** -- Famous German-American piano builder and founder in 1853 of Steinway and Sons

1803   **John Augustus Sutter** -- Pioneer settler on whose land gold was discovered, precipitating the 1849 California Gold Rush

1809   **Cyrus Hall McCormick** -- American inventor noted for the invention in 1831 of the mechanical reaping machine that revolutionized agriculture

1811   **Domingo Faustino Sarmiento** -- Argentine statesman, educator, and writer, noted for works such as *Civilization and Barbarism: Life of Juan Facundo Quiroga* (1845)

1812   **Charles Lewis Tiffany** -- American jeweler and founder of Tiffany's jewelry company, whose reputation became so great that his name now stands for the highest quality in jewelry

1817   **Charles Francois Daubigny** -- French painter and etcher noted for works such as *Lever de Lune* (1877)

1820   **Susan B. Anthony** -- American reformer and pioneer crusader for woman suffrage

1843   **Russell Herman Conwell** -- American lawyer, clergyman, and author of the famous lecture, "Acres of Diamonds"

1845   **Elihu Root** -- American lawyer, statesman, and cabinet officer, who won the 1912 Nobel Peace Prize

1861   **Alfred North Whitehead** – English mathematician and philosopher who with Bertrand Russell wrote the monumental work, *Principia Mathematica* (1910-1913)

1875   **Sir Ernest Shackleton** -- Irish Antarctic explorer, who led a British expedition to within 97 miles of the South Pole in 1908

1880   **Joseph Hergesheimer** -- American novelist noted for works such as *Java Head* (1919)

1882   **John Barrymore** – The youngest of the "Fabulous Barrymores" and the greatest actor of his day

1886   **Sir Cyril Newall** -- British Air Marshal

1892   **James V. Forrestal** -- First U.S. secretary of defense, 1947-1949, and secretary of the Navy, 1944-1947, who helped to build the United States Fleet into the largest in the world

1893   **Walter Donaldson** – American composer and pianist noted for songs such as "How Ya Gonna Keep 'em Down on the Farm?" "Yes, Sir, That's My Baby," and "My Blue Heaven"

1897   **Earl Blaik** -- American college football coach who coached the great Army football teams of the World War II era

1900   **George Earnshaw** -- Professional baseball player

1905   **Harold Arlen** -- Noted American composer of some 500 songs such as "That Old Black Magic," "Stormy Weather," and his greatest hit, "Over the Rainbow"

1907   **Cesar Romero** -- American motion-picture and television actor and "Latin lover" of the 1930s and 1940s, with a career of over 50 years

1911   **Leonard Woodcock** -- American labor leader and president of the United Automobile Workers, 1970-1977

1914   **Kevin McCarthy** -- American stage, screen, and television actor, and brother of writer Mary McCarthy

1922   **John B. Anderson** -- U.S. congressman and third-party presidential candidate in 1980

1922   **Herman Kahn** -- American futurologist and author of *On Thermonuclear War*

1927   **Harvey Korman** – American stage, screen, and television actor

1929   **Graham Hill** -- British automobile racing driver and twice winner of the Grand Prix

1929   **James Schlesinger** -- First secretary of the Department of Energy

1931   **Claire Bloom** -- English stage, screen, and television actress

1933   **Adolfo (Sardina)** -- Cuban-born fashion expert

1935   **Susan Brownmiller** -- American writer and feminist leader

1935   **Roger B. Chaffee** – U.S. astronaut who was killed in 1967 when fire and smoke swept through his Apollo spacecraft during a ground test

1940   **John Hadl** -- Professional football player
1941   **Brian Holland** -- American musician and songwriter whose Holland-Dozier-Holland partnership had over 30 hits
1948   **Marisa Berenson** -- American model and motion-picture actress
1948   **Ron Cey** -- Professional baseball player
1949   **Ken Anderson** -- Professional football player
1951   **Melissa Manchester** -- American rock and roll singer
1953   **Pat Tilley** -- Professional football player

FEBRUARY 15 -- EVENTS

360 AD The first Cathedral of Santa Sophia in Constantinople was dedicated.
1145   Eugenius III was elected Roman Catholic pope.
1288   Nicholas IV was elected Roman Catholic pope.
1493   Christopher Columbus arrived aboard the *Nina* at Santa Maria Island in the Azores, on his return trip from discovering America.
1643   Johann Bjornsson Printz and his predominately Finnish colonists landed in Port Christina in what is now Wilmington, Delaware, joining the Swedes who had founded the colony.
1764   St. Louis was established by French fur trader Pierre Laclede Liguest and his stepson Rene Auguste Chouteau.
1862   The construction of the *Monitor*, the first ironclad vessel of the United States Navy, was completed.
1867   The first performance of "On the Beautiful Blue Danube," the famous waltz of Johann Strauss Jr., created a sensation in Vienna.
1898   The U.S. battleship *Maine* blew up in Havana harbor, leading to the Spanish-American War.
1933   President Franklin D. Roosevelt narrowly escaped assassination in Miami when a fanatic fired at him and killed Mayor Anton J. Cermak of Chicago, who was riding with Roosevelt.
1942   Singapore surrendered in World War II to the Japanese, who had come in from the Malayan interior, a feat considered impossible, rather than from the sea.
1971   Great Britain adopted a decimal currency system, ending the 1,000-year history of the pence-and-pound currency.
1978   Leon Spinks defeated Muhammad Ali to become the heavyweight champion of the world.

FEBRUARY 16 -- BIRTHDAYS

1497 **Philip Melanchthon** -- German humanist and scholar who was Martin Luther's chief associate in starting and leading the Protestant Reformation

1519 **Gaspard de Coligny** – French statesman and "Admiral of France," who as a leading Huguenot was the first to be killed in the massacre on St. Bartholomew's Day in 1572

1620 **Frederick William** -- Ruler of Brandenburg, 1640-1688, known as the "Great Elector," who laid the foundations for the military greatness of Prussia

1740 **Giambattista Bodoni** -- Italian printer and type designer who introduced the "classical" typeface into bookmaking

1812 **Henry Wilson** -- U.S. vice president under President U.S. Grant and one of the founders of the Republican Party

1834 **Ernst Heinrich Haeckel** -- Noted German zoologist and evolutionist and author of the widely read book, *The Riddle of the Universe* (1899)

1838 **Henry Adams** – American historian and philosopher, noted for the Pulitzer Prize-winning book, *The Education of Henry Adams*

1840 **Henry Watterson** -- American newspaper editor associated with the Louisville *Courier-Journal* for over 50 years

1848 **Hugo De Vries** -- Dutch botanist and geneticist, known primarily for his "mutation theory"

1858 **Lon Myers** -- American track star who at one time held all U.S. records for distances from 50 yards to a mile

1876 **George Macauley Trevelyan** -- Famous British historian, noted for *History of England* (1926) and *England Under Queen Anne* (1930-1934)

1884 **Robert J. Flaherty** -- American motion-picture director and "father of the documentary"

1886 **Van Wyck Brooks** -- American critic, biographer, and historian, noted for the monumental work, *Makers and Finders: A History of the Writer in America, 1800-1915*

1886 **Sliding Billy Hamilton** -- Hall of Fame baseball player who was the pre-modern-era stolen-base king

1888 **Harold R. Medina** -- Noted U.S. federal judge who won fame for his fair conduct of the trial of 11 American Communist party leaders in 1949

1895 **Louis Calhern** -- American motion-picture actor noted for his romantic leading man roles in the 1920s and for his powerful character roles in the 1950s

1898   **Katharine Cornell** -- One of the greatest American stage actresses of the 1920s and 1930s
1901   **Wayne King** -- American composer, clarinetist, and bandleader of the Big Band Era, known as the "Waltz King," and known also for the song, "The Waltz You Saved for Me"
1903   **Edgar Bergen** -- Noted American ventriloquist and creator of Charlie McCarthy and Mortimer Snerd
1904   **George F. Kennan** -- American diplomat and architect of the U.S. containment policy of the 1950s
1907   **Alec Wilder** -- American composer
1909   **Hugh Beaumont** -- American motion-picture and television actor
1914   **Jimmy Wakely** -- American actor, singer, and songwriter
1920   **Patti Andrews** -- One of the singing Andrews Sisters, a highly popular trio in the 1940s
1934   **Marlene Bauer** -- Noted professional golfer
1935   **Sonny Bono** -- American singer, comedian, and member of the Sonny and Cher television team
1940   **Tracy Carter** -- American motion-picture and television actress
1943   **Anthony Dowell** -- American ballet dancer
1944   **Roger Dowdeswell** -- Professional tennis player from Zimbabwe
1952   **John Feaver** -- English tennis player
1959   **Kelly Tripucka** -- Professional basketball player
1959   **John McEnroe** -- American tennis player and superstar
1961   **Andy Taylor** -- Guitarist with the Duran Duran musical group

FEBRUARY 16 -- EVENTS

1786   James Monroe married Elizabeth Kortright.
1804   U.S. naval officer Stephen Decatur, in a daring raid, led a picked band into Tripoli harbor and set fire to the U.S.N. frigate *Philadelphia*, captured by the Tripoli pirates.
1862   Ft. Donelson surrendered unconditionally to Union General U.S. Grant in the Civil War, after Grant had refused to accept any other terms.
1868   The Benevolent and Protective Order of Elks was organized in New York City.
1937   Dr. Wallace H. Carothers, a chemist of the Du Pont company, patented nylon.
1938   Austrian Chancellor Kurt von Schuschnigg bowed to pressure and admitted Austrian Nazis into his cabinet, as the prelude to the overthrow of his government by the Germans.

1945   American paratroopers landed on Corregidor in the Philippines in World War II. Within 2 weeks the Americans retook the fortress from the Japanese.

1947   American Admiral Richard Byrd flew over the South Pole for the second time.

1959   Fidel Castro took power as premier of Cuba, following the overthrow of Fulgencio Batista.

1972   Wilt Chamberlain, the basketball superstar, became the first NBA player in history to score 30,000 points.

1978   Japan and China signed an eight-year $20-billion trade pact.

FEBRUARY 17 -- BIRTHDAYS

1653   **Arcangelo Corelli** -- Italian composer and one of the earliest musicians to use the violin, which was replacing the viol in his time

1740   **John Sullivan** -- American Revolutionary War hero who seized military supplies from a British fort in New Castle, N.H., in one of the first armed actions by colonists against the British

1740   **Horace Benedict de Saussure** -- French physicist and Alpinist

1774   **Raphaelle Peale** -- American artist and son of artist Charles Willson Peale

1781   **Rene Theophile Hyacinthe Laennec** — French physician who in 1816 invented the stethoscope

1796   **Giovanni Pacini** -- Italian composer

1836   **Gustavo Adolfo Becquer** -- Spanish poet and writer

1837   **Pierre Auguste Cot** — French painter noted for works such as *The Storm*

1843   **Aaron Montgomery Ward** -- American pioneer in the mail-order business and founder in 1872 of the Montgomery Ward Company

1854   **Friedrich Alfred Krupp** -- Grandson of the founder of the great German Krupp works, and father of Bertha Krupp, for whom the "Big Bertha" long-range guns of World War I were named

1856   **Frederick E. Ives** -- American inventor who developed the Ives halftone process of photoengraving

1857   **Samuel Sidney McClure** — American editor and publisher, who founded the McClure Syndicate in New York City in 1884, one of the first newspaper syndicates

1877   **Andre Maginot** -- French statesman for whom the heavily fortified French Maginot Line was named

1880   **Alvaro Obregon** -- Mexican statesman, soldier, and twice president of Mexico

1889	**H.L. Hunt** -- American oil producer who became one of the world's richest men
1892	**Bob Neyland** -- One of the greatest college football coaches
1899	**Harvey Oliver Brooks** -- American composer noted for such songs as "A Little Bird Told Me"
1902	**Marian Anderson** -- American contralto of whom the famous conductor Arturo Toscanini said, "A voice like hers comes once in a century"
1904	**Hans J. Morgenthau** -- German-born political scientist and historian
1906	**Billy Hayes** -- American composer, author, and guitarist, noted for songs such as "Blue Christmas"
1907	**Charlie Spivak** -- American orchestra leader and trumpet player of the Big Band Era
1907	**Buster Crabbe** -- American motion-picture and television actor and gold medal swimmer in the 1932 Olympics
1908	**Red Barber** -- Noted American sportscaster
1914	**Arthur Kennedy** -- American stage and motion-picture actor
1919	**Joseph Hunt** -- American Hall of Fame tennis player
1924	**Margaret Truman Daniel** -- Daughter of U.S. President Harry S Truman
1925	**Hal Holbrook** -- American stage, screen, and television actor
1934	**Alan Bates** -- English stage, screen, and television actor
1935	**Jimmy Brown** -- Professional football superstar whose career record 12,312 yards gained lasted from 1966 to 1984
1939	**John Leyton** -- British musician
1939	**Mary Ann Mobley** -- American actress and beauty queen
1942	**Huey P. Newton** -- American political activist
1955	**Stanley Morgan** -- Professional football player
1959	**Neil Lomax** -- Professional football player
1963	**Michael Jordan** -- Professional basketball player and superstar

FEBRUARY 17 -- EVENTS

1621	Miles Standish was appointed military commander of the Plymouth Colony.
1673	Moliere, the noted French playwright, died in Paris at age 51.
1801	The U.S. House of Representatives, after 35 ballots, broke the tie in the electoral vote between Thomas Jefferson and Aaron Burr, electing Jefferson the third president.
1817	Baltimore city streets were illuminated by gas lights, the first time gas had been used for this purpose in America.

1856	Heinrich Heine, the great German writer, died in Paris at age 58.

1856   Heinrich Heine, the great German writer, died in Paris at age 58.

1876   The first sardines were canned, by the Wolff and Reesing cannery in Eastport, Maine.

1897   The National Congress of Mothers, the forerunner of the Parent-Teacher Association, first met, in Washington, D.C.

1904   Giacomo Puccini's great opera, *Madama Butterfly*, premiered at Milan's La Scala.

1906   Alice Roosevelt, the daughter of President Theodore Roosevelt, married Congressman Nicholas Longworth in the East Room of the White House.

1909   Geronimo, the famous Apache Indian chief, died at approximately 80 years of age.

1933   *Newsweek* magazine had its beginnings in a weekly news magazine published under the name *News-Week* by journalist Thomas John Cardel Martyn.

1936   The comic strip, *The Phantom*, by Lee Falk and Ray Moore, first appeared.

1944   American troops landed on Eniwetok Island and naval forces raided Truk Island in World War II.

1958   The comic strip, *B.C.*, by Johnny Hart, appeared for the first time.

1959   The U.S. launched *Vanguard 2*, the first satellite to send weather information back to earth.

1964   The U.S. Supreme Court issued its "one man, one vote" decision, ruling that congressional districts must be roughly equal in population.

1979   China invaded Vietnam.

FEBRUARY 18 -- BIRTHDAYS

1516   **Mary I ("Bloody Mary")** – Daughter of Henry VIII and Catherine of Aragon, and first reigning queen of England, 1553-1558, who got her famous nickname because of the persecutions she caused

1589   **Sir Henry Vane (the Elder)** -- English statesman

1609   **Edward Hyde Clarendon** – English earl who played a leading role in restoring the monarchy in England in 1660

1745   **Count Alessandro Volta** -- Italian nobleman, noted as the inventor of the electric battery

1775   **Thomas Girtin** -- English painter

1795   **George Peabody** -- American philanthropist for whom George Peabody College was named

1838   **Ernst Mach** -- Austrian physicist for whom "Mach 1," the speed of sound, was named

1848   **Louis Comfort Tiffany** -- American artist, son of the founder of Tiffany's jewelry store, and developer of Tiffany Favrile glass

1857   **Max Klinger** -- German artist

1859   **Sholem Aleichem** -- Russian-born writer whose real name was Solomon Rabinowitz, and who is the most widely read of all Yiddish writers

1860   **Anders Leonhard Zorn** -- Swedish painter and etcher, noted for works such as *Summer in Sweden* and *Portrait of Ernest Renan*

1885   **Nikos Kazantzakis** -- Greek author, dramatist, poet, and philosopher, noted for the epic poem "The Odyssey: A Modern Sequel" and the novel *Zorba the Greek*

1890   **Edward Arnold** -- American stage and motion-picture actor, in some 150 films

1890   **Adolphe Menjou** -- American stage and motion-picture actor, noted for debonair man-of-the-world roles

1892   **Wendell L. Willkie** -- U.S. presidential candidate in 1940

1894   **Andres Segovia** -- One of the greatest guitarists of the 20th century

1895   **George Gipp** -- First Notre Dame All-American football player

1897   **Edward McNall Burns** -- American historian, teacher, and writer, noted for *Western Civilizations: Their History & Their Culture*

1898   **Luis Munoz-Marin** -- Four-time governor of Puerto Rico

1909   **Wallace Stegner** -- American novelist and critic, noted for works such as *On a Darkling Plain* (1940) and *A Shooting Star* (1961)

1910   **John Jacob Loeb** -- American composer and author, noted for songs such as "Boo Hoo," "Rosie the Riveter," and "Seems Like Old Times"

1913   **Dane Clark** -- American stage, screen, and television actor

1915   **Joe Gordon** -- Professional baseball player and manager

1920   **Bill Cullen** -- American television personality and show host

1920   **Jack Palance** -- American stage, screen, and television actor

1922   **Helen Gurley Brown** -- American author noted for *Sex and the Single Girl*

1925   **George Kennedy** -- American motion-picture and television actor who won an Academy Award for *Cool Hand Luke* (1967)

1927   **John W. Warner** -- U.S. senator

1931   **Toni Morrison** -- American novelist noted for works such as *Song of Solomon* (1977) and *Beloved*, which won the Pulitzer Prize in 1987

1931   **Johnny Hart** -- American cartoonist who created *B.C.* and, with Brant Parker, *The Wizard of Id*

1933   **Yoko Ono** -- Japanese filmmaker, singer, and wife of Beatle John Lennon

1938	**Manny Mota** -- Professional baseball player
1945	**Judy Rankin** -- Professional golfer
1950	**Bruce Kison** -- Professional baseball player
1950	**John Mayberry** -- Professional baseball player
1950	**Cybill Shepherd** -- American model and motion-picture actress
1951	**Dick Stockton** -- American tennis player
1952	**Maurice Lucas** -- Professional basketball player
1954	**John Travolta** -- American motion-picture and television actor
1957	**Vanna White** -- American television personality noted for her role on the TV game show, *Wheel of Fortune*
1959	**Rafael Ramirez** -- Professional baseball player
1961	**Alycia Moulton** -- American tennis player
1964	**Matt Dillon** -- American motion-picture and television actor

FEBRUARY 18 -- EVENTS

1546	Martin Luther, the great Protestant Reformation leader, died in Eisleben in Saxony at age 62.
1564	Michelangelo (Buonarroti), the great Italian artist, died in Rome at age 88.
1678	John Bunyan's great work, *The Pilgrim's Progress*, was licensed for publication only a few months after Bunyan was released from prison.
1685	French explorer Robert Cavalier, Sieur de La Salle, founded Fort Saint Louis, a few miles inland from Matagorda Bay, the first white settlement in Texas.
1735	*Flora, or Hob in the Well*, the first opera presented in the U.S., was performed in Charleston, South Carolina.
1861	Jefferson Davis was sworn in as provisional president of the Confederate States of America.
1885	Mark Twain's famous novel, *The Adventures of Huckleberry Finn*, was first published in the U.S. (It had already appeared in Britain and Canada in 1884.)
1915	Frank James, brother of notorious outlaw Jesse James, died in Excelsior Springs, Missouri, where he had been living as a respectable farmer.
1924	The comic strip, *Boots and Her Buddies*, by Edgar Martin, first appeared.
1930	The planet Pluto was discovered by astronomer Clyde W. Tombaugh, working at the Lowell Observatory in Flagstaff, Arizona.
1939	San Francisco's Golden Gate International Exposition opened.

1953   Lucille Ball and Desi Arnaz were awarded an $8 million con-
       tract, an enormous figure for the time, to continue their televi-
       sion program, *I Love Lucy.*
1972   The California Supreme Court ended capital punishment, call-
       ing it cruel and unusual punishment.

FEBRUARY 19 -- BIRTHDAYS

1473   Nicolaus Copernicus -- Polish astronomer famous for the discov-
       ery that the earth rotates around a stationary sun
1526   **Carolus Clusius** -- Dutch botanist who helped establish
       modern botany
1717   **David Garrick** -- One of the greatest English actors of all time
1818   **Lydia Pinkham** -- American housewife who patented "Mrs.
       Lydia E. Pinkham's Vegetable Compound" in 1876
1819   **William III** -- King of the Netherlands, 1849-1890
1843   **Adelina Patti** -- Spanish-born coloratura soprana, noted as one
       of the world's greatest operatic singers
1846   **Charles Simon Clermont-Ganneau** -- French orientalist
1859   **Svante August Arrhenius** -- Swedish Nobel Prize-winning chem-
       ist and physicist
1865   **Sven Anders Hedin** – Swedish explorer of Asia who provided
       the first maps and information about central Asia
1888   **John G. Adolfi** -- American motion-picture director of the silent
       as well as the talking era
1893   **Sir Cedric Hardwicke** -- Noted English stage and motion-picture
       actor with a career of some 50 years
1895   **Semen Timoshenko** -- One of the greatest Russian generals in
       World War II
1896   **Andre Breton** – French poet, novelist, and leader of the surre-
       alist movement in Paris in the 1920s and 1930s
1911   **Merle Oberon** -- Tasmanian-born leading lady of Hollywood
       and British films of the 1920s and 1930s
1912   **Saul Chaplin** – American composer, musical director, and pro-
       ducer, noted for *An American in Paris* (1951) and *West Side
       Story* (1961)
1912   **Ceil Chapman** -- American fashion designer
1912   **Stan Kenton** -- American bandleader of the Big Band Era
1916   **Eddie Arcaro** – Famous American jockey with five Kentucky
       Derby winners and two Triple Crown winners: Whirlaway in
       1941 and Citation in 1948
1924   **Lee Marvin** -- American stage, screen, and television actor

1940	**Smokey Robinson** -- American singer, composer, and producer
1953	**Corrado Barazzutti** -- Italian tennis player
1954	**Billy Waddy** -- Professional football player
1956	**Marita Redondo** -- American tennis player
1957	**Dave Stewart** -- Professional baseball player
1959	**Sarah Ferguson** -- Wife of Prince Andrew of England
1960	**Prince Andrew** -- Second son of Queen Elizabeth II of England
1962	**Hana Mandlikova** -- Czechoslovakian tennis player
1966	**Justine Bateman** – American motion-picture and television actress

FEBRUARY 19 -- EVENTS

1405   Tamerlane, the fierce Mongol leader, died of fever on his way to conquer China. He was 68 years old.

1594   Sigismund III was crowned King of Sweden.

1674   The Treaty of Westminster ceded New York (formerly New Amsterdam) to the British from the Dutch.

1861   The Emancipation Act of Czar Alexander II freed the Russian serfs.

1864   The Knights of Pythias was founded in Washington, D.C., by Justus Henry Rathbone.

1878   Thomas A. Edison patented the phonograph.

1881   Kansas became the first state to prohibit alcoholic beverages.

1922   Ed Wynn, "The Perfect Fool" of vaudeville, became the first big show business name to sign up for a starring role in a regular radio program.

1942   President Franklin D. Roosevelt signed the executive order that made possible the detention of Japanese-American citizens in World War II.

1945   The U.S. marines landed on Iwo Jima in World War II.

1977   The U.S. space shuttle *Enterprise* made its first test flight above a Boeing 747 airplane.

FEBRUARY 20 -- BIRTHDAYS

1500   **Charles V** -- King of Spain, 1516-1558, Holy Roman Emperor, 1519-1558, and ruler of the Netherlands and the Burgundian lands in 1506

1751   **Johann Heinrich Voss** -- German poet and translator of Homer

1829   **Joseph Jefferson** -- American comedian and one of the most beloved figures in the American theater

1834   **George Du Maurier** -- English novelist and artist, and grandfather of writer Daphne du Maurier

1844   **Ludwig Eduard Boltzmann** -- Austrian theoretical physicist, noted for the Stefan-Boltzmann law of radiated energy and for his contributions to the kinetic theory of gases

1887   **Vincent Massey** -- The first native-born governor-general of Canada, 1952-1959

1888   **Marie Rambert** -- Polish-born founder of the Ballet Rambert

1898   **Enzo Ferrari** -- Italian sports car manufacturer

1899   **Cornelius Vanderbilt Whitney** -- One of the founders of Pan American Airways

1902   **Ansel Adams** -- Noted American landscape photographer

1904   **Aleksei Kosygin** -- Russian premier, 1964-1980

1907   **Malcolm Atterbury** -- American motion-picture and television actor

1912   **Muriel Buck Humphrey** – U.S. senator and wife of Vice President Hubert Humphrey

1913   **Tommy Henrich** -- Professional baseball player

1914   **John Daly** -- American television personality and moderator of the long-running panel show, *What's My Line?*

1918   **Don Hesse** -- American editorial cartoonist

1924   **Sidney Poitier** -- American stage and motion-picture actor and director, who was Hollywood's number one black actor in the 1950s and 1960s

1924   **Gloria Vanderbilt** – American heiress and noted clothes designer

1925   **Robert Altman** -- American motion-picture and television director, noted for *M*A*S*H* (1970)

1927   **Hubert de Givenchy** -- Influential French fashion designer who designed clothes for First Lady Jackie Kennedy and other celebrities, and who by the 1980s was one of the greatest in his field

1928   **Elroy Face** -- Professional baseball pitcher with an 18-1 won-lost record in 1959

1929   **Amanda Blake** -- American motion-picture and television actress who played Miss Kitty in the long-running television series, *Gunsmoke*

1934   **Bobby Unser** -- American racing car driver who won the 1968 Indianapolis 500

1937   **Nancy Wilson** -- American popular music singer

1941   **Buffy Sainte-Marie** -- American singer

1942   **Philip Esposito** -- Professional hockey superstar who scored a record 152 points in 1970-1971

1946   **Sandy Duncan** – American stage, screen, and television actress

1946	**J. Geils** -- American rock guitarist and bandleader
1947	**Peter Strauss** -- American television and motion-picture actor
1948	**Jennifer O'Neill** -- American model and television and motion-picture actress
1951	**Edward Albert** -- American motion-picture actor and son of actors Eddie Albert and Margo
1954	**Glynis Coles** -- English tennis player
1954	**Patty Hearst** -- American heiress and noted fugitive of the 1970s
1963	**Charles Barkley** -- Professional basketball player

FEBRUARY 20 -- EVENTS

1839	Congress prohibited dueling in the District of Columbia.
1872	The Metropolitan Museum of Art in New York was opened to the public.
1878	Leo XIII was elected Roman Catholic pope.
1921	The motion picture, *The Four Horsemen of the Apocalypse*, starring Rudolph Valentino, was released for the first time.
1933	The U.S. House of Representatives voted to repeal Prohibition.
1938	Anthony Eden resigned as British foreign secretary in protest against the "appeasement" policy toward Hitler of Prime Minister Neville Chamberlain.
1962	U.S. astronaut John Glenn became the first American to orbit the earth, circling it three times in less than five hours.
1965	U.S. satellite *Ranger 8* photographed and then landed on the moon.
1976	The Southeast Asia Treaty Organization was formally disbanded in ceremonies in Manila.

FEBRUARY 21 -- BIRTHDAYS

1728	**Peter III** -- Czar of Russia for a short time in 1762 before being succeeded by Catherine the Great
1794	**Antonio Lopez de Santa Anna** -- Three-time president-dictator of Mexico who presided over the loss of Texas and the American Southwest to the United States
1801	**John Henry Cardinal Newman** -- British Catholic churchman and man of letters, noted for the famous hymn, "Lead, Kindly Light"
1821	**Charles Scribner** -- American publisher who with Isaac D. Baker founded the New York publishing house of Baker and Scribner in 1846, the forerunner of Charles Scribner's Sons

1836   Leo Delibes – French composer known for his opera *Lakme* and his two ballets *Coppelia* and *Sylvia*

1866   **August von Wassermann** -- German physician and bacteriologist known for the Wassermann test to detect venereal disease

1876   **Constantin Brancusi** -- Romanian sculptor who ranks as one of the greatest sculptors of the 20th century

1895   **Henrik Dam** -- Danish biochemist who discovered vitamin K

1903   **Anais Nin** -- French-born writer of poetic novels such as *The House of Incest* (1936) and *Ladders to Fire* (1946)

1903   **Tom Yawkey** -- Owner of the Boston Red Sox baseball team for over 40 years

1907   **W.H. Auden** -- English-born poet, known for his ballads, blues, limericks, sonnets, nonsense verse, and dramas, and who won the 1948 Pulitzer Prize for his poem *The Age of Anxiety*

1910   **Douglas Bader** -- Britain's most famous air ace who fought in World War II with two artificial legs

1915   **Ann Sheridan** – American motion-picture and television actress and "Oomph Girl" of the 1940s

1921   **Albert Axelrod** -- Professional fencer

1924   **Robert Mugabe** -- First president of Zimbabwe

1925   **Sam Peckinpah** -- American motion-picture and television director and screenwriter, noted for such scripts as television's long-running *Gunsmoke*

1927   **Erma Bombeck** -- American columnist, writer, and humorist

1927   **Guy Mitchell** -- American singer noted for "Singing the Blues"

1935   **Rue McClanahan** -- American television and stage actress

1936   **Barbara Jordan** – American congresswoman and political leader

1937   **Prince Harald** -- Crown prince of Norway

1937   **Ron Clarke** -- Noted Australian runner and holder of 19 world records

1940   **John Lewis** -- American civil rights leader

1946   **Tricia Nixon Cox** -- Daughter of President Richard M. Nixon

1951   **Erik Van Dillen** -- American tennis player

1958   **Alan Trammell** -- Professional baseball player

1961   **Christopher Atkins** -- American motion-picture actor

FEBRUARY 21 -- EVENTS

1598   Boris Godunov was elected czar of Russia.

1779   Captain James Cook, the great British explorer, was buried at sea, after being killed by the Hawaiian Islanders.

1807   Martin Van Buren married Hannah Hoes.

1848 John Quincy Adams collapsed on the floor of the House of Representatives, went into a coma, and died two days later.

1852 Nikolai Gogol, the great Russian writer, died in Moscow at age 42.

1853 Three-dollar gold pieces were authorized by the U.S. government.

1866 Lucy B. Hobbs became the first black woman graduate of a dental school, the Ohio College of Dental Surgery in Cincinnati.

1878 The world's first telephone directory was issued, by the New Haven, Connecticut, Telephone Company. It listed 50 names.

1885 The Washington Monument was dedicated in Washington, D.C.

1904 The National Ski Association of America was founded.

1916 Germany began the World War I Battle of Verdun, which was defended by French General Henri Petain, who made the famous vow, "They shall not pass!"

1925 The *New Yorker* magazine was first published.

1947 American inventor Edwin Land first publicly demonstrated his Polaroid Land camera, which produced an instant photograph in 60 seconds.

1965 Malcolm X, U.S. Black Muslim leader, was assassinated in New York City at age 39.

1972 President Richard M. Nixon arrived in Peking for his historic talks with the Chinese Communist leaders.

1975 President Nixon's aides John D. Ehrlichman, H.R. Haldeman, and John Mitchell were sentenced to from 2½ to 8 years in prison for their parts in the Watergate cover-up.

1978 China spared the "Gang of Four," including Mao Tse-tung's widow, from execution.

FEBRUARY 22 -- BIRTHDAYS

1403 **Charles VII** – King of France, 1422-1461, and "one of the most contemptible creatures" ever to disgrace the title of king

1440 **Ladislaus V** -- King of Bohemia and Hungary

1715 **Charles N. Cochin the Younger** – The outstanding French engraver of the 18th century

1732 **George Washington** -- First U.S. president, "Father of His Country," and one of the greatest Americans in history

1778 **Rembrandt Peale** -- American painter who painted hundreds of famous portraits and who was the son of the noted painter Charles Willson Peale

1785 **Jean Charles Athanase Peltier** -- French physicist who discovered the Peltier effect that current at a juncture of two dissimilar metals will produce heat or cold

1788   Arthur Schopenhauer -- German philosopher noted for his main work, *The World as Will and Idea* (1819, 1844)

1805   Sarah Flower Adams -- Writer of the hymn, "Nearer My God to Thee" (1841), which became famous when Lowell Mason later set it to music

1810   Frederic Chopin -- Polish composer and pianist, and one of the great masters of piano composition

1819   James Russell Lowell -- American poet and diplomat noted for his *Biglow Papers* and the famous poem, "The Vision of Sir Launfal" (1848)

1857   Lord Robert Baden-Powell -- British soldier who in 1907 founded the Boy Scout movement

1857   Heinrich Rudolph Hertz -- German physicist who discovered electromagnetic waves (between 1886 and 1888), and for whom the frequency unit hertz (cycles per second) was named

1868   Ren Shields -- American composer, author, and actor, noted for songs such as "In the Good Old Summertime" and "Frankie and Johnnie"

1874   Bill Klem -- Noted professional baseball umpire

1879   Uncle Charlie Moran -- Major league baseball pitcher, catcher, and umpire, and professional football coach

1892   David Dubinsky -- American labor leader and president of the International Ladies' Garment Workers' Union, 1932-1966

1892   Edna St. Vincent Millay -- American poet noted for works such as "A Few Figs from Thistles" and "The Ballad of the Harp Weaver"

1896   Nacio Herb Brown -- American composer noted for such songs as "You Were Meant for Me," "Singin' in the Rain," and "Temptation"

1900   Luis Bunuel -- Spanish motion-picture director with a career of some 50 years and a ranking among cinema's all-time greats

1901   Charles Newman -- American lyricist noted for songs such as "Six Lessons from Madam La Zonga" and "Why Don't We Do This More Often?"

1904   Peter Hurd -- American painter and illustrator

1906   Leon Henderson -- American economist and educator who headed the Office of Price Administration during World War II

1907   Sheldon Leonard -- American stage, screen, and television actor

1907   Robert Young -- American motion-picture and television actor who appeared in some 100 films and starred in two long-running television series, *Father Knows Best* and *Marcus Welby, M.D.*

1908   John Mills -- British stage and motion-picture actor with a 50-year career

1908   **Romulo Betancourt** -- President of Venezuela, 1958-1964
1915   **Gus Lesnevich** -- Light heavyweight boxing champion, 1941-1948
1918   **Charles O. Finley** -- American financier and colorful owner in the 1970s of the Oakland A's baseball team
1918   **Robert Pershing Wadlow** — Tallest man who ever lived, at 8 feet 11 inches
1918   **Sid Abel** -- Professional hockey player
1921   **Jean Bedel Bokassa** -- Army colonel who overthrew the government of the Central African Republic in 1966 and proclaimed himself Bokassa I, Emperor of the Central African Empire
1926   **Bunker Hunt** -- American entrepreneur and son of billionaire H.L. Hunt
1929   **Ryne Duren** — Professional baseball player and drug and alcohol consultant
1932   **Edward M. Kennedy** -- U.S. senator and brother of President John F. Kennedy
1934   **Sparky Anderson** -- Professional baseball manager who in 1984 became the first to manage World Series champions from each of the two major leagues
1937   **Tommy Aaron** -- Professional golfer
1943   **Dick Van Arsdale** — Professional basketball player and brother of basketball player Tom Van Arsdale
1944   **Tom Okker** -- Dutch tennis player
1944   **Tom Van Arsdale** -- Professional basketball player and brother of basketball player Dick Van Arsdale
1949   **Niki Lauda** — Austrian racing driver known as the "Austrian Ace"
1950   **Julius "Dr. J." Erving** -- Professional basketball superstar
1956   **John Turner** -- Professional football player
1956   **Joe Lefebvre** -- Professional baseball player
1964   **Gigi Fernandez** -- Puerto Rican tennis player

FEBRUARY 22 -- EVENTS

1276   Innocent V was crowned Roman Catholic pope.
1630   The Massachusetts Bay colonists tasted their first popcorn at their first Thanksgiving dinner.
1819   Spain agreed to turn over Florida to the United States in exchange for a U.S. agreement to pay some $5 million to American citizens in Florida for property damages.
1847   "General Taylor never surrenders," was the American response to the Mexican demand that they surrender in the Battle of Buena Vista in the Mexican War.

1848   The February Revolution of 1848 began in Paris, forcing the abdication of French King Louis Philippe two days later.

1862   Jefferson Davis was inaugurated as regular president of the Confederacy. He had been provisional president before this.

1879   The first "five cent" store was opened, by F.W. Woolworth in Utica, New York.

1892   Oscar Wilde's play, *Lady Windermere's Fan*, premiered at St. James Theatre in London.

1924   Calvin Coolidge delivered the first presidential radio broadcast from the White House.

1931   One hundred women in Miami, Florida, organized a "Carry Nation Brigade" to fight against bootleggers and gamblers.

1943   An American commercial plane carrying a company of American entertainers crashed in the Tagus River in Portugal, killing 24 people. One of the survivors was singer Jane Froman.

1973   The United States and the People's Republic of China agreed to establish liaison offices in Washington and Peking.

1980   The unranked U.S. Olympic hockey team, in a stunning upset, defeated the heavily favored Russians, 4-3, at Lake Placid, New York.

FEBRUARY 23 -- BIRTHDAYS

1395   **Johannes Gutenberg** -- German printer who invented the type mold, which made movable metallic type practical for the first time, and who used his method to print the magnificent Gutenberg Bible

1440   **Matthias Corvinus** -- Powerful king of Hungary, known as Matthias I, who ruled between 1458 and 1490

1564   **Christopher Marlowe** -- The first great Elizabethan writer of tragedy, noted for works such as *The Tragical History of Doctor Faustus* (the date is a guess based on his baptismal date)

1633   **Samuel Pepys** -- English author of the most famous diary in the history of the world

1649   **John Blow** -- English composer who wrote the anthem, "I Was Glad When They Said," for the opening of Christopher Wren's Choir of St. Paul's Cathedral in London in 1697

1685   **George Frederick Handel** -- German-English composer who wrote the famous oratorio *Messiah*, one of the most popular works in music

1726   **Sir William Chambers** -- English architect

1744   **Mayer Amschel Rothschild** -- German banker and financier, who founded the famous House of Rothschild in the late 18th century

1787	**Emma Hart Willard** -- The first American woman publicly to support higher education for women, and who wrote the famous poem, "Rocked in the Cradle of the Deep" (1830)
1817	**George Frederic Watts** -- English painter noted for his portraits of famous men of his time and for works such as *Sir Galahad*
1865	**Barney Dreyfuss** — American baseball owner and originator of the modern world series
1868	**W.E.B. Du Bois** -- One of the most important leaders of black protest in the United States and a co-founder in 1909 of the NAACP
1883	**Karl Jaspers** -- German philosopher and author, and leading proponent of existentialism
1904	**William L. Shirer** -- American journalist and author of the epic work, *The Rise and Fall of the Third Reich* (1959)
1905	**Sally Victor** -- American hat designer
1913	**Jon Hall** -- American motion-picture and television actor and producer
1927	**Regine Crespin** -- French dramatic soprano
1929	**Elston Howard** -- Professional baseball player
1938	**Sylvia Chase** -- American broadcast journalist
1939	**Peter Fonda** -- American motion-picture actor and director, and son of actor Henry Fonda
1940	**Jackie Smith** -- Professional football player
1943	**Frederick Biletnikoff** -- Professional football player
1944	**Johnny Winter** -- American rock and blues guitarist
1951	**Ed "Too Tall" Jones** -- Professional football player
1955	**Howard Jones** -- British musician, synthesizer, and singer
1958	**David Sylvian** -- British singer with the musical group Japan
1958	**John Shelby** -- Professional baseball player
1960	**Naruhito Hironomiya** -- Crown prince of Japan
1963	**Bobby Bonilla** -- Professional baseball player

FEBRUARY 23 -- EVENTS

303 AD	Roman Emperor Diocletian ordered a general persecution of the Christians.
532 AD	Work began on the third Cathedral of Santa Sophia in Constantinople.
1505	Christopher Columbus was granted a license to ride a mule in Spain.
1723	Sir Christopher Wren, the great English architect, died in London at age 90.

1792   Sir Joshua Reynolds, the noted English painter, died in London
        at age 68.
1821   John Keats, the great English poet, died of tuberculosis in Rome
        at age 25.
1822   Boston was granted a charter to incorporate as a city.
1836   The Mexican Army under General Santa Anna began its siege of
        the Alamo.
1847   U.S. General Zachary Taylor defeated Mexico's General Santa
        Anna in the Battle of Buena Vista in the Mexican War.
1848   John Quincy Adams died of a stroke in Washington, D.C., at
        age 80.
1870   Mississippi was readmitted to the Union.
1905   The first Rotary Club was founded by Paul P. Harris in Chicago.
1917   The Smith-Hughes Act was passed by Congress, setting up the
        Federal Board of Vocational Education.
1930   Nazi thug Horst Wessel died of blood poisoning after having
        been shot in a street brawl, inspiring the Nazis to make a martyr
        of him in their "Horst-Wessel-Lied."
1932   Franklin D. Roosevelt announced his candidacy for the Demo-
        cratic presidential nomination.
1942   A Japanese submarine fired on an oil refinery near Santa
        Barbara, California, the only time in World War II that any state
        received hostile fire.
1945   The U.S. Marines planted the American flag atop Mount Suribachi
        in Iwo Jima. Joe Rosenthal's picture showing the action is
        considered the best picture of World War II.
1954   The first mass inoculations of children with the anti-polio Salk
        vaccine began in Pittsburgh.
1967   The 25th Amendment to the Constitution was proclaimed,
        providing for presidential succession and for filling a vacancy in
        the office of vice president.

FEBRUARY 24 -- BIRTHDAYS

1463   **Giovanni Pico della Mirandola** -- Florentine Platonist philosopher
1597   **Vincent Voiture** -- French poet
1613   **Mattia Preti** -- Italian painter
1619   **Charles Le Brun** – One of the two outstanding French craftsmen
        (Andre Charles Boulle was the other) employed to create the
        Louis XIV furniture of the post-Renaissance period
1663   **Thomas Newcomen** -- English inventor of one of the first prac-
        tical steam engines in 1712

1709   **Jacques de Vaucanson** -- Noted French toymaker who specialized in extraordinary lifelike creations

1766   **Samuel Wesley** -- English composer and organist

1772   **William Harris Crawford** -- U.S. senator, statesman, and candidate for president in 1824

1786   **Wilhelm Karl Grimm** -- German writer who with his brother Jakob was noted for the famous Grimm's *Fairy Tales* (1812, 1815)

1836   **Winslow Homer** -- American painter noted for paintings of the sea, such as *The Gulf Stream* (1899), and of rural American life scenes

1840   **John Philip** Holland -- Irish-American inventor, who was largely responsible for the submarine

1842   **Arrigo Boito** -- Italian composer, librettist, and poet, noted for works such as the opera *Mefistofele* (1868)

1852   **George Augustus Moore** -- Irish author noted for works such as *Confessions of a Young Man* (1888) and *Heloise and Abelard* (1921)

1872   **John Jarvis** -- British swimming champion who held 108 titles

1874   **Honus Wagner** -- Hall of Fame baseball player considered by many experts to be baseball's greatest shortstop

1876   **Victor Moore** -- American actor and comedian of vaudeville, the stage, and motion pictures with a 40-year career

1877   **Rudolph Ganz** -- Swiss-American pianist, composer, and conductor

1880   **Sir Samuel Hoare** -- English statesman

1885   **Chester W. Nimitz** -- U.S. admiral and commander in chief of the American Pacific Fleet in World War II

1890   **Marjorie Main** -- American stage and motion-picture actress and co-star of the Ma and Pa Kettle series of movies

1896   **Richard Thorpe** -- American motion-picture director noted for hundreds of films in a 45-year career

1914   **Zachary Scott** -- American stage, screen, and television actor

1919   **Richard "Dick" Charles Krieg** -- American composer and author, noted for songs such as "Along the Navajo Trail" and "Mad About Him, Sad About Him Blues"

1921   **Abe Vigoda** -- American actor noted for his role as Fish in the long-running television series *Barney Miller*

1927   **Mark Lane** -- American lawyer and author

1928   **Michael Harrington** -- American political activist and writer

1931   **James Abourezk** -- U.S. senator

1932   **Michel Legrand** -- French singer and movie composer who won an Oscar for the score of *The Summer of '42* (1971)

1935   **Renata Scotto** -- American opera singer

1938   James Farentino -- American stage, screen, and television actor
1940   Jimmy Ellis -- World heavyweight boxing champion, 1968-1970
1946   Barry Bostwick -- American stage, screen, and television actor
1947   Rupert Holmes -- English-born composer, author, and record-
         ing artist, noted for writing and arranging for the Drifters, the
         Platters, Gene Pitney, and the Carol Burnett TV show
1952   Sharon Walsh -- American tennis player
1955   Eddie Johnson -- Professional basketball player
1956   Eddie Murray -- Professional baseball player

FEBRUARY 24 -- EVENTS

303 AD   The first Roman edict for persecution of the Christians was
         published on the order of Emperor Diocletian.
1525   Holy Roman Emperor Charles V defeated French King Francis
         I in the famous Battle of Pavia (Italy), which established the
         superiority of firearms over infantry lance and pike.
1582   Pope Gregory XIII issued the papal bull outlining the reforms of
         the Gregorian Calendar, which went into effect the following
         October and is still in use today.
1761   American patriot James Otis, in a speech protesting English
         search and seizure tactics, coined the famous phrase, " A man's
         home is his castle."
1785   John Adams was appointed first United States minister to
         Great Britain.
1803   The U.S. Supreme Court issued its landmark *Marbury v. Madi-
         son* decision, ruling that the court was the final interpreter of
         constitutional issues.
1821   Mexico declared its independence from Spain.
1848   Louis Philippe abdicated as King of France as a result of the
         Paris Revolution of 1848.
1868   The U.S. House of Representatives voted 128 to 47 to impeach
         President Andrew Johnson.
1903   The U.S. leased Guantanamo Bay from Cuba for the site of the
         Guantanamo Naval Station.
1922   Henri Desire Landru, known as "Bluebeard," was executed in
         Versailles, France, for murdering ten of his mistresses.
1942   The Voice of America made its first broadcast.

FEBRUARY 25 -- BIRTHDAYS

1510   Francisco Vasquez de Coronado -- Spanish explorer of the
         American Southwest in 1540, whose expedition discovered the
         Continental Divide and the Grand Canyon

1682	Giovanni Battista Morgagni -- Italian anatomist and pathologist, and "the father of pathologic anatomy," noted for his great book, *On the Seats and Causes of Diseases* (1761)
1707	**Carlo Goldoni** -- Italian playwright noted for works such as *The Servant of Two Masters* (1745) and *The Liar* (1750)
1746	**Charles Cotesworth Pinckney** -- American statesman, Revolutionary War soldier, and twice Federalist candidate for president
1778	**Jose de San Martin** -- South American liberator of Argentina, Chile, and Peru
1841	**Pierre Auguste Renoir** -- One of the most brilliant painters of the French Impressionist movement
1842	**Karl May** -- German adventure story writer, who wrote vividly of the American West though he never laid eyes on it
1848	**Edward Henry Harriman** – American financier, one of the leading railroad magnates of the late 19th century, and father of statesman W. Averell Harriman
1866	**Benedetto Croce** -- Perhaps the most distinguished Italian philosopher of the 20th century, and author of such works as *Aesthetic* (1902) and *Logic* (1905)
1871	**Oliver Samuel Campbell** -- American Hall of Fame tennis player
1873	**Enrico Caruso** -- Italian operatic tenor with one of the most brilliant voices in the history of music
1883	**Princess Alice** – Granddaughter of England's Queen Victoria, Countess of Athlone, and the last of the Royal Victorians
1888	**John Foster Dulles** -- U.S. secretary of state under President Eisenhower
1890	**Dame Myra Hess** – English pianist noted for her playing of the works of Bach, Mozart, and Scarlatti
1895	**Bert Bell** -- Professional football player, coach, and Commissioner of the National Football League
1896	**John McClellan** -- U.S. senator, 1943-1977
1901	**Zeppo Marx** – American comedian and member of the Marx Brothers comedy group
1904	**Adelle Davis** -- American writer and expert on diet
1908	**Frank G. Slaughter** -- American physician and author
1910	**Millicent Fenwick** -- U.S. congresswoman in the 1980s
1913	**Jim Backus** -- American stage, screen, and television actor, and voice of cartoon character Mr. Magoo
1916	**Ralph Baldwin** -- Harness racing driver who set 11 major world records
1917	**Anthony Burgess** -- English novelist noted for works such as *A Clockwork Orange* (1962) and *Nothing Like the Sun* (1964)

1918   **Bobby Riggs** -- American Hall of Fame tennis player and 1939 Wimbledon singles champion
1919   **Monte Irvin** -- Hall of Fame baseball player
1920   **Philip Habib** -- American career diplomat
1921   **Andy Pafko** -- Professional baseball player
1929   **Tommy Newsom** -- American musician noted for his role on *The Tonight Show*
1932   **Faron Young** -- American country singer
1934   **Tony Lema** -- Professional golfer
1937   **Bob Schieffer** -- American broadcast journalist
1937   **Tom Courtenay** -- English stage and motion-picture actor
1938   **Diane Baker** -- American motion-picture and television actress and director
1943   **George Harrison** -- Member of the Beatles musical group
1947   **Lee Evans** -- Professional runner
1951   **Cesar Cedeno** -- Professional baseball player
1958   **Kurt Rambis** -- Professional basketball player
1959   **Mike Peters** -- Welsh singer, guitarist, and harmonica player with the Alarm musical group
1975   **Drew Barrymore** -- American actress and granddaughter of the great actor John Barrymore

FEBRUARY 25 -- EVENTS

1570   Queen Elizabeth I of England was excommunicated by Pope Pius V.
1792   President George Washington met with government department heads at his home in the first U.S. cabinet meeting.
1804   Thomas Jefferson was nominated for a second term as president by his party, the Democratic-Republicans.
1820   Congressman Felix Walker from Buncombe County, N.C., in a long-winded speech about his county, caused the coining of the words *bunk* and *buncombe*, meaning nonsense.
1836   Samuel Colt obtained a U.S. patent on his famous revolver.
1870   Hiram R. Revels became the first black U.S. senator, as he was sworn in to serve out the unexpired term of Mississippi Senator Jefferson Davis.
1901   The United States Steel company was incorporated by Elbert Gary and J.P. Morgan.
1908   The North Tunnels, the first tunnels built under the Hudson River in New York City, were opened to the public.

1913　The 16th Amendment to the Constitution was proclaimed, establishing the income tax.

1919　Oregon became the first state to tax gasoline.

1932　Adolf Hitler acted hastily to become a citizen of Germany in time to run for president in an election to be held some two weeks later.

1933　The *Ranger*, the first U.S. aircraft carrier built expressly for that purpose, was launched.

1948　The Communists, in a bloodless coup, seized complete control of the government of Czechoslovakia.

1956　Soviet premier Nikita Khrushchev denounced the late dictator Josef Stalin in a speech before a Communist Party congress in Moscow.

1964　Cassius Clay (Muhammad Ali) knocked out Sonny Liston in the seventh round in Miami Beach to win the heavyweight boxing championship.

1986　President Ferdinand Marcos fled the Philippines in the wake of a tainted election and pressure from the United States. Corazon Aquino succeeded him.

FEBRUARY 26 -- BIRTHDAYS

1361　**Wenceslaus** -- One of the last kings of Germany before the Hapsburgs gained control in 1438

1531　**David Chytraeus** – The last of the "Fathers of the Lutheran Church"

1802　**Victor Hugo** – Noted French writer, whose novels *The Hunchback of Notre Dame* (1831) and *Les Miserables* (1862) rank among the world's most popular fiction

1808　**Honore Daumier** -- French artist and caricaturist who was imprisoned for six months for drawing a caricature of King Louis Philippe entitled "Gargantua"

1846　**William F. "Buffalo Bill" Cody** -- U.S. army scout, Indian fighter, and "Wild West Circus" owner

1861　**Ferdinand** – Bulgarian prince who in 1908 declared Bulgaria independent and made himself king

1869　**Nadezhda Krupskaya** -- Wife of Vladimir I. Lenin, the founder of the Russian Communist dictatorship

1877　**Rudolph Dirks** -- American cartoonist and creator in 1897 of *The Katzenjammer Kids* comic strip

1878　**Emmy Destinn** -- Czechoslovakian soprano

1882　**Husband E. Kimmel** – American admiral in command of the U.S. Naval fleet at Pearl Harbor when the Japanese attacked in 1941

1887   **Grover Cleveland Alexander** -- One of the greatest pitchers in baseball history, with 373 victories and 90 shutouts in a 20-year career

1887   **William Frawley** -- American motion-picture, stage, and television actor, noted for his role as a regular in the long-running TV series, *I Love Lucy*

1890   **Chance Milton Vought** -- American aeronautical engineer

1906   **Madeleine Carroll** -- English stage, screen, and television actress

1914   **Robert Alda** -- American stage, screen, and television actor, and father of actor Alan Alda

1915   **Preacher Roe** -- Professional baseball player

1916   **Jackie Gleason** -- American stage, screen, and television actor and comedian, and star of the long-running television series, *The Honeymooners*

1920   **Tony Randall** -- American stage, screen, and television actor and comedian

1921   **Betty Hutton** -- American stage and motion-picture singer and actress, and "The Blonde Bombshell" of the 1940s

1922   **Margaret Leighton** -- English stage and motion-picture actress

1928   **Fats Domino** -- American rock and roll pianist and singer

1931   **Robert Novak** -- Member of the Evans and Novak team of political columnists

1932   **Johnny Cash** -- American country-music singer and composer

1933   **Godfrey Cambridge** -- American stage, screen, and television comedian and actor

1950   **James Bertelsen** -- Professional football player

1954   **Bili Sparrow** -- American composer, author, and performer, noted for "Star Wars (That's the Politics)"

1954   **Ted McKnight** -- Professional football player

FEBRUARY 26 -- EVENTS

1564   Christopher Marlowe, the great Elizabethan writer and contemporary of William Shakespeare, was baptized, presumably at age 3 days, as was the custom.

1815   Napoleon Bonaparte escaped from Elba, where he had been in exile, to return to power in France.

1848   The French Second Republic was proclaimed, after the overthrow of King Louis Philippe in the Revolution of 1848.

1855   The first public school system was established in the South, in Nashville, Tennessee.

1919   The Grand Canyon National Park in Arizona was established by Congress.

1951   James Jones' great novel, *From Here to Eternity*, was published in New York.

1951   The 22nd Amendment to the U.S. Constitution was ratified, limiting a president to two terms in office.

FEBRUARY 27 -- BIRTHDAYS

280 AD **Constantine I (the Great)** --Roman emperor, A.D. 306-337, who made Christianity the religion of the empire, and in A.D. 315 built the Arch of Constantine, which is still a landmark of Rome

1691   **Edward Cave** -- English printer who published *Gentleman's Magazine*, the first modern English magazine, in 1731

1744   **John Lawrence Geib** -- American piano maker

1807   **Henry Wadsworth Longfellow** -- The most popular American poet of the 19th century, noted for works such as "Evangeline, A Tale of Acadie," "The Song of Hiawatha," and "The Cross of Snow"

1823   **Ernest Renan** -- French historian and religious scholar, noted for his *Life of Jesus* (1863)

1848   **Dame Ellen Terry**--The greatest actress on the English stage for fifty years in the late 19th and early 20th centuries

1850   **Henry Edwards Huntington** -- American railway and transportation system builder, and founder of the Henry E. Huntington Library and Art Gallery in San Marino, California

1878   **Manuel Ugarte** -- Argentine writer who coined the term, "Colossus of the North," in reference to the United States

1888   **Lotte Lehmann** -- German operatic soprano, noted for her interpretations of the music of Richard Wagner and Richard Strauss

1888   **Arthur M. Schlesinger** -- American historian, teacher, and author, who became known as the dean of American historians

1891   **David Sarnoff** -- American pioneer in the development of radio and television broadcasting, and president or chairman of the board of RCA from 1930 to 1970

1892   **William Demarest** -- American stage, screen, and television actor who played over 100 character roles in a 50-year career

1898   **Allison Danzig** -- Dean of U.S. tennis writers, who wrote for the New York *Times* for 45 years, and was the first writer to be inducted into the tennis Hall of Fame

1899   **Charles Herbert Best** -- Canadian physiologist and co-discoverer in 1921 with Sir Frederick G. Banting of insulin for the treatment of diabetes

1902   **John Steinbeck** -- American novelist, noted for works such as *The Winter of Our Discontent*, *Of Mice and Men*, and one of the most famous books of the 20th century, *The Grapes of Wrath*

1902   **Gene Sarazen** – American golf immortal who in the 1920s and early 1930s won the Masters, the British Open, the U.S. Open (twice), and the PGA (three times)

1904   **James T. Farrell** -- American writer noted for the *Studs Lonigan* trilogy (1932-1935)

1905   **Franchot Tone** -- American stage, screen, and television actor

1910   **Joan Bennett** -- American stage, screen, and television actress, and daughter of actor Richard Bennett and sister of actresses Constance and Barbara Bennett

1910   **Peter DeVries** -- American novelist, noted for works such as *The Tunnel of Love, The Mackerel Plaza,* and *The Blood of the Lamb*

1912   **Lawrence Durrell** – English novelist noted for *The Alexandria Quartet: Justine* (1957), *Balthazar* (1958), *Mountolive* (1959), and *Clea* (1960)

1913   **Irwin Shaw** -- American playwright and novelist, noted for works such as *Bury the Dead* (1936) and *The Young Lions* (1948)

1917   **John B. Connally** -- Governor of Texas, 1963-1969, and secretary of the treasury under President Nixon

1925   **Kenneth Koch** -- American poet and playwright

1927   **James Leo Herlihy** -- American actor, playwright, and novelist

1930   **Joanne Woodward** -- American stage, screen, and television actress, who won the Academy Award in 1957 for *The Three Faces of Eve*

1932   **Elizabeth Taylor** -- English-American motion-picture actress, who won the Academy Award in 1960 for *Butterfield 8* and in 1966 for *Who's Afraid of Virginia Woolf?*

1933   **Malcom Wallop** -- U.S. senator

1933   **Raymond Berry** -- Professional football player

1934   **Ralph Nader** -- American lawyer, writer, and social crusader for public health and safety, noted for the book, *Unsafe at Any Speed* (1965), which led to new safety standards for cars

1935   **Mirella Freni** -- Italian operatic soprano

1937   **Jay Silvester** -- Champion discus thrower

1948   **Munawar Igbal** -- Pakistani tennis player

1951   **Steve Harley** -- English musician and songwriter

1961   **James Worthy** -- Professional basketball player and superstar

FEBRUARY 27 -- EVENTS

1801   The District of Columbia was placed under the jurisdiction of the U.S. Congress.

1860 Abraham Lincoln made his famous address at Cooper Union in New York, ending with "Let us have faith that right makes might, . . . and dare to do our duty as we understand it."

1883 Oscar Hammerstein, the grandfather of noted lyricist Oscar Hammerstein II, patented the first practical cigar-rolling machine.

1900 England's Labour Party was founded.

1932 The neutron was discovered by English physicist Sir James Chadwick.

1933 The Nazis burned the Reichstag building in Berlin, and, to consolidate their power, accused the Communists of the act.

1939 The U.S. Supreme Court outlawed sit-down strikes.

1939 Great Britain and France recognized the regime of Generalissimo Francisco Franco in Spain.

1942 The Japanese routed an Allied fleet in the Battle of the Java Sea in World War II.

1959 The Boston Celtics scored a record 173 points in an NBA basketball game against Minneapolis.

1972 President Nixon and Chinese Premier Chou En-lai issued the Shanghai Communique at the conclusion of Nixon's visit to the People's Republic of China.

1973 Members of the American Indian Movement occupied Wounded Knee, S.D., the site of the 1890 Sioux Indian massacre, and remained there until early May.

FEBRUARY 28 -- BIRTHDAYS

1533 **Michel de Montaigne** – French author who wrote 107 essays and is considered by many to be the creator of the personal essay

1683 **Rene Antoine Ferchault de Reaumur** -- French scientist

1797 **Mary Lyon** -- American pioneer in providing higher education for women and the founder of Mount Holyoke College, which opened in 1837 as Mount Holyoke Seminary in South Hadley, Massachusetts

1820 **Sir John Tenniel** -- English illustrator and cartoonist, who illustrated Lewis Carroll's *Alice's Adventures in Wonderland* (1865) and *Through the Looking-Glass* (1872)

1824 **Charles Blondin** – French tightrope walker who crossed Niagara Falls three times on a tightrope

1859 **Florian Cajori** -- Swiss-American mathematician

1865 **Sir Wilfred Grenfell** -- British medical missionary, known as "Grenfell of Labrador," who devoted his life to serving people in Newfoundland, Labrador, and near the Arctic Circle

1865   **Arthur Symons** -- English poet and critic

1876   **John Alden Carpenter** -- American composer

1890   **Vaslav Nijinsky** -- Russian ballet dancer and the most famous male dancer of his time

1894   **Ben Hecht** -- American novelist, playwright, screenwriter, and director, noted for works such as *The Front Page* (with Charles MacArthur) and some 70 screenplays

1901   **Linus Pauling** -- American chemist who was the only person besides Marie Curie to win two Nobel Prizes (the 1954 prize in chemistry and the 1962 Peace Prize)

1906   **Bugsy Siegel** -- Well-known American racketeer of the 1940s

1907   **Milton Caniff** -- American comic strip artist who created *Terry and the Pirates* and *Steve Canyon*

1909   **Stephen Spender** -- English poet and writer noted for "The Express" and the autobiography *World Within World* (1951)

1910   **Vincente Minnelli** – American motion-picture director and father of actress Liza Minnelli, noted for directing films such as *An American in Paris*, which won the 1951 best picture Academy Award

1910   **Josef Myrow** -- Russian-born composer and pianist, noted for songs such as "On the Boardwalk in Atlantic City," "You Make Me Feel So Young," and "Marianne"

1915   **Zero Mostel** -- American stage and motion-picture actor who won three Tony Awards in four years (1961, 1963, and 1964)

1923   **Charles Durning** -- American stage and motion-picture actor

1926   **Svetlana Alliluyeva** -- Daughter of Russian dictator Joseph Stalin

1930   **Frank Malzone** -- Professional baseball player

1931   **Gavin MacLeod** – American television actor noted for his role as the captain in the long-running series, *The Loveboat*

1939   **John Fahey** -- American blues guitarist

1940   **Mario Andretti** -- Italian-American automobile racing driver who won the 1969 Indianapolis 500

1942   **Brian Jones** -- British guitarist with the Rolling Stones musical group

1945   **Bubba Smith** -- Professional football player

1948   **Bernadette Peters** – American motion-picture and television actress

1949   **Evan Williams** -- Professional golfer

1951   **Gustave Theoni** -- Professional skier

1952   **Fred Dean** -- Professional football player

1953   **Roland Harper** -- Professional football player

1956   **Adrian Dantley** -- Professional basketball player

FEBRUARY 28 -- EVENTS

590 AD Gregory I became Roman Catholic pope.
1632 Portland, Maine, was first settled.
1827 The Baltimore and Ohio Railroad had its beginnings in a charter granted to build a 380-mile railroad to the West to compete with the Erie Canal.
1844 The U.S. secretary of state and secretary of the Navy were killed when a new "Peacemaker" cannon exploded on the USS *Princeton*. President John Tyler escaped unharmed.
1845 The U.S. House and Senate passed a joint resolution inviting Texas to join the Union. Its acceptance started the Mexican War later in the year.
1849 The first forty-niners (the gold-rushers of 1849) reached San Francisco aboard the steamer *California*.
1854 Antislavery Whigs passed a resolution at Ripon, Wisconsin, calling for a new party--the Republican Party--if Congress passed the Kansas-Nebraska Bill.
1916 Henry James, the great American novelist, died in London at age 72.
1942 Japanese troops landed on Java in World War II.
1952 Vincent Massey was sworn in as the first Canadian-born governor-general of Canada.
1971 Jack Nicklaus won the PGA Tournament, making him the first golfer to win the world's four major titles--the U.S. Open, the British Open, the Masters, and the PGA--twice.
1972 President Richard Nixon returned to the United States and described his visit to China as the trip that "changed the world."
1974 The United States and Egypt re-established diplomatic relations after a 7-year break.

FEBRUARY 29 -- BIRTHDAYS

1468 **Paul III**—Roman Catholic pope, 1534-1549, who summoned the Council of Trent, restored the Inquisition, excommunicated Henry VIII, and made Michelangelo chief architect of the Vatican
1712 **Marquis de Montcalm** — French general who was killed in the Battle of Quebec in the French and Indian War
1736 **Ann Lee** -- English religious leader who founded the Society of Shakers in America
1756 **Christian F. Hansen** -- Noted Danish architect
1792 **Gioacchino Rossini** -- Italian operatic composer, noted for *The Barber of Seville* (1816), perhaps the greatest farce opera ever written, and *William Tell* (1829), with its famous overture

1808   **Charles Pritchard** -- Noted British astronomer
1860   **Herman Hollerith** -- American inventor who pioneered the processing of data in the U.S. census office by the use of punched cards, which were the forerunners of computer cards
1864   **Josef Svatopluk Machar** -- Czechoslovakian poet
1900   **Jean Negulesco** -- Rumanian-born motion-picture director noted for films such as *Johnny Belinda* (1948) and *Three Coins in the Fountain* (1954)
1904   **Jimmy Dorsey** -- American bandleader of the Big Band Era of the 1930s and 1940s, and brother of bandleader Tommy Dorsey
1904   **Pepper Martin** -- Professional baseball player and star of the 1934 St. Louis Cardinals' "Gas House Gang"
1908   **Balthus** -- French painter
1916   **Howard Nemerov** -- American poet and writer who won the Pulitzer Prize for poetry in 1978 for *The Collected Poems of Howard Nemerov*
1920   **Arthur Franz** -- American stage, screen, and television actor
1920   **Michele Morgan** -- The most popular movie actress in France before World War II
1924   **Al Rosen** -- Professional baseball player and executive
1924   **William Dodd Hathaway** -- U.S. senator
1928   **Joss Akland** -- English motion-picture actor
1948   **Willi Smith** -- American fashion designer
1952   **Reyno Seegers** -- South African tennis player

FEBRUARY 29 -- EVENTS

1288   A law was passed in Scotland making it legal for women to propose to men.
1504   Columbus used the total eclipse of the moon, which he knew from his almanac would occur, to scare the Jamaica natives into supplying him with food on his 4th voyage to America.
1872   England's Queen Victoria narrowly missed death at the hands of a would-be assassin, Albert O'Connor, an 18-year-old revolutionary.
1944   Allied soldiers landed in the Admiralty Islands in World War II.
1956   President Dwight D. Eisenhower announced his candidacy for reelection.
1956   The great blizzard of 1956 in Western Europe finally ended. It had lasted the entire month of February and resulted in 1,000 deaths.
1960   Agadir, Morocco, was hit by a major earthquake, a tidal wave, and fire, resulting in 12,000 deaths.

3

March

March, the third month of the year, was originally the first month of the ancient Roman calendar. Its Latin name was *Martius*, chosen to honor Mars, the Roman god of war. March was the first month of the year until 45 B.C., when Caesar made it the third month of his Julian Calendar. The running battle continued, however, as to which month, January or March, would be first, until the issue was finally settled by the Gregorian Calendar in 1582. Except for a brief period when Romulus issued the first Roman calendar, March has always had 31 days.

St. Patrick's Day is celebrated on March 17, and four American presidents--James Madison, Andrew Jackson, John Tyler and Grover Cleveland--were born in March. One of the most noteworthy events in world history, the assassination of Caesar, also occurred in the month (on the Ides of March--March 15--in 44 B.C.).

The March birthstones are the bloodstone and the aquamarine, and the special flower is the jonquil. Notable birthdays and events follow.

MARCH 1 -- BIRTHDAYS

1812   **Augustus Welby Northmore Pugin** — English architect, designer, author, and noted participant in the English Roman Catholic and Gothic revivals

1837   **William Dean Howells** — American novelist, editor, and critic, noted for works such as *The Rise of Silas Lapham* (1885) and *Criticism and Fiction* (1891)

1848   **Augustus Saint-Gaudens** -- Foremost American sculptor of the late 19th century, whose work is noted for its lifelike qualities

1880   **Julian Myrick** – American Hall of Fame tennis player and leader in the development of the game

1880   **Lytton Strachey** -- English biographer, essayist, and critic, noted for works such as *Eminent Victorians* (1918) and *Queen Victoria* (1921)

1883   **Thomas Shelvin** -- Yale end who ranked second to Jim Thorpe in 1926 as the greatest college football player of all time

1886   **Oskar Kokoschka** -- Austrian painter noted for works such as *The Tempest* and *View of the Thames*

1904   **Glenn Miller** -- One of the most notable of the American bandleaders of the Big Band Era of the 1930s and 1940s

1909   **David Niven** – English-American motion-picture and television actor and author, who won an Academy Award in 1958 for *Separate Tables*

1914   **Sidney Lippman** -- American composer, author, and publisher, noted for songs such as "A-You're Adorable" and "My Sugar Is So Refined"

1917   **Robert Lowell** -- A leading American poet of the 20th century, who won the 1947 Pulitzer Prize for "Lord Weary's Castle"

1917   **Dinah Shore** – American radio, motion-picture, and television singer and actress

1919   **Harry Caray** -- American baseball telecaster noted for his coverage of the St. Louis Cardinals and the Chicago Cubs

1921   **Terence Cardinal Cooke** -- Archbishop of New York who was appointed a cardinal of the Roman Catholic Church in 1969

1921   **Richard Wilbur** -- American poet whose volume *Things of This World* won the 1957 Pulitzer Prize for poetry

1924   **Donald K. Slayton** -- U.S. astronaut

1926   **Pete Rozelle** -- Commissioner of the National Football League

1927   **Harry Belafonte** -- American stage, screen, and television singer and actor

1934   **Jean-Michel Folon** -- Belgian painter and illustrator

1935   **Robert Conrad** – American motion-picture and television actor

1935   **Judith Rossner** -- American novelist, noted for works such as *Looking for Mr. Goodbar*

1942   **Joan Hackett** -- American motion-picture and television actress

1945   **Roger Daltrey** -- British singer with the Who musical group

1950   **Riley Odoms** -- Professional football player

1952   **Brian Winters** -- Professional basketball player

1953   **Jose Higueras** -- Spanish tennis player

1953   **Thomas "Hollywood" Henderson** -- Professional football player

1954	**Ron Howard** -- American television and motion-picture actor and director
1954	**Catherine Bach** -- American television actress noted for her role in the long-running TV series, *The Dukes of Hazzard*
1957	**Johnny Ray** -- Professional baseball player
1958	**Nik Kershaw** -- British singer and guitarist

MARCH 1 -- EVENTS

1638	The first Swedish settlers, and the first to build log cabins in America, arrived at the present site of Wilmington, Delaware.
1781	The Articles of Confederation became effective as the governing documents of the United States as Maryland became the 13th state to sign them.
1790	The first U.S. Census was authorized by Congress.
1803	Ohio was admitted to the Union as the 17th state.
1845	President John Tyler signed a joint House and Senate resolution admitting Texas to the Union. Texas formally joined in December, 1845.
1864	Rebecca Lee became the first black woman to receive a medical degree, from the New England Female Medical College in Boston.
1867	Nebraska was admitted to the Union as the 37th state.
1872	Yellowstone became America's first national park by an act of Congress setting aside a 2 million acre tract of wilderness in the Wyoming Territory.
1913	The United States income tax law took effect.
1932	Colonel Charles A. Lindbergh's baby was kidnapped from his bed in the Lindberghs' New Jersey home. He was later found dead.
1949	The great heavyweight boxer Joe Louis announced his retirement from the ring after an all-time record of over 11 years as champion.
1951	The 22nd Amendment to the U.S. Constitution was proclaimed, limiting a president to two terms in office.
1954	The United States detonated its first deliverable megaton-class hydrogen bomb, the Bravo.
1961	The Peace Corps was established by President John Kennedy.
1962	The first K-Mart store opened, in Garden City, Michigan.
1974	The Watergate grand jury indicted seven of President Nixon's presidential aides, and named Nixon himself as an unindicted co-conspirator.

MARCH 2 -- BIRTHDAYS

1316	**Robert II** -- King of Scotland who succeeded Robert Bruce's son David II

1545   **Sir Thomas Bodley** -- English diplomat who rebuilt the Oxford University library (now known as the Bodleian Library) after it was destroyed by King Edward VI in 1550

1578   **George Sandys** -- English traveler, poet, and colonizer

1769   **De Witt Clinton** -- Governor of New York who promoted the building of the Erie Canal

1793   **Sam Houston** -- American statesman who played a leading role in winning the independence of Texas from Mexico

1810   **Leo XIII** -- Roman Catholic pope, 1878-1903, best known for his famous encyclical *Rerum Novarum*, which upheld the rights of the working class

1824   **Bedrich Smetana** -- Bohemian composer noted for works such as *The Bartered Bride* (1866) and *My Country*, which contains his famous work, "The Moldau"

1829   **Carl Shurz** -- American statesman of the post-Civil War era

1862   **John Jay Chapman** -- American writer

1876   **Pius XII** -- Roman Catholic pope, 1939-1958

1897   **Max Lincoln Schuster** -- American publisher who with Richard Leo Simon founded the publishing house of Simon and Schuster in 1924

1900   **Kurt Weill** -- German composer of music for the stage and motion-picture scores, such as *Lady in the Dark* and *One Touch of Venus*

1902   **Edward U. Condon** -- American physicist noted for his application of new quantum theories to radioactive processes

1904   **Dr. Seuss (Theodor Seuss Geisel)** -- Noted American author of children's books, such as *The Cat in the Hat*, *Green Eggs and Ham*, and *How the Grinch Stole Christmas*

1909   **Mel Ott** -- Hall of Fame baseball player and first National Leaguer to hit over 500 career home runs

1913   **Mort Cooper** -- Professional baseball player

1917   **Desi Arnaz** -- American motion-picture and television actor and musician, who with his wife Lucille Ball formed Desilu Productions

1917   **Jim Konstanty** -- Professional baseball player

1919   **Jennifer Jones** -- American motion-picture actress who won the 1943 Academy Award for best actress in *The Song of Bernadette*

1927   **John Brademas** -- U.S. congressman, 1959-1981

1931   **Mikhail S. Gorbachev** -- General secretary of the Russian Communist Party and leader of the Soviet government, who succeeded Konstantin Chernenko in 1985

1942   **John Irving** -- American novelist

1950   **John Reaves** -- Professional football player

1950   **Karen Carpenter** -- American singer of the Carpenters brother and sister duo

| 1954 | **Pete Johnson** -- Professional football player |
| 1957 | **Earnest Gray** -- Professional football player |

MARCH 2 -- EVENTS

1415 Pope John XXIII (the antipope) abdicated under pressure from the Council of Constance.

1791 John Wesley, the founder of the Methodist Church, died in London at age 87.

1836 Texas declared its independence from Mexico.

1867 Russian composer Peter Tchaikovsky made his first appearance as a conductor, in St. Petersburg.

1877 The disputed presidential election of 1876 was decided by a commission, two days before inauguration day. The vote was 8-7 along party lines for Republican Rutherford B. Hayes.

1917 Puerto Ricans became citizens of the U.S. by the second Organic Act, or Jones Act.

1923 *Time* magazine was first published, in New York by Henry Luce and Briton Hadden.

1930 D.H. Lawrence, the noted English novelist, died in Vence, France, at age 44.

1939 Pius XII was elected Roman Catholic pope.

1949 The U.S. superfortress *Lucky Lady 2* completed the first non-stop round-the-world flight in 94 hours, 1 minute.

1962 Superstar Wilt Chamberlain made a record 100 points in an NBA basketball game between Philadelphia and New York at Hershey, Pennsylvania.

1969 The Concorde, the supersonic transport developed by France and England, made its first test flight.

1972 American jockey Willie Shoemaker rode his 555th lifetime winner, breaking Eddie Arcaro's record.

1972 The U.S. launched *Pioneer 10* on an unmanned flight that will take it past the planet Jupiter and then out of the solar system, where it will travel for 2 million years.

MARCH 3 -- BIRTHDAYS

1549 **Henric Laurenszoon Spieghel** -- Dutch poet

1606 **Edmund Waller** -- English poet best known for "Go, Lovely Rose" (1655)

1652 **Thomas Otway** -- English playwright best known for *Venice Preserved, or A Plot Discovered* (1682)

1756   **William Godwin** -- English philosopher and writer, who wrote the influential book *Political Justice* (1793), and who was the father of Mary Godwin Shelley, the wife of the poet Percy B. Shelley

1793   **Charles William Macready** -- English actor, stage manager, and diarist

1831   **George Mortimer Pullman** -- American inventor and businessman who popularized the Pullman sleeping car

1845   **Georg Cantor** -- German mathematician and father of set theory

1847   **Alexander Graham Bell** -- American scientist and inventor noted for the invention of the telephone (in 1875)

1860   **Monte Ward** -- Hall of Fame baseball player and manager

1869   **Sir Henry Wood** -- British composer and conductor

1872   **Willie Keeler** -- Hall of Fame baseball player whose philosophy was "Hit 'em where they ain't," and who hit .432 in 1897

1873   **William Green** -- American labor leader who succeeded William Gompers as president of the American Federation of Labor in 1924 and held that position until his death in 1952

1878   **Edward Thomas** -- Welsh poet and novelist, noted for works such as *The Happy-Go-Lucky Morgans* (1913)

1884   **Fontaine Fox** -- American cartoonist who created *Toonerville Folks,* with its famous Toonerville trolley, and drew the strip for 40 years until he retired himself and it in 1955

1895   **Matthew B. Ridgway** -- American general who succeeded General Douglas MacArthur as commanding general of the U.N. forces in the Korean War

1898   **Emil Artin** -- Noted Austrian-American mathematician

1902   **Isabel Bishop** -- American artist

1903   **Adrian** -- American costume designer

1911   **Jean Harlow** -- American motion-picture superstar and sex symbol of the 1930s

1920   **Ronald Searle** -- English cartoonist and writer, who created the appalling girls' school, St. Trinian's

1920   **Julius Boros** -- Professional golfer who won the U.S. Open in 1952 and 1963

1921   **Diana Barrymore** -- American stage and motion-picture actress, and daughter of the noted actor John Barrymore

1928   **Dave Dudley** -- American musician and songwriter, noted for "Six Days on the Road"

1933   **Lee Radziwell** -- American interior decorator and sister of Jackie Kennedy Onassis

1947   **Dennis Shaw** -- Professional football player

1950   **Ed Marinaro** -- Professional football player and television actor noted for his role in *Hill Street Blues*

1962   **Jackie Joyner-Kersee** -- American 1988 Olympic champion jumper

1962   **Herschel Walker** -- Professional football superstar

MARCH 3 -- EVENTS

1493   Christopher Columbus, on board the *Nina,* reached Lisbon on his return from the first voyage to America.

1820   The U.S. Congress passed the Missouri Compromise, admitting Maine to the Union as a free state and allowing Missouri to form a state constitution.

1845   Florida was admitted to the Union as the 27th state.

1849   The Department of the Interior was established.

1861   Czar Alexander II emancipated the serfs in Russia.

1863   The first draft law in U.S. history was passed by Congress.

1875   Georges Bizet's famous opera *Carmen* premiered at the Opera-Comique in Paris.

1915   D.W. Griffith's *The Birth of a Nation,* one of the world's greatest silent movies, had its world premiere in New York.

1918   The Bolsheviks of Russia signed the Treaty of Brest Litovsk with Germany, in which Russia agreed to withdraw from World War I.

1931   "The Star-Spangled Banner" was officially designated by Congress as the national anthem of the United States.

1934   John Dillinger, the notorious American criminal, escaped from the Crown Point Prison in Indiana, using a fake pistol he had carved out of wood and colored with shoe polish.

1974   Commercial aviation's worst air crash in history occurred as 346 people were killed in the crash of a Turkish DC-10 jumbo jet in a forest near Paris.

1978   Prime Minister Ian D. Smith of Rhodesia and three black leaders signed an agreement to transfer power to Rhodesia's black majority by December 31, 1978.

MARCH 4 -- BIRTHDAYS

1394   **Prince Henry the Navigator** -- Portuguese nobleman who was the leading promoter of exploration and the study of geography in the 15th century

1678   **Antonio Vivaldi** -- Italian violin virtuoso and composer who wrote nearly fifty operas

1748   **Count Casimir Pulaski** – Polish soldier who fought and was killed in the service of the American colonies in the Revolutionary War

1756   **Sir Henry Raeburn** – Perhaps the most famous Scottish painter of all time, who was known for works such as the famous *Boy with Rabbit*

1888   **Knute Rockne** -- One of the greatest football coaches of all time, who with Notre Dame, 1918-1931, won 105 games and lost 12, and made the forward pass an integral part of the game

1891   **Dazzy Vance** -- Hall of Fame baseball pitcher who led the National League in strikeouts for seven straight years

1897   **Lefty O'Doul** -- Professional baseball player and manager

1901   **Charles H. Goren** -- One of the foremost American bridge experts and columnists of the 20th century

1904   **George Gamow** -- Russian-American physicist and author, noted for works such as *The Birth of the Sun* (1940), *One, Two, Three . . . Infinity* (1947), and *A Planet Called Earth* (1963)

1906   **Phil Davis** -- American cartoonist who with Lee Falk created the comic strip, *Mandrake the Magician*

1913   **John Garfield** -- American stage and motion-picture actor

1918   **Margaret Osborne DuPont** -- American tennis player and superstar of the 1940s

1921   **Joan Greenwood** -- British stage and motion-picture actress

1924   **Kenneth O'Donnell** -- American government official and aide to President Kennedy

1927   **Dick Savitt** -- American tennis player and 1951 Wimbledon singles champion

1936   **Jim Clark** -- Scottish racing car driver and superstar, who won the Indianapolis 500 in 1965 and the Grand Prix in 1963 and 1965

1939   **Barbara McNair** -- American singer and actress

1939   **Paula Prentiss** -- American motion-picture and television actress

1939   **Joanne Gunderson Carner** -- Professional golfer

1944   **Mary Wilson** -- American musician with the Supremes musical group

1948   **Chris Squire** -- American rock musician

1953   **Kay Lenz** -- American motion-picture and television actress

1954   **Barbara Downs** -- American tennis player

1954   **Annette Coe** -- English tennis player

MARCH 4 -- EVENTS

1461   King Henry VI of England was deposed by the Yorkists. He ruled again briefly ten years later before he was murdered.

1681   William Penn was granted a charter by King Charles II to found the colony of Pennsylvania.

1789   The United States Constitution went into effect as the first Congress met in New York City.

1791   Vermont was admitted to the Union as the 14th state.

1793	Washington became the first president to be inaugurated on March 4, the original inauguration date. The date was moved to January 20 by the 20th Amendment beginning in 1937.
1801	Thomas Jefferson became the first president to be inaugurated in Washington, D.C.
1829	The mob at Andrew Jackson's inauguration broke White House furniture and china before being induced to leave by punch served on the White House lawn.
1837	Chicago, with a population of 4,000, was incorporated as a city.
1865	Abraham Lincoln, at his second inaugural, pleaded for national unity, "With malice toward none, with charity for all."
1902	The American Automobile Association was founded.
1917	Jeannette Rankin of Montana, the first woman to be elected to the House of Representatives, took her seat as a member of Congress.
1933	Franklin D. Roosevelt, at his first inaugural, said, "The only thing we have to fear is fear itself."
1946	The comic strip, *Rip Kirby,* by Alex Raymond, first appeared.
1952	Ronald Reagan married movie actress Nancy Davis.
1968	Joe Frazier knocked out Buster Mathis in the 11th round in New York to become in several states the heavyweight champion. (Other states recognized Jimmy Ellis.)
1974	British Prime Minister Edward Heath resigned and was succeeded by Labour Party leader Harold Wilson.
1976	John Pezzin made a record 33 consecutive strikes in a bowling match at Toledo, Ohio.

MARCH 5 -- BIRTHDAYS

1324	**David II** -- King of Scotland in 1329, and son of Scotland's great king, Robert Bruce
1326	**Louis I (the Great)** -- King of Hungary, 1343-1370
1512	**Gerhardus Mercator** – The greatest mapmaker of the 16th century and inventor of the Mercator projection
1658	**Antoine de la Mothe Cadillac** -- French soldier and explorer of North America, who in 1701 founded Detroit and in 1711 was governor of Louisiana
1696	**Giovanni Battista Tiepolo** – Italian painter of the Venetian group, noted for works such as *The Meeting of Antony and Cleopatra*
1817	**Sir Austen Henry Layard** – English archaeologist noted for excavations at Nimrod and Kiyunik in Iraq which revealed the remains of the palaces of the Assyrian kings of Nineveh
1824	**James Merritt Ives** -- Noted American lithographer who with Nathaniel Currier published the famous Currier and Ives color pictures

1853   **Howard Pyle** — American painter and illustrator, noted for works such as *The Merry Adventures of Robin Hood* (1883) and *The Story of King Arthur and His Knights* (1903)

1870   **Frank Norris** — American novelist noted for works such as *McTeague* (1899) and *The Octopus* (1901)

1882   **Egbert Anson Van Alstyne** — American composer and pianist, noted for songs such as "In the Shade of the Old Apple Tree," "Pretty Baby," and "Drifting and Dreaming"

1887   **Heitor Villa-Lobos** — Brazilian composer, conductor, and educator, noted for the forms *Bachiana Brasileira* and *Choros* in which he wrote his works

1891   **Daniel R. Fitzpatrick** — American political cartoonist who won the Pulitzer Prize for cartooning in 1926

1891   **Chic Johnson** — American comic actor who with Ole Olsen formed the Olsen and Johnson comedy act in vaudeville and the movies

1903   **Irving Kahal** — American lyricist, noted for songs such as "Let a Smile Be Your Umbrella," "Wedding Bells Are Breaking Up That Old Gang of Mine," and "The Night Is Young and You're So Beautiful"

1908   **Rex Harrison** — English stage and motion-picture actor who won the 1964 Academy Award for *My Fair Lady*

1918   **Paul Christman** — Hall of Fame football player

1921   **Elmer Valo** — Professional baseball player

1927   **Jack Cassidy** — American stage, screen, and television actor, singer, and dancer

1929   **J.B. Lenoir** — American blues singer

1930   **Del Crandall** — Professional baseball player

1930   **Loren Maazel** — Musical prodigy and conductor

1931   **Barry Tuckwell** — The world's premier horn player

1935   **Mal Anderson** — Australian tennis superstar

1936   **Dean Stockwell** — American stage, screen, and television actor who made the transition from child star to adult leading man

1937   **Olusegun Obasanjo** — Head of Nigeria's military government in the 1970s

1938   **Fred Williamson** — Professional football player and actor

1939   **Samantha Eggar** — English motion-picture actress

1945   **Randy Matson** — American shot-putter who set the world's record of 71 feet 5½ inches for a 16-pound shot put in 1967

1946   **Rocky Bleier** — Professional football player

1947   **Kent Tekulve** — Professional baseball player

1950   **Eugene Nicholas Fodor** — American concert violinist

1958   **Andy Gibb** — Australian singer and teenage idol

MARCH 5 -- EVENTS

493 AD German barbarian leader Odovacar (Odoacer), who had ended the Western Roman Empire in A.D. 476, was executed at age 59 by the Ostrogoths.

1625 Charles I succeeded to the English throne upon the death of his father James I.

1770 The Boston Massacre occurred, in which British troops fired into a crowd on King's Street, leaving five people dead.

1821 President James Monroe was inaugurated for his second term. (The date was moved because March 4 fell on a Sunday.)

1868 The U.S. Senate was organized into a Court of Impeachment to hear the charges against President Andrew Johnson.

1900 The Hall of Fame of Great Americans was established at New York University by Henry Mitchell MacCracken, a former chancellor of the university.

1933 The Nazis won 44% of the popular vote and 52% of the Reichstag seats in the last "free" election in Germany until after World War II.

1945 Marshal Tito became absolute ruler of Yugoslavia.

1946 Winston Churchill, in a speech at Fulton, Missouri, originated the term "Iron Curtain."

1953 Soviet dictator Joseph Stalin died in Moscow at age 73.

1960 Elvis Presley, the rock and roll idol, was released from the U.S. Army.

1979 U.S. space vehicle *Voyager 1* came within 172,000 miles of Jupiter and sent back spectacular photographs to the earth.

MARCH 6 -- BIRTHDAYS

1405 **John II** -- King of Castile, 1406-1454

1475 **Michelangelo (Buonarroti)** -- Great leader of the Italian Renaissance and one of the most famous artists in history

1619 **Savinien de Cyrano de Bergerac** -- French author and soldier, noted for his skill in sword fighting and for his long nose

1806 **Elizabeth Barrett Browning** -- Wife of English poet Robert Browning and poet in her own right, best known for "Sonnets from the Portuguese" (1850)

1831 **Philip H. Sheridan** -- Union cavalry general in the Civil War who fought at Chickamauga, the Battle of Chattanooga, and the Shenandoah Valley

1870 **Oscar Straus** -- Austrian composer best known for *The Chocolate Soldier* and *The Waltz Dream*

1885   **Ring Lardner** -- American sports reporter and author of humorous short stories, such as "Alibi Ike" and *You Know Me, Al*

1892   **Clark Daniel Shaughnessy** -- American football coach who revived the T formation

1896   **Jack Stern** -- American composer and author, noted for songs such as "Too Beautiful for Words," "When You're in Love," and "Remember Pearl Harbor"

1897   **John D. MacArthur** -- Noted American billionaire

1899   **Richard Leo Simon** -- American publisher who with Max Lincoln Schuster founded the publishing house of Simon and Schuster in 1924

1900   **Lefty Grove** -- Hall of Fame baseball pitcher who won 300 career games

1905   **Bob Wills** -- American bandleader, fiddler, and composer, noted for songs such as "San Antonio Rose," "Take Me Back to Tulsa," and "Time Changes Everything"

1906   **Lou Costello** -- American actor and member of the famed Abbott and Costello comedy team

1923   **Ed McMahon** -- American television performer and sidekick of Johnny Carson on the *Tonight Show*

1924   **William H. Webster** -- Director of the F.B.I. under Presidents Carter and Reagan, and Director of the C.I.A. under President Reagan

1924   **Sarah Caldwell** -- American conductor and first woman to conduct a major symphony orchestra

1926   **Alan Greenspan** -- American economist, advisor to Presidents Nixon and Ford, and Chairman of the Board of Governors of the Federal Reserve System

1927   **L. Gordon Cooper Jr.** -- One of the original team of seven U.S. astronauts and participant in the *Gemini 5* mission in 1965

1937   **Valentina Vladimirovna Tereshkova** -- Russian cosmonaut and first woman to travel in space (1963)

1941   **Willie Stargell** -- Professional baseball superstar

1943   **Bobby Fischer** -- First American to win the world chess title (1972-1975)

1945   **Robert Trumpy Jr.** -- Professional football player

1945   **Rob Reiner** -- American actor, son of actor Carl Reiner, and one of the stars of the long-running television comedy, *All in the Family*

1948   **Stephen Schwartz** -- American composer-lyricist, noted for *Godspell*

1952   **Jimmy Allen** -- Professional football player

1957   **Vagas Ferguson** -- Professional football player

MARCH 6 -- EVENTS

1521   Magellan landed on Guam in his round-the-world voyage.

1629   Holy Roman Emperor Ferdinand II issued the Edict of Restitution, providing that all church possessions acquired by the Protestants were to be returned to the Catholics.

1834   The city of York in the Canadian province of Upper Canada changed its name and was incorporated as Toronto.

1836   The Alamo at San Antonio fell to Mexican General Santa Anna after an 11-day siege. Its entire garrison was killed, including Davy Crockett and Jim Bowie.

1857   Chief Justice Roger B. Taney announced the Dred Scott Decision, refusing the slave Dred Scott the right to sue for his freedom.

1858   The Missionary Society of Saint Paul the Apostle, or the "Paulists," was founded in New York City by Father Isaac Thomas Hecker.

1896   Charles Brady King drove his "Horseless Carriage" on the streets of Detroit, the first automobile to appear in the Motor City.

1924   The Egyptian government officially opened Tutankhamen's mummy case.

1930   The first frozen foods--developed by Clarence Birdseye--were sold in grocery stores, in Springfield, Massachusetts.

1933   President Franklin D. Roosevelt proclaimed the national bank holiday to save the country's tottering banks.

1935   Oliver Wendell Holmes Jr., the great Supreme Court justice, died in Washington, D.C., two days before his 94th birthday.

1953   Georgi Malenkov succeeded Joseph Stalin as Soviet premier.

1957   The former British African colonies of Togoland and the Gold Coast became the independent nation of Ghana.

1967   Svetlana Alliluyeva, Joseph Stalin's daughter, appeared at the U.S. embassy in India to defect to the West. She returned to Russia in 1984.

MARCH 7 -- BIRTHDAYS

1556   **Guillaume du Vair** -- French philosopher and writer

1671   **Ellis Wynne** -- English clergyman and author

1693   **Clement XIII** -- Roman Catholic pope, 1758-1769

1707   **Stephen Hopkins** -- Governor of Rhode Island and signer of the Declaration of Independence

1785   **Alessandro Manzoni** — One of Italy's greatest novelists because of his only novel, *The Betrothed* (1827), which set the standard for modern Italian prose style

1792   **Sir John Herschel** — British astronomer, son of noted British astronomer Sir William Herschel, and pioneer in the use of hypo in photography

1802   **Sir Edwin Landseer** -- The most popular English artist of his time, noted for works such as *Dignity and Impudence* (1839) and *The Stag at Bay* (1846)

1844   **Anthony Comstock** -- American crusader against obscenity and imagined obscenity in literature

1845   **Daniel David Palmer** -- Founder of chiropractic

1849   **Luther Burbank** -- American plant breeder who developed numerous new trees, flowers, vegetables, and grasses, such as the Shasta daisy and the spineless cactus

1850   **Champ Clark** -- Speaker of the U.S. House of Representatives, 1911-1919, and chief opponent of Woodrow Wilson for the Democratic nomination for president in 1912

1850   **Tomas Masaryk** -- First president and chief founder of Czechoslovakia

1872   **Piet Mondrian** -- Dutch painter known for his rigidly geometric style

1875   **Maurice Ravel** -- French composer noted for works such as *Bolero* and *Daphnis et Chloe*

1889   **Ben Ames Williams** -- American novelist

1893   **Milton Avery** -- American painter noted for works such as *Swimmers and Sunbathers* (1945)

1908   **Anna Magnani** -- Egyptian-Italian stage, screen, and television actress, referred to by director Vittorio De Sica as "Italy's greatest actress"

1930   **Anthony Armstrong-Jones** -- English photographer and former husband of Princess Margaret

1934   **Willard Scott** -- American television weatherman on NBC's *Today* show

1934   **King Curtis** -- American rock and roll saxophone player

1938   **Janet Guthrie** -- American automobile racing driver

1938   **Homero Blancos** -- Professional golfer

1940   **Daniel J. Travanti** -- American television actor noted for his role in the popular series *Hill Street Blues*

1945   **John Heard** -- English motion-picture actor

1946   **Peter Wolf** -- American rock singer

1950   **Franco Harris** -- Professional football superstar and the second player in history after Jim Brown to rush for over 12,000 yards in a career

1950   **Billy Joe DuPree** -- Professional football player

1952   **Lynn Swann** -- Professional football superstar

1955   **Tommy Kramer** -- Professional football player

1957   **Kenny King** -- Professional football player

1960   **Joe Carter** -- Professional baseball player

1960   **Ivan Lendl** -- Czechoslovakian tennis player and superstar

1963   **Kim Ung-Yong** -- South Korean native with an I.Q. of 210, a world's record

MARCH 7 -- EVENTS

161 AD Roman Emperor Antoninus Pius died of fever at age 75, and was succeeded by Marcus Aurelius.

1274   St. Thomas Aquinas, one of the greatest Christian theologians, died at an approximate age of 49.

1277   Christian Averroism (studying questions from philosophical rather than from religious premises) was condemned by Bishop Etienne Tempier, on instructions of Pope John XXI.

1815   Napoleon Bonaparte was acclaimed by soldiers sent to arrest him on his return to France from the island of Elba, where he had been in exile.

1850   U.S. Senator Daniel Webster made a three-hour "Union-saving" speech, endorsing the Compromise of 1850.

1876   Alexander Graham Bell was granted a patent for his telephone.

1936   Adolf Hitler ordered German troops into the Rhineland, defying the Treaty of Versailles. Even he was amazed that the French offered no opposition.

1945   The Allies crossed the Rhine into Germany in World War II, using a bridge at Remagen that was still intact in spite of German efforts to blow it up.

1965   Civil rights demonstrators, in an attempted march on Montgomery, Alabama, were confronted in Selma by state troopers who used clubs and tear gas to break up the demonstration.

MARCH 8 -- BIRTHDAYS

1494   **Rosso Fiorentino** -- Florentine Mannerist painter

1714   **Carl Philipp Emanuel Bach** -- German composer and second surviving son of the great composer, Johann Sebastian Bach

1748   **William V** -- Prince of Orange

1783   **Hannah Hoes Van Buren** -- Wife of President Martin Van Buren

1787   **Karl von Grafe** -- Father of plastic surgery

1788   **Sir William Hamilton** -- Scottish metaphysical philosopher

1799   **Simon Cameron** -- Powerful Pennsylvania political boss of the 1800s whose definition of an honest politician was "one who when bought, stays bought"

1841   **Oliver Wendell Holmes Jr.** -- Noted U.S. Supreme Court justice, 1802-1832, and son of the famous novelist and writer

1858   **Ruggiero Leoncavallo** – Italian opera composer, best known for *Pagliacci* (1892)

1859   **Kenneth Grahame** – Scottish writer noted for the great children's classic, *The Wind in the Willows* (1908)

1865   **Frederic William Goudy** -- American type designer and printer noted for types such as Goudy Old Style, Forum, and Kennerley

1879   **Otto Hahn** -- German radiochemist who with Fritz Strassmann reported the splitting of the uranium atom in 1938

1891   **Sam Jaffe** -- American stage, screen, and television actor

1902   **Jennings Randolph** -- U.S. senator

1902   **Louise Beavers** – American motion-picture and television actress

1909   **Claire Trevor** -- American stage, screen, and television actress

1920   **Douglass Wallop** – American author noted for *The Year the Yankees Lost the Pennant* (1954), on which the hit musical *Damn Yankees* was based

1921   **Cyd Charisse** -- American motion-picture and television dancer and actress

1922   **Carl Furillo** -- Professional baseball player

1936   **Sue Ane Langdon** -- American actress

1938   **Charley Pride** -- American country music singer

1939   **Jim Bouton** – Professional baseball player and author of *Ball Four*

1939   **Lynn Seymour** -- Canadian dancer

1942   **Dick Allen** -- Professional baseball player

1943   **Lynn Redgrave** -- English stage, screen, and television actress, and daughter of English actor Sir Michael Redgrave

1944   **Susan Clark** -- Canadian-born motion-picture actress

1945   **Mickey Dolenz** -- American musician with the Monkees musical group

1953   **Jim Rice** -- Professional baseball player and superstar

MARCH 8 -- EVENTS

1702   Queen Anne, the last English monarch of the House of Stuart, ascended the throne upon the death of William III.

1869   Hector Berlioz, the noted French composer, died in Paris at age 65.

1874   Millard Fillmore died in Buffalo, New York, at age 74.

1894   New York became the first state to pass a dog licensing law.

1917   Rioting in St. Petersburg marked the beginning of the Russian February (by the old calendar) Revolution. It would end a week later with the abdication of the czar.

1917   Count Ferdinand von Zeppelin, German pioneer in lighter-than-air vehicles, died at age 78.

1917   The U.S. Senate voted to limit filibusters by adopting the cloture rule.

1930	William Howard Taft died in Washington, D.C., at age 72.

1930   William Howard Taft died in Washington, D.C., at age 72.
1942   The Japanese captured Rangoon, Burma, during World War II.
1950   Russia announced that it possessed the atomic bomb. They had tested their first bomb the previous August.
1965   The first American ground combat unit landed in South Vietnam. The unit consisted of some 3,500 marines.
1971   Joe Frazier defeated Muhammad Ali at Madison Square Garden in 15 rounds to retain his heavyweight championship.

MARCH 9 -- BIRTHDAYS

1291   **Can Grande della Scala** -- Military leader of Verona
1451   **Amerigo Vespucci** -- Italian merchant-explorer for whom the Americas were named
1629   **Alexis (Mikhailovich)** – Czar of Russia, 1645-1676, and son of Michael Romanov, the first of the Romanov czars
1749   **Comte de Mirabeau** -- French statesman, orator, and one of the principal leaders of the French Revolution
1758   **Franz Joseph Gall** – German anatomist who founded the pseudoscience of phrenology and co-authored the 4-volume work, *Anatomy and Physiology of the Nervous System* (1810-1820)
1763   **William Cobbett** – English writer, reformer, and publisher, who attacked the Industrial Revolution as an enemy of the working people
1773   **Isaac Hull** -- American naval commodore who commanded the USS *Constitution* when it defeated the British *Guerriere* in the War of 1812 and got the famous nickname "Old Ironsides"
1824   **Leland Stanford** -- American statesman, railroad builder, and founder in 1885 of Stanford University
1856   **Edward Goodrich Acheson** -- American inventor who developed the method of making graphite from coke in 1896
1856   **Eddie Foy** – Famous American vaudeville comedian and father of the *Seven Little Foys* of the movie by that name
1883   **James Kendis** – American composer, author, and publisher, noted for lyrics such as "I'm Forever Blowing Bubbles"
1890   **V.M. Molotov** -- Foreign minister of Russia until he was demoted in 1957 by Nikita Khrushchev
1898   **Luther H. Hodges** -- Governor of North Carolina and secretary of commerce under President Kennedy
1900   **Howard Hathaway Aiken** -- Harvard University professor who in 1944 built the Mark I, the first digital computer
1902   **Will Geer** -- American stage, screen, and television actor, noted for his role as Grandpa in the long-running television series, *The Waltons*

1902   **Edward Durrell Stone** -- American architect who designed the John F. Kennedy Center for the Performing Arts in Washington, D.C., and the Museum of Modern Art in New York City

1904   **Reinhard Heydrich** -- Feared Nazi "Hangman of Europe," whose assassination in 1942 led the Germans to kill 300 Czechs and destroy the town of Lidice for revenge

1905   **Rex Warner** -- English poet, novelist, and notable translator of the plays of ancient Greece

1906   **David Smith** -- American sculptor noted for works with metals, such as *Cubi XIX* (1964)

1910   **Samuel Barber** -- American composer noted for works such as *Vanessa* (1958) and his *Piano Concerto No. 1* (1963)

1912   **Arky Vaughan** -- Professional baseball player

1914   **Fred Clark** -- American stage and motion-picture actor

1918   **George Lincoln Rockwell** -- American Nazi leader

1918   **Mickey Spillane** -- American novelist noted for works such as *I, the Jury* (1946) and as the creator of detective Mike Hammer

1920   **Carl Betz** -- American stage, screen, and television actor

1923   **James Buckley** -- U.S. senator in the 1970s and brother of columnist William F. Buckley

1925   **G. William Miller** -- Chairman of the Board of Governors of the Federal Reserve System in the 1970s

1927   **Jackie Jensen** -- Professional baseball player

1934   **Yuri Gagarin** -- Russian cosmonaut and the first man to travel in space (on April 12, 1961)

1934   **Joyce Van Patten** -- American stage, screen, and television actress, who made the transition from child star to leading lady

1936   **Marty Ingels** -- American stage, screen, and television actor and comedian

1940   **Raul Julia** -- Puerto Rican stage, screen, and television actor

1942   **Bert Campaneris** -- Professional baseball player

1945   **Trish Van Devere** -- American stage, screen, and television actress, and wife of actor George C. Scott

1950   **Danny Sullivan** -- American race car driver who won the Indianapolis 500 in 1985

1950   **Andy North** -- Professional golfer

1951   **Billy Freer** -- South African tennis player

1955   **Fernando Bujones** -- American ballet dancer

1958   **Martin Fry** -- American singer with the ABC musical group

MARCH 9 -- EVENTS

1074   Pope Gregory VII excommunicated all married Roman Catholic priests.

1152	Frederick Barbarossa was crowned King of Germany at Aix-la-Chapelle.
1776	The British economist Adam Smith published his monumental work, *The Wealth of Nations.*
1796	Napoleon married Josephine de Beauharnais in Paris.
1822	Charles M. Graham of New York was granted a patent for false teeth.
1862	The *Monitor* and the *Merrimack,* in the first naval battle of ironclads, fought to a draw at Hampton Roads, Virginia, in the Civil War.
1864	General U.S. Grant was made commander-in-chief of the Northern armies in the Civil War.
1916	Pancho Villa, the Mexican bandit chieftain, led a raid across the American border, killing sixteen people in Columbus, New Mexico.
1954	Newsman Edward R. Murrow, on his TV show, *See It Now,* criticized Senator Joseph R. McCarthy's anti-Communist campaign, helping to bring about McCarthy's later downfall.
1961	*Sputnik IX,* carrying a dog, was launched by Russia.

MARCH 10 -- BIRTHDAYS

1452	**Ferdinand V** – King of Spain who with his wife, Queen Isabella, financed Columbus's voyage of discovery of America
1503	**Ferdinand I** -- Holy Roman Emperor, 1556-1564
1628	**Marcello Malpighi** -- Italian anatomist who discovered the capillary blood vessels that carry blood between the arteries and the veins
1730	**George Ross** -- Member of the Continental Congress and signer from Pennsylvania of the Declaration of Independence
1768	**Domingos de Sequeira** -- Portuguese painter
1772	**Friedrich von Schlegel** -- German poet and critic
1776	**Louise of Mecklenburg-Strelitz** – Queen of Prussia who ruled with her husband Frederick William III, 1797-1810, and supplied the backbone to resist Napoleon's attacks on her country
1788	**Joseph Karl von Eichendorff** -- German poet
1810	**Sir Samuel Ferguson** -- English poet
1845	**Alexander III** -- Czar of Russia, 1881-1894
1858	**Henry Watson Fowler** – English lexicographer and expert on the English language, noted for his *Dictionary of Modern English Usage* (1926)
1867	**Lillian D. Wald** – American social worker and pacificist who founded the Henry Street Settlement for nurses and who was largely responsible for the American system of public-school nursing
1880	**Mike Jacobs** -- Noted American boxing promoter, most famous for his promotion of Joe Louis

1885   **Tamara Karsavina** -- Noted Russian ballerina
1886   **Fred Waller** -- American inventor noted for cinerama in 1952
1888   **Barry Fitzgerald** -- Irish-born stage and motion-picture actor and one of Hollywood's prime character actors of the 1940s and 1950s
1888   **Oscar Gottfried Mayer** -- American meat packer and son of the founder of the Oscar Mayer company
1892   **Arthur Honegger** -- One of the foremost composers of his time, and one of *Les Six,* a famous group of French composers of the 1920s
1898   **Bert Bacharach** -- American syndicated columnist and father of songwriter Burt Bacharach
1900   **Peter De Rose** -- American composer and pianist noted for songs such as "Wagon Wheels," "Somebody Loves You," "Deep Purple," and "Moonlight Mood"
1909   **Two Ton Tony Galento** -- American heavyweight boxer during Joe Louis's reign as champion
1911   **Warner Anderson** -- Child star of silent movies and Broadway plays, and a solid supporting player as an adult in motion pictures and television
1912   **John Fischer** -- Professional golfer
1918   **Pamela Mason** -- American motion-picture actress
1920   **Jack Kent** -- American artist and writer, and creator in 1950 of the comic strip *King Aroo*
1940   **Chuck Norris** -- American movie actor and ex-world middle-weight karate champion
1940   **David Rabb** -- Noted American playwright
1940   **Leroy Ellis** -- Professional basketball player
1941   **Sandra Palmer** -- Professional golfer
1947   **Bob Greene** -- American newspaper columnist
1948   **Austin Carr** -- Professional basketball player
1958   **Steve Howe** -- Professional baseball player
1964   **Prince Edward** -- Youngest son of England's Queen Elizabeth II

MARCH 10 -- EVENTS

1496   Columbus concluded his second visit to the New World as he left Hispaniola for Spain.
1629   Charles I of England dissolved Parliament. It would not meet again until 1640.
1812   English poet Lord Byron published the first two cantos of *Childe Harold's Pilgrimage,* which immediately established his fame.
1813   King Frederick William III created the Iron Cross, Germany's first and highest decoration for military valor.

1831   The French Foreign Legion, one of the world's most colorful fighting forces, was created by King Louis Philippe for service outside France.

1862   The first paper money was issued by the United States.

1876   Alexander Graham Bell said his famous words, "Mr. Watson, come here. I want you!" It was the first intelligible sentence ever carried on the telephone.

1888   John L. Sullivan and Charlie Mitchell fought 44 rounds to a draw in a boxing match in Apremont, France.

1935   The comic strip, *Smokey Stover,* by Bill Holman, first appeared.

1948   Czech foreign minister Jan Masaryk was found dead in Prague. He either was murdered by the Communists or committed suicide in protest of the Communist takeover of Czechoslovakia.

1949   "Axis Sally" was convicted of treason for her Nazi propaganda broadcasts for the Germans in World War II.

MARCH 11 -- BIRTHDAYS

1544   **Torquato Tasso** – The greatest Italian poet of the late Renaissance, noted for works such as "Jerusalem Delivered" (1575)

1819   **Sir Henry Tate** -- English manufacturer and philanthropist

1885   **Sir Malcolm Campbell** -- English automobile racing champion

1887   **Henry Dixon Crowell** -- American composer

1887   **Raoul Walsh** – American pioneer motion-picture director and actor who began both careers with D.W. Griffith in 1912 and for 50 years was one of Hollywood's most prolific directors

1890   **Vannevar Bush** -- American electrical engineer who was active in U.S. weapons research in World War II and who invented the differential analyzer, an electronic calculating machine, in 1930

1895   **Wanda Gag** -- American author and illustrator of children's books, such as *Millions of Cats*

1898   **Dorothy Gish** -- American actress with a 60-year career, who with her sister Lillian Gish appeared in such movie classics as *Orphans of the Storm* (1922) and *Hearts of the World* (1918)

1899   **Frederick IX** -- King of Denmark, 1947-1972

1903   **Dorothy Schiff** -- American editor and publisher of the New York *Post*

1903   **Lawrence Welk** – American bandleader noted for his long-running television show

1914   **Ralph Ellison** – American author best known for his powerful novel *Invisible Man* (1952)

1916   **Sir Harold Wilson** -- Prime minister of Great Britain, 1964-1970

1923   **Louise Brough** – American tennis player who won four Wimbledon singles titles and was one of the greatest women players of all time

1926	**Ralph Abernathy** -- Co-founder with Martin Luther King Jr. of the Southern Christian Leadership Conference
1931	**Rupert Murdoch** -- Australian-born newspaper publisher
1934	**Sam Donaldson** -- American broadcast journalist
1936	**Antonin Scalia** -- U.S. Supreme Court Justice
1938	**Joseph Brooks** -- American songwriter noted for works such as "You Light Up My Life"
1945	**Dock Ellis** -- Professional baseball player
1948	**Cesar Geronimo** -- Professional baseball player
1961	**Mike Percy** – British bassist with the Dead or Alive musical group
1961	**Bruce Watson** -- Irish guitarist with the Big Country musical group

MARCH 11 -- EVENTS

1513	Leo X was elected Roman Catholic pope.
1702	The London *Daily Courant,* the first English daily newspaper, was published by Elizabeth Mallett.
1847	Johnny Appleseed (John Chapman), legendary planter of apple trees along the Ohio River, died at age 72.
1861	The Confederate Congress, meeting in Montgomery, Alabama, adopted the Constitution of the Confederacy.
1888	The famous "Blizzard of '88" struck the northeastern United States, eventually causing the death of some 400 people.
1917	Czar Nicholas II ordered the Duma (the Russian parliamentary body) to disband, but it refused, and the Russian February Revolution continued.
1941	The Lend-Lease Act became law, enabling the U.S. to help Britain in World War II by transferring weapons and equipment to nations fighting the Axis powers.
1942	General Douglas MacArthur left Bataan in World War II and flew to Australia, promising that "I shall return."
1954	The U.S. Army charged that Senator Joseph McCarthy had used pressure to obtain favored treatment for a former consultant to his subcommittee.
1970	Erle Stanley Gardner, American novelist and creator of Perry Mason, died at age 80.

MARCH 12 -- BIRTHDAYS

1626	**John Aubrey** -- English biographer and antiquary
1630	**Andre Le Notre** – French landscape architect who created most of the famous gardens of his day, such as Kensington Gardens in London, Versailles gardens in France, and the Vatican gardens

1685   **George Berkeley** -- Irish bishop and philosopher who tried to reconcile the doctrines of Christianity with the science of his day

1710   **Thomas Arne** -- English composer who wrote *Rule, Britannia* (1741)

1790   **John Frederic Daniell** -- English chemist and inventor of the Daniell battery

1795   **William Mackenzie** -- Canadian politician who led the unsuccessful December Rebellion in upper Canada in 1837

1806   **Jane Means Appleton Pierce** -- Wife of President Franklin Pierce

1818   **John L. Worden** -- Commander of the Union *Monitor* in 1862 in the famous Civil War battle with the Confederate *Merrimack,* the first between two ironclad ships

1821   **Sir John Joseph Caldwell Abbott** -- Prime minister of Canada, 1891-1892

1824   **Gustav Robert Kirchhoff** -- German physicist who formulated Kirchhoff's Laws for electric circuits

1831   **Clement Studebaker** -- Co-founder with his brother Henry of the Studebaker Brothers Manufacturing Company (1868), which evolved into the automobile company

1832   **Charles Cunningham Boycott** -- English land agent in the 1800s who was so harsh with his Irish tenants that his neighbors refused to associate with him, leading to the coining of the word "boycott"

1838   **Sir William Henry Perkin** -- English chemist who founded the aniline dye industry

1858   **Adolph Simon Ochs** -- American newspaperman who rose from newsboy to become the publisher of the New York *Times*

1863   **Gabriele D'Annunzio** -- Italian poet and novelist, noted for works such as *The Flame of Life* (1900), based on his love affair with the famous actress Eleonora Duse

1871   **Ralph Hodgson** -- English poet

1880   **Kemal Ataturk** -- Turkish patriot who founded the Republic of Turkey and served as its president from 1923 until his death in 1938

1894   **Joseph Meyer** -- American composer noted for songs such as "California, Here I Come" and "If You Knew Susie"

1905   **Allan Roberts** -- American composer, author, and pianist, noted for songs such as "You Always Hurt the One You Love," "Into Each Life Some Rain Must Fall," "Good, Good, Good," and "Tampico"

1910   **Masayoshi Ohira** -- Post-World War II prime minister of Japan

1912   **Les Brown** -- American bandleader of the Big Band Era of the 1940s, whose band was known as the "Band of Renown," and who wrote the popular song, "Sentimental Journey"

1912   **James Callaghan** -- Prime minister of Britain, 1976-1979

1912   **Paul Weston** -- American composer, author, and conductor, noted for songs such as "Shrimp Boats," "No Other Love," and "Day by Day"

1921   **Gordon MacRae** -- American stage and motion-picture actor and singer

1922   **Jack Kerouac** – American poet and novelist, noted for works such as *On the Road* (1956), a novel about the "beat generation," and *Big Sur* (1963)

1922   **Lane Kirkland** – President of the AFL-CIO, who succeeded George Meany

1923   **Walter M. Schirra Jr.** -- U.S. astronaut who was the command pilot of *Gemini 6* and *Apollo 7*

1925   **Georges Delerue** – French composer and leading cinema scorer, noted for his prolific output

1928   **Edward Albee** -- American playwright noted for works such as *The American Dream* (1961) and *Who's Afraid of Virginia Woolf?* (1962)

1930   **Vernon Law** -- Professional baseball player

1932   **Andrew Young** -- U.S. ambassador to the United Nations under President Carter and Mayor of Atlanta

1939   **Neil Sedaka** -- American popular singer and songwriter

1941   **Barbara Feldon** – American motion-picture and television actress

1942   **Paul Kantner** -- American guitarist with the Jefferson Airplane and the Jefferson Starship

1946   **Liza Minnelli** – American stage and motion-picture actress and singer, and daughter of actress Judy Garland and director Vincente Minnelli

1948   **Mark Moseley** -- Professional football player

1956   **Dale Murphy** -- Professional baseball superstar

1957   **Marlon Jackson** -- American singer with the Jackson 5 musical group

1962   **Darryl Strawberry** -- Professional baseball superstar

MARCH 12 -- EVENTS

1507   Cesare Borgia, the notorious Italian nobleman and subject of Machiavelli's famous book, *The Prince,* was killed in battle at age 32, fighting for the king of Navarre.

1664   New Jersey became a British colony as King Charles II gave the newly acquired area from Holland to his brother, James, Duke of York.

1912   Juliette Gordon Low founded the Girl Guides, which later became the Girl Scouts of America.

1912	American Army captain Albert Berry made the first parachute jump from an airplane, at Jefferson Barracks, Missouri.
1914	George Westinghouse, the noted American inventor, died at age 67.
1925	The first transatlantic radio broadcast was made.
1933	President Franklin D. Roosevelt broadcast his first "Fireside Chat" on the radio.
1938	German troops crossed the Austrian border after the Austrian government had resigned, accepting Hitler's invasion of the country.
1939	Pius XII was formally installed as Roman Catholic pope.
1940	Finland surrendered to the Soviet Union in the first Russo-Finnish War.
1947	President Harry S Truman announced the Truman Doctrine, proposing aid to Greece and Turkey against Communist aggression.
1951	The comic strip, *Dennis the Menace,* by Hank Ketchum, first appeared.

MARCH 13 -- BIRTHDAYS

1615	**Innocent XII** -- Roman Catholic pope, 1691-1700
1733	**Joseph Priestley** -- English clergyman and chemist who shares the credit with Carl Wilhelm Scheele for the discovery of oxygen
1741	**Joseph II** -- Holy Roman Emperor and King of Austria
1774	**Pierre-Narcisse Guerin** -- French painter
1781	**Karl Friedrich Schinkel** -- German architect
1781	**Johann Rudolf Wyss** -- Swiss writer who edited and published *The Swiss Family Robinson,* which was written by his father, Johann David Wyss
1798	**Abigail Powers Fillmore** -- Wife of President Millard Fillmore, who was also his former teacher
1855	**Percival Lowell** -- American astronomer best known for his belief in the possibility of life on Mars and in the existence of Martian canals
1860	**Hugo Wolf** -- Austrian composer who brought the 19th-century German *Lied* to its highest point of development
1870	**William James Glackens** -- American painter and illustrator noted for works such as *Chez Mouquin* (1905), and who was one of the original members of *The Eight,* a group of realistic artists
1884	**Sir Hugh Seymour Walpole** -- One of the most popular English novelists of the early 20th century, best known for the *Herries Chronicles* (1930-1933)

1886   **Frank "Home Run" Baker** -- Hall of Fame baseball player who,
        in spite of his nickname, never hit more than twelve home runs
        in a season
1908   **Paul Stewart** -- American stage, screen, and television actor
1908   **Walter Annenberg** – American publisher (*TV Guide*) and diplomat
1910   **Sammy Kaye** – American bandleader of the Big Band Era
        whose "Swing and Sway with Sammy Kaye" music spanned a
        career of 40 years
1914   **Bob Haggart** -- American composer and bass player
1916   **Lindy Boggs** -- U.S. congresswoman
1930   **Doug Harvey** -- Professional hockey player
1931   **Rosalind Elias** -- American opera singer
1948   **James Taylor** -- American rock singer and songwriter
1953   **Andy Bean** -- Professional golfer
1960   **Adam Clayton** -- Irish bassist of the U2 musical group
1964   **Will Clark** -- Professional baseball player

MARCH 13 -- EVENTS

1639   Harvard University was named for John Harvard, a Massachu-
        setts clergyman who gave the college its first large gift.
1781   Sir William Herschel, the English astronomer, discovered the
        planet Uranus, the first planet discovered since prehistoric times.
1791   Thomas Paine's *The Rights of Man* was published in London.
1852   "Uncle Sam" was portrayed in cartoon form representing the
        United States for the first time, in the New York weekly *Dioge-
        nes, Hys Lantern.*
1868   The impeachment trial of President Andrew Johnson began in
        the U.S. Senate.
1881   Czar Alexander II of Russia, the "czar liberator" who freed the
        serfs, was assassinated at age 62.
1884   Standard time was established in the United States.
1925   Tennessee's law against teaching evolution in the schools went into
        effect. It would lead later in the year to the famous Scopes trial.
1930   The planet Pluto was discovered by Clyde W. Tombaugh, an
        astronomer at the Lowell Observatory in Flagstaff, Arizona.
1933   Banks in the United States began reopening after a "holiday"
        declared by President Franklin D. Roosevelt.
1938   Seyss-Inquart, installed by the Nazis as Chancellor of Austria,
        and his cabinet agreed to the annexation of Austria by Germany.
1969   *Apollo 9* splashed down in the Pacific with astronauts McDivitt,
        Schweickart, and Scott aboard, after a ten-day flight in space.

MARCH 14 -- BIRTHDAYS

1681   **Georg Philipp Telemann** -- A leading German composer of the late Baroque period, and a contemporary of Johann Sebastian Bach

1804   **Johann Strauss the Elder** -- Austrian composer of some 250 pieces, such as the "Radetzsky March," and father of the "Waltz King," Johann Strauss Jr.

1813   **Joseph P. Bradley** – U.S. Supreme Court justice whose vote is generally considered the swing vote in deciding the disputed 1876 presidential election in favor of Rutherford B. Hayes

1820   **Victor Emmanuel II** -- King of Sardinia who played a principal role in uniting Italy before becoming its first king, 1861-1878

1844   **Humbert I** – King of Italy, 1878-1900, who was assassinated by a revolutionary

1848   **Theodore A. Metz** -- German-born composer, author, and conductor, noted for songs such as "There'll Be a Hot Time in the Old Town Tonight" and "Ta-ra-ra-Boom-de-ree"

1854   **Thomas R. Marshall** – U.S. vice president under President Wilson

1854   **Paul Ehrlich** – Nobel Prize-winning German bacteriologist who founded chemotherapy and in 1910 discovered a remedy for syphilis

1864   **Casey Jones** -- American railroad engineer who gave his life to save the lives of his passengers and crew in the famous wreck in Vaughan, Mississippi, in 1900

1865   **Filoteo Alberini** -- Italian film pioneer and inventor, noted for the Kinetograph (1894 and 1895)

1871   **Olive Fremstad** -- American operatic soprano

1879   **Albert Einstein** -- One of the greatest scientists of all time, best known for his theory of relativity (1905), which revolutionized physics and laid the foundation for splitting the atom

1894   **Osa Johnson** -- Wife of explorer Martin Johnson, who collaborated with him in his discoveries and documentary filmmaking

1898   **Richard L. Strout** -- American journalist who for nearly 40 years was the author of the noted TRB column in the *New Republic*

1898   **Reginald Marsh** – American artist and illustrator noted for his realistic pictures of American city life

1903   **Adolph Gottlieb** -- American painter noted for works such as *Thrust* (1959)

1907   **Edward Heyman** -- American lyricist and producer, noted for songs such as "You Oughta Be in Pictures," "Body and Soul," and "Boo-Hoo"

1911   **Edward Seiler** – Austrian-born lyricist, noted for songs such as "I Don't Want to Set the World on Fire," "When the Lights Go on Again All Over the World," and "Till Then"

1919   **Max Shulman** -- American humorist
1920   **Hank Ketchum** -- American cartoonist and creator of *Dennis the Menace*
1928   **Frank Borman** — American astronaut who commanded the *Apollo 8* space flight that first circled the moon (1968), and who later became an executive with Eastern Air Lines
1929   **Bob Goalby** -- Professional golfer
1933   **Michael Caine** -- English stage, screen, and television actor
1933   **Quincy Jones** -- American jazz musician
1934   **Eugene Andrew Cernan** -- American astronaut on the *Gemini 9* (1966) and *Apollo 10* (1969) flights
1942   **Rita Tushingham** -- English stage and motion-picture actress
1944   **Clyde Lee** -- Professional basketball player
1944   **Wes Unseld** -- Professional basketball player
1947   **Billy Crystal** -- American motion-picture and television actor and comedian
1956   **Butch Wynegar** -- Professional baseball player
1958   **Prince Albert Alexander** — Son of Prince Rainier and Princess Grace, and heir to the throne of Monaco
1961   **Kirby Puckett** -- Professional baseball player

MARCH 14 -- EVENTS

1743   The first Town Meeting in America was held at Faneuil Hall in Boston.
1794   Eli Whitney patented his cotton gin.
1874   "Taps," the Army's bugle call, was copyrighted by its composers, General Daniel Butterfield and his aide-de-camp, Oliver Wilcox.
1883   Karl Marx, the founder of Communism, died at age 64.
1893   New York's Waldorf Hotel opened on Fifth Avenue and 33rd Street.
1923   Warren G. Harding became the first U.S. President to file an income tax report.
1933   The U.S. Congress approved the sale and manufacture of 3.2 beer.
1938   Adolf Hitler entered Vienna in triumph after the annexation of Austria by Germany.
1951   The United Nations forces recaptured the South Korean capital of Seoul in the Korean War.
1964   A Dallas jury found Jack Ruby guilty of murdering Lee Harvey Oswald, President Kennedy's assassin.
1967   President John F. Kennedy's body was moved to its permanent memorial location in Arlington National Cemetery.

MARCH 15 -- BIRTHDAYS

1733	**Johann Zoffany** -- English painter
1767	**Andrew Jackson** -- 7th U.S. president and hero of the Battle of New Orleans in the War of 1812
1779	**William Lamb Melbourne** -- British prime minister, 1834-1841
1852	**Lady Isabella Augusta Gregory** -- Irish playwright noted for works such as *The Rising of the Moon* and *The Workhouse Ward*
1867	**Lionel Pigot Johnson** -- English poet and critic
1874	**Harold L. Ickes** -- American social activist and secretary of the interior under Presidents Franklin D. Roosevelt and Harry S. Truman
1877	**Malcolm Whitman** -- American tennis player and National Singles Champion in 1898, 1899, and 1900
1904	**George Brent** -- Irish-American stage and motion-picture actor
1911	**Ivan Allen Jr.** -- Mayor of Atlanta in the 1970s
1913	**MacDonald Carey** -- American stage, screen, and television actor
1913	**Lew Wasserman** -- President of MCA, Inc.
1915	**David Schoenbrun** -- American news correspondent
1916	**Harry James** -- American bandleader of the Big Band Era of the 1940s
1919	**Lawrence Tierney** -- American motion-picture actor
1926	**Norman Van Brocklin** -- Professional football superstar and coach
1932	**Alan L. Bean** -- U.S. astronaut who piloted the lunar module *Intrepid* on the *Apollo 12* mission
1941	**Mike Love** -- American singer with the Beach Boys musical group
1944	**William Masters** -- Professional football player
1945	**Mark Green** -- American lawyer, author, social activist and television commentator
1946	**Bobby Bonds** -- Professional baseball player
1949	**Jim Kern** -- Professional baseball player
1955	**Dee Snider** -- American singer with the Twisted Sister musical group
1955	**Mickey Hatcher** -- Professional baseball player
1957	**Mary Jean Carillo** -- American tennis player and sportscaster
1959	**Harold Baines** -- Professional baseball player
1959	**Elliott Teltscher** -- American tennis player
1961	**Terry Cummings** -- Professional basketball player
1962	**Steve Coy** -- British drummer with the Dead or Alive musical group

MARCH 15 -- EVENTS

44 BC	Julius Caesar was stabbed to death by Brutus, Cassius, and a group of Roman aristocrats, as he entered a Senate meeting in Rome.

1493   Christopher Columbus arrived in Palos, Spain, completing his first voyage to America. He was aboard the *Nina,* and the *Pinta,* which was feared lost, arrived a few hours later.

1820   Maine was admitted to the Union as the 23rd state.

1836   The U.S. Senate confirmed the nomination of Roger B. Taney as Chief Justice of the Supreme Court.

1875   John McCloskey, the Roman Catholic Archbishop of New York, was named the first American cardinal by Pope Pius IX.

1892   New York became the first state to authorize voting machines.

1913   President Woodrow Wilson held the first regular presidential press conference.

1917   Czar Nicholas II abdicated as a result of the February (by the old calendar) Revolution, and a democratic government was set up in Russia.

1919   The American Legion was founded in Paris by 1,000 veterans of the American Expeditionary Force.

1939   German troops occupied Prague, completing the annexation of Czechoslovakia. Hitler, who arrived in Prague at dusk, proclaimed that "Czechoslovakia has ceased to exist."

1964   Actors Richard Burton and Elizabeth Taylor were married in Montreal. It was her fifth marriage and his second.

1976   Egypt's People's Assembly voted 307 to 2 to end the 1971 treaty of friendship and cooperation with Russia.

MARCH 16 -- BIRTHDAYS

1568   **Juan Martinez Montanes** -- Spanish sculptor

1665   **Giuseppe Maria Crespi** – Italian painter known as Lo Spagnuolo

1739   **George Clymer** – Signer of the Declaration of Independence from Pennyslvania and member of the first U.S. House of Representatives

1751   **James Madison** – 4th U.S. president and "Father of the Constitution"

1787   **Georg Simon Ohm** -- German physicist who discovered Ohm's Law of electric circuits (1826), and for whom the *ohm,* the unit of electrical resistance, was named

1822   **Rosa Bonheur** -- French painter and sculptor, noted for works such as *The Horse Fair* and *Buffalo Bill*

1822   **John Pope** -- Union general in the Civil War who commanded the Northern forces in the Second Battle of Bull Run

1839   **Rene Francois A. Sully Prudhomme** -- Nobel Prize-winning French poet noted for works such as "Les Epreuves" (1866) and "Les Solitudes" (1869)

1846   **Magnus Gosta Mittag-Leffler** – Noted Swedish mathematician
1878   **Reza Shah Pahlavi** -- Shah of Iran, 1925-1941, and father of Shah Mohammed Reza Pahlavi
1892   **Cesar Vallejo** – Peruvian poet noted for works such as "The Dark Messengers" (1918) and "Take Thou This Cup from Me" (1940)
1892   **James Caesar Petrillo** -- President of the American Federation of Musicians (1940-1958), who forced recording companies in 1942 to pay a royalty to musicians for every record they sold
1897   **Conrad Nagel** -- Matinee idol of the American stage and leading man in scores of Hollywood films in the 1920s and 1930s, and a co-founder of the Academy of Motion Picture Arts and Sciences
1903   **Mike Mansfield** – U.S. senator and Majority Leader, 1961-1977, and U.S. Ambassador to Japan in the late 1970s and 1980s
1906   **Lloyd Waner** -- Hall of Fame baseball player who hit a record .355 as a rookie
1909   **Don Raye** – American composer, author, and singer, noted for songs such as "Cow Cow Boogie," "Mister Five by Five," "Beat Me Daddy Eight to the Bar," and "Irresistible You"
1912   **Pat Nixon** -- Wife of President Richard Nixon
1914   **Oscar Gustave Mayer** -- American meat packer and grandson of the founder of the Oscar Mayer company
1915   **Sammy Gallop** -- American composer noted for songs such as "Elmer's Tune," "Holiday for Strings," "Count Every Star," and "Vagabond Shoes"
1920   **Leo McKern** – Australian-British stage and motion-picture actor
1926   **Jerry Lewis** -- American comedian, actor, and director, with a career of some 40 years
1927   **Daniel Patrick Moynihan** – American educator, expert on urban affairs, and U.S. senator
1932   **R. Walter Cunningham** -- U.S. astronaut on the *Apollo 7* flight (1968)
1935   **Teresa Berganza** -- Spanish opera and concert singer
1937   **William Armstrong** -- U.S. senator
1940   **Bernardo Bertolucci** – Italian film director noted for such works as *The Grim Reaper* (1962) and *Last Tango in Paris* (1972)
1942   **Jerry Jeff Walker** -- American country singer and guitarist
1942   **MacArthur Lane** -- Professional football player
1949   **Erik Estrada** -- American television actor
1951   **Kate Nelligan** -- English motion-picture and television actress
1954   **Sammy White** -- Professional football player
1954   **Hollis Stacy** -- Professional golfer
1954   **Nancy Wilson** -- American rock singer with the group Heart

MARCH 16 -- EVENTS

1521   Ferdinand Magellan discovered the Philippine Islands on the first around-the-world trip.

1802   The United States Military Academy was founded at West Point, New York.

1850   Nathaniel Hawthorne's great novel, *The Scarlet Letter,* was first published.

1910   The famous American racer, Barney Oldfield, in a Benz car, set a land speed record of 131.7 miles per hour at Daytona Beach, Florida.

1918   Tallulah Bankhead, the great American actress, made her New York debut in the play, *Squab Farm.*

1935   Adolf Hitler effectively scrapped the Treaty of Versailles, proclaiming universal military service and a peacetime German army of 300,000 men.

1945   The U.S. Marines took Iwo Jima after nearly a month of heavy fighting in World War II.

1959   John B. Salling of the Army of the Confederate States of America died at age 113, the oldest age to which a veteran soldier has lived.

1966   U.S. spacecraft *Gemini 8* docked with an Agena rocket while in orbit.

1971   Thomas E. Dewey, New York governor and twice unsuccessful candidate for president, died eight days before his 69th birthday.

MARCH 17 -- BIRTHDAYS

1473   James IV -- King of Scotland, 1488-1513

1578   Francesco Albano -- Italian painter

1777   Roger B. Taney -- Fifth Chief Justice of the U.S. Supreme Court, 1836-1864, and one of its greatest

1781   Ebenezer Elliott – British agitator known as the "Corn Law Rhymer"

1787   Edmund Kean -- English Shakespearean actor considered the greatest poetic actor of the early 19th century

1804   Jim Bridger -- One of the greatest American frontiersmen of all time and one of the first whites to see the site of the present Yellowstone National Park

1834   Gottlieb Daimler -- German engineer who developed the automobile internal-combustion engine and produced the Mercedes automobile (named for his daughter), the forerunner of today's Mercedes-Benz

1846   Kate Greenaway -- Noted English illustrator of children's books such as *Under the Window* (1879) and *A--Apple Pie* (1886)

1884   Frank Buck — American wild animal authority and collector with the motto, "Bring 'Em Back Alive," the title of a book he wrote in 1931

1894   Paul Eliot Green -- American playwright noted for works such as *The Lost Colony* (1937) and the Pulitzer Prize-winning *In Abraham's Bosom* (1926)

1895   **Shemp Howard** -- Member of the slapstick vaudeville comedy act that later became the Three Stooges

1899   **Charlie Root** -- Professional baseball pitcher who threw the pitch that Babe Ruth hit for a "called" home run in the 1932 World Series

1901   **Alfred Newman** -- American composer, conductor, concert pianist, and one of Hollywood's most prolific film scorers, who was associated with some 200 films and won nine Academy Awards

1902   **Bobby Jones** -- American golf immortal who won the U.S. Open four times and the British Open three times, and in 1950 was voted "the outstanding golfer of the years 1900 to 1949"

1903   **Marquis Childs** -- Noted American newspaper columnist

1907   **John Pastore** -- The first person of Italian descent to win election as a state governor (Rhode Island, 1945-1950) and a U.S. senator (1950-1977)

1910   **Bayard Rustin** -- American civil rights leader and chief organizer of the 1963 March on Washington

1914   **Sammy Baugh** -- One of the greatest quarterbacks in college and professional football history

1918   **Mercedes McCambridge** -- American stage, screen, and radio actress, called by actor Orson Welles "the world's greatest living radio actress"

1919   **Nat King Cole** -- Noted American singer and jazz pianist

1919   Hank Sauer -- Professional baseball player who hit over 50 home runs in 1952

1920   **Pete Reiser** -- Professional baseball player

1930   **James Benson Irwin** -- U.S. astronaut who with David R. Scott drove an automobile on the moon in a 66-hour stay in 1971 (*Apollo 15*)

1938   **Rudolf Nureyev** — Noted Russian-born ballet dancer and actor

1944   **John Sebastian** -- American singer and guitarist with the Lovin' Spoonful musical group

1949   **Patrick Duffy** — American actor noted for his role in the long-running television series *Dallas*

1951   **Kurt Russell** -- American actor

1953   **Chuck Muncie** -- Professional football player

1954   **Lesley-Anne Down** — British motion-picture and television actress

1959   **Danny Ainge** -- Professional basketball player

1964   Rob Lowe -- American motion-picture actor

MARCH 17 -- EVENTS

44 BC   The conspirators in Julius Caesar's murder were granted amnesty in a short-lived reprieve before Mark Antony stirred the people to take revenge on them.

180 AD Marcus Aurelius, the great Roman emperor, died in Vindobona (now Vienna) at age 58.

461 AD St. Patrick, the patron saint of Ireland and a saint of the Roman Catholic Church, died in Ireland at an approximate age of 72. The date is celebrated as St. Patrick's Day.

1680   Francois La Rochefoucauld, the noted French writer, died in Paris at age 66.

1762   New York City had its first St. Patrick's Day parade.

1776   With General George Washington's men occupying Dorchester Heights above the city, British general Howe evacuated Boston in the Revolutionary War.

1861   Italy, previously united by Garibaldi and Cavour, proclaimed itself a kingdom with Victor Emanuel II as the first king.

1871   The National Association of Professional Baseball Players, the forerunner of baseball's National League, was established.

1897   Bob Fitzsimmons defeated Gentleman Jim Corbett in the 14th round in Carson City, Nevada, to win the heavyweight crown.

1905   Franklin D. Roosevelt married Eleanor Roosevelt, his distant cousin and a niece of President Theodore Roosevelt, who gave the bride away.

1912   The Camp Fire Girls was founded by Luther Halsey Gulick and his wife Charlotte, who held many of the first meetings at their summer home in Sebago Lake, Maine.

1941   The National Gallery of Art opened in Washington, D.C.

1942   General Douglas MacArthur arrived in Australia, during World War II, to become supreme commander of the Allied forces in the southwest Pacific.

1958   The United States launched its second earth satellite, *Vanguard 2*, which resulted in the discovery that the earth is pear-shaped.

MARCH 18 -- BIRTHDAYS

1578   **Adam Elsheimer** -- German painter and etcher noted for works such as "Flight into Egypt" (1609)

1609   **Frederick III** -- King of Norway and Denmark during the 17th century when Norway was a province of Denmark

1690   **Christian Goldbach** -- Prussian mathematician noted for Goldbach's conjecture that any even number is the sum of two prime numbers, a conjecture made in 1742 but which is still unproved

1782　John C. Calhoun -- American statesman, orator, vice president under President Jackson, and the only person to resign the vice presidency other than Spiro Agnew

1796　Jakob Steiner -- Swiss mathematician noted as one of the founders of synthetic geometry

1813　Joshua Ballinger Lippincott – American publisher who founded J.B. Lippincott & Co. in 1835

1837　Grover Cleveland – Only U.S. president to serve two nonconsecutive terms (1885-1889 and 1893-1897)

1842　Stephane Mallarmé – French poet, essayist, and translator, best known for his dream poem, "The Afternoon of a Faun" (1876)

1844　Nikolai Rimsky-Korsakov -- Russian composer noted for such works as *Scheherazade,* "Song of India," and "Flight of the Bumblebee"

1858　Rudolf Diesel -- German engineer noted for the diesel engine, which he patented in 1892

1869　Neville Chamberlain -- British prime minister, 1937-1940, noted for his appeasement policy toward Adolf Hitler, that led, not to "peace in our time," as Chamberlain hoped, but to World War II

1884　Joseph A. Burke -- American composer noted for songs such as "Tip Toe Through the Tulips," "Moon Over Miami," "Carolina Moon," and "American Patrol"

1885　Ed G. Nelson -- American composer, conductor, and pianist, noted for songs such as "I Apologize" and "Auf Wiedersehen, My Dear"

1886　Edward Everett Horton -- American stage and motion-picture actor in some 150 films

1893　Wilfred Owen -- British poet who was awarded the Military Cross for gallantry in World War I and was later killed in action at age 25

1897　Betty Compson -- One of the most popular American movie stars of the Roaring Twenties

1901　Johnny Cooney -- Professional baseball player

1903　Count Galeazzo Ciano -- Italian diplomat in the 1930s and 1940s, and son-in-law of Italian dictator Benito Mussolini

1905　Robert Donat -- English stage and motion-picture actor who won an Academy Award in 1939 for *Goodbye, Mr. Chips*

1911　Smiley Burnette – American stage and screen actor, and Gene Autry's comic sidekick Frog Milhouse in 81 motion pictures

1916　Elbie Fletcher -- Professional baseball player

1924　William Arthur Fredricks -- American composer, author, and singer noted for songs such as "You Can Trust Your Car to the Man Who Wears the Star"

1925　Peter Graves – American motion-picture and television actor and brother of actor James Arness

1927   **George Plimpton** -- American editor and television personality
1932   **John Updike** -- American novelist noted for works such as *The Poorhouse Fair, Rabbit, Run,* and *Couples*
1941   **Wilson Pickett** -- American soul singer
1942   **Jeff Mullins** -- Professional basketball player
1956   **Ingemar Stenmark** -- Professional skier
1959   **Irene Cara** -- American motion-picture actress and singer
1961   **Curt Warner** -- Professional basketball player
1963   **Vanessa Williams** -- First black Miss America (1984)

MARCH 18 -- EVENTS

1314   Jacques de Molay, the last grand master of the Order of Knights Templars, was burned at the stake in Paris.
1455   Fra Angelico, the famous Italian painter, died in Rome at age 55.
1584   Ivan the Terrible, the first czar of Russia, died at age 53.
1612   Bartholomew Legate became the last person burned in England for his religious beliefs.
1766   The British Parliament repealed the notorious Stamp Act.
1768   Laurence Sterne, the noted English novelist, died of pleurisy in London at age 54.
1902   Enrico Caruso, the great Italian singer, made his first phonograph recording, for the Gramophone Company.
1911   "Alexander's Ragtime Band," by American songwriter Irving Berlin, was published.
1931   Schick, Inc. marketed the world's first electric razor.
1940   Adolf Hitler and Benito Mussolini met at the Brenner Pass in the Tyrol, where Mussolini secretly promised to enter World War II on the side of Germany.
1965   Russian cosmonaut Aleksei Leonov became the first man to walk in space.
1974   Seven Arab countries lifted their oil embargo on the United States, in effect since October, 1973.

MARCH 19 -- BIRTHDAYS

1488   **Johannes Magnus** – Roman Catholic archbishop and historian
1519   **Henry II** – King of France, 1547-1559, who persecuted the Huguenots and took away their land
1593   **Georges de La Tour** – French painter noted for works such as *The Fortune Teller*
1601   **Alonso Cano** -- Spanish painter, sculptor, and architect

1603   **John IV** -- Portuguese nobleman, the duke of Braganza, who drove out the Spanish rulers of Portugal in 1640 and became the first king of Portugal of the House of Braganza

1721   **Tobias Smollett** -- One of the great early English novelists, best known for his classic novel, *The Expedition of Humphry Clinker* (1771)

1725   **Richard Howe** -- British admiral prominent in the American Revolutionary War

1734   **Thomas McKean** -- A Delaware signer of the Declaration of Independence, member of the Continental Congress, and governor of Pennsylvania

1813   **David Livingstone** -- Famous Scottish missionary and African explorer to whom explorer Henry Morton Stanley said the famous line when they met, "Dr. Livingstone, I presume?"

1821   **Sir Richard Burton** -- British explorer, author, and scholar, whose translation of *The Arabian Nights* is a literary classic

1844   **Minna Canth** -- Finnish novelist and dramatist

1847   **Albert Pinkham Ryder** -- American painter noted for works such as *Toilers of the Sea* (1891)

1848   **Wyatt Earp** – Noted frontiersman and lawman in the American West

1860   **William Jennings Bryan** -- American politician and three-time candidate for president

1864   **Charles M. Russell** -- American painter, sculptor, and "cowboy artist" who specialized in life of the Old West

1871   **Iron Man Joe McGinnity** -- Hall of Fame baseball pitcher who pitched a record 434 innings in 1903

1872   **Sergei Diaghilev** -- Russian ballet master and the greatest director in ballet history

1873   **Max Reger** -- German composer and organist who wrote over 260 songs

1882   **Gaston Lachaise** – French sculptor noted for rounded, classic figures, which were both robust and delicate, an example of which is *Georgia O'Keeffe* (1927)

1883   **Joseph "Vinegar Joe" Stilwell** -- American World War II general who commanded the U.S. forces in the China-Burma-India area

1888   **Josef Albers** -- German-born American painter noted for his series of square paintings *Homage to the Square*

1891   **Earl Warren** -- U.S. Supreme Court Chief Justice, 1953-1969

1892   **James A. Van Fleet** -- American World War II general who trained the armed forces which checked Communist aggression in Greece and Korea

1894   **"Moms" Mabley** -- American singer and comedienne

1904   **John J. Sirica** -- American judge noted for the Watergate trials

1905	**Albert Speer** -- Nazi World War II Minister of Armaments and War Production, and author of *Inside the Third Reich* (1970)
1907	**Kent Smith** -- American stage and motion-picture actor
1916	**Irving Wallace** -- American novelist
1919	**Peter Abrahams** -- Most prolific of South Africa's black prose writers
1927	**Richie Ashburn** -- Professional baseball player
1928	**Patrick McGoohan** -- American-born British stage, screen, and television actor and director
1930	**Ornette Coleman** -- American avant-garde musician
1932	**Gay Brewer** -- Professional golfer
1933	**Philip Roth** – American novelist and short-story writer, noted for works such as *Goodbye, Columbus* (1959) and *Portnoy's Complaint* (1969)
1936	**Ursula Andress** -- Swiss-born motion-picture actress
1938	**Joe Kapp** -- Professional football player
1944	**Lynda Bird Johnson (Robb)** -- Daughter of President Lyndon B. Johnson and wife of Virginia governor Charles Robb
1947	**Glenn Close** -- American motion-picture and television actress
1955	**Mike Norris** -- Professional baseball player
1955	**Bruce Willis** -- American stage and television actor
1956	**Chris O'Neill** -- Australian tennis player

MARCH 19 -- EVENTS

235 AD	Maximinus Thrax was proclaimed Emperor of Rome.
1452	Frederick III became the last Holy Roman emperor to be crowned by the pope.
1687	The great French explorer Sieur de La Salle was shot and killed by his own men at the Trinity River in Texas at age 43.
1859	Charles Gounod's opera *Faust* premiered at the Theatre Lyrique in Paris.
1917	The U.S. Supreme Court upheld the eight-hour work day for railroads.
1918	The U.S. Congress approved Daylight Saving Time.
1920	The U.S. Senate rejected the Versailles Treaty providing for a League of Nations.
1931	The Nevada legislature made gambling legal in the state.
1932	The comic strip *Henry,* by Carl Anderson, first appeared.
1942	All men in the United States between the ages of 45 and 62 were ordered to register for nonmilitary duty during World War II.
1951	Herman Wouk's novel, *The Caine Mutiny,* was published.
1953	The Academy Awards ceremony was telecast for the first time. The best picture was *The Greatest Show on Earth.*

1979 The U.S. House of Representatives began televising its day-to-day activities.

MARCH 20 -- BIRTHDAYS

43 BC **Ovid (Publius Ovidius Naso)** – The most versatile of the Roman poets, noted for works such as "Metamorphoses" and "Art of Love"

1680 **Emanuele Astorga** -- Spanish composer

1741 **Jean Antoine Houdon** -- Great French sculptor of the 18th century, noted for statues and busts of Washington, Franklin, Jefferson, and Voltaire, and for the *Diana Nue* in the Louvre Museum

1770 **Friedrich Holderlin** -- German poet

1796 **Edward Gibbon Wakefield** -- British statesman who colonized New Zealand

1804 **Neal Dow** – One of the principal leaders in Maine in passing the first prohibition law of any state (1851)

1810 **John Cardinal McCloskey** – Roman Catholic archbishop of New York, 1864-1885, and the first American cardinal (1875)

1811 **Napoleon II** -- King of Rome, Duke of Reichstadt, and only son of Napoleon Bonaparte

1811 **George Caleb Bingham** -- American painter noted for works such as *Daniel Boone Coming Through the Cumberland Gap* and *Stump Speaking*

1820 **Ned Buntline** – American publisher (born Edward Z.C. Judson) who founded the magazine *Ned Buntline's Own,* and gave the Know-Nothing party its name

1828 **Henrik Ibsen** – Norwegian playwright known as the father of modern drama, who wrote works such as *A Doll's House* (1879), *Hedda Gabler* (1890), and *Peer Gynt* (1867)

1834 **Charles W. Eliot** -- American educator, who as its president (1869-1909) made Harvard into one of the great universities of the world

1856 **Frederick Winslow Taylor** -- American engineer and efficiency expert for whom "Taylorism," the efficiency movement, was named

1882 **Rene Coty** – Last President of the Fourth French Republic, 1954-1959

1890 **Lauritz Melchior** -- Danish operatic tenor noted for his performances in Richard Wagner's operas

1892 **Stefan Banach** -- Ukrainian mathematician and founder of modern functional analysis

1892 **Mort Dixon** -- American composer noted for songs such as "That Old Gang of Mine," "Bye, Bye Blackbird," and "I'm Looking Over a Four Leaf Clover"

1900   **Urho Kekkonen** -- President of Finland, 1956-1980
1903   **Vincent Richards** -- American Hall of Fame tennis player, and youngest player to win a national championship (at age 15)
1906   **Abraham Beame** -- Mayor of New York City, 1974-1977
1907   **Ozzie Nelson** -- American actor and bandleader, who with his wife Harriet Hilliard starred in *The Adventures of Ozzie and Harriet,* one of television's longest-running hits
1908   **Frank Stanton** -- American television broadcaster
1908   **Sir Michael Redgrave** -- British stage and screen actor and superstar, and father of actors Corin, Lynn, and Vanessa Redgrave
1914   **Wendell Corey** -- American stage and motion-picture actor
1920   **Werner Klemperer** -- German motion-picture and television actor, and son of the famed conductor, Otto Klemperer
1922   **Larry Elgart** -- American bandleader
1922   **Ray Goulding** -- Ray of the Bob and Ray comedy team
1922   **Carl Reiner** – American comedy writer, actor, producer, and director
1922   **Jack Kruschen** -- American stage, screen, and television actor
1925   **John D. Ehrlichman** – Domestic affairs adviser to President Nixon, imprisoned for his role in the Watergate scandal
1928   **Fred M. Rogers** -- American television producer and host of *Mr. Rogers' Neighborhood*
1931   **Hal Linden** – American actor and star of the long-running television show, *Barney Miller*
1937   **Jerry Reed** -- American country singer
1939   **Brian Mulroney** -- Prime Minister of Canada
1945   **Pat Riley** -- Professional basketball player and highly successful coach
1948   **Bobby Orr** -- Professional hockey superstar and first defenseman to win the National Hockey League scoring title, with 120 points in 1969-1970
1950   **William Hurt** -- American motion-picture actor
1952   **Anand Amritraj** -- Indian tennis player
1952   **Rick Langford** -- Professional baseball player
1956   **Bill Manson** -- American tennis player

MARCH 20 -- EVENTS

1413   King Henry IV of England, the first king of the House of Lancaster, died in London's Westminster Abbey at age 46.
1727   Sir Isaac Newton, the great English physicist, died at age 84.
1815   King Louis XVIII fled Paris as Napoleon entered the city on his return to power from exile on Elba.

1852	Harriet Beecher Stowe's famous novel, *Uncle Tom's Cabin,* was published for the first time in book form.
1854	A committee was appointed at Ripon, Wisconsin, to form the new Republican Party.
1899	Martha M. Place of New York City was executed at Sing Sing for the murder of her stepdaughter. She was the first woman to be put to death by electrocution.
1940	Edouard Daladier resigned as French premier and was replaced by Paul Reynaud, as the German Armies were positioning themselves for an assault on the West in World War II.
1942	General MacArthur, on his safe arrival in Australia from the Philippines in World War II, vowed that "I shall return."
1969	John Lennon, the noted Beatle, married Yoko Ono in Gibraltar.

MARCH 21 -- BIRTHDAYS

1685	**Johann Sebastian Bach** -- German organist, "greatest genius of baroque music," and one of the two or three greatest composers in world history
1736	**Claude Nicolas Ledoux** -- French architect
1763	**Johann Paul Richter** -- German writer (known also as Jean Paul), humorist, and master of satire, noted for works such as *The Invisible Loge* (1793) and *The Titan* (1800-1803)
1768	**Jean Baptiste Joseph Fourier** -- French mathematician, noted for, among other things, the Fourier Series
1771	**Thomas Dibdin** -- English dramatist and songwriter
1806	**Benito Juarez** -- The national hero of Mexico
1821	**Frank Leslie** -- English-American publisher noted for *Frank Leslie's Illustrated Weekly*
1839	**Modest Mussorgsky** – Russian composer, noted for the great opera *Boris Godunov* and such other works as *Pictures at an Exhibition*
1869	**Florenz Ziegfeld** -- American theatrical producer, noted for the *Ziegfeld Follies* (first produced in 1907)
1880	**Hans Hofmann** -- Bavarian-born American abstract painter noted for works such as *The Golden Wall* (1961)
1884	**George David Birkhoff** -- One of the foremost American mathematicians of the early 20th century
1887	**Eric Mendelsohn** -- German architect, famed for his free and imaginative approach
1897	**Jack Meskill** -- American composer and author, noted for songs such as "On the Beach At Bali-Bali" and "Smile, Darn Ya, Smile"
1897	**Dorothy M. Stewart** -- Australian-born composer, author, and pianist, noted for songs such as "Now Is the Hour"

1903   Edgar Buchanan – American motion-picture and television actor
1905   Phyllis McGinley -- American author of children's books and
        Pulitzer Prize-winning poet
1906   John D. Rockefeller III -- Head of the Rockefeller Foundation
        and grandson of philanthropist John D. Rockefeller
1923   Mort Lindsey -- American bandleader
1929   James Coco -- American stage, screen, and television actor
1929   Jules Bergman -- American television newsman
1937   Tom Flores – Professional football player and coach who led the
        Oakland Raiders to two Superbowl championships (1984
        and 1987)
1939   Tommy Davis -- Professional baseball player
1944   Manny Sanguillen -- Professional baseball player
1945   Charles E. Greene -- Professional sprinter
1946   Timothy Dalton -- British motion-picture actor
1962   Matthew Broderick -- American motion-picture actor

MARCH 21 -- EVENTS

47 BC   Julius Caesar defeated Ptolemy XII, Cleopatra's brother and
        rival, at Alexandria, Egypt, thus restoring Cleopatra to the throne.
1556   Archbishop Thomas Cranmer was burned at the stake on orders
        of the Queen of England, Bloody Mary.
1621   The first Indian treaty by American colonists was made, between
        Governor Carver of the Plymouth Colony and Massasoit, chief
        of the Wampanoags.
1790   Thomas Jefferson became the first U.S. secretary of state.
1800   Pius VII was crowned Roman Catholic pope.
1804   The Code Napoleon went into effect in France and its
        occupied territories.
1918   Germany launched the first of its final offensives of World War
        I along the Somme.
1945   Seven thousand Allied planes dropped 12,000 tons of explosives
        on Germany in full daylight in World War II.
1946   The United Nations set up temporary headquarters at Hunter
        College in New York.
1963   The Alcatraz federal penitentiary in San Francisco Bay was closed
        after the U.S. government decided it was too expensive to maintain.
1965   The Selma-to-Montgomery civil rights march began in Ala-
        bama, led by the Reverend Martin Luther King Jr.
1972   The U.S. Supreme Court ruled that states could not require a
        one-year residency for voting eligibility.

MARCH 22 -- BIRTHDAYS

1459   **Maximilian I** -- Holy Roman Emperor, 1493-1519
1517   **Gioseffo Zarlino** -- Italian composer and greatest theorist of the mid-16th century
1599   **Sir Anthony Van Dyck** -- Most prominent Flemish painter of the 17th century
1797   **Wilhelm I** -- King of Prussia and first emperor of modern Germany, 1871-1888
1846   **Randolph Caldecott** -- English illustrator who began a new era in children's picture books, and for whom the Caldecott Medal, for the year's outstanding children's picture book, was named
1868   **Robert A. Millikan** -- American physicist who with his oil drop experiment first measured the charge of an electron
1869   **Emilio Aguinaldo** -- Filipino freedom fighter who led the struggle for Philippine independence from Spain and later from the United States
1884   **Arthur H. Vandenburg** -- U.S. senator and statesman of the Truman era
1887   **Chico Marx** -- American comedian and one of the Marx Brothers comedy group
1907   **James Gavin** -- American World War II general
1908   **Maurice Stans** -- Secretary of commerce under President Nixon
1908   **Louis L'Amour** -- American best-selling author of 86 Western novels
1910   **Nicholas Monsarrat** -- English novelist noted for *The Cruel Sea* (1951) and *The Tribe That Lost Its Head* (1956)
1914   **Karl Malden** -- American motion-picture and television actor
1914   **John Stanley** -- American comic strip writer and creator of *Little Lulu*
1917   **Ed Furgol** -- Professional golfer
1918   **Virginia Grey** -- American motion-picture actress
1923   **Marcel Marceau** -- Pre-eminent mime of the 20th century
1926   **Billy Goodman** -- Professional baseball player
1928   **Ed Macauley** -- Professional basketball player with over 11,000 career points
1930   **Derek Curtis Bok** -- President of Harvard University in the 1960s and 1970s
1930   **Pat Robertson** -- American minister and television evangelist
1931   **Burton Richter** -- American Nobel Prize-winning physicist
1931   **William Shatner** -- American motion-picture and television actor noted for his role as Captain Kirk in the long-running television series *Star Trek*

1936   **May Britt** -- Swedish motion-picture actress
1946   **Don Chaney** -- Professional basketball player
1948   **Andrew Lloyd Webber** -- British composer
1954   **Ross Browner** -- Professional football player

MARCH 22 -- EVENTS

1622   Indians massacred some 350 colonists at Jamestown, Virginia.
1765   The British Parliament passed the Stamp Act, the first direct tax on the American Colonies.
1794   Congress passed a law prohibiting American ships from supplying slaves to other countries.
1820   Commodore Stephen Decatur was mortally wounded in a duel with Commodore James Barron outside Washington.
1832   Johann Wolfgang von Goethe, the greatest German writer of all time, died in Weimar at age 82.
1882   The U.S. Congress outlawed polygamy.
1894   The first Stanley Cup game was played in Montreal, with Montreal beating Ottawa, 3-1.
1895   The first theater showing of a motion picture took place in Paris, using the cinematograph of inventors Louis and Auguste Lumiere.
1934   The first Masters Golf tournament began, in Augusta, Georgia.
1941   The Grand Coulee Dam on the Columbia River began producing electric power.
1977   Indira Gandhi resigned as prime minister of India after her party's defeat. She returned to power two elections later.
1979   The Israeli Parliament approved the peace treaty with Egypt.

MARCH 23 -- BIRTHDAYS

1430   **Margaret of Anjou** -- Queen consort of England's Henry VI
1736   **Arthur St. Clair** -- Scottish-American soldier and statesman and member of the Continental Congress
1749   **Marquis Pierre Simon de Laplace** -- French mathematician noted for the Laplace transform
1769   **William Smith** -- Father of English geology
1823   **Schuyler Colfax** -- U.S. Vice President under President Grant
1835   **Edward Caird** -- English philosopher and leader of the Neo-Hegelian school
1857   **Fannie Farmer** -- Noted American cooking expert and candy maker
1881   **Roger Martin Du Gard** -- Nobel Prize-winning French novelist noted for *Jean Barois* (1913) and *The World of the Thibaults* (1922-1940)

1887	**Sidney Hillman** -- American labor leader and organizer of the Amalgamated Clothing Workers of America
1887	**Juan Gris** -- Spanish-born painter and one of the pioneers of "cubism"
1900	**Erich Fromm** -- German psychoanalyst and social philosopher
1903	**Jay W. Johnson** -- American composer, author, and entertainer, noted for songs such as "Blue Christmas"
1908	**Joan Crawford** -- American stage and motion-picture actress and superstar for nearly 50 years
1912	**Wernher von Braun** -- German-American rocket and space expert who helped develop the German World War II V-2 rocket and the rockets that sent the first American into space
1917	**John Albert Guarnieri** -- American composer, author, and pianist, noted for songs such as "Blue Mood"
1922	**Marty Allen** -- American comedian and actor
1927	**Johnny Logan** -- Professional baseball player
1929	**Roger Bannister** -- British runner who in 1954 became the first man to run the mile in less than 4 minutes
1937	**Craig Breedlove** -- American automobile racer who set the world land speed record in 1963 at Bonneville Salt Flats in Utah at 407.45 mph, and in 1965 drove a car 600.6 mph at Bonneville
1938	**Maynard Jackson** -- First black mayor of Atlanta
1939	**Rosie Darmon** -- French tennis player
1943	**Lee May** -- Professional baseball player
1951	**Ron Jaworski** -- Professional football player and superstar
1953	**Chaka Khan** -- American rock singer
1954	**Moses Malone** -- Professional basketball superstar

MARCH 23 -- EVENTS

1540	Waltham Abbey, last remaining monastery in England, was dissolved.
1603	Queen Elizabeth I of England died in London at age 69.
1729	British artist James Hogarth eloped with Jane Thornhill.
1743	Handel's *Messiah* was heard for the first time by a theater audience in London. King George II was in the audience and inaugurated a precedent by rising to his feet to applaud.
1775	In a fiery oration, Patrick Henry said, "Give me liberty or give me death."
1840	The American slang expression "O.K." was first used in print in the New York *New Era*. It came from "Old Kinderhook," a nickname of then President Martin Van Buren.
1842	Stendhal (Marie Henri Beyle), the great French novelist, died in Paris at age 59.

1903   The Wright brothers applied for a patent on their airplane.
1933   The Enabling Act of 1933 passed, establishing Hitler's dictatorship in Germany.
1956   Pakistan became an independent republic within the British Commonwealth.
1973   Watergate burglar James McCord, in testimony to Judge Sirica, implicated higher-ups in the Watergate break-in, which led to the opening up of the case.
1983   Dr. Barney Clark died at the University of Utah Medical Center 112 days after receiving the world's first artificial heart.

MARCH 24 -- BIRTHDAYS

1490   **Georgius Agricola** -- German physician and scientist, known as the father of mineralogy
1688   **John Smibert** -- American painter
1755   **Rufus King** -- One of the founding fathers of the United States
1809   **Joseph Liouville** -- Noted French mathematician
1820   **Fanny J. Crosby** -- Blind American hymn writer noted for such works as "Pass Me Not, O Gentle Savior," "Safe in the Arms of Jesus," "Rescue the Perishing," and over 5,000 other poems and hymns
1834   **William Morris** -- English poet, artist, and reformer, who designed the Morris chair and in 1891 founded the Kelmscott Press
1834   **John Wesley Powell** -- American geologist who in 1869 was the first to explore the Grand Canyon
1835   **Josef Stefan** -- Austrian physicist and co-formulator of the Stefan-Boltzmann Law of radiant heat energy
1855   **Andrew Mellon** -- American financier and secretary of the treasury, 1921-1932
1866   **Jack McAuliffe** -- American Hall of Fame boxer
1874   **Harry Houdini** -- Sensational escape artist and one of the greatest magicians of his time
1885   **Charles Daniels** -- America's first great swimmer
1886   **Edward Weston** -- One of the most influential 20th-century photographers
1887   **Fatty Arbuckle** -- American comic actor, director, and screenwriter
1893   **George Sisler** -- Hall of Fame baseball player and one of the game's greatest hitters, with a .340 lifetime batting average
1894   **Al Espinosa** -- Professional golfer
1897   **Wilhelm Reich** -- German Freudian Marxist psychologist
1899   **Allen Saunders** -- American comic strip writer and one of the creators of *Mary Worth*

1902 **Thomas E. Dewey** -- Twice candidate for U.S. president, in 1944 and 1948
1903 **Malcolm Muggeridge** -- English journalist and television interviewer
1907 **Lauris J. Norstad** -- American general and early commander of the Strategic Air Command
1909 **Clyde Barrow** -- Notorious American robber and murderer who with his accomplice Bonnie Parker terrorized the American countryside in the 1930s
1915 **Richard Conte** -- American motion-picture actor
1920 **Gene Nelson** -- American dancer and actor
1925 **Norman Fell** -- American motion-picture and television actor
1928 **Vanessa Brown** -- Austrian-born motion-picture actress
1928 **Byron Janis** -- American concert pianist
1930 **Steve McQueen** -- American motion-picture and television actor
1940 **Bob Mackie** -- American fashion designer
1942 **Jesus Alou** -- Professional baseball player
1951 **Patty Bradley** -- Professional golfer
1954 **Donna Pescow** -- American television and motion-picture actress
1954 **Robert Carradine** -- American motion-picture actor and son of actor John Carradine
1956 **Gary Templeton** -- Professional baseball player
1958 **Bruce Hurst** -- Professional baseball player
1959 **Renaldo "Skeets" Nehemiah** -- Professional football player

MARCH 24 -- EVENTS

1603 James I, the first Stuart king of England, ascended to the throne, succeeding Queen Elizabeth I, who had died the previous day.
1765 England enacted the Quartering Act, requiring American colonists to provide temporary housing to British soldiers.
1882 Professor Robert Koch announced in Berlin his discovery of the pathogenic germs of tuberculosis.
1882 American poet Henry Wadsworth Longfellow died in Cambridge, Massachusetts, at age 75.
1905 Jules Verne, the great French novelist, died in Amiens at age 77.
1934 The United States granted the Philippines its independence, effective July 4, 1946.
1958 Rock and roll singer Elvis Presley was inducted into the U.S. Army in Memphis, Tennessee.
1964 The first U.S. John F. Kennedy half dollars were issued.
1971 The U.S. Senate voted to end sponsorship of the supersonic transport.

1973   Anwar Sadat became president of Egypt.
1989   The Exxon supertanker *Valdez* plowed into a rocky reef off
        Valdez, Alaska, spilling 240,000 barrels of oil into Prince Wil-
        liam Sound, in the worst oil disaster in American waters.

MARCH 25 -- BIRTHDAYS

1133   **Henry II** -- King of England, 1154-1189
1252   **Conrad the Younger** -- King of Jerusalem and Sicily
1347   **Catherine of Siena** -- Patron Saint of Italy
1614   **Juan Carreno de Miranda** -- Spanish painter
1771   **Joachim Murat** -- Most famous of Napoleon's cavalry commanders
1867   **Arturo Toscanini** -- One of the greatest virtuoso conductors of
        the first half of the twentieth century
1871   **Gutzon Borglum** -- American sculptor who planned the Mount
        Rushmore Memorial in South Dakota
1879   **William S. Knudsen** -- American industrialist who conceived the
        idea of the conveyer belt in mass producing automobiles, and
        who directed U.S. war production during World War II
1881   **Bela Bartok** -- Hungarian composer and pianist, and one of the
        giants of the 20th century
1900   **Robert B. Reed** -- American composer, conductor, and organist,
        noted for songs such as "Rise Up, O Men of God" and "Let Us
        Now Praise Famous Men"
1901   **Ed Begley** -- American stage, screen, and television actor
1903   **Frankie Carle** -- American composer noted for songs such as
        "Oh What It Seemed to Be" and "Sunrise Serenade" (song of
        the year in 1938)
1905   **Binnie Barnes** -- English-born motion-picture actress
1908   **David Lean** -- English motion-picture director
1909   **Dutch Leonard** -- Professional baseball player
1912   **Jean Vilar** -- French actor and director
1914   **Aline Saarinen** -- American television newswoman
1920   **Howard Cosell** -- American television sports announcer
1921   **Simone Signoret** -- French motion-picture actress who won an
        Academy Award for *Room at the Top* (1958)
1925   **Flannery O'Connor** -- American novelist and short story writer,
        noted for such works as *Everything That Rises Must Converge*
1928   **James Arthur Lovell Jr.** -- U.S. astronaut and participant in the
        record-breaking 14-day orbit of *Gemini 7* in December 1965
1932   **Wes Santee** -- American champion miler
1932   **John Willard Marriott Jr.** -- American restaurant executive and
        son of the founder of the Marriott Corporation

1934 **Gloria Steinem** -- Noted American feminist and editor
1940 **Anita Bryant** -- American singer and television personality
1942 **Aretha Franklin** -- American soul singer
1943 **Paul Michael Glaser** -- American actor
1947 **Elton John** -- American rock singer and composer
1955 **Lee Mazzilli** -- Professional baseball player
1960 **Steve Norman** -- British musician with the Spandau Ballet musical group

MARCH 25 -- EVENTS

708 AD Constantine I was elected pope.
1306 Robert Bruce was crowned King of Scotland.
1616 William Shakespeare called in his lawyer, Francis Collins, to revise his will. He died less than a month later.
1634 Lord Baltimore's colonists landed in Maryland.
1668 The first recorded horse race was held in America, at Hempstead, New York.
1776 The Continental Congress conferred the first medal awarded by the colonies upon General George Washington.
1807 The British Parliament abolished slave trade.
1894 Coxey's Army, led by Jacob S. Coxey, started out for Washington, D.C., from Massillon, Ohio, to "save the country" from the Panic of 1893.
1900 The Socialist Party of the United States was organized in Indianapolis.
1913 The Palace Theatre, the home of vaudeville, opened in New York City.
1918 Claude Debussy, the French composer, died of cancer in Paris at age 55.
1934 Horton Smith won the first Masters golf tournament.
1954 RCA began its commercial production of television sets equipped to transmit in color.
1957 The Treaty of Rome established the European Common Market.
1958 Sugar Ray Robinson won the middleweight boxing title for a record fifth time, in a 15-round decision in Chicago over Carmen Basilio.
1964 Britain set aside an acre of land at Runnymede, where the Magna Carta was signed in 1215, as a memorial for John F. Kennedy.
1965 The Reverend Martin Luther King Jr. led 25,000 marchers to the state Capitol in Montgomery, Alabama, completing the civil rights march from Selma.
1971 Civil war erupted in East Pakistan, leading to the creation of the independent state of Bangladesh.

1972   Bobby Hull scored his 600th career goal, becoming the only
        National Hockey League player besides Gordie Howe to reach
        this mark.
1975   King Faisal of Saudi Arabia was shot to death by a mentally
        ill nephew.

MARCH 26 -- BIRTHDAYS

1516   **Konrad von Gesner** -- Pioneer Swiss zoologist
1753   **Sir Benjamin Thompson** -- American-born English physicist and
        statesman who helped found the British Royal Institute in 1800
1850   **Edward Bellamy** -- American journalist and author, noted for
        the novel *Looking Backward* in 1888.
1859   **A.E. Housman** -- British poet and scholar, noted for *A Shropshire
        Lad* in 1896
1868   **Fuad I** -- King of Egypt
1874   **Robert Frost** -- The most popular American poet of his time
1874   **Conde Nast** -- American publisher and early owner of *Vogue* and
        House and Garden magazines
1879   **Othmar Herman Ammann** -- Designer of the Verazano-Nar-
        rows Bridge over New York harbor
1880   **Duncan Hines** -- American businessman and author, who be-
        came an authority on eating and lodging establishments
1893   **James B. Conant** -- American scientist and president of Harvard
        University, 1933-1953
1893   **Palmiro Togliatti** -- Leader of the Italian Communist Party after
        World War II
1907   **Leigh Harline** -- American composer and conductor, noted for
        songs such as "When You Wish Upon a Star" and "Jiminy
        Cricket"
1908   **Betty MacDonald** -- American novelist and author of *The Egg
        and I*
1911   **Tennessee Williams** -- American playwright noted for such
        works as *The Glass Menagerie* and *A Streetcar Named Desire*
1914   **William Westmoreland** -- U.S. general in the Vietnam War
1916   **Sterling Hayden** -- American actor and writer
1923   **Bob Elliott** -- Bob of the Bob and Ray comedy team
1925   **Pierre Boulez** -- French composer, pianist, and conductor of the
        New York Philharmonic
1930   **Gregory Corso** -- American poet and member of the Beat
        movement
1930   **Sandra Day O'Connor** -- First woman appointed to the U.S.
        Supreme Court

1931	**Leonard Nimoy** -- American motion-picture and television actor noted for his role as Spock in *Star Trek*
1934	**Alan Arkin** -- American motion-picture actor
1934	**Gino Cappelletti** -- Professional football player
1937	**Wayne Embry** -- Professional basketball player and executive
1939	**James Caan** -- American motion-picture actor
1942	**Erica Jong** -- American novelist and author of *Fear of Flying*
1943	**Bob Woodward** -- American newspaper reporter who with reporter Carl Bernstein helped the Washington *Post* win a Pulitzer Prize for its exposure of the Watergate scandals
1944	**Diana Ross** -- American singer and member of the Supremes singing group
1949	**Vicki Lawrence** -- American actress and comedienne
1956	**Ilano Kloss** -- South African tennis player
1960	**Marcus Allen** -- Professional football player

MARCH 26 -- EVENTS

1645	Oliver Cromwell's victory at Stowe-on-the-Wold ended the four-year civil war in England.
1804	The Louisiana Purchase was divided into the Territory of Orleans and the District of Louisiana.
1827	Ludwig van Beethoven died in Vienna at age 56. On his death bed the deaf master said, "I shall hear in heaven."
1892	Walt Whitman, the great American poet, died in Camden, New Jersey, five days before his 73rd birthday.
1900	The comic strip, *Happy Hooligan*, by Fred Opper, first appeared.
1918	General Ferdinand Foch of France was appointed commander of all Allied armies in World War I.
1923	Sarah Bernhardt, the noted stage actress, died in Paris in the arms of her son Maurice at age 81.
1953	Dr. Jonas Salk announced the discovery of the Salk vaccine.
1958	The U.S. Army launched *Explorer 3*, America's third successful satellite.
1971	East Pakistan proclaimed its independence, assuming the name Bangladesh.
1979	Egypt and Israel signed a treaty in Washington ending 31 years of war.

MARCH 27 -- BIRTHDAYS

| 1416 | **St. Francis of Paola** -- Founder of the Minim Friars |

1785   **Louis XVII** -- Son of the guillotined Louis XVI and King of France who never reigned because he was kept in prison during his two-year tenure as king

1797   **Alfred de Vigny** -- French poet, dramatist, and novelist

1813   **Nathaniel Currier** -- Senior member of the Currier and Ives print team

1845   **Wilhelm Roentgen** -- German physicist who discovered X-rays and in 1901 received the first Nobel Prize in Physics

1851   **Vincent D'Indy** -- French composer, organist, and conductor

1855   **Sir Alfred Ewing** -- English physicist who discovered hysteresis

1863   **Sir Henry Royce** -- Co-founder of Rolls-Royce, Ltd.

1879   **Miller Huggins** -- Manager of the great New York Yankee baseball teams of the Babe Ruth era

1879   **Edward Steichen** -- Pioneer of American photography

1886   **Ludwig Mies Van Der Rohe** -- A leading German architect of the early 20th century

1899   **Gloria Swanson** -- American motion-picture actress whose career spanned over sixty years

1901   **Sato Eisaku** -- Prime minister of Japan, 1964-1972

1910   **John Robinson Pierce** -- American engineer and father of the communications satellite

1914   **Budd Schulberg** -- American novelist and screenwriter

1914   **Snooky Lanson** -- American singer

1916   **Albert T. Frisch** -- American composer, pianist, and saxophonist, noted for songs such as "Two Different Worlds" and "Come Out Wherever You Are"

1917   **Cyrus Vance** -- American secretary of state under President Carter

1922   **Barnaby Conrad** -- American bullfighter and author

1924   **Sarah Vaughan** -- American jazz singer

1931   **David Janssen** -- American motion-picture and television actor

1939   **Cale Yarborough** -- American automobile racer

1942   **Michael York** -- British stage, screen, and television actor

1952   **Maria Schneider** -- French stage and motion-picture actress

1953   **Annemarie Proell** -- Austrian ski racer

MARCH 27 -- EVENTS

47 BC   Ptolemy XIII, King of Egypt and brother of Cleopatra, drowned in the Nile, probably with an assist by Julius Caesar, who thereby made Cleopatra queen.

30 AD   Jesus was condemned to be crucified by Pontius Pilate. The date is said to have been set down on a copper plate discovered in 1810 in the ancient city of Aquileia.

1513	Ponce de Leon discovered the east coast of Florida in his quest for the fountain of youth. He landed on the island of Bimini and reached the mainland on April 2.
1625	Charles I ascended to the throne of England, Scotland, and Ireland, upon the death of James I.
1794	President Washington signed the act creating the U.S. Navy.
1814	Andrew Jackson defeated the Creek Indians in the Battle of Horseshoe Bend in Alabama.
1836	The first Mormon temple was dedicated in Kirtland, Ohio.
1846	General Winfield Scott took Vera Cruz in the Mexican War.
1884	The first long-distance telephone call was made, between New York and Boston.
1917	The Seattle Metropolitans became the first U.S. team to win the Stanley Cup, defeating the Montreal Canadiens.
1920	Mary Pickford, "America's Sweetheart," married the swashbuckling actor, Douglas Fairbanks.
1958	Nikita Khrushchev became the head of the Soviet government.
1968	Russian cosmonaut Yuri Gagarin, the first man to orbit the earth, was killed in a plane crash.
1977	A KLM Boeing 747 crashed into a Pan Am 747 on a runway on the Canary Island of Tenerife, killing over 580 people, in the worst disaster in aviation history.

MARCH 28 -- BIRTHDAYS

1472	**Fra Bartolommeo** -- Italian painter
1515	**St. Teresa of Avila** – One of the great mystics of the Roman Catholic Church and a patron saint of Spain
1592	**John Amos Comenius** – Czech bishop whose textbook *Orbis Sensualium Pictus* was the first in which pictures were as important as the text
1660	**George I** -- First Hanoverian king of England, 1714-1727
1750	**Francisco de Miranda** – A Venezuelan patriot who fought in the American, French, and Spanish-American revolutions
1818	**Wade Hampton** -- Confederate general in the Civil War
1836	**Frederick Pabst** -- German-American brewer who co-founded Pabst Beer in 1864
1862	**Aristide Briand** – Nobel Peace Prize-winning French statesman who served as Premier of France eleven times and was largely responsible for the peaceful separation of church and state in France
1868	**Maxim Gorki** – Russian novelist and the foremost literary artist of his time in the Soviet Union
1875	**Helen Westley** -- American motion-picture actress

1878   Herbert Henry Lehman -- American philanthropist, governor of
        New York, and U.S. senator
1890   **Paul Whiteman** -- American bandleader and the "King of Jazz"
1893   **Spyros P. Skouras** -- Greek motion-picture mogul
1894   **Octave Blake** -- Harness racing Hall of Famer
1899   **August Busch Jr.** -- Head of the Anheuser-Busch beer company
        and owner of the St. Louis Cardinals baseball team
1902   **Dame Flora Robson** — Superb character actress of the British
        stage and screen
1903   **Rudolf Serkin** -- Czechoslovakian-born pianist and teacher
1906   **Bob Allen** -- American stage, screen, and television actor
1909   **Nelson Algren** -- American novelist and author of *The Man with
        the Golden Arm*
1909   **Lon Warneke** -- Professional baseball player and umpire
1914   **Edmund Muskie** — U.S. senator and secretary of state under
        President Carter
1915   **Jay Livingston** -- American composer and lyricist, noted for such
        songs as "Mona Lisa," "Buttons and Bows," "Silver Bells," and
        the theme song for the TV show *Bonanza*
1919   **Vic Raschi** -- Professional baseball player
1921   **Dirk Bogarde** -- English motion-picture actor
1924   **Freddie Bartholomew** -- Noted American child actor
1928   **Zbigniew Brzezinski** -- National security adviser under Presi-
        dent Carter
1933   **Frank Murkowski** -- U.S. senator
1937   **Liz Trotta** -- American broadcast journalist
1940   **Kevin Loughery** -- Professional basketball player and coach
1941   **James Turner** -- Professional football player
1941   **Alf H. Clausen** -- American composer noted for his music for TV
        variety shows, comedy shows, and dramatic shows, such as the
        Mary Tyler Moore Comedy Hour and *Charlie's Angels*
1942   **Jerry Sloan** -- Professional basketball player
1944   **Rick Barry** -- Professional basketball player and one of the
        game's superstars
1944   **Ken Howard** -- American motion-picture actor
1948   **Sam Lacey** -- Professional basketball player
1951   **Karen Kain** -- Canadian ballerina
1952   **James Scott** -- Professional football player
1955   **Reba McIntire** -- American country singer
1956   **Kurt Thomas** -- American gymnast and television commentator
1961   **Glenn Davis** -- Professional baseball player
1976   **Jennifer Capriati** -- American tennis player

MARCH 28 -- EVENTS

193 AD Emperor Pertinax of Rome was murdered by the Praetorian Guard.

1797 Nathaniel Briggs of New Hampshire received a patent for a washing machine.

1834 President Andrew Jackson was censured by the U.S. Senate for removing federal deposits from the U.S. Bank.

1854 Britain and France declared war on Russia, beginning the Crimean War.

1881 Modest Mussorgsky, the Russian composer, died of alcoholism in St. Petersburg at age 42.

1930 The name of Constantinople was officially changed to Istanbul. It had been called Istanbul unofficially since 1453 when the Turks brought down the eastern Roman Empire.

1939 Generalissimo Francisco Franco captured Madrid from the Spanish Loyalists, virtually ending the Spanish Civil War.

1953 Jim Thorpe, one of the greatest athletes of all time, died at age 64.

1969 Ex-President Dwight D. Eisenhower died in Walter Reed Hospital in Washington, D.C., at age 78.

1979 A cooling system malfunctioned at Pennsylvania's Three Mile Island power plant, leaking radioactivity into the air. It was the worst nuclear accident in history at the time.

MARCH 29 -- BIRTHDAYS

1790 **John Tyler** -- Tenth U.S. president and first to succeed to office because of the death of the president

1819 **Edwin Laurentine Drake** -- Driller of the first productive United States oil well, at Titusville, Pennsylvania

1840 **Sir John Keltie** -- English geographer

1859 **Oscar F. Mayer** -- Bavarian-born meat packer who with his brother Oscar Gottfried opened the first Oscar Mayer store, in 1883 in Chicago

1867 **Cy Young** -- Winningest pitcher in baseball with a career total of 511 victories, and for whom the Cy Young Award was named

1869 **Sir Edwin Landseer Lutyens** -- English architect who designed the British embassy in Washington, D.C., in the 1920s

1875 **Lou Henry Hoover** -- Wife of President Herbert Hoover

1878 **Albert Von Tilzer** -- American composer noted for songs such as "I'll Be With You in Apple Blossom Time," "Take Me Out to the Ball Game," and "Put Your Arms Around Me, Honey"

1881 **Raymond Mathewson Hood** -- Architect of some of America's most striking skyscrapers, such as the Chicago Tribune Tower and Rockefeller Center

1889   Howard Lindsay -- American playwright, actor, and author of a dramatization of Clarence Day's *Life with Father*

1891   **Warner Baxter** -- American motion-picture actor

1892   **Josef Cardinal Mindszenty** -- Hungarian Roman Catholic Church cardinal who became a symbol of the Hungarian resistance to Communism in the 1948 revolt

1899   **Lavrenty P. Beria** – Head of the Russian secret police under Stalin

1902   **Sir William Walton** -- English composer noted for such works as the oratorio *Belshazzar's Feast* and the opera *Troilus and Cressida*

1908   **Arthur O'Connell** -- American stage and motion-picture actor

1910   **Bill Dietrich** -- Professional baseball player

1911   **Philip Ahn** -- American stage, screen, and television actor

1916   **Eugene J. McCarthy** -- U.S. senator and opponent of the Vietnam War policy in the 1960s

1917   **Tommy Holmes** -- Professional baseball player

1918   **Pearl Bailey** -- American singer and actress

1919   **Eileen Heckart** -- American stage, motion-picture, and television actress

1921   **Ferris Fain** -- Professional baseball player

1937   **Billy Carter** -- Brother of President Jimmy Carter

1942   **Larry Pressler** -- U.S. senator

1943   **Vangelis (Papathanasiou)** -- Greek composer and pianist

1943   **Eric Idle** -- British comedian and actor

1944   **Denny McLain** -- Professional baseball pitcher who won 31 games in 1968

1945   **Walt Frazier** -- Professional basketball player

1949   **Joe Ehrmann** -- Professional football player

1955   **Earl Campbell** -- Professional football player

MARCH 29 -- EVENTS

1461   Edward IV of England defeated ex-King Henry VI at Towton Moor in the War of the Roses. The victory gave Edward the English throne.

1812   The first wedding took place in the White House when Mrs. Lucy Payne Washington, sister of Dolley Madison, married Justice Thomas Todd of the Supreme Court.

1813   Future president John Tyler married Letitia Christian.

1848   Niagara Falls stopped flowing for the first time in recorded history when tons of ice jammed the river near Buffalo. The local residents feared that the world was coming to an end.

1867   The British North America Act was passed, establishing the Dominion of Canada.

1882   The Knights of Columbus was chartered in Connecticut.
1917   The great race horse, Man O' War, was born at Nursery Stud,
        Kentucky. He went on to win 20 of 21 races before being put out
        to stud at age 4.
1927   Major Henry Segrave drove an automobile 203 miles per hour
        at Daytona Beach, Florida, the first time a motor-driven vehicle
        exceeded 200 mph.
1932   Comedian Jack Benny made his radio debut as a guest on the Ed
        Sullivan program.
1951   Ethel and Julius Rosenberg were found guilty of sabotage. They
        later became the only convicted spies to be executed by sentence
        of a U.S. civilian court.
1971   First Lieutenant William Calley was found guilty by a U.S. court-
        martial jury of murdering civilians at My Lai, South Vietnam.
1973   The last American troops left South Vietnam, ending U.S.
        involvement in the Vietnam War.

MARCH 30 -- BIRTHDAYS

1135   **Maimonides** -- Jewish philosopher who tried to harmonize
        Judaism with the teachings of Aristotle in his principal work, *The
        Guide of the Perplexed,* in 1190
1568   **Sir Henry Wotton** -- English poet and diplomat
1719   **Sir John Hawkins** -- Author of the first history of music in English
1727   **Tommaso Traetta** -- Italian composer
1746   **Francisco Goya** -- Spanish painter and one of the first masters of
        modern art
1842   **John Fiske** -- American philosopher and historian who helped
        spread Darwin's theory of evolution
1844   **Paul Verlaine** -- French poet of the symbolist movement of the
        late 19th century
1848   **Don Carlos II** -- Claimant to the Spanish throne
1853   **Vincent van Gogh** -- Dutch painter second in importance only to
        Rembrandt
1858   **De Wolf Hopper** -- American actor and singer of the 1880s
1863   **Joseph Caillaux** -- French statesman and fiscal expert
1880   **Sean O'Casey** -- The greatest Irish playwright of his time
1883   **Jo Davidson** -- American portrait sculptor whose greatest works
        include portraits of General John J. Pershing and Franklin
        D. Roosevelt
1894   **Sergey Vladimirovich Ilyushin** -- Russian aircraft designer
1913   **Richard Helms** -- American ambassador and director of the
        C.I.A. under President Nixon

1913   **Frankie Laine** – American actor, composer, author, and singer, with 16 Golden Records to his credit
1914   **Sonny Boy Williamson** -- American blues musician
1919   **McGeorge** Bundy -- Advisor to Presidents Kennedy and Lyndon Johnson
1920   **Turhan Bey** -- Austrian-born motion-picture actor
1923   **Dr. Frank Field** -- Television weatherman and media superstar
1930   **John Astin** -- American stage, screen, and television actor
1937   **Warren Beatty** – American motion-picture actor and producer and brother of actress Shirley MacLaine
1940   **Jerry Lucas** -- Professional basketball player
1945   **Eric Clapton** -- British guitarist and singer

MARCH 30 -- EVENTS

317 BC Phocion, Athenian general and statesman, died.
1191   Celestine III was crowned pope.
1533   Henry VIII of England divorced Catherine of Aragon, his first of six wives.
1842   Dr. Crawford Long became the first physician to use ether as an anesthetic in surgery.
1856   The Treaty of Paris ended the Crimean War.
1858   Hyman Lipman of Philadelphia patented the first pencil equipped with an eraser.
1867   Secretary of State Seward signed the agreement purchasing Alaska from Russia for $7 million--about two cents per acre. Americans roundly condemned the deal as "Seward's Folly."
1870   The Fifteenth Amendment to the Constitution was ratified, guaranteeing the right to vote regardless of race, color, or previous condition of servitude.
1945   Russian troops entered Austria, forcing a Nazi retreat on all fronts in World War II.
1953   Albert Einstein announced his revised Unified Field Theory, aimed at combining gravitational and electromagnetic equations in a single theory.
1981   President Reagan was shot on a Washington, D.C., street by a would-be assassin. Reagan's wound was minor and he became the first president to be shot and survive.

MARCH 31 -- BIRTHDAYS

1499   **Pius IV** -- Roman Catholic Pope, 1559-1563
1596   **Rene Descartes** -- French mathematician and "father of modern philosophy," noted for the rectangular, or Cartesian, coordinate system

1621	**Andrew Marvell** -- English poet whose works include such classics as "To His Coy Mistress"
1732	**Joseph Haydn** -- One of the greatest Austrian composers and "father of the symphony"
1809	**Edward FitzGerald** -- English writer and translator of the most famous version of *The Rubaiyat* of Omar Khayyam
1809	**Nikolai Gogol** -- Russian novelist and dramatist, noted for *The Inspector-General* (1836), perhaps the greatest Russian play, *Dead Souls,* and *The Overcoat* (both in 1842)
1811	**Robert Wilhelm Bunsen** -- German chemist who invented the Bunsen burner
1835	**John La Farge** -- American painter often called "the father of mural painting in America"
1844	**Andrew Lang** -- Scottish poet, historian, and anthropologist, noted for his book *Myth, Ritual, and Religion* (1887)
1870	**James M. Cox** -- U.S. presidential candidate in 1920
1878	**Jack Johnson** -- First black world heavyweight champion, 1908-1915
1895	**Vardis Fisher** -- American novelist known for such works as *The Children of God* (1939), a fictional history of the Mormons
1895	**John J. McCloy** -- American statesman of the post-World War II era
1903	**Arthur Godfrey** -- American television entertainer
1915	**Henry Morgan** -- American motion-picture and television actor and comedian
1918	**Tommy Bolt** -- Professional golfer
1922	**Richard Kiley** -- American stage, screen, and television actor
1927	**Cesar Chavez** -- U.S. labor leader and president of the United Farm Workers
1928	**Gordie Howe** – Professional hockey player whose record of the most points scored in National Hockey League history stood until Wayne Gretzky broke it in 1989
1928	**Lefty Frizzell** -- American country singer and musician
1931	**Miller Barber** -- Professional golfer
1934	**Shirley Jones** -- American singer and actress
1935	**Herb Alpert** -- American musician and leader of the Tiajuana Brass
1935	**Richard Chamberlain** – American motion-picture and television actor
1945	**Gabe Kaplan** -- American television actor
1948	**Albert Gore Jr.** -- U.S. senator, son of former senator Albert Gore, and candidate for the Democratic nomination for President in 1988

MARCH 31 -- EVENTS

1084   Henry VI of Germany, after deposing Pope Gregory VII, was crowned Holy Roman Emperor by Gregory's successor, Pope Clement III.

1631   John Donne, the English poet, died in London at age 59.

1829   Pius VIII was elected Roman Catholic pope.

1837   John Constable, the noted English painter, died in London at age 60.

1854   Commodore Matthew Perry signed a treaty opening Japan to trade with the United States.

1855   Charlotte Bronte, the English novelist, died in Haworth at age 38.

1870   Thomas Peterson-Mundy of Perth Amboy, New Jersey, became the first black man to vote in America, one day after the 15th Amendment made it possible.

1889   The Eiffel Tower in Paris was officially opened to the public.

1917   The United States took possession of the Virgin Islands by purchase from Denmark.

1931   Knute Rockne, the celebrated Notre Dame football coach, was killed in a plane crash in Kansas.

1932   The Ford Motor Company introduced the V-8 engine in its 1932 models.

1939   Prime Minister Neville Chamberlain pledged British support for Poland in the event of a Nazi invasion.

1973   Ken Norton defeated Muhammad Ali in a 12-round split decision, breaking Ali's jaw in the process.

1979   Iranians voted for a Muslim republic.

1981   De Witt Wallace, founder of *Reader's Digest,* died at age 91.

4

April

Our fourth month, April, got its name from *Aprilis*, a Latin word meaning *to open*, referring to the opening of leaves and buds during the month. April was the second month in the original Roman calendar, but it became the fourth month with the establishment of the Julian Calendar. April has always had 30 days except for a brief time in the calendar of Numa Pompilius when it had 29.

Special days of April include April Fools' Day (April 1), Pan American Day (April 14) and Patriot's Day, the anniversary of the beginning of the American Revolution in 1775 (April 19). Also, Easter and Good Friday occur most often in April, and the month has given us four Presidents: Thomas Jefferson, James Monroe, James Buchanan and U.S. Grant.

The birthstone of April is the diamond, and the special flowers are the sweet pea and the daisy. Notable birthdays and events of April are as follows.

APRIL 1 -- BIRTHDAYS

1578   **William Harvey** -- English physicist who discovered the nature of the circulation of the blood

1697   **Abbe Prevost** -- French novelist

1755   **Anthelme Brillat-Savarin** -- French jurist, writer, and gastronome

1815   **Otto von Bismarck** -- Prussian statesman who united the German states into one empire, and became known as the Iron Chancellor of Germany

199

1834   **Jim Fisk** -- American financier known as the "Barnum of Wall Street"
1866   **Ferruccio Benvenuto Busoni** -- Italian conductor and composer and one of the greatest pianists since Franz Liszt
1868   **Edmond Rostand** -- French dramatist and poet and author of *Cyrano de Bergerac* (1897)
1873   **Sergei Rachmaninoff** -- Russian composer and conductor, and one of the greatest pianists of all time
1875   **Edgar Wallace** -- English novelist and detective story writer
1883   **Lon Chaney** -- American actor who specialized in macabre characterizations
1886   **Wallace Beery** -- American stage and motion-picture actor
1895   **Alberta Hunter** – One of the great ladies of the golden age of jazz
1901   **Johnny Farrell** -- Hall of Fame golfer
1909   **Eddie Duchin** -- American bandleader and pianist
1922   **William Manchester** -- American writer and biographer
1928   **Herbert Klein** -- Assistant to President Nixon, 1969-1974
1929   **Jane Powell** -- American singer and actress
1929   **Bo Schembechler** -- Highly successful college football coach
1931   **George Baker** – Bulgarian-born motion-picture and television actor
1931   **Rolf Hochhuth** -- German author and playwright noted for *The Deputy* (1963), an attack on Pope Pius XII as a supposed silent accomplice in Hitler's treatment of the Jews
1932   **Debbie Reynolds** -- American motion-picture and television actress and singer
1939   **Ali MacGraw** -- American motion-picture actress
1939   **Rudolph Isley** -- American singer with the Isley Brothers
1939   **Phil Niekro** -- Professional baseball pitcher who won over 300 career games
1944   **Rusty Staub** -- Professional baseball player
1947   **Norm Van Lier** -- Professional basketball player
1948   **Willie Montanez** -- Professional baseball player

APRIL 1 -- EVENTS

1548   Parliament ordered the *Book of Common Prayer* printed in English.
1564   The French began calling those celebrating April 1 as New Year's (in opposition to the new Gregorian calendar) "April Fools," marking the beginning of April Fools' Day.
1789   The U.S. House of Representatives held its first meeting, in New York City. Frederick A. C. Muhlenberg of Pennsylvania was elected first Speaker of the House.

1885   Swift & Company, one of the world's leading meat-packing companies, was founded by Gustavus Franklin Swift.

1902   Claude Debussy's *Prelude to the Afternoon of a Faun* was played for the first time in America.

1918   The Royal Air Force was founded in Great Britain.

1939   The United States recognized Generalissimo Franco's Nationalist government in Spain, following the end of the Spanish Civil War.

1945   U.S. marines invaded Okinawa in World War II.

1954   The U.S. Congress authorized the establishment of the Air Force Academy.

1960   *Tiros 1*, the first satellite to take detailed weather pictures, was launched from Cape Canaveral, Florida.

1972   Major league baseball players struck for the first time in 102 years of organized baseball.

1973   The last of the United States prisoners of war returned home from North Vietnam.

1979   Iran proclaimed itself an Islamic Republic, following the downfall of the Shah.

APRIL 2 -- BIRTHDAYS

742 AD **Charlemagne** -- King of the Franks from A.D. 768 to 814, first Holy Roman Emperor from A.D. 800 to 814, and the greatest ruler of the early Middle Ages

1798   **August Heinrich** Hoffman -- Lyricist of "Deutschland, Deutschland, uber Alles"

1805   **Hans Christian Andersen** -- Master of the fairy tale and Denmark's most famous author

1827   **Holman Hunt** -- English painter

1834   **Frederic Bartholdi** -- French sculptor who designed the Statue of Liberty

1840   **Emile Zola** -- French novelist and critic, noted for such works as *Nana* (1880) and *Germinal* (1885)

1862   **Nicholas Murray Butler** – American educator and political figure, who helped found the Carnegie Endowment for International Peace

1869   **Hugh Jennings** – Professional baseball player and Hall of Famer

1875   **Walter Percy Chrysler** -- A founder and first president of Chrysler Corporation

1891   **Max Ernst** -- German painter and pioneer in the dada and surrealism movements

1907   **Luke Appling** – Hall of Fame baseball player who once hit a home run at age 75 in an Old Timers game

1908   **Buddy Ebsen** -- American dancer and actor
1912   **Herbert Mills** -- American singer and member of the Mills Brothers group
1914   **Sir Alec Guinness** -- British stage and motion-picture actor
1920   **Jack Webb** -- American actor, producer, and director
1924   **Bobby Avila** -- Professional baseball player
1926   **Jack Brabham** -- Australian automobile racing driver who won the Grand Prix three times
1927   **Billy Pierce** -- Professional baseball player
1927   **Carmen Basilio** -- World middle weight champion, 1957-1958
1939   **Marvin Gaye** -- American gospel and rhythm and blues singer
1941   **Leon Russell** -- American rock singer and musician
1943   **Larry Coryell** -- American jazz guitarist
1945   **Reggie Smith** -- Professional baseball player
1945   **Don Sutton** -- Professional baseball pitcher who won over 300 career games
1945   **Linda Hunt** -- American stage and motion-picture actress
1948   **Roy Gerela** -- Professional football player
1952   **David Humm** -- Professional football player
1964   **Pete Incaviglia** -- Professional baseball player

APRIL 2 -- EVENTS

999 AD Sylvester II was elected pope.
1250   The Seventh Crusade surrendered to the Turks in Egypt and its leader, French King Louis IX, was taken prisoner. He was released after he agreed to pay a huge ransom.
1513   Ponce de Leon landed on the Florida mainland near the present site of St. Augustine, seeking the Fountain of Youth.
1559   The Treaty of Cateau-Cambresis was signed for England. It committed England, Spain, and France to end the war between the late Holy Roman Emperor Charles V and France.
1589   Henry IV, the first Bourbon king, ascended the throne of France.
1792   The United States Mint was established by Congress.
1810   Napoleon married Archduchess Marie Louise of Austria, after divorcing Josephine.
1865   Confederate troops evacuated Richmond and Petersburg in the Civil War. The Confederacy surrendered a week later.
1902   Thomas L. Tally opened the first movie theater in Los Angeles.
1917   President Wilson asked Congress to declare war on Germany, saying, "The world must be made safe for democracy."
1956   The television soap operas *As the World Turns* and *The Edge of Night* premiered on CBS.

1963   American satellite *Explorer 17* was launched from Cape Canaveral. It was the first satellite to study the atmosphere.

1980   The U.S. prime interest rate hit a record 20 percent.

APRIL 3 -- BIRTHDAYS

1245   **Philip III** -- King of France, 1270-1285

1593   **George Herbert** -- A leading English poet of the 1600s

1753   **Simon Willard** -- American clockmaker and creator of the banjo clock

1778   **Pierre Bretonneau** -- First doctor to perform a tracheotomy for diphtheria

1783   **Washington Irving** -- First American man of letters and author of such works as *Rip Van Winkle* and *The Legend of Sleepy Hollow*

1822   **Edward Everett Hale** -- Author of *The Man Without a Country*

1823   **William Marcy Tweed** -- American political boss and head of the infamous "Tweed ring"

1837   **John Burroughs** -- American naturalist and writer

1859   **Reginald De Koven** -- American composer of light operas and of popular songs such as "Oh, Promise Me"

1863   **Henry van de Velde** -- Belgian architect

1881   **Alcide De Gasperi** -- Premier of Italy following World War II

1885   **Bud Fisher** -- American cartoonist and creator of *Mutt and Jeff*

1885   **Allan Dwan** -- Motion-picture director credited with over 400 films

1885   **Roger Lewis** -- American composer noted for songs such as "One Dozen Roses" and "Down Home Rag"

1898   **George Jessel** -- American singer and actor

1898   **Henry R. Luce** -- Co-founder in 1923 of *Time* magazine and one of the most prominent editors and publishers of his time

1901   **Larry Spier** -- American publisher and composer, noted for songs such as "Memory Lane" and "Put Your Little Foot Right Out"

1916   **Herb Caen** -- American newspaper columnist and humorist

1919   **Ervin Drake** -- American composer noted for songs such as "I Believe" and "It Was a Very Good Year"

1923   **Jan Sterling** -- American stage and motion-picture actress

1924   **Doris Day** -- American singer and actress

1924   **Marlon Brando** -- American stage and motion-picture actor and superstar

1926   **Virgil I. Grissom** -- Second American astronaut to travel in space (January 27, 1967)

1927   **Alex Grammas** -- Professional baseball player

1930   **Lawton Chiles** -- U.S. senator

1930   **Helmut Kohl** -- President of West Germany in the 1980s
1933   **Rod Funseth** -- Professional golfer
1934   **Jim Parker** -- Professional football player
1942   **Wayne Newton** -- American singer and nightclub performer
1943   **Jan Berry** -- Singer of the Jan and Dean duo
1943   **Marsha Mason** -- American stage and motion-picture actress
1944   **Tony Orlando** -- American singer
1949   **Lyle Alzado** -- Professional football player
1954   **Mike Pruitt** -- Professional football player
1961   **Eddie Murphy** -- American motion-picture and television actor and comedian

APRIL 3 -- EVENTS

1559   The Treaty of Cateau-Cambresis among England, Spain, and France was signed for Spain and France. (England had signed earlier.)
1776   George Washington received an honorary doctor of laws degree from Harvard College.
1800   Congress authorized Martha Washington, widow of George Washington, to send her mail postage free.
1860   The Pony Express postal service was started as two riders simultaneously left St. Joseph, Missouri, and Sacramento, California.
1865   Union forces occupied Richmond, the Confederate capital during the Civil War.
1882   Jesse James, the notorious outlaw, was shot and killed in St. Joseph, Missouri, by Robert Ford, a member of the James gang.
1897   Johannes Brahms, the great German composer, died in Vienna at age 63.
1936   Bruno Hauptmann was electrocuted in Trenton, New Jersey, for the kidnapping and murder of Charles A. Lindbergh Jr.
1946   Japanese general Masaharu Homma was executed for ordering the "Death March" of Americans captured in Bataan in World War II.
1948   President Harry S Truman signed the legislation implementing the Marshall Plan, which provided aid to Western Europe after World War II.
1953   *TV Guide* began publication.
1961   The 23rd Amendment to the U.S. Constitution was proclaimed, giving residents of the District of Columbia the right to vote in presidential elections.

APRIL 4 -- BIRTHDAYS

186 AD   Caracalla – Emperor of Rome, A.D. 211-217, whose public baths are among the most splendid of the Roman ruins existing today

1648   **Grinling Gibbons** -- English decorative wood carver and sculptor who was noted for much of the beautiful Restoration furniture of the Cromwell era

1752   **Nicola Antonio Zingarelli** -- Italian opera composer

1758   **John Hoppner** -- English painter

1758   **Pierre-Paul Prud'hon** -- French draftsman and painter

1780   **Edward Hicks** – American painter, best known for *The Peaceable Kingdom,* a depiction of the Isaiah prophecy that the lion would lie down with the lamb

1792   **Thaddeus Stevens** -- Radical Republican leader during the Reconstruction period who favored harsh treatment for the defeated South

1802   **Dorothea Dix** -- American prison and asylum reformer

1821   **Linus Yale** -- Designer of the Yale lock

1823   Sir Wilhelm Siemens -- German-born inventor of a regenerative gas-fired furnace in 1856 that led to the open-hearth steelmaking process

1843   Hans Richter -- Hungarian-born musician and one of the founders of modern orchestral conducting

1858   **Remy de Gourmont** -- French novelist and critic

1875   **Pierre Monteux** -- One of the leading 20th-century French-American conductors

1876   **Maurice de Vlaminck** – French painter and leader of the *fauvist* movement of the 1900s

1888   **Tris Speaker** -- One of the greatest outfielders in baseball history, with a graceful fielding form and a .344 lifetime batting average

1895   **Arthur Murray** -- American dancing teacher and founder of Arthur Murray Studios

1896   **Robert E. Sherwood** -- American playwright, journalist, and biographer, noted for works such as *The Petrified Forest*

1906   **John Cameron Swayze** – American reporter and commercial spokesman

1908   **Anthony Tudor** -- One of the most musically sophisticated choreographers in the annals of ballet

1914   **Frances Langford** -- American actress and singer

1915   **Muddy Waters** – American blues musician and singer (born McKinley Morganfield)

1920   **Eric Rohmer** -- French writer and filmmaker

1922   **Robert Abplanalp** -- American industrialist

1922   **Elmer Bernstein** -- One of Hollywood's most versatile and prolific composers, whose work includes the Oscar-winning original score for the movie *Thoroughly Modern Millie*
1924   **Gil Hodges** -- Professional baseball player and manager
1932   **Anthony Perkins** -- American motion-picture actor
1932   **Richard G. Lugar** -- U.S. senator
1938   **A. Bartlett Giamatti** -- Baseball commissioner who succeeded Peter Ueberroth in 1989
1942   **Jim Fregosi** -- Professional baseball player and manager
1947   **Ray Fosse** -- Professional baseball player
1956   **Tommy Herr** -- Professional baseball player

APRIL 4 -- EVENTS

527 AD Justinian I was crowned Emperor of the Byzantine Empire.
1581   Queen Elizabeth I of England knighted Sir Francis Drake after he had sailed around the world.
1818   Congress adopted the flag with 13 stripes and one star for each state.
1841   President William Henry Harrison died of pneumonia at age 68, just one month after taking office.
1844   Charles Bulfinch, the great American architect, died in Boston at age 80.
1850   Los Angeles was incorporated as an American city.
1887   Susanna Medora Salter was elected mayor of Argonia, Kansas, becoming the first woman to be elected mayor of any American community.
1914   The first showing of *The Perils of Pauline* took place in New York City.
1932   Professor C. G. King of the University of Pittsburgh became the first to isolate vitamin C.
1949   The North Atlantic Treaty Organization (NATO) was formed as 12 nations signed the treaty in Washington, D.C.
1968   Martin Luther King Jr., the great civil rights leader, was assassinated in Memphis at age 39.

APRIL 5 -- BIRTHDAYS

1588   **Thomas Hobbes** -- English philosopher and author of the monumental work *Leviathan* in 1651
1649   **Elihu Yale** -- English businessman and benefactor of Yale University

1725   **Giovanni Jacopo Casanova** -- Italian writer, soldier, adventurer, and the greatest of romantic lovers

1732   **Jean Honore Fragonard** -- French artist who painted in the highly ornamental style of the Rococo period

1811   **Jules Dupre** -- French painter

1827   **Joseph Lister** -- English medical scientist and founder of antiseptic surgery

1834   **Frank Richard Stockton** -- American author known for his short fairy tales for children and for his short stories such as "The Lady or the Tiger?" (1882)

1837   **Algernon Charles Swinburne** -- One of the major English poets of the 1800s, noted for such works as "The Garden of Proserpine"

1856   **Booker T. Washington** -- American educator and reformer who spent his life working to win equality for blacks

1871   **Pop Warner** -- American college football coach with a career of 47 seasons

1900   **Spencer Tracy** -- One of Hollywood's greatest actors

1901   **Chester Bowles** -- American ambassador and statesman

1901   **Melvin Douglas** -- American stage and motion-picture actor

1904   **Richard Eberhart** -- American poet who won the Bollingen Prize in poetry in 1962 and the Pulitzer Prize in 1966 for his *Selected Poems (1930-1965)*

1908   **Bette Davis** -- The "First Lady of the American Screen" and two-time Academy Award winner as the best leading actress

1908   **Herbert von Karajan** -- One of the leading symphony orchestra conductors of the mid-1900s

1911   **John Revolta** -- Professional golfer

1916   **Gregory Peck** -- American motion-picture actor and superstar, who won the best actor Academy Award for *To Kill a Mockingbird* (1962)

1920   **Arthur Hailey** -- American novelist and author of *Airport*

1922   **Gale Storm** -- American motion-picture and television actress

1923   **Nguyen Van Thieu** -- The last president of South Vietnam before the Communist takeover in 1975

1934   **Frank Gorshin** -- American actor and impressionist

1951   **Brad Van Pelt** -- Professional football player

1952   **Sandy Mayer** -- American tennis player

APRIL 5 -- EVENTS

1291   A Moslem army attacked Acre in the tiny Latin kingdom of Jerusalem, beginning the end of the history of the Crusader states in the East.

1614   Pocahontas, daughter of Indian chief Powhatan, married the English colonist John Rolfe in Virginia.

1621   The *Mayflower* left Plymouth on the return trip to England and though times were very hard, not a single Pilgrim was aboard.

1697   Sweden's great king Charles XII ascended to the throne at the age of 15 upon the death of his father Charles XI.

1768   The first American Chamber of Commerce was founded in New York City.

1792   President George Washington cast his first veto, rejecting a Congressional bill for apportioning representatives among the states.

1818   Chilean troops under Bernardo O'Higgins defeated the Spanish at the Maipo River to win independence for Chile.

1829   Pius VIII was crowned Roman Catholic pope.

1869   The last surviving soldier of the Revolutionary War, Daniel F. Bakeman, died in Freeman, New York, at age 109.

1887   Teacher Anne Sullivan achieved a major breakthrough with her blind and deaf pupil, Helen Keller, by teaching her the word *water* as spelled out in the Manual Alphabet.

1915   Jess Willard knocked out Jack Johnson in the 26th round at Havana, Cuba, to become the world heavyweight champion.

1933   President Franklin D. Roosevelt ordered the surrender of all private stores of gold in the United States.

1955   Sir Winston Churchill resigned as English prime minister at age 81.

1964   General Douglas MacArthur died at age 84.

1976   Howard Hughes, the famous recluse reputed to be the richest man in America, died at age 72.

1980   The world's most valuable stamp, an 1856 British Guiana one-cent magenta, was auctioned in New York to an anonymous buyer for $850,000.

1984   Kareem Abdul-Jabbar scored career point number 31,421, topping Wilt Chamberlain's record and becoming the highest-scoring basketball player in NBA history.

APRIL 6 -- BIRTHDAYS

1483   **Raphael (Raffaello Sanzio)** -- Painter, architect, and one of the masters of the Italian Renaissance

1671   **Jean Baptiste Rousseau** -- French dramatist and poet

1773   **James Mill** -- English philosopher and statesman and father of the great philosopher and economist John Stuart Mill

| 1810 | **Edmund H. Sears** -- Composer of "It Came Upon a Midnight Clear" |

1810   **Edmund H. Sears** -- Composer of "It Came Upon a Midnight Clear"

1823   **Joseph Medill** -- A crusading American editor and publisher of the Chicago *Tribune* from 1855 to 1899

1826   **Gustave Moreau** -- French painter noted for works such as *Oedipus and the Sphinx* (1864)

1860   **Rene Lalique** -- French jeweler and glassmaker

1866   **Lincoln Steffens** -- American journalist, writer, political philosopher, and "muckraker"

1884   **Walter Huston** -- American stage and motion-picture performer and brilliant character actor

1890   **Anthony Fokker** – Dutch-German pioneer aircraft manufacturer

1892   **Lowell Thomas** -- American news commentator, author, and explorer

1892   **Donald Wills Douglas** -- American aircraft designer and founder of Douglas Aircraft Company

1900   **Leo Robin** – American lyricist noted for songs such as "Beyond the Blue Horizon," "Prisoner of Love," "Blue Hawaii," "Thanks for the Memory," "Ebb-Tide," and "Love Is Just Around the Corner"

1903   **Charles R. Jackson** -- Author of *The Lost Weekend*

1903   **Mickey Cochrane** -- Hall of Fame baseball player and one of the greatest catchers in baseball history

1904   **Kurt Kiesinger** -- Chancellor of West Germany, 1966-1969

1905   **Bix Reichner** – American composer and author, noted for songs such as "Stop Beating 'Round the Mulberry Bush" and "Papa Loves Mambo"

1908   **Ernie Lombardi** -- Professional baseball player

1909   **Denver Darling** -- American composer noted for songs such as "Sioux City Sue" and "Choo Choo Ch-Boogie"

1914   **Ted Mossman** – American composer, author, and pianist, noted for songs such as "Till the End of Time" and "Full Moon and Empty Arms"

1925   **Arthur Larson** -- American Hall of Fame tennis player

1926   **Alexander Butterfield** -- U.S. government official who first revealed to the Watergate committee the existence of the Nixon tapes

1927   **Gerry Mulligan** -- American jazz musician

1929   **Andre Previn** -- German-born composer, arranger, and conductor of the London Symphony Orchestra

1936   **Roy Thinnes** -- American motion-picture and television actor

1937   **Merle Haggard** -- American country musician, songwriter, and singer

1951   **Burt Blyleven** -- Professional baseball player
1953   **Janet Lynn** -- American ice skater

APRIL 6 -- EVENTS

1199   Richard the Lion-Hearted died at age 32 of a crossbow bolt wound.
1520   Raphael, the Italian painter, died in Rome on his 37th birthday.
1528   Albrecht Durer, the German painter, died in Nuremberg at age 56.
1614   El Greco, the Spanish painter, died in Toledo, Spain, at age 73.
1748   The buried city of Pompeii was discovered by an Italian peasant digging in a vineyard.
1830   Joseph Smith founded the Church of Jesus Christ of Latter-day Saints (the Mormons) at Fayette, New York.
1841   John Tyler became U.S. president, the first vice president to succeed to the office. He was shooting marbles with his children when he learned of President Harrison's death.
1862   The Battle of Shiloh (Tennessee) began in the Civil War.
1866   The Grand Army of the Republic (GAR) was organized by Union army veterans at Decatur, Illinois.
1896   Ex-President Benjamin Harrison married his second wife, Mrs. Mary Dimmick.
1896   The first modern Olympic games were formally opened in Athens, Greece.
1909   American explorer Robert Peary reached the North Pole, the first man to do so.
1917   George M. Cohan wrote his famous World War I song, "Over There."
1917   The United States declared war on Germany in World War I by a Senate vote of 82-6.
1936   The comic strip *Mickey Finn,* by Lank Leonard, first appeared.
1941   Germany invaded Yugoslavia and Greece in World War II.
1965   *Early Bird*, the first commercial communications satellite, was launched by the U.S.

APRIL 7 -- BIRTHDAYS

1613   **Gerard Dou** -- Dutch painter
1770   **William Wordsworth** -- One of the most important of the English romantic poets

1780 William Ellery Channing – American clergyman and founder in 1825 of the American Unitarian Association

1859 Walter Chauncey Camp – "Father of American football," who threw the first forward pass and who named the All-America teams from 1889 to 1924

1860 W.K. Kellogg -- "King of the corn flakes" and founder of the W.K. Kellogg cereal company

1873 John McGraw – Professional baseball player and one of the greatest of all major league managers, with 10 pennant winners to his credit

1882 Kurt von Schleicher – One of Hitler's chief political opponents in Germany in 1932-1933

1884 Bronislaw Malinowski -- Founder of social anthropology

1889 Gabriela Mistral -- Chilean poet and educator and the first Latin-American writer to win the Nobel Prize for literature

1891 Sir David Low -- English political cartoonist

1893 Allen W. Dulles -- Director of the C.I.A. under President Eisenhower

1893 Irene Castle -- Noted American dancer who with her husband Vernon Castle formed the internationally famous ballroom dancing team of the 1910s

1897 Walter Winchell -- American newspaper and radio reporter and gossip columnist from the 1930s through the 1960s

1899 Robert Marcel Casadesus -- French pianist and composer

1908 Percy Faith -- Canadian bandleader, pianist, and composer

1908 Frank Fitzsimmons -- American labor leader who became president of the Teamsters union when Jimmy Hoffa became missing

1912 Jack Lawrence -- American composer and author, noted for songs such as "If I Didn't Care," "All or Nothing at All," "Hold My Hand," "Sunrise Serenade," "Sleepy Lagoon," "Symphony," and "Johnson Rag"

1915 Billie Holiday -- Outstanding jazz singer of her time

1918 Bobby Doerr -- Professional baseball player

1920 Ravi Shankar -- Indian sitar virtuoso

1928 James Garner -- American motion-picture and television actor

1931 Donald Barthelme -- American short-story writer

1934 Wayne Rogers – American television actor who starred as Trapper in the long-running series *M*A*S*H*

1935 Hodding Carter III -- American journalist and State Department spokesman under President Carter

1936 Preston Jones -- American playwright and actor

1938   Edmund "Jerry" Brown Jr. -- Governor of California, 1974-1982
1939   Francis Ford Coppola -- American motion-picture director and screenwriter
1939   David Frost -- English television performer and interviewer
1954   Tony Dorsett -- Professional football player

APRIL 7 -- EVENTS

30 AD   Christ was crucified on the hill of Calvary, according to his disciple John.
451 AD Attila the Hun plundered Metz, France.
1449   Felix V, the last antipope, abdicated his office.
1521   Magellan landed at Cebu in the Philippines, where he was later killed. Afterwards his crew completed the first trip around the world that he began.
1739   Dick Turpin, celebrated English robber, was hanged in York for stealing horses.
1827   The first friction matches were sold, in England.
1862   The Battle of Shiloh ended with heavy losses on both sides with the North claiming victory. Confederate general Albert Sydney Johnston was mortally wounded in the battle.
1880   The American Society of Mechanical Engineers was formed.
1927   The first U.S. demonstration of television was given when a New York audience saw Commerce Secretary Herbert Hoover at his desk in Washington, D.C.
1939   Italian troops invaded Albania, a prelude to World War II that was to start in September.
1947   Henry Ford, the great auto pioneer, died in Dearborn, Michigan, at age 83.
1949   The musical play *South Pacific* opened in New York at the Majestic Theater.
1959   The first atomic-generated electricity was produced, in Los Alamos, New Mexico.
1963   Jack Nicklaus won the Masters golf tournament at age 23, the youngest player ever to win it.

APRIL 8 -- BIRTHDAYS

1582   Phineas Fletcher -- English poet
1605   Philip IV -- King of Spain, 1621-1665

1692	**Giuseppe Tartini** -- Great Italian master of the violin, noted composer, and teacher who started the use of thicker strings and lighter bows
1726	**Lewis Morris** -- American Revolutionary War general, Continental Congressman, and signer from New York of the Declaration of Independence
1805	**Hugo von Mohl** -- German botanist who coined the word *protoplasm* and helped develop the "Cell Theory"
1842	**Elizabeth Custer** -- Wife of the American general, George Custer, who was killed in "Custer's Last Stand"
1869	**Harvey Williams Cushing** -- American physician and one of the world's greatest brain surgeons
1875	**Albert I** -- King of Belgium, 1909-1934, and a heroic military leader in World War I
1898	**E.Y. "Yip" Harburg** -- American playwright and lyricist, noted for songs such as "Over the Rainbow," "April in Paris," "It's Only a Paper Moon," and "Brother, Can You Spare a Dime?"
1902	**Joseph Krips** -- Austrian-born conductor
1905	**Ilka Chase** – American novelist and stage and motion-picture actress
1912	**Sonja Henie** – Norwegian-American actress and world champion figure skater at age 15
1914	**Irving Taylor** -- American composer and author, noted for lyrics such as "Mambo Jambo," "Three Little Sisters," and "Onezy-Twozy"
1918	**Betty Ford** -- Wife of President Gerald Ford
1919	**Ian Smith** -- First native-born prime minister of Rhodesia (now Zimbabwe)
1923	**Franco Corelli** -- Italian tenor
1929	**Jacques Brel** -- French composer, lyricist, and singer
1935	**John Gavin** -- American motion-picture actor and ambassador to Mexico under President Reagan
1940	**John Havlicek** – Professional basketball player and one of the game's superstars
1940	**Peggy Lennon** -- One of the singing Lennon Sisters
1943	**John Hiller** -- Professional baseball player
1944	**Jimmy Walker** -- Professional basketball player
1952	**Kim Warwick** -- Australian tennis player
1954	**Gary Carter** -- Professional baseball player
1955	**Ricky Bell** -- Professional football player
1957	**Fred Smerlas** -- Professional football player

1963   **Julian Lennon** – English rock musician and son of Beatle John
         Lennon and his first wife Cynthia

APRIL 8 -- EVENTS

1341   Petrarch was crowned Poet Laureate in Rome.

1378   Urban VI was elected Roman Catholic pope.

1492   Lorenzo the Magnificent, the most famous of the Medicis, died
         at age 43.

1513   Spanish explorer Ponce de Leon claimed Florida for Spain six
         days after reaching the mainland.

1730   The first Jewish congregation in the U.S. consecrated its syna-
         gogue in New York City.

1865   General Grant asked General Lee to surrender, which he did the
         following day, ending the Civil War.

1904   The Entente Cordiale was signed, establishing a diplomatic
         partnership between Great Britain and France.

1943   Wendell Willkie's book *One World* was published.

1952   President Truman seized the steel industry to forestall a
         general strike.

1974   Hank Aaron hit his 715th career home run, breaking Babe
         Ruth's record of 714.

1981   General Omar Bradley, American World War II hero and first
         chairman of the Joint Chiefs of Staff, died in New York at age 88.

APRIL 9 -- BIRTHDAYS

1738   **Rufus Putnam** -- Revolutionary War general and founder and
         father of Ohio

1821   **Charles Baudelaire** -- Best known and most widely translated
         French poet

1835   **Leopold II** – King of Belgium and founder of the Congo Free State

1865   **Charles Proteus Steinmetz** – German-American scientist and
         one of the world's foremost electrical engineers

1869   **Elie-Joseph Cartan** -- Noted French mathematician

1872   **Leon Blum** -- French Socialist premier before World War II

1888   **Sol Hurok** -- Ukrainian-born impresario and moviemaker

1889   **Efrem Zimbalist** -- Russian-born American violinist

1893   **Mary Pickford** -- "America's Sweetheart" of the silent screen

1893   **Charles Ephraim Burchfield** – American painter noted for his
         landscapes and rural life scenes

1894	**Tommy Manville** -- Often-married American heir of the Johns-Manville fortune
1895	**Mance Lipscomb** -- American blues musician
1895	**Michel Simon** -- French character actor
1898	**Paul Robeson** -- American singer and actor
1898	**Curly Lambeau** -- Hall of Fame football player and coach
1904	**Ward Bond** -- American motion-picture and television actor who appeared in some 200 films
1905	**J. William Fulbright** -- U.S. senator and initiator of the Fulbright educational program
1909	**Claude Passeau** -- Professional baseball player
1910	**Abraham Ribicoff** -- U.S. senator of the 1960s and 1970s
1919	**John Presper Eckert** -- Co-inventor of the ENIAC, the first electronic computer
1925	**Linda Goodman** -- Noted American astrologer and author of the best-selling book, *Sun Signs* (1968)
1926	**Hugh Hefner** -- Founder of *Playboy* magazine
1928	**Paul Arizin** -- Professional basketball player who scored over 16,000 career points
1928	**Tom Lehrer** -- American songwriter, performer, and mathematician, noted for comic songs such as "Be Prepared," "Poisoning Pigeons in the Park," and "The Masochism Tango"
1932	**Carl Perkins** -- American rockabilly musician
1933	**Jean-Paul Belmondo** -- French motion-picture actor
1939	**Michael Learned** -- American television actress noted for her role in the long-running series *Little House on the Prairie*
1942	**Brandon De Wilde** -- American stage, screen, and television actor
1954	**Dennis Quaid** -- American motion-picture actor
1957	**Severiano Ballesteros** -- Professional golfer

APRIL 9 -- EVENTS

491 AD	Eastern Roman Emperor Zeno died.
1483	King Edward IV of England died at age 40.
1555	Marcellus II was elected pope. He died 22 days later.
1626	Sir Francis Bacon, the great English philosopher, died at Highgate at age 65.
1682	La Salle, the great French explorer, reached the mouth of the Mississippi River and claimed all the land drained by it for France.

1865   General Robert E. Lee surrendered to General U.S. Grant at Appomattox Court House, Virginia, essentially ending the Civil War.

1928   Mae West made her debut in New York in the risque play, *Diamond Lil.*

1939   Some 75,000 people gathered at the Lincoln Memorial in Washington, D.C., to hear black singer Marian Anderson perform after the D.A.R. denied her the use of Constitution Hall.

1940   Germany attacked Denmark and Norway in World War II.

1941   The Professional Golfers' Association announced the creation of its Hall of Fame, with the first members selected being Bobby Jones, Francis Ouimet, Walter Hagen, and Gene Sarazen.

1942   U.S. troops on the Bataan peninsula surrendered to the Japanese in World War II.

1945   Dietrich Bonhoeffer, the noted theologian, was executed in a Nazi concentration camp on orders of Heinrich Himmler, only days before he would have been liberated by the Allies.

1959   Frank Lloyd Wright, the great American architect, died in Phoenix at age 89.

1959   NASA announced the selection of America's first astronauts: Scott Carpenter, Gordon Cooper, John Glenn, Gus Grissom, Wally Schirra, Alan Shepard, and Donald Slayton.

1965   The first baseball game, an exhibition between the Houston Astros and the New York Yankees, was played in the newly built Houston Astrodome.

APRIL 10 -- BIRTHDAYS

1512   **James V** -- King of Scotland, 1513-1542

1583   **Hugo Grotius** -- Dutch lawyer, theologian, statesman, poet, and the founder of international law

1647   **John Wilmot** -- Second Earl of Rochester and English poet

1755   **Samuel F. Christian Hahnemann** -- German physician and founder of homeopathy (the treating of a disease with medicines that produce symptoms of that disease)

1778   **William Hazlitt** -- One of the best essayists and critics in English literature

1794   **Matthew C. Perry** -- U.S. naval officer who opened trade with Japan, 1853-1854

1827   **Lew Wallace** -- American soldier, novelist, and author of *Ben Hur*

1829   **William Booth** -- Founder of the Salvation Army

1847 **Joseph Pulitzer** -- American newspaper publisher who established the Pulitzer Prizes

1867 **Æ (George William Russell)** -- Irish mystical poet and painter

1868 **George Arliss** -- British stage and screen actor

1879 **John Daniel Hertz** -- Founder of the Hertz car rental agency

1882 **Frances Perkins** -- Secretary of labor under President Franklin D. Roosevelt and the first woman cabinet member in the United States

1885 **Sigmund Gottfried Spaeth** -- American musician, author, and authority on opera

1891 **Tim McCoy** -- American motion-picture actor and one of Hollywood's most popular Western stars

1894 **Ben Nicholson** -- English painter noted for his abstract works which feature geometric forms and pale colors

1903 **Clare Booth Luce** -- American playwright, congresswoman, and diplomat

1912 **Roy Hofheinz** -- Principal builder of the Houston Astrodome

1915 **Harry Morgan** -- American motion-picture and television actor

1921 **Chuck Connors** -- Professional baseball player and actor

1924 **Kenneth Noland** -- American painter of the Abstract Expressionist school

1929 **Max von Sydow** -- Swedish stage and motion-picture actor

1932 **Omar Sharif** -- Egyptian motion-picture actor and expert bridge player

1934 **David Halberstam** -- American correspondent and author

1936 **John Madden** -- Professional football coach and sports commentator

1938 **Don Meredith** -- Professional football player and sports announcer

1941 **Paul Theroux** -- American writer and novelist

1946 **Bob Watson** -- Professional baseball player

1949 **Lee Lacy** -- Professional baseball player

1950 **Ken Griffey** -- Professional baseball player

1951 **Mike Roth** -- American bowler who won 26 professional championships

APRIL 10 -- EVENTS

1606 Sir Walter Raleigh sold his interest in the colony to be established at Jamestown, Virginia.

1790   The United States patent system was created by Congress.

1841   Horace Greeley published the first issue of the New York *Tribune.*

1849   Walter Hunt of New York patented his invention of the safety pin.

1866   The American Society for the Prevention of Cruelty to Animals was chartered in New York.

1938   Austrians voted for annexation to Germany in a plebiscite controlled by Hitler. The percentage for Anschluss was 99.73.

1945   The notorious Nazi concentration camp at Buchenwald was liberated by the U.S. 80th Division.

1953   The first feature length 3-D movie in color, *House of Wax,* premiered in New York City.

1963   The U.S. nuclear submarine *Thresher* mysteriously sank off Cape Cod, Massachusetts, claiming 129 lives.

1972   The United States, the U.S.S.R., and some 70 other nations signed an agreement banning biological warfare.

APRIL 11 -- BIRTHDAYS

146 AD **Lucius Septimius Severus** -- Emperor of Rome, A.D. 193-211

1357   **John I** -- King of Portugal, 1385-1433, and father of Prince Henry the Navigator

1492   **Marguerite d'Angouleme** -- French writer and Queen of Navarre

1586   **Pietro della Valle** -- Italian traveler and writer

1755   **James Parkinson** -- Physician and researcher on palsy, or Parkinson's disease

1794   **Edward Everett** -- Great American orator and chief speaker at Gettysburg on November 19, 1863, the day Lincoln delivered his famous Gettysburg Address

1857   **John Davidson** -- Scottish poet

1862   **Charles Evans Hughes** -- U.S. presidential candidate in 1916 and Supreme Court Justice

1869   **Gustav Vigeland** -- One of Norway's greatest sculptors and creator of some 150 works in Oslo's Frogner Park

1888   **Francesca Bertini** -- Italian stage and motion-picture actress

1893   **Dean Acheson** -- American secretary of state under President Truman

1898   **Lou Holtz** -- American comedian

1902   **Quentin Reynolds** -- American author and reporter

1913   **Oleg Cassini** -- French fashion designer

1916   **Alberto Ginastera** -- Argentine composer noted for his highly dramatic operas *Don Rodrigo* (1964) and *Bomarzo* (1967)

1919   **Hugh Carey** -- Governor of New York, 1975-1983

1928   **Ethel Kennedy** -- Wife of Senator Robert F. Kennedy

1939   **Louise Lasser** -- American television actress known for the title role in *Mary Hartman! Mary Hartman!*

1964   **Bret Saberhagen** -- Professional baseball player

APRIL 11 -- EVENTS

328 AD   The oldest stele (monolith with ornamentations) at Uaxactun, Guatemala, was put in place by the Mayas.

1814   Napoleon abdicated at Fontainebleau and Louis XVIII was crowned King of France. Napoleon returned to power the next year, however, before his final exile.

1865   President Lincoln made his last public speech, addressing a group of citizens at the White House.

1898   President McKinley asked Congress to declare war on Spain.

1921   Iowa became the first state to impose a cigarette tax.

1947   Jackie Robinson became the first black major league baseball player, in an exhibition game between the New York Yankees and his team, the Brooklyn Dodgers.

1951   President Truman fired General Douglas MacArthur as U.S. commander in Korea.

1953   Mrs. Oveta Culp Hobby became the first secretary of the Department of Health, Education and Welfare.

1970   *Apollo 13*, the manned lunar flight that had to be aborted, was launched at Cape Kennedy.

APRIL 12 -- BIRTHDAYS

1539   **Garcilaso de la Vega** -- One of the greatest Spanish chroniclers of the 16th century

1724   **Lyman Hall** -- American Revolutionary War statesman and signer of the Declaration of Independence

1744   **Francois Joseph Belanger** -- French architect

1777   **Henry Clay** --American statesman and three times candidate for president

1791   **Francis P. Blair** -- One of the founders of the Republican Party in the 1850s, who, however, returned to the Democratic Party after the Civil War

1857   **John Thomas Underwood** -- American merchant who in 1895
        founded the Underwood Typewriter Company
1878   **Charles Neil Daniels** -- American composer noted for songs
        such as "Moonlight and Roses," "Yearning," and "Dark Eyes"
1880   **Addie Joss** -- Hall of Fame baseball pitcher with a lifetime
        earned run average of 1.88, the second lowest in baseball history
1883   **Imogen Cunningham** -- American photographer
1885   **Robert Delaunay** -- French painter
1892   **Johnny Dodds** -- American jazz clarinetist
1904   **Lily Pons** -- French operatic soprano and actress
1904   **Frankie Masters** -- American composer, author, and conductor,
        noted for songs such as "Scatterbrain" and "Moonlight and
        You"
1905   **Warren Magnuson** -- U.S. senator
1913   **Lionel Hampton** -- American bandleader of the Big Band Era
1919   **Ann Miller** -- American dancer and actress
1926   **Jane Withers** -- American stage and motion-picture actress
        noted for her roles as a child actress
1930   **John Landy** -- Australian track star who set a world record of 3
        minutes 58 seconds for the mile run in 1954, breaking Roger
        Bannister's record set a month earlier
1940   **Herbie Hancock** -- American jazz pianist and composer
1944   **John Kay** -- Canadian singer with Steppenwolf
1944   **Mike Garrett** -- Professional football and baseball player
1947   **David Letterman** -- American late-night television host
1950   **Jerry Tagge** -- Professional football player
1950   **David Cassidy** -- American singer and television actor

APRIL 12 -- EVENTS

1204   The Fourth Crusaders captured Constantinople and mercilessly
        sacked it.
1606   England adopted the Union Jack as its flag.
1633   Galileo was put on trial in Rome by the Inquisition.
1858   The first American billiards championship was played in Detroit.
1861   Confederate troops attacked Fort Sumter, starting the Ameri-
        can Civil War.
1877   The first catcher's mask was worn in a baseball game, by James
        Alexander Tyng, in Lynn, Massachusetts.

1878	William Marcy Tweed, political boss of the notorious Tweed Ring, died in prison.
1922	The trial of Fatty Arbuckle, motion-picture comedian, ended with the jury convicting him of manslaughter in the death of a Hollywood starlet.
1945	President Franklin D. Roosevelt died of a cerebral hemorrhage at age 63 in Warm Springs, Georgia.
1955	The Salk anti-polio vaccine was pronounced effective and safe by the University of Michigan Vaccine Evaluation Center. It was the first effective vaccine against polio.
1961	Yuri Gagarin, sent into orbit in *Vostok 1* by the Russians, became the first man in space.
1981	Joe Louis, the great heavyweight boxing champion, died of a heart attack at age 66.
1981	The U.S. space shuttle *Columbia,* with astronauts John Young and Robert Crippen aboard, lifted off at Cape Canaveral.

APRIL 13 -- BIRTHDAYS

1519	**Catherine de Medici** -- Queen consort of King Henry II of France and mother of three French kings
1721	**John Hanson** -- Early American patriot, signer of the Articles of Confederation, and president in 1781 of the Continental Congress
1743	**Thomas Jefferson** -- Author of the Declaration of Independence and third United States president
1769	**Sir Thomas Lawrence** – English painter noted for works such as *The Calmady Children* (1823-1824)
1771	**Richard Trevithick** -- English inventor and engineer who designed the first high-pressure steam engine
1795	**James Harper** – One of the four Harper brothers who founded the famous publishing house of Harper and Brothers
1852	**F.W. Woolworth** -- American merchant who developed the F.W. Woolworth chain of stores
1860	**James Sidney Ensor** – Belgian painter who founded the exhibiting society Les Vingt at Brussels
1866	**Butch Cassidy** -- American cattle rustler and robber of the old West
1873	**Theodore Morse** -- American composer noted for songs such as "Keep On the Sunny Side," "M-O-T-H-E-R," and "Hail, Hail, the Gang's All Here"
1899	**Alfred Mosher Butts** -- American architect noted for his invention of the famous word game *Scrabble*

1906   **Samuel Beckett** -- Irish-born Nobel Prize-winning playwright and novelist, who often wrote in French and translated his works into English

1907   **Harold Stassen** -- Governor of Minnesota and candidate for the Republican nomination for president on numerous occasions

1909   **Eudora Welty** -- American short-story writer and novelist known for such works as *Losing Battles* (1970)

1919   **Howard Keel** -- American singer and actor

1919   **Madalyn Murray O'Hair** -- American atheist whose Supreme Court suit in 1963 resulted in outlawing school prayers

1927   **Mari Blanchard** -- American motion-picture actress

1929   **Marilynn Smith** -- Professional golfer

1937   **Lanford Wilson** -- American playwright

1939   **Christian Kuhnke** -- West German tennis player

1946   **Al Green** -- American soul singer

1970   **Ricky Schroder** -- American television actor

APRIL 13 -- EVENTS

1436   King Charles VII of France drove the English out of Paris in the Hundred Years' War.

1598   The Edict of Nantes, one of the most famous decrees in history, was signed by Henry IV of France. It gave freedom of worship and equal rights as citizens to the Huguenots.

1605   Boris Godunov, Czar of Russia during "The Time of Troubles," died at age 52.

1759   George Frederick Handel, Anglo-German composer of *Messiah,* died in London at age 74.

1846   The Pennsylvania Railroad was incorporated by the Pennsylvania legislature.

1941   Russia and Japan signed a five-year neutrality pact.

1943   President Franklin D. Roosevelt dedicated the Thomas Jefferson Memorial in Washington, D.C., as "a shrine to freedom."

1945   Harry S Truman, still stunned by the death of Franklin D. Roosevelt, making him president the previous day, likened his situation to "a load of hay or a bull" falling on him.

1986   U.S. jets attacked targets in Tripoli and Benghazi, Libya, in retaliation for terrorist attacks on Americans attributed to Libyan strongman Moammar Khadafy.

APRIL 14 -- BIRTHDAYS

1527   **Abraham Ortelius** -- Flemish mapmaker and publisher of the first modern atlas

1578   **Philip III** -- King of Spain, 1598-1621

1629   **Christian Huygens** -- Dutch physicist who discovered the polarization of light, founded the wave theory of light, and invented the hairspring, which made watches possible

1724   **Gabriel de Saint-Aubin** -- French printmaker

1810   **Justin S. Morrill** -- American legislator noted for the Morrill Act of 1862, which established the Land-Grant Colleges and Universities

1879   **James Branch Cabell** -- American novelist and author of *Jurgen* (1919)

1889   **Arnold Toynbee** -- English historian and author of the 12-volume outline of the civilizations of the world, *A Study of History*

1898   **Lee Tracy** -- American stage, screen, and television actor, with a 40-year career

1904   **Sir John Gielgud** -- One of the greatest British actors of the 20th century

1907   **Francois "Papa Doc" Duvalier** -- Dictator of Haiti in the 1950s and 1960s

1917   **Marvin Julian Miller** -- President of the major league baseball players union

1917   **Norman Luboff** -- American composer and conductor

1918   **Mary Healy** -- American actress and singer, and wife of actor Peter Lind Hayes

1925   **Rod Steiger** -- American motion-picture and television actor

1930   **Bradford Dillman** -- American motion-picture and television actor

1932   **Loretta Lynn** -- American country music singer

1935   **Erich Von Daniken** -- Swiss writer noted for *The Ancient Astronauts*

1936   **Bobby Nichols** -- Professional golfer

1941   **Pete Rose** -- Professional baseball superstar, who holds the record of career hits, and who, except for Ty Cobb, is the only player to have over 4,000

1941   **Julie Christie** -- English motion-picture actress

1949   **Jill Cooper** -- English tennis player

1966   **Greg Maddux** -- Professional baseball player

1968   **Anthony Michael Hall** -- American motion-picture actor

APRIL 14 -- EVENTS

73 AD   After two years of defending the fortress of Masada, the Jews committed mass suicide rather than surrender to the Roman Tenth Legion.

1828   Noah Webster copyrighted the first edition of his great lexicon, *An American Dictionary of the English Language.*

1865   Abraham Lincoln was shot in Ford's Theatre in Washington, D.C., by John Wilkes Booth, while attending a performance of *Our American Cousin.* He died the following day.

1890   The Pan-American Union (now the Organization of American States) was formed by delegates of 18 republics of North, South, and Central America, meeting in Washington, D.C.

1910   President William Howard Taft started the tradition of throwing out the first ball to open the baseball season.

1912   The British *Titanic,* the largest ship in the world, and considered to be unsinkable, struck an iceberg just before midnight and sank in 2½ hours in the North Atlantic.

1931   The 20 millionth Ford automobile rolled off the assembly line in Detroit.

1968   The Russian linking space vehicle, *Cosmos 212,* was launched.

1969   The Montreal Expos defeated the St. Louis Cardinals, 8-7, at Jarry Park in Montreal in the first major league baseball game ever played outside the U.S.

1981   The U.S. space shuttle *Columbia* landed safely at Edwards Air Force Base, California, after two days in space. It was the first conventional landing by a space vehicle.

APRIL 15 -- BIRTHDAYS

1452   **Leonardo da Vinci** -- Italian Renaissance painter, sculptor, and scientist, and one of the greatest geniuses of all time

1642   **Suleiman II** -- Ottoman sultan, 1687-1691

1707   **Leonhard Euler** -- The most prolific mathematician of the 18th century and perhaps of all time (a Swiss society has published 47 volumes of his work but much still remains)

1710   **Marie Camargo** -- French opera ballerina

1741   **Charles Willson Peale** -- American painter noted for portraits of Revolutionary War heroes

1812   **Theodore Rousseau** -- French painter

1814   John Lothrop Motley -- American historian and diplomat noted for his historical writings on the Netherlands

1843   Henry James -- One of America's greatest writers, whose most famous story is the psychological horror tale, *The Turn of the Screw*

1874   George Harrison Shull -- American geneticist and father of hybrid corn

1875   James Jackson Jeffries -- World heavyweight champion, 1899-1905

1888   Florence Bates -- American motion-picture actress

1889   A. Philip Randolph -- American labor union leader

1890   Billy De Beck -- American cartoonist and creator of *Barney Google* and *Snuffy Smith*

1894   Bessie Smith -- American singer and songwriter and one of the finest blues singers in the history of jazz

1897   Molly McGee -- American actress who was actor Fibber McGee's wife in real life and on the long-running radio show, *Fibber McGee and Molly*

1901   Rene Pleven -- Twice premier of the French Fourth Republic

1912   Kim Il Sung -- President of North Korea during the Korean War

1915   Walter Washington -- Mayor of Washington, D.C.

1916   Alfred Bloomingdale -- Father of the credit card

1922   Harold Washington -- First black mayor of Chicago, 1983-1988

1922   Michael Ansara -- American stage, screen, and television actor

1933   Roy Clark -- American musician, comedian, and country singer

1933   Elizabeth Montgomery -- American motion-picture and television actress

1933   Gloria Caldwell -- American composer noted for songs such as "La Paloma"

1939   Claudia Cardinale -- Italian motion-picture actress

1940   Woody Fryman -- Professional baseball player

1944   Dave Edmunds -- American rock singer and guitarist

1946   Ted Sizemore -- Professional baseball player

1951   Heloise (Heloise B. Reese) -- American columnist specializing in household hints and information

APRIL 15 -- EVENTS

1446   Filippo Brunelleschi, the first important architect of the Italian Renaissance, died in Florence at age 69.

1764	Madame de Pompadour, mistress of King Louis XVI of France, died in Versailles at age 42.
1850	The city of San Francisco was incorporated.
1861	President Lincoln issued his first call for troops in the American Civil War.
1865	Abraham Lincoln died in Washington, D.C., at age 56, the day after he was shot by the assassin John Wilkes Booth while attending a play at Ford's Theatre.
1900	Laborers working on the Cornell Dam at Croton, N.Y., went on strike demanding a raise from their current daily wage of $1.25 to $1.50.
1912	The British liner *Titanic* sank in the early morning 2½ hours after striking an iceberg in the North Atlantic the previous night, with 1500 people losing their lives.
1920	A robbery at a shoe company in South Braintree, Mass., resulted in the deaths of two persons, and in the arrest and subsequent execution of anarchists Sacco and Vanzetti.
1940	British troops landed in Norway to try to stop the German invaders in World War II.
1945	Franklin D. Roosevelt was buried in the rose garden of his Hyde Park, N.Y., estate.
1947	Jackie Robinson, baseball's first black player, appeared in his first major league game.

APRIL 16 -- BIRTHDAYS

1319	**John II** – King of France, 1350-1364, known as "John the Good"
1646	**Jules Hardouin Mansart** -- French architect
1815	**Henry Austin Bruce Aberdare** -- British statesman
1827	**Octave Cremazie** -- Father of French-Canadian poetry, whose "Le Drapeau de Carillon" is today one of the best-loved songs of French Canada
1844	**Anatole France** – Nobel Prize-winning French novelist and author of such works as *Penguin Island, The Gods Are Athirst,* and *The Revolt of the Angels*
1850	**Herbert Baxter Adams** -- American historian and educator
1867	**Wilbur Wright** -- American inventor who with his brother Orville built and flew the world's first airplane, at Kitty Hawk, North Carolina, on December 17, 1903
1871	**John Millington Synge** -- Irish playwright noted for works such as *In the Shadow of the Glen* (1903) and *Riders to the Sea* (1904)

1880   **George A. Norton** -- American lyricist and pianist, noted for songs such as "My Melancholy Baby" and "Memphis Blues"

1885   **Leo Weiner** -- Austrian composer

1889   **Charlie Chaplin** -- Outstanding motion-picture artist and greatest film comedian of all time

1897   **Milton Cross** -- American opera commentator

1903   **Paul Waner** -- Hall of Fame baseball player who had 3152 career hits

1904   **Clifford Case** -- U.S. senator, 1955-1979

1921   **Peter Ustinov** -- English motion-picture and television actor and writer

1921   **Clark Mollenhoff** -- American journalist and author

1922   **Kingsley Amis** -- English novelist and author of *Lucky Jim* (1954)

1924   **Henry Mancini** -- American composer and conductor, noted for songs such as "Moon River," "Days of Wine and Roses," and "Two for the Road"

1929   **Edie Adams** -- American motion-picture actress

1934   **Robert Stigwood** -- Australian-born movie producer noted for works such as *Saturday Night Fever* and *Grease*

1935   **Bobby Vinton** -- American singer and musician

1940   **Margrethe II** -- Queen of Denmark

1947   **Kareem Abdul Jabbar** -- Professional basketball superstar with the most career points in NBA history (38,387 in regular season play and 5,762 in the playoffs)

1951   **Henry Childs** -- Professional football player

APRIL 16 -- EVENTS

1503   Columbus left Veragua in Central America to start his return home on his fourth and last voyage to America.

1789   President-elect George Washington left Mount Vernon, Va., for New York for his inauguration.

1828   Francisco Goya, the great Spanish painter, died in Bordeaux at age 82.

1859   Alexis de Tocqueville, French historian, died in Cannes at age 53.

1862   President Lincoln signed into law a bill ending slavery in the District of Columbia.

1916   The Chicago Cubs beat the Cincinnati Reds, 7-6, in eleven innings, in the first baseball game played in Chicago's Wrigley Field.

1917   Vladimir Lenin arrived in Petrograd from exile in Germany, receiving a hero's welcome from his Russian supporters.

1935   *Fibber McGee and Molly,* the classic radio comedy show, premiered on NBC.

1938   Britain and Italy signed an agreement recognizing Italian control of Ethiopia in return for the withdrawal from Spain of all Italian "volunteers" in the Spanish Civil War.

1940   Bob Feller pitched an opening-day no-hitter as Cleveland beat Chicago, 1 to 0.

1942   The British government presented the entire island of Malta the George Cross for the gallant deed of resisting the German attempts to take the island in World War II.

1947   A French freighter exploded at a dock in Texas City, Texas, causing one of the worst disasters in American history with thousands killed and wounded.

1972   *Apollo 16* was launched on the first manned flight to the mountains of the moon.

APRIL 17 -- BIRTHDAYS

1622   **Henry Vaughan** -- One of the leading English poets of the 1600s

1731   **G.P. Cauvet** -- French ornament designer

1741   **Samuel Chase** -- U.S. Supreme Court justice who was impeached in 1804 for malfeasance, but acquitted the following year

1806   **William Gilmore Simms** -- Outstanding Southern man of letters in the 19th century

1820   **Alexander Joy Cartwright** -- New York surveyor who designed the game of baseball almost exactly as it is played today, and who organized the New York Knickerbockers, one of the first professional teams

1837   **J.P. Morgan** -- One of the greatest financiers in the history of the United States and founder of the U.S. Steel Corporation

1851   **Cap Anson** -- One of the greatest baseball players of all time with a career total of 3524 hits, third only to Ty Cobb and Pete Rose, and a batting average of .421 in 1887

1863   **C.P. Cavafy** -- Greek poet

1870   **Ray Stannard Baker** -- American editor and historian

1880   **Sir Leonard Woolley** -- English archaeologist who excavated the ancient Sumerian city of Ur

1894   **Nikita Khrushchev** -- Premier of the Soviet Union, 1958-1964

1897	**Thornton Wilder** -- Pulitzer Prize-winning American novelist and playwright, and author of *The Bridge of San Luis Rey* and *Our Town*
1903	**Gregor Piatigorsky** -- Famous Russian-born cellist
1915	**Rebekah Harkness** -- American patroness of the dance
1916	**Sirimavo R.D. Bandaranaike** -- World's first woman prime minister, of Sri Lanka in 1960
1918	**Anne Shirley** – Child star of silent movies and a leading actress of the talkies
1918	**William Holden** – American motion-picture and television actor
1923	**Harry Reasoner** -- American television newscaster
1948	**Geoff Petrie** -- Professional basketball player
1950	**Kevin Porter** -- Professional basketball player
1951	**Delvin Williams** -- Professional football player
1951	**Pam Teeguarden** -- American tennis player
1951	**Olivia Hussey** -- Argentine-born motion-picture and television actress

APRIL 17 -- EVENTS

1524	Florentine navigator Giovanni da Verrazano discovered the Narrows and New York harbor.
1605	Leo XI was crowned Roman Catholic pope.
1790	Benjamin Franklin died in Philadelphia at age 84. About 20,000 people, almost half the population of the city, honored him at his funeral.
1860	The first world heavyweight championship bout was held at Farnesworth, N.H., between John Heenan and Tom Sayers. The crowd stopped it after 42 rounds because it was so bloody.
1861	Virginia seceded from the Union.
1895	Japan took Formosa from China in the Treaty of Shimonoseki.
1916	Congress issued a charter to the American Academy of Arts and Letters.
1929	Babe Ruth married Claire Hodgson, his second wife, in the Church of St. Gregory the Great in New York City.
1961	The Bay of Pigs invasion by Cuban exiles was crushed by Castro.

APRIL 18 -- BIRTHDAYS

1480	**Lucretia Borgia** – Italian noblewoman and central figure of the notorious Borgia family

1570   **Thomas Middleton** -- English playwright of Shakespeare's time, noted for works such as *The Honest Whore* (with Thomas Dekker) and *A Chaste Maid in Cheapside*

1819   **Franz von Suppe** -- Yugoslavian operatic composer

1857   **Clarence Darrow** -- Famous American lawyer noted for dramatic criminal trials such as the Scopes trial and the Leopold and Loeb murder trial

1864   **Richard Harding Davis** -- American author of romantic novels and the best known reporter of his time

1880   **Sam Crawford** -- Hall of Fame baseball player

1881   **Max Weber** -- Russian-born American pioneer modern painter noted for works such as *Athletic Contest* (1915)

1882   **Leopold Stokowski** – English-born American virtuoso conductor

1884   **Ludwig Meidner** -- German painter

1901   **Al Lewis** – American composer, author, and publisher, noted for songs such as "No! No! A Thousand Times No!" "Blueberry Hill," and "Rose O'Day"

1902   **Harry Owen** -- American composer and author, noted for songs such as "Sweet Leilani" and "Down Where the Tradewinds Blow"

1902   **Wynn Bullock** -- American photographer

1911   **Huntington Hartford** -- American publisher, philanthropist, and heir to the A and P fortune

1912   **Wendy Barrie** -- English stage and motion-picture actress

1917   **Frederika** -- Queen Mother of Greece

1922   **Barbara Hale** – American motion-picture and television actress noted for her role as Della Street in the long-running TV series *Perry Mason*

1936   **Don Ohl** -- Professional basketball player with over 10,000 career points

1946   **Hayley Mills** -- English motion-picture actress

1946   **Catfish Hunter** -- Professional baseball pitcher who pitched a perfect game in 1968

1947   **James Wood** -- American motion-picture and television actor

1948   **Nate Archibald** -- Professional basketball player

APRIL 18 -- EVENTS

1328   Holy Roman Emperor Louis IV proclaimed Pope John XXII deposed for heresy and "lese majesty."

1521	Martin Luther appeared before the Diet of Worms and said, in refusing to retract his teachings, "Here I stand. I can do nothing else. God help me! Amen."
1775	Paul Revere rode across the Massachusetts countryside from Charlestown to Lexington, warning the American colonists that the British were coming.
1906	The San Francisco earthquake occurred, followed by 3 days of fires. It was the greatest such disaster in U.S. history, with 700 persons killed and 497 blocks of buildings razed.
1923	Yankee Stadium officially opened before 62,281 people, the largest crowd ever to see a baseball game at that time. The Yankees beat Boston on Babe Ruth's 3-run home run.
1932	Henry Ford introduced his Ford Model B, the last of the original 4-cylinder cars.
1934	The first "Washateria" in the U.S. opened, in Fort Worth, Texas.
1942	U.S. B-25 bombers from the carrier *Hornet* under Major Jimmy Doolittle bombed Tokyo for the first time in World War II.
1945	Ernie Pyle, beloved American war correspondent, was killed by a Japanese bullet in the Ryuku Islands.
1949	The Irish Republic was proclaimed.
1953	Mickey Mantle, New York Yankee superstar, hit a 565-foot home run in Griffith Stadium in Washington, D.C., the longest home run ever measured.
1955	Albert Einstein died in Princeton, New Jersey, at age 76.
1956	Prince Rainier III of Monaco married American actress Grace Kelly in a civil ceremony. A church wedding was performed on the following day.
1981	Tom Seaver of the Cincinnati Reds, and formerly of the New York Mets, struck out his 3,000th career batter.

APRIL 19 -- BIRTHDAYS

1721	**Roger Sherman** -- The only man to sign all four of these famous documents: the Articles of Association, the Declaration of Independence, the Articles of Confederation, and the U.S. Constitution
1772	**David Ricardo** -- The leading British economist of the early 1800s
1793	**Ferdinand I** -- Austrian emperor deposed in the Revolution of 1848
1832	**Lucretia Rudolph Garfield** -- Wife of President James A. Garfield

1836   **Augustus Juilliard** — American merchant, philanthropist, and patron of music, who left his fortune to support the Juilliard School in New York City

1883   **Getulio Vargas** -- President of Brazil, 1930-1945 and 1950-1954

1887   **John Taylor Arms** -- American printmaker

1900   **Constance Talmadge** -- American actress, comedienne, and star of the silent film era

1900   **Richard Hughes** -- Welsh writer noted for novels such as *A High Wind in Jamaica* (1929)

1909   **Bucky Walters** -- Professional baseball player

1912   **Glenn Theodore Seaborg** -- American nuclear chemist

1915   **Joseph Perkins Greene** — American composer and conductor, noted for songs such as "Across the Alley from the Alamo" and the lyrics for "And Her Tears Flow'd Like Wine"

1925   **Hugh O'Brian** -- American motion-picture and television actor

1927   **Don Adams** — American motion-picture and television actor and comedian

1928   **Alexis Korner** -- French blues musician

1933   **Jayne Mansfield** -- American motion-picture actress

1933   **Dick Sargent** -- American actor

1935   **Dudley Moore** -- English actor, musician, and composer

1942   **Alan Price** — English singer and songwriter with the Animals musical group

1946   **Tim Curry** -- English stage and motion-picture actor

1948   **Rick Miller** -- Professional baseball player

1952   **Mark Van Eeghen** -- Professional football player

1956   **Sue Barker** -- English tennis player

1960   **R.J. Reynolds** -- Professional baseball player

1960   **Frank Viola** -- Professional baseball player and Cy Young Award winner in 1988

APRIL 19 -- EVENTS

1775   The American Revolution began with the Battles of Lexington and Concord.

1782   The Netherlands recognized American independence.

1783   Congress ratified the preliminary peace treaty, ending the Revolutionary War.

1824   George Gordon, Lord Byron, the great English poet, died of fever at Missolonghi, Greece, at age 36.

| 1827 | Rene Caillie, French African explorer, began his trek to Timbuktu. |

1827 Rene Caillie, French African explorer, began his trek to Timbuktu.

1865 Funeral services were conducted in the East Room of the White House for Abraham Lincoln.

1891 Herman Melville, the great American writer, finished his novel *Billy Budd.* "End of Book, April 19, 1891," was on the last page of the manuscript, discovered 28 years later.

1898 The U.S. Congress passed a resolution asserting that Cuba was independent of Spain.

1933 The U.S. abandoned the gold standard by proclamation of President Franklin D. Roosevelt.

1943 Thousands of Jews living in the Warsaw ghetto began their famous fight against Nazi occupation in World War II.

1945 *Carousel,* the noted Rodgers and Hammerstein musical, opened on Broadway.

1951 General MacArthur, addressing Congress after being fired by President Truman, said, "Old soldiers never die; they just fade away."

1981 The Oakland A's won their eleventh straight game at the beginning of the season, a major league record at the time. The Atlanta Braves broke the record the following year.

APRIL 20 -- BIRTHDAYS

1492 **Pietro Aretino** -- Italian poet and writer noted for his attacks on the powerful

1494 **Johannes Agricola** -- Lutheran reformer and advocate of antinomianism

1745 **Philippe Pinel** -- French physician and pioneer in the movement for humane treatment for the mentally ill, whose theories became the basis for Freud's psychoanalytic treatment

1805 **Franz Xaver Winterhalter** -- German painter

1808 **Napoleon III** -- Emperor of the French, 1852-1870, and the last member of Napoleon Bonaparte's family to rule France

1850 **Daniel C. French** -- American sculptor noted for the statue of Abraham Lincoln in the Lincoln Memorial in Washington, D.C.

1860 **Charles Gordon Curtis** -- American inventor who developed the modern steam turbine in the early 1900s, which revolutionized power production

1871 **William Henry Davies** -- English poet

1889 **Adolf Hitler** -- Nazi dictator of Germany, 1933-1945

1893   **Harold Lloyd** -- American motion-picture actor and one of the kings of comedy

1893   **Joan Miro** -- Spanish artist and a leader of the Surrealist movement

1898   **Harvey Firestone Jr.** -- President of Firestone Tire and Rubber Company

1905   **Stanley Marcus** -- "Merchant Prince of Dallas" and son of the founder of the Neiman-Marcus stores

1910   **Robert F. Wagner** -- Mayor of New York City, 1954-1965

1920   **John Paul Stevens** -- U.S. Supreme Court justice

1923   **Tito Puente** -- American bandleader, composer, and percussionist

1924   **Nina Foch** -- Dutch-born motion-picture and television actress

1927   **Phil Hill** -- American automobile racing driver

1941   **Ryan O'Neal** -- American motion-picture and television actor

1945   **Steve Spurrier** -- Professional football player

1949   **Jessica Lange** -- American motion-picture actress

1961   **Don Mattingly** -- Professional baseball player

APRIL 20 -- EVENTS

1534   Jacques Cartier left France on instructions of French king Francis I to explore and claim Canada for France and to find a new sailing route to China.

1653   The Rump Parliament was dissolved by Oliver Cromwell, who entered it at the head of a troop of soldiers.

1812   Vice President George Clinton died in Washington at the age of 73--the first vice president to die in office.

1828   Rene Caillie, French African explorer, arrived in Timbuktu after a long trek across the Sahara Desert.

1861   Robert E. Lee resigned his commission in the U.S. Army in order to join the Confederate forces.

1898   Marie and Pierre Curie discovered the element radium.

1903   Andrew Carnegie presented $ 1.5 million for the construction of the Hague Peace Palace.

1934   Shirley Temple began her career as a child movie star in the film *Stand Up and Cheer.*

1945   The U.S. 7th Army captured the German city of Nuremberg in World War II.

1948   Walter Reuther, president of the United Automobile Workers, was seriously wounded by an unknown assailant with a shotgun.

1962	Russia and China signed a pact of friendship.
1971	The U.S. Supreme Court upheld the use of busing to achieve racial desegregation in the schools.
1972	The U.S. lunar module of *Apollo 16* landed on the moon with astronauts John Young and Charles Duke aboard, while Thomas Mattingly remained in the command module.

APRIL 21 -- BIRTHDAYS

1555	Lodovico Carracci -- Italian painter
1671	John Law — Scottish financier and gambler, noted for the "Mississippi Scheme," a land speculation deal in colonial Louisiana
1696	Francesco de Mura -- Italian painter
1782	Friedrich Froebel -- German educator who founded the kindergarten system in 1837
1816	Charlotte Bronte — English novelist whose most famous work, *Jane Eyre,* is one of the great works of world literature
1818	Josh Billings -- American humorist and cracker-barrel philosopher
1828	Hippolyte Taine — French historian, critic, and writer, who greatly influenced the naturalist movement in literature
1838	John Muir -- Scottish-born American naturalist, explorer, writer, and great national park advocate
1846	William Henry Goodyear — American art historian and archaeologist and son of Charles Goodyear, the discoverer of the process of vulcanizing rubber
1857	Paul Dresser -- American composer noted for songs such as "My Gal Sal" and "On the Banks of the Wabash"
1864	Max Weber — German sociologist and political economist, and one of the founders of modern sociology
1869	Edwin S. Porter -- American motion-picture pioneer director and the most prominent innovator in American cinema during its beginning years
1887	Joe McCarthy -- One of the greatest professional baseball managers and winner of 7 world series
1898	Steve Owen -- Professional football player and coach
1899	Randall Thompson -- American composer
1905	Edmund "Pat" Brown -- Governor of California, 1958-1966
1909	Rollo May -- American psychologist and author
1916	Anthony Quinn — Mexican-born stage, screen, and television actor

1926   Elizabeth II -- Queen of Great Britain and head of the British Commonwealth of Nations

1932   Elaine May -- American comedienne, screenwriter, and director

1935   Charles Grodin -- American motion-picture and television actor

1941   David Boren -- U.S. senator

1947   Al Bumbry -- Professional baseball player

1949   Patti LuPone -- American stage, screen, and television actress, who received a Tony Award for her title role in the Broadway musical *Evita* (1979)

1951   Tony Danza -- American motion-picture and television actor

1957   Jesse Orosco -- Professional baseball player

APRIL 21 -- EVENTS

753 BC Rome was founded, according to tradition.

1699   Jean Racine, the great French playwright, died at Port-Royal at age 59.

1836   The Texans under General Sam Houston defeated the Mexicans at the Battle of San Jacinto, ending the Texas war of independence.

1910   Mark Twain died in Redding, Connecticut, at age 74.

1918   Manfred von Richthofen, Germany's Red Baron ace flyer, was shot down and killed in World War I.

1924   The comic strip, *Wash Tubbs,* by Roy Crane, first appeared.

1960   Brasilia became the new capital of Brazil, replacing Rio de Janeiro.

APRIL 22 -- BIRTHDAYS

1451   Isabella I -- Queen of Castile and Aragon, and sponsor of Columbus in his discovery of America

1707   Henry Fielding -- English novelist, playwright, and author of *The History of Tom Jones, a Foundling,* one of the world's great novels

1711   Eleazar Wheelock -- Founder and first president of Dartmouth College

1722   Christopher Smart -- English poet

1724   Immanuel Kant -- One of the greatest philosophers of all time, and author of the *Critique of Pure Reason*

1766   Madame de Stael -- French political propagandist, conversationalist, and woman of letters

1840   Odilon Redon -- French artist

1866	Hans von Seeckt -- German general and head of the Reichswehr, 1920-1926
1870	**Vladimir I. Lenin** -- Founder of the Russian Communist Party and leader of the Bolshevik Revolution in 1917
1874	**Ellen Glasgow** -- American novelist and author of such works as *Barren Ground* and the Pulitzer Prize-winning *In This Our Life*
1876	**Ole Rolvaag** -- Norwegian-American novelist and author of *Giants in the Earth*
1881	**Alexander Kerensky** -- Premier of the first Russian government after the overthrow of the czar in 1917
1904	**J. Robert Oppenheimer** -- American physicist known as the man who built the atomic bomb
1908	**Eddie Albert** -- American motion-picture and television actor
1916	**Yehudi Menuhin** -- American violin virtuoso
1918	**Mickey Vernon** -- Professional baseball player
1937	**Jack Nicholson** -- American motion-picture actor and superstar
1938	**Deane Beman** -- Professional golfer
1938	**Glen Campbell** -- American musician, singer, and television entertainer
1949	**Spencer Haywood** -- Professional basketball player
1950	**Peter Frampton** -- British singer and guitarist
1959	**Freeman McNeil** -- Professional football player

APRIL 22 -- EVENTS

960 AD	Basil II was crowned Emperor of the Byzantine Empire.
1445	King Henry VI of England married Margaret of Anjou.
1500	Pedro Alvares Cabral, Portuguese explorer, discovered Brazil.
1509	Henry VII of England died at age 52, and was immediately succeeded by his 17-year-old son Henry VIII.
1836	Texas was granted its independence from Mexico.
1864	Congress authorized the U.S. Mint to use the motto, "In God We Trust," on all coins.
1876	Boston beat Philadelphia, 6-5, in the first National League baseball game.
1889	The Oklahoma Land Rush began when Oklahoma was officially opened for settlement at noon. By evening over 50,000 people had moved in.
1915	The Germans became the first nation to use poison gas in warfare, in the Second Battle of Ypres in World War I.
1944	Allied soldiers invaded New Guinea in World War II.

1945   Russian troops entered Berlin, the first Allied soldiers to do so, in World War II.

1954   The Senate Army-McCarthy hearings began and were shown on television.

APRIL 23 -- BIRTHDAYS

1484   **Julius Caesar Scaliger** -- French classical scholar and botanist

1500   **Johannes Stumpf** -- One of the most important theologians of the Swiss Protestant Reformation

1564   **William Shakespeare** -- The greatest writer of all time

1775   **Joseph M.W. Turner** -- English artist, who ranks with John Constable as one of the two greatest English landscape painters

1791   **James Buchanan** -- Fifteenth U.S. president

1813   **Stephen A. Douglas** -- American political leader and orator, who participated with Abraham Lincoln in the Lincoln-Douglas debates in 1858

1818   **James Anthony Froude** – English historian, biographer, and essayist, who wrote the 12-volume *History of England* (1856-1870)

1852   **Edwin Markham** – American poet and lecturer, best known for "The Man with the Hoe" (1899)

1858   **Max Planck** – German theoretical physicist, whose law of radiation laid the foundation for the quantum theory, and for whom Planck's constant was named

1891   **Sergei Prokofiev** -- Important Russian composer, best known perhaps for *Peter and the Wolf* (1936)

1897   **Lucius D. Clay** -- U.S. World War II general and director of the Berlin Airlift in 1948

1897   **Lester B. Pearson** -- Prime minister of Canada, 1963-1968

1899   **Vladimir Nabokov** – Russian-born novelist and author of *Lolita* (1955)

1899   **Ngaio Marsh** -- New Zealand theatrical producer and prolific mystery story writer

1900   **Jim Bottomley** -- Hall of Fame baseball player and manager

1904   **Duncan Renaldo** -- American motion-picture and television actor

1907   **Dolf Camilli** -- Professional baseball player

1921   **Janet Blair** -- American motion-picture actress and singer

1921   **Warren Spahn** -- Winningest left-handed pitcher in baseball history with 363 career victories

1926	**J.P. Donleavy** -- American-born Irish novelist
1928	**Shirley Temple (Black)** -- Most successful child movie star in Hollywood history
1932	**Halston (Roy Halston Frowick)** -- American fashion designer
1932	**Jim Fixx** -- American writer, editor, and author of a best-selling book on running to keep fit
1936	**Roy Orbison** -- American rockabilly singer
1937	**Don Massengale** -- Professional golfer
1940	**David Birney** -- American television actor
1942	**Sandra Dee** -- American motion-picture and television actress
1942	**Lee Majors** -- American motion-picture and television actor
1943	**Tony Esposito** -- Professional hockey player and one of the leading goalkeepers of the 1970s
1943	**Gail Goodrich** -- Professional basketball player
1944	**Marty Fleckman** -- Professional golfer
1947	**Bernadette Devlin** -- Irish civil rights worker
1948	**Vladimir Korotkov** -- Russian tennis player
1949	**Joyce De Witt** -- American actress
1950	**Joe Ferguson Jr.** -- Professional football player
1960	**Valerie Bertinelli** -- American television actress

APRIL 23 -- EVENTS

1016	Edmund Ironside succeeded his father Ethelred the Unready as king of England.
1349	King Edward III of England instituted the Order of the Garter.
1616	Miguel de Cervantes, the great Spanish novelist, died in Madrid at age 68.
1616	William Shakespeare died in Stratford-upon-Avon on his 52nd birthday.
1789	President-elect and Mrs. George Washington moved into the first "Presidential Mansion" at the corner of Franklin and Cherry Streets in New York City.
1850	William Wordsworth, the great English poet, died at Rydal Mount at age 80.
1896	Thomas A. Edison presented the first public showing of a motion picture in the United States, at Koster and Bial's Music Hall in New York City.
1946	Ed Head pitched a no-hitter as Brooklyn beat Boston, 5-0.

1964   Ken Johnson pitched a no-hitter but lost as Cincinnati beat Houston, 1-0.

1968   The United Methodist Church was formed as a merger of the Methodist Church and the Evangelical United Brethren Church in a ceremony in Dallas.

1969   Sirhan Sirhan was sentenced to death for the murder of Senator Robert F. Kennedy. The sentence later was reduced to life imprisonment.

APRIL 24 -- BIRTHDAYS

1743   **Edmund Cartwright** -- English inventor and clergyman, who invented a wool combing machine and a steam-powered loom for weaving cotton

1750   **John Trumbull** -- American poet and jurist, noted for works such as "The Progress of Dulness," a poetic satire of college education

1766   **Robert Bailey Thomas** -- American printer who in 1792 founded the *Farmer's Almanac*

1796   **Karl Leberecht Immerman** -- German poet

1815   **Anthony Trollope** -- English novelist and author of *The Warden* (1855) and *Barchester Towers* (1857)

1856   **Henri Philippe Petain** -- French World War I hero discredited in World War II as a Nazi collaborator

1882   **Tony Sarg** -- German puppet maker and showman, whose famous production, *The Rose and the Ring,* helped revive puppetry in the United States

1889   **Sir Stafford Cripps** -- British World War II statesman about whom Churchill said, "There but for the grace of God goes God."

1893   **Leslie Howard** -- English stage and screen actor

1894   **Howard Ehmke** -- Professional baseball player

1904   **Willem de Kooning** -- Dutch-born abstract expressionist artist, noted for his hectic and violent paintings and swirling patterns

1905   **Robert Penn Warren** -- American writer and Pulitzer Prize-winning author of *All the King's Men*

1934   **Shirley MacLaine** -- American stage and motion-picture actress and sister of actor Warren Beatty

1936   **Jill Ireland** -- English motion-picture actress

1942   **Barbra Streisand** -- American singer and actress

1944   **Bill Singer** -- Professional baseball player

1949   **Bob Chandler** -- Professional football player
1954   **Vince Ferragamo** -- Professional football player

APRIL 24 -- EVENTS

858 AD Nicholas I (the Great) was elected Roman Catholic pope.
1585   Sixtus V was elected Roman Catholic pope.
1792   "La Marseillaise," the French national anthem, was composed by French army officer Claude Joseph Rouget de Lisle.
1800   The Library of Congress was established with an appropriation of $5000 and Thomas Jefferson's entire private library.
1814   The British burned Washington, D.C., in the War of 1812.
1898   Spain declared war on the United States after rejecting America's ultimatum to withdraw from Cuba.
1945   Former senator A.B. "Happy" Chandler of Kentucky was elected baseball commissioner.
1947   Willa Cather, the American novelist, died at age 70.
1953   Winston Churchill was knighted by Queen Elizabeth II. He was made a knight of the Order of the Garter, Britain's highest order of knighthood.

APRIL 25 -- BIRTHDAYS

1214   **Louis IX (Saint Louis)** -- King of France, 1227-1270, noted for his fairness to all his subjects
1284   **Edward II** -- King of England, 1307-1327
1533   **William I (the Silent)** -- Prince of Orange and father of the Dutch Republic
1599   **Oliver Cromwell** -- British soldier and statesman of the English Civil War, and ruler of England, 1649-1658
1652   **Giovanni Battista Foggini** -- Italian sculptor
1792   **John Keble** -- English divine and poet who started the Oxford Movement, a revival in the Church of England in 1833
1822   **James Pierpont** -- American composer noted for "Jingle Bells" (1850), one of the two or three most popular songs ever written
1873   **Howard R. Garis** -- Creator of *Uncle Wiggly*
1873   **Walter De la Mare** -- English poet and novelist, noted for his poetry of childhood and for his novel, *Memoirs of a Midget*
1874   **Guglielmo Marconi** -- Italian physicist and one of the chief developers of the radio

1891   Sid Richardson -- American oil executive
1898   Fred Haney -- Professional baseball player and manager
1900   Wolfgang Pauli -- Austrian physicist and discoverer of the "Pauli exclusion principle" of electron position in an atom
1904   Georges Schreiber -- Belgian artist
1906   William J. Brennan Jr. -- U.S. Supreme Court justice
1908   Edward R. Murrow -- American broadcast journalist of the 1940s and 1950s
1910   Joseph Hirsch -- American artist
1914   Marcos Perez Jimenez -- President of Venezuela, 1952-1958
1914   Bob Russell -- American composer and author, noted for lyrics such as "No Other Love," "Frenesi," "Maria Elena," "Brazil," "Do Nothin' Till You Hear From Me," and "Ballerina"
1916   Jerry Barber -- Professional golfer
1918   Ella Fitzgerald -- American singer
1923   Albert King -- American blues singer and guitarist
1923   Arnold Miller -- President of the United Mine Workers
1928   Melissa Hayden -- Canadian ballerina
1932   Meadowlark Lemon -- One of the top stars of the Harlem Globetrotters basketball team
1940   Al Pacino -- American motion-picture actor
1946   Talia Shire -- American motion-picture actress
1955   Christopher Mottram -- English tennis player

APRIL 25 -- EVENTS

404 BC Athens surrendered to Sparta, ending the Peloponnesian War.
1507   "America" was first used for the New World in Martin Waldseemuller's geography book, *Cosmographiae Introductio.*
1719   The first edition of Daniel Defoe's *Robinson Crusoe* was published.
1792   Nicolas-Jacques Pelletier, a highwayman, became the first person under French law to be executed by the guillotine.
1846   Mexican troops crossed the Rio Grande and attacked a small U.S. cavalry group, giving President Polk the opportunity to declare war. War was declared on May 13, 1846.
1859   Construction began on the Suez Canal.
1898   The United States declared war on Spain, beginning the Spanish-American War.

1901 New York became the first state to require automobile license plates. The tax was one dollar.

1915 Allied troops landed on the Gallipoli Peninsula in World War I.

1945 A conference of delegates from 50 countries met in San Francisco to organize the United Nations.

1945 American and Russian troops joined forces at Torgau, on the Elbe, cutting Germany in two in World War II.

1945 Benito Mussolini and his mistress, Clara Petacci, escaped from Milan as U.S. troops entered the city in World War II.

1959 The St. Lawrence Seaway was opened to traffic.

1962 *Ranger 4* became the first U.S. space probe to strike the moon.

1980 The mission to rescue the 52 American hostages in Iran failed because of malfunctioning helicopters.

APRIL 26 -- BIRTHDAYS

121 AD **Marcus Aurelius** -- Roman Emperor, A.D. 161-180, noted also for his philosophy, contained in his diary, *Meditations*

1228 **Conrad I** -- King of Germany

1573 **Marie de Medicis** -- Queen consort of King Henry IV of France

1718 **Esek Hopkins** -- First Commodore of the U.S. Navy and the commander of the Continental Navy from 1775-1778

1785 **John James Audubon** -- American naturalist and artist, and one of the first to study and paint the birds of the United States

1787 **Ludwig Uhland** -- German poet

1798 **Eugene Delacroix** -- The leader of the Romantic movement in French painting

1812 **Baron Friedrich von Flotow** -- German composer

1812 **Alfred Krupp** -- German industrialist who developed the Krupp Works in Essen from a firm with four workers to one with 20,000

1822 **Frederick Law Olmsted** -- American landscape architect, who helped design New York's Central Park, the first great American park

1834 **Artemus Ward** -- American humorist and contemporary of Abraham Lincoln

1875 **Syngman Rhee** -- President of South Korea, 1948-1960

1877 **Sir Alliott Verdon-Roe** -- First Englishman to design, build, and fly an airplane

1891 **Paul G. Hoffman** -- American industrialist and statesman

1893 **Anita Loos** -- American screenwriter, playwright, and novelist, best known for *Gentlemen Prefer Blondes* (1925)

1894   **Rudolf Hess** -- Adolf Hitler's deputy party leader, who flew to Scotland during World War II to persuade Great Britain to get out of the war

1899   **Guinn "Big Boy" Williams** -- American motion-picture actor, who appeared in numerous supporting roles with Tom Mix, Harry Carey, and Roy Rogers

1900   **Hack Wilson** -- Hall of Fame baseball player who in 1930 hit 58 home runs and drove in a record 190 runs

1900   **Charles Richter** -- American geophysicist and developer of the Richter scale for measuring earthquake intensities

1914   **Bernard Malamud** -- American novelist and short story writer noted for works such as *The Natural* (1952)

1914   **Paul Norris** -- American cartoonist and creator of *Power Nelson, Futureman* and *Yank and Doodle*

1916   **Morris West** -- Australian novelist

1917   **Sal Maglie** -- Professional baseball player

1919   **Virgil Trucks** -- Professional baseball pitcher who pitched two no-hit games in 1952

1927   **Granny Hamner** -- Professional baseball player

1933   **Carol Burnett** -- American television and motion-picture comedienne and actress

1937   **Bob Boozer** -- Professional basketball player

1944   **Martha Rockwell** -- Professional skier

1947   **Amos Otis** -- Professional baseball player

1955   **Mike Scott** -- Professional baseball player

1960   **Roger Taylor** -- Drummer with the Duran Duran musical group

APRIL 26 -- EVENTS

1564   William Shakespeare was baptized at Stratford-on-Avon in the parish church.

1607   John Smith and his colonists reached the Chesapeake Capes after 18 weeks at sea. Eighteen days later they landed at the site they called Jamestown after King James I.

1731   Daniel Defoe, English novelist and author of the famous adventure story, *Robinson Crusoe,* died in London at age 70.

1768   England's Royal Academy opened its first art exhibit.

1865   John Wilkes Booth, assassin of Abraham Lincoln, was caught and killed by federal troops near Port Royal, Virginia.

1865   Mrs. Sue Landon Vaughn led a group to decorate Confederate graves in Vicksburg, Miss., causing the day to be celebrated as Confederate Memorial Day.

1910   President William Howard Taft dedicated the Pan-American Union building in Washington, D.C.

1937   Nazi planes annihilated the defenseless Basque town of Guernica in the Spanish Civil War, making Guernica a symbol of antifascism and inspiring Pablo Picasso's famous painting.

1954   A nationwide test of the new Salk anti-polio vaccine began in 45 states.

1965   The African nations of Tanganyika and Zanzibar merged to form Tanzania.

1983   The Dow-Jones industrial average closed above 1,200 for the first time in history.

1986   A power plant reactor caught fire at Chernobyl, near the Soviet city of Kiev, leading to a meltdown and the worst nuclear accident in world history.

APRIL 27 -- BIRTHDAYS

1759   **Mary** Wollstonecraft **Godwin** -- English writer noted for her book, *A Vindication of the Rights of Women* (1792)

1791   **Samuel F.B. Morse** -- Inventor of the electric telegraph and the Morse code

1820   **Herbert Spencer** -- English philosopher and early evolutionist

1822   **Ulysses S. Grant** -- U.S. Civil War general and 18th president

1840   **Edward Whymper** -- First man to climb the Matterhorn, in 1865

1896   **Rogers Hornsby** -- Hall of Fame baseball player and greatest right-handed hitter of all time, with a .358 lifetime batting average

1898   **Ludwig Bemelmans** -- American humorous writer and painter, who wrote and illustrated books for children and adults

1900   **Walter Lantz** -- American animator and cartoon film producer noted especially for his creation of Woody Woodpecker

1904   **Arthur Burns** -- American economist and chairman of the Federal Reserve System

1913   **Philip Hauge Abelson** -- Noted American physical chemist

1916   **Enos Slaughter** -- Professional baseball player

1918   **John Scali** -- American journalist and diplomat

1922   **Jack Klugman** -- American motion-picture and television actor

1927	**Coretta Scott King** — Wife of civil rights leader Martin Luther King Jr.

1927   **Coretta Scott King** — Wife of civil rights leader Martin Luther King Jr.

1931   **Igor Oistrakh** -- Russian-born virtuoso violinist

1932   **Anouk Aimee** -- French motion-picture actress

1937   **Sandy Dennis** -- American motion-picture actress

1938   **Earl Anthony** -- American bowler, who was Bowler of the Year in 1974, 1975, and 1976

1941   **Judith Blegen** -- American operatic soprano

1948   **Georges Goven** -- French tennis player

1949   **Guy Walkingstick** -- Professional golfer

1951   **Gary Huff** -- Professional football player

1952   **George Gervin** -- Professional basketball player

1957   **Willie Upshaw** -- Professional baseball player

1967   **Prince Willem Alexander** -- First male heir to the Dutch throne in three generations

APRIL 27 -- EVENTS

1296   Edward I of England defeated the Scots in the Battle of Dunbar, enabling him to seize the Stone of Scone, the symbol of Scottish authority, and make himself king of Scotland.

1509   The city of Venice was excommunicated by Pope Julius II.

1521   Spanish navigator Ferdinand Magellan was killed by tribesmen on the island of Mactan in the Philippines. His crew later completed the first trip around the world.

1667   The great English poet John Milton sold his *Paradise Lost* copyright for 10 English pounds.

1777   Benedict Arnold defeated the British at Ridgefield, Conn., in the American Revolutionary War.

1814   Napoleon was made King of Elba, a tiny island off the coast of Italy, where he supposedly was exiled.

1867   Pi Beta Phi, the first national fraternity for women, was founded at Monmouth College, Monmouth, Illinois.

1882   Ralph Waldo Emerson, the great American philosopher, died in Concord, Massachusetts, at age 78.

1941   German troops occupied Athens in World War II.

1947   "Babe Ruth Day" was observed throughout the United States, honoring the seriously ill Babe, who died a year later.

1958   The comic strip, *Rick O'Shay,* by Stan Lynde, first appeared.

1965   The noted broadcast journalist Edward R. Murrow died in Pawling, New York, at the age of 57.

1968   Jimmy Ellis beat Jerry Quarry in a 15 round decision in Oakland, California, to become heavyweight champion.

APRIL 28 -- BIRTHDAYS

32 AD   **Marcus Salvius Otho** -- Emperor of Rome for less than a year, A.D. 69

1442   **Edward IV** -- King of England, 1461-1469 and 1471-1483

1753   **Franz Achard** -- Discoverer in 1793 of beet sugar extraction

1758   **James Monroe** -- Fifth U.S. president

1874   **Sidney Toler** -- American stage and motion-picture actor, who played the title role of the *Charlie Chan* movie series

1878   **Lionel Barrymore** -- American stage, radio, and screen actor, and member of the famous Barrymore family of actors

1889   **Antonio de Oliveira Salazar** -- Dictator of Portugal, 1932-1968

1892   **John Jacob Niles** -- American folksinger

1897   **Felix Bernard** -- American composer noted for songs such as "Dardanella," "I'd Rather Be Me," and "Winter Wonderland"

1917   **Robert Anderson** -- American playwright noted for works such as *Tea and Sympathy* and *I Never Sang for My Father*

1921   **Rowland Evans Jr.** -- Member of the Evans and Novak team of political columnists

1921   **Karl Suessdorf** -- American composer and author, noted for songs such as "Moonlight in Vermont," "Key Largo," and "The Good Humor Man"

1924   **Kenneth Kaunda** -- Zambian patriot who led the British colony of Northern Rhodesia to independence in 1964 as the Republic of Zambia, and became its first president

1926   **Harper Lee** -- American author who won the Pulitzer Prize for her novel, *To Kill a Mockingbird* (1960)

1930   **James A. Baker** -- White House Chief of Staff and Secretary of the Treasury under President Reagan and Secretary of State under President Bush

1933   **Carolyn Jones** -- American motion-picture and television actress

1941   **Ann-Margret (Olsson)** -- Swedish-born motion-picture and television actress

1943   **Ivan Nagy** -- Hungarian ballet dancer

1950   **Jay Leno** -- American comedian and actor

APRIL 28 -- EVENTS

1429   The forces of Joan of Arc entered Orleans in the Hundred Years' War. Orleans was captured from the English five days later.

1521   Hernando Cortes, the Spanish conquistador, began a 75-day siege of Tenochtitlan, the Aztec city on the site of modern Mexico City.

1788   Maryland became the seventh state of the Union.

1789   The sailors mutinied on the British ship *Bounty* and cast Captain Bligh adrift in a small boat with 18 of his men.

1881   Billy the Kid, the notorious Western outlaw, killed two deputies and escaped from jail, where he was waiting to be hanged.

1945   Benito Mussolini and his mistress Clara Petacci were shot at Lake Como by Italian partisans, and their bodies were taken to Milan and later hung by the heels in front of a garage.

1947   Thor Heyerdahl's *Kon-Tiki* was towed out to sea from Peru in preparation for its departure for Polynesia.

1952   World War II officially ended between the United States and Japan with a treaty signed in San Francisco.

1969   Charles de Gaulle resigned as president of France.

1988   The Baltimore Orioles lost their 21st straight game, giving them a 0-21 record, the worst start in baseball history.

APRIL 29 -- BIRTHDAYS

1745   **Oliver Ellsworth** -- Third chief justice of the U.S Supreme Court (1796-1800)

1792   **Matthew Vassar** -- American brewer who founded Vassar College

1818   **Alexander II** -- Czar of Russia, 1855-1881, who liberated the serfs in 1861

1837   **Georges Boulanger** -- French general, minister, and politician

1854   **Henri Poincare** -- French mathematician, noted as one of the greatest of modern times

1860   **Lorado Taft** -- American sculptor noted for *The Spirit of the Great Lakes* at the Art Institute of Chicago

1863   **William Randolph Hearst** -- U.S. newspaper publisher and founder of the Hearst chain

1879   **Sir Thomas Beecham** -- Internationally acclaimed British conductor

1893   Harold Urey – American physicist and discoverer of deuterium

1899   Duke Ellington – American composer and jazz orchestra leader

1901   Hirohito -- Emperor of Japan

1904   Fletcher Martin -- American artist

1904   Russ Morgan -- American composer and bandleader, noted for songs such as "Please Think of Me," "Somebody Else Is Taking My Place," and his theme song, "Does Your Heart Beat for Me?"

1907   Fred Zinnemann -- American motion-picture director noted for works such as *High Noon, From Here to Eternity,* and *A Man for All Seasons*

1909   Tom Ewell -- American motion-picture and television actor

1912   Richard Carlson -- American motion-picture and television actor

1915   Donald Mills -- American singer and member of the Mills Brothers group

1919   Celeste Holm -- American stage, screen, and television actress

1922   George Allen -- Professional football player and coach

1933   Rod McKuen -- American poet and author, noted for songs for films, television, operas, and ballets

1934   Luis Aparicio -- Hall of Fame baseball player

1936   Zubin Mehta -- Indian symphony orchestra conductor

1944   Jim Hart -- Professional football player

1947   Johnny Miller -- Professional golfer

1947   Jim Ryun -- American runner who ran the mile in 3:51.1

1948   James Otis -- Professional football player

1966   Ed Correa -- Professional baseball player

1970   Andre Agassi -- American tennis player

APRIL 29 -- EVENTS

1770   Captain James Cook discovered Botany Bay in Australia.

1862   A Union fleet under Admiral Farragut captured New Orleans in the Civil War.

1894   Coxey's Army, with Jacob S. Coxey at its head, arrived in Washington, D.C., to petition Congress for relief legislation.

1900   Casey Jones brought his Illinois Central *Cannonball* into Memphis the night before the famous wreck.

1913   Gideon Sundback of Hoboken, New Jersey, patented the zipper under the name "separable fastener."

1945   Adolf Hitler and Eva Braun were married in an underground
        bunker in Berlin, one day before committing suicide.

1945   The bodies of Benito Mussolini and his mistress Clara Petacci
        were hung up by the heels and displayed to the populace in
        Milan, Italy.

1945   American soldiers in World War II liberated 32,000 prisoners in
        the notorious Nazi concentration camp in Dachau, Germany,
        where untold thousands of victims had been killed.

1947   Thor Heyerdahl, the Norwegian scientist, left Peru on his raft
        Kon-Tiki to test the theory that pre-Incan Indians had drifted
        across the ocean to colonize Polynesia.

1974   President Richard Nixon announced the release of transcripts of
        the Watergate tapes. The transcripts, though edited, were
        damaging enough to help destroy his presidency.

1981   Steve Carlton, Philadelphia Phillies' pitcher, struck out his 3,000th
        career batter.

1986   Roger Clemens of the Boston Red Sox struck out a record 20
        batters in a 9-inning game, as Boston beat Seattle, 3-1.

APRIL 30 -- BIRTHDAYS

1309   **Casimir III (the Great)** -- King of Poland, 1333-1370, who
        established the first system of laws in Europe

1504   **Francesco Primaticcio** -- Italian painter

1662   **Mary II** – Queen of England, 1689-1694, who with her husband
        ruled as William and Mary following the Glorious Revolution of
        1688

1777   **Karl Friedrich Gauss** – Perhaps the greatest mathematician of
        all time

1823   **Henry Oscar Houghton** -- American publisher who in 1864
        founded Hurd and Houghton, which later became Houghton
        Mifflin Company

1845   **Martins Joaquin Pedro de Oliveira** -- Portuguese writer

1870   **Franz Lehar** -- Hungarian composer of light operas, noted for
        such lilting music as *The Merry Widow Waltz*

1877   **Alice B. Toklas** -- Companion and secretary of writer Gertrude
        Stein

1893   **Joachim von Ribbentrop** -- Adolf Hitler's top diplomatic figure

1904   **John T. Benson Jr.** -- American composer noted for "Love
        Lifted Me"

1909   **Juliana** -- Queen of the Netherlands, 1948-1980

1912   **Eve Arden** -- American motion-picture, television, and radio actress and comedienne noted for the title role in the long-running radio series *Our Miss Brooks*

1916   **Robert Shaw** -- American choral conductor and one of the most outstanding of his time

1918   **Donald McNeill** -- American Hall of Fame tennis player

1924   **Sheldon Harnick** -- American popular songwriter

1925   **Corinne Calvet** -- French motion-picture actress

1926   **Cloris Leachman** -- American stage, motion-picture, and television actress

1933   **Willie Nelson** -- American country singer and composer

1944   **Jill Clayburgh** -- American stage and screen actress

1946   **Donald Schollander** -- American swimmer who set the 200-meter freestyle record of 1 minute 54.3 seconds in 1968

1949   **Karl Meiler** -- West German tennis player

1961   **Isiah Thomas** -- Professional basketball player

APRIL 30 -- EVENTS

1380   Saint Catherine of Siena, patron saint of nurses, died in Rome at age 33.

1789   George Washington was inaugurated in New York City as the first president of the United States.

1803   The Louisiana Purchase was completed from France by the United States. The treaty was signed by both countries two days later.

1812   Louisiana was admitted to the Union as the 18th state.

1879   Sarah Josepha Hale, author of "Mary Had a Little Lamb," died at age 91.

1883   Edouard Manet, the great French impressionist painter, died in Paris at age 51.

1900   Casey Jones, the "brave engineer" of the famous folk song, was killed at Vaughan, Mississippi, when his Engine 382 collided with a freight train.

1939   The National Broadcasting Company (NBC) began regular television broadcasts.

1945   Adolf Hitler committed suicide in a bunker 30 feet below the ruins of the Reich Chancellery in Berlin at age 56. Shortly afterwards the Russians captured the city.

1961   Willie Mays of the San Francisco Giants hit four home runs in a single baseball game.

1970   President Nixon announced the invasion of Cambodia by U.S. forces in Vietnam, for the purpose of clearing out sanctuaries used by the North Vietnamese.

1973   President Nixon announced the resignation of H.R. Haldeman, John Ehrlichman, and Richard Kleindienst, and the firing of John Dean, because of the Watergate scandals.

1974   The White House released edited transcripts of the Watergate tapes, creating shock, dismay, and outrage in Congress and among the people.

1975   The South Vietnamese capital of Saigon fell to Communist forces, as the Vietnam War ended in the unconditional surrender of South Vietnam.

1980   Beatrix became Queen of the Netherlands, succeeding her mother, Juliana, who abdicated in her favor.

5

May

May, the fifth month, was the third month in the early Roman calendar, and it gets its name from the Latin *Maius*, the origin of which is debatable. The most widely accepted story is that the name honored Maia, the Roman goddess of spring and growth, and the mother of Mercury. Many scholars maintain that May was named in tribute to the *majores*, the Latin word for "older men." Thus May would be the month sacred to the majores, as June is to the *juniores* ("younger men"). May was one of the four named months of the calendar of Romulus, at which time it had 30 days, but since then it has always had 31 days.

May Day (May 1) is a special day observed as a festival of spring in many countries. For the ancient Romans it was sacred to Flora, the goddess of flowers, and they celebrated the day with flower-decked parades. In the United States, May 1 is celebrated as Law Day. Other special days of May are Mother's Day, the second Sunday of the month, Armed Forces Day, the third Saturday of the month, and Memorial Day, a legal holiday on the last Monday in May honoring those who died in America's wars. Also, the most famous horse race in the United States, the Kentucky Derby, takes place on the first Saturday of May at Churchill Downs in Louisville, Kentucky.

Two American Presidents, Harry S Truman and John F. Kennedy, were born in May, as was Queen Victoria of England, whose birthday on May 24 is celebrated in the United Kingdom as Commonwealth Day.

The birthstone for May is the emerald and the flowers are the lily of the valley and the hawthorn. Notable birthdays and events of May are as follows.

MAY 1 -- BIRTHDAYS

1218   **Rudolf I** -- King of Germany, 1254-1273, and founder of the Hapsburg dynasty in Austria, which ruled until 1918

1672   **Joseph Addison** -- English essayist, best known for *The Spectator* series published in 1711 and 1712 with Sir Richard Steele

1764   **Benjamin Henry Latrobe** -- The first professionally trained architect to practice in the United States, and designer of the south wing of the U.S. Capitol after the British burned the original

1769   **Duke of Wellington** -- British general and conqueror of Napoleon at the Battle of Waterloo in 1815

1808   **Gerard de Nerval** -- French writer whose translation at age 19 of Goethe's *Faust* was praised by Goethe himself

1825   **George Inness** -- Noted American landscape painter

1827   **Jules Adolphe Breton** -- French painter noted for the famous picture *Return of the Gleaners*

1830   **Mary Harris "Mother" Jones** -- Irish-American labor leader who wrote her autobiography at age 95 and whose motto was "Pray for the dead and fight like hell for the living"

1845   **George Harrison Mifflin** -- American publisher

1852   **Calamity Jane (Martha Jane Canary)** -- American frontierswoman and companion of Wild Bill Hickok

1862   **Marcel Prevost** -- French novelist

1887   **Edwin Muir** -- Scottish novelist, poet, and critic, noted for works such as *Poor Toni* (1932)

1889   **Alfonso Reyes** -- Mexican writer

1896   **Mark Clark** -- U.S. World War II general, who commanded the Fifth Army in Italy

1900   **Ignazio Silone** -- Italian novelist, noted for the intensely human novel, *Bread and Wine*

1904   **Valentina** -- Russian-born American fashion designer

1907   **Kate Smith** -- Noted American popular singer

1908   **Carl Albert** -- U.S. Representative and Speaker of the House, 1971-1977

1910   **J. Allen Hynek** -- American astronomer and UFO authority

1916   **Glenn Ford** -- American motion-picture and television actor and superstar in over 200 movies

1916   **Jane Jacobs** -- American urbanologist and writer

1917   **John Berardino** -- Professional baseball player and actor

1917   **Danielle Darrieux** -- French stage and motion-picture actress

1918	**Jack Paar** – American television personality and early host of the *Tonight Show*
1923	**Joseph** Heller -- American novelist and author of *Catch-22* (1961)
1925	**M. Scott Carpenter** -- Second U.S. astronaut to make an orbital space flight, in *Aurora 7* in 1962
1928	**Terry Southern** -- American writer
1930	**Ollie Matson** -- Professional football player
1930	**Little Walter (Jacobs)** -- American blues musician
1939	**Frank Beard** -- Professional golfer
1939	**Judy Collins** -- American folk and pop singer
1960	**Steve Cauthen** – American jockey and Kentucky Derby winner when he was a teenager

MAY 1 -- EVENTS

305 AD	Roman emperor Diocletian abdicated at age 60. He was unpopular because the government had grown too big and he had raised taxes.
1045	Pope Benedict IX sold the papacy to John Gratianus, Gregory VI.
1316	Edward Bruce was crowned King of Ireland.
1429	Joan of Arc began raising the English siege of Orleans.
1464	King Edward IV of England secretly married Elizabeth Woodville.
1625	King Charles I of England married France's Henrietta Maria by proxy.
1700	John Dryden, the noted English writer, died in London at age 68.
1786	Wolfgang Amadeus Mozart's famous opera *The Marriage of Figaro* premiered in Vienna.
1851	The London Crystal Palace Exhibition, the first world's fair, opened.
1873	Penny postcards were placed on sale for the first time by the United States Post Office.
1884	Construction began on the first skyscraper, the Home Insurance Building in Chicago. It had 10 stories and was designed by architect William Le Baron Jenney.
1898	U.S. Commodore George Dewey's Asiatic Squadron of six ships destroyed the entire Spanish fleet in the Battle of Manila Bay in the Spanish-American War.
1931	The Empire State Building was dedicated by New York's former governor Al Smith.

1931   Singer Kate Smith began her long-running radio program on CBS, on her 24th birthday.

1941   The great motion picture, *Citizen Kane,* directed by and starring Orson Welles, premiered in New York City.

1945   Radio Hamburg announced the death of Adolf Hitler, who had committed suicide two days earlier.

1948   Eddie Arcaro became the first jockey to ride four Kentucky Derby winners, winning with Citation.

1960   An American U-2 spy plane was shot down deep inside Russia, and the pilot, Gary Powers, was taken prisoner.

MAY 2 -- BIRTHDAYS

1659   **Alessandro Scarlatti** -- A leading composer of early Italian opera

1729   **Catherine the Great** -- Empress of Russia, 1762-1796

1752   **Humphrey Repton** -- English landscape architect whose informal style has become identified with English landscape gardening

1772   **Novalis (Friedrich von Hardenberg)** -- German Romantic poet, noted for such works as "Hymns to the Night" (1800)

1779   **John Galt** -- Scottish novelist

1792   **Rufus Porter** -- Founder of *Scientific American* magazine

1835   **John Heenan** -- Hall of Fame boxer

1859   **Jerome Klapka Jerome** -- British writer and author of *Three Men in a Boat* (1889)

1860   **Theodor Herzl** -- Austrian writer who founded the Zionist movement, whose aim was to set up a Jewish national home in Palestine

1870   **Lewis J. Selznick** -- Russian-American film executive, founder of the Selznick Company, and father of film notables David O. and Myron Selznick

1887   **Eddie Collins** -- Hall of Fame baseball player, with 3,313 career hits

1887   **Vernon Castle** -- English-born dancer who with his wife Irene Castle formed the internationally famous ballroom dancing team of the 1910s

1892   **Manfred von Richthofen** -- Germany's "Red Baron" and top aviator in World War I

1895   **Lorenz Hart** -- American lyricist who with Richard Rodgers wrote nearly 400 songs, such as "Blue Moon," "With a Song in My Heart," "You Are Too Beautiful," and "Bewitched, Bothered and Bewildered"

1895   **Peggy Bacon** -- American printmaker

1897   **John Frederick Coots** -- American composer noted for songs such as "Santa Claus Is Coming to Town" and "Love Letters in the Sand"

1902   **Brian Aherne** -- English-born motion-picture actor

1903   **Dr. Benjamin Spock** -- Noted American pediatrician and author

1904   **Bing Crosby** -- American singer, actor, and one of the most versatile entertainers in American history

1924   **Theodore Bikel** -- Austrian-born actor and writer

1935   **Faisal II** -- King of Iraq, 1953-1958

1945   **Bianca Jagger** -- American model and wife of musician Mick Jagger

1952   **John Andrews** -- American tennis player

1953   **Jamaal Wilkes** -- Professional basketball player

1954   **Keith Moreland** -- Professional baseball player

MAY 2 -- EVENTS

1519   Leonardo da Vinci died at the Chateau de Cloux near Amboise, France, at age 66.

1670   The Hudson Bay Company was chartered by King Charles II of England.

1803   The Louisiana Purchase agreement, completed 3 days earlier, was formally signed in Paris by American envoys James Monroe and Robert Livingston.

1808   The Spanish populace attacked Napoleon's French guard in the Dos de Mayo insurrection in Madrid.

1863   General Stonewall Jackson was shot accidentally by his own soldiers outside Chancellorsville, Virginia. He died eight days later.

1865   The first paid fire department was established, in New York City.

1876   Ross Barnes of the Chicago White Stockings and Baby Jones of the Cincinnati Reds hit the first home runs in major league history, as Chicago won, 15-9.

1885   *Good Housekeeping* magazine was first published by Clark W. Bryan in Holyoke, Massachusetts.

1933   Adolf Hitler abolished labor unions throughout Germany.

1939   Lou Gehrig took himself out of the New York Yankee lineup after a record 2,130 consecutive games, because of the rare paralysis he was stricken with.

1945	The Germans surrendered Berlin to the Russians and Nazi troops in Italy surrendered unconditionally to the Allies in World War II.
1954	Stan Musial of the St. Louis Cardinals hit a record five home runs in a doubleheader.
1972	J. Edgar Hoover, first and only FBI director in its first 48-year history, died at age 77.

MAY 3 -- BIRTHDAYS

1469	**Niccolo Machiavelli** -- Florentine statesman and writer noted for *The Prince,* one of the great works of world literature
1761	**August Kotzebue** -- German writer whose murder in 1819 as an alleged Russian spy led the Prussian government to issue the repressive Carlsbad Decrees
1849	**Jacob August Riis** -- American newspaperman, social reformer, and "America's first photojournalist"
1874	**Francois Coty** -- Noted French perfume manufacturer
1877	**Karl Abraham** -- German psychoanalyst
1891	**Eppa Rixey** -- Hall of Fame baseball player
1892	**Beulah Bondi** -- American stage, screen, and television actress
1897	**V.K. Krishna Menon** -- Indian nationalist
1898	**Golda Meir** -- Prime minister of Israel, 1969-1974
1902	**Walter Slezak** – Austrian-born stage and motion-picture actor
1904	**Red Ruffing** -- Hall of Fame baseball player
1906	**Mary Astor** -- American motion-picture actress
1907	**Earl Wilson** -- American columnist on show business activities
1913	**Earl Blackwell** -- American publisher and social arbiter
1913	**William Inge** – American playwright and screenwriter noted for works such as *Come Back, Little Sheba; Picnic; Bus Stop;* and *The Dark at the Top of the Stairs*
1915	**Richard Lippold** -- American sculptor noted for delicate abstract and geometric work such as *Variation Number 7: Full Moon*
1919	**Pete Seeger** -- American folk protest singer and songwriter
1919	**Betty Comden** -- American playwright, lyricist, and songwriter
1920	**John Lewis** -- American pianist and composer
1920	**Sugar Ray Robinson** – Welterweight and six times middleweight world champion and one of the greatest boxers in history
1921	**Alida Valli** -- Italian motion-picture actress
1921	**Goose Tatum** -- Basketball star of the Harlem Globetrotters

1927   **Mell Lazarus** -- American comic strip artist noted for *Miss Peach* and *Momma*
1931   **Joe Layton** -- American choreographer and director
1936   **James Brown** -- American soul singer
1937   **Engelbert Humperdinck** -- British singer
1937   **Frankie Valli** -- American singer with the Four Seasons
1946   **Davey Lopes** -- Professional baseball player
1948   **Garfield Heard** -- Professional basketball player
1948   **Peter Oosterhuis** -- Professional golfer

MAY 3 -- EVENTS

1429   Joan of Arc liberated Orleans from the English in the Hundred Years' War.
1471   Edward IV won the Battle of Tewkesbury in the Wars of the Roses to wrest the throne of England from Henry VI.
1494   Columbus discovered the island of Jamaica on his second voyage to America, and named it Santiago.
1765   The first American medical school was established, in the College of Philadelphia, now the University of Pennsylvania.
1802   Washington, D.C., was incorporated as a city.
1810   English poet Lord Byron swam the Hellespont in 1 hour and 10 minutes.
1921   West Virginia imposed the first state sales tax.
1937   Margaret Mitchell won a Pulitzer Prize for *Gone With the Wind.*
1952   The first big commercial jet plane, the De Havilland Comet, began passenger service in Great Britain.
1979   Margaret Thatcher became the first woman prime minister of the United Kingdom.
1980   Genuine Risk won the Kentucky Derby, becoming the second filly in history to do so. Regret was the first, in 1915.

MAY 4 -- BIRTHDAYS

1622   **Juan de Valdes Leal** -- Spanish Baroque painter
1655   **Bartolommeo Cristofori** -- Italian harpsichord maker who developed the principle of striking a hammer against strings in 1709, which led to the piano
1770   **Charlotte Smith** -- English novelist and poet
1770   **Baron Francois Pascal Simon Gerard** -- French painter
1796   **Horace Mann** -- Father of American public education

1796   **William Hickling Prescott** -- American historian and writer, whose works rank as classics in the study and writing of history

1825   **Thomas Henry Huxley** -- British scientist and humanist, who helped advance Darwin's theory of evolution, and who coined the words *agnostic* and *biogenesis*

1826   **Frederick Edwin Church** -- American artist and one of the best-known landscape painters in the mid-1800s, noted for works such as *Scene in the Catskill Mountains*

1827   **John Hanning Speke** -- English African explorer who in 1862 confirmed that Lake Victoria is the source of the Nile

1872   **Harold Bell Wright** -- American minister and author, noted for *The Shepherd of the Hills* (1907) and *The Winning of Barbara Worth* (1911)

1886   **Shelton Brooks** -- American composer noted for "The Darktown Strutters' Ball"

1889   **Francis Cardinal Spellman** -- Outstanding U.S. leader of the Catholic Church

1903   **Elmer Layden** -- Football player known as one of the Four Horsemen of Notre Dame

1909   **Howard Da Silva** -- American stage and motion-picture actor

1928   **Maynard Ferguson** -- Canadian-born virtuoso jazz trumpeter

1928   **Betsy Rawls** -- Hall of Fame golfer

1928   **Hosni Mubarak** -- Egyptian president who succeeded Anwar Sadat

1929   **Audrey Hepburn** -- English stage and motion-picture actress

1930   **Roberta Peters** -- American operatic soprano

1932   **Tammy Wynette** -- American country singer

1936   **El Cordobes (Manuel Benitez Perez)** -- Spanish bullfighter who was the highest paid in history

1941   **George F. Will** -- American newspaper columnist

1942   **Juan Gisbert** -- Spanish tennis player

1947   **Butch Beard** -- Professional basketball player

1949   **Laura Dupont** -- American tennis player

1951   **Jackie Jackson** -- American singer and guitarist with the Jackson 5

1956   **Ken Oberkfell** -- Professional baseball player

MAY 4 -- EVENTS

1328   England recognized Robert Bruce as king of Scotland in the Treaty of Northampton.

1493	Pope Alexander VI drew the Line of Demarcation, dividing the disputed lands of Spain and Portugal.
1626	Peter Minuit, the Dutch colonizer, landed on Manhattan Island, which he later bought from the Indians for $24.
1776	Rhode Island declared its independence from England, the first American colony to do so.
1814	Napoleon arrived on the island of Elba for his first exile.
1863	The Battle of Chancellorsville ended in victory for the South, but they lost their great general Stonewall Jackson, who was shot accidentally by his own men two days earlier.
1886	The Haymarket riot took place in Chicago during a meeting of anarchists to protest police tactics against strikers.
1902	The comic strip, *Buster Brown,* by R.F. Outcault, first appeared.
1904	The United States took over the Panama Canal Zone.
1919	The comic strip, *Harold Teen,* by Carl Ed, first appeared.
1927	The Academy of Motion Picture Arts and Sciences was formed.
1932	Gangster Al Capone was jailed in Atlanta for income-tax evasion.
1942	The Battle of the Coral Sea began between the United States and Japan in World War II.
1970	Ohio National Guardsmen opened fire on 1,000 Kent State students protesting the Vietnam War, killing four students and wounding eight others.
1980	Marshal Tito (Josip Broz), Yugoslavia's president for 35 years, died three days before his 88th birthday.
1981	Ron Davis, New York Yankees' pitcher, struck out eight straight batters, tying the American League record.

MAY 5 -- BIRTHDAYS

1210	**Alfonso III** -- One of the earliest kings of Portugal
1282	**Don Juan Manuel** -- Most important prose writer of 14th-century Spain
1747	**Leopold II** -- Holy Roman Emperor
1813	**Soren Kierkegaard** -- Danish philosopher and religious thinker, and one of the founders of existentialism
1818	**Karl Marx** -- German sociologist and economist whose ideas formed the basis for Marxism, or Communism
1826	**Eugenie Bonaparte** -- Wife of Napoleon III of France
1830	**John Batterson Stetson** -- The leading American hat manufacturer in the late 1800s, whose most famous creation was his ten-gallon hat

1846   **Henryk Sienkiewicz** -- Popular Polish novelist and author of *A Prophet in His Own Country*

1867   **Nellie Bly** -- Newspaper writer famous for an around-the-world race

1883   **Chief Bender** -- Hall of Fame baseball player

1883   **Archibald Percival Wavell** -- English World War II general

1890   **Christopher Morley** — American literary journalist and author of *Kitty Foyle* (1939)

1895   **Charles MacArthur** – American director, screenwriter, and playwright

1899   **Freeman Gosden** -- American actor who played Amos on the *Amos 'n' Andy* radio show

1903   **James Beard** -- American gourmet

1911   **Max Frisch** -- Swiss author and one of the leading writers of the German-speaking world after World War II

1912   **Alice Faye** -- American stage and motion-picture actress and superstar

1913   **Tyrone Power** -- American motion-picture actor and leading man of the 1930s and 1940s

1915   **Richard Rovere** -- American writer and journalist

1927   **Pat Carroll** -- American motion-picture and television actress

1947   **Larry Hisle** -- Professional baseball player

1949   **Larry Steele** -- Professional basketball player

1956   **Ron Oester** -- Professional baseball player

MAY 5 -- EVENTS

1645   King Charles I of England surrendered himself to the Scots following the end of the English Civil War.

1821   Napoleon died of cancer at Longwood on the island of Saint Helena at age 51.

1847   The American Medical Association was organized in Philadelphia.

1862   French troops, trying to keep Archduke Maximilian in power in Mexico, were routed by the Mexicans near Puebla. The anniversary is celebrated in Mexico as Cinco de Mayo Day.

1864   The Battle of the Wilderness between generals Lee and Grant began in northern Virginia in the Civil War.

1904   Cy Young, the winningest pitcher in baseball, pitched a perfect game (no man reached base) for the Boston Red Sox against Philadelphia.

| 1920 | Nicola Sacco and Bartolomeo Vanzetti were arrested for the murder of two payroll guards in South Braintree, Mass. The ensuing trial became one of the most famous in U.S. history. |

1920   Nicola Sacco and Bartolomeo Vanzetti were arrested for the murder of two payroll guards in South Braintree, Mass. The ensuing trial became one of the most famous in U.S. history.

1925   John T. Scopes was arrested for teaching evolution in Dayton, Tennessee, leading to the famous Scopes trial which tested the right to teach evolution in the schools.

1929   The comic strip, *Napoleon,* by Clifford McBride, first appeared.

1936   The Italian army under Marshal Pietro Badoglio captured Addis Ababa, the capitol of Ethiopia.

1956   Jim Bailey ran the mile in 3 minutes 58.6 seconds, the first to run the mile in under 4 minutes in the United States.

1961   Alan B. Shepard in *Freedom 7* made the first U.S. manned space flight.

1973   Secretariat won the Kentucky Derby in the record time of 1 minute, 59^2/s seconds.

MAY 6 -- BIRTHDAYS

973 AD   **Henry II (the Saint)** -- Emperor of Germany of the Saxon dynasty

1501   **Marcellus II** -- Roman Catholic pope who served for less than a year in 1555

1758   **Maximilien Robespierre** -- Most famous and most controversial leader of the French Revolution

1830   **Abraham Jacobi** -- Founder of U.S. pediatrics

1856   **Robert Edwin Peary** -- American Arctic explorer who led the first expedition to the North Pole in 1909

1856   **Sigmund Freud** -- Austrian physician famous as the founder of psychoanalysis

1861   **Rabindranath Tagore** -- Indian poet, philosopher, and nationalist

1888   **Perry Jones** -- American Hall of Fame tennis player

1888   **Ernst Ludwig Kirchner** -- German painter

1895   **Rudolph Valentino** -- American motion-picture actor idolized in the 1920s as the "Great Lover"

1902   **Harry Golden** -- American publisher and author of *Only in America*

1902   **Max Ophuls** -- German-born French motion-picture director

1907   **Weeb Ewbank** -- The only professional football coach to coach champions in the National Football League, the American Football League, and the Super Bowl

1913   **Carmen Cavallaro** -- American bandleader of the Big Band Era of the 1940s

1913   **Stewart Granger** -- English motion-picture and television actor
1914   **Randall Jarrell** -- American poet and novelist
1915   **Orson Welles** -- American actor, director, and writer, noted for his role in the great movie *Citizen Kane* and for scaring an entire nation with his 1938 radio show *War of the Worlds*
1915   **Theodore White** -- American editor, novelist and writer, noted for his books on U.S. elections, notably *The Making of the President, 1960*
1916   **Ross Hunter** -- American motion-picture producer
1931   **Willie Mays** -- Hall of Fame baseball player and second after Babe Ruth to hit 600 career home runs
1933   **Jimmie Rodgers** -- American country music singer and guitarist
1951   **Samuel K. Doe** -- Head of state of Liberia
1953   **Mark Farrell** -- English tennis player
1954   **Tom Abernethy** -- Professional basketball player

MAY 6 -- EVENTS

1628   The Petition of Right was drawn up by the English Parliament, which declared unconstitutional certain actions of King Charles I.
1835   The New York *Herald* newspaper was first published.
1840   The famous "penny black" stamp was issued in England, the first postage stamp in history.
1851   Dr. John Gorrie of Apalachicola, Florida, received a patent for the manufacture of ice by mechanical means.
1862   Henry David Thoreau, American writer and philosopher, died of tuberculosis in Concord, Massachusetts, at age 44.
1864   The Battle of the Wilderness ended indecisively with heavy losses in both Northern and Southern ranks in the Civil War.
1915   Babe Ruth, a Boston Red Sox pitcher at the time, hit his first major league home run, off New York Yankee pitcher Jack Warhop at the Polo Grounds in New York.
1937   The German zeppelin *Hindenburg* burst into flames and exploded while approaching Lakehurst, New Jersey, killing 36 of the 97 people on board.
1941   Dictator Joseph Stalin dismissed V.M. Molotov and named himself premier of Russia.
1942   American composer Irving Berlin published his classic "White Christmas," which was destined to become the best-selling record of all time.
1942   The U.S. garrison at Corregidor in the Philippines in World War II surrendered to the Japanese.

1953   Bobo Holloman, in his first major league start, pitched a no-hitter, as the St. Louis Browns beat the Philadelphia Athletics, 6-0.

1954   Roger Bannister, British athlete, became the first man to run the mile in less than four minutes (3 minutes 59.4 seconds), at Oxford, England.

MAY 7 -- BIRTHDAYS

1574   **Innocent X** -- Roman Catholic pope, 1644-1655

1694   **Pierre Jean Mariette** -- French print publisher

1711   **David Hume** -- Scottish philosopher who strongly influenced the development of the philosophical schools of skepticism and empiricism

1812   **Robert Browning** -- One of the greatest poets of Victorian England

1826   **Varina Davis** -- Second wife of Confederate president Jefferson Davis

1833   **Johannes Brahms** -- One of the greatest composers in history

1840   **Peter Ilich Tchaikovsky** -- The first Russian composer to gain international fame, and whose works include *Marche Slave, Symphony No. 6* (the *Pathetique*), and the famous *Nutcracker Suite*

1851   **Adolf von Harnack** -- German New Testament scholar noted for books such as *The Essence of Christianity* (1904) and *Epistles of Saint Paul* (1926)

1870   **Marcus Loew** -- Pioneer American motion-picture theater owner

1885   **George "Gabby" Hayes** -- Comic motion-picture sidekick of William Boyd and Roy Rogers who played in over 200 Western movies

1892   **Archibald MacLeish** -- Pulitzer Prize-winning American poet and playwright noted for works such as "Conquistador" (1932) and *J.B.* (1959)

1892   **Tito (Josip Broz)** -- Yugoslav World War II hero and head of state, 1945-1980

1901   **Gary Cooper** -- American motion-picture actor and one of Hollywood's all-time great stars

1909   **Edwin Herbert Land** -- American inventor best noted for the Polaroid Land camera

1914   **Jack Elliott** -- American composer noted for such songs as "It's So Nice to Have a Man Around the House" and "Sam's Song"

1919   **Eva Peron** – Argentine film actress and wife of President Juan Peron

1922   **Darren McGavin** – American motion-picture and television actor

1923   **Anne Baxter** – American motion-picture actress and grand-daughter of noted architect Frank Lloyd Wright

1928   **Dick Williams** -- Professional baseball player and manager, who piloted the Oakland Athletics to three consecutive world championships in 1972, 1973, and 1974

1930   **Babe Parilli** -- Professional football player

1931   **Teresa Brewer** -- American singer

1933   **Johnny Unitas** – One of the greatest professional football quarterbacks in history, who threw at least one touchdown pass in each of 47 consecutive games, 1956-1960

1942   **Bob Weiss** -- Professional basketball player

1946   **Marvin Hubbard** -- Professional football player

1949   **Bill Lloyd** -- Australian tennis player

1950   **Janis Ian** -- American singer

1955   **Peter McNamara** -- Australian tennis player

MAY 7 -- EVENTS

1536   Archbishop Thomas Cranmer annulled the marriage of King Henry VIII and Anne Boleyn.

1789   The first President's Inaugural Ball was held in honor of George Washington in the Assembly Rooms in New York.

1915   The British passenger liner *Lusitania* sank off the coast of Ireland after it was torpedoed by a German submarine.

1939   Germany and Italy announced the formation of the Rome-Berlin Axis, a prelude to World War II, which was to follow in September.

1943   Tunis and Bizerte surrendered to the Americans in World War II, effectively ending Axis resistance in Africa.

1945   Germany surrendered, ending World War II in Europe after 2,075 days of the bloodiest and costliest war in history.

1954   The Vietminh forces of Ho Chi Minh captured Dien Bien Phu from the French after a 55-day siege.

1977   Seattle Slew won the Kentucky Derby. He went on from there to win horse racing's Triple Crown.

MAY 8 -- BIRTHDAYS

1668 **Alain Rene Lesage** -- French novelist and dramatist, noted for the witty novel, *Gil Blas,* a satire on life in Paris

1737 **Edward Gibbon** — The greatest English historian of his century and author of *The History of the Decline and Fall of the Roman Empire*

1753 **Miguel Hidalgo y Costilla** -- Mexican priest, called "The Father of Mexican Independence," who rang the church bells in Dolores calling for Mexico to rebel against Spain

1821 **William Henry Vanderbilt** -- American philanthropist and son of Cornelius Vanderbilt, the founder of the Vanderbilt fortune

1828 **Jean Henri Dunant** -- Swiss banker and founder of the International Red Cross

1847 **Oscar Hammerstein** — German-American theatrical manager, financier, and grandfather of lyricist Oscar Hammerstein II

1855 **John Warne "Bet a Million" Gates** -- First of the giant gamblers, who gambled billions of dollars in his lifetime

1858 **Dan Brouthers** -- Hall of Fame baseball player

1884 **Harry S Truman** -- 33rd U.S. president

1885 **Thomas B. Costain** -- Canadian-American novelist and historian, noted for such works as *The Silver Chalice* (1952)

1892 **Ezio Pinza** -- Italian opera singer and star of the long-running play, *South Pacific*

1893 **Edd Roush** -- Hall of Fame baseball player

1895 **Edmund Wilson** -- American writer and literary and social critic

1895 **Fulton J. Sheen** -- Roman Catholic bishop and television personality of the 1950s

1895 **Jose Gomez** -- One of the greatest matadors of all time

1903 **Fernandel (Fernand Constandin)** — French stage and motion-picture actor

1906 **Roberto Rossellini** -- Italian motion-picture director

1919 **Lex Barker** -- American motion-picture actor

1920 **Sloan Wilson** — American novelist and author of *The Man in the Gray Flannel Suit*

1926 **Don Rickles** -- American comedian and actor

1928 **Theodore Sorenson** -- American author and speechwriter for President Kennedy

1930 **Gary Snyder** -- American poet of the "Beat" movement

1932 **Sonny Liston** -- World heavyweight champion, 1962-1964

1936   **James R. Thompson** -- Governor of Illinois
1940   **Peter Benchley** -- American writer noted for *Jaws* and *The Deep*
1940   **Rick Nelson** -- American actor and singer
1942   **Angel Cordero** -- American jockey
1943   **Toni Tennille** -- American singer
1945   **Robert Grim** -- Professional football player
1951   **Dennis Leonard** -- Professional baseball player
1954   **David Keith** -- American television and motion-picture actor
1959   **Ronnie Lott** -- Professional football player
1964   **Melissa Gilbert** -- American television actress

MAY 8 -- EVENTS

1541   Spanish explorer Hernando De Soto discovered the Mississippi River at a point near the present site of Memphis, Tenn.
1660   England's civil war ended as Charles II was proclaimed king.
1823   The famous song, "Home, Sweet Home," by John Howard Payne and Sir Henry Bishop, was first sung publicly in the opera *Clari, or The Maid of Milan.*
1846   The first major battle of the Mexican War was fought at Palo Alto, Texas, resulting in victory for American general Zachary Taylor.
1879   George B. Selden of Rochester, New York, filed for the first automobile patent, which led to the famous dispute resulting in the cross-licensing system used by auto makers today.
1880   Gustave Flaubert, French novelist, died at Croisset at age 58.
1886   Coca-Cola first went on sale, at Jacob's Pharmacy in Atlanta. Pharmacist John S. Pemberton had formulated the syrup, which remained unchanged until 1985.
1903   Paul Gauguin, French painter, died in the Marquesas Islands at age 54.
1914   The U.S. Senate approved the observance of Mother's Day annually on the second Sunday in May.
1942   The Battle of the Coral Sea ended in a decisive American victory over Japan in World War II.
1945   The world celebrated V-E Day (Victory in Europe), following the German surrender on the previous day.
1961   The comic strip, *Apartment 3-G,* by Nicholas Dallis, Harold Anderson, and Alex Kotzky, appeared for the first time.
1968   Catfish Hunter pitched a perfect game (no man reached base) as Oakland beat Minnesota, 4-0.

MAY 9 -- BIRTHDAYS

1439　**Pius III** -- Roman Catholic pope, who served less than a year in 1503

1800　**John Brown** -- Radical abolitionist who led the raid on the United States arsenal at Harpers Ferry on October 16, 1859

1843　**Belle Boyd** -- "The Rebel Spy" for the South in the Civil War

1855　**Francois Pompon** -- French sculptor noted for works such as *Polar Bear* (1922)

1860　**Sir James Barrie** -- Scottish novelist and playwright, noted for *Peter Pan* (1904)

1870　**Harry Vardon** -- The first of the great modern golfers, and winner of the British Open six times between 1896 and 1914

1873　**Howard Carter** -- English archaeologist who discovered the tomb of Egyptian king Tutankhamon in 1922

1882　**Henry J. Kaiser** -- Noted American shipbuilder during World War II and co-founder of the Kaiser-Frazer automobile corporation

1883　**Jose Ortega y Gasset** -- Spanish philosopher

1893　**William Moulton Marston** -- Creator of *Wonder Woman*

1895　**Richard Barthelmess** -- American motion-picture actor

1905　**Lili D'Alvarez** -- Spain's greatest woman tennis player

1908　**Bill Jurges** -- Professional baseball player

1909　**Jim Hagerty** -- American radio and television executive and press secretary for President Eisenhower

1912　**Pedro Armendariz** -- Mexican motion-picture actor

1914　**Carlo Maria Giulini** -- Italian-born conductor

1914　**Hank Snow** -- American country singer

1918　**Mike Wallace** -- American television interviewer and co-host of the *Sixty Minutes* program

1919　**Betty Jameson** -- Hall of Fame golfer

1921　**Daniel Berrigan** -- American priest and social activist

1928　**Pancho Gonzales** -- American Hall of Fame tennis player, and one of the top players of the post-World War II era

1936　**Albert Finney** -- English motion-picture actor

1936　**Glenda Jackson** -- English stage and motion-picture actress

1937　**David Prater** -- American soul singer of the Sam and Dave duo

1939　**Ralph Boston** -- Professional long jumper and 1960 Olympic gold medal winner

1939　**Ion Tiriac** -- Romanian tennis player

1946   **Candice Bergen** -- American motion-picture actress, photojour-
         nalist, and daughter of ventriloquist Edgar Bergen
1948   **Calvin Murphy** -- Professional basketball player
1948   **John Mahaffey** -- Professional golfer
1949   **Billy Joel** -- American singer, songwriter, and musician, noted
         for songs such as "Just the Way You Are"
1954   **Balazs Taroczy** -- Hungarian tennis player
1960   **Tony Gwynn** -- Professional baseball player
1962   **Dave Gahan** -- English lead vocalist with the Depeche Mode
         musical group

MAY 9 -- EVENTS

1502   Christopher Columbus set sail from Cadiz, Spain, on his fourth
         and last voyage to America.
1754   Benjamin Franklin's famous *Join or Die* cartoon became the first
         newspaper cartoon in America, appearing in the Pennsylvania
         Gazette.
1864   Union general John Sedgwick, shortly after saying, "They couldn't
         hit an elephant at this distance," was killed by a Confederate
         sharpshooter at Spotsylvania, Virginia.
1907   An annual Mother's Day was publicly suggested by Miss Anna
         Jarvis of Philadelphia.
1926   Admiral Richard E. Byrd and Floyd Bennett became the first
         men to fly to the North Pole.
1933   The first of the Nazi book burnings took place as 25,000 books
         were burned in a bonfire in Berlin.
1936   Ethiopia was formally annexed to Italy by Benito Mussolini.
1949   Prince Rainier III became ruler of Monaco.
1974   Impeachment hearings of the U.S. House Judiciary Committee
         began against President Nixon.

MAY 10 -- BIRTHDAYS

1837   **Pinckney** Benton Stewart **Pinchback** -- Only black to serve as
         governor of any state (35 days as governor of Louisiana in 1872)
         until Douglas Wilder of Virginia in 1990
1838   **John Wilkes Booth** -- Assassin of Abraham Lincoln
1838   **James Bryce** -- British historian, statesman, and author of *The
         American Commonwealth*

1843   **Benito Perez Galdos** -- Spanish novelist and playwright

1850   **Sir Thomas Johnstone Lipton** -- Founder of the Lipton tea empire

1868   **Ed Barrow** -- Professional baseball general manager who switched Babe Ruth from a pitcher to an outfielder

1885   **Fritz von Unruh** -- German dramatist, poet, and novelist

1886   **Karl Barth** -- One of the most influential theologians of the 20th century

1888   **Max Steiner** -- Austrian-born composer and conductor, noted for songs such as "A Summer Place," "As Long as I Live," "Sugarfoot," and "So Big"

1890   **Alfred Jodl** -- Nazi World War II general who signed the terms of Germany's unconditional surrender

1895   **Abe Tuvim** -- American lyricist noted for songs such as "A Gay Ranchero" and "Chile Con Conga"

1898   **Ariel Durant** -- American historian and wife of Will Durant, with whom she co-authored the last four volumes of the ten-volume series, *The Story of Civilization*

1899   **Fred Astaire** -- American stage and motion-picture star noted for his graceful, imaginative dancing and acting in over 35 movies in a 50-year career

1902   **David O. Selznick** -- American motion-picture producer, whose greatest work was *Gone With the Wind*

1910   **Jimmy Demarest** -- First professional golfer to win three Masters tournaments

1917   **Margo** -- Mexican-born stage and motion-picture actress

1919   **Ella T. Grasso** -- Governor of Connecticut, 1975-1980, and first woman to be elected governor who did not follow her husband

1920   **Richard Adams** -- English novelist noted for *Watership Down* (1972) and *Shardik* (1974)

1922   **Nancy Walker** -- American stage, screen, and television actress

1927   **Mike Souchak** -- Professional golfer

1936   **Gary Owens** -- American comedian and TV personality noted as the comic announcer on the long-running television show, *Laugh In*

1938   **Manuel Santana** -- Spanish tennis player

1946   **Donovan (Donovan Leitch)** -- Scottish folk and pop singer

1955   **Mark David Chapman** -- Assassin of the famous singer John Lennon

MAY 10 -- EVENTS

1744   King Louis XV of France died of smallpox at age 69 and was succeeded by his grandson, the ill-fated Louis XVI.

1775   Ethan Allen and his Green Mountain Boys captured Fort Ticonderoga from the British in the American Revolution.

1818   Paul Revere, the great American Revolutionary War hero, died at age 83.

1857   The Sepoy Rebellion began at Meerut, near Delhi, India, resulting in British rule of India the following year.

1863   Confederate general Stonewall Jackson died after being shot accidentally by his own men on May 2.

1865   Union forces captured Confederate president Jefferson Davis in Irwinville, Georgia, following the end of the Civil War.

1869   The first transcontinental railway in America was completed at Promontory Point, Utah, where the tracks of the Union Pacific and the Central Pacific were joined.

1871   The Treaty of Frankfurt was signed, formally ending the Franco-Prussian War.

1924   J. Edgar Hoover was named the first director of the F.B.I.

1933   Nazi storm troopers and students staged a massive book burning in Berlin of works of authors considered offensive to the state.

1940   German troops invaded Belgium and Holland, ending the "phony war" in the West in World War II.

1940   Winston Churchill succeeded Neville Chamberlain as prime minister of Great Britain.

1941   Rudolf Hess, Hitler's second in command, parachuted into Glasgow, Scotland, to "save humanity."

1948   The comic strip, *Rex Morgan, M.D.,* by Nicholas Dallis, Frank Edgington, and Marvin Bradley, first appeared.

1954   "Rock Around the Clock," by Bill Haley and the Comets, was released, the first big rock and roll record.

1968   The Vietnam peace talks began in Paris.

1980   The U.S. government gave condition approval to $1.5 billion in federal loan guarantees to Chrysler Corporation.

MAY 11 -- BIRTHDAYS

482 AD   **Justinian I (the Great)** -- Byzantine (East Roman) emperor, A.D. 527-565

1811	**Chang and Eng Bunker** — The original Siamese twins (so-called because they were born in Meklong, Siam)
1823	**Alfred Stevens** -- Belgian painter noted for works such as *After the Ball* (1874)
1852	**Charles W. Fairbanks** -- U.S. vice president under Theodore Roosevelt
1854	**Ottmar Mergenthaler** -- Inventor of the Linotype typesetting machine
1888	**Irving Berlin** — One of the greatest American popular songwriters, noted for such songs as "White Christmas," "God Bless America," "Alexander's Ragtime Band," and "Always"
1891	**Henry Morgenthau Jr.** — Secretary of the Treasury under Franklin D. Roosevelt
1892	**Dame Margaret Rutherford** -- English stage and motion-picture actress
1893	**Martha Graham** -- American dancer and choreographer, who pioneered the modern dance movement
1894	**Ellsworth Bunker** — American diplomat and last ambassador to South Vietnam
1895	**William Grant Still** -- First black to conduct a professional symphony orchestra in the United States
1902	**Bidu Sayao** -- Brazilian soprano
1903	**Charlie Gehringer** -- Hall of Fame baseball player
1904	**Salvador Dali** -- Spanish surrealist painter and one of the most publicized figures in modern art
1907	**Rip Sewell** -- Professional baseball player
1912	**Phil Silvers** -- American stage, screen, and television actor and comedian
1912	**Foster Brooks** -- American actor and comedian
1920	**Denver Pyle** -- American motion-picture and television actor
1921	**Gene Hermanski** -- Professional baseball player
1924	**Antony Hewish** -- English astronomer who discovered pulsars in 1967
1926	**Mort Sahl** -- American comedian and actor
1932	**Valentino (Garavani)** -- Italian dress designer
1934	**Jack Twyman** -- Professional basketball superstar with over 15,000 career points
1935	**Doug McClure** -- American motion-picture and television actor
1939	**Milt Pappas** -- Professional baseball player
1940	**Butch Hartman** -- American auto racer

1941   **Eric Burdon** -- Singer with the Animals musical group
1945   **Thomaz Koch** -- Brazilian tennis player
1946   **Robert K. Jarvik** -- American physician and inventor of the Jarvik heart, the first mechanical heart to be permanently implanted in a human being
1950   **Dane Iorg** -- Professional baseball player

MAY 11 -- EVENTS

330 AD Constantinople was dedicated as the new capital of the Roman Empire during the reign of Constantine the Great.

1647   Peter Stuyvesant took over as governor of New Amsterdam.

1792   American explorer Robert Gray discovered the mouth of the Columbia River.

1846   President Polk asked Congress to declare war on Mexico.

1858   Minnesota was admitted to the Union as the 32nd state.

1862   The Confederates scuttled their ironclad, the *Merrimack*, to keep it from being captured by the Union in the Civil War.

1900   Jim Jeffries knocked out Gentleman Jim Corbett in round 23 to retain the heavyweight boxing championship.

1910   Glacier National Park in Montana was established.

1911   The National Health Insurance Bill was introduced in Parliament by Prime Minister Herbert Henry Asquith of Britain.

1943   American forces landed on Japanese-occupied Attu Island in the Aleutians in World War II. The island was retaken three weeks later.

1949   Israel was admitted to the United Nations.

1949   Siam changed its name to Thailand.

MAY 12 -- BIRTHDAYS

1496   **Gustavus I** -- King of Sweden, 1523-1560, who established the Lutheran faith as Sweden's state religion

1755   **Giovanni Battista Viotti** -- Italian violinist and composer, considered by some to be the father of modern violin playing

1812   **Edward Lear** -- English landscape painter and writer of nonsense verse, a good example of which is "The Owl and the Pussy-Cat"

1820   **Florence Nightingale** -- Founder of the nursing profession and one of the greatest women of England's Victorian Age

1828	**Dante Gabriel Rossetti** -- One of England's most famous poets and painters of the 1800s
1842	**Jules Massenet** -- French composer noted for his operas, the best known of which is *Manon* (1884)
1845	**Gabriel Faure** -- French composer and organist, who played one of the biggest roles in freeing French music from German influences
1850	**Henry Cabot Lodge** -- U.S. senator, 1893-1924, who led the fight against America's joining the League of Nations
1880	**Lincoln Ellsworth** -- American Arctic and Antarctic explorer, who with Roald Amundsen made the first aerial crossing of the vast North Polar Basin in 1925
1895	**Harold Olsen** -- Hall of Fame basketball player and coach
1902	**Philip Wylie** -- American writer and author of *Generation of Vipers* (1942)
1910	**Gordon Hill Jenkins** -- American composer and author, noted for songs such as "San Fernando Valley"
1914	**Howard K. Smith** -- American newscaster and commentator
1918	**Julius Rosenberg** -- U.S. citizen who with his wife Ethel was the first to be executed for espionage during peacetime
1925	**Yogi Berra** -- Hall of Fame baseball player and one of the three or four greatest catchers in history
1925	**John Simon** -- American writer and critic
1929	**Burt Bacharach** -- American composer noted for songs such as "Raindrops Keep Falling on My Head" and "What the World Needs Now"
1935	**Felipe Alou** -- Professional baseball player
1936	**Tom Snyder** -- American television talk show host
1936	**Frank Stella** -- American artist
1938	**George Carlin** -- American comedian
1939	**Ron Ziegler** -- Press secretary for President Nixon
1941	**Susan Hampshire** -- English motion-picture and television actress
1948	**Steve Winwood** -- English singer, musician, and songwriter with the Traffic group
1953	**Kevin Grevey** -- Professional basketball player
1955	**Colin Dowdeswell** -- Zimbabwean tennis player
1957	**Lou Whitaker** -- Professional baseball player
1959	**Kevin Bass** -- Professional baseball player
1962	**Emilio Estevez** -- American motion-picture actor and son of actor Martin Sheen

MAY 12 -- EVENTS

1621   The first wedding took place in Plymouth Colony, Massachu-
       setts, as Edward Winslow married Susanna White.

1780   The entire Continental Army of 2,500 soldiers surrendered to
       the British at Charleston, South Carolina, in the American
       Revolution.

1789   The Society of Tammany was formed in New York City by
       William Mooney.

1875   The first shut-out in major league baseball occurred, as Chicago
       beat St. Louis, 1-0, in the National Association of Professional
       Baseball Players, later the National League.

1926   Roald Amundsen and Lincoln Ellsworth crossed the North Pole
       by dirigible, only a few days after Admiral Byrd's historic flight.

1932   Charles A. Lindbergh's kidnapped baby son was found dead in
       Hopewell, New Jersey.

1937   George VI was crowned King of England in Westminster Abbey,
       succeeding Edward VIII, who had abdicated.

1943   The last organized Axis army force in Africa in World War II
       surrendered in southern Tunisia.

1949   The Russians called off the Berlin blockade after 328 days,
       during which time the United States and Britain supplied the city
       by means of the Berlin Airlift.

MAY 13 -- BIRTHDAYS

1655   **Innocent XIII** -- Roman Catholic pope, 1721-1724

1717   **Maria Theresa** -- Empress, Archduchess of Austria, Queen of
       Hungary, and mother of French queen Marie Antoinette

1729   **Henry William Stiegel** -- Early American iron and glass manu-
       facturer, best known for Stiegel glass, considered by many ex-
       perts today as the most beautiful glass ever blown

1792   **Pius IX** -- Roman Catholic pope, 1846-1878, who had the longest
       reign in papal history

1840   **Alphonse Daudet** -- French novelist sometimes called the "French
       Dickens"

1842   **Sir Arthur Sullivan** -- One of the most famous English composers
       of his day and co-composer with Sir William Gilbert of the
       Gilbert and Sullivan operettas

1877   **Joseph Stella** -- American painter

1882   **Georges Braque** -- French artist, who, with Pablo Picasso, led the
       development of cubism in the early 1900s

1907 **Daphne Du Maurier** -- English writer of popular romantic novels, such as *Rebecca* and *Jamaica Inn*

1913 **William R. Tolbert Jr.** -- President of Liberia, 1937-1980

1914 **Joe Louis** -- Heavyweight boxing champion, 1937-1949, and one of the all-time greats of the ring

1926 **Bea Arthur** -- American television actress

1927 **Fred Hellerman** -- American singer, guitarist, and songwriter, with the Weavers musical group

1927 **Clive Barnes** -- American drama critic

1927 **Herbert Ross** -- American director and choreographer noted for films such as *Carmen Jones* and *Funny Girl*

1941 **Marshall Field V** -- American newspaper publisher

1949 **Franklin Ajaye** -- American actor

1950 **Stevie Wonder** -- American blind-from-birth pop rock musician, singer, and composer, noted for songs such as "You Are the Sunshine of My Life" and "Living for the City"

1953 **Pat Gregg** -- Australian tennis player

1965 **Jose Rijo** -- Professional baseball player

MAY 13 -- EVENTS

1783 Society of the Cincinnati, the oldest military organization in the United States, was founded, with George Washington as its first president.

1787 British captain Arthur Phillip sailed from Portsmouth, England, with 11 ships and a cargo of convicts bound for settlement in Australia.

1846 The Mexican War began, as Congress declared war.

1854 The first American billiard match of importance was held at Malcolm Hall in Syracuse, N.Y., as Joseph N. White defeated George Smith for the $200 purse by a score of 500 to 484.

1867 Jefferson Davis, the ex-Confederate president, was released from prison in Ft. Monroe, Virginia, where he had been held for two years awaiting trial.

1917 Three peasant children reported seeing near Fatima, Portugal, a vision of the Virgin Mary, since known as Our Lady of Fatima.

1918 The first United States air mail stamps were issued.

1940 Winston Churchill made his first speech as British prime minister, saying, "I have nothing to offer but blood, toil, tears, and sweat."

1954 President Dwight D. Eisenhower signed the bill authorizing construction of the St. Lawrence Seaway.

1981   Pope John Paul II was shot twice in an assassination attempt in Rome. He later fully recovered.

MAY 14 -- BIRTHDAYS

1686   **Gabriel Daniel Fahrenheit** -- German physicist who developed the Fahrenheit temperature scale

1710   **Adolf Frederick** -- King of Sweden, 1751-1771

1727   **Thomas Gainsborough** -- One of the greatest English painters of all time, whose most famous work is *The Blue Boy*

1752   **Timothy Dwight** -- American religious leader during the Jeffersonian era

1771   **Robert Owen** -- Welsh-born social reformer who set up the famous New Harmony community in Indiana in 1825

1771   **Thomas Wedgwood** -- The first person to conceive the basic process of modern photography, and the son of Josiah Wedgwood, the famous English pottery designer

1852   **Alton B. Parker** -- U.S. presidential candidate in 1904

1853   **Sir Thomas Henry Hall Caine** -- English novelist

1881   **Ed Walsh** -- Hall of Fame baseball pitcher who pitched a record 464 innings in one season

1885   **Otto Klemperer** -- Famous German conductor and composer, who directed the Kroll Opera in Berlin, the Los Angeles Philharmonic Orchestra, and the New York Philharmonic Orchestra

1891   **Grant Clarke** -- American composer noted for songs such as "Ragtime Cowboy Joe" and "I Hate to Lose You"

1899   **Earle Combs** -- Hall of Fame baseball player, who with Babe Ruth and Bob Meusel constituted the great 1927 New York Yankees' "perfect outfield"

1900   **Billie Dove** -- "The American Beauty" of the silent and early sound screen

1907   **Mohammad Ayab Khan** -- President of Pakistan, 1958-1969

1925   **Les Moss** -- Professional baseball player

1925   **Patrice Munsel** -- American operatic soprano

1936   **Bobby Darin** -- American songwriter and actor

1937   **Dick Howser** -- Professional baseball player and manager

1942   **Tony Perez** -- Professional baseball player

1943   **Jack Bruce** -- Bassist and singer with the musical group Cream

1944   **George Lucas** -- American motion-picture director and writer

1955   **Dennis Martinez** -- Professional baseball player

MAY 14 -- EVENTS

1607 Captain John Smith and his colonists landed at Jamestown, Virginia, and established the first permanent English colony in America.

1610 Henry IV, the great king of France who issued the Edict of Nantes, was murdered at age 56 by the fanatic Francois Ravaillac.

1643 Louis XIV, the "Grand Monarch" of France, became king upon the death of his father Louis XIII.

1787 Delegates began gathering in Philadelphia for the convention to draw up the U.S. Constitution.

1796 Edward Jenner, the great English physician, performed the first vaccination against smallpox, on an 8-year-old boy.

1804 Meriwether Lewis and William Clark left St. Louis on their journey to explore the Northwest, the famous Lewis and Clark Expedition.

1851 Gail Borden, of Brooklyn, New York, applied for a patent for condensed milk.

1874 The first real football game with rules similar to those of the modern game was played between Harvard and McGill Universities.

1904 The first Olympic games to be held in the United States opened in St. Louis.

1940 The Dutch armies surrendered to the Germans in World War II.

1942 Congress established the WAAC's, the Women's Auxiliary Army Corps.

1948 Great Britain ended her 31-year rule in Palestine, followed immediately by a proclamation in Tel Aviv of the birth of the state of Israel.

1965 The John F. Kennedy Memorial was dedicated at Runnymede, England.

1973 *Skylab 1* was launched, the first American manned space station.

1975 U.S. forces recaptured the American merchant ship *Mayaguez* in a raid off the Cambodian island of Koh Tang.

MAY 15 -- BIRTHDAYS

1265 **Dante (Alighieri)** -- Italy's greatest poet, whose epic work, the *Divine Comedy,* ranks among the greatest works of world literature

1625 **Carlo Maratti** -- Italian painter

1773   **Klemens von Metternich** -- Austrian statesman who helped defeat Napoleon and reshape Europe after 1815

1788   **James Gadsden** -- U.S. minister to Mexico who negotiated the Gadsden Purchase from Mexico of the land along the southern bank of the Gila River

1813   **Stephen Heller** -- Hungarian pianist and composer

1845   **Elie Metchnikoff** -- Noted Russian biologist and 1908 Nobel Prize winner for his studies of the white blood cells

1856   **Lyman Frank Baum** -- American writer and author of *The Wonderful Wizard of Oz* (1900)

1859   **Pierre Curie** -- French physicist and co-discoverer, with his wife Marie Curie, of the element radium

1860   **Ellen Louise Axson** -- First wife of President Woodrow Wilson

1862   **Arthur Schnitzler** -- Austrian playwright and novelist, whose best-known story is the short novel *Leutnant Gustl* (1901)

1890   **Katherine Anne Porter** -- American novelist and short-story writer, noted for her Pulitzer Prize-winning *Collected Short Stories* (1965) and *Ship of Fools* (1962)

1902   **Richard J. Daley** -- Mayor of Chicago, 1955-1976

1904   **Clifton Fadiman** -- American critic, author, and radio and television master of ceremonies

1905   **Joseph Cotten** -- American stage and motion-picture actor

1909   **James Mason** -- English stage and motion-picture actor

1914   **Turk Broda** -- Hall of Fame hockey player

1915   **Paul Samuelson** -- American Nobel Prize-winning economist, writer, and author in 1948 of the best-selling economics textbook in the world

1918   **Eddy Arnold** -- American country music singer

1923   **Richard Avedon** -- A leading 20th century photographer

1930   **Jasper Johns** -- American "pop artist"

1931   **Ken Venturi** -- Professional golfer

1931   **Joseph Califano Jr.** -- Secretary of Health, Education, and Welfare under President Carter

1936   **Anna Maria Alberghetti** -- Italian actress and singer

1937   **Trini Lopez** -- American musician, actor, and bandleader

1940   **Don Nelson** -- Professional basketball player

1940   **Roger Ailes** -- Communications consultant and advisor to George Bush in the 1988 presidential election

1948   **Brian Eno** -- Avant-garde rock musician

1953   **George Brett** -- Professional baseball player and superstar

MAY 15 -- EVENTS

1485	Ferdinand, King of Aragon, captured Ronda (Spain) from the Moors.
1602	Bartholomew Gosnold, the English navigator, discovered Cape Cod.
1862	Congress created the Department of Agriculture.
1885	Canadian rebel Louis Riel surrendered to Canadian government forces, ending the *metis* rebellion, or the Riel Rebellion. He was later hanged.
1886	Emily Dickinson, the great American poet, died in Amherst, Massachusetts, at age 55.
1917	General Ferdinand Foch was named chief of staff of the French Army in World War I.
1918	The U.S. Post Office launched the first air mail service, between Washington, Philadelphia, and New York.
1930	United Air Lines hired the first stewardess in airlines history, Miss Ellen Church, who served on a flight between San Francisco and Cheyenne, Wyoming.
1940	The first nylon stockings went on sale in the United States.
1941	Joe DiMaggio, the great New York Yankee baseball player, singled off Chicago White Sox pitcher Ed Smith to begin his famous 56-game hitting streak.
1948	The new state of Israel was attacked by Egyptian planes and invaded in the north and east by troops from Lebanon and Transjordan.
1953	Rocky Marciano knocked out Jersey Joe Walcott in the first round to retain his heavyweight championship.
1972	Alabama governor George C. Wallace was shot and left paralyzed in Laurel, Md., while campaigning for president. The would-be assassin, Arthur Bremer, was later sent to prison.
1981	Len Barker pitched a perfect game (no one reached base) as Cleveland beat Toronto, 3-0.

MAY 16 -- BIRTHDAYS

1763	**Louis Nicholas Vauquelin** -- French chemist who discovered the elements chromium and beryllium
1782	**John Sell Cotman** -- English landscape painter and etcher, noted for works such as *Greta Bridge* (1805)
1801	**William H. Seward** -- U.S. secretary of state, 1862-1869, noted for promoting the purchase of Alaska from Russia in 1867

1804   Elizabeth Peabody -- Founder of one of the first U.S. kindergartens, in Boston in 1860

1821   Pafnuty Lvovich Chebyshev -- Russian mathematician noted for the Chebyshev polynomials

1827   Norman Jay Colman -- First U.S. Secretary of Agriculture (1889)

1831   Edward David Hughes -- American scientist who invented the first real microphone, in 1878

1832   Philip Danforth Armour -- Co-founder of Armour and Company

1905   Henry Fonda -- American stage, motion-picture, and television actor, and top-ranking star for over 50 years

1911   Margaret Sullavan -- American stage and motion-picture actress

1912   Studs Terkel -- American journalist and author noted for works such as *Hard Times* (1970)

1913   Woody Herman -- American saxophone player and bandleader

1919   Liberace (Wladziu V. Liberace) -- American pianist and television performer

1920   Dave Philley -- Professional baseball player

1921   Harry Carey Jr. -- American motion-picture actor

1924   Frank Mankiewicz -- American columnist and author

1928   Billy Martin -- Professional baseball player and manager

1929   John Conyers Jr. -- U.S. congressman

1931   Lowell Weicker -- U.S. senator

1940   Lainie Kazan -- American nightclub and television singer

1943   Donny Anderson -- Professional football player

1944   Billy Cobham -- American jazz drummer

1949   Rick Reuschel -- Professional baseball player

1952   Pierce Brosnan -- American television and motion-picture actor, noted for his title role in the series *Remington Steele*

1953   Rick Rhoden -- Professional baseball player

1955   Jack Morris -- Professional baseball player

1955   Olga Korbut -- Russian gymnast

1960   Yannick Noah -- French tennis player

MAY 16 -- EVENTS

1532   Sir Thomas More resigned as Lord Chancellor because of his disapproval of Henry VIII's plan to marry Anne Boleyn.

1605   Paul V was elected pope of the Roman Catholic Church.

1866   Congress authorized the first U.S. five-cent piece, first called the half-dime and later referred to as the nickel because of its content of 25% nickel and 75% copper.

1868   The U.S. Senate failed by one vote to convict President Andrew Johnson in his impeachment trial.

1903   George A. Wyman left San Francisco on the trip in which he became the first person to cross the North American continent by motorcycle. Two months later he reached New York.

1920   Joan of Arc was canonized as a saint by Pope Benedict XV.

1927   The Supreme Court ruled that bootleggers must file income tax returns.

1929   The first Oscars were awarded by the Motion Picture Academy. Winners were Janet Gaynor, best actress, Emil Jannings, best actor, and *Wings* was the best picture.

1940   German units penetrated the northwest extension of France's Maginot Line in World War II.

MAY 17 -- BIRTHDAYS

1740   **John Penn** -- A North Carolina delegate to the Continental Congress and a signer of the Declaration of Independence

1749   **Edward Jenner** --British physician and discoverer of vaccination as a means of preventing smallpox

1768   **Caroline** -- Wife of King George IV of England

1803   **Robert Smith Surtees** -- English novelist

1866   **Erik Satie** -- French composer and pianist whose bold harmonies influenced Maurice Ravel and several other composers

1868   **Horace Elgin Dodge** -- One of the Dodge brothers who developed the Dodge automobile

1875   **Jean Angelo** -- French stage and motion-picture actor

1886   **Alfonso XIII** -- The last king of Spain, 1902-1931, before the Spanish Civil War

1899   **Del Webb** -- American builder and baseball executive with the New York Yankees during their glory years of the 1950s

1903   **Cool Papa Bell** -- Hall of Fame baseball player

1906   **Zinka Milanov** -- Yugoslav soprano

1911   **Maureen O'Sullivan** -- Irish-born motion-picture actress

1911   **Clark Kerr** -- Noted American educator

1912   **Archibald Cox** -- American law professor and first Watergate special prosecutor

1914   **Stewart Alsop** -- American newspaper columnist
1916   **Richard W. Bolling** -- U.S. congressman
1918   **Birgit Nilsson** -- Swedish dramatic soprano and one of the finest singers of heroic roles in the operas of Richard Wagner
1919   **Merle Miller** -- American writer and biographer
1920   **Harriet Van Horne** -- American columnist and author
1921   **Bob Merrill** -- American composer noted for songs such as "Honeycomb," "Love Makes the World Go Round," "How Much Is That Doggie in the Window?" and "If I Knew You Were Coming I'da Baked a Cake"
1932   **Billy Hoeft** -- Professional baseball player
1934   **Earl Morrall** -- Professional football player
1936   **Dennis Hopper** -- American motion-picture actor and director, noted for *Easy Rider* (1969)
1938   **Paolo Bortoluzzi** -- Italian ballet dancer
1941   **Ronald Tavel** -- American writer
1945   **Tony Roche** -- Australian tennis player and superstar
1950   **Wendy Paish** -- Australian tennis player
1955   **Debra Winger** -- American motion-picture actress
1956   **Sugar Ray Leonard** -- Welterweight boxing champion
1957   **Linda Mottram** -- English tennis player
1957   **Pascual Perez** -- Professional baseball player

MAY 17 -- EVENTS

352 AD   Liberius became pope of the Roman Catholic Church.
885 AD   Stephen V became pope of the Roman Catholic Church. He was Stephen VI at the time, but in 1961 Stephen II was dropped from the list of popes.
1510   Sandro Botticelli, the great Italian painter, died in Florence at age 65.
1792   The New York Stock Exchange had its real beginning in a meeting of 24 brokers under a buttonwood tree on the present site of 68 Wall Street.
1814   Norway adopted its present constitution, which was accepted by Sweden, but the Swedes refused to grant Norway its independence and continued to rule the country until 1905.
1827   Andrew Johnson married Eliza McCardle.
1875   The first Kentucky Derby was run, at Churchill Downs in Louisville. The winner was Aristides and the purse was $2,850.

1939   King George VI visited Canada, the first reigning British monarch to do so.

1940   The Germans occupied Brussels in World War II.

1954   The U.S. Supreme Court ruled unanimously that racial segregation in the public schools was unconstitutional, and ordered it ended with "all deliberate speed."

1969   The Russian space vehicle *Venera 6* landed on Venus.

1973   The Senate Select Committee opened hearings on the Watergate affair under the chairmanship of Senator Sam Ervin.

MAY 18 -- BIRTHDAYS

1610   **Stefano della Bella** -- Italian printmaker

1742   **Lionel Lukin** -- Inventor of lifeboats

1836   **Wilhelm Steinitz** -- World chess champion who reigned from 1866 to 1885

1850   **Oliver Heaviside** -- English physicist and mathematician

1862   **Josephus Daniels** -- U.S. Secretary of the Navy during World War I

1868   **Nicholas II** – The last czar of Russia, who was executed in 1918 by the Bolsheviks

1872   **Bertrand Russell** -- English mathematician and philosopher and coauthor with Alfred North Whitehead of the monumental work, *Principia Mathematica*

1883   **Walter Gropius** -- German architect and founder of the famous Bauhaus school of design in Germany

1889   **Thomas Midgley Jr.** -- American chemist who first discovered lead as an anti-knock additive to gasoline

1897   **Frank Capra** – Italian-born motion-picture director, noted for the classic, *It Happened One Night,* among many others

1902   **Meredith Willson** – American composer, author, and flutist, noted for songs such as "76 Trombones," "Iowa," "May the Good Lord Bless and Keep You," and "It's Beginning to Look Like Christmas"

1904   **Jacob Javits** -- U.S. senator in the 1960s and 1970s

1909   **Fred Perry** -- British tennis player and Wimbledon singles champion, 1934-1936

1912   **Richard Brooks** -- American screenwriter and motion-picture director, noted for such films as *The Blackboard Jungle* (1955), *The Brothers Karamazov* (1958), and *Elmer Gantry* (1960)

1912   **Dan Topping** -- American baseball executive and principal owner of the New York Yankees during their glory years of the 1950s

1913   **Perry Como** – American singer and actor with a career of over 40 years as a star

1914   **Pierre Balmain** -- French fashion designer

1919   **Dame Margot Fonteyn** – England's leading ballerina of the 20th century, and one of the first English dancers to achieve an international reputation

1920   **John Paul II** -- Roman Catholic pope

1921   **Patrick Dennis** -- American writer and author of *Auntie Mame*

1924   **"Choo Choo" Charlie Justice** -- Professional football player

1930   **Pernell Roberts** -- American television actor

1931   **Robert Morse** -- American motion-picture actor

1934   **Dwayne Hickman** -- American motion-picture and television actor

1937   **Brooks Robinson** -- Hall of Fame baseball player

1946   **Reggie Jackson** -- Professional baseball player and superstar

1951   **Jim Sundberg** -- Professional baseball player

MAY 18 -- EVENTS

1291   The Crusaders abandoned Tyre to the Moslems, the prelude to the end of the final Crusade.

1642   Montreal, Canada, was founded by a small Roman Catholic missionary group headed by Paul de Chomedey, Sieur de Maisonneuve.

1643   The Battle of Rocroi was won by the great French commander, the Prince de Conde, over the Spanish, destroying the myth of the "invincible Spanish infantry."

1804   Napoleon Bonaparte was proclaimed Emperor of France by the French senate.

1852   Massachusetts became the first state to make school attendance compulsory.

1860   Abraham Lincoln was nominated for president on the third ballot by the Republican convention in Chicago.

1863   General U.S. Grant began the siege of Vicksburg in the Civil War. The siege lasted until July 4, when the defenders surrendered.

1910   Halley's Comet neared the earth, after passing over the sun in late April, frightening hundreds of thousands of people in the U.S., who thought the world was coming to an end.

1933   The Tennessee Valley Authority was created by Congress.
1940   Nazi forces in Belgium broke through toward the coast, capturing Antwerp in World War II.
1953   American aviatrix Jacqueline Cochran became the first woman to fly faster than the speed of sound, in an F-86 sabrejet at 652.3 miles per hour.
1974   India joined the nuclear club by exploding its first atomic bomb.
1980   The Mount Saint Helens volcano in Washington State erupted, killing 60 persons and dumping 600,000 tons of ash on the surrounding area.

MAY 19 -- BIRTHDAYS

1593   **Jacob Jordaens** -- Flemish painter
1593   **Claude Vignon** -- French painter
1611   **Innocent XI** -- Pope of the Roman Catholic Church, 1676-1689
1762   **Johann Gottlieb Fichte** -- German philosopher, who strongly influenced German nationalism in the late 18th and early 19th centuries
1795   **Johns Hopkins** -- American financier and philanthropist, who financed the founding of Johns Hopkins University
1860   **Vittorio Emanuele Orlando** -- Italian World War I prime minister
1861   **Dame Nellie Melba** -- Australian soprano for whom Peach Melba was named, and who was said to have had "as many lovers as she gave encores"
1890   **Ho Chi Minh** -- President of North Vietnam, 1954-1969, and leader in North Vietnam's successful fight for independence from France
1897   **Lady Astor (Nancy Langhorne)** -- First woman to serve in the British Parliament
1909   **Bruce Bennett** -- American actor and Olympic shot-putter
1925   **Malcolm X (Malcolm Little)** -- Leader of the Black Muslims in the 1950s and 1960s
1928   **Dolph Schayes** -- Professional basketball player with over 19,000 career points
1929   **Gil McDougald** -- Professional baseball player
1929   **Curt Simmons** -- Professional baseball player
1934   **Jim Lehrer** -- American television newsman and commentator on the *MacNeil-Lehrer News Hour*
1935   **David Hartman** -- American actor and television host
1941   **Nora Ephron** -- American writer

1942   **Frank Froehling III** -- American tennis player
1945   **Pete Townshend** -- British guitarist and songwriter for the Who musical group
1949   **Archie Manning** -- Professional football player
1950   **Patrick Caddell** -- American public opinion analyst and pollster
1952   **Dan Ford** -- Professional baseball player
1952   **Joey Ramone** -- American musician with the Ramones musical group
1955   **Ed Whitson** -- Professional baseball player

MAY 19 -- EVENTS

715 AD Gregory II (Saint Gregory) was elected Roman Catholic pope.
1342   Clement VI was crowned Roman Catholic pope. He was one of the French popes who resided at Avignon.
1536   Anne Boleyn, the second queen of England's King Henry VIII, was beheaded on Henry's orders on charges of adultery.
1571   Manila was founded by Spanish conquistador Miguel Lopez de Legazpe.
1643   Massachusetts, Plymouth, Connecticut, and New Haven formed the "United Colonies of New England."
1649   The Commonwealth of England was established following the overthrow of King Charles I.
1795   James Boswell, Dr. Samuel Johnson's famous biographer, died in London at age 54.
1864   Nathaniel Hawthorne, the noted American writer, died in Plymouth, New Hampshire, at age 59.
1884   The five Ringling Brothers founded their famous circus, in Baraboo, Wisconsin.
1935   Lawrence of Arabia (T.E. Lawrence) was killed in a motorcycle accident at Clouds Hill, Dorset, at age 46.
1940   General Maxime Weygand was appointed commander-in-chief of Allied forces in World War II, replacing General Gamelin, in the face of advancing Nazi forces in France.
1945   Four hundred U.S. Superfortress bombers attacked Tokyo in World War II.

MAY 20 -- BIRTHDAYS

1364   Sir Henry Percy -- English rebel who led an uprising against King Henry IV

1663 **William Bradford** -- American printer who established New York's first newspaper, the New York *Gazette*

1764 **Johann Gottfried Schadow** -- German sculptor

1768 **Dolley Payne Madison** -- Wife of President James Madison

1772 **Sir William Congreve** -- English artillery officer, who invented the rocket used by British troops against Napoleon, and whose "rockets' red glare" was referred to in "The Star-Spangled Banner"

1799 **Honore de Balzac** -- French writer and one of the most important novelists of the 1800s, noted for works such as *Pere Goriot* and *Eugenie Grandet*

1806 **John Stuart Mill** -- English philosopher and economist, noted for his *System of Logic* (1843), which ranks with Aristotle's works on logic

1808 **Thomas Dartmouth Rice** -- Father of the U.S. minstrel show

1818 **William George Fargo** -- Co-founder of the gold-rush express company of Wells, Fargo & Company

1851 **Emile Berliner** -- American inventor of the practical telephone transmitter in 1877 and the "lateral-cut" recording disc in 1887

1856 **Henri Edmond Cross** -- French painter

1882 **Sigrid Undset** -- Nobel Prize-winning Norwegian novelist, noted for the epic trilogy, *Kristin Lavransdatter* (1920-1922)

1899 **John Marshall Harlan** -- U.S. Supreme Court justice, 1955-1971

1908 **Jimmy Stewart** -- American stage, screen, and television actor, and star performer for over 40 years

1915 **Moshe Dayan** -- Israeli soldier and statesman, who commanded the Israeli forces in the Arab-Israeli war of 1956 and the Six-Day War against Egypt, Jordan, and Syria in 1967

1919 **George Gobel** -- American comedian and television performer

1921 **Hal Newhouser** -- Professional baseball pitcher who won 29 games in 1945

1927 **Bud Grant** -- Professional football player and coach

1931 **Ken Boyer** -- Professional baseball player and manager

1937 **Dave Hill** -- Professional golfer

1940 **Sadaharu Oh** -- Japanese baseball player with over 800 career home runs in Japan

1940 **Stan Mikita** -- Professional hockey player who won the National Hockey League trophies for most valuable player, leading scorer, and sportsmanship in 1966-1967 and 1967-1968

1942 **Frew McMillan** -- South African tennis player

1944 **Joe Cocker** -- British rock singer

1946   **Bobby Murcer** -- Professional baseball player
1946   **Cher (Cherilyn Sakisian)** -- American singer, television per-
        former, and motion-picture actress
1951   **Cullen Bryant** -- Professional football player
1952   **Rickie Upchurch** -- Professional football player
1954   **Jimmy Henderson** -- American rock musician
1958   **Ron Reagan** -- American dancer and son of President Reagan

MAY 20 -- EVENTS

1498   Vasco da Gama anchored at Calicut, India, after his historic
        voyage around the Cape of Good Hope.
1506   Christopher Columbus died in Valladolid, Spain, at age 54. The
        "Discoverer of America and Admiral of the Ocean Sea" died in
        a humble dwelling in poverty.
1536   King Henry VIII of England married Jane Seymour one day
        after he had beheaded his first wife Anne Boleyn.
1830   The first railroad timetable was published, in the newspaper
        Baltimore *American.*
1861   North Carolina seceded from the Union. It was among the last
        of the Southern states to do so.
1861   The capital of the Confederacy was moved from Montgomery,
        Alabama, to Richmond, Virginia.
1862   President Lincoln signed the Homestead Act, opening millions
        of acres of Western land to settlers.
1882   The Triple Alliance was formed in Vienna between Germany,
        Austria, and Italy.
1927   Charles A. Lindbergh left New York's Roosevelt Field in his
        Spirit of St. Louis on the first nonstop solo trip across the Atlantic.
        He landed in Paris the next day.
1932   Amelia Earhart began the first solo flight by a woman across the
        Atlantic Ocean. She made the trip from Newfoundland to
        Londonderry in 15 hours.
1939   The Pan American Airways *Yankee Clipper* took off from Port
        Washington, N.Y., for Europe, inaugurating regular transatlan-
        tic air service.
1941   German paratroops invaded Crete in World War II.

MAY 21 -- BIRTHDAYS

1471   **Albrecht Durer** -- German painter, engraver, and designer, and
        one of the foremost artists of his country during the Renaissance

1527   **Philip II** -- King of Spain, 1556-1598, during whose reign Spain conquered Portugal, but was defeated by the English in the destruction of Spain's "Invincible Armada" in 1588

1688   **Alexander Pope** — Great English poet and brilliant satirist whose works are the most often quoted of any English author except Shakespeare

1780   **Elizabeth Gurney Fry** -- Pioneer British prison reformer, who was among the first to insist that prisoners need help rather than punishment in becoming good citizens

1792   **Gustave Gaspard de Coriolis** — French mathematician noted for analyzing the Coriolis force on moving objects due to the earth's rotation

1844   **Henri Rousseau** -- French "primitive" painter whose works strongly influenced the surrealism movement of the 1920s

1873   **Richard Bennett** -- American stage and screen actor, leading matinee idol of his day, and father of actresses Barbara, Constance, and Joan Bennett

1878   **Glenn Curtiss** -- American inventor and pioneer in the development of aircraft

1884   **Sir Claude Auchinleck** -- British World War II field marshal

1889   **Mario Bonnard** -- Italian motion-picture actor and director

1890   **Harry Austin Tierney** -- American composer and pianist, noted for songs such as "Alice Blue Gown"

1898   **Armand Hammer** -- American financier, manufacturer, and art collector

1902   **Earl Averill** — Professional baseball player who hit the ball that injured Dizzy Dean's toe and ultimately ended his career

1904   **Fats Waller** -- American pianist, composer, and jazz musician

1904   **Robert Montgomery** -- American motion-picture actor and director

1912   **Monty Stratton** -- Professional baseball player

1916   **Harold Robbins** -- Highly popular American novelist

1917   **Dennis Day** -- American singer and actor

1917   **Raymond Burr** -- American television and motion-picture actor noted for the long-running series *Perry Mason*

1921   **Andrei Dmitriyevich Sakharov** -- Russian physicist and noted dissident who shared the 1958 Nobel Prize in physics

1923   **Ara Parseghian** -- American football coach and sportscaster

1925   **Peggy Cass** -- American stage and television actress

1926   **Robert Creeley** — American poet and founder of the "Black Mountain" movement of the 1950s

1941   **Ronald Isley** -- American singer with the Isley Brothers
1944   **Peter Banaszak** -- Professional football player
1948   **Jurgen Fassbender** -- West German tennis player
1960   **Kent Hrbek** -- Professional baseball player
1961   **Tim Lever** -- British keyboardist and saxophonist with the Dead or Alive musical group

MAY 21 -- EVENTS

1542   Hernando de Soto, the Spanish explorer, died and was buried in the Mississippi River, which he had discovered the previous year.

1819   The first bicycle was ridden on the streets of New York. It was considered such a hazard that a city law was passed forbidding "velocipedes in public places."

1832   The first Democratic National Convention was held, in Baltimore. President Andrew Jackson was nominated for a second term.

1854   Lawrence, Kansas, was sacked by pro-slavery "border ruffians."

1881   Clara Barton founded the American Association of the Red Cross, which later became the American Red Cross.

1924   Fourteen-year-old Bobby Franks was murdered by two students, Nathan Leopold Jr. and Richard Loeb, resulting later in the famous Leopold-Loeb trial.

1927   Charles A. Lindbergh arrived at Le Bourget Field near Paris, France, completing the first solo nonstop flight across the Atlantic Ocean.

1932   Amelia Earhart landed in Londonderry, Ireland, completing the first woman's solo nonstop transatlantic flight.

1940   Berlin Radio claimed the annihilation of the French Ninth Army in World War II.

1972   Michelangelo's *Pieta,* one of the world's sculptural masterpieces, was severely damaged in St. Peter's Basilica by Lazlo Toth, a Hungarian emigre.

1977   Seattle Slew won the Preakness Stakes at Pimlico.

MAY 22 -- BIRTHDAYS

1733   **Hubert Robert** -- French painter

1783 **William Sturgeon** – English electrical engineer who devised the first electromagnet capable of supporting more than its own weight

1813 **Richard Wagner** -- One of the world's four or five greatest composers

1820 **Worthington Whittredge** -- American landscape painter

1845 **Mary Cassatt** -- One of America's greatest women painters, noted for works such as *The Cup of Tea, The Bath,* and *Woman and Child Driving*

1859 **Sir Arthur Conan Doyle** – British writer and creator of Sherlock Holmes, the world's best-known detective

1891 **Edwin B. Edwards** -- American composer, violinist, and trombonist, noted for such songs as "Tiger Rag"

1902 **Al Simmons** -- Hall of Fame baseball player

1907 **Sir Laurence Olivier** -- One of the most exciting and versatile actors in the English-speaking world

1908 **Horton Smith** – Hall of Fame golfer, and first to win the Masters Tournament (in 1934)

1914 **Vance Packard** -- American writer and author of *The Hidden Persuaders*

1915 **George Baker** -- American cartoonist and creator of *The Sad Sack*

1922 **Judith Crist** -- American film critic

1924 **Charles Aznavour** -- French lyric writer, singer, and actor

1928 **T. Boone Pickens Jr.** – American business executive and "corporate raider," noted for his takeover attempts of U.S. corporations

1930 **Marisol** -- American sculptor

1934 **Peter Nero** -- American pianist

1934 **Garry Wills** – American writer and author of political biography

1938 **Susan Strasberg** -- American stage and motion-picture actress and daughter of actor and director Lee Strasberg

1938 **Richard Benjamin** -- American motion-picture actor

1941 **Paul Edward Winfield** -- American motion-picture and television actor

1942 **Barbara Parkins** -- Canadian-born television and motion-picture actress

1943 **Tommy John** -- Professional baseball player

1947 **Chuck Baltazar** -- American jockey

1955 **Nancy Yeargin** -- American tennis player

MAY 22 -- EVENTS

337 AD Roman emperor Constantine the Great died at age 49, after being baptized a Christian on his deathbed.

1819 The USS *Savannah* set out from Savannah, Georgia, on the first successful transatlantic voyage by a steamship. It docked in Liverpool, England, on June 20.

1849 Abraham Lincoln was granted a patent titled "Buoying Vessels over Shoals," making him the only president of the United States to hold a patent.

1885 Victor Hugo, the great French novelist, died in Paris at age 83.

1906 Wilbur and Orville Wright were granted a patent on their airplane.

1923 The comic strip, *The Nebbs,* by Sol Hess, first appeared.

1939 Adolf Hitler and Benito Mussolini concluded their "Pact of Steel," allying Germany and Italy in a prelude to World War II.

1960 The world's strongest assessable earthquake, 9.5 on the Richter scale, occurred south of Concepcion, Chile.

1972 President Nixon arrived in Moscow, the first U.S. president to visit the Russian capital.

1979 Joseph Clark was elected the youngest prime minister in the history of Canada.

MAY 23 -- BIRTHDAYS

1707 **Carolus Linnaeus** – Swedish botanist who established the modern scientific method of naming plants and animals by their genus (group) and species (kind)

1734 **Franz Mesmer** -- Austrian physician who pioneered in the practice of hypnotism, and for whom the word *mesmerism* (animal magnetism) was named

1799 **Thomas Hood** -- English poet and humorist, who excused himself for working so hard by punning, "So that I may earn my livelihood I have to be a lively Hood"

1810 **Margaret Fuller** – American journalist, social reformer, and a leader of the philosophical movement called *transcendentalism*

1820 **James Buchanan Eads** -- American engineer and inventor, who designed and built the steel-arch Eads Bridge in St. Louis

1824 **Ambrose Everett Burnside** – Civil War Union general whose whiskers on the side of his face gave rise to the term *burnsides,* which later became *sideburns*

1828   **Edward Hitchcock** -- First professor of physical education in the United States, in 1861 at Amherst

1850   **Virginia Knight Logan** -- American composer and author (songs such as "A Song for You and Me," "Rose of My Heart," and "Moonlight Waltz"), and mother of composer Frederick Logan

1883   **Douglas Fairbanks** -- American stage and motion-picture actor and one of the superstars of Hollywood in the 1920s

1886   **James Gleason** -- American stage and screen actor in over 100 films

1888   **Zack Wheat** -- Hall of Fame baseball player

1890   **Herbert Marshall** -- English stage and motion-picture actor

1898   **Frank McHugh** -- American stage, screen, and television actor in over 100 movies

1908   **Max Abramovitz** -- American architect

1908   **John Bardeen** -- American physicist and co-inventor of the transistor

1910   **Artie Shaw** -- American bandleader of the Big Band Era of the 1930s and 1940s

1910   **Franz Kline** -- American abstract painter noted for his large black-and-white paintings

1912   **John Payne** -- American motion-picture and television actor

1921   **James Benjamin Blish** – American author noted for his books about *Star Trek*

1928   **Rosemary Clooney** -- American actress and singer

1933   **Joan Collins** -- English motion-picture and television actress

1933   **John Browning** -- American pianist

1934   **Mason Rudolph** -- Professional golfer

1934   **Robert A. Moog** -- Inventor of the Moog electronic synthesizer

1944   **John Newcombe** -- Australian tennis player and Wimbledon singles champion, 1970-1971

1946   **David Graham** -- Professional golfer

1949   **James Braxton** -- Professional football player

1951   **Anatoly Karpov** -- Russian grand master of chess

1952   **Marvin Hagler** -- Middleweight boxing champion known as Marvelous Marvin

MAY 23 -- EVENTS

1430   Joan of Arc was captured by the Burgundians at Compiegne and sold to the English for the equivalent of $3,000.

1498	Girolamo Savonarola, Italian friar and fiery religious reformer, was hanged and his body burned for heresy on orders of Pope Alexander VI.
1533	Archbishop Cranmer divorced King Henry VIII of England from Catherine of Aragon so that Henry's earlier secret marriage to Anne Boleyn would have validity.
1618	The "Defenestration of Prague" occurred, in which prominent Protestant leaders in Prague were seized and thrown out of a castle window, marking the start of the Thirty Years' War.
1701	Captain William Kidd was hanged in London for piracy and murder.
1785	Benjamin Franklin, in a letter to George Whatley, first described the bifocal eyeglasses he had just invented.
1788	South Carolina entered the Union as the 8th state.
1873	The Royal Canadian Mounted Police was established.
1906	Henrik Ibsen, the great Norwegian playwright, died in Oslo at age 78.
1911	The New York Public Library building at Fifth Avenue and 42nd Street was dedicated by President William Howard Taft.
1915	Italy declared war on Austria-Hungary, thus entering World War I on the side of the Allies.
1922	*Abie's Irish Rose,* a new comedy by Anne Nichols, opened at the Fulton Theater in New York.
1934	Clyde Barrow and Bonnie Parker, the notorious outlaws, were killed in a hail of bullets near Shreveport, Louisiana.
1945	Heinrich Himmler, the notorious Nazi Gestapo chief, died by biting a cyanide capsule hidden in his mouth, 3 days after his capture by British troops.
1951	The Chinese Communists annexed Tibet.

MAY 24 -- BIRTHDAYS

1494	**Jacopa da Pontormo** -- Italian painter
1544	**William Gilbert** -- English physician and pioneer researcher in electricity and magnetism
1616	**John Maitland** -- Scottish statesman and Duke of Lauderdale
1693	**Georg Raphael Donner** -- Austrian sculptor
1743	**Jean Paul Marat** -- One of the most radical leaders of the French Revolution, who, with Danton and Robespierre, was responsible for the Reign of Terror

1816   **Emanuel Gottlieb Leutze** -- German painter known for his American historical works, such as his masterpiece, *Washington Crossing the Delaware*

1819   **Victoria** -- Queen of England, 1837-1901, and one of the greatest rulers in English history

1854   **Richard Mansfield** -- One of the best-known actors in the United States during the 1890s

1870   **Jan Christiaan Smuts** -- South African soldier, scholar, and World War II prime minister

1878   **Harry Emerson Fosdick** -- One of the best known Protestant ministers in the United States in the first half of the 20th century

1895   **Samuel I. Newhouse** -- American newspaper publisher

1899   **Suzanne Langlen** -- French tennis player, six times Wimbledon singles champion, and one of the greatest women players in history

1903   **Dwight B. Latham** -- American composer, author, and singer, noted for songs such as "MacNamara's Band" and "I'm My Own Grandpaw"

1909   **Wilbur Mills** -- U.S. congressman prominent during the 1950s and 1960s

1914   **Lilli Palmer** -- German-born stage and motion-picture actress

1918   **Coleman Young** -- Mayor of Detroit

1925   **Mai Zetterling** -- Swedish motion-picture and television actress

1927   **John B. Kelly Jr.** -- U.S. Olympic champion and brother of Princess Grace of Monaco

1934   **Jane M. Byrne** -- Mayor of Chicago who succeeded Richard Daley

1941   **Bob Dylan** -- American folk singer, musician, and composer, noted for songs such as "Blowin' in the Wind" (1962) and "Like a Rolling Stone" (1965)

1946   **Francisco "Pancho" Guzman** -- Ecuadorian tennis player

1947   **Cecilia Martinez** -- American tennis player

1950   **Jo Ann Washam** -- Professional golfer

1953   **Michael Strachan** -- Professional football player

MAY 24 -- EVENTS

1626   Peter Minuit, the Dutch colonial governor, bought the island of Manhattan from the Indians for the equivalent of $24.

1738   John Wesley was given "saving faith" during a Moravian meeting in Aldersgate Street, London, which eventually led him to establish Methodism.

1830   The first division of the Baltimore & Ohio Railroad was completed, a 13-mile link from Baltimore to Ellicott Mills.

1844   "What hath God wrought!" was sent by Samuel F.B. Morse from the Supreme Court room in the Capitol to Baltimore, as the first public telegraph message.

1859   "Ave Maria," by Charles Gounod, was sung for the first time at a concert in Paris.

1883   The Brooklyn Bridge was opened to traffic, linking Brooklyn and Manhattan.

1935   The first major league night baseball game was played, at Crosley Field in Cincinnati, with the Reds defeating the Philadelphia Phillies, 2-1.

1940   Adolf Hitler ordered the German armored units to halt mop-up operations and head toward Paris in World War II. This move saved 336,000 British soldiers trapped at Dunkerque.

1941   The British HMS *Hood,* the world's largest warship at the time, was sunk by the German battleship *Bismarck* between Iceland and Greenland in World War II.

1950   Sweetwater Clifton joined the New York Knickerbockers, becoming the first black National Basketball Association player.

1962   U.S. astronaut Scott Carpenter made a three-orbit flight in *Aurora 7,* the second orbital flight by an American.

MAY 25 -- BIRTHDAYS

1616   **Carlo Dolci** -- Italian painter

1803   **Ralph Waldo Emerson** -- American poet and essayist and a leading figure in the thought and literature of American civilization

1803   **Edward George Bulwer-Lytton** -- English historical novelist and playwright, whose most famous novel is *The Last Days of Pompeii* (1834)

1818   **Jakob Burckhardt** -- Swiss historian, art critic, and author of the four-volume work *A Cultural History of Greece* (1898-1902)

1825   **Daniel Baird Wesson** -- American firearms manufacturer and co-founder with Horace Smith of Smith and Wesson Revolver Company

1845   **Lip Pike** -- Baseball's first professional player

1878   **Bojangles Robinson** -- American dancer and actor of vaudeville, the musical stage, and motion-pictures

1886   **Philip Murray** -- American labor leader and second president of the CIO, 1940-1952

1889	**Igor Sikorsky** -- Russian-born pioneer in aircraft design, who produced the world's first four-engine airplane in 1913
1897	**Gene Tunney** -- World heavyweight champion, 1926-1928, who defeated Jack Dempsey for the crown
1898	**Bennett Cerf** -- American publisher and television personality
1905	**Joseph Harsch** -- American journalist and commentator
1908	**Robert Morley** -- English actor and playwright
1908	**Theodore Roethke** -- American poet who received the Pulitzer Prize in 1954 for *The Waking: Poems 1933-1953*
1916	**Lindsey Nelson** -- American sportscaster
1916	**Ginny Simms** -- American singer and radio performer
1917	**Steve Cochran** -- American stage and motion-picture actor
1917	**Theodore Hesburgh** -- American priest, president of the University of Notre Dame, and civil rights champion
1918	**Claude Akins** -- American stage, screen, and television actor
1921	**Hal David** -- American songwriter and lyricist who collaborated with Burt Bacharach on such songs as "Raindrops Keep Falling on My Head" and "What the World Needs Now"
1923	**John Weitz** -- German-American fashion designer, author, and sportsman, who served as a World War II spy for the United States
1925	**Jeanne Crain** -- American motion-picture actress
1926	**Bill Sharman** – Greatest free thrower in the history of professional basketball
1926	**Miles Davis** -- American trumpeter and pioneer of cool jazz
1927	**Robert Ludlum** -- American novelist noted for works such as *The Icarus Agenda, The Bourne Supremacy,* and *The Osterman Weekend*
1929	**Beverly Sills** -- American operatic soprano
1932	**K. C. Jones** -- Professional basketball player and coach, noted for his tenure with the Boston Celtics
1934	**Ron Nesson** -- American newsman and press secretary for President Ford
1935	**Cookie Gilchrist** -- Professional football player
1936	**Tom T. Hall** -- American singer and songwriter
1943	**Leslie Uggams** -- American singer and actress
1947	**Jessi Colter** -- American country singer
1947	**Karen Valentine** -- American television actress
1950	**John Montefusco** -- Professional baseball player
1954	**Bob Knepper** -- Professional baseball player

MAY 25 -- EVENTS

1787	The Constitutional Convention opened in Independence Hall in Philadelphia to draft a constitution for the United States.
1810	Buenos Aires overthrew Spanish authority and set up its own self-government. The rest of Argentina declared its independence eight years later.
1878	The world premiere of Gilbert and Sullivan's operetta *HMS Pinafore* was held in London.
1914	The Irish Home Rule Bill was passed by the British Parliament.
1927	Henry Ford announced the discontinuance of the Model T and plans to replace it with the Model A.
1935	Jesse Owens, America's future Olympic star, broke five world's records and tied a sixth at the Big Ten Championships at Ann Arbor, Mich. He did all six in 45 minutes.
1935	Babe Ruth hit the last home run of his career, number 714, at Forbes Field in Pittsburgh.
1938	The Soviet ambassador to the U.S. declared that Moscow was "ready to defend Czechoslovakia in the event of aggression" by Adolf Hitler.
1943	Roosevelt and Churchill concluded their Washington *Trident* conference after agreeing on the future strategies of World War II.
1945	The U.S. Chiefs of Staff set November 1 as the date for the launching of Operation Olympic, the invasion of Japan in World War II.
1961	President John F. Kennedy called for the nation to put a man on the moon by the end of the 1960s.
1979	A DC-10 jet crashed in Chicago, killing all 272 persons aboard, in the worst disaster in the history of American aviation.
1985	A hurricane roared in from the Bay of Bengal and devastated Bangladesh coastal communities, leaving some 20,000 dead.

MAY 26 -- BIRTHDAYS

1602	**Philippe de Champaigne** -- French painter
1650	**Duke of Marlborough** -- One of England's greatest generals
1667	**Abraham De Moivre** – Noted French mathematician best known for De Moivre's Theorem
1822	**Edmond de Goncourt** -- French novelist, art critic, and diarist, who with his brother Jules provided the basis for the realist and naturalist literary movements in France

1886 **Al Jolson** -- American singer, actor, and most popular recording artist of his time

1894 **Paul Lukas** -- Hungarian stage and motion-picture actor whose career spanned over 50 years

1897 **Norma Talmadge** -- One of the most popular idols of the American screen in the 1920s, who appeared in over 200 silent films

1907 **John Wayne** -- American motion-picture actor and superstar who appeared in some 250 films in a career of over 40 years

1910 **Laurance Rockefeller** -- American millionaire and conservationist

1910 **Adolfo Lopez Mateos** -- President of Mexico, 1958-1964

1911 **Ben Alexander** -- American motion-picture and television actor

1912 **Janos Kadar** -- Premier of Hungary after the Hungarian Revolt of 1956

1920 **Peggy Lee** -- American singer and actress

1923 **James Arness** -- American motion-picture actor and star of television's long-running series *Gunsmoke*

1927 **Jacques Bergerac** -- French motion-picture actor

1932 **Ranan R. Lurie** -- American cartoonist and most widely syndicated columnist in the world

1937 **Jack R. Murphy** -- Noted American jewel thief known as "Murph the Surf"

1939 **Brent Musburger** -- American sportscaster

1941 **Cliff Drysdale** -- South African tennis player and sportscaster

1947 **Darrell Evans** -- Professional baseball player

1949 **Dan Pastorini** -- Professional football player

1949 **Hank Williams Jr.** -- American country singer

1951 **Sally Ride** -- First American woman astronaut

1955 **Wesley Walker** -- Professional football player

MAY 26 -- EVENTS

735 AD The Venerable Bede, the learned English writer, died at an age of approximately 63.

1521 The Diet of Worms, a special meeting of princes, nobles, and clergymen, outlawed Martin Luther and his followers, after Luther refused to retract his teachings.

1583 Susanna, the first child of William Shakespeare and Anne Hathaway, was baptized.

1703   Samuel Pepys, the noted English diarist, died in London at age 70.
1865   General Edmund Kirby-Smith surrendered the last Confederate army still in the field, finally ending the Civil War fighting.
1927   The Ford Motor Company turned out its 15 millionth car.
1940   British prime minister Winston Churchill made the decision to evacuate Dunkerque in Operation Dynamo in World War II.
1954   The funeral ship of the Egyptian pharaoh Cheops was unearthed in a limestone chamber near the Great Pyramid of Giza.
1959   Harvey Haddix pitched 12 perfect innings but lost in the 13th as Milwaukee beat Pittsburgh, 1-0.

MAY 27 -- BIRTHDAYS

1626   **William II** -- Prince of Orange
1629   **Pierre Legros** -- French sculptor
1699   **Giovanni Antonio Guardi** -- Italian painter
1794   **Cornelius Vanderbilt** -- American shipping and railroad magnate and founder of the Vanderbilt fortune, one of the greatest in America
1818   **Amelia Jenks Bloomer** -- American temperance reformer and women's rights advocate, who, because of her famous "Turkish pantaloons," caused the word *bloomers* to be added to the language
1819   **Julia Ward Howe** -- American poet and social reformer who wrote "The Battle Hymn of the Republic"
1836   **Jay Gould** -- American financier and founder of the Gould fortune
1837   **James Butler "Wild Bill" Hickok** -- American frontier scout and peace officer in the West
1867   **Arnold Bennett** -- English novelist and playwright, whose best-known work is *The Old Wives' Tale* (1908)
1871   **Georges Rouault** -- French painter, printmaker, and ceramicist, noted for such works as *The Old King* and *Miserere*
1878   **Isadora Duncan** -- American dancer who greatly influenced dancing in the 1900s
1894   **Louis Ferdinand Celine** -- French novelist noted for works such as *Journey to the End of the Night* (1932)
1894   **Dashiell Hammett** -- American detective fiction writer and creator of Sam Spade (in *The Maltese Falcon*) and Nick and Nora Charles (*The Thin Man*)

1907   **Rachel Carson** -- American marine biologist and science writer, and author of *The Sea Around Us* (1951) and *Silent Spring* (1962)

1908   **Harold Jacob Rome** -- American composer and author, noted for lyrics such as "All of a Sudden My Heart Sings" and "On the Avenue"

1909   **Pinky Higgins** -- Professional baseball player

1911   **Hubert H. Humphrey** – U.S. Vice President, 1965-1969, and presidential candidate in 1968

1911   **Vincent Price** -- American motion-picture actor

1912   **Sam Snead** – Professional golfer who won over 130 tournaments

1912   **John Cheever** -- American novelist and short-story writer

1915   **Herman Wouk** – American novelist who won a Pulitzer Prize in 1952 for *The Caine Mutiny*

1915   **Fred Wise** -- American lyricist noted for songs such as "A-You're Adorable" and "Let Me Go, Lover"

1923   **Henry Kissinger** -- U.S. secretary of state under Presidents Nixon and Ford

1928   **Thea Musgrave** -- Scottish composer and conductor

1930   **John Barth** -- Highly original American novelist, whose best-known work is *The Sot-Weed Factor* (1960)

1935   **Lee Meriweather** -- American television actress

1941   **Allan Carr** -- American show business producer noted for *La Cage aux Folles*

1950   **Michael Siani** -- Professional football player

1954   **Catherine Carr** -- Professional swimmer

1956   **Mark Clear** -- Professional baseball player

MAY 27 -- EVENTS

1564   John Calvin, the great Swiss religious leader, died in Geneva at age 57.

1679   The Act of Habeas Corpus, one of the basic guarantees of personal freedom in English and American law, was passed by the English Parliament.

1703   The construction of St. Petersburg (Leningrad), Russia, was begun by Peter the Great.

1840   Niccolo Paganini, the great Italian violinist, died of cancer at age 57, after a legendary deathbed performance on his Guarnerius violin.

1905   The naval battle of Tsushima Strait between Japan's island of
        Kyushu and Korea began in the Russo-Japanese War. The
        result was the near annihilation of the Russian fleet.

1929   Charles A. Lindbergh, the hero of the solo Atlantic flight,
        married Anne Morrow.

1935   The U.S. Supreme Court ruled the National Industrial Recovery
        Act unconstitutional.

1936   The Cunard Line's *Queen Mary* began its transatlantic maiden
        voyage.

1937   The Golden Gate Bridge was opened to the public.

1941   The British navy sank the powerful German battleship *Bismarck*
        off the coast of France, in one of the most important naval
        actions of World War II.

1942   Reinhard Heydrich, the "Hangman of Czechoslovakia," was
        murdered by patriots in Prague during World War II. In revenge
        the Nazis destroyed the town of Lidice.

1949   Robert Ripley, founder of Ripley's *Believe It or Not,* died at age
        56.

1964   Jawaharlal Nehru, India's first prime minister, died at the age of
        74.

MAY 28 -- BIRTHDAYS

1738   **Joseph Guillotin** – French physician and inventor of the guillo-
        tine in 1792

1743   **Louis Jean Desprez** -- French architect

1759   **William Pitt the Younger** -- British prime minister, 1783-1801
        and 1804-1806, and the youngest person ever to hold the post

1779   **Thomas Moore** -- Irish poet, satirist, and composer of "Believe
        Me If All Those Endearing Young Charms"

1807   **Louis Agassiz** -- Swiss-born naturalist, geologist, and educator

1818   **Pierre G.T. Beauregard** -- Confederate general who directed
        the bombardment of Fort Sumter, which started the Civil War,
        and who also fought at the first Battle of Bull Run and at Shiloh

1853   **Carl Larsson** -- Swedish illustrator

1884   **Eduard Benes** – Co-founder of Czechoslovakia in 1918 and
        president at the time of the Nazi takeover in 1938

1888   **Jim Thorpe** -- One of the most accomplished all-around athletes
        in history

1895   **Warren Giles** -- President of baseball's National League in the
        1950s and 1960s

1896	**Dick Sanford** -- American author and singer, noted for lyrics such as "Purple Shadows," "The Singing Hills," and "Mention My Name in Sheboygan"
1900	**Jack Little** -- English-born composer, author, and producer, noted for songs such as "A Shanty in Old Shanty Town"
1908	**Ian Fleming** -- English novelist and creator of James Bond
1912	**David Barbour** -- American composer noted for songs such as "Manana" and "It's a Good Day"
1916	**Walker Percy** -- American novelist and essayist noted for works such as *Love in the Ruins*
1917	**Barry Commoner** -- American biologist, environmentalist, and presidential candidate in 1980
1925	**Dietrich Fischer-Dieskau** -- German baritone
1931	**Stephen Birmingham** -- American writer and novelist
1931	**Carroll Baker** -- American motion-picture actress
1934	**Dionne** quintuplets -- Annette, Cecille, Emilie, Marie, and Yvonne Dionne, the first quintuplets to survive infancy
1938	**Jerry West** -- Professional basketball superstar
1944	**Gladys Knight** -- American singer
1945	**John Fogerty** -- American singer, songwriter, and guitarist with Creedence Clearwater Revival
1947	**Sondra Locke** -- American actress
1947	**Beth Howland** -- American actress
1957	**Kirk Gibson** -- Professional baseball player
1958	**Bill Doran** -- Professional baseball player

MAY 28 -- EVENTS

1291	Acre, in the Kingdom of Jerusalem, fell to the Moslems, ending the Crusades.
1533	Archbishop Thomas Cranmer pronounced King Henry VIII's marriage to Anne Boleyn valid.
1628	The English Parliament presented the Petition of Right to King Charles I, declaring unconstitutional certain actions of the king.
1863	The first black regiment from the North left Boston to fight in the Civil War.
1905	Japan completed the destruction of the Russian fleet begun the previous day in Tsushima Strait in the Russo-Japanese War.
1918	Units of the U.S. First Division launched the first American offensive in France in World War I, capturing Cantigny from the Germans.

1929   The first color movie, *On With the Show,* was released by Warner Brothers.

1934   The Dionne quintuplets, the first in history to survive infancy, were born in Callender, Ontario, Canada.

1937   Neville Chamberlain became prime minister of Britain.

1940   King Leopold III surrendered the 300,000-man Belgian army to the Nazis in World War II, and in turn was disowned by his cabinet.

1972   The Duke of Windsor, formerly King Edward VIII of England, died at age 77.

MAY 29 -- BIRTHDAYS

1630   **Charles II** -- King of England, 1660-1685, and the first of the restored Stuart line after the end of the Commonwealth

1698   **Edme Bouchardon** -- French sculptor

1736   **Patrick Henry** -- American orator and revolutionary, who said "Give me liberty or give me death" in 1775 before the Virginia Provincial Convention

1826   **Ebenezer Butterick** -- Inventor of paper patterns for clothing

1860   **Isaac Manuel Francisco Albeniz** -- Spanish pianist and composer and founder of contemporary Spanish music

1874   **G.K. Chesterton** -- English critic and author, known as "The Prince of Paradox"

1880   **Oswald Spengler** -- German philosopher of history noted for *The Decline of the West* (1918-1922)

1892   **Max Brand** -- American writer of Western novels such as *Destry Rides Again,* who in his prime turned out roughly two books per month

1894   **Josef von Sternberg** -- Austrian-American motion-picture director and one of the great masters of the American screen

1898   **Beatrice Lillie** -- English actress and one of the brightest and most natural comediennes of her time

1900   **Jack Palmer** -- American composer and author, noted for songs such as "Jumpin' Jive" and "Sentimental Baby"

1903   **Bob Hope** – American stage, screen, and television actor, and one of America's top comedians for over 50 years

1906   **T.H. White** -- English novelist and satirist

1913   **Iris Adrian** -- American motion-picture actress in some 100 films

1913   **Tony Zale** – Middleweight boxing champion, 1940-1947 and 1948

1917   **John F. Kennedy** -- 35th U.S. president

1918   **Herb Shriner** -- American humorist and television personality in the 1950s

1928   **Felix Rohatyn** -- American financier who helped rescue New York City from bankruptcy in the 1970s

1932   **Paul Ehrlich** -- American population biologist and author of *The Population Bomb*

1932   **Richie Guerin** -- Professional basketball player with over 14,000 career points

1939   **Al Unser** -- American racing car driver who won the Indianapolis 500 four times

1944   **Helmut Berger** -- Austrian motion-picture actor

1950   **Lesley Hunt** -- Australian tennis player

1955   **John W. Hinckley Jr.** -- Attempted assassin of President Reagan in 1981

MAY 29 -- EVENTS

1453   Constantinople fell to the Turkish sultan Mohammed II, marking the end of the Eastern Roman Empire or, as it was then called, the Byzantine Empire.

1649   England was declared a Commonwealth with Oliver Cromwell as Lord Protector

1660   Charles II entered London, achieving the Restoration of the Stuart monarchy in England after Oliver Cromwell's death.

1724   Benedict XIII was elected pope of the Roman Catholic Church.

1765   Patrick Henry made his famous speech to the Virginia House of Burgesses, in which he said, "If this be treason, make the most of it."

1790   Rhode Island became the last of the original 13 colonies to ratify the U.S. Constitution and thus became the 13th state.

1848   Wisconsin was admitted to the Union as the 30th state.

1867   The Austrian Compromise was forced upon Emperor Francis Joseph I, creating the Dual Monarchy of Austria-Hungary.

1911   Sir William Gilbert, the great English composer of Gilbert and Sullivan fame, died at Harrow Weald, Middlesex, at age 74.

1932   World War I veterans known as the "bonus army" began arriving in Washington to demand cash bonuses they were supposed to receive 13 years later.

1940   The British began the evacuation of Dunkerque in World War II, an operation in which 336,000 soldiers were rescued.

1953   Edmund Hillary of New Zealand and Tenzing Norgay of Nepal became the first men to climb Mt. Everest, the world's highest mountain.

MAY 30 -- BIRTHDAYS

1846   **Peter Carl Faberge** -- Noted Russian jeweler

1875   **Giovanni Gentile** -- "Philosopher of Fascism"

1885   **Karl Behr** -- American Hall of Fame tennis player

1887   **Alexander Archipenko** -- Russian-born sculptor noted for using solids and hollows in portraying the human form

1888   **James A. Farley** -- Franklin D. Roosevelt's campaign manager in 1932 and 1936, and postmaster general of the United States, 1933-1940

1891   **Ben Bernie** -- American composer and violinist noted for "Sweet Georgia Brown"

1896   **Howard Hawks** -- American motion-picture director and screenwriter, who directed such films as *The Road to Glory, Sergeant York,* and *The Big Sleep*

1899   **Irving Thalberg** -- American motion-picture director and "Boy Wonder of Hollywood" in the 1920s

1901   **Cornelia Otis Skinner** -- American stage actress and writer

1902   **Stepin Fetchit** -- First black actor to receive featured billing in American motion pictures

1906   **Norris Goff** -- American actor who played Abner Peabody on the radio program, *Lum and Abner,* of the 1930s and 1940s

1908   **Mel Blanc** -- American actor and voice specialist, who supplied the voice of numerous cartoon characters

1909   **Benny Goodman** -- American bandleader whose career spanned the Big Band Era of the 1930s and 1940s to the 1980s

1913   **Pee Wee Erwin** -- American trumpeter and composer

1915   **Frank Blair** -- Television newscaster who spent 20 years on the *Today* show

1920   **George London** -- American bass-baritone famous for his strong, masculine voice

1926   **Christine Jorgensen** -- Noted American transsexual

1934   **Aleksei Leonov** -- Russian cosmonaut and first man to walk in space

1936   **Keir Dullea** -- American stage, screen, and television actor

1939   **Michael J. Pollard** -- American stage and motion-picture actor

1943   **Gale Sayers** -- Professional football superstar

1949 **Lydell Mitchell** -- Professional football player
1964 **Wynonna Judd** -- American country singer who with her mother Naomi formed the singing Judds duo

MAY 30 -- EVENTS

1431 Joan of Arc was burned at the stake in the Old Market Square of Rouen by the English.
1498 Christopher Columbus departed from Sanlucar, Spain, on his third voyage to America.
1588 The Spanish Armada of 130 ships, commanded by the Duke of Medina Sidonia, sailed from Lisbon to prepare to engage the English.
1593 Christopher Marlowe, the great English playwright, was killed in a tavern brawl in Deptford at age 29.
1640 Peter Paul Rubens, the noted Flemish painter, died in Antwerp at age 62.
1744 Alexander Pope, the great English poet, died at Twickenham, outside London, at age 56.
1778 Voltaire, the greatest French philosopher of all time, died in Paris at age 83.
1878 The future great French artist, Henri Toulouse-Lautrec, fell at age 13 and broke his leg. A year later he broke the other leg, causing him to grow up deformed and dwarfish.
1894 Robert Lowe of the Boston Red Sox hit four home runs in four consecutive times at bat.
1896 The first automobile accident occurred, in New York City.
1911 The first Indianapolis 500 auto race was held; it was won by Ray Harroun driving a 1911 Marmon Wasp at an average speed of 74.59 miles per hour.
1922 The Lincoln Memorial was dedicated in Washington, D.C., by Chief Justice William Howard Taft.
1942 Cologne, Germany, was raided by the RAF in the first 1,000-bomber attack.
1961 Rafael Trujillo, the tyrannical dictator of the Dominican Republic, was assassinated, ending 31 years of harsh and severe rule.
1971 The U.S. Martian probe, *Mariner 9,* was launched.

MAY 31 -- BIRTHDAYS

1443 **Margaret Beaufort** -- Mother of King Henry VII of England and founder of St. John's and Christ's Colleges, Cambridge

1469   **Manuel I (the Fortunate)** -- King of Portugal, 1495-1521, who was in power when Portuguese heroes Vasco da Gama sailed around the Cape of Good Hope to India and Pedro Alvares Cabral discovered Brazil.

1622   **Jan Abrahamsz Beerstraaten** -- Dutch painter noted for works such as *Skating at Slooten*

1773   **Ludwig Tieck** -- German writer

1819   **Walt Whitman** -- American poet and essayist whose *Leaves of Grass* is considered one of the world's major literary works

1819   **William Worrall Mayo** -- Founder with his two sons of the Mayo Clinic in 1889 at St. Mary's Hospital in Rochester, Minnesota

1857   **Pius XI** -- Roman Catholic pope, 1922-1939, who settled the "Roman Question" with Italy, whereby the pope was granted temporal sovereignty over Vatican City

1860   **Walter Richard Sickert** -- Most important of the British Impressionist painters

1883   **Frances Alda** -- New Zealand soprano

1888   **Jack Holt** -- American motion-picture hero of some 100 Hollywood silents and talkies, and father of actors Jennifer, Tim, and David Holt

1894   **Fred Allen** -- American comedian and actor

1898   **Norman Vincent Peale** -- American minister noted also for his books and radio and television programs

1908   **Don Ameche** -- American motion-picture and television actor, and leading man in more than 40 films

1912   **Henry Jackson** -- U.S. senator from the 1960s to the early 1980s

1920   **Edward Bennett Williams** -- American lawyer and defender of controversial clients

1923   **Rainier III** -- Prince of Monaco

1923   **Ellsworth Kelly** -- American painter

1924   **Patricia Harris** -- Secretary of Housing and Urban Development under President Carter

1930   **Clint Eastwood** -- American television and motion-picture actor and director

1933   **Shirley Verrett** -- American mezzo-soprano

1938   **Peter Yarrow** -- American singer and guitarist with the Peter, Paul, and Mary musical group

1943   **Joe Namath** -- Professional football superstar and actor

1947   **John Bonham** -- British drummer with the Led Zeppelin musical group

1950   **Tippy Martinez** -- Professional baseball player

1955   **Laura Baugh** -- Professional golfer
1965   **Brooke Shields** -- American motion-picture and television actress

MAY 31 -- EVENTS

1594   Tintoretto, the great Venetian painter of the Italian Renaissance, died in Venice at age 76.
1669   Samuel Pepys, the great English writer, ended his famous *Diary*.
1740   Frederick the Great ascended the Prussian throne.
1790   The U.S. copyright law was enacted by Congress.
1809   Franz Joseph Haydn, the great Austrian composer, died in Vienna at age 77.
1889   Johnstown, Pennsylvania, suffered a disastrous flood after heavy rains caused the Conemaugh Dam to burst. More than 2,000 people were killed in its wake.
1902   The Treaty of Vereeniging ended the Boer War, with the two defeated republics, the Orange Free State and the South African Republic (the Transvaal), becoming British colonies.
1907   A flotilla of "taximeter cabs" arrived in New York from Paris, the first taxis to be seen in any American city.
1910   The Union of South Africa was founded.
1913   Amendment 17 to the Constitution went into effect, providing for the direct election of U.S. senators.
1916   The Battle of Jutland, the greatest naval battle of World War I, began in the North Sea.
1927   The last Model T Ford was produced, to make way for Henry Ford's new Model A. Over 15 million of the "Tin Lizzies" had been built since their introduction in 1908.
1962   Adolf Eichmann was hanged by Israel for World War II crimes against humanity.
1979   Rhodesia got black-majority rule and changed its name to Zimbabwe-Rhodesia, which later became Zimbabwe.
1983   Jack Dempsey, the legendary boxing great, died in New York City at age 78.
1989   Representative Jim Wright resigned his post as Speaker of the House under the cloud of ethics charges, becoming the first speaker in U.S. history to quit in mid-term.

6

June

June, our sixth month, was originally the fourth month in the ancient Roman calendar, and has always had 30 days, except for a brief time under Numa Pompilius, when it had 29. Most scholars believe that its Latin name *Junius* was chosen to honor the young men of Rome (the *juniores*). Other authorities believe that June was named for Juno, the patron goddess of marriage. Both beliefs have some credibility, since it is known that the Romans dedicated the month to the young men of Rome, and for centuries June has been known as a favorable month for marriages.

The United States celebrates Flag Day on June 14, commemorating the day in 1777 when the Stars and Stripes was adopted as the official flag. Another special June day is Father's Day, celebrated on the third Sunday. President George Bush was born in June, and June is also the birth month of Jefferson Davis, the President of the Confederacy, and Amerigo Vespucci, for whom the American continents were named.

The birthstones for June are the pearl, the moonstone and the alexandrite. Its special flowers are the rose and the honeysuckle. June's notable birthdays and events follow.

JUNE 1 -- BIRTHDAYS

1503   **Wilhelm Von Grumbach** -- German knight and adventurer

1637   **Jacques Marquette** -- French missionary and North American explorer, who, with Louis Joliet, discovered that the Mississippi River flowed into the Gulf of Mexico

1780   Carl von Clausewitz -- Influential Prussian military strategist and author of *On War,* one of the most important books on military matters

1793   **Henry Francis Lyte** -- British clergyman and hymnalist remembered for "Abide With Me" and "Jesus, I My Cross Have Taken"

1801   **Brigham Young** -- Successor to Joseph Smith as head of the Church of Jesus Christ of Latter-day Saints, who led the Mormons to Utah and established their church in the Great Salt Lake valley

1804   **Mikhail Ivanovich Glinka** -- The first important Russian composer, and the founder of a distinctly Russian type of music

1831   **John B. Hood** -- Confederate general in the Civil War

1833   **John Marshall Harlan** -- Noted U.S. Supreme Court justice, 1877-1911

1878   **John Masefield** -- English writer and 16th poet laureate of England from 1930 to 1967

1882   **John Drinkwater** -- English playwright, poet, and biographer, and author of *Abraham Lincoln* and *Robert E. Lee*

1887   **Clive Brook** -- English stage and motion-picture actor with a 40-year career

1890   **Frank Morgan** -- American stage and motion-picture actor in over 100 films

1907   **Sir Frank Whittle** -- English pioneer developer of the turbojet engine, whose Whittle engine powered the first British jet plane in 1941 and was the model for the first U.S. turbojets

1908   **Billy Werber** -- Professional baseball player

1921   **Nelson Riddle** -- American composer and musician

1922   **Joan Caulfield** -- American stage, screen, and television actress

1926   **Andy Griffith** -- American motion-picture and television actor

1926   **Marilyn Monroe** -- American actress and sex symbol of the 1950s

1926   **Richard S. Schweiker** -- U.S. senator and secretary of Health and Human Services under President Reagan

1930   **Edward Woodward** -- English stage, screen, and television actor

1933   **Alan "The Horse" Ameche** -- Hall of Fame football player and superstar

1934   **Pat Boone** -- American singer, actor, and author

1937   **Red Grooms** -- American artist

1947   **Ron Wood** -- British rock guitarist with the Rolling Stones

1953   **David Berkowitz** -- American murderer who left the message, "Son of Sam," with each of his victims

1963   **Alan Wilder** -- British keyboardist and songwriter with the
         Depeche Mode musical group

JUNE 1 -- EVENTS

1789   President George Washington signed the first act of Congress,
         concerning the administration of oaths.

1792   Kentucky was admitted to the Union as the 15th state.

1796   Tennessee was admitted to the Union as the 16th state.

1812   President James Madison asked Congress to declare war on
         Great Britain.

1813   Captain James Lawrence was mortally wounded in a sea battle
         in the War of 1812, and uttered the famous words that would
         become the U.S. Navy's password: "Don't give up the ship!"

1868   Ex-President James Buchanan died in Lancaster, Pennsylvania,
         at age 77.

1916   The Battle of Jutland ended in a draw with Britain losing 14 ships
         and Germany 11. But British sea supremacy endured, and the
         German fleet was inactive for the rest of World War I.

1925   The comic strip *Ella Cinders,* by Bill Conselman and Charlie
         Plumb, first appeared.

1925   Lou Gehrig, the great New York Yankees' first baseman, began
         his record string of playing in 2,130 consecutive games.

1958   General Charles de Gaulle became premier of France.

1968   Helen Keller, the great blind and deaf writer, died at age 87.

JUNE 2 -- BIRTHDAYS

1535   **Leo XI** -- Roman Catholic pope (1605)

1731   **Martha Custis Washington** -- Wife of George Washington

1740   **Marquis de Sade** -- French author of erotic writings, whose use
         of torture gave to the language the term *sadism*

1773   **John Randolph** — American statesman, whose biting tongue
         made him the most feared orator of his time

1788   **Solomon Willard** -- American architect

1835   **Pius X** -- Roman Catholic pope, 1903-1914, who was beatified in
         1951 and canonized in 1954

1840   **Thomas Hardy** -- English novelist and poet, known for such
         works as *Far from the Madding Crowd, The Return of the Native,*
         and *Jude the Obscure*

1845   **Arthur MacArthur** -- American general and father of General Douglas MacArthur

1849   **Albert Besnard** -- French painter

1852   **Charles B. Lawlor** -- Irish-born composer and singer, noted for songs such as "The Sidewalks of New York"

1857   **Sir Edward Elgar** -- British composer, best known for *Pomp and Circumstance,* a set of five marches

1863   **Wilbert Robinson** -- Hall of Fame baseball player and manager

1875   **Charles Stewart Mott** -- American automotive pioneer and early executive in the General Motors Corporation

1887   **Howard E. Johnson** -- American lyricist noted for songs such as "M-O-T-H-E-R" and "When the Moon Comes Over the Mountain"

1890   **Hedda Hopper** -- American gossip columnist and actress

1895   **Alex Gerber** -- American composer and author, noted for songs such as "My Home Town Is a One-Horse Town"

1899   **Edwin Way Teale** -- American naturalist, writer, and photographer

1904   **Johnny Weissmuller** -- American swimmer and actor who played the motion-picture role of Tarzan from 1932 to 1948

1929   **Ken McGregor** -- American tennis player

1930   **Charles Conrad Jr.** -- U.S. astronaut and commander of the *Apollo 12* flight to the moon in 1969

1938   **Gene Michael** -- Professional baseball player and manager

1938   **Sally Kellerman** -- American motion-picture actress

1940   **Constantine II** -- King of Greece, 1964-1967

1940   **Jim Maloney** -- Professional baseball pitcher who pitched two no-hit games in 1965

1941   **Charlie Watts** -- British drummer with the Rolling Stones

1941   **Stacy Keach** -- American stage and motion-picture actor

1944   **Marvin Hamlisch** -- American composer and pianist, who won a record 3 Oscars in one night--one for the score of *The Sting* and two (for the score and for the title song) for *The Way We Were*

1944   **Garo Yepremian** -- Professional football player

1950   **Lawrence McCutcheon** -- Professional football player

JUNE 2 -- EVENTS

597 AD   Saxon King Ethelbert was converted to Christianity and baptized by St. Augustine of Canterbury.

1420   King Henry V of England married Catherine, the daughter of King Charles VI of France.

1851   Maine passed the first prohibition law in United States history. It stayed on the books until 1934.

1875   Alexander Graham Bell discovered the secret of the telephone in an attic electrical workshop in Boston.

1886   Grover Cleveland married Frances Folsom in the White House, the first time that a U.S. president had married in the executive mansion.

1896   Guglielmo Marconi patented his wireless telegraphy in Great Britain.

1924   Congress conferred citizenship upon all American Indians.

1941   Lou Gehrig, the New York Yankees' great first baseman, died at age 37, of Lou Gehrig's disease, a rare form of paralysis.

1953   Queen Elizabeth II of England was crowned in Westminster Abbey in London.

JUNE 3 -- BIRTHDAYS

1736   **Augustin de Saint-Aubin** -- French printmaker

1771   **Sydney Smith** -- English clergyman, gourmet, wit, and one of the foremost preachers of his day

1808   **Jefferson Davis** -- President of the Confederate States of America during the Civil War

1819   **Johan Barthold Jongkind** -- Dutch painter and etcher

1844   **Garret A. Hobart** -- U.S. vice president in President McKinley's first term

1864   **Ransom Eli Olds** -- American pioneer automobile inventor and manufacturer for whom the Oldsmobile and the Reo (his initials) were named

1865   **George V** -- King of England, 1910-1936

1877   **Raoul Dufy** -- French artist best known for his lively, decorative paintings, of which *Le Haras du Pin* is a good example

1883   **Harold F. Orlob** -- American composer and author, noted for songs such as "I Wonder Who's Kissing Her Now"

1887   **Roland Hayes** -- American lyric tenor and winner of the 1924 Spingarn Medal

1891   **Mary K. Browne** -- Professional golfer and tennis champion

1901   **Maurice Evans** -- English stage, screen, and television actor with a career of some 50 years

1904   **Jan Peerce** -- One of the most successful American opera and concert tenors of the 20th century

1906   **Josephine Baker** -- American singer, motion-picture actress, and nightclub entertainer

1911	**Paulette Goddard** -- American motion-picture actress
1913	**Ellen Corby** -- American motion-picture and television actress
1915	**Leo Gorcey** -- American stage and motion-picture actor who starred in the movies of the Dead End Kids and the Bowery Boys
1923	**Charles Sifford** -- Professional golfer
1925	**Tony Curtis** -- American stage, screen, and television actor
1926	**Allen Ginsberg** -- American poet of the Beat generation
1926	**Colleen Dewhurst** -- Canadian stage and motion-picture actress
1931	**Bert Lance** -- Budget director under President Carter
1931	**Raul Castro** -- First Cuban vice premier and brother of Cuban revolutionary leader Fidel Castro
1942	**Curtis Mayfield** -- American soul singer
1945	**Hale Irwin** -- Professional golfer
1946	**Jaime Fillol** -- Chilean tennis player
1952	**Lief Johansson** -- Swedish tennis player
1954	**Sue Stap** -- American tennis player

JUNE 3 -- EVENTS

1539	Spanish explorer Hernando de Soto landed in the Tampa Bay area and claimed Florida for Spain. (Ponce de Leon had already claimed Florida for Spain in 1513, however.)
1864	General Lee held off General Grant with heavy losses in the Battle of Cold Harbor in the Civil War. Grant lost 6,000 men in one hour, forcing him to withdraw and change his tactics.
1871	Jesse James robbed the newly opened Obocock Bank in Corydon, Iowa, escaping with $15,000.
1875	Georges Bizet, the noted French composer, died at Bougival, France, at age 36, exactly three months after the first performance of his great opera *Carmen.*
1888	"Casey at the Bat," the immortal baseball classic written by Ernest L. Thayer, was published for the first time, in the San Francisco *Examiner.*
1899	Johann Strauss Jr., the "Waltz King," died in Vienna at age 73.
1924	Franz Kafka, the noted Austrian writer, died of tuberculosis in Klosterneuberg, Austria, at age 40.
1932	Lou Gehrig of the New York Yankees hit four home runs in one game against the Philadelphia Athletics.
1935	The French liner *Normandie* set a record on its maiden voyage, crossing the Atlantic in less than 4 days and 12 hours.

1937   The Duke of Windsor, formerly King Edward VIII of England,
        married Mrs. Wallis Warfield Simpson in Monts, France. He
        had abdicated the English throne in order to marry her.
1948   The world's largest telescope, the 200-inch Hale reflector, was
        dedicated at Mount Palomar Observatory, California.
1963   Pope John XXIII died in Rome at age 81.
1965   Astronaut Edward White spent 21 minutes outside his spacecraft,
        Gemini 4, becoming the first American to walk in space.
1989   Chinese soldiers stormed Tiananmen Square in Beijing and
        crushed a 3-week student sit-in for democracy, firing machine
        guns and killing 500 to 2,000 people.

JUNE 4 -- BIRTHDAYS

1738   **George III** -- King of England, 1760-1820, who reigned during
        the American Revolutionary War
1862   **Bob Fitzsimmons** -- World middleweight champion, 1891-1897,
        heavyweight champion, 1897-1899, and light-heavyweight cham-
        pion, 1903-1905
1867   **Carl Gustav Mannerheim** -- Finnish World War II general, and
        one of the founders of the Republic of Finland in 1919
1880   **Clara Blandick** -- American motion-picture actress who played
        Judy Garland's aunt in *The Wizard of Oz*
1881   **Nathalie Gontcharova** -- Russian painter
1891   **Erno Rapee** -- Hungarian-born composer and conductor, noted
        for songs such as "Charmaine" and "Rockettes on Parade"
1903   **Luther Adler** -- American stage and screen actor
1908   **Rosalind Russell** -- American stage and motion-picture actress
1916   **Gaylord Nelson** -- U.S. senator in the 1960s and 1970s
1917   **Charles Collingwood** -- American television news reporter
1917   **Howard Metzenbaum** -- U.S. senator
1919   **Robert Merrill** -- Noted American baritone
1920   **Russell Errol Train** -- Noted American conservationist
1922   **Samuel Lea Gravely Jr.** -- First black admiral in the history of the
        U.S. Navy
1924   **Dennis Weaver** -- American motion-picture and television ac-
        tor, who played Chester in the long-running series, *Gunsmoke*
1936   **Bruce Dern** -- American motion-picture and television actor
1946   **Bettina Gregory** -- American broadcast journalist
1948   **Sandra Post** -- Professional golfer

1952	**Parker Stevenson** – American motion-picture and television actor
1953	**Mike Barber** -- Professional football player
1956	**Terry Kennedy** -- Professional baseball player
1957	**Tony Pena** -- Professional baseball player
1965	**Andrea Jaeger** -- American tennis player

JUNE 4 -- EVENTS

1070	The process of making Roquefort cheese was discovered by an anonymous shepherd in a cave near Roquefort, France.
1260	Kublai Khan, the grandson of Genghis Khan, became the leader of the Mongol dynasty that ruled China for a century.
1543	The second of the New Laws of Spain was passed to prevent the establishment of a Spanish-American nobility in America.
1658	English and French troops defeated a Spanish relief force in the Battle of the Dunes, resulting in the surrender of Dunkerque to the English after a long siege.
1798	Giovanni Jacopo Casanova, the greatest of romantic lovers, died in Bohemia at age 73.
1800	The White House, though as yet unfinished, was declared ready for occupancy by President and Mrs. John Adams.
1893	The Anti-Saloon League of America was organized in Ohio.
1896	Henry Ford drove the first Ford car out of a brick shed at 58 Bagley Avenue, Detroit, and conducted a trial run around the city.
1940	The evacuation of Dunkerque was completed, with 336,000 Allied soldiers rescued by the British Navy in World War II.
1942	The Battle of Midway, one of the most decisive naval battles in history, began between the United States and Japan in World War II.
1944	The Allies captured Rome, which became the first Axis capital to fall in World War II.
1970	Sonny Tufts, the American motion-picture actor, died at age 58.

JUNE 5 -- BIRTHDAYS

1718	**Thomas Chippendale** -- The most famous English cabinetmaker of his time
1723	**Adam Smith** -- Scottish social philosopher, author of *The Wealth of Nations* (1776), and the founder of modern economics

1771   **Asher Benjamin** -- American architect

1819   **John Couch Adams** -- Co-predictor with Urbain J.J. Leverrier of the position of the planet Neptune (1845)

1874   **Jack Chesbro** -- Hall of Fame baseball pitcher who won 41 games in 1904

1877   **Pancho Villa** -- Mexican revolutionary and bandit chieftain, who sought unsuccessfully to control Mexico after the fall of President Profirio Diaz in 1910

1883   **John Maynard Keynes** -- Father of Keynesian economics and one of the most important economists of all time

1897   **Madame Chiang Kai-shek** -- Wife of Chinese premier Chiang Kai-shek, the leader of mainland China from 1926 to 1949

1898   **Frederico Garcia Lorca** -- One of the greatest Spanish poets, who with Miguel de Cervantes is the most widely translated Spanish author

1898   **William Boyd** -- American actor, producer, and star of 54 Hopalong Cassidy episodes

1911   **George Vaughn Horton** -- American composer, author, and arranger, noted for songs such as "Mockin' Bird Hill" and "Choo Choo Ch' Boogie"

1915   **Alfred Kazin** -- Russian-born writer, critic, and educator

1921   **Cornelius Ryan** -- Irish-born American author

1929   **Robert Lansing** -- American motion-picture and television actor

1934   **Bill Moyers** -- American broadcast journalist

1939   **Charles Joseph "Joe" Clark** – Youngest prime minister in Canada's history (1979-1980)

1954   **Ernie Ewart** -- Australian tennis player

JUNE 5 -- EVENTS

1294   Saint Celestine V was elected Roman Catholic pope. He was unhappy, however, with the office, and abdicated before the year was out.

1783   The brothers Jacques and Joseph Montgolfier sent up the first balloon, a large smoke-filled cloth bag, at Annonay, France.

1917   More than 9 million American men, between the ages of 21 and 30, registered for the draft under the Selective Military Conscription Act.

1933   President Franklin D. Roosevelt signed the bill taking the United States off the gold standard.

1940   The Germans began the Battle of France in World War II.

1947 The Marshall Plan for saving Western Europe's economy was described by Secretary of State George C. Marshall at the commencement exercises at Harvard University.

1967 The Six-Day War began as Israeli planes launched a lightning attack on airfields in Egypt, Jordan, and Syria, almost completely destroying the Arab air forces.

1968 Senator Robert F. Kennedy was shot in Los Angeles after a campaign speech. He died the following day.

1975 Egypt reopened the Suez Canal to shipping exactly eight years after it was closed during the Six-Day War.

JUNE 6 -- BIRTHDAYS

1436 **Regiomontanus (Johann Muller)** -- German astronomer responsible for the revival of trigonometry in Europe

1599 **Diego Velazquez** -- The major Spanish painter of the 17th century

1606 **Pierre Corneille** -- Father of French classical tragedy and the founder of French heroic comedy

1625 **Domenico Guidi** -- Italian sculptor

1714 **Joseph I** -- A minor king of Portugal in the 18th century

1755 **Nathan Hale** -- American Revolutionary War officer who immortalized the words, "I only regret that I have but one life to lose for my country," before being hanged by the British as a spy

1756 **John Trumbull** -- American painter, best known for his small, dramatic paintings of Revolutionary War scenes

1799 **Alexander Pushkin** -- Russia's most celebrated poet, novelist, and dramatist, noted for such works as the poem, "Eugene Onegin," and the play, *Boris Godunov*

1804 **Louis Antoine Godey** -- Founder in 1830 of *Godey's Lady's Book*, the first woman's magazine in the United States

1872 **Alexandra** -- Wife of Nicholas II, the last czar of Russia

1875 **Thomas Mann** -- German-American novelist and 1929 Nobel Prize winner, noted for such works as *Buddenbrooks* (1901) and *Confessions of Felix Krull, Confidence Man* (1954)

1886 **Paul Dudley White** -- Heart specialist and personal physician of President Dwight D. Eisenhower

1898 **Walter Abel** -- American stage and motion-picture actor

1901 **Sukarno** -- First president of Indonesia and leader of the Indonesian independence movement

1902 **Jimmy Lunceford** -- American jazz musician and bandleader of the Big Band Era

1903   **Aram Khachaturian** -- Russian composer, noted for the ballet *Gayne,* which includes the famous "Sabre Dance"

1907   **Bill Dickey** -- Hall of Fame baseball player and manager, and one of the two or three greatest catchers in the history of baseball

1917   **Kirk Kerkorian** -- American corporation executive and chairman of Metro-Goldwyn-Mayer

1926   **T.K. (Tom) Ryan** – American cartoonist and creator of *Tumbleweeds*

1932   **David R. Scott** -- U.S. astronaut who with astronaut James B. Irwin drove the moon car Rover on the surface of the moon on the *Apollo 15* mission

1932   **Billie Whitelaw** -- British stage, screen, and television actress

1934   **Roy Innis** -- American civil rights leader and national director of CORE

1939   **Gary U.S. Bonds** -- American singer and songwriter

1956   **Bjorn Borg** -- Swedish tennis player, winner of five straight Wimbledon singles titles, and one of the greatest players in history

1959   **Amanda Pays** -- British motion-picture and television actress

JUNE 6 -- EVENTS

1660   The Peace of Copenhagen ended the Danish-Swedish War, resulting in Sweden's taking all the Danish territory in what is now Sweden.

1844   The Young Men's Christian Association (YMCA) was founded in London by George Williams.

1918   The World War I Battle of Belleau Wood began. It would end in victory for the U.S. Marines over the Germans 19 days later.

1925   The Chrysler Corporation was created by Walter Chrysler, by a reorganization of the Maxwell Motor Company.

1933   The first motion-picture drive-in theater opened, in Camden, New Jersey.

1934   The Securities and Exchange Commission was established.

1941   Louis Chevrolet, organizer of the Chevrolet Motor Company in 1911, died at age 63.

1942   The Battle of Midway ended in disaster for Japan. It also ended Japanese threats to Hawaii and the United States.

1944   The largest air, sea, and land operation in history was carried out on D Day, as the Americans and British invaded the beaches of Normandy in France in World War II.

1956	Elvis Presley, the rock singer, appeared on television for the first time, on the *Ed Sullivan Show*.

1956   Elvis Presley, the rock singer, appeared on television for the first time, on the *Ed Sullivan Show*.

1968   Senator Robert F. Kennedy died in Los Angeles from a gunshot wound inflicted the previous day.

1974   The White House admitted that President Nixon was named an unindicted co-conspirator in the Watergate case by the grand jury.

1978   California voters approved Proposition 13, cutting property taxes 57%.

JUNE 7 -- BIRTHDAYS

1502   **Gregory XIII** -- Roman Catholic pope, 1572-1585, who in 1582 established the Gregorian calendar, which is still in use today

1778   **Beau Brummell** -- English dandy and fashion leader in the early 1800s

1848   **Paul Gauguin** – French painter noted for his colorful and decorative style, and for his paintings of the South Sea Island people

1868   **Charles Rennie Mackintosh** -- Scottish architect

1879   **Knud Rasmussen** – Danish Arctic explorer and writer, who in 1910 founded the trading station of Thule in Greenland

1894   **Alexander de Seversky** -- Russian-American pilot, aircraft designer, and military authority, who founded the Seversky Aero Corporation in 1922

1896   **Imre Nagy** -- Premier of Hungary at the time of the 1956 Hungarian revolt against the Russians

1908   **Lew Quadling** -- American composer and author, noted for songs such as "Sam's Song"

1909   **Jessica Tandy** -- English stage and motion-picture actress

1909   **Peter Rodino** -- U.S. congressman and chairman of the committee investigating charges against President Nixon in the Watergate affair in 1973-1974

1917   **Dean Martin** -- American motion-picture and television singer and actor

1917   **Gwendolyn Brooks** -- American poet who won the 1950 Pulitzer Prize for *Annie Allen*, her second collection of poems

1922   **Rocky Graziano** -- World middleweight champion, 1947-1948

1933   **Herb Score** -- Professional baseball player

1934   **Philippe Entremont** -- French pianist and conductor

1940   **Tom Jones** -- Welsh-American singer whose earliest hit was "The Green, Green Grass of Home"

1944   **Cazzie Russell** -- Professional basketball player
1947   **Don Money** -- Professional baseball player
1947   **David Lundstrom** -- Professional golfer
1947   **Thurman Munson** -- Professional baseball player
1959   **Prince** -- American rock and roll soul singer

JUNE 7 -- EVENTS

1576   Martin Frobisher, the English navigator, left England on his first trip to seek a Northwest Passage to India. He never succeeded, but he discovered Frobisher Bay on Baffin Island.

1628   King Charles I of England formally accepted the Petition of Right from Parliament. He continued his autocratic rule, however, until it led to his execution in 1649.

1769   Daniel Boone first set eyes on Kentucky. The date is now celebrated as Boone Day by the Kentucky State Historical Society.

1776   Richard Henry Lee of Virginia introduced in the Continental Congress the resolution calling for the declaration of independence from England.

1832   The Reform Act of 1832 was passed by the British Parliament, giving most men of the middle class the right to vote.

1864   Abraham Lincoln was renominated for president at his party's convention in Baltimore.

1909   Mary Pickford, the great American movie star, made her debut in the film, *The Violin Maker of Cremona.*

1917   The International Association of Lions Clubs was founded in Chicago.

1937   Jean Harlow, the famous American motion-picture actress, died of cerebral edema at age 26.

1940   After 62 days of bitter fighting, the Germans finally drove the Allies out and completed their occupation of Norway in World War II.

1948   President Eduard Benes of Czechoslovakia resigned rather than sign a new Communist-dictated constitution for his country.

1981   Israeli planes destroyed a nuclear power plant in Iraq.

JUNE 8 -- BIRTHDAYS

1772   **Robert Stevenson** -- Scottish engineer and noted lighthouse builder, who invented the flashing light used in lighthouses

1810   **Robert Schumann** -- Noted German composer and pianist who ranks with Franz Liszt and Frederic Chopin in developing the techniques of romantic piano music

1814   **Charles Reade** -- English novelist and author of *The Cloister and the Hearth* (1861), considered by some to be the greatest historical novel in English

1829   **Sir John Everett Millais** -- English painter and a founder of the Pre-Raphaelite Brotherhood in 1848

1867   **Frank Lloyd Wright** -- One of America's greatest and most influential architects, noted for his Prairie Style of buildings and for such projects as New York's Guggenheim Museum

1876   **Richard H. Gerard** -- American composer noted for songs such as "Sweet Adeline"

1903   **Ralph Yarborough** -- U.S. senator in the 1960s

1911   **Van Lingle Mungo** -- Professional baseball player

1916   **Francis H.C. Crick** -- Nobel Prize-winning British biologist who helped build the Watson-Crick model of the molecular structure of DNA, the substance that transmits genetic information

1917   **Byron R. "Whizzer" White** -- American football player and U.S. Supreme Court justice

1918   **Robert Preston** -- American motion-picture and stage actor

1921   **Suharto** -- Second president of Indonesia, after Sukarno

1921   **Alexis Smith** -- Canadian-born motion-picture actress

1923   **Malcolm Boyd** -- American priest, author and Freedom Rider

1924   **Lyn Nofziger** -- Republican Party strategist

1925   **Barbara Pierce Bush** -- Wife of President George Bush

1930   **Dana Wynter** -- English motion-picture and television actress

1933   **Joan Rivers** -- American comedienne

1936   **James Darren** -- American motion-picture and television actor

1939   **Herbert Adderly** -- Professional football player

1940   **Nancy Sinatra** -- American singer and actress and daughter of singer Frank Sinatra

1943   **Willie Davenport** -- American Olympic champion hurdler

1944   **Mark Belanger** -- Professional baseball player

1952   **Dave Jennings** -- Professional football player

1962   **Nick Rhodes** -- Keyboardist with the Duran Duran musical group

JUNE 8 -- EVENTS

632 AD   The prophet Mohammed, the founder of the Islamic religion, died in Medina at age 63.

1191   Richard the Lion-Hearted of England arrived at the port of Acre in the Holy Land during the third Crusade. He captured Acre, but could not recapture Jerusalem from the Turks.

1504   Michelangelo's statue of David was set in place in the Palazzo in Florence.

1809   Thomas Paine, the great American Revolutionary patriot, died in New Rochelle, New York, at age 72.

1830   The USS *Vincennes* returned to New York, becoming the first warship to circumnavigate the globe.

1845   Andrew Jackson died at the Hermitage at age 78.

1861   Tennessee became the last state to secede from the Union.

1869   Ives W. McGaffey of Chicago patented the vacuum cleaner, described by him as a "sweeping machine."

1915   Secretary of State William Jennings Bryan resigned, protesting the firm notes of President Wilson to the Germans in connection with the sinking of the *Lusitania.*

1953   The Supreme Court ruled that restaurants in the District of Columbia could not refuse to serve blacks.

1965   The Russian moon shot *Luna 6* was launched.

1966   The merger of the National and American football leagues was announced, to take effect in 1970.

1967   The Israelis occupied the Gaza Strip, the Sinai Peninsula, and Jordanian territory west of the River Jordan in the Six-Day War.

JUNE 9 -- BIRTHDAYS

1595   **Wladyslaw IV Vasa** — Swedish nobleman of the House of Vasa, chosen by the ruling Polish *szlachta* to be king of Poland, 1632-1648

1597   **Pieter Jansz Saenredam** — Dutch pioneer of the "church portrait"

1672   **Peter the Great** -- Czar of Russia, 1682-1725, who founded the city of St. Petersburg (now Leningrad), and started Russia on the path of modernization

1768   **Samuel Slater** -- Founder of the U.S. cotton textile industry

1781   **George Stephenson** -- English inventor known as the "Founder of Railways" and "Engine Doctor" because of the many locomotives and railroads he built

1785 **Sylvanus Thayer** -- American army officer known as the father of West Point because of his long service as superintendent of the United States Military Academy

1791 **John Howard Payne** -- American playwright, actor, and diplomat, who wrote the lyrics for the famous song, "Home, Sweet Home"

1865 **Carl August Nielsen** -- Danish composer best known for six symphonies and the comic opera, *Maskerade* (1906)

1892 **Cole Porter** -- American composer of popular music, noted for such songs as "Begin the Beguine," "Night and Day," and "So in Love Am I"

1900 **Fred Waring** -- American bandleader of the Big Band Era of the 1930s and 1940s

1911 **Frank McCormick** -- Professional baseball player

1912 **Buddy Feyne** -- American composer noted for songs such as "Tuxedo Junction," "Jersey Bounce," and "The Shadow Knows"

1916 **Robert S. McNamara** -- U.S. secretary of defense, 1961-1968, and president of the World Bank

1922 **George Axelrod** -- American novelist and playwright, noted for works such as *The Seven-Year Itch*

1923 **Les Paul** -- American singer and electric guitar and recording pioneer

1926 **Mona Freeman** -- American motion-picture and television actress

1931 **Bill Virdon** -- Professional baseball player and manager

1934 **Jackie Mason** -- American comedian and actor

1938 **Barry Phillips-Moore** -- Australian tennis player

1951 **Dave Parker** -- Professional baseball player

1961 **Michael J. Fox** -- Canadian-born motion picture and television actor

JUNE 9 -- EVENTS

68 AD Roman emperor Nero committed suicide at age 31 after being sentenced to death by the Senate.

1156 Frederick Barbarossa, King of Germany and Holy Roman Emperor, married Beatrix of Upper Burgundy.

1534 Jacques Cartier, the French explorer, sailed into the St. Lawrence River, so named by him because he discovered it on St. Lawrence's feast day.

1815   The Vienna Settlement, under the leadership of Austria's Prince Metternich, reshaped Europe after the final defeat of Napoleon.

1870   Charles Dickens, the great English novelist, died of a stroke at Gadshill, Kent, at age 58.

1899   Jim Jeffries knocked out Bob Fitzsimmons at Coney Island, New York, to win the heavyweight boxing championship.

1940   Norway surrendered to the Nazis in World War II.

1943   Congress passed the "Pay-As-You-Go" income tax deduction law, authorizing employers to withhold income taxes.

1959   The *George Washington,* the first ballistic-missile submarine, was launched by the United States.

1960   Bing Crosby was awarded the first ever platinum disc for selling two hundred million records.

1973   Secretariat won the Belmont Stakes in New York to become horse racing's first Triple Crown winner since Citation in 1948.

1978   One of the 21 known complete copies of the Gutenberg Bible was sold in London for 2.4 million dollars, a record price for a printed book.

JUNE 10 -- BIRTHDAYS

1741   **Joseph Warren** -- American patriot who sent Paul Revere on his famous ride to alert the countryside that the British were coming

1819   **Gustave Courbet** – French painter famous for his efforts to develop realism in French painting in the 1800s

1832   **Nikolaus August Otto** -- German engineer who, with Eugen Langen, built the world's first four-stroke internal combustion engine

1854   **Francois Curel** -- French dramatist and novelist

1875   **James MacDermid** -- American composer and organist, noted for songs such as "My Love Is Like the Red Red Rose"

1880   **Andre Derain** – French artist, and one of the leaders of the *fauves*, a noted group of painters of the early 1900s

1887   **Harry Flood Byrd** -- Powerful United States senator from Virginia, 1933-1965

1889   **Sessue Hayakawa** – Japanese motion-picture actor noted for his role in *The Bridge on the River Kwai*

1904   **Frederick Loewe** -- Austrian-American composer, who, with lyricist Alan Jay Lerner, wrote the hits for such Broadway musicals as *My Fair Lady, Camelot, Gigi,* and *Paint Your Wagon*

1908	Robert "Bob" Cummings -- American motion-picture and television actor
1910	Howlin' Wolf (Chester Burnett) -- American blues guitarist
1915	Saul Bellow -- Canadian-American novelist noted for works such as *Dangling Man, The Victim, Humboldt's Gift,* and *Mr. Sammler's Planet*
1921	Prince Philip -- Duke of Edinburgh and husband of Queen Elizabeth II of England
1922	Judy Garland -- American singer, actress, and superstar
1925	Nat Hentoff -- American newspaper columnist
1926	June Haver -- American stage, screen, and television actress
1928	Maurice Sendak -- American illustrator and writer of children's books, the best known of which is *Where the Wild Things Are*
1929	James A. McDivitt -- U.S. astronaut on the flight of *Gemini 4* in 1965
1933	F. Lee Bailey -- Noted American trial lawyer
1943	Jon McGlocklin -- Professional basketball player
1943	Jeff Greenfield -- American broadcast commentator and newspaper columnist
1947	Ken Singleton -- Professional baseball player
1950	John Gianelli -- Professional basketball player
1951	Danny Fouts -- Professional football player
1951	Jackie Fayter -- English tennis player
1953	Dean Joubert -- South African tennis player
1955	Floyd Bannister -- Professional baseball player

JUNE 10 -- EVENTS

1190	Holy Roman Emperor Frederick Barbarossa drowned at age 67 while crossing the River Calycadnus in Cilicia during the Third Crusade.
1610	The first Dutch settlers arrived on Manhattan Island.
1692	Bridget Bishop became the first of the Salem, Massachusetts, "witches" to be hanged.
1776	The Continental Congress appointed a committee to draft a declaration of independence.
1801	Tripoli declared war on the United States to force the payment of more tribute money for the protection of American shipping.
1847	The Chicago *Tribune* began publication.
1865	The world premiere of Richard Wagner's *Tristan und Isolde* took place in Munich.

1935   Alcoholics Anonymous was founded by Bill Wilson, a stockbroker, and Bob Smith, a physician.

1940   With the French on the verge of collapse in World War II, Italian premier Mussolini declared war and invaded France from the south.

1942   In retaliation for the assassination of Nazi "Hangman" Reinhard Heydrich, the Germans burned the Czech town of Lidice, shot its 173 males, and imprisoned its women and children.

1959   Rocky Colavito of the Cleveland Indians hit four home runs in one game.

1967   The Israelis captured Syria's Golan Heights in the Six-Day War.

1983   The Northern and Southern branches of the Presbyterian Church reunited after being separated since the Civil War began in 1861.

JUNE 11 -- BIRTHDAYS

1555   **Ludovico Zacconi** -- Italian Renaissance writer on music

1572   **Ben Jonson** -- English dramatist and poet of the Elizabethan era, noted for such works as *The Alchemist* and the famous song, "Drink to Me Only With Thine Eyes"

1758   **Kamehameha I** -- King and founder of the Kingdom of Hawaii

1769   **Anne Newport Royall** -- America's first female crusading journalist

1776   **John Constable** — One of the greatest English landscape artists

1815   **Julia Margaret Cameron** — One of the greatest portrait photographers of the 19th century

1838   **Mariano Fortuny y Carbo** -- Spanish painter

1864   **Richard Strauss** -- German composer and conductor, noted for such works as *Der Rosenkavalier* (1910) and *Capriccio* (1941)

1867   **Edward Bradford Fitchener** — Co-founder of experimental psychology in the United States

1879   **Roger Bresnahan** -- Hall of Fame baseball player

1880   **Jeannette Rankin** -- First woman to be elected to the U.S. Congress, and the only member of the House to vote against America's entering World War II (she also opposed entering World War I)

1883   **Frank King** -- American comic strip cartoonist and creator of *Gasoline Alley*

1895   **Nikolai Bulganin** -- Russian premier, 1955-1958

1900   **Lawrence Spivak** — Longtime moderator of the radio and television program *Meet the Press*

1910	**Jacques-Yves Cousteau** -- Noted French underseas explorer and writer
1912	**James Algar** -- Director and screenwriter with Walt Disney Productions
1913	**Rise Stevens** -- American operatic soprano
1913	**Vince Lombardi** -- Noted professional football coach, who led the Green Bay Packers to five National Football League titles
1919	**Richard Todd** -- Irish stage and motion-picture actor
1925	**William Styron** -- American novelist and 1968 Pulitzer Prize winner for *The Confessions of Nat Turner*
1929	**Frank Thomas** -- Professional baseball player
1930	**Charles Rangel** -- U.S. representative
1935	**Gene Wilder** -- American actor, scriptwriter, and director
1936	**Chad Everett** -- American motion-picture and television actor
1939	**Jackie Stewart** -- Most successful Grand Prix driver in history, with a record total of 27 career wins
1954	**Gary Fencik** -- Professional football player
1956	**Joe Montana** -- Professional football player and superstar

JUNE 11 -- EVENTS

1509	King Henry VIII of England married Catherine of Aragon, the first of his six wives.
1580	Buenos Aires was founded by Spanish conquistador Juan de Garay.
1861	A convention met in Wheeling to protest Virginia's seceding from the Union and to form the new state of West Virginia. Its final name, however, was not chosen until 1862.
1895	The Duryea brothers Charles and Frank were granted a patent on the first successful gasoline-powered automobile in the United States.
1927	President Coolidge presented the first Distinguished Flying Cross to Charles A. Lindbergh.
1934	The comic strip, *Mandrake the Magician,* by Lee Falk and Phil Davis, first appeared.
1938	Johnny Vander Meer pitched the first of two consecutive no-hitters, as Cincinnati beat Boston, 3-0.
1940	The French cabinet withdrew to Tours as German troops neared Paris in World War II.

1950   Ben Hogan won the U.S. Open golf championship in a miracu-
        lous comeback after suffering near-fatal injuries in an earlier car
        accident.
1977   Seattle Slew won the Belmont Stakes to win the Triple Crown.
1989   Michael Chang defeated Stefan Edberg in 5 sets to become at 17
        the youngest man ever to win the French Open tennis title and
        the first American to do so since 1955.

JUNE 12 -- BIRTHDAYS

1512   **Paulus Manutius** -- Founder of the Aldine press in Venice
1720   **Isaac Pinto** -- Translator of the first Jewish prayerbook pub-
        lished in America
1733   **Alessandro Longhi** -- Italian painter
1806   **John Augustus Roebling** -- American civil engineer who de-
        signed the Brooklyn Bridge
1819   **Charles Kingsley** -- English novelist, clergyman, and author of
        Westward Ho! (1855)
1827   **Johanna Spyri** -- Swiss author of children's stories, best known
        for *Heidi* (1881)
1851   **Pol Plancon** -- French bass
1851   **Sir Oliver Joseph Lodge** -- English physicist whose electric wave
        research helped in developing the radio
1874   **Charles McNary** -- U.S. senator and vice presidential candidate
        with Wendell Willkie in 1940
1876   **Thomas Clark Hinkle** -- American author of children's books
1897   **Anthony Eden** -- Prime minister of Great Britain, 1955-1957
1899   **Anni Albers** -- American textile designer
1912   **Dick Manning** -- Russian-born composer and author, noted for
        songs such as "Takes Two to Tango," "Allegheny Moon," and
        "Papa Loves Mambo"
1912   **Russell Hayden** -- American Western movie actor and television
        director
1915   **David Rockefeller** -- Chairman of the board of Chase Manhat-
        tan Bank
1924   **George Herbert Walker Bush** -- 41st U.S. President and vice
        president under President Reagan
1928   **Vic Damone** -- American singer and actor
1929   **Anne Frank** -- German-Jewish girl who wrote a vivid diary while
        hiding from the Nazis during World War II

1933   **Jim Nabors** -- American singer and actor
1935   **Nicole Berger** -- French motion-picture actress

JUNE 12 -- EVENTS

1458   The College of St. Mary Magdalen was founded at Oxford, England.
1775   The American sloop *Unity* captured the British schooner *Margaretta* in the first naval battle of the Revolutionary War.
1776   George Mason drafted the Virginia Bill of Rights, as part of the new Virginia constitution.
1839   Abner Doubleday, an American army officer, invented the game of baseball at Cooperstown, N.Y. (Others give the credit to Alexander Joy Cartwright, who established the early rules.)
1864   Emperor Maximilian arrived in Mexico City from France to take over the Mexican government.
1878   William Cullen Bryant, America's first important poet, died in New York at age 83.
1880   John Richmond pitched the first perfect game (not a runner reached base) in major league history, as Worcester beat Cleveland, 1-0.
1917   The Secret Service extended its protection of the president to his family as well.
1930   Max Schmeling won the heavyweight championship, defeating Jack Sharkey in four rounds in New York.
1939   The Baseball Hall of Fame was established at Cooperstown, New York.
1979   Bryan Allen, a 26-year-old cyclist, flew a man-powered aircraft, the *Gossamer Albatross,* across the English Channel.
1981   Major league baseball players went on strike for the first time in history during a regular season.

JUNE 13 -- BIRTHDAYS

37 AD   **Gnaeus Julius Agricola** -- Roman general noted for conquering all of England and part of Scotland from A.D. 77 to 84
823 AD **Charles I (the Bald)** -- Grandson of Charlemagne who with his two half brothers divided Charlemagne's empire into 3 parts, with Charles becoming the first king of France, A.D. 843-877
1692   **Joseph Highmore** -- English portrait painter

1752   **Fanny Burney** -- English novelist and diarist noted for *Evelina, or the History of a Young Girl's Entry into the World* (1778), where she coined the phrase, "I'd do it as soon as say Jack Robinson"

1786   **Winfield Scott** -- American general and hero of the Mexican War, officer in the War of 1812 and briefly in the Civil War, and presidential candidate in 1852

1854   **Sir Charles Algernon Parsons** -- English engineer and inventor of the first marine steam turbine

1865   **William Butler Yeats** -- Irish poet ånd dramatist thought by some to be the greatest poet of his time

1879   **Robert Elkington Wood** -- American businessman who from 1928 to 1954 made Sears, Roebuck and Company into the world's largest merchandising firm

1880   **Vincent Rose** -- Italian-born composer, conductor, and pianist, noted for songs such as "Avalon," "Whispering," "Linger Awhile," and "Blueberry Hill"

1892   **Basil Rathbone** -- British stage and motion-picture actor with a 50 year career

1892   **Richard M. Jones** -- American composer, author, and conductor, noted for songs such as "Trouble in Mind" and "Red Wagon"

1894   **Watson Washburn** -- American Hall of Fame tennis player

1894   **Mark Van Doren** -- American poet, writer, and teacher, who won the Pulitzer Prize in 1940 for his *Collected Poems*

1897   **Paavo Nurmi** -- Finnish track star who dominated long-distance running in the 1920s

1899   **Carlos Chavez** -- Mexican composer and conductor, noted for such works as *Sinfonia India* (1936)

1903   **Red Grange** -- The "Galloping Ghost" of football, and one of the greatest football players of all time

1908   **Marie Vieira da Silva** -- Portuguese painter

1911   **Luis Alvarez** -- American nuclear physicist who won the 1968 Nobel Prize for contributions to the knowledge of subatomic particles

1913   **Ralph Edwards** -- Host of the television show, *This Is Your Life*

1915   **Don Budge** -- American Hall of Fame tennis player, and the first man in history to win the Grand Slam (1938)

1920   **Ben Johnson** -- American motion-picture actor

1922   **Mel Parnell** -- Professional baseball player

1926   **Paul Lynde** -- American motion-picture and television actor and comedian

1931   **Jay MacPherson** -- Canadian lyric poet

1935   **Christo (Javacheff)** -- Bulgarian artist
1936   **Larry Adams** -- American jockey
1947   **Zeljko Franulovic** -- Yugoslavian tennis player
1948   **Brian Fairlie** -- New Zealand tennis player
1951   **Fred Saunders** -- Professional basketball player
1951   **Richard Thomas** -- American stage, screen, and television actor
1962   **Ally Sheedy** -- American motion-picture actress
1963   **Bettina Bunge** -- German tennis player

JUNE 13 -- EVENTS

323 BC   Alexander the Great died of a fever in Babylon at age 33.

49 AD   Pope Leo I (the Great) presented his *Tome,* affirming the reality of the two natures of Christ (human and divine) to Flavian, the Bishop of Constantinople.

1231   Saint Anthony of Padua, the noted Franciscan scholar, died in Vercelli, Italy, at age 36.

1877   The last Russo-Turkish War began.

1927   Charles A. Lindbergh was honored for his historic transatlantic flight in a ticker tape parade in New York City.

1935   Jim Braddock won the heavyweight boxing title from Max Baer in a 15-round decision at Long Island City, New York.

1935   Senator Huey Long of Louisiana spoke 15 hours and 35 minutes on the Senate floor, setting a filibuster record.

1940   The French army abandoned Paris in World War II in the face of advancing German troops.

1944   Germany's World War II "secret weapon," the V-1 rocket, or flying bomb, was dropped on London for the first time.

1955   The worst accident in the history of auto racing occurred at LeMans, France, as 77 spectators and a driver were killed by an out-of-control car.

1966   The Supreme Court issued its landmark *Miranda v. Arizona* decision, saying that an accused cannot be questioned without his consent and he must be advised of his rights.

1967   President Lyndon B. Johnson nominated Thurgood Marshall to become the first black justice on the U.S. Supreme Court.

1971   The New York *Times* began publication of "The Pentagon Papers," based on secret Pentagon studies of the Vietnam War.

1983   The U.S. space probe *Pioneer 10* crossed Neptune's orbit and left the solar system for parts unknown.

JUNE 14 -- BIRTHDAYS

1716   Peter Harrison -- American architect

1736   **Charles Augustin de Coulomb** -- French physicist known for Coulomb's Law of force between two electrical charges

1811   **Harriet Beecher Stowe** -- American author noted for *Uncle Tom's Cabin,* one of the most famous novels in American history

1820   **John Bartlett** -- American publisher known chiefly for the book *Familiar Quotations*

1850   **Horatio Herbert Kitchener** -- Noted English field marshal who distinguished himself as governor-general of the Sudan, commander of the Egyptian army, and victorious commander in the Boer War

1855   **Robert M. La Follette** -- U.S. senator and leader of the Progressive movement of the first quarter of the 20th century

1856   **Andrey Andreyevich Markov** -- Russian mathematician noted for the theory of stochastic processes and Markov chains

1874   **"Major" (Edward) Bowes** -- American radio broadcaster and master of ceremonies of the 1930s and 1940s

1895   **May Allison** -- American motion-picture actress and a leading star of Hollywood silent films

1906   **Margaret Bourke-White** -- American photographer and writer who was the first accredited woman correspondent to go overseas in World War II

1908   **John Scott Trotter** -- American composer and conductor, who recorded the fantastically successful "White Christmas" record with Bing Crosby

1909   **Burl Ives** -- American actor and folk singer

1914   **Yuri Andropov** -- Soviet Communist party chairman and premier who succeeded Leonid Brezhnev in 1983

1918   **Dorothy McGuire** -- American stage and motion-picture actress

1919   **Sam Wanamaker** -- American motion-picture actor and director

1921   **Gene Barry** -- American motion-picture and television actor

1922   **Kevin Roche** -- American architect

1925   **Pierre Salinger** -- American journalist and press secretary for President John Kennedy

1926   **Don Newcombe** -- Professional baseball player

1928   **Ernesto "Che" Guevara** -- Cuban revolutionary and second most powerful man in Fidel Castro's Cuban government

1946   **Marla Gibbs** -- American actress

1946   **Donald Trump** -- American businessman and real estate tycoon

1950	**Fred Hemmes** -- Dutch tennis player
1952	**Eddie Mekka** -- American actor
1955	**Laurie Rowley** -- American tennis player
1955	**Vince Evans** -- Professional football player
1958	**Eric Heiden** -- American speed skater and winner of five gold medals in the 1980 Olympics
1969	**Steffi Graf** -- West German tennis player who won the grand slam (all 4 of the major tournaments) in 1988

JUNE 14 -- EVENTS

1645	Oliver Cromwell defeated the forces of Charles I at the Battle of Naseby.
1775	The U.S. Army was founded by the Continental Congress.
1777	The Continental Congress adopted the Stars and Stripes as the official flag of the United States.
1800	After a famous march across the Alps, Napoleon defeated the Austrians at Marengo, Italy, consolidating his political position in France.
1807	Napoleon routed the Russian armies at Friedland, forcing Czar Alexander I to make peace.
1825	Pierre Charles L'Enfant, designer of the United States capital, died in Green Hill, Maryland, at age 70.
1846	California was proclaimed a republic, as the Bear Flag was hoisted at Sonoma.
1866	The Seven Weeks' War began between Austria and Prussia. It was engineered by Otto von Bismarck, chancellor of Prussia, to make Prussia the dominant power in Germany.
1917	American general John J. Pershing and his staff arrived in Paris, symbolizing America's entry into World War I. The American Expeditionary Forces arrived on June 26.
1919	John Alcock and Arthur Whitten-Brown left St. John's, New-foundland, in a twin-engine Vickers on the first transatlantic flight. They landed in Ireland the next day.
1922	President Warren G. Harding made the first presidential radio broadcast.
1934	Max Baer knocked out Primo Carnera in the 11th round in Long Island City, New York, to win the heavyweight championship.
1936	G.K. Chesterton, the noted English writer, died in Beaconsfield, Buckinghamshire, at age 62.
1940	The Germans occupied Paris in World War II.

1963   The Russian manned space flight *Vostok 5* was launched.

1982   Argentine forces on the Falkland Islands surrendered to the British, ending the war over the islands.

1985   Lebanese Shiite hijackers seized an Athens-to-Rome TWA plane and took the 153 people aboard hostage. The last of them were finally released 17 days later.

JUNE 15 -- BIRTHDAYS

1330   **Edward (the Black Prince)** -- One of the most famous warriors in English history, noted for his exploits in the Hundred Years' War

1605   **Thomas Randolph** -- English poet and dramatist

1728   **Shah Alam** -- Ruler of the Mogul Empire in India

1843   **Edvard Grieg** – Norwegian composer, pianist, and conductor, noted for works such as *Concerto in A minor* and *Peer Gynt*

1861   **Ernestine Schumann-Heink** -- Greatly admired Czechoslovakian contralto

1887   **Malvina Hoffman** -- American sculptor

1892   **Tex Owens** – American composer, author, and singer, noted for works such as Eddy Arnold's theme song, "Cattle Call"

1900   **Otto Luening** -- American composer, conductor, and flutist

1912   **Babe Dahlgren** -- New York Yankee first baseman who replaced Lou Gehrig at the end of his famous streak of 2,130 consecutive games

1914   **Saul Steinberg** -- Romanian-American cartoonist and illustrator noted for his small-scale pen-and-ink drawings

1921   **Erroll Garner** -- American jazz pianist and composer, noted for such songs as "Misty" and "Gaslight"

1922   **Morris Udall** -- U.S. congressman

1932   **Mario Cuomo** -- Governor of New York

1937   **Waylon Jennings** -- American country singer

1938   **Billy Williams** -- Professional baseball player and superstar

1941   **Harry Nilsson** -- American singer and songwriter

1949   **Dusty Baker** -- Professional baseball player

1956   **Lance Parrish** -- Professional baseball player

1958   **Wade Boggs** -- Professional baseball player and superstar

JUNE 15 -- EVENTS

1094	El Cid, the great Spanish national hero, captured Valencia from the Moors.
1215	The Magna Carta was approved at Runnymede by King John of England.
1521	Pope Leo X denounced Martin Luther's writings and ordered Luther to recant.
1752	Benjamin Franklin demonstrated the relationship between electricity and lightning when he launched a kite at Philadelphia during a summer storm.
1775	The Continental Congress appointed George Washington commander in chief of the colonial forces.
1836	Arkansas was admitted to the Union as the 25th state.
1844	Charles Goodyear was granted a patent for rubber vulcanization.
1846	The English Parliament repealed the Corn Law, which had severely restricted the import of corn and other grain.
1846	The United States and Great Britain signed the Oregon Treaty setting the boundary between Canada and the U.S. at the 49th parallel.
1849	James K. Polk died in Nashville, Tennessee, at age 53.
1853	Stephen Foster's famous song, "My Old Kentucky Home, Good Night," made its debut.
1903	Barney Oldfield, the great American automobile racer, became the first to drive an automobile a mile a minute, in Indianapolis.
1919	John Alcock and Arthur Whitten-Brown landed near Clifden, Ireland, completing the world's first transatlantic flight.
1938	Johnny Vander Meer pitched his second consecutive no-hitter, a fantastic feat, as Cincinnati beat Brooklyn, 6-0.
1944	American troops invaded Saipan in the Mariana Islands in World War II.

JUNE 16 -- BIRTHDAYS

1514	**Sir John Cheke** -- English humanist
1762	**Giuseppe Bernardino Bison** -- Italian painter
1858	**Gustavus V** -- King of Sweden, 1907-1950
1890	**Stan Laurel** -- Member of the Laurel and Hardy comedy team, the most successful comedy duo in screen history
1895	**Lew Pollack** — American composer, author, and singer, noted for songs such as "Charmaine" and "The Right Somebody to Love"

1903   Helen Traubel -- American operatic singer
1910   Ilona Massey -- Hungarian-born actress and singer
1917   Irving Penn -- Influential American photographer
1917   Katherine Graham -- Publisher of the Washington *Post*, 1969-
        1979
1935   Jim Dine -- American artist
1937   Erich Segal -- American writer noted for *Love Story* and
        Oliver's Story
1938   Joyce Carol Oates -- American novelist, poet, and short-story writer
1946   Derek Sanderson -- Professional hockey player
1946   Ivan Molina -- Colombian tennis player
1951   Roberto Duran -- World welterweight champion in 1980
1952   Ron LeFlore -- Professional baseball player
1962   Wally Joyner -- Professional baseball player

JUNE 16 -- EVENTS

1464   Roger van der Weyden, the famous Flemish painter who helped
        found the Flemish movement in painting, died in Brussels at
        age 64.

1845   The Congress of the Republic of Texas agreed to annexation by
        the United States.

1845   The American premiere of Gioacchino Rossini's famous opera
        William Tell took place in New York City.

1846   Pius IX was elected Roman Catholic pope. He served for 32
        years, the longest reign in papal history.

1858   Abraham Lincoln made his famous speech which included the
        line: "A house divided against itself cannot stand."

1903   The Ford Motor Company was founded by Henry Ford.

1940   Marshal Henri Philippe Petain replaced Paul Reynaud as pre-
        mier of France, as the Germans pierced the Maginot Line and
        were poised to overrun France in World War II.

1963   The Russians launched the first woman cosmonaut, Valentina
        Tereshkova, into space in *Vostok 6*.

JUNE 17 -- BIRTHDAYS

1239   Edward I -- King of England, 1272-1307, of the Plantagenet line,
        and son of King Henry III

1682   Charles XII -- One of the greatest kings and military leaders in
        Sweden's history, reigning from 1697, at age 15, until he was
        killed in battle in 1718

1703 **John Wesley** – English religious leader and founder of the Methodist Church

1818 **Charles Gounod** – French composer, whose best-known work is the opera *Faust* (1859, revised in 1869), noted for its familiar "Soldiers' Chorus"

1832 **Sir William Crookes** – English chemist noted for the invention of the Crookes tube and for the discovery of the element thallium

1882 **Igor Stravinsky** – Russian composer noted for such works as *The Firebird* (1910) and *The Rite of Spring* (1913)

1888 **Heinz Guderian** – One of the greatest German generals of World War II, and the architect of *Blitzkrieg,* which was so successful in the early stages of the war

1902 **Sammy Fain** – American composer, singer, and pianist noted for songs such as "Let a Smile Be Your Umbrella," "Secret Love," "Love Is a Many Splendored Thing," and "I'll Be Seeing You"

1904 **Ralph Bellamy** – American stage, screen, and television actor

1907 **Charles Eames** – American designer

1910 **Red Foley** – American country singer and musician

1914 **John Hersey** – American Pulitzer Prize-winning novelist, noted for such works as *A Bell for Adano* (1945) and *Hiroshima* (1946)

1919 **Kingman Brewster Jr.** – President of Yale and U.S. ambassador to Great Britain

1923 **Elroy "Crazylegs" Hirsch** – Professional football player

1929 **Tigran Vartanovich Petrosyan** – Russian chess master and world champion, 1966-1969

1944 **Chris Spedding** – British session guitarist

1948 **Dave Concepcion** – Professional baseball player

1951 **Joe Piscopo** – American comedian and television and motion-picture actor

JUNE 17 – EVENTS

1673 Father Jacques Marquette and Louis Joliet began exploring the Mississippi River.

1682 The city of Philadelphia was founded by William Penn.

1775 The British won the Battle of Bunker Hill, with heavy losses due to American Col. William Prescott's order, "Don't fire until you see the whites of their eyes."

1794 Fifty-four people were guillotined in the "Reign of Terror" of the final stages of the French Revolution.

1856   The first Republican National Convention was held, in Philadelphia.   John C. Fremont was nominated as the party's first candidate for president.

1880   John Ward pitched the second perfect game (not a runner reached base) in major league history, as Providence beat Buffalo, 5-0.

1928   Amelia Earhart became the first female passenger on a transatlantic flight, from Newfoundland to Burry Port, Wales, in a plane piloted by Wilmer Stultz.

1939   Eugen Weidmann, a French murderer, became the last person to be publicly guillotined.

1940   Russia invaded Estonia, Latvia, and Lithuania in a prelude to World War II.

1940   Marshal Henri Petain, who had just taken over as head of the French government, agreed to surrender to Germany in World War II.

1942   The term "G.I. Joe" first appeared, in Dave Breger's comic strip in *Yank*.

1944   Iceland officially gained independence from Denmark, and the Republic of Iceland was founded.

1953   East Germans rebelled against Russian rule, but German rock throwers were no match for Soviet tanks, and the revolt was quickly crushed.

1954   Rocky Marciano retained his heavyweight title, defeating former champion Ezzard Charles.

1963   The Supreme Court prohibited the reading of biblical verses and the recitation of the Lord's Prayer in public schools.

1967   Communist China exploded its first hydrogen bomb.

1972   Five men were arrested by Washington, D.C., police in the Watergate Hotel break-in that led ultimately to the destruction of the Nixon presidency.

JUNE 18 -- BIRTHDAYS

1618   **Jean Lepautre** -- French designer
1621   **Allart van Everdingen** -- Dutch painter
1716   **Joseph Vien** -- French painter
1803   **Robert W. Weir** -- American painter
1812   **Ivan Alexandrovich Goncharov** -- Russian novelist noted for works such as *Fregat Pallada* (1858) and *Oblomov* (1859)

1854   **Edward Wyllis Scripps** -- Famous American newspaper publisher who started the first newspaper chain and founded the United Press Associations, now United Press International

1857   **Henry Clay Folger** -- Founder in 1930 of the Folger Shakespeare Library in Washington, D.C.

1877   **James Montgomery Flagg** – Illustrator of the World War I recruiting poster with the caption, "I want you"

1884   **Edouard Daladier** -- French premier at the beginning of World War II

1895   **Blanche Sweet** -- American stage and screen actress and a favorite D.W. Griffith leading lady of the silent period

1901   **Jeanette MacDonald** -- American singer and actress, especially noted for the films she made with Nelson Eddy in the most successful singing partnership in musical film history

1901   **Jimmy Dale** -- American composer noted for songs such as "I Hate to See the Evening Sun Go Down"

1903   **Raymond Radiguet** -- French poet and novelist

1904   **Keye Luke** – Chinese-American stage, screen, and television actor, noted for his role as the "Number One Son" in the Charlie Chan movies

1906   **Kay Kyser** -- American musician and bandleader of the Big Band Era

1908   **Sam Martin** – American composer and author, noted for songs such as "You Call Everybody Darling"

1910   **E.G. Marshall** -- American motion-picture and television actor

1910   **Ray McKinley** -- American composer, author, and bandleader, noted for lyrics such as "Beat Me Daddy, Eight to the Bar"

1913   **Sylvia Porter** -- American financial columnist and writer

1913   **Sammy Cahn** -- American lyricist noted for such songs as "Three Coins in the Fountain," "I'll Walk Alone," "Let It Snow, Let It Snow, Let It Snow," and "High Hopes"

1916   **Richard Boone** -- American motion-picture and television actor

1924   **George Mikan** -- Professional basketball player who dominated the game in the 1940s and 1950s

1926   **Eva Bartok** -- Hungarian motion-picture actress

1926   **Tom Wicker** -- American journalist and author

1937   **John D. Rockefeller IV** – Governor of West Virginia and U.S. senator

1939   **Lou Brock** -- Hall of Fame baseball player who stole a record 118 bases in 1974 and broke Ty Cobb's career record of 892 in 1977

1942   **Paul McCartney** -- Member of the Beatles musical group

1947   **Barry Manilow** -- American pop singer and songwriter
1952   **Carol Kane** -- American stage and motion-picture actress
1952   **Isabella Rossellini** -- Italian-born motion-picture actress and daughter of actress Ingrid Bergman and director Roberto Rossellini
1956   **Kathy May** -- American tennis player
1961   **Allison "Alf" Moyet** -- British vocalist with the Yaz musical group
1961   **Andres Galarraga** -- Professional baseball player

JUNE 18 -- EVENTS

1155   Frederick Barbarossa was crowned Holy Roman Emperor.
1778   American forces occupied Philadelphia as the British withdrew in the Revolutionary War.
1798   Concluding a toast to John Marshall at O'Eller's Tavern in Philadelphia, U.S. Rep. Robert Goodloe Harper said, "Millions for defense, but not one cent for tribute!"
1812   Congress declared war on Great Britain, marking the beginning of the War of 1812.
1815   In one of history's most decisive battles, Napoleon was defeated in the Battle of Waterloo by an allied army under the Duke of Wellington, ending Napoleon's remarkable career.
1873   Susan B. Anthony, the noted American suffragette, was fined $100 for trying to vote in Rochester, New York, in the 1872 presidential election.
1902   Samuel Butler, the noted English novelist, died in London at age 66.
1940   On the eve of the Battle of Britain, Winston Churchill said, "If the British Empire and its Commonwealth last for a thousand years, men will still say, 'This was their finest hour.'"
1941   Joe Louis knocked out Billy Conn in the 13th round in New York to retain his heavyweight title. Conn was ahead on points and would have won had he avoided a knockout.
1963   Russian cosmonaut Valentina Tereshkova, the first woman in space, completed her flight.
1979   President Jimmy Carter and Russian president Leonid Brezhnev signed the SALT II treaty in Vienna. The U.S. Senate, however, failed to ratify it.
1983   Sally Ride became America's first woman astronaut in space as she and four colleagues blasted off aboard the space shuttle *Challenger*.

1986 Pitcher Don Sutton won his 300th career game, as California defeated Texas, 5-1.

JUNE 19 -- BIRTHDAYS

1507 **Annibale Caro** -- Italian poet noted for translating Virgil's *Aeneid*

1566 **James I** -- The first Stuart king of England, 1603-1625, successor to Queen Elizabeth I, and the king who sponsored the translation known as the King James Version of the Bible

1623 **Blaise Pascal** -- French philosopher, mathematician, scientist, and author, noted for the great work *Pensees*

1783 **Thomas Sully** -- One of the finest U.S. portrait painters of the 19th century

1856 **Elbert Green Hubbard** -- American author, biographer, and publisher, who died in the sinking of the *Lusitania* in 1915

1861 **Douglas Haig** -- Commander in chief of the British forces in France in World War I, who directed the attack that broke Germany's Hindenburg Line and led to the end of the war

1865 **Dame May Whitty** -- English stage and motion-picture actress with a career of over 60 years

1877 **Charles Coburn** -- American stage and motion-picture actor in nearly 100 films

1881 **Jimmy Walker** -- Mayor of New York City, 1926-1932

1884 **Eddie Cicotte** -- One of the top baseball pitchers of his day, and one of the Chicago White Sox players implicated in the 1919 "Black Sox" scandal

1896 **Wallis Warfield Simpson** -- The Duchess of Windsor and wife of former King Edward VIII of England, who abdicated his throne to marry her

1897 **Moe Howard** -- American comedian and actor and one of the original Three Stooges

1902 **Guy Lombardo** -- American bandleader of the Big Band Era whose career extended into the 1980s

1903 **Lou Gehrig** -- One of baseball's all-time greatest players, and "Iron Horse," who played in a record 2,130 consecutive games

1908 **Quentin Burdick** -- U.S. senator

1908 **Mildred Natwick** -- Gifted character actress of the American stage and screen, whose career spanned 45 years

1909 **Osamu Dazai** -- Foremost Japanese novelist of his day

1910 **Abe Fortas** -- Supreme Court justice, 1965-1969

1912	**Martin Gabel** -- American stage, screen, and television actor
1914	**Alan Cranston** -- U.S. senator
1919	**Louis Jourdan** -- French motion-picture actor
1921	**Howell Heflin** -- U.S. senator
1932	**Marisa Pavan** -- Italian-born motion-picture actress and twin sister of actress Pier Angeli
1932	**Pier Angeli** -- Italian-born motion-picture and twin sister of actress Marisa Pavan
1934	**Gena Rowlands** -- American stage, screen, and television actress
1941	**Harold Elschenbroich** -- West German tennis player
1943	**Malcolm McDowell** -- English motion-picture actor
1949	**Jerry Reuss** -- Professional baseball player
1954	**Johnnie LeMaster** -- Professional baseball player
1955	**Bruce Harper** -- Professional football player

JUNE 19 -- EVENTS

1215	The articles of the Magna Carta, agreed to by King John four days earlier, were written out in legal form, or engrossed, as a royal charter.
1586	English colonists left Roanoke Island, N.C., for home, after failing to establish the first permanent English colony in America.
1588	The Spanish Armada anchored at Corunna, Spain, to pick up provisions and regroup after a violent storm on the Portuguese coast, before proceeding to engage the English fleet.
1846	Alexander Joy Cartwright brought the New York Knickerbockers and the New York Nine to Hoboken, N.J., to play the first game of baseball. The Nine won, 23-1.
1856	The Republicans adjourned their first National Convention after nominating John C. Fremont as their first presidential candidate.
1865	Word finally reached the piney woods of East Texas that the slaves were freed. The date was thereafter celebrated as Freedom Day by American blacks.
1867	Maximilian, the usurper Emperor of Mexico, was executed by a firing squad of troops of the Mexican Republic.
1886	William Howard Taft married Helen Herron.
1910	Father's Day was first observed. It was started by Mrs. John Bruce Dodd of Spokane, Washington.
1912	The U.S. government adopted the eight-hour day for its employees.

1923   The comic strip, *Moon Mullins,* by Frank Willard, first appeared.

1934   The Federal Communications Commission was created.

1936   Max Schmeling knocked out Joe Louis in the 12th round at New York's Yankee Stadium.

1944   The Battle of the Philippine Sea began between the United States and Japan in World War II. It ended decisively in the Americans' favor on the following day.

1953   Ethel and Julius Rosenberg were executed for spying for the Russians. They were the first Americans given a death sentence for espionage by a United States civilian court.

1978   The comic strip, *Garfield,* by Jim Davis, first appeared.

JUNE 20 -- BIRTHDAYS

1566   Sigismund III -- King of Poland, 1587-1632, of the House of Vasa

1615   **Salvator Rosa** -- Italian painter noted for works such as *Prometheus* (1635) and *L'Umana Fragilita* (1656)

1819   **Jacques Offenbach** -- French composer best known for his opera, *The Tales of Hoffmann*

1858   **Charles W. Chesnutt** -- First important black American novelist

1858   **Medardo Rosso** -- Italian sculptor

1873   **Alberto Santos-Dumont** -- Brazilian-born French aviation pioneer in both lighter-than-air and heavier-than-air machines

1891   **John Costello** -- Prime minister of the Republic of Ireland, 1948-1951 and 1954-1957

1894   **George Delacorte** -- American publisher and philanthropist

1903   **Glenna Collett Vare** -- Sportswoman who dominated U.S. women's golf in the 1920s and 1930s

1905   **Lillian Hellman** -- America's foremost woman playwright, noted for such works as *The Children's Hour* (1934) and *The Little Foxes* (1939)

1909   **Errol Flynn** -- Tasmanian-born motion-picture actor and dashing hero of the 1940s

1911   **Gail Patrick** -- American actress and producer

1921   **Pancho Segura** -- Ecuadorian tennis player

1924   **Audie Murphy** -- American World War II hero and motion-picture actor

1924   **Chet Atkins** -- American guitarist

1925   **Doris Hart** -- American Hall of Fame tennis player, who ranked in the top ten for 14 consecutive years, 1942-1955

1935   **Leonard Dawson** -- Professional football player

1942   **Brian Wilson** -- American singer and composer with the Beach Boys musical group
1946   **Andre Watts** -- American pianist
1953   **Paul Ramirez** -- Mexican tennis player
1953   **Cyndi Lauper** -- American rock singer
1958   **Dickie Thon** -- Professional baseball player
1960   **John Taylor** -- Bassist of the Duran Duran musical group

JUNE 20 -- EVENTS

404 AD The first Cathedral of Santa Sophia in Constantinople was burned to the ground by rioters.

1389   The Turks defeated the Serbs on the Kossovo Plain, destroying the Serbian Empire and resulting in Turkish rule of Serbia for 400 years.

1530   The Diet of Augsburg opened. It was called by Holy Roman Emperor Henry V to end the quarrels between Catholics and Protestants.

1632   The second Lord Baltimore received a grant from the king of England for the tract of land on which he founded the colony of Maryland.

1756   The Black Hole of Calcutta, a suffocating dungeon, got its name when a number of British prisoners were locked in it overnight and died of suffocation.

1782   Congress adopted the Great Seal of the United States.

1789   The Tennis Court Oath pledging the Third Estate to a new constitution was taken, marking the beginning of the French Revolution.

1793   Eli Whitney applied for a patent on his cotton gin.

1837   Queen Victoria of England began her 64-year reign.

1863   West Virginia was admitted to the Union as the 35th state.

1893   Lizzie Borden was found not guilty of murdering her father and stepmother, who were hacked to death in Fall River, Massachusetts, on August 4, 1892.

1910   Fanny Brice made her debut in the *Ziegfeld Follies of 1910.*

1944   The Battle of the Philippine Sea ended with a decisive U.S. victory over Japan in World War II. The Americans lost 27 planes while the Japanese lost 402.

1948   Ed Sullivan's television variety show, *Toast of the Town,* made its debut. It ran for nearly 23 years.

1960   Floyd Patterson regained the heavyweight boxing title, knocking out Ingemar Johansson in the 5th round in New York.

JUNE 21 -- BIRTHDAYS

1002   Leo IX – Roman Catholic pope, 1049-1054, known as Saint Leo

1639   **Increase Mather** – Puritan minister and scholar of colonial Massachusetts, and father of Puritan minister Cotton Mather

1640   **Abraham Mignon** -- German painter

1676   **Anthony Collins** -- English deist and freethinker

1774   **Daniel D. Tompkins** – U.S. vice president under President Monroe

1781   **Simeon-Denis Poisson** -- Noted French mathematician

1839   **Joaquim Maria Machado de Assiz** -- The greatest figure in Brazilian literature, and the founder in 1897 of the Brazilian Academy of Letters

1850   **Daniel Carter Beard** -- American naturalist and illustrator, and an early pioneer in shaping the Boy Scouts of America

1859   **Henry Ossawa Tanner** -- American painter noted for works such as *Daniel in the Lions' Den* (1896)

1863   **Max Wolf** -- German astronomer and discoverer of 228 asteroids

1879   **Henry Creamer** – American composer noted for songs such as "Way Down Yonder in New Orleans" and "After You've Gone"

1882   **Rockwell Kent** -- American painter, illustrator, printmaker, and author

1892   **Reinhold Niebuhr** -- One of the most important American theologians of the 20th century

1903   **Al Hirschfield** -- American cartoonist and artist

1904   **Mack Gordon** -- Polish-American composer noted for songs such as "I've Got a Gal in Kalamazoo," "Chattanooga Choo-Choo," "You'll Never Know," "Mam'selle," and "I Can't Begin to Tell You"

1905   **Jean-Paul Sartre** -- French existential philosopher, novelist, and playwright

1906   **Harold Spina** – American composer and author, noted for songs such as "It's So Nice to Have a Man Around the House"

1912   **Mary McCarthy** – American novelist, critic, essayist, and author of *The Group* (1963)

1913   **Willie Mosconi** -- Noted American billiard player, and 15 times world pocket billiards open champion

1918   **Eddie Lopat** -- Professional baseball player and manager

1919   **Paolo Soleri** -- Italian architect, designer, and city planner

1921   **Gower Champion** -- American dancer, director, and choreographer

1921   **Jane Russell** -- American motion-picture and television actress

1922   **Judy Holliday** -- American motion-picture actress

1925   **Maureen Stapleton** -- American stage, screen, and television actress

1931   **Margaret Heckler** -- American congresswoman and secretary of Health and Human Services under President Reagan

1935   **Francoise Sagan** -- French novelist and author of *Bonjour Tristesse*

1941   **Mariette Hartley** -- American motion-picture and television actress and morning show hostess

1944   **Ray Davies** -- British singer and guitarist with the Kinks musical group

1947   **Meredith Baxter** -- American television actress

1947   **Michael Gross** -- American television actor

1949   **Duane Thomas** -- Professional football player

1953   **Charlie Moore** -- Professional baseball player

1956   **Rick Sutcliffe** -- Professional baseball player

1957   **Mark Brzezicki** -- Irish drummer with the Big Country musical group

1982   **Prince William** -- Son of Charles and Lady Diana, Prince and Princess of Wales

JUNE 21 -- EVENTS

1631   John Smith, one of the founders of Jamestown, Virginia, died at age 51.

1788   New Hampshire ratified the U.S. Constitution, the ninth state to do so, which made it operative.

1810   Zachary Taylor married Margaret Mackall Smith.

1834   Cyrus McCormick was granted a patent for an improved version of his reaper, originally invented in 1831.

1879   F.W. Woolworth opened his first five-and-ten-cent store, in Lancaster, Pennsylvania.

1932   Jack Sharkey won the heavyweight title from Max Schmeling in 15 rounds in Long Island City, New York.

1939   Baseball fans were saddened as they learned that Lou Gehrig had a rare type of paralysis and would never play again.

1940	Richard Nixon married Pat Ryan.
1945	The U.S. marines took Okinawa in World War II after nearly three months of fighting.
1948	CBS demonstrated the first long-playing 33⅓ rpm records. Two of the first releases were Mendelssohn's *Violin Concerto* and Tchaikovsky's *Fourth Symphony*.
1954	John Landy of Australia established a new world's record in running the mile in 3 minutes, 58 seconds, in Turku, Finland.
1963	Paul VI became Roman Catholic pope.
1964	Jim Bunning pitched a perfect game (no man reached base) as the Philadelphia Phillies beat the New York Mets, 6-0.
1982	John Hinckley Jr. was found innocent by reason of insanity for attempting to assassinate President Reagan.

JUNE 22 -- BIRTHDAYS

1555	**Francisco de Ribalta** -- Spanish painter
1758	**George Vancouver** – British navigator and explorer for whom Vancouver, Canada, was named
1805	**Giuseppe Mazzini** -- Italian patriot and pioneer in the struggle to unite Italy in the 1830s and 1840s
1844	**Margaret Sidney** -- Author of *The Five Little Peppers and How They Grew*
1856	**Sir Henry Rider Haggard** -- Highly successful English writer of the late 1800s and author of *King Solomon's Mines* (1885) and *She* (1887)
1869	**Hendrikus Colijn** -- Dutch prime minister during the Great Depression
1882	**William M. Scholl** -- American medical school graduate and former shoemaker who developed Dr. Scholl's arch support and promoted corn and bunion pads to ease aching feet
1887	**Julian Huxley** -- British biologist, writer, and grandson of the famous zoologist, T.H. Huxley
1898	**Erich Maria Remarque** -- German-American novelist and author of *All Quiet on the Western Front* (1929), one of the most famous war stories of all time
1903	**Carl Hubbell** -- Hall of Fame baseball pitcher who won 16 consecutive games in 1936
1906	**Anne Morrow Lindbergh** -- American poet and wife of aviator hero Charles A. Lindbergh, noted for such works as *Gift from the Sea* (1955)

1906   **Billy Wilder** -- Austrian-born motion-picture director, noted for
        such films as *Stalag 17* (1953) and *Witness for the Prosecu-*
        tion (1958)

1907   **Michael Todd** — American motion-picture producer and show-
        man, noted for such shows as *Oklahoma!* (1955) and *Around the*
        World in 80 Days (1956)

1909   **Buddy Adler** -- American motion-picture producer who won an
        Academy Award in 1953 for *From Here to Eternity*

1915   **Cornelius Warmerdam** -- American athlete and the first man to
        pole vault 15 feet (15 feet 1^1/$_8$ inches in 1940)

1921   **Joseph Papp** -- One of Broadway's greatest producers, noted for
        some 100 plays, among which are *Electra* (1964), *Hair* (1967), *A*
        Chorus Line (1975), and *The Pirates of Penzance* (1980)

1922   **Bill Blass** -- American fashion designer

1933   **Dianne Feinstein** -- Mayor of San Francisco

1937   **Kris Kristofferson** -- American singer and motion-picture actor

1941   **Ed Bradley** -- American television personality, noted as a regu-
        lar on the long-running show, *Sixty Minutes*

1947   **Robert Douglass** -- Professional football player

1948   **Pete Maravich** -- Professional basketball player

1948   **Todd Rundgren** -- American rock musician

1949   **Meryl Streep** -- American stage, screen, and television actress,
        who won Academy Awards for best actress in *Sophie's Choice*
        and *Kramer vs. Kramer*

1949   **Lindsay Wagner** -- American motion-picture and television
        actress

1954   **Freddie Prinze** -- American television actor and comedian

JUNE 22 -- EVENTS

1527   Niccolo Machiavelli, the great Italian writer, died in Florence at
        age 58.

1611   The famous explorer Henry Hudson, his son, and 7 loyal sailors
        were set adrift in a small boat in Hudson Bay by mutineers and
        were never heard of again.

1633   Galileo was forced by the Court of Inquisition to confess the
        "falsehood" of the Copernican theory of planetary motion.

1812   Napoleon crossed the Neman River with his Grande Armee of
        600,000 men, opening his campaign against Russia.

1815   After his defeat at the Battle of Waterloo, Napoleon abdicated
        for the second and last time.

1846	Adolphe Sax patented the saxophone, his invention of a few years earlier.
1870	Congress created the Department of Justice.
1937	Joe Louis knocked out Jim Braddock in the 8th round at Comiskey Park in Chicago to become heavyweight champion of the world.
1938	Joe Louis knocked out Max Schmeling in the first round to retain his heavyweight championship. The victory avenged an earlier loss to Schmeling, the only loss Louis had in his prime.
1940	France surrendered to Germany in World War II.
1941	More than 150 German and other Axis divisions invaded Russia in Operation Barbarossa in World War II.
1944	The GI Bill of Rights became law, under which more than 7,800,000 World War II veterans studied or trained.
1949	Ezzard Charles defeated Joe Walcott in a 15 round decision to become heavyweight champion.
1969	Judy Garland, the noted American actress, was found dead at age 47.
1973	The *Skylab 1* astronauts returned to earth after 28 days in space.

JUNE 23 -- BIRTHDAYS

1625	**John Fell** -- English clergyman and scholar
1763	**Josephine de Beauharnais** -- Wife of Napoleon Bonaparte
1859	**Edouard Michelin** -- Co-founder of the Michelin Tire Company
1875	**Carl Wilhelm Emil Milles** -- Swedish-American sculptor, noted for fountains such as *Meeting of the Waters* in St. Louis
1876	**Irvin S. Cobb** -- American journalist, humorist, and actor
1889	**Anna Akhmatova** -- The greatest woman poet in Russian literature
1894	**Alfred Charles Kinsey** -- American physician and student of human sexual behavior, whose books on the subject were considered sensational in the 1940s
1894	**Prince Edward** -- The Duke of Windsor, formerly King Edward VIII of England, who abdicated his throne in 1936 to marry the woman he loved
1895	**Norman R. Raine** -- Creator of *Tugboat Annie*
1895	**George Weiss** -- Professional baseball general manager, whose tenure with the New York Yankees produced their great teams of the 1950s and 1960s

1898   Charles Francis Kenny -- American composer and author, noted for such songs as "Love Letters in the Sand" and "There's a Gold Mine in the Sky"

1910   **Jean Anouilh** -- Popular French playwright known for his polished dramas

1910   **Edward P. Morgan** -- American broadcast journalist

1913   **William Rogers** -- U.S. secretary of state under President Nixon

1915   **Dennis Price** -- English stage and motion-picture actor

1927   **Bob Fosse** -- American dancer, choreographer, and director, noted for such hits as *Damn Yankees* and *Cabaret*

1929   **June Carter Cash** -- American country singer and wife of singer Johnny Cash

1933   **Dave Bristol** -- Professional baseball player and manager

1936   **Richard David Bach** -- American writer noted for *Jonathan Livingston Seagull*

1940   **Wilma Rudolph** -- American sprinter and winner of three gold medals in the 1960 Olympic Games

1956   **Tony Hill** -- Professional football player

JUNE 23 -- EVENTS

1483   King Edward V of England, age 12, and his younger brother, the Duke of York, were murdered in the Tower of London, probably on orders of their uncle, the future Richard III.

1683   William Penn signed a friendship treaty with the Leni-Lenape Indians on the Delaware River, shortly after he arrived in the Pennsylvania region.

1713   Queen Anne of England ordered French descendants in Nova Scotia to take an oath of allegiance to England within a year, or leave.

1860   The United States Secret Service was established, for the purpose of protecting the president and his family.

1863   French historian Ernest Renan published his *Life of Jesus*.

1868   Christopher Latham Sholes, Carlos Glidden, and Samuel W. Soule patented their Type-Writer, the first such machine that was practical.

1947   Congress overrode President Truman's veto to enact the Taft-Hartley Act.

1967   President Lyndon Johnson met Russia's premier Aleksei Kosygin at the Glassboro, New Jersey, summit conference.

1967   Jim Ryun, the United States runner, ran the mile in a record 3 minutes, 51.1 seconds.

JUNE 24 -- BIRTHDAYS

1542 **St. John of the Cross** -- Spanish poet, Juan de Yepis y Alvarez

1616 **Ferdinand Bol** -- Dutch painter

1693 **Michael Rysbrack** -- English sculptor

1771 **E.I. Du Pont** -- French-American industrialist who founded the powder works in 1802 in Delaware that formed the beginning of the Du Pont Company of today

1795 **Ernst Heinrich Weber** -- German anatomist and physiologist

1813 **Henry Ward Beecher** -- Noted Congregational minister and Protestant spokesman, and brother of Harriet Beecher Stowe, the author of *Uncle Tom's Cabin*

1839 **Gustavus Franklin Swift** -- American industrialist who in 1885 founded Swift & Company

1842 **Ambrose Bierce** -- American misanthropic writer and journalist, and author of *Can Such Things Be?* (1893) and *The Devil's Dictionary* (1911)

1848 **Brooks Adams** -- American historian, critic of capitalism, and grandson of John Quincy Adams

1852 **Victor Adler** -- Creator of the Austrian Socialist Party

1879 **Agrippina Vaganova** -- Russian ballerina and teacher

1895 **Jack Dempsey** -- One of the most popular world heavyweight boxing champions of all time (1919-1926)

1906 **Phil Harris** -- American actor and musician

1907 **Rollie Hemsley** -- Professional baseball player

1911 **Juan-Manuel Fangio** -- World champion automobile racer who won the Grand Prix five times, four times in succession (1954-1957)

1912 **Norman Cousins** -- Editor of *The Saturday Review* for 32 years

1915 **Sir Fred Hoyle** -- English mathematician and astronomer

1916 **John Ciardi** -- American poet and longtime poetry editor of *The Saturday Review*

1928 **Larry Foust** -- Professional basketball player

1931 **Billy Casper** -- Professional golfer

1933 **Doug Sanders** -- Professional golfer

1933 **Sam Jones** -- Professional basketball superstar with over 14,000 career points

1935 **Pete Hamill** -- American newspaper columnist

1942 **Mick Fleetwood** -- English rock musician of the Fleetwood Mac musical group

1944   **Arthur Brown** -- British rock singer
1944   **Jeff Beck** -- British rock and jazz guitarist
1945   **Betty Stove** -- Dutch tennis player
1948   **Steve Patterson** -- Professional basketball player
1957   **Doug Jones** -- Professional baseball player

JUNE 24 -- EVENTS

217 AD Hannibal defeated the Romans at Lago di Trasimeno in the Second Punic War.

541 AD Attila the Hun raised his siege of Orleans, France, in a prelude to his being pushed out of France by a combined army of Romans and barbarians.

1314   The Battle of Bannockburn was fought in which Scotland's Robert Bruce defeated England's King Edward II, taking Stirling Castle, the last English foothold in Scotland.

1497   John Cabot completed his historic voyage for England to the New World, landing on the North American coast at what is believed to be either Newfoundland or Nova Scotia.

1519   Lucretia Borgia, the central figure in the notorious Borgia family, died at age 39.

1540   Henry VIII of England divorced his fourth wife, Anne of Cleves.

1665   Thomas Willett, the first mayor of New York City, was installed in office.

1885   Woodrow Wilson married his first wife, Ellen Louise Axson.

1898   The United States defeated the Spanish in the Battle of Las Guasimas, Cuba, the first land engagement of the Spanish-American War.

1908   Grover Cleveland died in Princeton, New Jersey, at age 71.

1948   The Russians initiated the Berlin Blockade, stopping all rail, water, and highway routes to West Berlin.

1956   Dean Martin and Jerry Lewis broke up their comedy team after ten years and sixteen films.

JUNE 25 -- BIRTHDAYS

1852   **Antonio Gaudi** -- Spanish architect noted for Barcelona's Casa Mila, completed in 1910

1865   **Robert Henri** -- American painter and art teacher, and the guiding spirit of The Eight, an informal association of painters in the early 20th century

1886   Henry H. "Hap" Arnold -- American general who developed the small U.S. Army Air Corps into the powerful U.S. Air Force of World War II, and the only man to serve as general of both the Army and Air Force

1887   **George Abbott** -- American playwright, director, producer, and screenwriter who wrote, directed, or produced more than 120 Broadway plays and was active at age 100

1900   **Lord Louis Mountbatten** -- English naval leader and statesman, and the last viceroy of India before its independence in 1947

1903   **George Orwell** -- British writer and author of *Animal Farm* (1945) and *1984* (1949)

1906   **Roger Livesey** -- English stage, screen, and television actor

1906   **Joe Kuhel** -- Professional baseball player

1913   **Adele Girard Marsala** -- American composer and harpist, noted for songs such as "Little Sir Echo"

1915   **Peter Lind Hayes** -- American actor, composer, and author

1918   **Sid Tepper** -- American composer and author, noted for songs such as "Red Roses for a Blue Lady," "The Naughty Lady of Shady Lane," and "Say Something Sweet to Your Sweetheart"

1923   **Sam Francis** -- American painter

1924   **Sidney Lumet** -- American motion-picture director, noted for such films as *Murder on the Orient Express* (1974), *Dog Day Afternoon* (1975), and *Network* (1976)

1925   **June Lockhart** -- American motion-picture and television actress

1933   **James Meredith** -- American civil rights advocate and first black graduate of the University of Mississippi

1942   **Willis Reed** -- Professional basketball player

1945   **Carly Simon** -- American pop rock singer

1949   **Phyllis George** -- American television personality and former Miss America

1963   **George Michael** -- British singer, composer, musician, and founder of the Wham! musical group

JUNE 25 -- EVENTS

1503   Two of Columbus's ships were beached in Jamaica, where he was marooned for a year on the return trip of his fourth voyage to America.

1630   Governor John Winthrop of the Massachusetts Bay Colony introduced the fork to America.

1788   Virginia ratified the Constitution, becoming the 10th state.

1876   The Battle of the Little Bighorn began between U.S. General
        Custer and Chief Crazy Horse. The battle, known as "Custer's
        Last Stand," ended in disaster for Custer the next day.

1886   Arturo Toscanini, a 19-year-old cellist, conducted the orchestra
        in a Rio de Janeiro performance of *Aida* so successfully that he
        became a conductor, the greatest of his time.

1916   Thomas Eakins, the American painter, died in Philadelphia at
        age 71.

1918   United States marines captured Belleau Wood in World War I.

1938   The Fair Labor Standards Act became law.

1950   The North Koreans invaded South Korea, starting the Ko-
        rean War.

1962   The U.S. Supreme Court declared prayer in the public schools
        unconstitutional.

1973   John Dean testified before the Select Senate Committee that
        President Nixon knew about the Watergate break-in as early as
        September 15, 1972.

JUNE 26 -- BIRTHDAYS

1742   **Arthur Middleton** – American Revolutionary War leader and
        one of the South Carolina signers of the Declaration of Inde-
        pendence

1763   **George Morland** -- English painter

1819   **Abner Doubleday** -- Inventor of baseball, who laid out the first
        diamond-shaped field in Cooperstown, New York, in 1839, and
        coined the word *baseball*

1824   **Lord Kelvin (William Thomson)** -- One of the greatest British
        physicists of the 1800s

1853   **Frederick Henry Evans** -- English photographer

1854   **Sir Robert L. Borden** -- Prime minister of Canada, 1911-1920,
        and one of the greatest of all time

1891   **Sidney Coe Howard** – American playwright noted for works
        such as *They Knew What They Wanted* (1924) and *Alien Corn* (1933)

1892   **Pearl Buck** -- Nobel Prize-winning American author noted for
        novels of life in China, such as *The Good Earth* (1932)

1894   **Jeanne Eagels** -- American stage and motion-picture actress

1894   **Clarence Lovejoy** -- Founder of the college guides

1897   **Hans Barth** -- German painter and composer

1898   **Willy Messerschmitt** -- German aircraft designer

1901   Stuart Symington -- U.S. senator in the 1950s, 1960s, and 1970s
1902   Bill Lear -- Father of the Lear jet plane
1903   Babe Herman -- Professional baseball player
1904   Peter Lorre -- Hungarian-American motion-picture actor
1906   Al Stillman -- American lyricist noted for songs such as "I Believe," "The Breeze and I," "Chances Are," "It's Not for Me to Say," "In Spain They Say 'Si Si'," and "Jukebox Saturday Night"
1908   Debs Garms -- Professional baseball player who won the National League batting championship in 1940
1914   Mildred "Babe" Didrikson Zaharias -- One of the greatest woman athletes in history, who excelled in basketball, baseball, tennis, and won 17 major women's golf tournaments in a row
1921   Howie Pollet -- Professional baseball player
1922   Eleanor Parker -- American motion-picture and television actress
1934   John Tunney -- U.S. senator and son of boxing great Gene Tunney
1936   Hal Greer -- Professional basketball superstar with over 15,000 career points
1939   Charles Robb -- Governor of Virginia, U.S. senator, and son-in-law of President Lyndon B. Johnson
1940   Billy Davis Jr. -- Member of the 5th Dimension singing group

JUNE 26 -- EVENTS

363 AD Emperor Julian, the last Roman emperor to oppose Christianity, died in Mesopotamia at age 32, while fighting the Persians.
1284   The Pied Piper of Hamelin, Germany, according to legend, lured 130 children of the town into oblivion.
1483   Richard III, the last Plantagenet king of England, assumed the throne.
1541   Spanish explorer Francisco Pizarro, the conquerer of Peru, was killed by a group of his enemies, who burst into his house while he was entertaining guests at dinner.
1844   John Tyler married his second wife, Julia Gardiner, becoming the first president to marry while in office.
1876   The Battle of the Little Bighorn ended with Crazy Horse wiping out General George Custer and his entire column of 208 men.
1906   The first French Grand Prix auto race began at Le Mans. It was completed the following day.
1916   The Cleveland Indians, in a game with the Chicago White Sox, appeared on the field with numbers on their uniforms, the first time numbers were used to identify baseball players.

1917   The first U.S. troops landed in France in World War I, under the command of General John J. Pershing.

1945   The United Nations Charter was signed by all 50 nations present at the San Francisco Conference.

1948   The United States announced the Berlin Airlift to fly cargo to West Berlin and nullify the Russian blockade.

1959   Ingemar Johansson knocked out Floyd Patterson in the third round in New York City to win the heavyweight championship.

1963   "Ich bin ein Berliner," President John F. Kennedy said to a cheering crowd in West Berlin.

JUNE 27 -- BIRTHDAYS

1462   **Louis XII** -- King of France, 1498-1515, known as "The Father of His People"

1550   **Charles IX** -- King of France, 1560-1574

1806   **Augustus De Morgan** -- English mathematician, noted for De Morgan's theorems of logic

1846   **Charles Stewart Parnell** -- Irish Nationalist leader of the 1870s and 1880s

1850   **Lafcadio Hearn** -- American author noted for works such as *Chita: A Memory of Last Island* (1889) and *In Ghostly Japan* (1899)

1859   **Mildred J. Hill** -- American composer, author, and pianist, noted for songs such as "Good Morning to All" and the most popular song of all time, "Happy Birthday to You"

1872   **Paul Laurence Dunbar** -- American novelist and poet, and one of the earliest U.S. black writers

1874   **John Golden** -- American playwright and songwriter

1880   **Helen Keller** -- Outstanding American author and educator who was blind and deaf

1895   **Joseph Patrick McEvoy** -- American novelist and creator of the comic strip, *Dixie Dugan*

1897   **Maceo Pinkard** -- American composer and author, noted for songs such as "Sweet Georgia Brown" and "Gimme a Little Kiss, Will Ya Huh?"

1900   **Otto E. Passman** -- U.S. congressman, 1947-1977

1907   **John McIntire** -- American motion-picture and television actor

1913   **Philip Guston** -- American painter noted for his melancholy city scenes such as *Martial Memory* (1940-1941)

1922   **Bob Keeshan** – American television actor who played Captain Kangeroo for thirty years (October 1955 to December 1984)

1929   **Peter Maas** -- American author

1930   **H. Ross Perot** -- American millionaire and philanthropist

1933   **Gary Crosby** -- American singer and son of singer Bing Crosby

1938   **Bruce Edward Babbitt** -- Governor of Arizona

1941   **Errol Mann** -- Professional football player

1943   **Rico Petrocelli** -- Professional baseball player and sports announcer

1944   **Bruce Johnston** -- American musician with the Beach Boys musical group

1945   **Catherine Lacoste** -- Professional golfer

1949   **Lionel Richie** -- American singer who won five Grammy Awards

JUNE 27 -- EVENTS

1787   Edward Gibbon, the great English historian, completed his monumental work, *The Decline and Fall of the Roman Empire,* at his house in Lausanne, Switzerland.

1844   Joseph Smith, founder of the Mormon Church, was murdered by a mob in Carthage, Illinois.

1847   New York and Boston were first linked by telegraph wires.

1861   The Central Pacific Railroad was organized in California.

1864   Confederate troops won the Battle of Kenesaw Mountain, Georgia, in the Civil War.

1921   The New York Curb Exchange became an indoor securities market as it opened its first building in New York City.

1941   The U.S. Army's four-engined B-19, the largest bomber in the world at the time, passed its first test flight in California.

1944   The Allies captured Cherbourg in World War II, giving them an excellent harbor for the upcoming liberation of France.

1947   Automobile workers received the first pension in automotive history as the Ford Motor Company agreed to finance their pension plan.

1950   President Harry S Truman ordered the U.S. air and naval forces under General Douglas MacArthur to help repel the North Korean invaders of South Korea.

1985   Tennis player Anne White appeared at Wimbledon in white leotards. She was allowed to play but was warned not to wear such dress again.

JUNE 28 -- BIRTHDAYS

1476   Paul IV -- Roman Catholic pope, 1555-1559

1491   Henry VIII -- King of England, 1509-1547, noted for establishing the Reformation in England and for his six wives

1503   Giovanni della Casa -- Italian bishop, poet, and translator

1577   Peter Paul Rubens -- The greatest Flemish painter of the 1600s and the most important baroque painter of northern Europe

1712   Jean Jacques Rousseau -- French philosopher, who was the most important writer of the Enlightenment movement of the 1700s, and whose political philosophy was the inspiration for the French Revolution

1795   Lambert Hitchcock -- American chairmaker

1858   Otis Skinner -- Distinguished American stage actor of the late 19th and early 20th centuries, and the father of actress Cornelia Otis Skinner

1867   Luigi Pirandello -- Nobel Prize-winning Italian dramatist noted for his philosophic plays

1874   Oley Speaks -- American composer and singer, noted for songs such as "On the Road to Mandalay" and "Now the Day Is Over"

1875   Henri Leon Lebesgue -- Distinguished French mathematician, noted for the Lebesgue integral

1883   Pierre Laval -- French politician who collaborated with the Nazis in World War II and served as premier in their puppet Vichy French regime

1894   Francis Townsend Hunter -- American Hall of Fame tennis player

1902   John Dillinger -- Notorious American criminal of the Depression era

1902   Richard Rodgers -- One of the greatest American composers of popular music, who wrote nearly 400 songs and composed the music for such hits as *Oklahoma!, South Pacific,* and *The Sound of Music*

1905   Ashley Montagu -- English anthropologist and writer

1909   Eric Ambler -- English author noted for his mystery novels of intrigue and international adventure

1914   Lester Raymond Flatt -- American guitarist and singer who with Earl Scruggs formed the Flatt and Scruggs musical duo

1915   Leonard C. MacKenzie Jr. -- American composer and author, noted for songs such as "Chiquita Banana"

1926   Mel Brooks -- American comedian, actor, and motion-picture director

1933	**Pat Morita** -- American motion-picture and television actor
1946	**Gilda Radner** -- American motion-picture and television actress
1948	**Raymond Chester** -- Professional football player
1949	**Don Nottingham** -- Professional football player
1949	**Clarence Davis** -- Professional football player
1949	**Don Baylor** -- Professional baseball player
1950	**Chris Speier** -- Professional baseball player
1952	**Joe Sambito** -- Professional baseball player
1954	**Mark Edmondson** -- Australian tennis player
1955	**Matt Robinson** -- Professional football player
1964	**Mark Grace** -- Professional baseball player
1969	**Danielle Brisebois** -- American television actress

JUNE 28 -- EVENTS

1461	King Edward IV of England was crowned at Westminster Abbey.
1519	Charles I of Spain became Charles V, Holy Roman Emperor, creating overnight a vast empire larger than any since ancient Rome.
1709	Peter the Great of Russia destroyed Sweden as a major power in the Battle of Poltava in the Great Northern War, one of the greatest military battles in history.
1778	Molly Pitcher took her mortally wounded husband's place at a cannon in the Battle of Monmouth, New Jersey, in the American Revolutionary War.
1836	James Madison died at Montpelier, his country estate in Virginia, at age 85.
1838	Queen Victoria was crowned at Westminster Abbey a year after she ascended the English throne.
1894	Congress made Labor Day a national holiday, designating it as the first Monday in September.
1907	New York catcher Branch Rickey, the future great baseball executive, in a game with the Washington Senators, allowed 13 stolen bases, an all-time record.
1914	Archduke Francis Ferdinand, heir to the throne of Austria-Hungary, and his wife Sophie were assassinated in Sarajevo, in the Austrian province of Bosnia, triggering World War I.
1919	The Treaty of Versailles was signed in the Hall of Mirrors of the Palace of Versailles, near Paris, ending World War I and establishing the League of Nations.

1919   Harry S Truman married Elizabeth Virginia "Bess" Wallace.
1948   The Communist Party Cominform denounced Marshal Tito of Yugoslavia for his anti-Soviet opinions.
1950   The North Koreans captured Seoul, South Korea's capital, in the Korean War.
1978   The U.S. Supreme Court ruled in the Bakke case that the University of California Medical School must admit Allan P. Bakke. Bakke, a white man, had charged "reverse discrimination."

JUNE 29 -- BIRTHDAYS

1798   **Count Giacomo Leopardi** -- Italian lyric poet and essayist of the early 19th century
1805   **Hiram Powers** -- The greatest American sculptor of the mid-1800s, noted for his statues of George Washington and Benjamin Franklin, and for his most famous work, *Greek Slave*
1830   **J.Q.A. Ward** -- American sculptor
1858   **George Washington Goethals** -- American civil engineer and army officer who directed the completion of the Panama Canal
1861   **William James Mayo** -- American physician who, with his father and brother, founded the Mayo Clinic in Rochester, Minnesota, in 1889
1868   **George E. Hale** -- American astronomer who founded the three largest U.S. observatories--Yerkes (1895), Mount Wilson (1904), and Palomar (dedicated in 1948)
1871   **Luisa Tetrazzini** -- Italian operatic soprano noted for her remarkable vocal agility in coloratura roles
1885   **John Storrs** -- American sculptor
1900   **Antoine de Saint-Exupery** -- French aviator and writer, who was the chief influence in the creation of the literature of aviation
1901   **Nelson Eddy** -- American singer and actor, who joined with Jeanette MacDonald to become the most popular screen duo of their day
1908   **Leroy Anderson** -- American songwriter, conductor, and composer of "The Blue Tango"
1908   **Joan Davis** -- American stage and motion-picture actress and comedienne
1910   **Frank Loesser** -- American composer and author, noted for songs such as "Heart and Soul," "Let's Get Lost," "On a Slow Boat to China," "Two Sleepy People," "Baby, It's Cold Outside," and "Thumbelina"

1911	**Prince Bernhard** -- Husband of Queen Juliana of Holland
1912	**John Willard Toland** -- American journalist, historian, and author, noted for books such as *The Rising Sun* and *Adolf Hitler*
1915	**Dizzy Trout** – Professional baseball player who won 27 games in 1945
1915	**Ruth Warrick** -- American stage, screen, and television actress and star of the television soap opera *All My Children*
1919	**Slim Pickens** -- American motion-picture and television actor
1934	**Carl Levin** -- U.S. senator
1936	**Harmon Killebrew** -- Hall of Fame baseball player who had 573 career home runs
1944	**Gary Busey** -- American actor
1949	**Valerie Ziegenfuss** -- American tennis player
1955	**Jimmy Rogers** -- Professional football player
1956	**Pedro Guerrero** -- Professional baseball player

JUNE 29 -- EVENTS

64 AD	The Apostle Peter was executed in the gardens of Nero at the foot of Vatican Hill (traditional date).
67 AD	The Apostle Paul was executed on the Via Ostia three miles from Rome.
1312	Henry VII of Germany was crowned Holy Roman Emperor in Rome.
1408	The Council of Cardinals met to end the Great Schism in the Roman Catholic Church.
1504	Columbus sailed from Jamaica for home on his fourth and last voyage to America.
1776	The Virginia state constitution was adopted, and Patrick Henry was elected as the first governor.
1852	Henry Clay, U.S. senator and secretary of state, died at age 75.
1861	Elizabeth Barrett Browning, the English poet, died in Florence at age 55.
1916	The Western Pacific Railroad was incorporated.
1933	Primo Carnera knocked out Jack Sharkey in the sixth round in Long Island City, New York, to win the heavyweight title.
1934	Zaro Agha died in Istanbul at age 164. He was alleged to be the oldest man in the world.
1949	South Africa began its racial segregation program of apartheid.

JUNE 30 -- BIRTHDAYS

1685   **John Gay** -- English playwright and poet, best known for *The Beggar's Opera* (1728)

1685   **Dominikus Zimmerman** -- German architect

1771   **Joseph Short** -- American cabinetmaker

1789   **Horace Vernet** -- French painter

1819   **William A. Wheeler** -- U.S. vice president under President Hayes.

1879   **Walter Hampden** -- American stage, screen, radio, and television actor with a career that spanned over 50 years

1884   **Georges Duhamel** -- French scientist, mathematician, and author

1893   **Walter Ulbricht** -- Premier of East Germany after World War II

1893   **Harold Laski** -- English political scientist and educator

1900   **Madge Bellamy** -- American motion-picture and stage actress

1905   **William Zeckendorf** -- American real estate empire builder

1906   **John William Van Ryn** -- One of the greatest doubles tennis players of the 1930s

1908   **Grady Watts** -- American composer and author, noted for songs such as "Blue Champagne" and "Daddy's Boy"

1915   **Harry M. Weese** -- American architect

1917   **Lena Horne** -- American singer and actress

1917   **Buddy Rich** -- American drummer

1918   **Susan Hayward** -- American motion-picture actress

1927   **Shirley Fry Irvin** -- American Hall of Fame tennis player who ranked in the top ten from 1944 through 1956

1938   **Geoffrey Moss** -- American cartoonist and illustrator

1966   **Mike Tyson** -- World heavyweight champion

JUNE 30 -- EVENTS

1604   King James I of England approved a list of 54 scholars to revise the Bible. Under the leadership of Richard Bancroft, they produced the King James Version seven years later.

1859   French acrobat Emile Blondin made the first tightrope crossing of Niagara Falls, a distance of 1,100 feet, as 5,000 people watched, 160 feet below him.

1882   Charles Guiteau was hanged for the assassination of President James A. Garfield.

1906   The Federal Food and Drug Act of 1906 was signed into law by President Theodore Roosevelt.

1918 Eugene V. Debs, U.S. socialist leader, was arrested for interference with army and navy recruiting. He subsequently served nearly 3 years of a 10-year jail sentence.

1924 The Teapot Dome scandals of the Harding Administration resulted in the indictment of Secretary of the Interior Albert Fall and two oilmen.

1934 On orders of Adolf Hitler, the Nazis exterminated their enemies in Germany on the "Night of the Long Knives."

1936 Margaret Mitchell published her famous novel, *Gone With the Wind.*

1940 The comic strip, *Brenda Starr,* by Dale Messick, appeared for the first time.

1950 President Harry S Truman ordered U.S. ground forces into the Korean War.

1963 Paul VI was crowned as the 262nd pope of the Roman Catholic Church.

1971 The 26th Amendment to the U.S. Constitution was ratified, making 18 years the minimum age for voting.

1971 Three Russian cosmonauts, who set a 24-day endurance record in orbit, became the first men to die in space, as their *Soyuz 11* vehicle burned on entering the earth's atmosphere.

7

July

July, the seventh month of the year, was originally the fifth month of the ancient Roman calendar. As such it was appropriately named *Quintilis*, the Latin word for *fifth*. To honor Julius Caesar, who gave the world the Julian Calendar, the name of the month was changed to *Julius*, or July. In the first calendar of Romulus, July had 30 days, but from the time of Numa Pompilius, it has had 31 days.

July 4 is Independence Day in the United States, commemorating the day in 1776 when the Declaration of Independence was adopted. Bastille Day, the French Independence Day, occurs on July 14, and Canada celebrates July 1 as Dominion Day, marking the anniversary of the establishment of the Dominion of Canada in 1867. The Philippines, Venezuela, Argentina, Peru, Belgium and the Netherlands all celebrate their Independence Day in July, as well. One other special day is Moon Day (July 20), the anniversary of the first landing on the moon in 1969. Four American Presidents, John Quincy Adams, James Garfield, Calvin Coolidge and Gerald Ford, were born in July, as was Caesar, himself, on July 12, 100 B.C.

The birthstone for July is the ruby, and the flowers are the water lily and the larkspur. Notable birthdays and events of July are as follows.

JULY 1 -- BIRTHDAYS

1506   **Louis II** -- King of Hungary and Bohemia (1516-1526)

1646   **Gottfried Wilhelm Leibnitz** – German mathematician and scholar who shares with Isaac Newton the distinction of inventing the calculus

1725   **Jean Baptiste Rochambeau** – French general who helped the Americans in the Revolutionary War

1742   **Georg Christoph Lichtenberg** -- German physicist and satirist

1802   **Gideon Welles** -- Secretary of the Navy under Presidents Lincoln and Andrew Johnson

1804   **George Sand** -- Highly popular French novelist of the 1800s, known also for her love affairs with the composer Frederic Chopin and the poet Alfred de Musset

1807   **Thomas G. Clemson** -- American mining engineer, for whom Clemson University was named

1857   **Roger Connor** -- Hall of Fame baseball player with a lifetime batting average of .325

1861   **John Clarkson** – Hall of Fame baseball pitcher who won 53 games in 1885

1872   **Louis Bleriot** -- French aviation pioneer, who made the first flight across the English Channel in 1909

1892   **James M. Cain** -- American novelist noted for such works as *The Postman Always Rings Twice*

1893   **Walter White** -- American writer and executive secretary of the NAACP, 1931- 1955

1899   **Charles Laughton** -- English stage and motion-picture actor, and master performer for 40 years

1902   **William Wyler** -- German-American motion-picture director, who won Academy Awards for *Mrs. Miniver* (1942), *The Best Years of Our Lives* (1946), and *Ben-Hur* (1959)

1907   **Bill Stern** -- Colorful American sports announcer

1907   **Ilya Bolotowsky** -- American painter and sculptor noted for the geometric style

1909   **Madge Evans** -- American child actress of the 1930s

1912   **David Brower** – American conservationist and president of Friends of the Earth

1916   **Olivia De Havilland** -- One of Hollywood's leading dramatic actresses of the 1930s and 1940s, whose film career spanned over 40 years and resulted in two Academy Awards for best actress

1925   **Farley Granger** -- American stage, screen, and television actor

1931   **Leslie Caron** -- French dancer and motion-picture actress

1931   **Tab Hunter** -- American motion-picture actor

1934   **Kirsten Simone** -- Prima ballerina of Denmark

1934   **Jean Marsh** -- English motion-picture and television actress and writer

1936   **Jamie Farr** -- American actor who played the role of Klinger in the long- running television show *M*A*S*H*

1941   **Sally Quinn** -- American journalist

1942   **Genevieve Bujold** -- Canadian stage and motion-picture actress

1942   **Karen Black** -- American stage and motion-picture actress

1946   **Debbie Harry** -- American rock singer for the Blondie musical group

1952   **Dan Aykroyd** -- Canadian motion-picture and television actor and comedian

1952   **Roger Carr** -- Professional football player

1959   **Ann Smith** -- American tennis player

1961   **Lady Diana Spencer** -- Wife of Prince Charles, the heir to the English throne

JULY 1 -- EVENTS

1543   Sir Thomas More, the noted English writer, was convicted of high treason against King Henry VIII on perjured evidence, and was condemned to death.

1642   Londoners revolted against King Charles I, marking the beginning of the English Civil War.

1847   The first U.S. adhesive postage stamps went on sale in the form of Benjamin Franklin 5-cent stamps and George Washington 10-cent stamps.

1862   The Battle of the Seven Days ended in General Robert E. Lee's saving Richmond from the Union forces in the Civil War.

1863   The Battle of Gettysburg, the greatest ever fought in the Western hemisphere, began in Gettysburg, Pennsylvania, in the Civil War.

1867   "On the Beautiful Blue Danube," the famous waltz of Johann Strauss Jr., was played in America for the first time, at a New York City concert.

1867   The British North America Act went into effect, creating the Dominion of Canada.

1896   Harriet Beecher Stowe, author of *Uncle Tom's Cabin,* died in Hartford, Connecticut, at age 85.

1898   Theodore Roosevelt and his "Rough Riders" occupied San Juan Hill in Cuba in the Spanish-American War.

1916   British troops attacked the Germans on the Somme front to relieve pressure on Verdun in World War I.

1916	Dwight D. Eisenhower married Mamie Geneva Doud.

1916   Dwight D. Eisenhower married Mamie Geneva Doud.

1932   Franklin D. Roosevelt was nominated for president at the Democratic Convention in Chicago.

1943   The "pay-as-you-go" system of income tax withholding began for American wage earners.

1966   Medicare went into effect in the United States.

1971   The 182-year-old U.S. Post Office Department was replaced by the U.S. Postal Service.

1980   "O Canada" was officially proclaimed the Canadian national anthem.

1983   Buckminster Fuller, the inventor of the geodesic dome, died at age 87.

JULY 2 -- BIRTHDAYS

419 AD **Valentinian III** -- Emperor of Rome, A.D. 425-455, who was crowned at the age of 6

1486   **Jacopo Sansovino** -- Florentine sculptor and architect

1489   **Thomas Cranmer** -- First Protestant archbishop of Canterbury, and supporter of King Henry VIII in his successful attempt to divorce his first wife, Catherine of Aragon

1714   **Christoph Willibald Gluck** -- German composer who reformed opera in the 1700s by achieving a balance between the music and the dramatic parts

1796   **Michael Thonet** -- Austrian furniture designer

1855   **Clarence W. Barron** -- Founder of *Barron's Financial Weekly*

1862   **Sir William Bragg** -- British physicist who shared the 1915 Nobel Prize for research on the structure of crystals

1877   **Hermann Hesse** – German novelist and poet, and 1946 Nobel Prize winner

1879   **Bob Zuppke** -- One of the most famous coaches in college football, who introduced the offensive huddle in the early 1930s

1898   **Anthony C. McAuliffe** – U.S. World War II general who said "Nuts!" to the Nazi ultimatum to surrender in the Battle of the Bulge

1903   **Sir Alexander Douglas-Home** -- British prime minister, 1963-1964

1903   **Olav V** -- King of Norway, who succeeded his father Haakon VII in 1957

1905   **Rene Lacoste** -- French tennis player and one of the greatest of the 1920s and 1930s, who won 2 Wimbledon titles, 2 U.S. titles, and 3 French titles

1908   **Thurgood Marshall** – The first black justice of the U.S. Supreme Court

1922   **Dan Rowan** -- American comedian and co-star of television's long-running *Laugh-in*

1925   **Medgar Evers** -- American civil rights leader

1925   **Patrice Lumumba** -- First prime minister of Zaire

1931   **Larry Costello** -- Professional basketball player

1935   **Ed Bullins** -- American playwright

1937   **Richard Petty** -- Most successful Grand National stock car driver in the U.S. in the 1970s and 1980s

1947   **Luci Baines Johnson** – Daughter of President Lyndon B. Johnson

1949   **Curtis Rowe** -- Professional basketball player

1954   **Victor Amaya** -- American tennis player

1961   **Jimmy McNichol** -- American motion-picture actor

1964   **Jose Canseco** -- Professional baseball player and first to hit 40 home runs and steal 40 bases in one season (1988)

JULY 2 -- EVENTS

1644   Oliver Cromwell defeated the Royalists in the Battle of Marston Moor in the English Civil War.

1776   The Continental Congress approved the Declaration of Independence, to be signed two days later.

1778   Jean Jacques Rousseau, the great French writer, died at Ermenonville, France, at age 66.

1881   President James A. Garfield was shot by the assassin Charles Guiteau. Garfield lived for over two months before dying on September 19.

1890   The Sherman Anti-Trust Act was passed by Congress, outlawing monopolies that hindered trade.

1903   Ed Delahanty, one of the greatest baseball players of all time, was swept over Niagara Falls and killed at age 35, in the prime of his career.

1904   Anton Chekhov, the great Russian playwright, died of tuberculosis in the German resort of Badenweiler at age 44.

1926   The United States Army Air Corps was established by Congress.

1932   Franklin D. Roosevelt accepted the Democratic Party's nomination for president, pledging "a new deal for the American people."

1937   Amelia Earhart, the noted American aviatrix, was lost in the Pacific Ocean. Her disappearance is still an unsolved mystery.

1941   Joe DiMaggio, the great Yankee outfielder, hit a home run to extend his hitting streak to 45 games, breaking the old record of 44 set by Wee Willie Keeler in 1897.

1961   Ernest Hemingway, the noted American writer, shot himself at Ketchum, Idaho, at age 58.

1964   President Lyndon Johnson signed the Civil Rights Act of 1964 into law. It was the strongest civil rights law in United States history.

1976   North and South Vietnam were officially reunited.

JULY 3 -- BIRTHDAYS

1423   **Louis XI** – King of France, 1461-1483, known as the "terrible king"

1567   **Samuel de Champlain** -- French explorer who founded Quebec and was called the "Father of New France"

1683   **Edward Young** -- English poet and essayist

1728   **Robert Adam** – Scottish architect and furniture designer famous with his brother James for the Adam style of architecture

1731   **Samuel Huntington** -- Connecticut signer of the Declaration of Independence

1738   **John Singleton Copley** -- The greatest portrait painter in colonial America

1746   **Henry Grattan** -- Irish statesman

1789   **Johann Friedrich Overbeck** -- German painter of Christian religious subjects

1881   **Leon Errol** -- Australian-born stage and screen actor and comedian

1883   **Franz Kafka** – Czechoslovakian-born Austrian novelist, noted for such works as *The Trial* and *In the Penal Colony*

1901   **Jean Dubuffet** – French painter noted for works such as *M. Plume, Portrait of Henri Michaux* (1947), *Corps de Dame* (1950), and *Les Vagabonds* (1954)

1903   **Dick Robertson** -- American composer, author, and singer, noted for songs such as "A Little on the Lonely Side" and "Goodnight, Wherever You Are"

1905   **Frank Layton Ryerson** -- American composer and author, noted for songs such as "Blue Champagne," and "The Boston Tea Party"

1906   **George Sanders** -- British stage and motion-picture actor

1909   **Earl Butz** -- Secretary of agriculture in the Nixon-Ford administration

1909   **Stavros Niarchos** -- Greek shipowner and tycoon

1913   **Dorothy Kilgallen** – American journalist and television entertainer

1927   **Ken Russell** -- English motion-picture director

1930   **Pete Fountain** -- American jazz musician
1940   **John Patrick Sears** -- American lawyer and political cam-
        paign manager
1943   **Geraldo Rivera** -- American broadcast journalist
1947   **Betty Buckley** -- American actress
1952   **Adriano Panatta** -- Italian tennis player
1953   **Frank Tanana** -- Professional baseball player
1955   **Matt Keough** -- Professional baseball player
1957   **Laura Branigan** -- American singer
1962   **Tom Cruise** -- American motion-picture actor

JULY 3 -- EVENTS

1608   French explorer Samuel de Champlain founded Quebec and
        gave it its name.
1775   General George Washington formally took command of the
        Continental Army at Cambridge, Massachusetts.
1863   The Battle of Gettysburg ended in General Lee's defeat and
        marked the turning point in the Civil War. General Pickett led
        his famous charge on this last day of the battle.
1890   Idaho was admitted to the Union as the 43rd state.
1898   The Spanish fleet in Santiago Bay, Cuba, was destroyed by U.S.
        Commodore Winfield Schley in the Spanish-American War.
1945   The first postwar civilian automobile left the Ford Motor Company
        assembly line.
1950   U.S. soldiers engaged the North Koreans for the first time in the
        Korean War.
1962   Algeria became independent after 132 years of French rule.
1976   Israeli commandos, in a daring raid, rescued 103 hostages being
        held by terrorists at Uganda's Entebbe Airport.

JULY 4 -- BIRTHDAYS

1477   **Aventinus (Johannes Turmair)** -- Bavarian humanist and historian
1756   **William Rush** -- American sculptor noted as the finest of the
        early wood carvers
1804   **Nathaniel Hawthorne** -- One of America's greatest writers and
        author of *The Scarlet Letter* (1850), a masterpiece of American
        literature

1807	**Giuseppe Garibaldi** -- Italian military hero and one of the principal leaders in the unification of Italy into a single kingdom
1816	**Hiram Walker** -- American distiller who founded Hiram Walker's Distillery in 1857
1819	**E.R. Squibb** -- American pharmacist who founded the forerunner of the pharmaceutical firm of E.R. Squibb and Sons in 1858
1826	**Stephen Foster** -- One of America's best-loved composers, who wrote over 200 songs, such as "Swanee River," "My Old Kentucky Home, Good Night," and "Jeanie with the Light Brown Hair"
1837	**Carolus-Duran** -- French painter
1847	**James A. Bailey** -- Partner with P.T. Barnum in the Barnum and Bailey Circus
1872	**Calvin Coolidge** -- 30th U.S. president
1878	**George M. Cohan** -- American actor, songwriter, and playwright, noted for "Give My Regards to Broadway" and "You're a Grand Old Flag," among others (his real birthday was July 3, but he claimed July 4)
1883	**Rube Goldberg** -- American cartoonist known for his complicated mechanical contrivances for accomplishing simple tasks and for his creation of the cartoon character *Boob McNutt*
1885	**Louis B. Mayer** -- Russian-born movie executive who in the 1930s developed Metro-Goldwyn-Mayer into one of the greatest Hollywood studios, with "more stars than there are in the heavens"
1889	**Joseph Young** -- American lyricist noted for songs such as "Rockabye Your Baby With a Dixie Melody," "Dinah," "I'm Sitting on Top of the World," and "In a Shanty in Old Shanty Town"
1895	**Irving Caesar** -- American composer noted for songs such as "Swanee," "Tea for Two," "Animal Crackers in My Soup," and "Is It True What They Say About Dixie?"
1898	**Gertrude Lawrence** -- Noted British stage and screen actress and comedienne
1900	**Louis Armstrong** -- American singer, musician, and bandleader, and one of the world's leading jazz performers, whose career spanned over half a century
1902	**George Murphy** -- American dancer, actor, and U.S. senator
1902	**Meyer Lansky** -- American mobster of the 1930s
1903	**Abe Saperstein** -- Professional basketball coach
1905	**Lionel Trilling** -- American writer, scholar, and critic
1911	**Mitch Miller** -- American oboist and conductor
1912	**Virginia Graham** -- American television talk show hostess

1916	Tokyo Rose (Iva Toguri d'Aquino) -- American World War II traitor who broadcast pro-Japanese propaganda during the war to American troops
1918	**Abigail Van Buren** -- American newspaper advice columnist and twin sister of columnist Ann Landers
1918	**Ann Landers** -- American newspaper advice columnist and twin sister of columnist Abigail Van Buren
1924	**Eva Marie Saint** -- American stage, motion-picture, and television actress
1927	**Neil Simon** -- American playwright and screenwriter, noted for such works as *Come Blow Your Horn* (1961) and *Barefoot in the Park* (1967)
1928	**Gina Lollobrigida** -- Italian motion-picture actress
1928	**Stephen Boyd** -- Irish motion-picture actor
1929	**Chuck Tanner** -- Professional baseball player and manager
1930	**George Steinbrenner** -- American industrialist and owner of the New York Yankees baseball team
1938	**Bill Withers** -- American singer and songwriter
1940	**Bob Carmichael** -- Australian tennis player
1943	**Emerson Boozer** -- Professional football player and sportscaster
1948	**Clamma Dale** -- American soprano
1948	**Wayne Nordhagen** -- Professional baseball player
1951	**John Alexander** -- Australian tennis player
1962	**Pam Shriver** -- American tennis player
1963	**Henri LeConte** -- French tennis player

JULY 4 -- EVENTS

1623	William Byrd, the noted English composer, died at Stondon Massey, Essex, at age 80.
1776	The Declaration of Independence was adopted in Independence Hall in Philadelphia, and signed by John Hancock "by order and in behalf of Congress."
1778	George Rogers Clark and his frontiersmen, the "Big Knives," captured the supply base of Kaskaskia in Illinois from the British during the Revolutionary War.
1798	George Washington was commissioned as "Lieutenant General and Commander in Chief of the Armies" by President John Adams.
1802	The United States Military Academy opened at West Point, New York.

1826   John Adams died in Quincy, Mass., at age 90. His last words were, "Thomas Jefferson still survives." By a remarkable coincidence, however, Jefferson died also, at age 83.

1831   James Monroe died in New York City at age 73. He was the third ex-President to die on Independence Day, five years after the deaths of John Adams and Thomas Jefferson.

1848   Francois Rene de Chateaubriand, the great French novelist, died in Paris at age 79.

1863   Vicksburg surrendered, after a long siege, to General U.S. Grant's Union army in the Civil War.

1884   The Statue of Liberty was presented to the United States by France in a Paris ceremony.

1895   The verses of "America the Beautiful," by Katherine Lee Bates, appeared for the first time, in *The Congregationalist,* a Boston magazine.

1917   "Lafayette, we are here!" announced Colonel Charles Stanton after U.S. troops arrived in France in World War I.

1919   Jack Dempsey won the heavyweight championship, knocking out Jess Willard in the third round in Toledo, Ohio.

1939   Baseball immortal Lou Gehrig said farewell to New York fans at Yankee Stadium honoring him on his special day.

1946   The Republic of the Philippines was established as an independent nation.

1976   The U.S. celebrated its 200th birthday throughout the land. In New York harbor President Ford struck the ship's bell of the USS *Forrestal* once for each original colony.

1984   Phil Niekro got career strikeout number 3,000, as he pitched the New York Yankees to a 5-0 win over the Texas Rangers. He was only the 9th pitcher in history to strike out 3,000 men.

JULY 5 -- BIRTHDAYS

1709   Etienne de Silhouette -- French minister of finance for whom the silhouette was named because of his reputation for stinginess

1753   **Jonathan Carter Hornblower** -- Inventor of the double-beat valve

1755   **Sarah Siddons** -- The greatest of English tragic actresses, whose striking beauty made her a subject of poets and painters

1801   **David Farragut** -- U.S. admiral who at the Civil War battle of Mobile Bay said, "Damn the torpedoes. Full speed ahead!"

1803   **George Borrow** -- English linguist, writer, and traveler

1810   **P.T. Barnum** -- The world's most famous showman, and founder in 1871 of the circus, "The Greatest Show on Earth"

1820   **William John Macquorn Rankine** -- Scottish engineer and a founder of thermodynamics, noted for the Rankine cycle

1853   **Cecil Rhodes** -- British diamond king, statesman, and empire builder, largely responsible for the development of the British Empire in Africa

1879   **Dwight Filley Davis** – American statesman and tennis enthusiast, who in 1900 established the Davis Cup, an annual award for the world champion tennis team

1879   **Wanda Landowska** – Noted Polish harpsichordist, pianist, and composer

1880   **Beatrix Hoyt** -- Noted professional golfer

1889   **Jean Cocteau** -- French playwright, novelist, artist, and avant-garde writer, noted for such works as *Les Enfants Terribles* (1929) and *Orpheus* (1950)

1902   **Henry Cabot Lodge** -- U.S. ambassador to the United Nations under President Eisenhower and vice presidential candidate in 1960

1904   **Milburn Stone** -- American motion-picture and television actor who played Doc Adams in the long-running television series *Gunsmoke*

1911   **Georges Pompidou** -- President of France, 1969-1974, who succeeded General de Gaulle

1917   **Manolete (Manuel L.R. Sanchez)** -- One of the greatest Spanish matadors in history

1923   **John McKay** -- Noted college and professional football coach

1937   **Shirley Knight** -- American stage and motion-picture actress

1943   **Mark Cox** -- English tennis player

1948   **Julie Nixon Eisenhower** – Daughter of President Richard Nixon

1950   **Gary Matthews** -- Professional baseball player

1951   **Goose Gossage** -- Professional baseball player

1956   **James Lofton** -- Professional football player

JULY 5 -- EVENTS

1632   Sir Anthony Van Dyck, the famous Flemish painter, was knighted by King Charles I in London.

1811   Venezuela declared its independence from Spain, the first of the South American countries to do so.

1865   William Booth, a former Methodist minister, founded in the slums of London the organization that in 1878 became the Salvation Army.

1935   The National Labor Relations Act was signed into law by President Franklin D. Roosevelt.

1940   Great Britain broke diplomatic relations with Vichy France during World War II.

1945   The Labour Party, in a great surprise, defeated the Conservative Party, resulting in British prime minister Winston Churchill's being replaced by Clement Attlee 21 days later.

1945   General Douglas MacArthur announced the liberation of the Philippines in World War II.

1946   The bikini, the shocking new bathing suit of designer Louis Reard, was first modeled at a Paris fashion show.

1948   England adopted the National Health Service Act, providing free medical service for all.

1971   The 26th Amendment to the Constitution was certified, lowering the voting age to 18.

JULY 6 -- BIRTHDAYS

1739   **Georges Jacob** -- French cabinetmaker

1747   **John Paul Jones** – American Revolutionary War hero and the "Father of the American Navy"

1755   **John Flaxman** -- English sculptor and illustrator, and one of the leaders of the neoclassical movement of the late 1700s

1796   **Nicholas I** -- Czar of Russia, 1825-1855, noted for his harsh rule and for putting down the Decembrist revolution in 1825

1832   **Maximilian** -- Archduke of Austria and Emperor of Mexico, 1864-1867

1892   **Jack Yellen** -- Polish-born composer noted for songs such as "Are You From Dixie?" "Ain't She Sweet," "Happy Days Are Here Again" (campaign song of FDR), and "Wonder What's Become of Sally"

1899   **Mignon Eberhart** -- American author of popular mystery novels

1909   **Andrei Gromyko** -- Russian foreign minister

1913   **Eleanor Clark** -- American writer

1913   **Gwyn Thomas** -- English novelist

1915   **LaVerne Andrews** – American singer and member of the Andrews Sisters singing group, a highly popular trio in the 1940s

1918   **Sebastian Cabot** -- English-born motion-picture and television actor

1919   **Dorothy Kirsten** -- American operatic soprano

1921   **Nancy Reagan** -- American actress and wife of President Ronald Reagan

1921   **Bill Haley** -- American pioneer rock and roll musician, noted for the first rock and roll record, "Rock Around the Clock"

1925   **Merv Griffin** -- American television talk show host

1927   **Pat Paulson** -- American comedian

1927   **Janet Leigh** -- American motion-picture actress

1932   **Della Reese** -- American singer and actress

1935   **The 14th Incarnate Dalai Lama** -- Religious leader and, until the Chinese invaded his country in 1950, the supreme ruler of Tibet

1946   **Sylvester Stallone** — American motion-picture actor and screenwriter noted for his roles in the *Rocky* and *Rambo* movies

1946   **James Wyeth** -- American painter and son of painter Andrew Wyeth

1948   **Brad Park** -- Professional hockey player

1952   **Shelley Hack** -- American model and actress

1952   **Grant Goodeve** -- American actor

1954   **Jason Thompson** -- Professional baseball player

1954   **Willie Randolph** -- Professional baseball player

1956   **Billy Taylor** -- Professional football player

JULY 6 -- EVENTS

1189   King Henry II of England died at age 55 and was succeeded by his son, Richard I, the Lion-Hearted.

1415   John Huss, whose teachings were forerunners of those of Martin Luther, was burned at the stake on a charge of heresy.

1535   Sir Thomas More, the great English writer, was beheaded in London at age 57 on orders of King Henry VIII.

1553   Mary I (Bloody Mary) became queen of England upon the death of her brother, Edward VI.

1701   Captain Kidd (William Kidd) was hanged in England for piracy.

1777   British troops captured Fort Ticonderoga from the Americans in the Revolutionary War.

1854   The delegates formally adopted the name Republican for their new party, at a party meeting in Jackson, Michigan.

1865   *The Nation,* a liberal weekly magazine, was founded in New York.

1885   Louis Pasteur administered the first antirabies vaccine to a person, Joseph Meister, who had been bitten by a rabid dog. Meister consequently survived.

1928   A preview of the first all-talking motion picture, *Lights of New York,* took place at the Strand Theater in New York.

1933   Baseball's first All-Star Game was played in Chicago, with the American League beating the National League, 4-2, on Babe Ruth's two-run home run.

1979   Martina Navratilova won the Wimbledon women's singles title for the second straight year.

1980   Bjorn Borg won the Wimbledon men's singles championship for the fifth straight year, an unprecedented feat.

1985   Martina Navratilova defeated Chris Evert Lloyd for her 4th consecutive Wimbledon singles championship.

JULY 7 -- BIRTHDAYS

1586   **Thomas Hooker** -- Congregational preacher and a founder of Connecticut

1752   **Joseph Marie Jacquard** -- French inventor who perfected the automatic pattern, or Jacquard, loom

1833   **Felicien Rops** -- Belgian painter

1884   **Lion Feuchtwanger** -- American novelist and playwright

1887   **Marc Chagall** -- Russian-born French painter and designer, noted for his dreamlike, fanciful paintings

1899   **George Cukor** -- American motion-picture director whose entertainment career spanned 60 years

1902   **Vittorio De Sica** -- Italian motion-picture actor and director

1906   **Satchel Paige** -- Professional baseball pitcher thought by some to have been the greatest of all time

1909   **Billy Herman** -- Professional baseball player

1911   **Gian Carlo Menotti** -- Italian-American opera composer, noted for such works as *Amahl and the Night Visitors* (1951), *The Consul* (1950), and *The Saint of Bleecker Street* (1954)

1917   **Lawrence F. O'Brien** -- Political strategist for President Kennedy and commissioner of the American Basketball Association

1919   **William Kunstler** -- Crusading American lawyer

1921   **Ezzard Charles** -- World heavyweight champion, 1950-1951

1922   **Pierre Cardin** -- French fashion designer

1927   **Doc Severinsen** -- American trumpeter and bandleader on the *Tonight Show* with Johnny Carson

1940   **Ringo Starr** -- Member of the Beatles musical group

1944   **Tony Jacklin** -- Professional golfer

1946   **Tadeusz Nowicki** -- Polish tennis player
1948   **Fred Brown** -- Professional basketball player
1950   **Shelley Duvall** -- American motion-picture actress
1955   **Len Barker** -- Professional baseball pitcher who pitched a per-
        fect game in 1981

JULY 7 -- EVENTS

1307   King Edward I of England died at age 68 on his way to subdue the
        new Scottish king, Robert Bruce.

1754   King's College (later Columbia University) had its beginnings
        when Samuel Johnson, its first president, enrolled eight students.

1846   Monterey, California, was captured from the Mexicans by a
        band of American settlers and proclaimed to be annexed to the
        United States.

1898   Hawaii was annexed by the United States.

1923   Warren G. Harding became the first U.S. president to visit Alaska.

1930   Sir Arthur Conan Doyle, the British novelist, died at Crowbor-
        ough, Essex, at age 71.

1937   The Japanese staged an "incident" near Peiping (Beijing) as an
        excuse for starting war with China.

1946   Jimmy Carter married Rosalynn Smith of Plains, Georgia.

1979   Bjorn Borg won his fourth straight Wimbledon singles title.

1984   Martina Navratilova won her third straight Wimbledon singles
        championship and her fifth in seven years.

1985   Boris Becker, a 17-year-old German, defeated Kevin Curren to
        win the Wimbledon singles championship, becoming the young-
        est player ever to win this or any Grand Slam tournament.

JULY 8 -- BIRTHDAYS

1478   **Giangiorgio Trissino** -- Italian philologist, dramatist, and poet
1621   **Jean de La Fontaine** -- French poet famous for his *Fables* (1668-
        1694) and a collection of racy stories called *Contes* (1664-1666)
1790   **Fitz-Greene Halleck** -- American poet
1837   **William Quantrill** -- Confederate guerrilla band captain in the
        Civil War
1838   **Ferdinand von Zeppelin** -- Famous German pioneer in lighter-
        than-air vehicles, and the first large-scale builder of dirigible
        balloons, which became known as zeppelins

1839   **John D. Rockefeller** -- American industrialist, founder of the Standard Oil Company, and at one time the world's richest man

1867   **Kathe Kollwitz** -- German painter, sculptor, and printmaker, noted for violent images of common people and for becoming, in 1919, the first woman elected to the Berlin Academy

1869   **William Vaughn Moody** – American poet, dramatist, teacher, and literary historian, noted for his landmark drama, *The Great Divide* (1906)

1872   **Harry Von Tilzer** – American composer noted for songs such as "A Bird in a Gilded Cage," "On a Sunday Afternoon," and "I Want a Girl Just Like the Girl That Married Dear Old Dad"

1882   **Percy Grainger** -- Australian-American composer, pianist, and conductor, noted as a leading interpreter of Edvard Grieg's piano music and for his own works such as "Marching Song of Democracy" (1917)

1890   **Stanton MacDonald-Wright** -- American painter

1892   **J. Russel Robinson** -- American composer and author, noted for songs such as "Mary Lou," "Singin' the Blues," "Margie," and "Memphis Blues"

1898   **Alec Waugh** -- English novelist and travel writer, noted for such works as *The Loom of Youth* (1917)

1906   **Philip Johnson** -- American architect

1907   **George Romney** -- Governor of Michigan, 1963-1969, and secretary of Housing and Urban Development under President Nixon

1908   **Nelson Rockefeller** -- Governor of New York, 1958-1974, and U.S. vice president under President Ford

1914   **Billy Eckstine** -- American singer

1917   **Fay Emerson** -- American motion-picture and television actress

1918   **Craig Stevens** -- American motion-picture and television actor

1918   **Irwin Hasen** -- American cartoonist and creator of *The Green Hornet* and *Green Lantern*

1926   **Elisabeth Kubler-Ross** -- Swiss-born psychiatrist and author of *On Death and Dying*

1926   **George H. Weyerhaeuser** – President of Weyerhaeuser Company

1931   **Roone Arledge** -- American television producer and executive

1935   **Steve Lawrence** -- American singer and actor

1946   **Cynthia Gregory** -- American ballet dancer

1951   **Alan Ashby** -- Professional baseball player

1956   **Terry Puhl** -- Professional baseball player

1961   **Andy Fletcher** -- British keyboardist with the Depeche Mode musical group

JULY 8 -- EVENTS

49 BC The city of Paris, France, was founded by the Parisii, a Celtic tribe of fishermen.

1497 Vasco da Gama, the Portuguese navigator, left Lisbon on the voyage that would make him the first man to sail around the Cape of Good Hope to India.

1663 King Charles II of England granted Rhode Island its second charter, which remained the law of the colony and state until 1843.

1776 The Liberty Bell rang out in Philadelphia to announce the adoption of the Declaration of Independence.

1822 Percy Bysshe Shelley, the great English poet, died in a sailing accident in the Gulf of Spezia, near Leghorn, Italy, at age 29.

1835 The famous crack in the Liberty Bell appeared as the bell was being rung during the funeral of Chief Justice John Marshall.

1889 John L. Sullivan fought the last bare-knuckle heavyweight championship fight, defeating Jake Kilrain in the 75th round to retain his title.

1889 The *Wall Street Journal* was first published.

1891 Warren G. Harding married Florence Kling DeWolfe.

1896 William Jennings Bryan made his famous "Cross of Gold" speech at the Democratic National Convention in Chicago.

1907 The first *Ziegfeld Follies* was staged on the roof garden of the New York Theater.

1919 The comic strip, *Toots and Casper,* by Jimmy Murphy, first appeared.

1950 General Douglas MacArthur was appointed United Nations commander in Korea.

1978 Bjorn Borg, the Swedish tennis star, won his third consecutive Wimbledon singles title.

1984 John McEnroe became the first American since Don Budge in 1938 to win two consecutive Wimbledon singles championships.

JULY 9 -- BIRTHDAYS

1562 **Orazio Gentileschi** -- Italian painter

1764 **Ann Radcliffe** -- English Gothic novelist

1819 **Elias Howe** -- American inventor, noted for his invention of the sewing machine, which he patented in 1846

1835 **Tomas Estrada Palma** -- First president of Cuba, 1902-1906

1856 **Daniel Guggenheim** -- American industrialist and philanthropist, who in 1924 set up the Daniel and Florence Guggenheim Foundation to promote "the well-being of mankind"

1856 **Nikola Tesla** – Hungarian-born engineer who invented the alternating-current induction motor and played the major role in establishing 60-hertz power in the U.S.

1878 **H.V. Kaltenborn** -- American radio commentator recognized as the "father" of his profession

1879 **Ottorino Respighi** -- One of the best-known Italian composers of the early 1900s, and composer of "The Fountains of Rome" (1917) and "The Pines of Rome" (1924)

1887 **Samuel Eliot Morison** -- American rear admiral, historian, and Pulitzer Prize winner in 1943 for his *Admiral of the Ocean Sea,* a biography of Columbus, and in 1960 for *John Paul Jones*

1890 **Walter Henry "Hy" Heath** – American composer and author, noted for songs such as "Mule Train"

1894 **Dorothy Thompson** – Noted American journalist and wife of the famous novelist Sinclair Lewis

1897 **Albert Wedemeyer** -- American World War II general

1901 **Barbara Cartland** -- World's all-time best-selling author of romantic fiction, with over 250 books that have sold over 100 million copies

1908 **Minor White** -- American photographer

1916 **Edward Heath** -- British prime minister, 1970-1974

1927 **Ed Ames** -- American singer and actor

1928 **Vince Edwards** -- American stage, screen, and television actor

1928 **Donald Joyce Hall** -- Chief executive officer of Hallmark Cards and son of its founder, Joyce Clyde Hall

1933 **Hedrick Smith** -- American journalist

1937 **David Hockney** -- English painter noted for works such as *Mt. Fuji and Flowers* (1972)

1945 **Mike Riordan** -- Professional basketball player

1947 **O.J. Simpson** -- Professional football player and superstar

1955 **Willie Wilson** -- Professional baseball player

1956 **Tom Hanks** -- American motion-picture actor

JULY 9 -- EVENTS

1540 The English Parliament declared the marriage of Henry VIII and Anne of Cleves null and void.

1755   English general George Braddock was decisively defeated by the French at Fort Duquesne in a battle in which his assistant, Colonel George Washington, distinguished himself.

1776   The Declaration of Independence was read aloud to General George Washington's troops in New York.

1797   Edmund Burke, the great British statesman, died at Beaconsfield at age 68.

1816   Argentina declared its independence of Spain, following the lead of Buenos Aires, which had been independent since 1810.

1850   President Zachary Taylor died in the White House at age 65 of a typhus infection.

1877   The world's first telephone company, the Bell Telephone Company, was founded.

1918   Congress authorized the Distinguished Service Medal.

1924   The Democrats nominated John W. Davis for president on the 103rd ballot, an all-time record number.

1963   The comic strip, *Fred Basset,* by Alex Graham, first appeared.

JULY 10 -- BIRTHDAYS

1509   **John Calvin** -- One of the chief leaders of the Protestant Reformation and the founder of the Presbyterian Church

1723   **Sir William Blackstone** -- English jurist whose *Commentaries on the Laws of England* became the most influential book in the history of English law

1792   **George Mifflin Dallas** -- U.S. vice president under President Polk, for whom the city of Dallas, Texas, was named

1792   **Frederick Marryat** -- English author whose novels about life at sea were widely read in the 1800s

1824   **Richard King** -- American cattleman who founded the famous King Ranch in Texas

1830   **Camille Pissarro** -- French impressionist painter, and perhaps the most popular and respected member of the impressionist group

1834   **James McNeill Whistler** -- The most original American artist of the 1800s, best known for his *Arrangement in Grey and Black,* commonly known as *Whistler's Mother*

1861   **Albert Bigelow Paine** -- American writer

1867   **Finley Peter Dunne** -- American writer, humorist, and creator of *Mr. Dooley*

1868   **Bobby "Link" Lowe** -- First major league baseball player to hit four home runs in one game (May 30, 1894)

1871 **Marcel Proust** – French novelist and author of the seven-part novel and masterpiece of world literature, *Remembrance of Things Past,* which contains *Swann's Way* (1913) and six other novels

1882 **Ima Hogg** -- Noted American philanthropist

1885 **Mary O'Hara** -- American writer and author of *My Friend Flicka* (1941)

1888 **Giorgio de Chirico** – Italian painter and founder of the Metaphysical School of painting

1889 **Noble Sissle** -- American author and conductor, noted for songs such as "I'm Just Wild About Harry" and "You Were Meant for Me"

1891 **Rexford Guy Tugwell** – Assistant secretary of agriculture under Franklin D. Roosevelt and one of FDR's original brain trusters

1892 **Slim Summerville** -- American comedian of the silent films and character actor of the talkies

1894 **Jimmy McHugh** -- American composer, noted for songs such as "I'm in the Mood for Love," "On the Sunny Side of the Street," "It's a Most Unusual Day," "Let's Get Lost," and "How Blue the Night"

1895 **John Gilbert** -- American actor and great screen idol of the silent movies, who teamed with Greta Garbo in a number of scorching screen romances

1908 **H.J. Heinz II** – Chairman of the board of the H.J. Heinz company

1914 **Joe Shuster** -- American comic book artist and co-creator with Jerry Siegel of *Superman*

1918 **Jack Easton** -- American composer, author, and pianist, noted for scores of numerous Broadway plays and for the NBC Peacock Theme

1920 **Owen Chamberlain** -- American physicist noted for co-discovering the antiproton

1920 **David Brinkley** -- American television newscaster and commentator

1921 **Jeff Donnell** -- American motion-picture actress

1921 **Jake LaMotta** -- Middleweight boxing champion, 1949-1951

1923 **Jean Kerr** -- American writer, author of *Please Don't Eat the Daisies,* and wife of writer Walter Kerr

1923 **Earl Henry Hamner Jr.** -- American author noted for the television story, *The Waltons*

1926 **Carleton Carpenter** -- American motion-picture actor, singer, and dancer

1926   **Fred Gwynne** -- American actor noted for his role in the long-running television show *The Munsters*
1931   **Del Insko** -- Professional harness racer
1931   **Nick Adams** -- American motion-picture actor
1933   **Jerry Herman** -- American popular songwriter, noted for works such as "Hello, Dolly!" (which won the 1965 Grammy Award) and "Mame"
1933   **Jan De Gaetani** -- American singer
1933   **Richard Gordon Hatcher** – One of the first black men to be elected mayor of a major U.S. city (Gary, Indiana, in 1967)
1940   **Gene Alley** -- Professional baseball player
1943   **Arthur Ashe** – American tennis player and Wimbledon singles champion in 1975
1945   **Toni Fritsch** -- Professional football player
1945   **Virginia Wade** -- English tennis player who won the Wimbledon singles title in 1977
1946   **Hal McRae** -- Professional baseball player
1947   **Arlo Guthrie** -- American guitarist, singer, songwriter, and son of singer Woody Guthrie
1949   **James Montgomery** -- Professional football player
1954   **Andre Dawson** -- Professional baseball player

JULY 10 -- EVENTS

138 AD Roman emperor Hadrian died at Baiae at age 62.
1460   The Duke of York defeated King Henry VI at Northampton, but Henry survived on the throne of England until the following year.
1850   Millard Fillmore became the 13th U.S. president, succeeding Zachary Taylor, who had died the previous day.
1890   Wyoming was admitted to the Union as the 44th state.
1923   Benito Mussolini secured his fascist dictatorship by dissolving Italy's nonfascist parties.
1925   The Scopes trial began in Dayton, Tenn., with John Scopes accused of teaching evolution in a public school. The opposing lawyers were Clarence Darrow and William Jennings Bryan.
1929   Congress made official the current size of U.S. paper money.
1936   Chuck Klein of the Philadelphia Phillies hit four home runs in a 10-inning baseball game.
1940   The Battle of Britain began, as the German *Luftwaffe* started the great World War II air raids on the British Isles that would continue until October 31.

1943 British, American, and Canadian troops invaded Sicily in World War II.

1951 Armistice talks began at Kaesong, aimed at ending the Korean War.

1962 The communications satellite *Telstar 1* was launched by the United States in Cape Canaveral, Florida, to relay TV and telephone signals between America and Europe.

JULY 11 -- BIRTHDAYS

1274 **Robert Bruce** – King of Scotland, 1328-1329, who spent most of his life in a gallant struggle to free his country from English rule

1657 **Frederick I** – First king of Prussia, 1701-1713, and son of the "great elector" of Brandenburg, Frederick William

1767 **John Quincy Adams** -- Sixth U.S. president and son of President John Adams

1819 **Susan Warner** -- American novelist, noted for *The Wide, Wide World* (1850), considered by many to be the first U.S. best-seller

1838 **John Wanamaker** -- American merchant and philanthropist and founder of John Wanamaker & Company, one of the largest department stores in the United States

1854 **Dr. Thomas Bowdler** -- Self-appointed cleanser of literature, whose "cleaned-up" version of Shakespeare gave to the language the new word *bowdlerize* (expurgate)

1861 **George W. Norris** -- American statesman, U.S. senator, and advocate of public ownership of hydroelectric power plants, such as TVA

1885 **Roger de La Fresnaye** -- French painter noted for works such as *The Artillery* (1912)

1890 **Arthur William Tedder** -- Marshal of the RAF and deputy supreme commander to General Dwight D. Eisenhower in World War II

1890 **Theodora "Dolly" Morse** -- American lyricist noted for songs such as "Three O'Clock in the Morning," "Hail, Hail, the Gang's All Here," and "Siboney"

1892 **Thomas Mitchell** -- American stage, screen, and television actor, and one of the screen's greatest character actors

1894 **Walter Wanger** -- American motion-picture producer

1897 **Johnny Marvin** -- American composer, author, and singer, who wrote such songs as "Goodbye Little Darlin'" for many Gene Autry films

1899   **E.B. White** -- American writer and author of *Stuart Little* (1945) and *Charlotte's Web* (1952)

1910   **Sally Blane** -- American motion-picture actress and sister of actress Loretta Young

1922   **Gene Evans** -- American motion-picture and television actor

1944   **Lou Hudson** -- Professional basketball player

1957   **Peter Murphy** — British rock musician with the Bauhaus musical group

JULY 11 -- EVENTS

1533   King Henry VIII of England was excommunicated by Pope Clement VII for marrying Anne Boleyn.

1598   San Juan de los Caballeros, the first settlement in New Mexico, was founded by Juan de Onate.

1798   The Marine Corps was re-created as a separate military service by an act of Congress.

1804   Alexander Hamilton was mortally wounded at age 49 in a duel with Vice President Aaron Burr at Weehawken, New Jersey. He died the following day.

1864   Confederate General Jubal Early invaded the outskirts of Washington. Lincoln watched the battle from a parapet, becoming the only president under enemy fire while in office.

1916   The Second Battle of the Somme began in World War I.

1936   Adolf Hitler guaranteed Austria's frontier in a treaty with the Austrians. (Two years later he annexed the country.)

1937   George Gershwin, the noted American composer, died in Hollywood at age 38.

1955   The U.S. Air Force Academy was dedicated at Lowry Air Base, Colorado. The academy moved to its permanent site near Colorado Springs in 1958.

1962   The first U.S. television programs were broadcast by the BBC via satellite.

1979   The doomed spaceship *Skylab* plummeted to earth after six years and 34,981 orbits in space.

1985   Nolan Ryan struck out his 4,000th career batter, becoming the first pitcher ever to reach that plateau.

JULY 12 -- BIRTHDAYS

100 BC **Julius Caesar** — Roman general and statesman, and one of the greatest men in the history of the world

1730   **Josiah Wedgwood** -- England's greatest potter and one of the most famous pottery designers of all time

1817   **Henry David Thoreau** -- American essayist, poet, celebrated practical philosopher, and the author of *Walden,* one of the world's great books

1824   **Eugene Louis Boudin** -- French painter

1849   **Sir William Osler** – Canadian physician and one of the greatest medical teachers

1854   **George Eastman** -- American inventor and manufacturer, who founded the Eastman Kodak Company

1863   **Albert Calmette** -- Bacteriologist and developer of a tuberculosis vaccine

1868   **Stefan George** -- German poet and a major representative of the European symbolism movement in poetry

1884   **Amedeo Modigliani** -- One of the greatest Italian artists of the 1900s

1886   **Jean Hersholt** – Danish radio and motion-picture actor and "elder statesman" of the film community

1895   **Kirsten Flagstad** – Norwegian operatic soprano, and the greatest Wagnerian soprano of the mid-20th century

1895   **Buckminster Fuller** -- American writer and designer of automobiles, cities, and geodesic domes

1895   **Oscar Hammerstein II** -- American lyricist and collaborator with composers Jerome Kern, George Gershwin, and Richard Rodgers, best known perhaps for "Ol' Man River"

1908   **Milton Berle** -- American motion-picture and television actor and comedian, known as "Mr. Television" in the 1950s

1910   **Edward Johnson** -- American composer, trombonist, and arranger, noted for songs such as "The Jersey Bounce"

1915   **Yul Brynner** -- American motion-picture and television actor

1917   **Andrew Wyeth** -- The most popular American painter of his time

1919   **Vera Ralston** -- Czechoslovakian motion-picture actress

1920   **Keith Andes** -- American motion-picture and television actor

1922   **Mark Hatfield** -- U.S. senator

1934   **Van Cliburn** -- American pianist who in 1958 won the International Tchaikovsky Competition in Moscow

1937   **Bill Cosby** – American actor and comedian noted for his television role in *The Bill Cosby Show,* one of the most popular of the 1980s

1938   **Ron Fairly** -- Professional baseball player

1943   **Paul Silas** -- Professional basketball player

1943	**Christine Perfect McVie** -- English singer and musician with the Fleetwood Mac musical group
1951	**Cheryl Ladd** -- American motion-picture and television actress
1953	**Tony Armas** -- Professional baseball player
1956	**Mario Soto** -- Professional baseball player

JULY 12 -- EVENTS

526 AD	Saint Felix IV became Roman Catholic pope.
1153	Anastasius IV was crowned Roman Catholic pope.
1536	Desiderius Erasmus, the great Dutch humanist, died in Basel, Switzerland, at an approximate age of 70.
1543	King Henry VIII of England married his sixth wife, Catherine Parr.
1690	England's William III defeated James II, the Catholic pretender, in the Battle of the Boyne, completing the Protestant conquest of Ireland.
1691	Innocent XII was elected Roman Catholic pope.
1730	Clement XII was elected Roman Catholic pope.
1812	General William Hull's American army of 2,000 men invaded Canada at a point near Detroit in the War of 1812.
1862	Congress authorized the Medal of Honor (sometimes called the Congressional Medal of Honor) and designated it as the United States' highest military award.
1863	General Jubal Early's Confederate army, which had bombarded the outskirts of Washington, D.C., was thrown back by Union forces in the Civil War.
1870	John Wesley Hyatt, an American printer, patented Celluloid, which he had invented the previous year.
1912	*Queen Elizabeth,* starring Sarah Bernhardt, became the first foreign film shown in America.
1933	The minimum wage in the United States was set at 40 cents an hour.
1941	German armies cracked the Stalin Line in Russia in World War II, and marched toward Moscow. They eventually penetrated its suburbs, but were never able to take it.
1961	Weather satellite *Tiros 3* was launched, which discovered Hurricane Esther over the Atlantic Ocean.
1984	Democratic candidate for president Walter Mondale announced his choice of Congresswoman Geraldine Ferraro as the first woman to run for vice president on a major party ticket.

JULY 13 -- BIRTHDAYS

1590	**Clement X** -- Roman Catholic pope, 1670-1676
1607	**Wenceslaus Hollar** -- English printmaker
1608	**Ferdinand III** -- Holy Roman emperor who signed the Peace of Westphalia, ending the Thirty Years' War
1793	**John Clare** -- English poet
1821	**Nathan Bedford Forrest** -- Confederate general in the Civil War, whose motto was "Git thar fustest with the mostest men"
1841	**Otto Wagner** -- Austrian architect
1859	**Sidney Webb** -- British economist and influential Fabian Socialist of the late 1800s and early 1900s
1863	**Mary Emma Woolley** -- American educator and first woman to receive a bachelor's degree from Brown University
1886	**Father Edward Joseph Flanagan** -- American priest who founded Boys Town in Nebraska in 1917
1889	**Stan Coveleski** -- Hall of Fame baseball player
1895	**Sidney Blackmer** -- American stage and motion-picture actor whose career spanned over 50 years
1901	**Mickey Walker** -- World welterweight champion, 1922-1926, and middleweight champion, 1926-1931
1913	**Dave Garroway** -- Original host of television's *Today Show*
1928	**Bob Crane** -- American motion-picture and television actor
1928	**Sven Davidson** -- Swedish tennis player
1931	**Frank Ramsey** -- Professional basketball player
1934	**Wole Soyinka** -- Nigerian dramatist and perhaps the foremost English-language poet and playwright of black Africa, who won the Nobel Prize for literature in 1986
1935	**Jack Kemp** -- Professional football player, U.S. congressman, and Secretary of Housing and Urban Development under President Bush
1937	**Charles Coody** -- Professional golfer
1942	**Roger McGuinn** -- American guitarist, singer, and founder of the Byrds musical group
1942	**Harrison Ford** -- American motion-picture actor noted for his roles as Indiana Jones, among others
1946	**Richard Anthony "Cheech" Marin** -- American writer, actor, and member with Tommy Chong of the Cheech and Chong comedy duo
1961	**Anders Jarryd** -- Swedish tennis player

JULY 13 -- EVENTS

1787   Congress passed the Northwest Ordinance, one of the most important laws ever adopted, providing for the governing of the Northwest Territory and subsequently all the U.S. territories.

1793   Jean Paul Marat, the notorious French revolutionary, was stabbed to death while sitting in his bathtub, by a young French girl, Charlotte Corday.

1798   William Wordsworth wrote his famous poem, "Tintern Abbey."

1837   Buckingham Palace in London's West End became the official residence of British royalty, as Queen Victoria became the first British monarch to occupy it.

1863   Rioting against the Civil War military draft erupted in New York City, resulting in the death of over 1,000 people over the next three days.

1865   In an editorial in the New York *Tribune,* Horace Greeley gave the famous advice, "Go West, young man, go West and grow up with the country."

1870   The "Ems Telegram" was sent to Otto von Bismarck, who condensed it deliberately to infuriate the French, leading, as he had hoped it would, to the Franco-Prussian War.

1896   Ed Delahanty of the Philadelphia Phillies hit four home runs in one game.

1900   Allied troops took Tientsin, China, in the Boxer Rebellion.

1972   The Paris peace talks on the Vietnam War resumed after a ten-week suspension.

1985   President Reagan underwent surgery to remove a large intestinal polyp. Vice President Bush was given unprecedented temporary acting powers under the 25th Amendment.

JULY 14 -- BIRTHDAYS

1454   **Angelo Poliziano** -- The best known of the brilliant group of writers gathered at the court of Lorenzo de Medici, who revived Italian literature in the second half of the 15th century

1602   **Jules Cardinal Mazarin** -- French statesman, clergyman, and chief minister of France after the death of Cardinal Richelieu in 1642

1658   **Camillo Rusconi** -- Italian sculptor

1750   **Aaron Arrowsmith** -- English geographer and cartographer

1794   **John Gibson Lockhart** -- Scottish writer

1852 **Dr. James Dwight** -- Father of American lawn tennis and early tennis great

1858 **Emmeline Goulden Pankhurst** -- English suffragette who was one of the foremost leaders in securing equal voting privileges for women in England

1860 **Owen Wister** – American novelist, best known for *The Virginian* (1902)

1862 **Gustav Klimt** -- Austrian painter

1883 **Monte Carlo** -- Danish-born composer noted for songs such as "Tangerine"

1890 **Ossip Zadkine** -- Russian sculptor

1894 **Ted Koehler** -- American lyricist noted for songs such as "Between the Devil and the Deep Blue Sea," "I Love a Parade," "Stormy Weather," "Let's Fall in Love," and "Animal Crackers in My Soup"

1899 **William J. Hill** -- American composer noted for songs such as "Empty Saddles," "Have You Ever Been Lonely?" "The Last Round-Up," "In the Chapel in the Moonlight," and "The Old Spinning Wheel"

1902 **Harry Haenigsen** -- American cartoonist and creator of the comic strips, *Our Bill* and *Penny*

1903 **Irving Stone** – American novelist and biographer, noted for *Lust for Life* (1934), a novel about Vincent Van Gogh, and for *The Agony and the Ecstasy* (1961), a biography of Michelangelo

1904 **Isaac Bashevis Singer** -- Polish-born Yiddish writer noted for works such as *Satan in Goray* and *Yentl*

1908 **Johnny Murphy** -- Professional baseball player

1909 **Annabella (Suzanne Charpentier)** – French dancer and actress

1910 **William Hanna** – American cartoonist and animator, noted with Joseph Barbera and Fred Quimby for creating the Tom and Jerry cartoons

1911 **Terry-Thomas** -- English stage, screen, and television actor and comedian

1912 **Woody Guthrie** -- Influential American folk singer and composer, who wrote more than 1,000 songs, including "This Land Is Your Land"

1912 **Willard Francis Motley** -- American novelist noted for *Knock On Any Door*

1913 **Gerald R. Ford** -- 38th U.S. president

1916 **Claude Harmon** -- Professional golfer

1918 **Ingmar Bergman** – Internationally-known Swedish motion-picture director

1923   **Dale Robertson** -- American motion-picture actor

1927   **John Chancellor** -- American television newscaster

1929   **Bob Purkey** -- Professional baseball player

1930   **Polly Bergen** -- American motion-picture and television actress

1932   **Roosevelt Grier** -- Professional football player and actor

1934   **Lee Elder** -- Professional golfer

1938   **Moshe Safdie** – Israeli architect who designed the master plan of Expo 67

1938   **Jerry Rubin** -- American political activist

1943   **Bob Unger** -- Professional golfer

1947   **Steve Stone** -- Professional baseball player and broadcaster

1948   **Kenneth Burrough** -- Professional football player

1961   **Boy George O'Dowd** -- Lead singer with the British musical group, Culture Club

JULY 14 -- EVENTS

1789   Parisians stormed the Bastille prison, marking the start of the French Revolution. The date has since been known as Bastille Day, the great national holiday of France.

1806   Meriwether Lewis and William Clark, of the Lewis and Clark Expedition, became the first white men in history to enter what is now Washington state from the east.

1830   Emma Hart Willard wrote "Rocked in the Cradle of the Deep" while at sea.

1853   Commodore Matthew Perry was received by the Lord of Toda on his mission to open trade between the U.S. and Japan.

1865   Edward Whymper became the first man to climb the Matterhorn, one of Europe's most ferocious peaks.

1881   Billy the Kid was killed in Fort Sumner, New Mexico, by Sheriff Pat Garrett.

1908   D.W. Griffith's first picture, *The Adventures of Dollie,* was released, and shown for the first time, at Keith & Proctor's Union Square Theater in New York.

1921   Nicola Sacco and Bartolomeo Vanzetti were convicted of murder in the famous Sacco-Vanzetti trial.

1965   Adlai E. Stevenson, twice a presidential candidate, died of a heart attack in London at age 65.

JULY 15 -- BIRTHDAYS

1573   **Inigo Jones** -- First major architect of the English Renaissance

1606   **Rembrandt (Harmenszoon van Rijn)** -- The Netherlands' greatest artist

1631   **Richard Cumberland** -- Father of English Utilitarianism

1704   **August Gottlieb Spangenberg** -- American bishop and founder of the Moravian Church of America

1779   **Clement Clarke Moore** -- American poet who in 1822 wrote the most popular of American Christmas poems, "A Visit from St. Nicholas," also known as "'Twas the Night Before Christmas"

1796   **Thomas Bulfinch** -- American historian and author of *Bulfinch's Mythology,* a collection of works such as *The Age of Fable* and *The Age of Chivalry*

1833   **Thomas Collier Platt** -- U.S. senator and New York political boss

1895   **Jane "Ginny" Bunford** -- Tallest woman in the world at 7 feet 11 inches, reduced to 7 feet 7 inches, because of a spine curvature disease

1903   **Walter D. Edmonds** -- American author, noted for novels such as *Drums Along the Mohawk* (1936)

1905   **Dorothy Fields** -- American lyricist noted for such songs as "The Way You Look Tonight," "I Can't Give You Anything But Love, Baby," "I'm in the Mood for Love," and "On the Sunny Side of the Street"

1906   **Richard Armour** -- American author and humorist noted for works such as *Light Armour* (1954), *The Classics Reclassified* (1960), and *The Academic Bestiary* (1974)

1919   **Iris Murdoch** -- British novelist noted for her complex and witty works, such as *A Fairly Honourable Defeat* (1970)

1933   **Julian Bream** -- English classical guitarist

1935   **Alex Karras** -- Professional football player, sportscaster, and actor

1939   **Patrick Wayne** -- American actor and son of actor John Wayne

1941   **Archie Clark** -- Professional basketball player

1946   **Linda Ronstadt** -- American country rock singer

1946   **Laura Rossouw** -- South African tennis player

1948   **Tom Leonard** -- American tennis player

1952   **Charles Lesley** -- English tennis player

JULY 15 -- EVENTS

971 AD Saint Swithin, the Bishop of Winchester, was reburied inside his cathedral. The day is celebrated in England as Saint Swithin's Day.

1099   The Crusaders captured Jerusalem, slaughtering 40,000 people and burning the mosques.

1870   Georgia became the last of the Confederate states to be readmitted to the Union.

1876   George Washington Bradley of the Washington baseball team pitched the first no-hit game in major league history, defeating Hartford, 2-0.

1883   Tom Thumb, 40 inch-tall midget in P.T. Barnum's circus, died at age 45.

1912   Jim Thorpe sparked the U.S. team to victory in the 1912 Olympics. He won 15 events and was called "the most wonderful athlete in the world" by Sweden's King Gustav.

1918   Germany launched its last offensive on the Marne in World War I.

1948   President Harry Truman was nominated for reelection by the Democrats in their convention in Philadelphia, in spite of widespread doubts that he could win in November.

1958   U.S. marines landed in Lebanon to prevent a Communist takeover.

1965   American scientists displayed close-up pictures of the planet Mars taken by the *Mariner 4* spacecraft.

1971   President Nixon announced that he would make a historic trip to Peking to confer with officials of the People's Republic of China.

1973   Nolan Ryan pitched his second no-hitter of the season as California beat Detroit, 6-0.

1985   His doctors announced that President Reagan had cancer in a portion of his large intestine that had been removed, and they were optimistic that he would recover completely.

JULY 16 -- BIRTHDAYS

1486   **Andrea del Sarto** – Outstanding painter of the Italian Renaissance

1661   **Pierre Lemoyne,** Sieur d' Iberville -- French-Canadian explorer and founder of the province of Louisiana

1723   **Sir Joshua Reynolds** -- One of the greatest English portrait painters of all time

1796   **Camille Corot** -- French landscape and figure painter

1821   **Mary Baker Eddy** -- Founder of Christian Science and the Church of Christ, Scientist

1848   Eben Rexford -- Composer of "Silver Threads Among the Gold"

1872   **Roald Amundsen** -- Norwegian explorer who discovered the South Pole in December of 1911

1880   **Kathleen Norris** -- American novelist

1883   **Charles Sheeler** -- American painter and photographer noted for paintings that blend realism with cubism

1887   **Shoeless Joe Jackson** -- Professional baseball player with a .356 lifetime batting average, who was banished from baseball in the 1919 "Black Sox" scandal

1888   **Percy Kilbride** -- American actor and co-star of the Ma and Pa Kettle films

1896   **Trygve Lie** -- First United Nations secretary-general

1903   **Carmen Lombardo** -- Canadian-born composer and singer, and brother of bandleader Guy Lombardo, noted for songs such as "Coquette," "Boo Hoo," and "Seems Like Old Times"

1907   **Barbara Stanwyck** -- American stage, screen, and television actress, and one of the top stars of the 1930s and 1940s

1911   **Ginger Rogers** -- American dancer and actress with a 40-year career, who won an Academy Award for her performance in *Kitty Foyle* (1940)

1911   **Sonny Tufts** -- American stage and motion-picture actor, whose name and statistics became favorites of trivia buffs

1915   **Barnard Hughes** -- American motion-picture and television actor

1920   **Jose Lopez Portillo** -- President of Mexico in the 1970s

1924   **Bess Myerson** -- American television personality and consumer official

1932   **Richard Thornburgh** -- Attorney General under Presidents Reagan and Bush

1942   **Margaret Smith Court** -- Australian tennis superstar and the second woman (after Maureen Connolly) to win the grand slam of tennis (1970)

1948   **Marianne Kindler** -- Swiss tennis player

1948   **Pinchas Zukerman** -- Israeli-born violin virtuoso

1952   **Stewart Copeland** -- American musician and drummer for the Police musical group

JULY 16 -- EVENTS

622 AD   Mohammed made his famous flight, or *Hegira,* from Mecca to Medina, marking the beginning of the Moslem calendar.

1054   Michael Cerularius, Patriarch of Constantinople, was excom-
        municated by delegates of Pope Leo IX, precipitating the schism
        between the Churches of Rome and Constantinople.

1769   The first mission in California was established in San Diego by
        Father Junipero Serra.

1790   The District of Columbia was established by Congress.

1862   David G. Farragut became the first rear admiral in the U.S. Navy.

1918   Ex-Czar Nicholas II of Russia and his family were murdered by
        the Bolsheviks in a cellar in Ekaterinburg (now Sverdlovsk).

1941   New York Yankee superstar Joe DiMaggio set his amazing
        record of hitting safely in 56 consecutive games, going 3 for 4
        against Cleveland.

1945   The first atomic bomb was exploded, near Alamogordo, New
        Mexico. It produced the equivalent of 17,000 tons of TNT.

1969   *Apollo 11* lifted off from Cape Kennedy, bound for the moon,
        with astronauts Armstrong, Aldrin, and Collins on board. Four
        days later it put the first men on the moon.

1973   White House aide Alexander Butterfield publicly revealed the
        existence of President Nixon's taping system in the White House.

JULY 17 -- BIRTHDAYS

1674   **Isaac Watts** -- English clergyman, noted for composing 761
        hymns and psalms, including such classics as "Joy to the World"
        and "O God, Our Help in Ages Past"

1744   **Elbridge Gerry** -- Massachusetts governor for whom *gerryman-
        der* was named, because he went to such lengths to redistrict the
        state that one district looked like a salamander, or *gerrymander*

1763   **John Jacob Astor** -- American fur magnate and founder of the
        famous Astor fortune

1827   **Sir Frederick Augustus Abel** -- British chemist and explosives
        expert

1860   **Gustav Mahler** -- Bohemian composer and one of the greatest
        conductors of his time

1871   **Lyonel Feininger** -- Internationally known American painter

1876   **Maxim Litvinov** -- Russian diplomat who negotiated the recog-
        nition of Russia by the United States in 1933

1877   **Edward Madden** -- American lyricist noted for songs such as "By
        the Light of the Silvery Moon," "Moonlight Bay," and "Silver Bell"

1878   **Harold Hackett** -- American Hall of Fame tennis player, who,
        with Fred Alexander, formed one of the most famous doubles
        teams of the early 1900s

1888	**Shmuel Yosef Agnon** – Hebrew novelist and short story writer, who shared the Nobel Prize for literature in 1966
1889	**Erle Stanley Gardner** -- American author, noted for the Perry Mason mystery novels
1899	**James Cagney** -- American stage and motion-picture superstar, with a career spanning over 60 years
1900	**Marcell Dalio** – French motion-picture actor with a 40-year career
1905	**John Carroll** -- American actor and singer
1905	**William Gargan** -- American stage and motion-picture actor
1909	**Hardy Amies** -- English fashion designer
1912	**Art Linkletter** -- American television personality and writer
1915	**Cass Daley** -- American actress, singer, and comedienne
1917	**Phyllis Diller** -- American comedienne and actress
1917	**Lou Boudreau** -- Hall of Fame baseball player and manager
1930	**Roy McMillan** -- Professional baseball player
1934	**Donald Sutherland** -- Canadian stage and motion-picture actor
1935	**Peter Schickele** -- American composer
1935	**Benjamin R. Civiletti** – Attorney general under President Carter
1935	**Diahann Carroll** -- American singer and motion-picture actress
1941	**Daryle Lamonica** -- Professional football player
1942	**Connie Hawkins** -- Professional basketball player
1953	**Mike Thomas** -- Professional football player

JULY 17 -- EVENTS

1453	The Hundred Years' War ended with the defeat of the English by the French at Castillon.
1821	Spain transferred Florida to the United States.
1841	*Punch,* the English humor periodical, published its first issue in London.
1861	The first U.S. paper money, or "greenbacks," was issued.
1898	U.S. troops captured Santiago, Cuba, in the Spanish-American War.
1903	James McNeill Whistler, the American painter, died in London at age 69.
1936	The Spanish Civil War began with the revolt of the military garrisons.
1938	"Wrong Way" Corrigan left Floyd Bennett Field, New York, for California and wound up the next day in Ireland.

1941   Joe DiMaggio's famous hitting streak was finally stopped at 56 consecutive games, as he went hitless against Cleveland's Al Smith and Jim Bagby Jr.

1955   Disneyland opened in California.

1975   U.S. astronauts and Soviet cosmonauts joined hands after linking their Apollo and Soyuz spacecrafts.

1987   The Dow-Jones Industrial Average closed at 2510.04, the first time in history it had closed above 2500.

JULY 18 -- BIRTHDAYS

1635   **Robert Hooke** -- English physicist who discovered the law of elasticity

1659   **Hyacinthe Rigaud** -- French painter

1811   **William Makepeace Thackeray** -- English Victorian novelist and author of *Vanity Fair,* one of the great books of world literature

1843   **Virgil W. Earp** -- American lawman of the old West and brother of Marshall Wyatt Earp

1845   **Tristan Corbiere** -- French poet

1852   **Gertrude Kasebier** -- American photographer

1853   **Henrik Antoon Lorentz** -- Dutch physicist noted for the electron theory of matter

1882   **Manuel Galvez** -- Argentine novelist and biographer

1882   **Hermann Hagedorn** -- American author and poet

1887   **Vidkun Quisling** -- Norwegian army officer whose collaboration with the Nazis in World War II established his name as a synonym for traitor

1891   **Gene Lockhart** -- American stage, screen, and television actor with a 60-year career

1893   **M.K. Jerome** – American composer and publisher, noted for songs such as "My Wild Irish Rose," "Just a Baby's Prayer at Twilight," and "Sweet Dreams, Sweetheart"

1894   **Richard Dix** -- American stage and motion-picture actor

1902   **Jessamyn West** -- American writer and novelist, best known for *Friendly Persuasion* (1945)

1903   **Chill Wills** – American vaudeville and motion-picture actor with a screen career of over 40 years

1906   **S.I. Hayakawa** – American university president and U.S. senator

1906   **Clifford Odets** -- Leading American dramatist of the theater of social protest of the 1930s

1911   **Hume Cronyn** -- Canadian stage and motion-picture actor

1913   Walter Kerr -- American newspaper columnist and writer, noted for works such as *Pieces at Eight* and *The Silent Clowns*
1913   **Red Skelton** -- American comedian and actor
1918   **Nelson Mandela** -- South African civil rights leader
1921   **John Glenn Jr.** -- First U.S. astronaut to orbit the earth (February 20, 1962), and U.S. senator
1929   **Screamin' Jay Hawkins** -- American singer and pioneer of rock theatrics
1929   **Dick Button** -- American champion figure skater
1940   **James Brolin** -- American motion-picture and television actor
1940   **Joe Torre** -- Professional baseball player and manager
1943   **Calvin Peete** -- Professional golfer
1957   **Nick Faldo** -- English professional golfer
1963   **Mike Greenwell** -- Professional baseball player

JULY 18 -- EVENTS

64 AD   Two-thirds of Rome burned while Emperor Nero allegedly fiddled.
1374   Petrarch, the great Italian poet, died in Arqua, Italy, two days before his 70th birthday.
1610   Michelangelo da Caravaggio, the Italian painter, died at Port Ercole at age 36.
1817   Jane Austen, the great English novelist, died in Winchester, England, at age 41.
1872   Britain introduced the concept of voting by secret ballot.
1918   France opened the Second Battle of the Marne in World War I.
1936   The Spanish Civil War began as army chiefs in Spanish Morocco headed by General Francisco Franco start a revolt against the Madrid government.
1938   "Wrong Way" Corrigan, who had left New York for California, arrived at Baldonnel Airport in Dublin, Ireland.
1940   President Franklin D. Roosevelt was nominated for an unprecedented third term by the Democratic convention in Chicago.
1944   Allied troops captured St.-Lo in World War II, opening the way for General Omar Bradley's U.S. First Army to break out of the Normandy peninsula and sweep across France.
1948   Pat Seerey of the Chicago White Sox hit four home runs in an 11-inning game.
1951   Jersey Joe Walcott knocked out Ezzard Charles in seven rounds in Pittsburgh to win the heavyweight championship.

1969   *Apollo 11* entered the moon's gravitational sphere two days before its occupants became the first men on the moon.

1969   A car driven by Senator Edward Kennedy plunged off a bridge on Chappaquiddick Island, resulting in the drowning of Mary Jo Kopechne.

1984   In the worst one-day massacre in American history, 21 people were shot to death in a McDonald's restaurant in San Ysidro, California, by James Oliver Huberty, an unemployed laborer.

JULY 19 -- BIRTHDAYS

1789   **John Martin** -- English painter

1814   **Samuel Colt** -- American inventor, known for the Colt revolver, the first successful repeating pistol

1834   **Edgar Degas** -- Noted French impressionist painter, famous for showing his figures in awkward or informal positions

1846   **Edward Charles Pickering** -- American astronomer who invented a meridian photometer to measure the brightness of the stars

1860   **Lizzie Borden** -- Alleged American murderess who, according to the poem, "took an axe and gave her mother forty whacks . . ."

1865   **Charles Horace Mayo** -- American physician and one of the founders of the Mayo Clinic in Rochester, Minnesota

1893   **Vladimir Vladimirovich Mayakovsky** -- Russian poet and playwright

1896   **Bob Meusel** -- Professional baseball player and member of the New York Yankees' 1927 "perfect outfield" of Babe Ruth, Earle Combs, and Meusel

1896   **A.J. Cronin** -- British physician and novelist, noted for such works as *The Citadel* (1937) and *The Keys to the Kingdom* (1942)

1898   **Herbert Marcuse** -- American philosopher and writer, noted for *One Dimensional Man* (1964)

1904   **Robert Todd Lincoln Beckwith** -- Great-grandson and last descendent of Abraham Lincoln

1916   **Phil Cavaretta** -- Professional baseball player

1917   **William Scranton** -- Governor of Pennsylvania, 1963-1967

1922   **George S. McGovern** -- U.S. senator and presidential candidate of the Democratic Party in 1972

1942   **Vicki Carr** -- American singer

1946   **Ilie Nastase** -- Romanian tennis player

1947   **Maria Nasuelli** -- Italian tennis player

1949   **Mike Estep** -- American tennis player
1954   **Alvan Adams** -- Professional basketball player

JULY 19 -- EVENTS

1318   Austria recognized the Three Forest Cantons, marking the beginning of modern Switzerland.
1553   Lady Jane Grey was deposed, and King Henry VIII's daughter Mary was proclaimed Queen of England.
1842   The SS *Great Britain* was launched, the first of the screw-propelled steamships.
1848   The first Women's Rights Convention was held, in Seneca Falls, New York.
1870   France declared war on Prussia, starting the Franco-Prussian War.
1918   German armies began a general retreat across the Marne River in France, after their last great World War I offensive failed.
1942   Arturo Toscanini conducted the NBC Symphony Orchestra in the first American performance of the *Seventh Symphony* by Dmitri Shostakovich.
1969   *Apollo 11* went into orbit around the moon, one day before it landed the first men on the moon.
1970   The Russian space vehicle, *Soyuz 9,* landed after a record 268 orbits around the earth.
1973   Both Republican and Democratic senior counsels to the House Judiciary Committee urged the panel to recommend that President Nixon be impeached.
1984   The Democratic Convention nominated Geraldine Ferraro to run for vice president with Walter Mondale. She was the first woman candidate for the office on a major party ticket.

JULY 20 -- BIRTHDAYS

1304   **Petrarch (Francesco Petracco)** -- Great Italian poet, scholar, and humanist
1519   **Innocent IX** -- Roman Catholic pope who served for less than a year in 1591
1785   **Mahmud II** -- Ottoman sultan, 1808-1839
1847   **Max Liebermann** -- German painter
1890   **Theda Bara** -- Early silent film star, known as the Vamp because of her sensational role in *A Fool There Was* (1915), based on Kipling's poem, "The Vampire"

1890   **Giorgio Morandi** -- Italian painter
1895   **Lazlo Moholy-Nagy** -- Hungarian artist
1901   **Heinie Manush** -- Hall of Fame baseball player
1909   **William "Fish Bait" Miller** -- U.S. Congressional doorkeeper
1919   **Sir Edmund Percival Hillary** – New Zealand mountain climber who was the first to reach the summit of Mt. Everest (1953)
1919   **Benson Ford** – American industrialist and grandson of noted automobile maker Henry Ford
1920   **Elliott Richardson** -- Holder of three cabinet posts under President Nixon
1921   **Fred Schroeder** – American Hall of Fame tennis player and 1949 Wimbledon singles champion
1925   **Lola Albright** -- American motion-picture and television actress
1930   **Sally Ann Howes** -- English stage, screen, and television actress
1938   **Natalie Wood** -- American motion-picture actress who made the transition from child star to adult star
1938   **Diana Rigg** -- English motion-picture and television actress
1939   **Judy Chicago** -- American artist
1940   **Tony Oliva** -- Professional baseball player
1947   **James L. Harris** -- Professional football player
1947   **Carlos Santana** -- Mexican rock and jazz guitarist
1950   **Nick Weatherspoon** -- Professional football player
1955   **Jim Smith** -- Professional football player
1956   **Mima Jausovec** -- Yugoslavian tennis player
1960   **Mike Witt** -- Professional baseball player

JULY 20 -- EVENTS

1605   French explorer Samuel Champlain reached Cape Cod during one of his eleven trips to Canada.

1796   Explorer Mungo Park first saw the River Niger in Africa.

1881   Indian chief Sitting Bull surrendered to the United States government and was put on a reservation for two years.

1917   Alexander Kerensky was named premier of Russia by the provisional government. His government lasted only a few months until Lenin seized power.

1925   Clarence Darrow cross-examined William Jennings Bryan as an expert witness on the Bible in the Scopes trial in Dayton, Tennessee. The result was a disaster for Bryan.

1942   The first detachment of WAAC's started their basic training at Fort Des Moines, Iowa, in World War II.

1944   Adolf Hitler was seriously injured and narrowly escaped death when a time bomb planted by a German officer exploded in Hitler's headquarters.

1945   The U.S. flag was raised over Berlin, as the first American troops prepared to participate in the occupation government following World War II.

1969   *Eagle,* of the *Apollo 11* mission, landed on the Sea of Tranquility, and Neil Armstrong became the first man to set foot on the moon. He was followed shortly by Edwin Aldrin Jr.

1976   U.S. space vehicle *Viking 1* landed on Mars and relayed crisp surface photographs to the earth.

JULY 21 -- BIRTHDAYS

1414   **Sixtus IV** -- Roman Catholic pope, 1471-1484

1664   **Matthew Prior** -- English poet

1673   **John Weaver** -- English dancer and ballet master

1816   **Paul Julius von Reuter** -- Founder of the first news agency, which still bears his name

1817   **Sir John Gilbert** -- English Romantic painter

1858   **Chauncey Olcott** -- American composer, author, and actor, noted for songs such as "My Wild Irish Rose," "When Irish Eyes Are Smiling," and "Mother Machree"

1863   **Sir C. Aubrey Smith** -- British stage and motion-picture actor in nearly 70 movies, best known for his memorable character roles

1864   **Frances Folsom Cleveland** – Wife of President Grover Cleveland

1881   **Johnny Evers** -- Hall of Fame baseball player and member of the famous Tinker-to-Evers-to-Chance double play combination

1885   **Frances Parkinson Keyes** -- American novelist

1895   **Ken Maynard** – One of Hollywood's most popular cowboy actors

1899   **Hart Crane** -- American poet, best known for "The Bridge"

1899   **Ernest Hemingway** – One of the most influential and most famous American writers of his time

1901   **Allyn Joslyn** -- American stage and motion-picture character comedian

1905   **Diana Trilling** -- American novelist

1905   **David M. Kennedy** -- U.S. secretary of the treasury under President Nixon

1911   **Marshall McLuhan** -- Canadian communications theorist and writer, noted for *Understanding Media* (1964) and *The Medium Is the Massage* (1967)

1920   **Isaac Stern** -- Russian-born violin virtuoso

1922   **Kay Starr** -- American singer

1924   **Don Knotts** -- American motion-picture and television actor

1926   **Paul Burke** -- American motion-picture and television actor

1930   **Gene Littler** -- Professional golfer

1933   **John Gardner** -- American novelist

1948   **Cat Stevens** -- English singer and songwriter, noted for "Morning Has Broken"

1949   **Al Hrabosky** -- Professional baseball player

1952   **Robin Williams** -- American motion-picture and television actor

JULY 21 -- EVENTS

365 AD A great earthquake struck the eastern Mediterranean and destroyed the Roman city of Kourion on the island of Cyprus.

1796   Robert Burns, the great Scottish poet, died in Dumfries at age 47.

1831   Leopold I was proclaimed King of the Belgians, as Belgium became independent of Holland.

1861   Northern troops retreated in disorder after the first Battle of Bull Run, at which Confederate general Thomas J. Jackson gained his nickname "Stonewall."

1873   Jesse James carried out the world's first train robbery, holding up the Rock Island Express at Adair, Iowa.

1918   Allied troops captured Chateau-Thierry in World War I.

1925   The Scopes trial ended in Dayton, Tennessee, as John Scopes was found guilty and fined $100 for teaching evolution in the public schools.

1944   Franklin D. Roosevelt was renominated for an unprecedented fourth term at the Democratic Convention in Chicago.

1954   The Indochinese War between France and Vietnam ended with a treaty granting North Vietnam its independence.

1959   The United States launched the *Savannah,* the world's first nuclear-powered merchant ship.

1961   U.S. astronaut Virgil Grissom became the second American in space, as *Liberty Bell 7* was launched for a suborbital flight of 16 minutes.

1963   Paul VI was elected Roman Catholic pope.

1969   Astronauts Neil Armstrong and Edwin Aldrin Jr. returned from the moon to the command module, rejoining astronaut Michael Collins.

JULY 22 -- BIRTHDAYS

1478   **Philip the Handsome** -- Archduke of Austria who became king of Spain by marrying Juana of Castile

1713   **Jacques Germain Soufflot** -- French architect

1784   **Friedrich Wilhelm Bessel** -- German astronomer and mathematician, noted for Bessel's equation and its solutions, the Bessel functions

1822   **Gregor Johann Mendel** -- Austrian botanist who discovered the principles of heredity

1833   **Benjamin R. Hanby** -- Composer of "Darling Nellie Gray"

1849   **Emma Lazarus** -- American poet who wrote the sonnet inscribed on the pedestal of the Statue of Liberty

1860   **Frederick William Rolfe** -- English writer

1870   **Tom Pendergast** -- Democratic party boss of Kansas City and leader of one of the largest political machines in the U.S. in the 1930s and 1940s

1878   **Ernest R. Ball** -- American composer noted for songs such as "Let the Rest of the World Go By" and "When Irish Eyes Are Smiling"

1882   **Edward Hopper** -- American painter who produced some of the finest realistic works of his time

1890   **Rose Fitzgerald Kennedy** – Mother of President John F. Kennedy

1892   **Arthur Seyss-Inquart** – Austrian Nazi leader during the Austrian *Anschluss* engineered by Adolf Hitler in 1937

1893   **Karl Menninger** -- American psychiatrist whose ideas widely influenced public attitudes toward mental illness

1893   **Jesse Haines** -- Hall of Fame baseball player

1898   **Alexander Calder** – One of the first American sculptors of international significance, and one of the best-known American artists of the mid-20th century

1898   **Stephen Vincent Benet** -- American poet, novelist, and short-story writer, noted for such works as *By the Waters of Babylon* and *John Brown's Body*

1901   **Charles Weidman** – Major innovator of the U.S. modern dance

1905   **Doc Cramer** -- Professional baseball player

1908   **Amy Vanderbilt** -- American expert on etiquette
1913   **Licia Albanese** -- American soprano
1917   **Adam Malik** -- Indonesian diplomat and president of the 26th
        U.N. General Assembly
1921   **William Roth** -- U.S. senator
1922   **Jason Robards Jr.** -- American motion-picture and television actor
1923   **Robert Dole** -- U.S. senator and Minority Leader
1928   **Orson Bean** -- American actor and comedian
1932   **Oscar De La Renta** -- American fashion designer
1934   **Louise Fletcher** -- American motion-picture actress
1941   **Susie Maxwell Berning** -- Professional golfer
1944   **Sparky Lyle** -- Professional baseball player
1944   **Joyce Hume** -- English tennis player
1947   **Cliff Johnson** -- Professional baseball player
1951   **Ron Turcotte** -- Canadian jockey
1956   **Scott Sanderson** -- Professional baseball player
1957   **Dave Stieb** -- Professional baseball player

JULY 22 -- EVENTS

1587   The second "Lost Colony" was established on Roanoke Island,
        off the North Carolina coast. It, like the first one, disappeared.
1588   After a month of regrouping at Corunna, Spain, the Spanish
        Armada headed toward the English Channel to engage the
        English fleet.
1613   Michael, the first Romanov Czar of Russia, was crowned. Six-
        teen more Romanov czars followed him to the Russian throne.
1796   Cleveland, Ohio, was founded by Moses Cleaveland, a surveyer,
        and a group of Connecticut settlers.
1871   The notorious "Tweed Ring," headed by New York boss Wil-
        liam Marcy Tweed, was exposed by the New York *Times*.
1933   American aviator, Wiley Post, in his plane, the *Winnie Mae,*
        completed the first round-the-world solo flight.
1934   John Dillinger, "Public Enemy Number One," was shot and
        killed by FBI agents as he left the Biograph Theater in Chicago.
1967   Carl Sandburg, the great American biographer and poet, died in
        Flat Rock, North Carolina, at age 89.
1969   *Apollo 11* left the moon's atmosphere bound for home, after
        placing the first men on the moon.

1975   Congress voted to restore the American citizenship of Confederate General Robert E. Lee.

JULY 23 -- BIRTHDAYS

1339   **Louis I** -- Duke of Anjou
1477   **Francesco Granacci** -- Italian painter noted for works such as *Scenes from the Life of Saint John the Baptist* (around 1510)
1777   **Philipp Otto Runge** -- German painter
1816   **Charlotte Saunders Cushman** -- First native-born American stage star
1823   **Coventry Patmore** -- English poet
1864   **F. Holland Day** -- American photographer
1883   **Sir Alan Francis Brooke, Viscount Alanbrooke** -- British World War II field marshal
1884   **Albert Warner** -- One of the Warner Brothers who founded the motion-picture company of the same name
1884   **Emil Jannings** -- Swiss-born motion-picture actor who was the first to win the Academy Award for best actor, in 1927-1928 for *The Last Command* and *The Way of All Flesh*
1888   **Gluyas Williams** -- American cartoonist, primarily for *The New Yorker* magazine
1888   **Raymond Chandler** -- American novelist, creator of detective Philip Marlowe, and author of *The Big Sleep* (1939)
1892   **Haile Selassie** -- Emperor of Ethiopia, 1930-1974
1894   **Arthur Treacher** -- English stage, screen, and television actor
1918   **Pee Wee Reese** -- Hall of Fame baseball player
1923   **Ray Boone** -- Professional baseball player
1924   **Gloria DeHaven** -- American stage, screen, and television actress
1926   **Johnny Groth** -- Professional baseball player
1930   **Moon Landrieu** -- Mayor of New Orleans and secretary of Health and Human Services under President Carter
1934   **Bert Convy** -- American television host and actor
1936   **Don Drysdale** -- Hall of Fame baseball player and sports announcer
1936   **Anthony McLeod Kennedy** -- U.S. Supreme Court justice
1947   **David Essex** -- English singer and drummer
1950   **Belinda J. Montgomery** -- American actress
1961   **Martin Gore** -- British keyboardist with the Depeche Mode musical group

JULY 23 -- EVENTS

685 AD   John V became Roman Catholic pope.

1803   Robert Emmett, Irish patriot, led an unsuccessful insurrection against the British in Ireland.

1829   William A. Burt of Mount Vernon, Michigan, patented his "typographer," claimed by many to be the first typewriter.

1904   The ice cream cone was invented by Charles E. Menches of St. Louis.

1914   Austria-Hungary issued an ultimatum to Serbia, demanding that Austrian officials participate in the trial of those accused of murdering Archduke Francis Ferdinand.

1942   The best seller, *See Here, Private Hargrove,* by Marion Hargrove, was first published.

1944   The Russians crossed the Curzon Line into Poland in World War II.

1945   Marshal Henri Philippe Petain, the French collaborator with the Nazis in World War II, went on trial for treason in Paris.

1951   Marshal Petain died in prison at age 95.

1984   Vanessa Williams became the first Miss America to give up her title, after shocking pictures of her appeared in *Penthouse* magazine.

JULY 24 -- BIRTHDAYS

1686   **Benedetto Marcello** -- Venetian composer and writer

1725   **John Newton** -- English clergyman and composer, in 1779, of "Amazing Grace"

1783   **Simon Bolivar** -- The great South American general who won independence from Spain for Bolivia, Colombia, Ecuador, Peru, and Venezuela

1802   **Alexandre Dumas** -- French novelist, noted for *The Three Musketeers* (1844) and *The Count of Monte Cristo* (1845), two of the most popular historical novels in world literature

1803   **Adolphe Charles Adam** -- Composer of "Holy Night"

1803   **Alexander Jackson Davis** -- American architect

1843   **Sir William de Wiveleslie Abney** -- British specialist in the chemistry of photography

1864   **Frank Wedekind** -- German playwright, noted for *Spring's Awakening* (1890-1891) and *Pandora's Box* (1894)

1871   **Giacomo Balla** -- Italian painter and sculptor

1878   **Lord Dunsany** -- Irish writer (born Edward John Plunkett), noted for his tales and for such plays as *The Gods of the Mountain* (1911)

1880   **Ernest Bloch** -- Swiss-American composer, noted for the opera *Macbeth* (1910) and the rhapsody "America" (1928)

1895   **Robert Graves** -- English author, poet, and translator, noted for works such as *I, Claudius* (1934), *The White Goddess* (1948), and 136 other novels and books of poetry

1897   **Amelia Earhart** -- American aviatrix and first woman to fly alone over the Atlantic Ocean

1900   **Zelda (Sayre) Fitzgerald** -- American writer and wife of novelist F. Scott Fitzgerald

1916   **John D. MacDonald** -- The "General Motors of American novelists," noted for some 75 books such as *The Executioners* (1958) and *Condominium* (1977)

1920   **Bella Abzug** -- U.S. congresswoman and advocate of women's rights

1921   **Billy Taylor** -- American pianist, composer, and conductor

1922   **Charles McC. Mathias Jr.** -- U.S. senator

1927   **Alex Katz** -- American painter

1932   **William D. Ruckelshaus** -- Director of the Environmental Protection Agency under Presidents Nixon and Reagan

1935   **Patrick Bruce Oliphant** -- American political cartoonist

1936   **Ruth Buzzi** -- American comedienne

1948   **Mack Herron** -- Professional football player

1951   **Lynda Carter** -- American actress and singer

1953   **Steve Grogan** -- Professional football player

JULY 24 -- EVENTS

1680   New Hampshire became a royal colony of the British crown.

1704   British naval forces captured Gibraltar from Spain, and have retained it to the present.

1847   Brigham Young and his Mormon followers settled Salt Lake City, Utah.

1862   Martin Van Buren died in Kinderhook, New York, at age 79.

1866   Tennessee became the first state of the Confederacy to be readmitted to the Union.

1945   The Potsdam Conference opened at Potsdam, near Berlin, following Germany's defeat in World War II. Attending were Harry S Truman, Winston Churchill, and Joseph Stalin.

1946   The United States made the first underwater test of an atomic bomb, at Bikini Atoll in the Pacific Ocean.

1959   Vice President Richard Nixon and Russian Premier Nikita Khrushchev engaged in their "Kitchen Debate" at a U.S. exhibition in Moscow.

1969   The *Apollo 11* mission, placing the first men on the moon, ended with a successful splashdown in the Pacific Ocean.

1974   The Supreme Court ruled 8-0 that President Nixon must produce the subpoenaed Watergate tapes.

JULY 25 -- BIRTHDAYS

1654   **Agostino Steffani** -- Italian composer and singer

1750   **Henry Knox** -- American Revolutionary War general, who directed Washington's troops when they crossed the Delaware, and who became the first U.S. secretary of war

1775   **Anna Symmes Harrison** -- Wife of President William Henry Harrison

1799   **Charles Coffin Little** -- American publisher who with James Brown founded Little, Brown & Co. in 1837

1844   **Thomas Eakins** -- One of the greatest American realist painters of the 1800s

1848   **Arthur James Balfour** — British prime minister, 1902-1905, noted for the Balfour Declaration of 1917, favoring the establishment of a national Jewish home in Palestine

1854   **David Belasco** -- American actor, playwright, and a leading theatrical producer for nearly 40 years

1870   **Maxfield Parrish** -- American painter and illustrator noted for Maxfield Parrish blue, the unusual shade of blue used in many of his paintings

1874   **Joaquin Torres-Garcia** -- Uruguayan painter

1894   **Walter Brennan** -- American motion-picture and television actor, and first to win three Academy Awards

1902   **Eric Hoffer** -- American writer and political scientist

1907   **Johnny Hodges** -- American composer and saxophonist, noted for songs such as "I'm Beginning to See the Light," "Wanderlust," and "Wonder of You"

1919   **Jack Gilford** -- American stage, screen, and television actor

1924   **Frank Church** -- U.S. senator in the 1960s and 1970s

1926   **Whitey Lockman** -- Professional baseball player

1927   **Stanley Dancer** -- American harness-racing driver

1929 **Peter Farb** -- American author and editor
1940 **John Pennel** -- American pole vaulter who set the world's record of 17 feet 10½ inches in 1969
1941 **Nate Thurmond** -- Professional football player
1945 **Donna Theodore** -- American singer
1954 **Walter Payton** -- Professional football player and superstar who broke Jimmy Brown's career rushing record in 1984
1957 **Gordon Jones** -- Professional football player

JULY 25 -- EVENTS

44 AD Saint James, the brother of John and the son of Zebedee, and one of the 12 apostles, became the first of the apostles to be martyred, when Herod Agrippa I had him killed.

215 AD Frederick II, called *Stupor Mundi* (the Amazement of the World), was crowned Holy Roman Emperor at Aix-la-Chapelle.

1593 King Henry IV of France, a Protestant, converted to Roman Catholicism in order to end the religious wars in his country.

1814 George Stephenson, the great British engineer, first successfully demonstrated a steam locomotive. His engine, *Puffing Billy,* pulled heavy loads of coal for years.

1834 Samuel Taylor Coleridge, the famous English poet, died in London at age 61.

1866 Ulysses S. Grant was named General of the Army, the first officer to hold that rank.

1909 French aviator Louis Bleriot made the first airplane flight across the English Channel.

1934 Chancellor Englebert Dollfus of Austria was murdered by the Nazis because he tried to prevent Adolf Hitler from taking over Austria.

1943 Benito Mussolini, the Fascist dictator of Italy, resigned and Marshal Badoglio took over as Italian chief of state, following Italy's collapse in World War II.

1944 U.S. forces broke out of Normandy and began the sweep across France in World War II.

1952 Puerto Rico became a self-governing commonwealth.

1956 The luxury liner *Andrea Dorea* and the steamer *Stockholm* collided 45 miles off Nantucket Island, resulting in 54 deaths.

1963 The United States, Russia, and Britain signed the test-ban treaty, prohibiting nuclear testing in the atmosphere, in space, or underwater.

1978   The world's first test tube baby (conceived outside a woman's womb) was born to John and Lesley Brown in Oldham, England.

JULY 26 -- BIRTHDAYS

1739   **George Clinton** -- Governor of New York and U.S. vice president, 1805-1812

1796   **George Catlin** -- American painter and student of Indian life

1799   **Isaac Babbit** -- American inventor, known for special alloys called Babbit metals, used to reduce friction in moving parts

1856   **George Bernard Shaw** – Most significant British playwright since the 17th century

1858   **Colonel Edward M. House** – Confidential adviser to President Woodrow Wilson

1874   **Serge Koussevitzky** -- Russian-born conductor and foremost double bass player of his time, known primarily for conducting the Boston Symphony Orchestra from 1924 to 1949

1875   **Carl Jung** – Swiss psychologist and psychiatrist who used the terms *introvert* and *extrovert* to describe personalities

1875   **Antonio Marchado y Ruiz** -- Spanish poet

1885   **Andre Maurois** -- French biographer and novelist, noted for such works as *Ariel* (1923), *The Life of Disraeli* (1927), and *The Titans* (1957)

1892   **Sad Sam Jones** -- Professional baseball player

1893   **George Grosz** -- German painter and graphic artist

1894   **Aldous Huxley** -- English novelist, poet, essayist, and author of *Brave New World* (1932) and *Point Counter Point* (1928)

1897   **Paul Gallico** -- American novelist and essayist

1902   **Gracie Allen** -- American comedienne who teamed with her husband, George Burns, to form the Burns and Allen comedy duo

1903   **Estes Kefauver** -- U.S. senator and vice presidential candidate in 1956 with Adlai Stevenson

1904   **Edwin Albert Link** – American inventor who developed the mechanical trainer, a machine that simulates flying conditions on the ground

1908   **Salvador Allende** -- Marxist president of Chile in the early 1970s

1914   **Erskine Hawkins** -- American trumpeter and bandleader

1914   **Ralph Blane Hunsecker** -- American composer noted for songs such as "Buckle Down, Winsocki!" "Have Yourself a Merry Little Christmas," "Skip to My Lou," "The Trolley Song," and "Pass That Peace Pipe"

1920	**Bob Waterfield** -- Professional football player
1922	**Blake Edwards** -- American motion-picture producer and author
1923	**Hoyt Wilhelm** -- Hall of Fame baseball pitcher who pitched in a record number of games and retired at age 49
1928	**Stanley Kubrick** -- American motion-picture director, noted for such films as *2001: A Space Odyssey* (1968) and *A Clockwork Orange* (1971)
1929	**Alexis Weissenberg** -- Bulgarian-born French pianist
1943	**Mick Jagger** -- British singer with the Rolling Stones musical group
1950	**Charlie Smith** -- Professional football player
1950	**Susan George** -- English motion-picture and television actress
1951	**Bobby Wadkins** -- Professional golfer
1954	**Vitas Gerulaitis** -- American tennis player
1956	**Dorothy Hamill** -- American ice-skating champion

JULY 26 -- EVENTS

1581	The Netherlands declared its independence from Spain.
1775	Benjamin Franklin became Postmaster General.
1788	New York ratified the Constitution, becoming the 11th state.
1847	Liberia was proclaimed an independent republic.
1908	The investigative agency which later became the F.B.I. was created on orders of U.S. Attorney General Charles J. Bonaparte.
1925	William Jennings Bryan died of a stroke in Dayton, Tenn., five days after his participation in the Scopes trial.
1945	The Potsdam conferees issued an ultimatum demanding the unconditional surrender of Japan in World War II.
1945	Clement Attlee replaced Winston Churchill as prime minister after the Labour Party's unexpected defeat of the Conservative Party in the British elections of July 5.
1947	President Harry S Truman signed the National Security Act, consolidating the Department of Defense.
1956	Egypt's president Gamal Abdel Nasser seized the Suez Canal from its British and French owners.
1971	*Apollo 15*, with three astronauts aboard, was launched from Cape Kennedy, and headed for the moon.

JULY 27 -- BIRTHDAYS

| 1672 | **Gilles Marie Oppenord** -- French architect |

1768   **Charlotte Corday** -- Young French girl who stabbed French revolutionary Jean Paul Marat to death while he was sitting in his bathtub

1835   **Giosue Carducci** -- Italian poet and critic

1842   **Hugo Henneberg** -- Austrian photographer

1861   **Louis Vivin** -- French painter

1870   **Hilaire Belloc** – British poet, novelist, and essayist, who wrote more than 150 books

1880   **Joe Tinker** -- Hall of Fame baseball player and member of the famed Tinker-to-Evers-to-Chance double play combination

1880   **Donald Crisp** -- Scottish-born motion-picture actor who appeared in 364 films in a 55-year career

1904   **Anton Dolin** -- First internationally famous English male dancer

1906   **Leo Durocher** – Professional baseball player and highly successful manager

1916   **Elizabeth Hardwick** -- American writer and editor

1916   **Keenan Wynn** -- American stage and motion-picture actor and son of actor Ed Wynn

1918   **Leonard Rose** -- American violincellist

1922   **Norman Lear** – American television producer, noted for the long-running comedy, *All in the Family*

1939   **Irv Cross** -- Professional football player and sportscaster

1942   **Dennis Ralston** -- American tennis player

1944   **Bobbie Gentry** – American country singer and songwriter, noted for songs such as "Ode to Billy Joe"

1946   **Haven Moses** -- Professional football player

1948   **Mack Calvin** -- Professional basketball player

1948   **Peggy Fleming** -- American ice figure skater and Olympic champion

1948   **Betty Thomas** -- American actress

1949   **Maureen McGovern** -- American singer and actress

1952   **Melvin Barnes** -- Professional basketball player

1952   **Bump Wills** -- Professional baseball player and son of baseball great Maury Wills

JULY 27 -- EVENTS

1694   The Bank of England was founded in London.

1789   The U.S. Department of Foreign Affairs, the forerunner of the Department of State, was established by Congress, and made an executive agency under the President.

1866	The first permanent Atlantic cable was laid by Cyrus W. Field, stretching from Valencia, Ireland, to Heart's Content, Newfoundland.
1909	Orville Wright set a record by staying aloft in an airplane for 1 hour, 12 minutes, and 40 seconds.
1921	Insulin was isolated for the first time by Dr. Frederick Banting and his assistant, Charles Best, at the University of Toronto Medical School.
1953	The Korean War ended with a truce agreement between the U.N. and North Korea.
1974	The U.S. House Judiciary Committee passed its first article of impeachment against President Richard Nixon.

JULY 28 -- BIRTHDAYS

1618	**Abraham Cowley** -- English poet and essayist whose first volume of verse, *Poetical Blossoms,* was published when he was 15
1746	**Thomas Heywood Jr.** -- American patriot, statesman, and soldier, and a South Carolina signer of the Declaration of Independence
1844	**Gerard Manley Hopkins** -- One of the major poets of Victorian England
1857	**Ballington Booth** -- Founder of the Volunteers of America and son of William Booth, the founder of the Salvation Army
1866	**Beatrix Potter** -- British author and illustrator, who created the *Peter Rabbit* children books, known all over the world
1887	**Marcel Duchamp** -- French painter of the cubist school, who was later influential in the Dada movement
1891	**Carl Spaatz** -- First chief of staff of the U.S. Air Force
1892	**Joe E. Brown** -- American actor and comedian
1898	**Charles William Mayo** -- American surgeon and son of Charles Horace Mayo, a founder of the Mayo Clinic
1901	**Freddie Fitzsimmons** -- Professional baseball player
1901	**Rudy Vallee** -- American actor, national radio singing idol of the 1920s, and composer, noted for songs such as "I'm Just a Vagabond Lover" and "There Is a Tavern in the Town"
1909	**Malcolm Lowry** -- English novelist and author of *Under the Volcano*
1910	**Richard Lewine** -- American composer, author, and producer, noted for songs such as "Love Makes the World Go Round"
1929	**Jacqueline Kennedy Onassis** -- Wife of President John F. Kennedy
1934	**Jacques D'Amboise** -- American ballet dancer and leading member of the New York City Ballet

1937   **Peter Duchin** -- American pianist and bandleader
1941   **Ricardo Muti** -- Italian conductor who succeeded Eugene Ormandy as director of the Philadelphia Orchestra in 1980
1943   **Mike Bloomfield** -- American blues musician
1943   **Bill Bradley** -- Professional basketball superstar and U.S. senator
1945   **Rick Wright** -- English keyboardist for the Pink Floyd musical group
1948   **Sally Struthers** -- American actress and one of the stars of the long-running television comedy, *All in the Family*
1949   **Vida Blue** -- Professional baseball player
1951   **Doug Collins** -- Professional basketball player
1957   **Charles Alexander** -- Professional football player

JULY 28 -- EVENTS

1402   Mongol leader Tamerlane defeated the Turks at the Battle of Angora in Anatolia.
1540   Thomas Cromwell, chief minister of King Henry VIII of England, was beheaded.
1540   King Henry VIII of England secretly married his fifth wife, Catherine Howard.
1750   Johann Sebastian Bach, the great composer, died in Leipzig at age 65.
1794   Maximilien Robespierre, the notorious French Revolutionary leader, was guillotined in Paris at age 36.
1821   Peru declared its independence from Spain.
1868   The 14th Amendment to the Constitution was ratified, extending citizenship to all persons born or naturalized in the United States.
1896   Miami, Florida, with 269 inhabitants, was incorporated.
1914   Austria-Hungary declared war on Serbia to begin World War I.
1930   The July Revolution in Paris ended with the overthrow of Charles X and the call to power of Louis Philippe, the Duke of Orleans.
1932   The Bonus Marchers, a 15,000-man "army" of World War I veterans, were dispersed with tanks, cavalry, and infantry by General Douglas MacArthur in Washington, D.C.
1973   *Skylab 3* was launched, beginning a 59-day mission plagued with defects that required emergency repairs by the astronauts themselves.
1976   Earthquakes rocked northern China, killing 655,000 people.

JULY 29 -- BIRTHDAYS

1580   **Francesco Mochi** -- Italian sculptor

1605   **Simon Dach** -- German poet of the early Baroque movement

1794   **Thomas Corwin** -- U.S. senator and author of Corwin's Law: "If you would succeed in life, you must be solemn, solemn as an ass."

1805   **Alexis de Tocqueville** -- French statesman and political philosopher, known for his book, *Democracy in America* (1835-1840)

1824   **Alexandre Dumas the Younger** -- French novelist, playwright, and son of novelist Alexandre Dumas

1824   **Eastman Johnson** -- American painter

1869   **Booth Tarkington** -- Pulitzer Prize-winning American novelist and dramatist, and author of *Monsieur Beaucaire* (1900) and *The Magnificent Ambersons* (1919)

1877   **William Beebe** -- American naturalist and writer, noted for his vivid accounts of tropical jungles, undersea explorations, and studies of birds

1878   **Donald Perry "Don" Marquis** -- American writer and newspaper columnist who created archy, the cockroach, and mehitabel, the cat

1883   **Benito Mussolini** -- Italian Fascist dictator, 1922-1943

1887   **Sigmund Romberg** -- Noted Hungarian-American composer of operettas, such as *The Student Prince* and *Blossom Time*

1889   **Ernst Reuter** -- Mayor of post-World War II West Berlin

1892   **William Powell** -- Smooth villain of Hollywood silents and leading man of the talkies, especially noted for the Thin Man series of movies with actress Myrna Loy

1900   **Don Redman** -- American saxophonist, composer and jazz orchestra pioneer

1900   **Owen Lattimore** -- American author and China expert

1905   **Dag Hammarskjold** -- Swedish statesman and second U.N. secretary general

1907   **Melvin Belli** -- Noted American trial lawyer

1918   **Edwin O'Connor** -- American novelist and author of *The Last Hurrah*

1921   **Richard Egan** -- American motion-picture actor

1924   **Mark Ethridge Jr.** -- Noted American publisher

1926   **Don Carter** -- Noted professional American bowler

1930   **Paul Taylor** -- American modern dancer and choreographer

1932   **Nancy Landon Kassebaum** -- U.S. senator and daughter of presidential candidate Alf Landon

1933   **Randy Sparks** -- American composer and author noted for film and television songs, such as "The Singing Nun"

1936   **Elizabeth Dole** -- Member of the Cabinet under Presidents Reagan and Bush, and wife of U.S. Senator Robert Dole

1938   **Peter Jennings** -- Canadian-born American television news correspondent and anchorman

1948   **Neal Walk** -- Professional basketball player

1951   **Dan Driessen** -- Professional baseball player

1952   **Scott Wedman** -- Professional basketball player

JULY 29 -- EVENTS

1030   King Olaf II, the patron saint of Norway, was killed in battle.

1565   Mary, Queen of Scots, married Henry Stuart, Lord Darnley.

1588   "We have time enough to finish the game and beat the Spaniards, too," said Sir Francis Drake during a game of bowls when told the Spanish Armada had been sighted near the Scilly Isles.

1703   Daniel Defoe, author of *Robinson Crusoe,* was put in a pillory for a political pamphlet he wrote.

1754   The first international boxing match in history took place as the British champion Jack Slack knocked out the French contender Jean Petit.

1778   The French fleet arrived at Rhode Island to help the American colonists in the Revolutionary War.

1856   Robert Schumann, the great German composer, died at Endenich, near Bonn, at age 46.

1890   Vincent van Gogh, the famous Dutch painter, died in Auers, France, after shooting himself two days earlier. He was 37 years old.

1945   An armada of U.S. B-29 bombers dropped 3,500 tons of fire bombs on six Japanese cities in World War II.

1968   Pope Paul VI issued his edict against artificial birth control.

1974   The U.S. House Judiciary Committee passed its second article of impeachment against President Nixon.

1981   Prince Charles, heir to the English throne, and Lady Diana Spencer were married in St. Paul's Cathedral in London.

JULY 30 -- BIRTHDAYS

1511   **Giorgio Vasari** -- Florentine Mannerist painter and writer

1763   **Samuel Rogers** -- English poet

1818   Emily Bronte—English novelist and author of *Wuthering Heights* (1847), a masterpiece of world literature

1857   **Thorstein Veblen** -- One of the most original and creative thinkers in the history of American economics, and author of the famous work, *The Theory of the Leisure Class* (1899)

1863   **Henry Ford** – American pioneer automobile industrialist, founder of the Ford Motor Company, and developer of the Model T and Model A automobiles

1880   **Robert R. McCormick** -- Editor of the Chicago *Tribune,* 1925-1955, who made it one of the nation's most important newspapers

1889   **Emanuel Haldeman-Julius** -- American publisher and founder of the E. Haldeman-Julius company noted for its Little Blue Books

1890   **Casey Stengel** -- Hall of Fame baseball player and one of the most successful managers in history, who managed the New York Yankees to ten pennants in twelve years

1898   **Henry Moore** -- English sculptor, noted for such works as *King and Queen* (1953) and *Reclining Figure* (1965)

1928   **Joe Nuxhall** -- Professional baseball player who began his major league career at age 15

1939   **Peter Bogdanovich** – American motion-picture director, producer, and screenwriter

1940   **Patricia Schroeder** -- U.S. Congresswoman who labeled Ronald Reagan "the Teflon President".

1941   **Paul Anka** -- Canadian-born singer, actor, and songwriter

1944   **Pat Kelly** -- Professional baseball player

1947   **William Atherton** -- American stage and motion-picture actor

1947   **Arnold Schwarzenegger**—Austrian-born bodybuilder, holder of Mr. World and Mr. Universe male physique titles, and actor

1948   **Jim Mandrich** -- Professional football player

1951   **Efren Herrera** -- Professional football player

1954   **Ellis Valentine** -- Professional baseball player

1957   **Eddie Lee Ivery** -- Professional football player

1957   **Steve Trout** -- Professional baseball player and son of baseball player Dizzy Trout

JULY 30 -- EVENTS

1502   Christopher Columbus reached the Bay Islands off the coast of Honduras on his fourth voyage to America.

1588   The Spanish Armada entered the English Channel and had its first engagement with the English fleet on the following day.

1619   The House of Burgesses of Virginia, the first representative legislative body in America, met for the first time in Jamestown.

1729   Baltimore Town, which later became Baltimore, was founded by the Maryland colonial government.

1771   Thomas Gray, the noted English poet, died at age 54.

1862   The term *Copperhead,* meaning a Northerner sympathetic to the South, first appeared, in the Cincinnati *Gazette.*

1898   Otto von Bismarck, Germany's Iron Chancellor, died at Friedrichsruh at age 83.

1918   Sergeant Joyce Kilmer, American poet and author noted for the famous poem "Trees," was killed in action in France in World War I.

1932   Vice President Charles Curtis officially opened the 1932 Summer Olympic Games in Los Angeles.

1942   President Franklin D. Roosevelt signed the bill creating the WAVES, the women's branch of the U.S. Navy.

1947   Thor Heyerdahl, on his raft *Kon-Tiki,* sighted Puka Island in eastern Polynesia, after a journey from Peru.

1965   President Lyndon B. Johnson signed the Medicare bill into law.

1974   The U.S. House Judiciary Committee passed its third article of impeachment against President Nixon.   .

JULY 31 -- BIRTHDAYS

1396   **Philip the Good** -- Duke of Burgundy

1803   **John Ericsson** -- Swedish-American engineer who invented the screw propeller and designed and built the *Monitor,* the famous ironclad warship of the Union in the Civil War

1875   **Jacques Villon** -- French painter

1883   **Erich Heckel** -- German painter

1900   **Elmo Roper** -- American marketing consultant and founder of the Roper Poll

1912   **Milton Friedman** -- American economist, columnist, and author of *Capitalism and Freedom,* in which he advocated a "negative income tax"

1912   **Irv Kupcinet** -- American journalist and television host, noted for *Kup's Show*

1916   **William Selden Todman** -- American television producer noted for his shows with Mark Goodson

1919   **Curt Gowdy** -- American television sportscaster

1920	**Ndabaningi Sithole** -- Clergyman and nationalist leader in Zimbabwe's struggle against white rule
1921	**Whitney M. Young Jr.** -- American civil rights leader and head of the National Urban League, 1961-1971
1922	**Hank Bauer** -- Professional baseball player and manager
1929	**Don Murray** -- American stage and motion-picture actor
1939	**Norman Snead** -- Professional football player
1939	**France Nuyen** -- French motion-picture actress
1943	**Susan Flannery** -- American actress
1944	**Geraldine Chaplin** – American actress and daughter of comedian Charlie Chaplin and granddaughter of playwright Eugene O'Neill
1946	**Bob Welch** – American rock musician with the Fleetwood Mac musical group
1951	**Evonne Goolagong Cawley** -- Australian tennis player and twice Wimbledon singles champion
1957	**Leon Durham** -- Professional baseball player

JULY 31 -- EVENTS

432 AD	Saint Sixtus III was elected Roman Catholic pope.
1485	William Caxton, the first English printer, published his version of Sir Thomas Malory's great romance of knighthood, *Morte D'Arthur.*
1498	Christopher Columbus discovered Trinidad on his third voyage to America.
1556	Saint Ignatius Loyola, founder of the Jesuits, died in Rome at age 65.
1588	The Spanish Armada made its first contact with the English, commanded by Lord Howard of Effingham. The first contact was a probing action, the actual battle beginning on the next day.
1777	The Marquis de Lafayette of France was commissioned a major general in the Continental Army in the Revolutionary War.
1790	The first United States patent was issued, for potash manufacture.
1875	Andrew Johnson died in Carter Station, Tennessee, at age 66.
1945	The French World War II traitor Pierre Laval surrendered to U.S. occupation authorities in Linz, Austria.
1948	New York's Idlewild Airport (now John F. Kennedy Airport) was dedicated by President Harry Truman.
1950	Joe Adcock of the Milwaukee Braves hit four home runs and a double in a single game.

1964   U.S. space probe *Ranger 7* landed on the moon and televised 4,308 pictures of the moon to the earth.

1972   Vice-presidential candidate Thomas Eagleton withdrew from Senator George McGovern's ticket following disclosures that Eagleton had once undergone psychiatric treatment.

1975   Teamsters ex-president Jimmy Hoffa was reported missing. He was never found.

1981   The seven-week major league baseball strike came to an end.

1988   The last Playboy Club in the U.S. closed, in Lansing, Michigan.

8

August

August, the eighth month of the year, was the sixth month of the ancient Roman calendar, and was appropriately called *Sextilis*, the Latin word for *sixth*. In the original calendar of Romulus, August had 30 days. This was changed to 29 by Numa Pompilius and changed again to 30 in the Julian Calendar. In 8 B.C. the Roman Senate changed the name of the month to *Augustus* (August) to honor the emperor Augustus. He had been born in September, but he chose Sextilis for his month because during it so many fortunate events had happened to him, such as his election as one of the two consuls, the conquest of Egypt, and the cessation of the civil wars. According to legend, Augustus took one day from February and added it to August, giving it its present total of 31 days. He wanted his month to have as many days as July, the month of his great uncle Julius Caesar.

Bolivia, Ecuador, India and Switzerland celebrate their national independence days in August, and V-J Day on August 14 marks the Allied victory over Japan in World War II in 1945. Two United States Presidents, Herbert Hoover and Lyndon B. Johnson, were born in August, and Christopher Columbus set sail from Palos, Spain, on August 3, 1492, to discover the new world.

The birthstones for August are the sardonyx and the peridot, and the August flowers are the poppy and the gladiolus. Notable August birthdays and events follow.

427

AUGUST 1 -- BIRTHDAYS

10 BC   Claudius I -- Emperor of Rome, A.D. 41-54, who built Rome's harbor at Ostia, and conquered parts of England and Thrace (now the Balkans)

126 AD Publius Helvius Pertinax -- Emperor of Rome who served for less than one year (A.D. 193)

1495   Jan van Scorel -- Dutch painter

1520   Sigismund II Augustus -- King of Poland, 1548-1572

1714   Richard Wilson -- British landscape painter

1744   Chevalier de Lamarck -- French biologist and botanist, noted for being one of the first to propose a theory of biological evolution

1770   William Clark -- American explorer, who with Meriwether Lewis led the famous Lewis and Clark exploration of the U.S. Northwest Territory from 1804 to 1806

1779   Francis Scott Key — American lawyer and poet who wrote the words to "The Star-Spangled Banner" during the War of 1812

1815   Richard Henry Dana Jr. -- American novelist and author of *Two Years Before the Mast* (1840)

1818   Maria Mitchell -- American astronomer noted for her studies of sunspots and as the first woman member of the American Academy of Arts and Sciences

1819   Herman Melville -- One of America's greatest writers, and author of *Moby-Dick* (1851), one of the great novels in literature, and *Billy Budd* (published in 1924 after Melville's death)

1843   Robert Todd Lincoln -- Eldest son of Abraham Lincoln and the only son of Lincoln to survive to manhood

1883   Jonathan M. Wainwright -- American World War II general and hero of Bataan and Corregidor

1898   William B. Ziff -- American publisher

1898   Morris Stoloff -- American composer, conductor, and violinist, noted for songs such as "A Song to Remember," and scores for movies such as *Cover Girl, The Jolson Story,* and *Song Without End*

1899   William Steinberg — Noted American conductor of the Pittsburgh Symphony and the Boston Symphony orchestras

1914   Lloyd Mangrum -- Professional golfer and winner of the U.S. Open in 1946

1921   **Jack Kramer** -- One of the all-time great tennis players

1922   **Arthur Hill** -- Canadian stage and motion-picture actor

1922   **C. Peter McColough** -- Chairman of Xerox Corporation

1929   **Ralph Kessler** -- American composer noted for the background music of such TV shows as *Buck Rogers, Quincy,* and *Barnaby Jones*

1930   **Geoffrey Holder** -- Trinidad-born choreographer and costume designer

1931   **Tom Wilson** -- American cartoonist and creator of *Ziggy*

1933   **Dom De Luise** -- American actor and comedian

1936   **Yves Saint-Laurent** -- French dress designer

1942   **Giancarlo Giannini** -- Italian motion-picture actor

1942   **Jerry Garcia** -- American guitarist with the Grateful Dead musical group

1948   **Cliff Branch** -- Professional football player

1950   **Milt May** -- Professional baseball player

1952   **Greg Gross** -- Professional baseball player

1973   **Tempestt Bledsoe** -- American television actress noted for her role in the *Bill Cosby Show*

AUGUST 1 -- EVENTS

1137   Louis VI (the Fat), King of France, died of dysentery.

1291   The three Swiss cantons signed the Perpetual Covenant, establishing the Swiss Confederation, which became known later as Switzerland.

1423   The English defeated the French at Crevant in the Hundred Years' War.

1498   Christopher Columbus, on his third voyage to America, sailed across the Gulf of Paria to the mainland of Venezuela. He did not actually land until August 5.

1588   The first day's battle between the Spanish Armada and the English fleet was indecisive, with both sides exchanging long-range gunfire.

1589   King Henry III of France was stabbed to death while sitting on the privy, by a fanatic monk, Jacques Clement.

1788   Thomas Gainsborough, the great English painter, died in London at age 61.

1790   The first U.S. census was completed, showing a population of 3,929,214 in 17 states.

1794   The Whiskey Rebellion began in Pennsylvania, in protest of the excise tax on alcoholic beverages.

1798   British admiral Horatio Nelson in the Battle of the Nile almost destroyed the French fleet, ending Napoleon's hopes of a vast Eastern conquest.

1876   Colorado was admitted to the Union as the 38th state.

1907   The U.S. Army established an Aeronautical Division, the fore-runner of the U.S. Air Force.

1914   Germany declared war on Russia in World War I.

1933   Carl Hubbell, the New York Giants' ace pitcher, pitched his 44th consecutive scoreless inning, a record.

1946   The U.S. Atomic Energy Commission was established.

1966   Charles Joseph Whitman, a lone gunman in a senseless act, killed 15 people from a tower on the campus of the University of Texas at Austin, before he was killed by the police.

1972   Nate Colbert of the San Diego Padres hit five home runs in a doubleheader.

AUGUST 2 -- BIRTHDAYS

1696   **Mahmud I** -- Ottoman sultan, 1730-1754

1754   **Pierre Charles L'Enfant** -- French engineer and architect, who planned the design of Washington, D.C.

1820   **John Tyndall** -- English physicist and natural philosopher, who first demonstrated the Tyndall effect, explaining why the sky is blue

1835   **Elisha Gray** -- American inventor, who claimed to have invented the telephone before Alexander Graham Bell, and who was a founder of the Western Electric Company

1865   **Irving Babbitt** -- American critic, teacher, and leader of the "new humanism" movement

1867   **Ernest Dowson** -- English poet, best known for "Cynara" (1891) and "The Days of Wine and Roses" (1896)

1868   **Constantine I** -- King of Greece, 1913-1917 and 1920-1923

1871   **John French Sloan** -- American painter and etcher, and member of the Eight, an association of painters in the early 20th century

1880   **Arthur Garfield Dove** -- American painter, whose paintings were among the earliest abstract works painted in America

1892   **John Kieran** -- American columnist and radio performer

1892   **Jack Warner** -- American motion-picture producer and co-founder of Warner Brothers in 1923

1894   **Westbrook Pegler** -- American journalist

1905   **Myrna Loy** -- American motion-picture actress, known especially for her starring roles opposite William Powell in The Thin Man series of movies

1915   **Gary Merrill** -- American stage and motion-picture actor

1918   **Beatrice Straight** -- American motion-picture and television actress

1922   **Paul Laxalt** -- U.S. senator

1924   **James Baldwin** -- American novelist, essayist, and playwright, noted for *The Fire Next Time* (1963) and *Another Country* (1962)

1925   **Carroll O'Connor** -- American stage, screen, and television actor, and star of the long-running television comedy, *All in the Family*

1932   **Lamar Hunt** -- American sports franchise owner and son of billionaire H.L. Hunt

1932   **Peter O'Toole** -- Irish motion-picture actor

1946   **Bob Beamon** -- American long jumper who set the world's record of 29 feet 2¼ inches in 1968

1952   **Mike Ivie** -- Professional baseball player

AUGUST 2 -- EVENTS

216 BC   The great Carthaginian general Hannibal and his elephants routed the Romans in the Battle of Cannae, a battle famous for Hannibal's use of "double envelopment," still used today.

47 BC   Upon defeating Pharnaces, King of Pontus, Julius Caesar said, "I came, I saw, I conquered."

1776   Members of the Continental Congress began the process of signing the Declaration of Independence. Fifty members signed on this day.

1824   New York City's Fifth Avenue was opened.

1832   The U.S. defeated Chief Black Hawk and his Sauk and Fox Indians in the Battle of Bad Axe, effectively ending the Black Hawk War.

1858	The first street letter boxes were set up, in Boston.

1876   Wild Bill Hickok was murdered at age 39 while playing poker and holding 2 aces and 2 eights, known ever since as a "dead man's hand."

1909   The first Lincoln pennies were issued.

1923   President Warren G. Harding died suddenly in San Francisco at age 57. He was succeeded the next day by Vice President Calvin Coolidge.

1927   "I do not choose to run," said President Calvin Coolidge, taking himself out of the 1928 presidential race.

1934   German president Paul von Hindenburg died, leaving Adolf Hitler free to consolidate his dictatorship.

1936   Jesse Owens, the great American athlete, set a new world's record for the 100-meter run in the Olympic Games in Berlin.

1939   The Hatch Act was passed by Congress, forbidding federal civil service employees from taking an active part in political campaigns.

1943   Navy Lieutenant John F. Kennedy rescued the members of his boat, *PT-109*, after it was sheared in two by a Japanese destroyer in the South Pacific.

1945   The Potsdam Conference ended with President Truman, Premier Stalin, and Prime Minister Attlee, who had replaced Churchill, calling for Germany's disarmament and Japan's surrender.

1956   Albert Woolson, the last Union veteran of the Civil War, died at age 109.

1978   The movie *Star Wars* surpassed *Jaws* as the all-time high money-maker.

1983   The House of Representatives voted overwhelmingly to make Dr. Martin Luther King Jr.'s birthday, January 15, a national holiday.

AUGUST 3 -- BIRTHDAYS

1746   **James Wyatt** -- English architect

1770   **Frederick William III** -- King of Prussia, 1797-1840, who was defeated by Napoleon at the Battles of Jena and Auerstadt in 1806

1801   **Joseph Paxton** -- English architect noted for his design of the Crystal Palace of the 1851 London Exhibition, one of the first buildings to have prefabricated parts made in factories

1811 **Elisha Graves Otis** -- American inventor, who built the first elevator protected by safety devices against accidentally falling

1867 **Stanley Baldwin** – Three times British prime minister, 1923-1924, 1924-1929, and 1935-1937

1872 **Haakon VII** -- First king of Norway after it gained its independence from Sweden in 1905

1886 **Russ Westover** -- American comic strip writer, and creator of *Tillie the Toiler* in 1921

1887 **Rupert Brooke** -- English poet, noted primarily for his sonnet sequence "1914"

1894 **Harry Heilmann** -- Hall of Fame baseball player who hit .403 in 1923

1900 **Ernie Pyle** – Beloved American World War II war correspondent who was killed on Okinawa in 1945

1901 **John C. Stennis** -- U.S. senator

1905 **Dolores Del Rio** -- Glamorous Mexican motion-picture actress, and one of the most beautiful women ever to grace the American screen

1905 **Maggie Kuhn** -- Founder of the Gray Panthers

1918 **James MacGregor Burns** -- American historian and writer, and author of *Roosevelt: The Lion and the Fox* (1956)

1920 **Jim Hegan** -- Professional baseball player

1920 **George C. Cory Jr.** -- American composer noted for songs such as "I Left My Heart in San Francisco" (with Ernest Altschuler)

1921 **Marilyn Maxwell** -- American actress and singer

1921 **Richard Adler** -- American songwriter

1923 **Jean Hagen** -- American motion-picture and television actress

1924 **Leon Uris** -- American novelist and author of *Exodus* (1958)

1926 **Tony Bennett** -- American singer

1931 **Alex Cord** -- American motion-picture actor

1935 **Richard Lamm** -- Governor of Colorado

1940 **Lance Alworth** -- Professional football player

1940 **Martin Sheen** -- American stage, screen, and television actor

1951 **Paulo Bertolucci** -- Italian tennis player

1960 **Sid Bream** -- Professional baseball player

1960 **Tim Mayotte** -- American tennis player

1964 **Kevin Elster** -- Professional baseball player

AUGUST 3 -- EVENTS

30 BC   Mark Antony committed suicide in Alexandria, Egypt, to which he had been pursued by Octavian after the Battle of Actium.

1291   The Crusaders abandoned Tortosa to the Moslems.

1422   King Henry V of England died of dysentery in France at age 34, after having won the entire northern half of France in the Hundred Years' War.

1492   Christopher Columbus sailed from Palos, Spain, on his first voyage to America, with a fleet of three ships--the *Santa Maria,* the *Pinta,* and the *Nina*--and 90 men.

1610   Henry Hudson, the great British sea captain and adventurer, discovered Hudson Bay in Canada.

1778   Milan's world-famous opera house, La Scala, opened for its first performance.

1858   John Hanning Speke, the English African explorer, discovered Lake Victoria.

1914   Germany declared war on France in World War I.

1923   Calvin Coolidge became president of the United States upon the death of President Harding. He was sworn in at 2:45 A.M. by the light of a kerosene lamp by his father, a notary public.

1924   Joseph Conrad, the great Polish-English novelist, died in Bishopsbourne, England, at age 66.

1948   Whittaker Chambers, the admitted ex-Communist, accused Alger Hiss of being a member of the Communist underground.

1958   The U.S. atomic submarine *Nautilus* crossed the North Pole under the Arctic ice.

AUGUST 4 -- BIRTHDAYS

1521   **Urban VII** – Roman Catholic pope, who served for less than one year in 1590

1755   **Nicholas Jacques Conte** -- French developer in 1795 of the pencil-making process that is still used in the manufacture of modern pencils

1792   **Percy** Bysshe Shelley -- One of the greatest English Romantic poets, noted for such poems as "Ode to the West Wind" (1819)

1816   **Russell Sage** -- American banker and philanthropist whose widow Margaret incorporated the Russell Sage Foundation to help remove the causes of poverty

1839   **Walter Horatio Pater** -- English essayist and critic, and author of *Marius the Epicurean* (1885)

1841   **William Henry Hudson** -- British author and naturalist, best noted for the novel, *Green Mansions* (1904)

1853   **John Henry Twachtman** -- One of the first U.S. Impressionist painters

1859   **Knut Hamsun** -- Nobel Prize-winning Norwegian novelist, best known for *The Growth of the Soil* (1917)

1861   **Jesse W. Reno** -- American inventor noted for the invention of the escalator

1870   **Sir Harry Lauder** -- Scottish comedian, ballad singer, and "Scotland's Goodwill Ambassador," who became one of the world's most beloved entertainers

1890   **Dolf Luque** -- Professional baseball player

1910   **William Howard Schuman** -- American composer and administrator, who won the Pulitzer Prize in 1943

1913   **Wesley Addy** -- American stage and screen actor

1920   **Helen Thomas** -- American journalist

1934   **Dallas Green** -- Professional baseball player, manager, and executive

1948   **John Grubb** -- Professional baseball player

1949   **John Riggins** -- Professional football superstar

1962   **Roger Clemens** -- Professional baseball pitcher who struck out a record 20 batters in a nine-inning game (April 29, 1986) and won both the Cy Young and Most Valuable Player Awards in 1986

AUGUST 4 -- EVENTS

1060   Philip I became king of France at age 8.

1578   Sebastian I of Portugal was killed and his army utterly defeated at Al-Kasr al-Kebir in Northwest Africa, ending for a time European excursions into Africa.

1735   John Peter Zenger won an acquittal of libel charges intended to censor his attacks on the Crown. The case established freedom of the press in America.

1790   Congress established the Revenue Cutter Service, later known as the United States Coast Guard.

1821   The weekly magazine *Saturday Evening Post* was founded.

1875   Hans Christian Andersen, the great Danish fairy tale writer, died in Copenhagen at age 70.

1892   Lizzie Borden's parents were murdered with an axe in Fall River, Massachusetts. It seemed obvious that "Lizzie Borden took an axe . . ." but she was later acquitted.

1903   Pius X was elected Roman Catholic pope.

1914   Germany invaded neutral Belgium and Great Britain declared war on Germany in World War I.

1916   Denmark and the United States signed a treaty transferring control of the Virgin Islands to the United States.

1944   Anne Frank and her family were betrayed to the Gestapo in Amsterdam, after two years of hiding, during which time she wrote her famous diary.

1985   Baseball greats Tom Seaver and Rod Carew reached career milestones, as Seaver won his 300th game and Carew got his 3,000th base hit.

AUGUST 5 -- BIRTHDAYS

1540   **Joseph Justus Scaliger** -- French philosopher and historian

1604   **John Eliot** -- English clergyman and "Apostle to the Indians," and the first minister to teach the Christian religion to the Indians of New England

1694   **Leonardo Leo** -- Italian composer and teacher

1749   **Thomas Lynch Jr.** -- South Carolina signer of the Declaration of Independence

1802   **Niels Henrik Abel** -- One of the greatest Norwegian mathematicians of all time

1813   **Ivar Aasen** -- Norwegian language scholar

1827   **Manuel Deodoro da Fonseca** -- First president of Brazil, who ruled for a few months in 1891

1850 **Guy de Maupassant** -- French author and one of the world's great short-story writers

1889 **Conrad Aiken** -- American poet, novelist, and critic, whose *Selected Poems* won the Pulitzer Prize in 1930

1890 **Naum Gabo** -- Russian-born sculptor

1906 **John Huston** -- Noted American motion-picture actor and director, and son of actor Walter Huston, who directed such films as *The Treasure of Sierra Madre* (1948) and *The African Queen* (1952)

1908 **Harold Edward Holt** -- Australian Prime Minister who mysteriously drowned while in office in Port Philip Bay, Australia

1911 **Robert Taylor** -- American motion-picture and television actor, and one of Hollywood's top stars for 30 years

1914 **David Brian** -- American stage and motion-picture actor

1918 **Tom Drake** -- American motion-picture actor

1920 **George Tooker** -- American painter noted for works such as *Government Bureau* (1956)

1923 **Richard Kleindienst** -- Attorney general under President Nixon

1930 **Neil Armstrong** -- U.S. astronaut and first man to set foot on the moon (July 20, 1969)

1940 **Roman Gabriel** -- Professional football player and superstar

1943 **Nelson Briles** -- Professional baseball player and announcer

1945 **Loni Anderson** -- American television actress

1950 **Bob McKinley** -- American tennis player

1950 **Holly Palance** -- American actress

1952 **Freddie Scott** -- Professional football player

1953 **Rick Mahler** -- Professional baseball player

AUGUST 5 -- EVENTS

1498 Columbus landed on the Paria Peninsula in Venezuela on his third voyage, and wrote in his log, "I believe that this is a very great continent which until today has been unknown."

1858 The first transatlantic cable was completed, between Trinity Bay, Newfoundland, and Valencia, Ireland. It failed, however, after only four weeks of service.

1861 Congress abolished flogging in the U.S. Army.

1864   Union admiral David Farragut won the Battle of Mobile Bay in the Civil War, after giving the order, "Damn the torpedoes! Full speed ahead!"

1886   The Republic of Colombia was founded.

1912   The Progressive Party, formed by Theodore Roosevelt, met to select a presidential candidate for the 1912 campaign.

1924   The comic strip, *Little Orphan Annie,* by Harold Gray, first appeared.

1957   The comic strip, *Andy Capp,* by Reginald Smythe, first appeared.

1962   Marilyn Monroe, the glamorous American actress, died in her bedroom from acute barbiturate poisoning.

1974   President Nixon released the "smoking gun" tape, showing him guilty of the Watergate cover-up. On the June 23, 1972, tape he ordered the FBI "to stay the hell out of this."

AUGUST 6 -- BIRTHDAYS

1644   **Louise de la Valliere** -- Mistress of King Louis XIV of France

1651   **Francois de La Mothe-Fenelon** -- French writer and archbishop, whose best known work is the novel *Telemachus* (1699)

1697   **Charles VII** -- The first Holy Roman emperor (1742-1745) in 300 years who was not a member of the Hapsburg family

1809   **Alfred, Lord Tennyson** -- One of the most important English poets of the 1800s and one of the supreme craftsmen in the English language

1828   **Andrew Taylor Still** -- American physician and founder of osteopathy

1851   **John Robertson Reid** -- English painter

1868   **Paul Claudel** -- One of the foremost French poets and play-wrights of the 1900s

1876   **Miller Hutchinson** -- Inventor of the Dictograph and the Klaxon horn

1880   **Leo Carrillo** -- American motion-picture and television actor

1881   **Sir Alexander Fleming** -- British bacteriologist who discovered penicillin in 1929

1888   **Arthur Fields** -- American composer noted for songs such as "And the Angels Sing" and "Aba Daba Honeymoon"

1892	**Hoot Gibson** – American actor and "World's All-Around Champion Cowboy" in 1912
1893	**Louella Parsons** -- American Hollywood gossip columnist
1893	**Wright Patman** -- U.S. congressman
1896	**Ray Blades** -- Professional baseball player and manager
1900	**Nat Simon** -- American composer, author, and conductor, noted for songs such as "Poinciana," "No Can Do," and "The Old Lamplighter"
1900	**Dutch Schulz** – American gangster and Prohibition era bootlegger
1908	**Helen Hull Jacobs** -- One of the greatest women tennis players in history and winner of the U.S. singles title four years in a row (1932-1935)
1911	**Lucille Ball** -- American comedienne, actress, and star of television's long-running comedy, *I Love Lucy*
1917	**Robert Mitchum** -- American motion-picture actor and veteran of more than sixty films
1919	**Pauline Betz** -- American tennis player who dominated the game during the middle 1940s
1922	**Doug Ford** -- Professional golfer
1922	**Sir Frederick A. Laker** -- Owner and founder of Laker Airways
1930	**Abbey Lincoln** -- American jazz singer and motion-picture actress
1938	**Bert Yancey** -- Professional golfer
1953	**Janet Newberry** -- American tennis player
1955	**Ron Davis** -- Professional baseball player
1957	**Bob Horner** -- Professional baseball player

AUGUST 6 -- EVENTS

1338	The Diet of Frankfurt issued the decree *Licet Juris,* marking the beginning of the papacy's exclusion from Imperial affairs.
1497	John Cabot landed in Bristol on his return from his North American voyage.
1588	The Spanish Armada anchored at Calais after an inconclusive six-day battle with the English. It remained there for two days before being attacked again by the English.
1623	Anne Hathaway, wife of William Shakespeare, died at age 67.

1637   Ben Jonson, English dramatist and poet, died in London at age 65.

1660   Diego Velazquez, the great Spanish painter, died in Madrid at age 61.

1806   The Holy Roman Empire came to an end, precipitated by the armies of Napoleon.

1825   Bolivia became independent of Spain and Peru.

1890   Cy Young, baseball's winningest pitcher, appeared in his first major league game.

1890   New York became the first state to electrocute a criminal, as William Kemmler was electrocuted for murder in Auburn, New York.

1926   Gertrude Ederle, a 20-year-old New Yorker, became the first woman to swim the English Channel.

1926   The first talking pictures were shown, at the Warner Theater in New York City.

1926   Harry Houdini, the great American escape artist, remained under water for 91 minutes in an airtight case and survived.

1940   Estonia was annexed as one of the republics of the Soviet Union.

1945   The first atomic bomb was dropped, on Hiroshima, Japan, by the *Enola Gay,* a high-flying U.S. B-29 bomber.

1945   Jamaica became independent of Great Britain.

1973   Vice President Spiro Agnew acknowledged he was being investigated for law violations. As a result he later became the second vice president to resign the office.

1978   Pope Paul VI died in the 15th year of his reign.

AUGUST 7 -- BIRTHDAYS

317 AD **Flavius Julius Constantius** -- Roman emperor, A.D. 337-361

1742   **Nathanael Greene** -- American Revolutionary War general, ranked second only to Washington as a military leader

1779   **Karl Ritter** -- German geographer and co-founder of modern geographical science

1783   **John Heathcoat** -- English inventor who developed a machine for making a kind of lace known as bobbinet

1867   **Emil Nolde** -- German impressionist painter noted for works such as *Harvest Day* (1904) and *The Life of Christ* (1912)

1876 **Mata Hari** -- French dancer who was executed as a Germany spy during World War I, and whose name has become a synonym for the seductive female spy

1881 **Francois Darlan** -- French World War II admiral

1885 **Billie Burke** -- American stage, screen, and television actress, with a 60-year career

1886 **Bill McKechnie** -- Professional baseball player and manager

1893 **C. Luckeyth "Luckey" Roberts** -- American composer, conductor, and pianist, noted for songs such as "Moonlight Cocktail"

1901 **Ann Harding** -- American stage and motion-picture actress, who was a leading lady in the 1930s and a veteran character actor in the 1940s and 1950s

1903 **Louis S.B. Leakey** -- English anthropologist and paleontologist, who discovered fossil remains in Africa of *Homo erectus* and others, ranging in age up to 1,750,000 years

1904 **Ralph Bunche** -- American United Nations diplomat

1910 **Freddie Slack** -- American composer, author, and bandleader, noted for songs such as "Cow Cow Boogie," "Beat Me Daddy Eight to the Bar," and "O Sole Mio"

1926 **Stan Freberg** -- American composer, author, and comedian

1927 **Edwin Edwards** -- Governor of Louisiana in the 1970s and 1980s

1929 **Don Larsen** -- Professional baseball pitcher who pitched a perfect game (no one reached base) in the 1956 World Series for the New York Yankees against the Brooklyn Dodgers

1942 **Garrison Keillor** -- American humorist noted for the long-running radio program *A Prairie Home Companion*

1944 **Lana Cantrell** -- Australian-born singer

1947 **Kerry Melville Reid** -- Australian tennis player

1950 **David James Wottle** -- American mile runner

1951 **Gary Hall** -- American swimmer who set the world record 400-meter individual medley of 4 minutes 31 seconds in 1970

1954 **Steve Kemp** -- Professional baseball player

AUGUST 7 -- EVENTS

1782 The Badge of Military Merit, which in 1932 became the Purple Heart, was established by George Washington.

1789   Congress created the United States War Department.

1882   The famous Hatfield-McCoy feud in West Virginia and eastern
          Kentucky broke out, leading eventually to 100 men, women, and
          children killed or wounded.

1912   The Progressive Party nominated Theodore Roosevelt for
          president, leading to a three-way race with Woodrow Wilson
          and incumbent president William Howard Taft.

1928   The comic strip, *Alley Oop,* by V.T. Hamlin, made its first
          appearance.

1928   New American dollars were issued in a size one-third smaller
          than the previous bills.

1942   U.S. troops landed on Guadalcanal in the Solomon Islands in
          World War II.

1947   Thor Heyerdahl, on the raft *Kon-Tiki,* landed in Tuamotu Archi-
          pelago in Polynesia, having drifted 4,000 miles from Peru in
          15 weeks.

1954   Dr. Roger Bannister defeated John Landy, as both ran the mile
          in less than four minutes. Bannister's time was 3 minutes 58.8
          seconds and Landy's was 3 minutes 59.6 seconds.

1964   The Gulf of Tonkin resolution was passed by Congress, giving
          the president powers to repel attacks on U.S. armed forces.

1971   *Apollo 15* splashed down in the Pacific Ocean after exploring the
          moon's surface.

AUGUST 8 -- BIRTHDAYS

1646   **Sir Godfrey Kneller** -- Anglo-German portrait painter

1763   **Charles Bulfinch** – The greatest architect in New England history

1799   **Nathaniel Brown Palmer** -- American sea captain believed to be
          the first explorer to sight Antarctica in 1820

1819   **Charles A. Dana** -- American editor who built the New York *Sun*
          into one of the most important newspapers of its time

1866   **Matthew Henson** – Only black member of Admiral Robert E.
          Peary's North Pole expedition

1879   **Emiliano Zapata** -- Mexican Indian leader of the Mexican
          Revolution in 1910

1879   **Dr. Bob (Robert Holbrook Smith)** – Co-founder with Bill W. of
          Alcoholics Anonymous in 1935

1884 **Sara Teasdale** -- American poet and author of "Flame and Shadow" (1920)

1896 **Marjorie Kinnan Rawlings** -- American novelist and author of *The Yearling* (1939)

1900 **Victor Young** -- American composer, conductor, and violinist, noted for songs such as "Sweet Sue," "Stella by Starlight," "I Don't Stand a Ghost of a Chance With You," and "Golden Earrings"

1901 **Ernest Orlando Lawrence** -- American Nobel Prize-winning atomic physicist, who helped develop the cyclotron

1902 **Paul A.M. Dirac** -- British Nobel Prize-winning physicist noted for his prediction of the existence of the positive electron, or positron

1908 **Arthur Goldberg** -- U.S. Supreme Court justice and U.N. ambassador under President Lyndon Johnson

1910 **Sylvia Sidney** -- American stage and motion-picture actress and one of the most popular leading ladies of the 1930s

1913 **Robert Stafford** -- U.S. senator

1913 **Axel Stordahl** -- American composer, conductor and arranger of the Big Band Era

1922 **Rudi Gernreich** – American fashion designer, noted for women's topless bathing suits and miniskirts

1923 **Rory Calhoun** -- American motion-picture and television actor

1923 **Esther Williams** -- American swimming star and motion-picture actress

1926 **Richard Anderson** -- American motion-picture and television actor

1926 **Webb Pierce** -- American country singer

1927 **Andy Warhol** -- American filmmaker and pop artist

1930 **Joan Adams Mondale** -- Wife of Vice President Walter Mondale

1932 **Mel Tillis** -- American country singer and songwriter

1936 **Frank Howard** -- Professional baseball player and manager

1937 **Dustin Hoffman** -- American motion-picture actor who won Academy Awards for best actor in *Kramer vs. Kramer* (1979) and *Rainman* (1989)

1938 **Connie Stevens** -- American singer and actress

1938 **Vada Pinson** -- Professional baseball player

1942   **Tory Ann Fretz** -- American tennis player
1947   **Jose Cruz** -- Professional baseball player
1949   **Brian Sipe** -- Professional football player

AUGUST 8 -- EVENTS

117 AD   Roman emperor Trajan died at Selinus at age 63.

1588   The English sent 8 burning ships into Calais harbor, driving the
         Spanish Armada out to sea, where it was badly defeated, with
         only 67 of its original 130 ships returning to Spain.

1815   Napoleon Bonaparte set sail for St. Helena to spend the rest of
         his days in exile.

1844   Brigham Young was chosen to lead the Mormon Church, follow-
         ing the murder of Joseph Smith.

1900   The first Davis Cup Tennis Tournament began, in Massachusetts.

1911   The membership of the House of Representatives was fixed
         at 435.

1918   The British broke the German line at Amiens in World War I.

1936   Jesse Owens won his fourth gold medal in the Berlin Olympics
         as the U.S. took first place in the 400-meter relay.

1940   In a move to increase India's contribution to the war effort,
         Britain promised a new constitution and partnership with India
         after World War II.

1945   Russia declared war on Japan in World War II, and invaded
         Manchuria.

1950   Florence Chadwick swam the English Channel in 13 hours, 28
         minutes, a new record for women.

1973   Vice President Spiro Agnew called reports that he had taken
         kickbacks from government contracts "damned lies." He was
         later forced to resign because they did not seem to be.

1974   President Nixon announced that he would resign at noon on the
         following day.

AUGUST 9 -- BIRTHDAYS

1593   **Izaak Walton** -- English author and critic, known for his classic
         on fishing, *The Compleat Angler* (1653)

1757 **Thomas Telford** -- Scottish civil engineer, noted for the Telford road construction method of using large flat stones for road foundations

1776 **Amedeo Avogadro** -- Italian physicist known for Avogadro's law of gases, and for the table of atomic weights

1819 **William Thomas Green Morton** -- American dentist, who introduced ether as an anesthetic for painless dentistry

1832 **Nathaniel Pitt Langford** -- Co-discoverer of the geysers at Yellowstone Park

1839 **Gaston Paris** -- The greatest French philologist of his time

1880 **Ramon Perez de Ayala** -- One of the greatest Spanish novelists of the 20th century

1901 **Charles Farrell** -- American silent film, talkies, and television actor

1905 **Zino Francescatti** -- French violinist noted for his concert performances in Europe and America

1905 **Leo Genn** -- English stage and screen actor

1913 **Herman Talmadge** -- Governor of Georgia, U.S. senator, and son of Georgia governor Eugene Talmadge

1919 **Ralph Houk** -- Professional baseball player and manager with a career spanning over 40 years

1927 **Robert Shaw** -- English stage and motion-picture actor and novelist

1928 **Bob Cousy** -- One of the greatest all-around players in professional basketball history, who led the Boston Celtics to 6 world championships

1931 **Hurricane Jackson** -- American professional boxer

1938 **Rod Laver** -- One of the greatest tennis players of all time, and the first to win the Grand Slam twice

1939 **Claude Osteen** -- Professional baseball player

1942 **Tommie Agee** -- Professional baseball player

1942 **David Steinberg** -- American comedian, actor, and writer

1945 **Ken Norton** -- American boxer

1946 **Jim Kiick** -- Professional football player

1949 **Ted Simmons** -- Professional baseball player

1952 **John Cappelletti** -- Professional football player

1954 **Henry Marshall** -- Professional football player

1955 **Doug Williams** -- Professional football player

1957   **Melanie Griffith** -- American motion-picture actress and daughter of actress Tippi Hedren

AUGUST 9 -- EVENTS

48 BC   Julius Caesar defeated Pompey in the Battle of Pharsalus, in Greece, but Pompey escaped to Egypt, where he was later murdered.

117 AD   Hadrian succeeded Trajan as Emperor of Rome.

1638   Jonas Bronck became the first European settler in what is now the Bronx, New York, which was named for his family, the Broncks.

1842   The Webster-Ashburton Treaty was signed in Washington, D.C., fixing the boundary between Canada and Maine, and settling other minor disputes.

1854   Henry David Thoreau published *Walden,* one of the world's great books.

1901   The coronation of Edward VII as King of England took place in London. Edward had become king following the death of his mother, Queen Victoria, in January.

1921   Franklin D. Roosevelt was stricken with polio on Campobello Island, off New Brunswick, Canada.

1937   Japanese troops captured Nanking, the capital of China, in the Sino-Japanese War.

1945   The American bomber *Bock's Car* dropped the second atomic bomb used in warfare, on Nagasaki, Japan.

1965   Singapore became independent of the Malaysian Federation.

1969   Actress Sharon Tate and four others were found brutally murdered in Bel Air, California. Charles Manson and others of the "Manson family" were later convicted of the crime.

1974   Richard M. Nixon became the first president in history to resign. He was succeeded by Vice President Gerald Ford.

AUGUST 10 -- BIRTHDAYS

1729   **William Howe** -- British general who ordered the hanging of Nathan Hale in the American Revolutionary War

1753	**Edmund Randolph** -- General George Washington's aide-de-camp during the Revolutionary War and one of the framers of the U.S. Constitution
1798	**Minard Lafever** -- American architect
1848	**William Harnett** -- The leading American still-life painter of the late 1800s
1865	**Alexander Konstantinovich Glazunov** -- Russian composer
1874	**Herbert Hoover** -- 31st U.S. president
1895	**Harry Richman** -- American composer, author, and singer, noted for songs such as "Walking My Baby Back Home" and "Cherie"
1897	**Larry Shay** -- American composer and conductor, noted for songs such as "When You're Smiling (The Whole World Smiles With You)," "Everywhere You Go," and "Highways Are Happy Ways"
1897	**Reuben Nakian** -- American sculptor
1900	**Norma Shearer** -- "First Lady of Hollywood" in the 1920s and 1930s
1908	**Claude Thornhill** – American composer, pianist, and bandleader of the Big Band Era
1914	**Jeff Corey** -- American motion-picture and television actor
1915	**Noah Beery Jr.** -- American motion-picture and television actor
1923	**Rhonda Fleming** -- American motion-picture actress
1924	**Martha Hyer** -- American motion-picture actress
1928	**Jimmy Dean** -- American singer and actor
1928	**Eddie Fisher** -- American singer
1933	**Rocky Colavito** -- Professional baseball player
1942	**Heide Orth** -- West German tennis player
1942	**Betsey Johnson** -- American fashion designer
1947	**Ian Anderson** -- Scottish singer, flutist, and songwriter for the Jethro Tull musical group
1956	**Rosanna Arquette** -- American motion-picture actress
1956	**Dianne Fromholtz** -- Australian tennis player
1956	**Gerald Small** -- Professional football player
1962	**Jon Farriss** – Australian drummer with the INXS musical group

AUGUST 10 -- EVENTS

1471   Sixtus IV was elected Roman Catholic pope.

1776   A committee of Benjamin Franklin, John Adams, and Thomas Jefferson suggested *E Pluribus Unum* as the motto for the Great Seal of the United States.

1790   The *Columbia,* under the command of Robert Gray, completed the first voyage around the world by a ship flying the U.S. flag.

1792   Paris rioters stormed the Tuileries, where King Louis XVI was under house arrest, and killed the king's famous Swiss Guard.

1821   Missouri was admitted to the Union as the 24th state.

1833   Chicago, with a population of 200, was incorporated as a town.

1846   Congress established the Smithsonian Institution, naming it for James Smithson, who bequeathed his fortune for its establishment.

1943   The Quebec Conference in World War II between President Roosevelt and Prime Minister Churchill began in the Citadel in Quebec.

1945   Japan offered to surrender in World War II if their emperor could keep his throne.

AUGUST 11 -- BIRTHDAYS

1657   **Pierre Etienne Monnot** -- French sculptor

1743   **David Roentgen** -- German cabinetmaker

1778   **Friedrich Ludwig Jahn** – German teacher who invented gymnastics

1819   **Martin Johnson Heade** -- American painter

1833   **Robert G. Ingersoll** -- American politician, lawyer, and writer, noted for his oratory and agnosticism

1837   **Sadi Carnot** -- French engineer noted for the Carnot cycle theory of heat engines

1862   **Carrie Jacobs Bond** -- American songwriter, noted for "I Love You Truly" (1906) and "A Perfect Day" (1910)

1865   **Gifford Pinchot** -- American statesman and pioneer of U.S. forestry and conservation

1867   **Hobart Bosworth** – American stage and motion-picture actor with a career of nearly 70 years

1902   **Lloyd Nolan** -- American stage, screen, and television actor with a career of over 50 years

1907   **Bobo Newsom** -- Professional baseball player

1912   **Jean Parker** -- Leading lady of the 1930s and 1940s Hollywood films

1914   **Hugh Martin** -- American composer, author, and singer, noted for songs such as "Buckle Down Winsocki," "The Trolley Song," "Have Yourself a Merry Little Christmas," and "Pass the Peace Pipe"

1918   **Dik Browne** -- American cartoonist and creator of *Hagar the Horrible,* one of the most popular comic strips of the 1980s

1921   **Alex Haley** -- American writer and author of *Roots*

1924   **Arlene Dahl** -- American stage and motion-picture actress

1925   **Mike Douglas** -- American television talk show host

1925   **Carl Thomas Rowan** -- American newspaper columnist

1926   **Claus von Bulow** -- Danish-born businessman who was acquitted in two sensational trials of attempted murder of his wife, heiress Sunny von Bulow

1933   **Jerry Falwell** -- American television clergyman

1941   **William Munson** -- Professional football player

1941   **Elizabeth Holtzman** -- American congresswoman and state attorney general

1942   **Otis Taylor Jr.** -- Professional football player

1944   **Clem Haskins** -- Professional basketball player

AUGUST 11 -- EVENTS

1492   Rodrigo Borgia, the head of the notorious Borgia family of Italy, was elected Roman Catholic pope, and crowned as Alexander VI.

1596   Hamnet, son of William Shakespeare and Anne Hathaway, died at age 11.

1834   The minstrel song, "Old Zip Coon," was introduced at the Bowery Theater in New York City.

1862   Sarah Bernhardt, the great French actress, made her debut at the Comedie-Francaise in Jean Racine's play, *Iphigenie.*

1902   Oliver Wendell Holmes was appointed associate justice of the U.S. Supreme Court by President Theodore Roosevelt.

1909   The first radio SOS in history was sent when the liner *Arapahoe* asked for help off Cape Hatteras, North Carolina.

1919   The Weimar Constitution was adopted at Weimar, creating a republican Germany.

1924   A newsreel motion-picture short was made of the presidential candidates for the first time in history. They were Calvin Coolidge, John W. Davis, and Robert La Follette.

1945   The Allies agreed for Emperor Hirohito to keep his throne in return for the surrender of Japan in World War II.

1952   Hussein I became King of Jordan.

1954   A formal peace announcement ended the Indo-China War between the victorious Vietminh and the French.

1956   Jackson Pollock, the great American artist, was killed in an automobile accident on Long Island, New York, at age 44.

1964   Pope Paul VI became the first Roman Catholic pope to ride in a helicopter.

1984   Carl Lewis, American runner, won his 4th gold medal in the Olympic Games in Los Angeles. The 4 events he won were the same ones won by Jesse Owens in the Olympics of 1936.

AUGUST 12 -- BIRTHDAYS

1753   **Thomas Bewick** -- English printmaker

1762   **George IV** -- King of England, 1820-1830

1774   **Robert Southey** -- English poet laureate during the time of Keats, Shelley, and Byron, and who popularized the fairy tale, "The Three Bears"

1781   **Robert Mills** — Early American architect and engineer, noted for his design of the Washington Monument

1849   **Abbott Thayer** -- American painter

1856   **Diamond Jim Brady** — Famous American gambler and gourmet

1862   **Julius Rosenwald** -- American philanthropist, who was president of Sears, Roebuck and Company, 1909-1924, and who gave over $63 million to worthy causes

1876   **Mary Roberts Rinehart** -- American novelist and playwright, noted for works such as *The Circular Staircase* (1908)

1880   **Christy Mathewson** -- One of the first five players chosen for the Baseball Hall of Fame, and winner of 373 career games as a pitcher

1881   **Cecil B. De Mille** -- American giant of the motion-picture industry, noted for directing over 200 films in a 60-year career, a notable example of which is *The Ten Commandments* (1923 and 1956)

1882   **George Wesley Bellows** -- A leading American artist of the early 1900s

1887 **Erwin Schrodinger** -- Austrian physicist noted for contributions to quantum mechanics, such as Schrodinger's equation

1892 **Ray Schalk** -- Hall of Fame baseball player

1897 **Charles O'Flynn** -- American lyricist noted for songs such as "Smile, Darn Ya, Smile"

1898 **Oscar Homolka** -- Austrian stage and motion-picture actor

1904 **Frank Ervin** -- Professional harness racer

1911 **Jane Wyatt** -- American stage, screen, and television actress

1911 **Cantinflas (Mario Moreno Reyes)** – Mexican actor and comedian with a 40-year career

1918 **Roy C. Bennett** -- American composer noted for songs such as "Red Roses for a Blue Lady" and "Naughty Lady of Shady Lane"

1919 **Fred Hutchinson** -- Professional baseball player and manager

1921 **Marjorie Reynolds** -- American motion-picture actress

1925 **Dale Bumpers** -- Governor of Arkansas and U.S. senator

1926 **John Derek** -- American motion-picture actor and director

1927 **Porter Wagoner** -- American country music singer

1929 **Buck Owens** -- American guitarist and television actor

1933 **Parnelli Jones** -- American automobile racing driver

1936 **John Poindexter** -- American admiral and National Security Adviser under President Reagan who claimed to act for the president without his knowledge in the Iran-Contra scandal of 1987

1939 **George Hamilton** -- American motion-picture actor

1946 **Robert Maud** -- South African tennis player

1949 **Mark Knopfler** -- British guitarist with the Dire Straits musical group

1950 **George McGinnis** -- Professional basketball player

AUGUST 12 -- EVENTS

1492 Christopher Columbus reached San Sebastian in the Canary Islands on his first voyage to America. He stayed there until September 6 before resuming his voyage.

1588 The English turned away, allowing the stricken Spanish Armada to sail north and eventually west around the British Isles back to Spain.

1658 The first police force in America was organized by the Dutch in New Amsterdam.

1676 King Philip, chief of the Wampanoag Indians, was killed by English colonists near Mt. Hope, R.I., ending King Philip's War, the most destructive Indian war in New England history.

1827   William Blake, the English poet, died in London at age 69.

1851   American inventor Isaac Singer put his sewing machine into production and organized his company.

1877   Thomas A. Edison, the great American inventor, invented the phonograph, one of the most original of all the world's inventions.

1898   The United States annexed the Hawaiian Islands.

1898   The U.S. and Spain signed an armistice, ending the Spanish-American War.

1937   Edith Wharton, the noted American novelist, died at St. Brice-sous-Foret, France, at age 75.

1941   President Franklin D. Roosevelt and Prime Minister Winston Churchill signed the Atlantic Charter on a cruiser off the coast of Newfoundland. It was made public two days later.

1953   The Russians exploded their first hydrogen bomb.

1955   Thomas Mann, the German writer, died in Zurich at age 80.

AUGUST 13 -- BIRTHDAYS

1422   **William Caxton** -- English merchant who introduced printing into England with *The Dictes or Sayings of the Philosophers* (1477), the first book printed in England

1655   **Johann Christoph Denner** -- German oboe maker

1757   **James Gillray** -- English illustrator

1814   **Anders Jonas Angstrom** -- Swedish physicist for whom the Angstrom unit of wave length was named

1818   **Lucy Stone** -- American pioneer in the women's rights movement, and perhaps the first married woman to keep her maiden name

1819   **Sir George Gabriel Stokes** -- Noted English physicist and mathematician

1820   **Sir George Grove** – English writer of music and Bible dictionaries

1851   **Felix Adler** -- American educator, reformer, and founder of the first free kindergarten in New York City

1860   **Annie Oakley** -- American markswoman who starred in Buffalo Bill's Wild West Show for 17 years

1867   **George Luks** – American painter and illustrator and one of the original members of the group of realistic painters called the Eight

1895   **Bert Lahr** – American stage and motion-picture actor and comedian, who played the Cowardly Lion in *The Wizard of Oz*

1898   **Jean Borotra** – One of France's famous Four Musketeers of tennis, who dominated the game in the late 1920s and early 1930s

1899   **Alfred Hitchcock** – English-American motion-picture director and master of suspense, noted for such films as *The Man Who Knew Too Much* (1934), *Psycho* (1960), and *The Birds* (1963)

1902   **Felix Wankel** -- Inventor of the Wankel engine

1904   **Buddy Rogers** -- American motion-picture actor

1908   **Gene Raymond** -- American motion-picture and television actor and leading man of the 1930s

1909   **John Beal** – American motion-picture actor with a 40-year career

1910   **Lou Finney** -- Professional baseball player

1912   **Salvador Luria** – Nobel Prize-winning Italian-American biologist

1912   **Ben Hogan** -- One of the all-time great golfers, who won the U.S. Open four times and the Masters Tournament twice

1913   **Archbishop Makarios** -- Religious and political leader of Cyprus, and its first president after gaining independence from Great Britain

1917   **Sid Gordon** -- Professional baseball player

1919   **George Shearing** -- Blind English pianist

1919   **Rex Humbard** -- American evangelist

1921   **Neville Brand** -- American motion-picture and television actor

1926   **Fidel Castro** -- Guerrilla leader and premier of Cuba after the overthrow of the Batista regime in 1959

1929   **Pat Harrington Jr.** -- American motion-picture and television actor noted for his role in the long-running series *One Day at a Time*

1930   **Don Ho** -- American singer

1935   **Mudcat Grant** -- Professional baseball player

1949   **Andre Thornton** -- Professional baseball player

1949   **Bobby Clarke** -- Professional hockey player

AUGUST 13 -- EVENTS

523 AD John I was elected Roman Catholic pope.

1099   Paschal II was elected Roman Catholic pope.

1521   Hernando Cortes, the Spanish conquistador, completed his conquest of Mexico with the surrender of Tenochtitlan (the present site of Mexico City) by Aztec ruler Montezuma.

1624   French King Louis XIII named Cardinal Richelieu his first minister.

1704   England's Duke of Marlborough routed the French, destroying their reputation for invincibility, in the Battle of Blenheim, one of the most decisive battles in European history.

1792   French revolutionaries imprisoned King Louis XVI and his family.

1863   Eugene Delacroix, the great French painter, died in Paris at age 65.

1923   Mustafa Kemal Ataturk was elected the first president of the new Republic of Turkey.

1928   The comic strip, *Tim Tyler's Luck,* by Lyman Young, first appeared.

1930   Frank Hawks, an American flier, set a new speed record by flying from Los Angeles to New York City in 12 hours, 25 minutes.

1946   H.G. Wells, the great English writer, died in London at age 79.

1960   The first two-way telephone conversation by satellite took place, using the first passive communications satellite, *Echo 1.*

1961   East German police started building the Berlin Wall, sealing off the East-West boundary of the two Germanys.

AUGUST 14 -- BIRTHDAYS

1714   **Joseph Vernet** -- French landscape and marine artist

1734   **Thomas Sumter** -- American Revolutionary War officer, nick-named the "Gamecock"

1734   **Pius VII** -- Roman Catholic pope, 1800-1823

1777   **Hans Christian Oersted** -- Danish physicist who discovered electromagnetism

1810   **Samuel Sebastian Wesley** — English composer, organist, and son of noted composer Samuel Wesley

1860   **Ernest Thompson Seton** -- English-American naturalist, popular writer and illustrator, and an active participant in founding the Boy Scouts of America

1867   **John Galsworthy** -- English novelist and playwright, noted for *The Forsythe Saga* (1906-1921)

1880   **Fred Alexander** -- American Hall of Fame tennis player, who, with Harold Hackett, formed one of the most famous doubles teams of the early 1900s

1903   **John Ringling North** -- American circus showman

1913   **Paul "Daffy" Dean** -- Professional baseball pitcher who with his famous brother Dizzy won over 50 games in 1934 to spark the St. Louis Cardinals "Gas House Gang" to the world championship

1919   **Ted Kroll** -- Professional golfer

1925   **Russell Baker** -- American newspaper columnist

1926   **Buddy Greco** -- American singer

1930   **Earl Weaver** -- Highly successful professional baseball manager and sportscaster

1935	**John Brodie** – Professional football superstar and sportscaster
1940	**Arthur Laffer** -- U.S. economist and supply-side theoretician
1941	**David Crosby** -- American singer and guitarist with the Crosby, Stills, Nash, and Young musical group
1944	**Robyn Smith** -- First female jockey at a major track
1946	**Susan St. James** – American motion-picture and television actress
1948	**Steve Martin** -- American motion-picture and television actor and comedian
1952	**Debbie Meyer** -- American freestyle swimmer and 1968 Olympic champion
1959	**Magic Johnson** -- Professional basketball player

AUGUST 14 -- EVENTS

1040	Duncan, King of Scots, was murdered by Macbeth, who became king.
1281	A Mongol armada with 150,000 men was destroyed by a typhoon, which ended 53 days of fighting with the Japanese.
1457	The *Mainz Psalter* was published, the first book printed in Europe to bear the name of its printers--Johann Fust and Peter Schoffer. (It was due, however, to Johannes Gutenberg.)
1756	American frontiersman Daniel Boone, at age 21, married 16-year-old Rebecca Bryan. Their marriage lasted 56 years and produced ten children.
1900	U.S. marines captured Peking, China, ending the Boxer Rebellion.
1917	China declared war on Germany and Austria in World War I.
1923	The comic strip, *Felix the Cat,* by Pat Sullivan, first appeared.
1935	The U.S. Social Security Act was passed by Congress.
1945	V-J Day finally arrived, as Japan accepted the Allies' World War II surrender terms, ending the greatest war in the history of the world.
1947	Pakistan became independent of India.
1973	The United States ended the bombing of Cambodia, officially terminating its involvement in Indochina.

AUGUST 15 -- BIRTHDAYS

| 1702 | **Francesco Zuccarelli** -- Italian painter |
| 1769 | **Napoleon Bonaparte** -- Emperor of the French, 1804-1815, the greatest military genius of his time, and one of the most celebrated personages in the history of the West |

1771   **Sir Walter Scott** -- Scottish romantic writer and author of *Ivan-hoe* (1819) and *The Lady of the Lake* (1810)

1785   **Thomas De Quincey** -- English essayist, noted for *Confessions of an English Opium-Eater* (1821)

1810   **Louise Colet** -- French poet and novelist

1845   **Walter Crane** -- English illustrator noted for works such as *Beauty and the Beast* (1874)

1859   **Charles A. Comiskey** -- Professional baseball player and early owner of the Chicago White Sox

1860   **Florence Kling DeWolfe Harding** -- Wife of President Warren G. Harding

1875   **Samuel Coleridge-Taylor** -- English composer

1879   **Ethel Barrymore** -- "First Lady" of the American theater, and member of the famous Barrymore family of actors

1881   **Ted Snyder** -- American composer and pianist, noted for songs such as "The Sheik of Araby" and "Who's Sorry Now?"

1885   **Edna Ferber** -- American novelist and playwright, noted for such works as *Cimarron, Show Boat,* and *Giant*

1888   **Albert Spalding** -- One of the leading American violinists of his day

1888   **Lawrence of Arabia** -- English soldier and writer, born Thomas Edward Lawrence, and one of the most adventurous personalities of World War I

1890   **Jacques Ibert** -- French composer noted for the orchestral suite, *Escales,* or *Ports of Call* (1922)

1892   **Sidney Clare** -- American composer noted for songs such as "Ma, He's Making Eyes at Me," "On the Good Ship Lollipop," and "Polly Wolly Doodle"

1894   **Harry Akst** -- American composer noted for songs such as "Baby Face" and "Guilty"

1898   **Lillian Carter** -- Mother of President Jimmy Carter

1898   **Charles Tobias** -- American composer noted for songs such as "Rose O'Day," "The Old Lamplighter," "No Can Do," "As Long As I Live," and "Get Out and Get Under the Moon"

1901   **Ned Washington** -- American lyricist noted for songs such as "I'm Getting Sentimental Over You," "La Cucaracha," "When You Wish Upon a Star," "High Noon," and "The Nearness of You"

1903   **Joseph C. Garland** -- American composer noted for songs such as "In the Mood"

1904   **Bil Baird** -- American puppeteer

1909 **Johnny Lange** -- American composer and author, noted for songs such as "Mule Train" and "Someone's in the Kitchen With Dinah"

1912 **Wendy Hiller** -- English stage, screen, and television actress, with a career of over 50 years

1912 **Julia Child** -- American cooking expert and television performer

1915 **Signe Hasso** -- Swedish stage, screen, and television actress

1924 **Phyllis Schlafly** -- American writer and political activist

1924 **Robert Bolt** -- English playwright

1925 **Oscar Peterson** -- Canadian jazz pianist and singer

1925 **Mike Connors** -- American television actor

1930 **Tom Mboya** -- Major political figure in Kenya's early days of independence

1933 **Lori Nelson** -- American motion-picture actress

1935 **Vernon Jordan** -- American civil rights leader and president of the National Urban League

1935 **Jim Dale** -- English stage and screen actor and composer, noted for the lyrics to "Georgy Girl"

1946 **Jim Webb** -- American contemporary music composer

1950 **Princess Anne** -- Daughter of Queen Elizabeth II of England

1950 **Samuel Cunningham Jr.** -- Professional football player

1958 **Joe Cowley** -- Professional baseball player

1959 **Pete Burns** -- British rock singer with the Dead or Alive musical group

AUGUST 15 -- EVENTS

1057 Macbeth, King of Scots, was killed by Malcolm Canmore, son of ex-king Duncan, while fleeing from the Battle of Dunsinane.

1237 Berlin was founded by fishermen and traders.

1534 Ignatius of Loyola founded the Jesuits (Society of Jesus) in Paris.

1812 Indian allies of the British massacred the soldiers and settlers of Fort Dearborn, near the present site of Chicago.

1914 The Panama Canal officially opened, as the SS *Ancon* went through.

1918 The United States and Russia broke diplomatic relations.

1920 The comic strip, *Peter Rabbit,* adapted by Harrison Cady, first appeared.

1935 Humorist Will Rogers and aviator Wiley Post were killed in a plane crash near Point Barrow, Alaska.

1944   U.S. and British troops invaded southern France in World War II, landing near Toulon.
1947   India became independent of Great Britain.
1948   The independent Republic of Korea was proclaimed with Seoul as its capital.
1960   The Congo became independent of Belgium.
1969   The Woodstock rock-music festival was staged near Bethel, New York, with some 500,000 fans attending.

AUGUST 16 -- BIRTHDAYS

1557   **Agostino Carracci** -- Italian painter
1645   **Jean de La Bruyere** -- French satirist noted for ridiculing the injustice and hypocrisy he saw in French life
1795   **Heinrich August Marschner** -- German composer
1798   **Mirabeau Buonaparte Lamar** -- Texan independence fighter and second president of the Texas Republic, 1838-1841
1831   **Henry Timken** -- Pioneer developer of differential gearing in the United States
1860   **Jules Laforgue** -- French writer
1861   **Edith Carow Roosevelt** -- Second wife of President Theodore Roosevelt
1861   **Arthur Cayley** -- English mathematician
1862   **Amos Alonzo Stagg** -- U.S. college football coach who had a 71-year career
1868   **Bernarr Macfadden** -- American physical culturist who founded *Physical Culture* and *True Story* magazines and once opened a New York restaurant at which most items sold for one cent
1877   **Karl Hoschna** -- Bohemian-American composer and oboist, noted for songs such as "Cuddle Up a Little Closer, Lovey Mine" and "Girl of My Dreams"
1884   **George Whiting** -- American singer and lyricist, noted for songs such as "My Blue Heaven" and "Strolling Through the Park One Day"
1888   **Armand John Piron** -- American composer and author, noted for songs such as "Day by Day" and "I Wish I Could Shimmy Like My Sister Kate"
1892   **Harold Foster** – American cartoonist and creator of *Prince Valiant*
1894   **George Meany** -- President of the AFL-CIO, 1955-1979
1898   **Jerome Irving Rodale** -- American author and publisher who founded *Prevention* magazine in 1950

1899   **Glenn Strange** -- American actor who played Frankenstein's monster in several films and the bartender Sam in the long-running television series *Gunsmoke*

1907   **Mae Clarke** -- Early motion-picture leading lady, noted as the recipient of the grapefruit in her face from James Cagney in *The Public Enemy* (1931)

1910   **Glenn J. Spencer** -- American composer, author, and conductor, noted for such works as the TV theme of *Gunsmoke*

1913   **Menachem Begin** -- Israeli prime minister in the late 1970s and early 1980s

1913   **Osie Penman Hawkins Jr.** -- American operatic baritone

1914   **Joseph J. Lilley** -- American composer, author, and director, noted for songs such as "Jingle Jangle Jingle"

1922   **Gene Woodling** -- Professional baseball player

1922   **William Alfred** -- American playwright and educator

1926   **Fess Parker** -- American motion-picture and television actor

1927   **Neil Edward Strawser** -- American broadcast journalist

1928   **Ann Blyth** -- American motion-picture actress

1930   **Tony Trabert** -- American Hall of Fame tennis player and sportscaster

1930   **Robert Culp** -- American motion-picture and television actor

1930   **Frank Gifford** – Professional football superstar and sportscaster

1932   **Eydie Gorme** -- American singer

1932   **Betsy von Furstenberg** -- German-born stage and motion-picture actress

1933   **Stuart A. Roosa** -- American astronaut and participant in the *Apollo 14* moon exploration mission

1935   **Julie Newmar** -- American stage, screen, and television actress

1945   **Joaquin Loro-Mayo** -- Mexican tennis player

1946   **Marie Pinterova** -- Czechoslovakian tennis player

1946   **Lesley Warren** – American motion-picture and television actress

1958   **Jose Luis Clerc** -- Argentine tennis player

1958   **Tim Farriss** – Australian guitarist with the INXS musical group

1958   **Madonna** -- American rock singer

1960   **Timothy Hutton** -- American motion-picture actor

AUGUST 16 -- EVENTS

1513   King Henry VIII of England defeated the French in the Battle of the Spurs at Guinegate.

1777   The Americans defeated the British in the Battle of Bennington in the Revolutionary War. The British had 900 casualties as compared to the Americans' 80.

1780   General Cornwallis almost completely destroyed the American army of General Gates in the Battle of Camden in the Revolutionary War.

1812   British and Indian forces captured Detroit in the War of 1812.

1858   "England and America are united by telegraphy. Glory to God in the highest" was the first transatlantic message, sent by Queen Victoria to President Buchanan over Cyrus Field's cable.

1903   Lt. General Samuel B.M. Young became the first U.S. Army chief of staff.

1923   Carnegie Steel Corporation established the eight-hour work day for its employees.

1948   Babe Ruth, perhaps baseball's greatest player, died in New York at age 53.

1962   The Beatles fired their drummer, Pete Best, and replaced him with Ringo Starr.

1963   Ralph Briggs Fuller, American cartoonist and creator of *Oaky Doaks,* died in Boothbay Harbor, Maine, at age 73.

1974   President Ford ordered all of President Nixon's White House tape recordings and other documents held in custody until the Watergate legal issues were settled.

1977   Elvis Presley, the rock and roll idol, died in Memphis at age 42.

AUGUST 17 -- BIRTHDAYS

1786   **Davy Crockett** -- Soldier, Congressman, and one of the most famous frontiersmen in United States history

1888   **Monty Woolley** -- American stage and motion-picture actor and director

1890   **Harry L. Hopkins** -- Closest personal advisor of President Franklin D. Roosevelt

1892   **Mae West** -- American vaudeville and motion-picture actress and one of the movies' true greats

1899   **Stephan Weiss** -- Austrian-born composer and author, noted for songs such as "Put Your Dreams Away" and "Sentimental Me"

1904   **John Hay Whitney** -- U.S. ambassador and publisher

1906   **Hazel Bishop** -- Noted American cosmetics manufacturer

1909   **Larry Clinton** -- American composer noted for songs such as "The Dipsy Doodle" and "My Reverie"

1913   **Rudy York** -- Professional baseball player

1914   **Franklin D. Roosevelt Jr.** -- U.S. congressman and son of President Roosevelt

1920   **Evelyn Ankers** -- English stage and motion-picture actress

1923   **Larry Rivers** -- American painter whose works suggest the speed and diversity of modern life by including seemingly unfinished parts

1929   **Francis Gary Powers** -- American U2 pilot captured on a reconnaissance mission deep inside Russia in 1960

1930   **Ted Hughes** -- British poet

1932   **Red Kerr** -- Professional basketball superstar with over 12,000 career points

1933   **Jim Davenport** -- Professional baseball player

1941   **Boog Powell** -- Professional baseball player

1943   **Robert De Niro** -- American stage and motion-picture actor

1952   **Guillermo Vilas** -- Argentine tennis player

1960   **Sean Penn** -- American motion-picture actor

AUGUST 17 -- EVENTS

1498   Cesare Borgia, a Cardinal at age 18 by appointment of his father, Pope Alexander VI, renounced his great office to marry a French princess.

1590   John White, the leader of the second expedition of English settlers to Roanoke Island, returned from a trip to England to find that the entire colony had vanished.

1786   Prussia's Frederick the Great died at Sans-Souci in Potsdam at age 74.

1807   Robert Fulton's famous steamboat, the *Clermont,* made its first run up the Hudson River from New York City to Albany.

1877   Billy the Kid, the notorious Western outlaw, killed his first man, F.P. Cahill, who earlier in the day had humiliated Billy by wrestling him to the floor in a saloon.

1896   Gold was discovered in the Klondike at Bonanza Creek, Alaska, by George W. Carmack and his Indian wife Kate.

1933   Lou Gehrig, New York Yankee baseball great, broke the record of consecutive games played when he appeared in his 1,308th game. He went on eventually to 2,130.

1940   The United States and Canada made formal arrangements for a joint defense of North America during World War II.

1942   U.S. bombers made their first independent raid on Europe in World War II, attacking Rouen, France.

1945   Indonesia proclaimed its independence from Holland.
1969   The Woodstock rock-music festival in Woodstock, New York, ended after three days.
1969   Hurricane Camille slammed into the Mississippi Gulf Coast, claiming more than 250 lives.
1978   The first transatlantic balloon crossing was successfully completed when the *Eagle II* landed in Normandy, after a five-day trip from the U.S.

AUGUST 18 -- BIRTHDAYS

1587   **Virginia Dare** -- The first English child born in America (on Roanoke Island, the Lost Colony off the coast of what is now North Carolina)
1685   **Brook Taylor** -- English mathematician noted for Taylor's series
1774   **Meriwether Lewis** -- American explorer, who with William Clark, led the Lewis and Clark Expedition that explored the Pacific Northwest, 1804-1806
1807   **Charles Francis Adams** -- Son of President John Quincy Adams, and an American diplomat considered second only to Benjamin Franklin
1830   **Francis Joseph I** -- Emperor of Austria and later of Austria-Hungary, 1848-1916, and member of the ancient ruling family of Hapsburg
1835   **Marshall Field** -- American merchant who developed the world-famous Marshall Field & Company department store in Chicago
1873   **Otto Abels Harbach** -- American lyricist noted for songs such as "Rose-Marie," "No, No, Nanette," "Cuddle Up a Little Closer, Lovey Mine," "I Won't Dance," and "Smoke Gets in Your Eyes"
1879   **Gus Edwards** -- German-American composer noted for songs such as "By the Light of the Silvery Moon," "In My Merry Oldsmobile," and "Jimmy Valentine"
1893   **Burleigh Grimes** -- Hall of Fame baseball player, and the last of the legal National League spitball pitchers before the pitch was banned
1896   **Alan Mowbray** -- English-born motion-picture actor who appeared in nearly 200 films
1897   **Stanley Marshall Rinehart Jr.** -- American book publisher
1917   **Caspar Weinberger** -- Secretary of Defense under President Reagan
1919   **Walter Joseph Hickel** -- Secretary of the Interior under President Nixon

1922   **Shelley Winters** -- American stage and motion-picture actress

1927   **Rosalynn Smith Carter** -- Wife of President Jimmy Carter

1933   **Roman Polanski** -- Polish motion-picture director and actor, who directed such films as *Rosemary's Baby* (1968) and *Chinatown* (1974)

1934   **Roberto Clemente** -- Hall of Fame baseball player

1935   **Rafer Johnson** – Professional football superstar and motion-picture actor

1937   **Robert Redford** -- American motion-picture actor and highly popular star of the 1970s and 1980s

1941   **Christopher Jones** -- American actor and singer

1951   **Gregory Pruitt** -- Professional football player

1955   **Bruce Benedict** -- Professional baseball player

1955   **Patrick Swayze** -- American motion-picture and television actor

AUGUST 18 -- EVENTS

328 AD Saint Helena, the mother of Roman Emperor Constantine the Great, died at age 82.

1227   Genghis Khan, the great Mongol conqueror, died at age 60.

1503   Pope Alexander VI died accidentally of poison, probably intended for a guest and probably administered from habit by one of his notorious children, Cesare or Lucretia Borgia.

1678   Andrew Marvell, the English poet, died in London at age 57.

1786   Reykjavik, Iceland, was founded.

1846   U.S. Brigadier General Stephen W. Kearny captured Santa Fe, New Mexico, in the Mexican War.

1850   Honore de Balzac, the great French novelist, died in Paris at age 51.

1856   Gail Borden patented the first successful milk-condensing process.

1880   Work began on the Washington Monument after the first false start in 1848.

1902   The first unassisted triple play in baseball was made by Henry O'Hagen.

1914   President Woodrow Wilson issued his Proclamation of Neutrality, aimed at keeping the U.S. out of World War I.

1919   The Anti-Cigarette League of America was organized in Chicago.

1923   Helen Wills, eighteen-year-old Californian and future superstar, won the Women's National Tennis Championship at Forest Hills, New York.

1963   James Meredith became the first black graduate of the University of Mississippi.

AUGUST 19 -- BIRTHDAYS

1398   Inigo Lopez de Mendoza Santillana -- Spanish poet and literary patron

1631   **John Dryden** -- The outstanding English writer of the Restoration period (the second half of the 17th century)

1646   **John Flamsteed** — "Astronomer royal" (director of the Royal Greenwich Observatory), 1675-1719, whose discoveries helped Isaac Newton formulate the laws of gravitation

1785   **Seth Thomas** -- Pioneer American clock maker

1796   **Agnes Strickland** -- English biographer

1843   **Charles Montagu Doughty** -- English writer and traveler

1856   **Harold Frederic** — American journalist and novelist, noted for *The Damnation of Theron Ware* (1896)

1858   **Edith Nesbit** -- English writer

1870   **Bernard Baruch** -- American financier and adviser to every U.S. president from Woodrow Wilson to Dwight D. Eisenhower

1871   **Orville Wright** -- One of the Wright brothers who made the world's first controlled airplane flight in 1903

1878   **Manuel Quezon** -- Philippine statesman and first president of the Philippine Commonwealth, 1935-1944

1883   **Gabrielle "Coco" Chanel** -- Parisian high-fashion dress designer

1889   **Stoddard King** -- American lyricist noted for songs such as "Listen to the Mocking Bird" and "There's a Long, Long Trail A-Winding"

1892   **Alfred Lunt** -- American stage and motion-picture actor, who with his wife Lynn Fontanne formed one of the most celebrated acting teams in the history of the theater

1898   **Eleanor Boardman** -- American leading lady and Kodak Girl of the silent movies of the 1920s

1899   **Bradley Walker Tomlin** — American abstract expressionist painter

1900   **Colleen Moore** -- American star of the Hollywood silents and early talkies, who "created the flapper" of the 1920s

1902   **Ogden Nash** -- American writer of humorous poetry, found in such books as *I'm a Stranger Here Myself* (1938)

1903   **James Gould Cozzens** -- Pulitzer Prize-winning American novelist, and author of *By Love Possessed* (1957)

1903   **Claude Dauphin** -- French stage and motion-picture actor

1906   **Philo T. Farnsworth** -- American developer of the image dissector, one of the pioneering inventions that led to television

1913   **Harry Mills** -- American singer and member of the Mills Brothers group

1915   **Ring Lardner Jr.** -- American writer and son of the famous author and sports reporter

1919   **Malcolm S. Forbes** -- Editor-in-chief of *Forbes Magazine*

1921   **Gene Roddenberry** -- American television producer noted for the long-running show *Star Trek*

1926   **Robert Schakne** -- American journalist

1931   **Willie Shoemaker** -- American jockey with over 6,000 winners

1933   **Debra Paget** -- American motion-picture actress

1934   **Renee Richards** -- American dentist and tennis player

1939   **Ginger Baker** -- English drummer with the Cream rock music group

1940   **Jill St. John** -- American motion-picture and television actress

1940   **Johnny Nash** -- American singer, recording artist, and composer, noted for songs such as "My Merry Go Round" and "I Can See Clearly Now"

1946   **Bill Clinton** -- Governor of Arkansas

1960   **Ron Darling** -- Professional baseball player

AUGUST 19 -- EVENTS

480 BC   The Battle of Thermopylae was won by the Persians under Xerxes. The main Greek force escaped, however, and they eventually won the war.

14 AD   Roman emperor Augustus died at Nola at age 76 after a 41-year reign.

312 AD   Roman emperor Constantine the Great supposedly saw a vision of a cross and the words, "In this sign conquer," causing him to eventually embrace Christianity.

1580   Andrea Palladio, the great Italian Renaissance architect, died in Venice at age 71.

1662   Blaise Pascal, the great French philosopher, died in Paris at age 39.

1700   Peter the Great of Russia declared war on Sweden, marking the beginning of the Great Northern War which destroyed Sweden as one of the world's major powers.

1812   The U.S. frigate *Constitution* defeated the British frigate *Guerriere* in a famous battle of the War of 1812, in which the *Constitution* won its nickname "Old Ironsides."

1819   James Watt, the inventor of the steam engine, died at age 83.

1862   The Second Battle of Bull Run began in the Civil War. The battle lasted two days and resulted in the South's regaining nearly all of Virginia.

1890   The Daughters of the American Revolution was founded in Washington, D.C.

1934   Germany voted almost 10 to 1 for Adolf Hitler to succeed the late President Hindenburg in an election overseen by Hitler's Nazis.

1942   Canadian, British, and American commandos tried out invasion tactics in a suicidal raid on the Nazi forces in Dieppe, France, in World War II.

1944   The U.S. Third Army under General George S. Patton reached the River Seine in France in World War II.

1945   Lieutenant General Jonathan Wainwright, hero of the Battle of Corregidor, was liberated from a Japanese World War II prison in Sian, Manchuria.

1951   Eddie Gaedel, a 3 feet 7 inch midget, pinch-hit and was walked for the St. Louis Browns against the Detroit Tigers.

1953   Premier Mohammed Mossadegh of Iran was ousted in a revolt that brought the Shah back to power.

1960   Gary Powers, pilot of a United States U2 reconnaissance plane downed deep inside Russia, was convicted of espionage by the Russians.

1977   American comedian Groucho Marx died at age 86, but his own epitaph was not used: "Here lies Groucho Marx, and lies, and lies, and lies."

AUGUST 20 -- BIRTHDAYS

1561   **Jacopo Peri** -- Italian composer

1745   **Francis Asbury** -- Early American circuit rider and the most important Methodist leader in America during the late 1700s and early 1800s

1778   **Bernardo O'Higgins** -- Liberator of Chile from Spain

1785   **Oliver Hazard Perry** -- U.S. naval officer, who after capturing the British fleet on Lake Erie in the War of 1812, reported, "We have met the enemy and they are ours."

1795   **Robert F. Stockton** -- U.S. naval officer who helped conquer California in the Mexican War

1807   **Narcisse Diaz de La Pena** -- French painter

1833   **Benjamin Harrison** -- 23rd U.S. president

1860   **Raymond Poincare** – French prime minister before World War I

1873   **Eliel Saarinen** -- Finnish-born architect noted for works such as the famous Helsinki railroad station and, with his son Eero, the Tabernacle Church of Christ in Columbus, Indiana

1881   **Edgar Guest** -- English-born American poet, noted for "A Heap o' Living" (1916) and "Life's Highway" (1933)

1886   **Paul Tillich** -- Noted German-American theologian

1890   **H.P. Lovecraft** -- American horror story writer and 20th century master of the Gothic tale, noted for works such as *The Dunwich Horror* and *At the Mountains of Madness*

1905   **Jack Teagarden** – American trombonist and first successful non-Negro blues singer

1908   **Al Lopez** -- Professional baseball player and highly successful manager

1910   **Eero Saarinen** -- Noted Finnish-American architect, and designer of the Gateway Arch along the Mississippi River in St. Louis

1913   **Donald Yetter Gardner** -- American composer noted for songs such as "All I Want for Christmas Is My Two Front Teeth"

1920   **Ralph Mallory Kovel** -- American columnist and antique authority

1926   **Jacqueline Susann** -- American writer and author of *Valley of the Dolls*

1942   **Fred Norman** -- Professional baseball player

1942   **Isaac Hayes** -- American popular songwriter

1944   **Graig Nettles** -- Professional baseball player

1944   **Rajiv Gandhi** -- Prime minister of India who succeeded his mother, Indira Gandhi, after her assassination in 1984

1947   **Robert Plant** – British singer with the Led Zeppelin musical group

1960   **Tom Brunansky** -- Professional baseball player

AUGUST 20 -- EVENTS

1741   Vitus Bering, a Danish sea captain commissioned by Peter the Great of Russia to probe for a land connection between Asia and North America, discovered Alaska, landing on Kayak Island.

1794   General Anthony Wayne defeated the Indians in the Battle of Fallen Timbers, ending 20 years of Indian warfare on the American frontier.

1837   Queen Victoria ascended the throne of England immediately following the death of her Uncle, King William IV.

1914   The Germans occupied Brussels in World War I.

1923   The comic strip, *Just Kids,* by Clare Briggs, appeared for the first time.

1934   The comic strip *Li'l Abner,* by Al Capp, first appeared.

1940   "Never in the field of human conflict was so much owed by so many to so few," said Winston Churchill in praising the RAF to the House of Commons during World War II.

1940   Leon Trotsky, exiled Soviet Bolshevist and arch rival of Joseph Stalin, was stabbed with an ice pick in Mexico by one of Stalin's agents. He died the following day.

1968   Russian and Russian satellite troops invaded Czechoslovakia to suppress a bold Czech move for more freedom.

AUGUST 21 -- BIRTHDAYS

1165   **Philip II (Philip Augustus)** -- The first great king of the Capetian dynasty in France

1725   **Jean Baptiste Greuze** -- French painter whose works were highly popular from 1750 to the French Revolution

1765   **William IV** -- King of England, 1830-1837, and son of King George III

1789   **Augustin Louis Cauchy** -- One of the greatest of modern mathematicians

1796   **Asher B. Durand** -- American painter and engraver

1798   **Jules Michelet** -- French historian

1865   **Charles B. Ward** -- English-born composer and singer noted for "Strike Up the Band" and "The Band Played On"

1872   **Aubrey Vincent Beardsley** -- English artist who illustrated stories and plays with elegant black-and-white line drawings

1892   **F. Dudleigh Vernor** -- American composer and organist, noted for songs such as "Sweetheart of Sigma Chi"

1895   **Benny Davis** -- American composer noted for songs such as "Margie," "Baby Face," "Yearning," "Carolina Moon," and "Make Believe"

1896   **Roark Bradford** -- American playwright and author of *Green Pastures* (1930)

1904   **Count Basie** -- American pianist, composer, and jazz band leader

1907   **Hy Zaret** -- American composer and author, noted for songs such as "Unchained Melody" and "So Long for Awhile" (theme song of *Hit Parade*)

1908   **Ray Berres** -- Professional baseball player

1916   **Murry Dickson** -- Professional baseball player
1920   **Gerry Staley** -- Professional baseball player
1929   **Herman Badillo** -- Puerto Rican-born lawyer and congressman
1930   **Princess Margaret** -- Sister of Queen Elizabeth II of England
1936   **Mart Crowley** -- American writer and author of *The Boys in the Band*
1936   **Wilt Chamberlain** -- One of the greatest offensive players in the history of professional basketball, who once made 100 points in a single game (in 1962)
1938   **Kenny Rogers** -- American country music singer
1945   **Patty McCormack** -- American motion-picture and television actress
1950   **Ray Wersching** -- Professional football player
1951   **Harry Smith** -- American television reporter and co-anchor of the CBS *This Morning* show

AUGUST 21 -- EVENTS

1621   "1 Widow and 11 Maides" were sent from London to the Jamestown, Virginia, colony to be sold to wife-seeking bachelors for 120 pounds of tobacco apiece.

1680   The Pueblo Indians, in revolt under their leader Pope, took possession of Santa Fe, New Mexico, after driving out the Spanish.

1745   Czar Peter III of Russia married Catherine the Great (as she became), who upon Peter's death became empress of Russia.

1835   Nat Turner's Rebellion, the largest slave revolt in American history, occurred near Jerusalem, Virginia. Fifty-one whites were killed and Nat Turner was captured and hanged.

1858   The first of the great Lincoln-Douglas debates was held at Ottawa, Illinois.

1887   Dan Casey of the New York Giants struck out in the ninth inning, providing Ernest L. Thayer with the inspiration for his famous poem, "Casey at the Bat."

1911   The priceless *Mona Lisa* painting of Leonardo da Vinci was stolen from the Louvre Museum in Paris by Vicenzo Peruggia. He was arrested and the painting was returned two years later.

1940   Leon Trotsky, the Russian revolutionary leader and arch rival of Joseph Stalin, died of wounds inflicted by an assassin the previous day in Mexico City.

1951   The U.S. ordered construction of the first atomic-powered submarine. The program resulted in 1955 in the *Nautilus,* the world's first nuclear-powered warship.

1959   Hawaii was admitted to the Union as the 50th state.

1968   The Russians seized Alexander Dubcek, Czechoslovakia's liberal Communist leader, putting an end to the Czech revolt.

AUGUST 22 -- BIRTHDAYS

1764   **Charles Percier** -- French architect

1769   **Leo XII** -- Roman Catholic pope, 1823-1819

1834   **Samuel Pierpont Langley** -- American astronomer, physicist, and pioneer in aeronautics, for whom Langley Air Force Base in Virginia is named

1851   **Daniel Frohman** -- American theatrical manager identified with the theater for over 60 years

1862   **Claude Debussy** -- One of the greatest French composers of the late 1800s

1891   **Jacques Lipchitz** -- Polish-American sculptor and modern artist

1893   **Dorothy Parker** -- American short-story writer and poet, and one of the great humorists of her time

1897   **Max Rich** -- American composer, author, and pianist, noted for songs such as "Smile, Darn Ya, Smile"

1902   **Leni Riefenstahl** -- German motion-picture actress and director, noted for her films dramatizing the Nazi movement

1917   **John Lee Hooker** -- One of the early American blues musicians

1920   **Ray Bradbury** -- Science fiction writer and television and movie scriptwriter noted for books such as *Fahrenheit 451*

1920   **Denton A. Cooley** -- American surgeon noted as a pioneer in heart transplant operations

1928   **F. Ray Marshall** -- Secretary of Labor under President Carter

1929   **Honor Blackman** -- American motion-picture actress

1934   **Diana Sands** -- American motion-picture actress

1935   **Morton Dean** -- American broadcast journalist

1939   **Carl Yastrzemski** -- Hall of Fame baseball player

1940   **Valerie Harper** -- American motion-picture and television actress

1942   **Kathy Lennon** -- One of the singing Lennon Sisters

1947   **Cindy Williams** -- American motion-picture and television actress

1949   **Diana Nyad** -- American world marathon swimming champion

1955   **Ann Kiyomura** -- American tennis player

1955 **Carrie Meyer** -- American tennis player
1956 **Paul Molitor** -- Professional baseball player
1956 **Wes Chandler** -- Professional football player
1964 **Mats Wilander** -- Swedish tennis player

AUGUST 22 -- EVENTS

1485 Henry Tudor (later Henry VII) killed Richard III at Bosworth Field, the last battle of the Wars of the Roses, to become the first Tudor king of England.

1762 Ann Franklin became America's first newspaper editor, with the Newport (Rhode Island) *Mercury.*

1787 John Fitch successfully demonstrated his side-paddled steamboat on the Delaware River.

1818 The USS *Savannah* was launched. The next year it was to become the first steamship to cross the Atlantic Ocean.

1848 U.S. Grant married Julia Dent.

1851 The U.S. yacht *America* won the America's Cup for the first time. An American yacht won every America's Cup race since then until 1984.

1903 Barney Dreyfuss, an American sportsman, proposed that baseball organize a World Series, resulting in the first World Series in October 1903 between Pittsburgh and Boston.

1903 Theodore Roosevelt became the first American president to ride in an automobile, in Hartford, Connecticut.

1942 "We are attacking Stalingrad and we shall take it," Hitler announced in the Sportpalast in Berlin. He did attack, but the Battle of Stalingrad was an eventual disaster for him.

1968 Pope Paul VI arrived in Bogota, Colombia, for the start of the first papal visit in history to Latin America.

AUGUST 23 -- BIRTHDAYS

1754 **Louis XVI** -- King of France, 1774-1793, who was on the throne at the beginning of the French Revolution, and who was beheaded in 1793 by the revolutionaries

1769 **Baron de Cuvier** -- French naturalist and founder of comparative anatomy

1849 **William Ernest** Henley -- English poet and critic, and author of "Invictus"

1869 **Edgar Lee Masters** -- American poet, novelist, and author of *Spoon River Anthology* (1915)

1882   **Will Hough** -- American lyricist noted for songs such as "I
        Wonder Who's Kissing Her Now" (with Joseph Edgar Howard)

1884   **Will Cuppy** -- American humorist and author of *The Decline and
        Fall of Practically Everybody* (1950)

1894   **Sholom Secunda** -- Russian-born composer and conductor,
        noted for songs such as "Bei Mir Bist Du Schon" and "Dana,
        Dana, Dana"

1895   **Florence Vidor** -- Popular star of Hollywood silents and wife of
        director King Vidor

1896   **Wendell Woods Hall** -- American composer and singer, noted
        for songs such as "It Ain't Gonna Rain No Mo'"

1904   **William Primrose** -- Scottish violinist and teacher

1905   **Ernie Bushmiller** -- American cartoonist and creator of *Fritzi
        Ritz* and *Nancy*

1908   **Arthur Adamov** -- One of the founders of the Theater of
        the Absurd

1912   **Gene Kelly** -- American dancer and motion-picture actor
        and director

1913   **Bob Crosby** -- American bandleader and brother of singer
        Bing Crosby

1922   **George Kell** -- Hall of Fame baseball player

1924   **Sherman Lollar** -- Professional baseball player

1929   **Vera Miles** -- American motion-picture and television actress

1932   **Howard B. Johnson** -- President of Howard Johnson's Restau-
        rant chain and son of the founder

1934   **Barbara Eden** -- American motion-picture and television actress

1934   **Sonny Jurgenson** -- Professional football player and sportscaster

1942   **Nancy Richey Gunter** -- American tennis player

1946   **Keith Moon** -- British drummer for musical group the Who

1949   **Rick Springfield** -- American singer

1949   **Stephanie Beacham** -- British motion-picture and television actress

1949   **Shelley Long** -- American motion-picture and television actress

1957   **Mike Boddicker** -- Professional baseball player

1970   **River Phoenix** -- American motion-picture actor

AUGUST 23 -- EVENTS

1500   Because of discontent and troubles among the Spanish settlers
        on Hispaniola, Columbus was put in chains and ordered back to
        Spain. He was later released by the king and queen.

1775	King George III of England declared all the colonies to be in rebellion, and ordered a naval blockade of the colonies.
1777	King Louis XVI of France finally consummated his 7-year marriage to Marie Antoinette, after undergoing surgery for a phimosis condition.
1838	Mount Holyoke Female Seminary in South Hadley, Mass., the first college for women, graduated its first students.
1902	Fannie Farmer opened her School of Cookery in Boston.
1914	Japan declared war on Germany in World War I.
1926	Hundreds of thousands of women mourned the death of Rudolph Valentino, the screen's "Great Lover"
1927	Nicola Sacco and Bartolomeo Vanzetti, the principals in the famous anarchist case, were executed in the Charlestown, Massachusetts, prison.
1939	German foreign minister Ribbentrop flew to Moscow to conclude a nonaggression pact with Joseph Stalin.
1947	Margaret Truman, daughter of President Harry Truman, gave her first public concert in the Hollywood Bowl.
1948	The World Council of Churches was founded in Amsterdam.
1970	Mark Spitz, American swimmer, broke the 100-meter freestyle record with a time of 51.9 seconds.

AUGUST 24 -- BIRTHDAYS

1113	**Geoffrey Plantagenet** -- Count of Anjou and ancestor of the Plantagenet kings of England
1580	**John Taylor** -- English novelist and poet
1591	**Robert Herrick** – English "Cavalier" poet who wrote the famous line, "Gather ye Rosebuds while ye may," in his well-known poem, "To the Virgins"
1724	**George Stubbs** -- English painter noted for works such as *Mares and Foals* (1762)
1759	**William Wilberforce** -- A leader in the fight to abolish slavery in the British Empire
1772	**William I** -- First king of the present-day kingdom of the Netherlands, 1815-1840
1784	**Joseph Emerson Worcester** -- American lexicographer
1847	**Charles Follen McKim** -- American architect who helped design the Boston Public Library and the Pennsylvania Railway Station in New York City
1852	**Jim O'Rourke** -- Hall of Fame baseball player and manager

1872   **Sir Max Beerbohm** – British writer and caricaturist, and author of *Zuleika Dobson* (1911)

1886   **William Francis Gibbs** -- Director of mass production of U.S. World War II cargo ships

1895   **Richard Cardinal Cushing** – American Roman Catholic cardinal

1895   **Tuanku Abdul Rahman** -- First chief of state of the Federation of Malaya

1897   **Fred Rose** -- American composer, author, and singer, noted for songs such as "Roly Poly," "Hang Your Head in Shame," and "Be Honest With Me"

1898   **Malcolm Cowley** -- American writer

1899   **Jorge Luis Borges** -- Argentine essayist, poet, and master of the short story

1903   **Graham Vivian Sutherland** -- English painter noted for his surrealistic landscapes

1924   **Louis Teicher** -- American pianist and composer with the musical team of Ferrante and Teicher

1946   **Ray Moore** -- South African tennis player

1956   **Antonio "Garcia" Bernazard** -- Professional baseball player

1956   **Gerry Cooney** -- American heavyweight boxer

1960   **Cal Ripken Jr.** -- Professional baseball player and son of player and manager Cal Ripken

AUGUST 24 -- EVENTS

79 AD   Mount Vesuvius erupted violently and buried the Roman cities of Pompeii and Herculaneum. Pliny the Elder died of asphyxiation at age 56 while witnessing the scene from the coast.

410 AD   Alaric, leader of the Visigoths, sacked Rome, but spared its churches.

1215   Pope Innocent III, on an appeal from King John of England, issued a bull annulling the Magna Carta, which, however, remained in effect.

1313   Henry VII, Holy Roman emperor, died at age 44.

1572   The Massacre of St. Bartholomew's Day began in Paris, in which thousands of French Huguenots (Protestants) were killed.

1814   British troops captured Washington, D.C., and burned the White House in the War of 1812.

1875   Matthew Webb became the first person to swim the English Channel, swimming from Dover to Cap Gris-Nez, France, in 21 hours.

1932   Amelia Earhart became the first woman to make a nonstop flight across the United States, flying from Los Angeles to Newark in just over 19 hours.

1939   The Nazi-Soviet nonaggression pact was announced to the world, which reacted in disbelief.

1949   The North Atlantic Treaty went into effect, organizing the U.S. and Western Europe in NATO to defend themselves against aggression.

1954   President Getulio Vargas of Brazil killed himself after his regime was overthrown by federal troops.

1959   Daniel K. Inouye was sworn in as the first Japanese-American U.S. congressman and Hiram L. Fong was sworn in as the first Chinese-American U.S. senator. Both were from Hawaii.

1968   France tested its first hydrogen bomb, in the South Pacific.

AUGUST 25 -- BIRTHDAYS

1530   **Ivan IV (the Terrible)** -- Czar of Russia who conquered Siberia, made Moscow the capital of the country, and who ranks second to Peter the Great as the greatest Russian czar.

1678   **Jacques Caffieri** -- French sculptor

1744   **Johann Gottfried von Herder** -- One of the most original and versatile German writers and philosophers, who inspired the great German writer Goethe and the other writers of the *Sturm und Drang* movement

1819   **Allan Pinkerton** -- American detective and founder in 1850 of the Pinkerton detective agency

1836   **Bret Harte** -- One of the greatest American story writers, noted for *The Luck of Roaring Camp* and *The Outcasts of Poker Flat*

1837   **Jacob Maris** -- Dutch painter

1850   **Bill Nye** -- American humorist who wrote comic histories, such as *Bill Nye's History of the United States* (1894)

1860   **George Fawcett** – Character actor of the silent screen in nearly 100 roles

1884   **Vincent Auriol** -- First president of the Fourth French Republic

1901   **Kjeld Abell** -- Danish dramatist and social critic

1905   **Clara Bow** -- American actress and "It" girl of the Roaring '20s

1909   **Ruby Keeler** -- Canadian motion-picture actress, dancer, and singer

1909   **Michael Rennie** -- English motion-picture actor

1912   **Theodore Key** -- American cartoonist and author, especially noted for his work in the *New Yorker* magazine

1913   **Walt Kelly** -- American cartoonist and creator of *Pogo*
1913   **Jill Jackson** -- American composer, author, and publisher, noted for lyrics such as "Let There Be Peace on Earth (Let It Begin With Me)"
1916   **Van Johnson** -- American motion-picture actor and leading man of the 1940s and 1950s
1917   **Don Defore** -- American motion-picture and television actor
1917   **Mel Ferrer** -- American motion-picture actor and director
1918   **Leonard Bernstein** -- American conductor, composer, and pianist, who wrote the music for *On the Waterfront* (1954) and *West Side Story* (1957)
1919   **George C. Wallace** – Governor of Alabama and candidate for president in 1968
1923   **Monty Hall** -- Canadian-born television game show host
1927   **Althea Gibson** -- American Hall of Fame tennis player, and Wimbledon singles champion in 1957 and 1958
1930   **Sean Connery** -- British actor and original star of the James Bond series of movies
1946   **Rollie Fingers** -- Professional baseball player
1948   **Anne Archer** -- American motion-picture actress
1953   **Bob Lacey** -- Professional baseball player

AUGUST 25 -- EVENTS

608 AD Boniface IV became Roman Catholic pope.
1270   King Louis IX of France (Saint Louis) died in northern Africa while leading the Eighth Crusade.
1572   The Massacre of St. Bartholomew's Day in Paris ended, but not before thousands of Huguenots were killed.
1580   Spain gained control of Portugal by winning the Battle of Alcantara near Lisbon.
1718   New Orleans, Louisiana, was founded by French governor Jean Baptiste le Moyne, Sieur de Bienville, and named in honor of the Duke of Orleans.
1825   Uruguay declared its independence from Brazil.
1835   Ann Rutledge, reportedly Abraham Lincoln's only true love, died in New Salem, Illinois, at age 22.
1867   Michael Faraday, the great English physicist, died at age 75.
1916   The National Park Service was established within the Department of the Interior.

1921	The United States signed a peace treaty with Germany, formally ending World War I hostilities between the two nations.
1928	Admiral Richard E. Byrd's first Antarctic expedition left New York.
1939	Great Britain signed a treaty to support Poland in case of a German attack.
1944	U.S. and French troops liberated Paris in World War II after four years of Nazi occupation.
1950	President Truman ordered the Army to seize the nation's railroads to avert a strike.
1952	Virgil Trucks pitched his second no-hit game of the season as Detroit beat New York, 1-0.

AUGUST 26 -- BIRTHDAYS

1676	**Robert Walpole** -- The most influential politician in England during the first half of the 18th century, and the first man to serve as prime minister
1740	**Joseph Michel Montgolfier** -- French balloonist who with his brother Jacques invented the first balloons to carry men into the air
1743	**Antoine Laurent Lavoisier** -- French chemist, considered the father of modern chemistry, noted for the law of conservation of matter, the present-day system of chemical names, and for the first modern textbook
1819	**Prince Albert** -- Prince of Saxe-Coburg-Gotha and husband of Queen Victoria of England
1869	**Jacques Emile Ruhlmann** -- French cabinetmaker
1873	**Lee De Forest** -- American inventor, noted for the triode vacuum tube that made radio possible
1874	**Andrew B. Sterling** -- American lyricist noted for songs such as "Wait Till the Sun Shines, Nellie," "Meet Me in St. Louis, Louis," "On a Sunday Afternoon," and "Strike Up the Band"
1880	**Guillaume Apollinaire** -- French poet and art critic, who coined the word *surrealism* in 1917
1885	**Jules Romains** -- French novelist, dramatist, and poet, best known for the satirical play *Dr. Knock* (1923) and the novels published under the general title of *Men of Good Will* (1913-1946)
1892	**Ruth Roland** -- Queen of Hollywood silent serials, billed when she was a child star on stage as Baby Ruth
1895	**Earl K. Long** -- Three-times governor of Louisiana, and brother of the noted Louisiana political boss, Huey P. Long

1901   **Maxwell D. Taylor** – American general in World War II and Vietnam

1904   **Christopher Isherwood** -- English-American novelist noted for works such as *Goodbye to Berlin* (1939)

1906   **Albert Sabin** – Russian-American developer of the Sabin polio vaccine approved for use in 1961

1915   **Jim Davis** -- American motion-picture and television actor

1920   **Brant Parker** -- American cartoonist who with Johnny Hart created *The Wizard of Id*

1921   **Benjamin Bradlee** -- American journalist and author

1922   **Irving R. Levine** -- American broadcast journalist

1931   **Guy Vander Jagt** -- U.S. congressman

1934   **Tom Heinsohn** -- Professional basketball player, coach, and sportscaster

1935   **Geraldine Ferraro** -- Democratic vice presidential candidate in 1984, and the first woman to run for the office on a major party ticket

1939   **Al Green** -- Professional golfer

1952   **Donnie Shell** -- Professional football player

AUGUST 26 -- EVENTS

1346   The Battle of Crecy in the Hundred Years' War established England as a great power. The hero was Edward, the Black Prince, 16-year-old son of Edward III of England.

1382   Moscow was burned by the Mongols.

1498   Michelangelo was commissioned to make the *Pieta,* which is now in St. Peter's Church in Rome, and is one of his most enduring works.

1666   Franz Hals, the great Dutch painter, died in Haarlem, the Netherlands, at age 86.

1797   John Quincy Adams married Louisa Catherine Johnson.

1801   Robert Morris, the financer of the American Revolution, was released after two years from debtor's prison.

1884   Ottmar Mergenthaler, the German-American inventor, received a patent for the Linotype machine.

1888   Peter Tchaikovsky, the great Russian composer, completed his *Fifth Symphony,* one of his finest works.

1918   In World War I Germany began a general retreat to the Hindenburg Line, "the Black Day" in the history of the German army, according to German general Ludendorff.

1920   The 19th Amendment to the Constitution was proclaimed, giving women the right to vote.

1948   Axis Sally (Mildred Elizabeth Gillars) was flown to the U.S. to face charges of treason for her wartime propaganda broadcasts for the Nazis in World War II.

1974   Russian cosmonaut Lev Demin became the first grandfather in space, when *Soyuz 15* was launched by the Soviets.

1978   John Paul I was elected Roman Catholic pope.

AUGUST 27 -- BIRTHDAYS

550 BC   **Confucius** -- Famous wise man of China whose teachings formed the basis for Confucianism (date uncertain)

1545   **Allesandro Farnese** -- Spanish Duke of Parma, whose failure to link up his forces with those of the Spanish Armada contributed to the Armada's defeat by the English

1725   **Charles Townshend** -- British chancellor of the exchequer whose taxation policies helped cause the American Revolution

1770   **Georg Wilhelm Friedrich Hegel** – German idealist philosopher and one of the most influential thinkers of recent times

1809   **Hannibal Hamlin** -- U.S. vice president in President Lincoln's first term

1825   **William Balfour Baikie** -- British explorer and philologist

1858   **Giuseppe Peano** -- Italian mathematician and a founder of symbolic logic

1865   **Charles G. Dawes** – U.S. vice president under President Coolidge

1871   **Theodore Dreiser** -- Foremost American novelist in the "naturalism movement," and author of *Sister Carrie* (1900) and *An American Tragedy* (1925)

1877   **Charles Stewart Rolls** -- English automobile manufacturer who with Frederick Henry Royce founded the Rolls-Royce company in 1906

1882   **Samuel Goldwyn** -- Pioneer American filmmaker who with Edgar Selwyn formed the Goldwyn company, and who was noted for unintentionally funny sayings like "Include me out"

1890   **Man Ray** -- American painter and photographer and one of the founders of New York's Societe Anonyme, Inc., in 1920

1896   **Morris Ankrum** -- American stage and motion-picture actor

1899   **C.S. Forester** -- English novelist who won fame for his fictional creation of Horatio Hornblower

1908   **Lyndon B. Johnson** -- 36th U.S. president

1908   **Frank Leahy** -- Highly successful coach of the Notre Dame
        football team during the World War II era
1909   **Pres Young** -- American saxophonist and jazz musician
1909   **Don George** -- American composer noted for such lyrics as "I'm
        Beginning to See the Light" and "The Wonder of You"
1910   **Mother Teresa** – Noted humanitarian and Nobel Peace Laureate
1916   **Martha Raye** – American motion-picture actress and comedienne
1929   **Ira Levin** --American novelist noted for works such as *Rose-
        mary's Baby* and *The Stepford Wives*
1937   **Tommy Sands** -- American rock-and-roll singer and guitarist
1943   **Tuesday Weld** – American motion-picture and television actress
1951   **Buddy Bell** -- Professional baseball player
1954   **John Lloyd** -- English tennis player

AUGUST 27 -- EVENTS

1576   Titian, the great Italian painter, died in Venice at an age of
        approximately 99.
1660   English poet John Milton's books were burned in London be-
        cause of his attacks on King Charles II.
1665   The first play, *Ye Bare and Ye Cubb,* was performed in the North
        American colonies, at Accomac, Virginia. Three local residents
        were fined for acting in it.
1776   The British defeated George Washington's patriots in the Battle
        of Long Island in the Revolutionary War.
1783   French physicist J.A.C. Charles sent up the first hydrogen bal-
        loon, in Paris. It climbed to about three thousand feet and
        remained in view for an hour.
1789   The Declaration of the Rights of Man was accepted by the
        French National Assembly.
1859   Edwin L. Drake struck oil in Titusville, Pennsylvania, marking
        the beginning of the oil industry.
1883   The island volcano Krakatoa blew up, causing tidal waves that
        claimed 36,000 lives in Java and Sumatra.
1904   The first automobile driver to be jailed for speeding was given a
        five-day sentence in Newport County, Rhode Island.
1912   *Tarzan,* Edgar Rice Burroughs famous novel, first appeared, in
        a magazine. (It appeared as a comic strip in 1929.)
1928   The Kellogg-Briand Pact was signed by 15 nations in Paris,
        condemning the use of war and calling for the peaceful settle-
        ment of disputes.

1945 Admiral Halsey led the U.S. Third Fleet into Sagami Bay near Tokyo in preparation for the signing by General MacArthur of the peace treaty with Japan, ending World War II.

1975 Haile Selassie, Ethiopia's last emperor, died in Addis Ababa at age 83, almost a year after his overthrow in a military coup.

AUGUST 28 -- BIRTHDAYS

1749 **Johann Wolfgang von Goethe** -- German author and one of the greatest writers of all time, whose masterpiece is the verse play *Faust*

1774 **Elizabeth Ann Bayley Seton** -- American religious leader known as Mother Seton who founded the Sisters of Charity in the United States and became the first person born in the U.S. to be canonized

1810 **Constant Troyon** -- French painter

1831 **Lucy Ware Webb Hayes** -- Wife of President Rutherford B. Hayes, who gained the nickname "Lemonade Lucy" because she refused to serve alcoholic beverages in the White House

1833 **Sir Edward Coley Burne-Jones** -- English painter and designer

1886 **Byron Gay** -- American composer and musician, noted for songs such as "The Vamp" and "Little Ford Rambled Right Along"

1894 **Karl Boehm** -- Austrian-born conductor

1897 **Charles Boyer** -- French-American motion-picture actor and "great lover" of the 1930s and 1940s

1898 **Charlie Grimm** -- Professional baseball player and manager

1906 **Sir John Betjeman** -- England's most popular 20th century poet

1907 **Sam Levene** -- American stage, screen, and television actor

1910 **Morris Graves** -- American painter noted for paintings that show the influence of oriental mysticism

1913 **Richard Tucker** -- The outstanding American operatic tenor of his time

1916 **C. Wright Mills** -- American sociologist and writer

1917 **Jack Kirby** -- American comic book artist and creator of *Captain America*

1921 **Nancy Kulp** -- American motion-picture and television actress, noted for her role in the long-running TV series, *The Beverly Hillbillies*

1930 **Ben Gazzara** -- American motion-picture and television actor

1939 **Catherine Mackin** -- American broadcast journalist

1940   **William Cohen** -- U.S. congressman and senator
1943   **Lou Piniella** -- Professional baseball player, manager, and executive
1946   **Mike Torrez** -- Professional baseball player
1950   **Ron Guidry** -- Professional baseball player
1958   **Scott Hamilton** -- American skater who won the gold medal in men's figure skating in the 1984 Winter Olympics

AUGUST 28 -- EVENTS

430 AD   Saint Augustine, the great Christian theologian, died at age 75.
476 AD   The western Roman Empire founded by Augustus in 27 B.C. ended at Ravenna, where Emperor Romulus Augustulus was deposed by the barbarian leader Odovacar (Odoacer).
1565   Spanish explorers, led by Don Pedro Menendez de Avilés, arrived at the present site of St. Augustine, Florida.
1609   Henry Hudson discovered Delaware Bay.
1811   English poet Percy Bysshe Shelley eloped with 16-year-old Harriet Westbrook.
1830   The first American-built locomotive, the *Tom Thumb,* by Peter Cooper, lost its famous race to a horse-drawn stagecoach at the last minute when a pulley belt slipped.
1833   Slavery was abolished in the British colonies by Parliament.
1850   Richard Wagner's famous opera *Lohengrin* was first performed, in Weimar, Germany.
1922   The first radio commercial was aired, an ad for the Queensboro Realty Company of Jackson Heights, New York, on station WEAF in New York.
1941   Japanese ambassador Nomura delivered a note to President Franklin D. Roosevelt declaring Japan's peaceful intentions.
1963   Some 200,000 persons staged a "Freedom March" on Washington, D.C., to demonstrate demands for civil rights.
1968   Police clashed with anti-war demonstrators in the streets of Chicago as the Democratic National Convention nominated Vice President Hubert H. Humphrey for president.

AUGUST 29 -- BIRTHDAYS

1609   **Il Sassoferrato** -- Italian painter
1619   **Jean Baptiste Colbert** -- French minister of finance to King Louis XIV for 22 years

1632	**John Locke** -- One of the greatest English philosophers of all time, whose work had a profound influence on Thomas Jefferson in writing the Declaration of Independence
1780	**Jean Auguste Dominique Ingres** -- French painter and the leading neoclassical painter of the early 1800s
1809	**Oliver Wendell Holmes** – American physician, poet, and humorist
1862	**Maurice Maeterlinck** -- Belgian poet and dramatist who won the Nobel Prize for literature in 1911
1871	**Jack Butler Yeats** – The leading Irish painter of the 20th century
1876	**Charles F. Kettering** – American inventor who developed automobile self-starters, leaded gasoline, a diesel engine for trains, and a high-compression automobile engine
1879	**Harry Williams** -- American lyricist noted for songs such as "In the Shade of the Old Apple Tree," "Good Night, Ladies," and "Mickey"
1891	**Joyce Clyde Hall** – American businessman who founded Hallmark Greeting Cards
1898	**Preston Sturges** -- American motion-picture director and playwright
1899	**Lyman L. Lemnitzer** -- American general and chairman of the Joint Chiefs of Staff, 1960-1962
1909	**George Macready** – American stage, screen, and television actor
1912	**Barry Sullivan** -- American stage, screen, and television actor
1915	**Ingrid Bergman** -- Swedish motion-picture actress and a superstar for 40 years
1916	**George Montgomery** -- American motion-picture actor
1920	**Charlie Parker** – American alto saxophonist and jazz musician
1923	**Richard Attenborough** -- English motion-picture actor and director noted for his direction of the Academy Award-winning picture *Gandhi* (1983)
1927	**Gary Gabelich** – American racing car driver, who set a record speed of 631 miles per hour in 1970
1934	**David Pryer** -- U.S. senator
1938	**Elliott Gould** -- American motion-picture and television actor
1940	**James Brady** -- White House press secretary who was shot in the attempt on President Reagan's life
1941	**Robin Leach** -- English-born reporter, columnist, and founder of *Go Magazine,* and the genius behind the TV shows, *Lifestyles of the Rich and Famous* and *Entertainment Tonight*
1947	**Bob Lutz** -- American tennis player
1950	**Doug De Cinces** -- Professional baseball player

1958   **Michael Jackson** -- American singer who started out with the Jackson 5 musical group

AUGUST 29 -- EVENTS

28 AD   John the Baptist was beheaded by Herod at the request of his stepdaughter Salome.

1261   Urban IV was elected Roman Catholic pope.

1484   Innocent VIII was elected Roman Catholic pope.

1526   The Battle of Mohacs (Hungary) ended in the victory of the Turks over the Hungarians, which destroyed the medieval kingdom of Hungary.

1533   Atahualpa, last ruler of the Inca Empire in Peru, was executed by Spanish conquistador Francisco Pizarro, after Atahualpa had purchased his freedom with a huge treasure.

1825   Portugal recognized Brazil's independence, completing without bloodshed the 3-year transition from a colony to an independent nation.

1831   Michael Faraday, the great English physicist, discovered induction, the principle on which electric generators and motors operate.

1842   The Treaty of Nanking ended the Opium War in China.

1852   Brigham Young proclaimed the "celestial law of marriage," signifying approval of polygamy among Mormons.

1877   Brigham Young, Mormon pioneer leader, died in Salt Lake City at age 76.

1910   Japan annexed Korea and made the Korean emperor a prince.

1944   Paris celebrated its liberation from the Nazis as 15,000 American troops marched down the Champs-Elysees in World War II.

1949   The Soviet Union tested its first atomic bomb.

1966   The Beatles played their last live show before a paying audience, in Candlestick Park, San Francisco.

AUGUST 30 -- BIRTHDAYS

1334   **Pedro the Cruel** -- King of Castile and Leon

1494   **Correggio (Antonio Allegri)** -- Italian artist who at the peak of the Renaissance ranked with Michelangelo and Titian

1609   **Artus Quellinus** -- Flemish sculptor

1748   **Jacques Louis David** -- The most celebrated French artist during the French Revolution and the Napoleonic era

1794   **Stephen Watts Kearny** -- American general who helped win California during the Mexican War

1797   **Mary Wollstonecraft Shelley** — Author of the famous horror novel *Frankenstein* (1818), and second wife of the English poet Percy Bysshe Shelley

1820   **George Frederick Root** -- American composer, noted for "The Battle Cry of Freedom" and "Tramp, Tramp, Tramp, the Boys Are Marching"

1837   **Ellen Lewis Herndon Arthur** -- Wife of President Chester A. Arthur

1871   **Lord Rutherford** -- English physicist (born Ernest Rutherford), the "father of nuclear science," who worked out the nuclear theory of the atom and discovered alpha and beta rays and protons

1892   **George Aiken** -- U.S. senator, 1940-1976, and "father of food stamps"

1893   **Huey P. Long** -- Founder of the Long political dynasty in Louisiana that began in the late 1920s and lasted until the 1960s

1896   **Raymond Massey** -- Canadian-born motion-picture actor who appeared in more than 60 films

1899   **Kiki Cuyler** -- Hall of Fame baseball player

1901   **Roy Wilkins** — American civil rights advocate and NAACP executive director, 1965-1977

1901   **John Gunther** -- American journalist and author of a series of nonfiction books such as *Inside Europe* (1936) and *Inside Asia* (1939)

1907   **John W. Mauchly** — Co-inventer of ENIAC, the first electronic computer, in 1946

1907   **Shirley Booth** -- American stage, motion-picture, and television actress

1908   **Fred MacMurray** -- American stage, screen, and television star, with a career of over 45 years

1912   **Joan Blondell** -- American motion-picture actress

1912   **Edward Mills Purcell** -- American physicist who shared the 1952 Nobel Prize for developing a method for determining the magnetic properties of nuclei

1914   **Julie Bishop** -- American motion-picture actress

1918   **Ted Williams** -- Hall of Fame baseball player who hit .406 in 1941 and was one of the greatest hitters of all time

1923   **Vic Seixas** -- American Hall of Fame tennis player and 1953 Wimbledon singles champion

1925   **Donald O'Connor** -- American actor, singer, and dancer

1927   **Geoffrey Beene** -- American fashion designer
1931   **John L. Swigert Jr.** -- U.S. astronaut and participant in the *Apollo 13* mission
1937   **Bruce McLaren** -- Automobile racing driver
1939   **Elizabeth Ashley** -- American motion-picture actress and author
1943   **Robert Crumb** -- American cartoonist and creator of *Felix the Cat,* a con man cat not to be confused with the earlier comic strip of the same name
1943   **Jean-Claude Killy** -- French daredevil skier
1944   **Tug McGraw** -- Professional baseball player
1950   **Timothy Bottoms** -- American motion-picture actor
1952   **Wojek Fibak** -- Polish tennis player
1953   **Jose Moreno** -- Spanish tennis player
1955   **Marvin Powell** -- Professional football player

AUGUST 30 -- EVENTS

257 AD   Sixtus III became Roman Catholic pope.
1462   Paul II was elected Roman Catholic pope.
1483   Louis XI of France, the "terrible king," died at age 60.
1637   Anne Hutchinson was banished from Massachusetts for "traducing the ministers and the ministry."
1682   William Penn sailed from England for America, to take over and open for settlement the land granted to him by the king, which was named Pennsylvania, meaning Penn's Woods.
1780   Benedict Arnold, the American Revolutionary War traitor, first conspired with the British to surrender the American fort at West Point.
1862   Generals Robert E. Lee and Stonewall Jackson led the Southern troops to victory in the second Battle of Bull Run in the Civil War.
1905   Ty Cobb, one of the greatest baseball players of all time, made his first major league appearance, hitting a double and driving in two runs for the Detroit Tigers.
1932   Hermann Goering, one of Hitler's underlings, was elected president of the German Reichstag, enabling him to frustrate democratic procedures and help Hitler gain power.
1941   The siege of Leningrad by German troops began during World War II.
1945   General Douglas MacArthur arrived in Yokohama to set up headquarters for the U.S. occupation of Japan following World War II.

1967	The U.S. Senate confirmed the appointment of Thurgood Marshall as the first black justice on the Supreme Court.
1968	The English musical group, the Beatles, released "Hey Jude," the first single on their own Apple record label.
1983	The U.S. shuttle *Challenger* blasted off from Cape Canaveral, Fla., with Guion S. Bluford Jr., the first black American astronaut to go into space, and four others aboard.
1984	U.S. space shuttle *Discovery* was launched at Cape Canaveral, Florida.

AUGUST 31 -- BIRTHDAYS

12 AD	**Caligula** – Emperor of Rome, A.D. 37-41, noted for his cruelty and insanity
161 AD	**Commodus** -- Emperor of Rome, A.D. 180-192 (born Lucius Aelius Aurelius)
1740	**Johann Friedrich Oberlin** -- Lutheran pastor for whom Oberlin College was named
1806	**Charles James Lever** -- Irish novelist
1811	**Theophile Gautier** -- French poet, novelist, and critic, noted for *Enamels and Cameos* (1852)
1821	**Hermann von Helmholtz**-- Noted German physicist who helped prove the law of conservation of energy
1870	**Maria Montessori** -- Italian educator, who developed the special method of teaching young children known as the Montessori Method
1875	**Eddie Plank** -- Hall of Fame baseball pitcher and winner of 327 career games
1879	**Yoshihito** -- Emperor of Japan, 1912-1926, and father of Emperor Hirohito
1880	**Wilhelmina** -- Queen of the Netherlands, 1890-1948
1885	**DuBose Heyward** – American novelist and poet, best known for the novel *Porgy* (1925), which George Gershwin used later as the basis for his opera *Porgy and Bess*
1886	**L. Wolfe Gilbert** -- Russian-born composer and author, noted for songs such as "Waiting for the Robert E. Lee," "Green Eyes," "Lily of the Valley," and "Down Yonder"
1897	**Fredric March** -- American stage and screen star and winner of two Academy Awards for Best Actor
1905	**Dore Schary** -- American motion-picture director and playwright, who shared an Academy Award for *Boys Town* (1938)

1907   **Ramon Magsaysay** -- President of the Philippines, 1953-1957
1908   **William Saroyan** -- American playwright and novelist, noted for such works as *The Daring Young Man on the Flying Trapeze* (1934) and *The Time of Your Life* (1939)
1910   **Jack Howard** -- President of the Scripps-Howard newspaper chain
1914   **Richard Basehart** -- American stage and motion-picture actor with a 40-year career
1916   **Daniel Schorr** -- American television news commentator
1918   **Alan Jay Lerner** -- American playwright and lyricist, who with Frederick Loewe composed the hits for *Brigadoon, My Fair Lady,* and *Camelot*
1924   **Buddy Hackett** -- American comedian and actor
1928   **James Coburn** -- American motion-picture actor
1931   **Jean Beliveau** -- Professional hockey player
1935   **Eldridge Cleaver** -- American civil rights activist
1935   **Frank Robinson** -- Hall of Fame baseball player and manager, who won the most valuable player award in each major league
1937   **Warren Berlinger** -- American motion-picture actor
1945   **Itzhak Perlman** -- Highly popular Israeli violinist
1945   **Van Morrison** -- Irish rock singer
1948   **Howard Porter** -- Professional basketball player
1949   **Richard Gere** -- American stage and motion-picture actor
1954   **Claudell Washington** -- Professional baseball player
1958   **Von Hayes** -- Professional baseball player

AUGUST 31 -- EVENTS

30 BC   Cleopatra, the famous queen of Egypt, killed herself, supposedly by clasping an asp to her breast.
1688   John Bunyan, the noted English writer and preacher, died at age 59.
1867   Charles Baudelaire, the great French poet, died in Paris at age 46.
1881   The U.S. Lawn Tennis Association held its first championship tournament, in Newport, R.I.
1886   The most disastrous American earthquake to occur east of the Mississippi River hit Charleston, South Carolina, killing 100 people.
1907   The Triple Entente was agreed to by Great Britain, France, and Russia.

1914 The Germans, under von Hindenburg, crushed the Russian Second Army in the Battle of Tannenberg in World War I.

1939 Adolf Hitler promised peace if Poland would accept sixteen conditions. Poland refused and World War II began the following day.

1949 The last meeting of the Grand Army of the Republic was held at Indianapolis with six of the surviving Civil War veterans attending.

1950 Gil Hodges of the Brooklyn Dodgers hit four home runs in a single game.

1969 Rocky Marciano, ex-heavyweight champion, was killed in a plane crash one day before his 46th birthday.

1976 Mexico floated the peso which immediately dropped 40% in value.

1980 Polish labor leaders signed agreements with the Communist government establishing the right to strike. The result was the Solidarity labor federation.

9

September

September, the ninth month of the year, was originally the seventh month in the ancient Roman calendar, accounting for its Latin name *Septembris*, meaning *seventh*. It originally had 30 days in the calendar of Romulus, but its length was reduced to 29 days by Numa Pompilius. The Julian Calendar increased its number of days to 31, and the emperor Augustus reduced it to its present number of 30 when he made several changes in order to increase his month, August, to one of 31 days.

Labor Day, the first Monday in September, is the only legal holiday to occur in the month, but the Jewish holidays of Rosh Hashanah, or New Year, and Yom Kippur, the Day of Atonement, also often fall in September. Another special day is Constitution Day on September 17, commemorating the signing of the Constitution on that date in 1787. Also, one United States President, William Howard Taft, was born in September.

The birthstone for September is the sapphire and the special flowers are the aster and the morning glory. Notable September birthdays and events follow.

SEPTEMBER 1 -- BIRTHDAYS

1529   **Taddeo Zuccaro** -- Italian painter and leader of the Mannerist school
1566   **Edward Alleyn** — One of the greatest actors of the Elizabethan stage

1854   **Engelbert Humperdinck** -- German composer noted for his opera *Hansel and Gretel* (1893)

1868   **Frank McKinney "Kin" Hubbard** -- American humorist, journalist, cartoonist, and creator of *Abe Martin*

1875   **Edgar Rice Burroughs** -- American author and creator of *Tarzan of the Apes* (1914), one of the most famous characters in fiction

1888   **Clement Wood** -- American lyricist noted for songs such as "Short'nin' Bread" and "De Glory Road"

1893   **Betty Blythe** -- American stage and motion-picture actress

1898   **Jimmy Hatlo** -- American cartoonist noted for his daily panel, *They'll Do It Everytime*

1899   **Richard Arlen** -- American motion-picture actor with a career of over 40 years

1904   **Johnny Mack Brown** -- Rose Bowl hero and motion-picture actor in over 200 films

1907   **Walter Reuther** -- American labor leader and president of the United Auto Workers, 1946-1970

1910   **Jack Hawkins** -- British stage and motion-picture actor

1922   **Yvonne De Carlo** -- Canadian-born motion-picture and television actress

1922   **Vittorio Gassman** -- Italian motion-picture actor

1922   **Melvin Laird** -- U.S. congressman and secretary of defense under President Nixon

1923   **Rocky Marciano** -- World heavyweight boxing champion, 1952-1956, who retired with 49 wins and no losses

1927   **Lloyd M. Bucher** -- Commander of the USS *Pueblo* when it was seized by the North Koreans in 1968

1933   **Conway Twitty** -- American country music singer

1935   **Guy Rodgers** -- Professional basketball player

1937   **Al Geiberger** -- Professional golfer

1938   **George Maharis** – American motion-picture and television actor

1939   **Lily Tomlin** -- American motion-picture and television actress

1941   **Rico Carty** -- Professional baseball player

1947   **Edward Podolak** -- Professional football player

1949   **Gary Maddox** -- Professional baseball player

1954   **Patrick DuPre** -- American tennis player

SEPTEMBER 1 -- EVENTS

1181   Lucius III became Roman Catholic pope.

1271   Gregory X was elected Roman Catholic pope.

1715   Louis XIV, the great French king, died in Paris four days before his 77th birthday.

1878   The first woman telephone operator, Miss Emma Nutt, was hired by the Telephone Dispatch Company in Boston.

1896   Chop suey was first concocted and served, not in China but in the U.S., by the chef of the visiting Chinese statesman Li Hung Chang.

1923   Japan suffered the worst earthquake in its history in which 143,000 persons were killed.

1939   World War II began at 5 A.M., as German troops smashed into Poland.

1972   Bobby Fischer became America's first world chess champion, defeating Russia's Boris Spassky in Reykjavik, Iceland.

1979   American space probe *Pioneer 11* flew past Saturn sending back information on two newly discovered rings.

1983   A Korean Air Lines Boeing 747 was shot down over the Sea of Japan by a Russian jet fighter, killing all 269 people on board.

1985   The *Titanic* was discovered by a team of French and American scientists on the ocean floor 13,000 feet below the surface and 400 miles south of Newfoundland.

SEPTEMBER 2 -- BIRTHDAYS

1838   **Liliuokalani** -- Queen of Hawaii, 1891-1893

1839   **Henry George** -- American social reformer, who first proposed the "single tax," and who wrote the classic book, *Progress and Poverty* (1879)

1840   **Giovanni Verga** -- Highly influential Italian novelist, playwright, and short story writer

1850   **Eugene Field** -- American poet and humorist, noted for "Little Boy Blue" and "Wynken, Blynken, and Nod"

1850   **Albert G. Spalding** -- Professional baseball player and manager, and sporting goods executive

1864   **Louis Seraphine** -- French painter

1901   **Adolph Rupp** -- Longtime basketball coach at the University of Kentucky

1905   **Vera Vague** -- American actress and comedienne

1914   **Romare Bearden** -- American painter

1917   **Cleveland Amory** -- American writer and columnist

1918   **Allen Drury** -- American editor and writer, who won the Pulitzer Prize in 1960 for his novel *Advise and Consent*

1918   **Martha Mitchell** -- Wife of attorney general and Watergate figure John Mitchell

1921   **Marge Champion** -- American dancer and actress

1937   **Peter Ueberroth** -- Commissioner of Baseball, 1984-1989

1948   **Terry Bradshaw** -- Professional football superstar

1950   **Lamar Johnson** -- Professional baseball player

1952   **Jimmy Connors** – American tennis player, 1974 Wimbledon singles champion, and the first man to win 100 singles titles

SEPTEMBER 2 -- EVENTS

44 BC   Cicero delivered his *First Philippic,* an attack on Mark Antony, in the Roman senate.

31 BC   Octavian's general, Agrippa, defeated the combined fleets of Antony and Cleopatra in the Battle of Actium, establishing Octavian as the ruler of the entire Roman world.

1666   The Great Fire of London broke out and within a week destroyed four-fifths of the city.

1789   The U.S. Department of the Treasury was established.

1864   Union troops under General Sherman entered Atlanta before continuing their "March to the Sea," in the Civil War.

1870   Napoleon III and his 80,000 troops surrendered to the Germans at Sedan in the Franco-Prussian War.

1901   Theodore Roosevelt, then vice president, said at the Minnesota State Fair, "Speak softly and carry a big stick; you will go far."

1930   The first nonstop flight from Europe to the United States was completed by French aviators Dieudonne Coste and Maurice Bellonte.

1945   The Allies and Japan signed the World War II surrender agreement on board the battleship *Missouri* in Tokyo Bay. President Truman proclaimed it V-J (Victory over Japan) Day.

SEPTEMBER 3 -- BIRTHDAYS

1499   **Diane de Poitiers** -- Duchess of Valentinois and mistress of King Henry II of France

1734   **Joseph Wright (Wright of Derby)** -- English painter

1814   **James Joseph Sylvester** -- Noted English mathematician

1849   **Sarah Orne Jewett** -- American novelist and short-story writer, noted for *The Country of the Pointed Furs* (1896)

1856   Louis Henri Sullivan -- One of America's greatest architects, and
        the pioneer of the skyscraper
1860   Edward Albert Filene -- American merchant and founder of the
        Twentieth Century Fund to study major economic problems
1907   Loren Eiseley -- American anthropologist and writer
1910   Dorothy Maynor -- American operatic soprano
1913   Alan Ladd -- American motion-picture actor in over 50 lead-
        ing roles
1914   Dixy Lee Ray -- Governor of Washington
1915   Kitty Carlisle -- American stage, screen, and television actress
1923   Mort Walker -- American cartoonist and creator of *Beetle Bailey*
1925   Hank Thompson -- American singer, guitarist, and bandleader
1926   Anne Jackson -- American stage, screen, and television actress
1926   Irene Papas -- Greek stage and screen actress and dancer
1935   Bob Ussery -- American jockey
1935   Eileen Brennan -- American stage, screen, and television actress
1942   Al Jardine -- Guitarist with the Beach Boys musical group
1943   Dave Eichelberger -- Professional golfer
1944   Valerie Perrine -- American actress and dancer
1952   Natalie Fuchs -- French tennis player
1965   Charlie Sheen -- American motion-picture actor and son of
        actor Martin Sheen

SEPTEMBER 3 -- EVENTS

1189   Richard the Lion-Hearted was crowned King of England.
1651   Oliver Cromwell, the English Commonwealth ruler, defeated
        the Royalists at Worcester, but Charles II, whom they were
        trying to restore to the throne, escaped to France.
1658   Oliver Cromwell, English Lord Protector, died at age 58.
1783   The Treaty of Paris recognized the independence of the thirteen
        American colonies, and established the boundaries of the new
        United States.
1826   The USS *Vincennes* left New York Harbor to circumnavigate the
        globe, the first warship to accomplish that feat.
1883   Ivan Turgenev, the great Russian writer, died in Bougival, near
        Paris, at age 64.
1894   The first Labor Day was celebrated as a legal holiday.
1914   Benedict XV was elected Roman Catholic pope.

1939   Great Britain and France declared war on Germany in World War II, two days after German dictator Adolf Hitler had attacked Poland.

1943   The Allies invaded the Italian mainland in World War II, landing at Calabria in southern Italy. The Italians signed an armistice later in the day.

1944   Canadian and British troops liberated Brussels in World War II.

1950   The comic strip, *Beetle Bailey,* by Mort Walker first appeared, on Walker's 27th birthday.

1951   The long-running TV soap opera *Search for Tomorrow* made its debut.

1969   Ho Chi Minh, North Vietnamese president, died at age 79.

1972   Mark Spitz, American swimmer, won the sixth of his seven gold medals in the 1972 Olympics in Munich, by winning the 100-meter freestyle.

1976   U.S. spacecraft *Viking 2* landed on Mars and began relaying to earth the first close-up, color photographs of the Martian surface.

SEPTEMBER 4 -- BIRTHDAYS

1768   **Francois Rene de Chateaubriand** – One of the most important figures in French romantic literature

1802   **Marcus Whitman** -- American pioneer, doctor, and missionary among the Indians

1804   **Thomas Ustick Walter** -- American architect who added the Senate and House wings and the large cast-iron dome to the United States Capitol

1824   **Anton Bruckner** -- Austrian composer and organist, best known for his nine symphonies

1824   **Phoebe Cary** -- American poet

1846   **Daniel Hudson Burnham** -- American architect who built the Railway Exchange Building in Chicago, one of the first skyscrapers in the U.S.

1848   **R.R. Bowker** -- American publisher, editor, and author

1888   **Peck Griffin** -- American Hall of Fame tennis player

1892   **Darius Milhaud** -- French-born composer noted for his works for the stage, such as *The Creation of the World* and *Christophe Colomb*

1893   **Frank Warshauer** – American composer, author, and conductor, noted for songs such as "It Isn't Fair" and "Rainy Day Blues"

1895   **Nigel Bruce** -- Mexican-born motion-picture actor

1905   **Mary Renault** -- English novelist noted for works such as *The Last of the Wine* (1956), *The King Must Die* (1958), and *The Bull from the Sea* (1962)

1908   **Richard Wright** – American novelist, short-story writer, and author of *Native Son* (1940) and *Black Boy* (1945)

1915   **Richard Thomas Goldhahn** -- American composer noted for songs such as "Sioux City Sue" and "Esmereldy"

1917   **Henry Ford II** -- President of the Ford Motor Company and grandson of Ford founder Henry Ford

1918   **Paul Harvey** -- American television commentator

1918   **Bill Talbert** – One of the world's outstanding doubles tennis players, ranking in the top ten 13 years

1926   **Donald Petersen** – Chairman and Chief Executive Office of Ford Motor Company

1929   **Thomas Eagleton** -- U.S. senator and 1972 candidate for vice president whose place was taken by Sargent Schriver because of Eagleton's history of mental treatment

1930   **Mitzi Gaynor** -- American actress and dancer

1933   **Richard Castellano** – American stage, screen, and television actor

1942   **Ray Floyd** -- Professional golfer

1949   **Tom Watson** – Professional golfer and one of the game's super-stars of the 1970s and 1980s

1950   **Doyle Alexander** -- Professional baseball player

1950   **Frank White** -- Professional baseball player

1951   **Judith Ivey** -- American stage, screen, and television actress

SEPTEMBER 4 -- EVENTS

1609   Henry Hudson, the famous British sea captain, discovered Manhattan Island.

1781   Los Angeles was founded by Felipe de Neve, the Spanish governor of Upper California.

1870   Revolutionists overthrew the Empire of Napoleon III and proclaimed the Third Republic in France, two days after Napoleon surrendered at Sedan in the Franco-Prussian War.

1882   America's first steam electric-power plant, the Pearl Street Station, built by Thomas A. Edison, went into operation in New York City.

1886   The famous Apache chief Geronimo surrendered to U.S. General Nelson Miles at Skeleton Canyon in Arizona.

1888   George Eastman patented the first hand-held roll-film camera, which he called a Kodak.

1929 The *Graf Zeppelin* completed the only round-the-world trip by an airship.

1939 The U.S. Navy received orders to shoot on sight any vessel that threatened American ships, as World War II raged in Europe.

1944 The Allies liberated Antwerp from Germany in World War II.

1948 After celebrating her Golden Jubilee in August, Queen Wilhelmina abdicated, making her daughter Juliana Queen of the Netherlands.

1957 The school integration crisis began in Little Rock, Arkansas, resulting eventually in President Eisenhower's sending in Federal troops to enforce the court integration orders.

1957 Ford Motor Company introduced the Edsel automobile, which was subsequently so unpopular its name became synonymous with failure.

1965 Albert Schweitzer, the great German philosopher, physician, and musician, died at age 90.

1972 American swimmer Mark Spitz won a record 7th Olympic gold medal in the 400-meter relay at the Munich Olympic Games.

SEPTEMBER 5 -- BIRTHDAYS

1187 **Louis VIII** -- Capetian king of France, 1223-1226

1568 **Tommaso Campanella** -- Italian Platonic philosopher, poet, and writer, best known for his socialistic work, *The City of the Sun* (1602)

1638 **Louis XIV** -- The "Sun King" of France, 1643-1715, who ruled in one of France's most brilliant periods

1735 **Johann Christian Bach** -- German composer and youngest son of Johann Sebastian Bach

1774 **Kaspar David Friedrich** -- German painter

1791 **Giacomo Meyerbeer** -- German composer who was one of the most popular opera composers of his day

1817 **Aleksey Konstantinovich Tolstoy** -- Russian poet and novelist

1847 **Jesse James** -- Notorious outlaw of the American West, who specialized in robbing trains and banks

1875 **Napoleon Lajoie** -- Hall of Fame baseball player, who hit .422 in 1901 and had 3,251 career hits

1897 **Arthur C. Nielsen** -- Founder of the Nielsen system of rating television shows

1897 **Morris Carnovsky** -- American stage and motion-picture actor with a career of over 55 years

1901 **Florence Eldridge** -- American stage and motion-picture actress with a career of over 40 years

1902   **Darryl F. Zanuck** – Flamboyant picture maker of Hollywood's Golden Age, who produced such classics as *The Grapes of Wrath* (1940) and *Tobacco Road* (1941)

1905   **Arthur Koestler** -- Yugoslavian novelist and essayist, noted for *Darkness at Noon* (1941)

1910   **Clyde D. Sandgren** -- American composer and author, noted for songs such as "Near You," "Little Girl," and "I'm Pretending"

1912   **John Cage** -- Highly original and controversial modern American composer, noted for seeking new sounds, such as by inserting objects between some of the piano strings

1913   **John Mitchell** -- U.S. attorney general, Watergate figure, and the first member of any president's cabinet to be imprisoned

1916   **Frank Yerby** -- American novelist and author of works such as *The Foxes of Harrow*

1921   **Jack Valenti** – President of the Motion Picture Association of America

1927   **Paul A. Volcker Jr.** -- Chairman of the board of governors of the Federal Reserve System under Presidents Carter and Reagan

1929   **Bob Newhart** -- American comedian and actor

1932   **Carol Lawrence** -- American actress and dancer

1933   **Katherine Helmond** -- American actress

1936   **Bill Mazeroski** -- Professional baseball player who hit the last pitch of the 1960 World Series for a home run to give the Pittsburgh Pirates the victory over the New York Yankees

1936   **John Danforth** -- U.S. senator

1939   **Bill Kilmer** -- Professional football superstar

1939   **William Devane** -- American stage, screen, and television actor

1940   **Raquel Welch** -- American motion-picture actress

1946   **Buddy Miles** -- American rock drummer

1950   **Cathy Lee Guisewite** – American cartoonist and creator of the comic strip *Cathy*

1960   **Candy Maldonado** -- Professional baseball player

SEPTEMBER 5 -- EVENTS

1316   John XXII, the second Roman Catholic pope to reside in Avignon, France, rather than Rome, was crowned.

1569   Pieter Bruegel the Elder, the great Flemish painter, died at age 44.

1698   Russian czar Peter the Great imposed a tax on beards.

1755   Six thousand Acadians were expelled by the British from Nova Scotia, providing the inspiration for Longfellow's famous poem "Evangeline"

1774   The First Continental Congress met at Philadelphia, with 56 delegates representing 12 colonies attending.

1791   Wolfgang Amadeus Mozart, the great composer, died in Vienna at age 35.

1836   Sam Houston was elected as first president of the Republic of Texas.

1882   Workers staged the first Labor Day parade, in New York City.

1885   Jake D. Gumper of Fort Wayne, Indiana, bought the first gasoline pump manufactured in the United States.

1905   The Treaty of Portsmouth ended the Russo-Japanese War.

1972   Arab terrorists killed 2 Israeli Olympic players and held 9 others hostage in Munich. The hostages and the terrorists were later killed in a police shoot-out.

1975   President Gerald Ford escaped assassination in Sacramento, California, when a Secret Service agent deflected a gun pointed at him by a woman named Squeaky Fromme.

1984   Space shuttle *Discovery* safely completed its flight as it landed at Edwards Air Force Base, California.

SEPTEMBER 6 -- BIRTHDAYS

1475   **Sebastiano Serlio** -- Italian Mannerist architect and painter

1666   **Ivan V** – Czar of Russia, 1682-1689, and weak-minded half brother of Peter the Great

1757   **Marquis de Lafayette** -- French soldier and statesman who fought with the Americans in the Revolutionary War

1766   **John Dalton** – English chemist who in 1802 formulated Dalton's Law, the law of partial pressures in gases

1805   **Horatio Greenough** – American sculptor noted for the famous statue of George Washington (1840) that stands in the Smithsonian Institution in Washington, D.C.

1835   **Justin Louis Emile Combes** – French premier during the Dreyfus Affair

1860   **Jane Addams** – American social worker and humanitarian, who founded Hull House in Chicago and shared the 1931 Nobel Peace Prize

1876   **Boardman Robinson** – American artist, mural painter, and illustrator, noted for his illustrations for Fyodor Dostoevsky's novel, *The Brothers Karamazov*

1885　　Otto Kruger -- American stage and motion-picture actor with a fifty-year career

1888　　Joseph P. Kennedy -- American ambassador, financier, and father of President John F. Kennedy

1888　　Red Faber -- Hall of Fame baseball player

1893　　John W. Bricker -- U.S. senator and vice presidential candidate in 1944

1899　　Billy Rose -- American theatrical impresario and pop song composer, noted for songs such as "Me and My Shadow," "The Night Is Young and You're So Beautiful," and "It's Only a Paper Moon"

1903　　"Slapsie" Maxie Rosenbloom -- American professional boxer and character comedian of Hollywood films

1908　　Raymond Firestone -- Chairman of the board of Firestone Tire and Rubber Company

1924　　John Melcher -- U.S. senator

1929　　Dow Finsterwald -- Professional golfer

1937　　Jo Ann Worley -- American actress and comedienne

1944　　Roger Waters -- Bass player for the Pink Floyd rock group

1944　　Swoosie Kurtz -- American stage, screen, and television actress

1947　　Jane Curtin -- American actress and comedienne

SEPTEMBER 6 -- EVENTS

1492　　Christopher Columbus left San Sebastian in the Canary Islands, resuming his first voyage westward to America.

1522　　The *Victoria,* the last surviving ship of Magellan's fleet, commanded by Sebastian del Cano, arrived in Sanlucar, Spain, completing the first trip around the world.

1628　　The Massachusetts Bay Colony was established in Salem, Massachusetts, by a group of 100 English Puritans led by John Endecott.

1898　　Queen Wilhelmina was crowned Queen of the Netherlands. She had been queen since 1890 with her mother, Queen Emma, ruling as regent until 1898.

1901　　President William McKinley was shot by the assassin Leon Czolgosz at the Pan-American Exposition in Buffalo. He died 8 days later.

1914　　The First Battle of the Marne began in France in World War I.

1948　　The coronation of Queen Juliana of the Netherlands took place in Amsterdam.

1978   Camp David summit talks began between Egypt's President Anwar Sadat, Israel's President Menachem Begin, and President Jimmy Carter.

SEPTEMBER 7 -- BIRTHDAYS

1492   **Jacopo Aconcio** -- Italian Protestant leader of the Reformation era

1533   **Elizabeth I** -- Queen of England, 1558-1603, during one of the most glorious periods in English history, and one of the greatest monarchs of all time

1707   **Georges Louis Leclerc de Buffon** -- French naturalist and writer, and one of the forerunners of Charles Darwin in considering the facts of evolution

1819   **Thomas A. Hendricks** -- U.S. vice president in President Cleveland's first term

1831   **Victorien Sardou** -- One of the most successful French playwrights of his time, whose *La Tosca* became the basis of Giacomo Puccini's noted opera of the same name

1860   **Grandma Moses** -- American primitive painter, Anna Mary Robertson Moses, who started painting at age 76 and painted 25 pictures after her 100th birthday

1867   **J.P. Morgan Jr.** -- American financier who succeeded his father as chairman of the board of U.S. Steel Corporation

1885   **Elinor Wylie** -- American poet, noted for "Jennifer Lorn" (1923)

1887   **Dame Edith Sitwell** -- English poet and literary critic

1897   **Al Sherman** -- Russian-born composer and author, noted for songs such as "On the Beach at Bali-Bali," "For Sentimental Reasons," and "No! No! A Thousand Times No!"

1900   **Taylor Caldwell** -- English-born American novelist noted for works such as *Dynasty of Death* (1938) and *This Side of Innocence* (1946)

1903   **Margaret Landon** -- Author of *Anna and the King of Siam*

1905   **Ivy Baker Priest** -- Treasurer of the United States under President Eisenhower

1908   **Paul Brown** -- Professional football player and coach, noted for his work with the Cleveland Browns (the only professional team ever named for its coach)

1908   **Michael Ellis De Bakey** -- American heart surgeon noted for his pioneering work in the treatment of cardiovascular disease

1909   **Elia Kazan** -- Turkish-born American motion-picture director, noted for films such as *Gentlemen's Agreement* (1947), *On the Waterfront* (1954), and *East of Eden* (1955)

1913   **Anthony Quayle** -- British motion-picture and television actor

1914   **James A. Van Allen** -- American physicist, who in 1958 discovered the Van Allen radiation belts that circle the earth

1923   **Louise Suggs** -- Professional golfer

1923   **Peter Lawford** -- American motion-picture actor

1924   **Daniel Inouye** -- First U.S. senator of Japanese ancestry

1929   **Clyde Lovellette** – Professional basketball player with 12,000 career points

1930   **Sonny Rollins** -- American saxophonist

1930   **Baudouin** -- King of Belgium who assumed the throne in 1951 when his father, Leopold III, abdicated

1936   **Buddy Holly** -- American singer, guitarist, and songwriter

1937   **John Phillip Law** -- American motion-picture actor

1942   **Richard Roundtree** -- American motion-picture actor

1946   **Joe Rudi** -- Professional baseball player

1948   **John Brockington** -- Professional football player

1951   **Bert Jones** -- Professional football player

1955   **Corbin Bernsen** -- American motion-picture and television actor noted for his role in the popular series *L.A. Law*

SEPTEMBER 7 -- EVENTS

70 AD   The Romans sacked Jerusalem, leaving only the "Wailing Wall" intact.

1502   Amerigo Vespucci, the Italian traveler for whom America was named, returned to Lisbon after his third trip to America.

1812   Napoleon defeated the Russians, led by Marshal Kutuzov, in the Battle of Borodino, and subsequently captured Moscow. In the process, however, his French Grande Armee was decimated.

1822   Brazil declared its independence from Portugal. The break was accomplished without bloodshed.

1825   The French hero of the American Revolution, the Marquis de Lafayette, gave his last farewell to President John Quincy Adams at the White House while on his famous U.S. tour.

1876   Jesse James and the Younger Brothers attempted to rob the First National Bank of Northfield, Minnesota, in a bungled holdup that destroyed the notorious James-Younger gang.

1892   Gentleman Jim Corbett knocked out John L. Sullivan in the 21st round of the first major prize fight fought under the Marquis of Queensberry rules.

1921   The first American beauty contest ever held was won by Margaret Gorham, who won the first Miss America Contest in Atlantic City, New Jersey.

1940   German planes blasted London, marking the beginning of the London Blitz in World War II in which the city was bombed 82 out of 85 nights.

1977   President Jimmy Carter and General Omar Torrijos Herrera, Panama's chief of government, signed the Panama Canal treaties providing for eventual return of the canal to Panama.

SEPTEMBER 8 -- BIRTHDAYS

1157   **Richard the Lion-Hearted** -- King of England, 1189-1199, known as Richard I, who was the first of the Plantagenet dynasty

1474   **Ludovico Ariosto** -- Italian Renaissance poet, noted for the long narrative poem, *Orlando Furioso* (1516), which influenced the works of Byron, Milton, and Shakespeare

1767   **August Wilhelm von Schlegel** -- German writer and critic, and translator of Shakespeare's plays

1804   **Eduard Morike** -- German lyric poet and novelist

1830   **Frederic Mistral** -- French Nobel Prize-winning poet, noted for works such as "Mireille" and "Song of the Rhine"

1841   **Antonin Dvorak** -- Czechoslovakian composer best known for his symphony *From the New World*

1886   **Siegfried Sassoon** -- English poet and writer

1889   **Robert A. Taft** -- U.S. senator, 1939-1953, and son of President William Howard Taft

1896   **Howard Dietz** -- American songwriter and publicity executive, who created the M-G-M trademark, Leo the Lion, and its Latin motto, *Ars Gratia Artis*

1896   **Frank Silver** -- American conductor, author, and drummer, noted for songs such as "Yes, We Have No Bananas"

1897   **Jimmy Rodgers** -- American composer, author, and singer, noted for songs such as "In the Jailhouse Now" and "Mississippi Moon"

1900   **Claude Pepper** -- U.S. senator and congressman who served in Congress and was a strong advocate for the elderly until his death in 1989

1901   Hendrik F. Verwoerd -- Prime minister of the Republic of South Africa, 1958-1966
1907   **Buck Leonard** -- Hall of Fame baseball player
1911   **Euell Gibbons** -- American writer and nutritional expert
1912   **Leo Cherne** -- American author, sculptor, and diplomat
1912   **Jacques Fath** -- French clothing designer
1916   **Hillary Brooke** -- American stage and motion-picture actress
1922   **Sid Caesar** -- American comedian and actor
1924   **Grace Metalious** -- American writer and author of *Peyton Place*
1924   **Wendell Ford** -- U.S. senator
1925   **Peter Sellers** -- English comedian and motion-picture actor
1930   **Nguyen Cao Ky** – South Vietnamese military and political leader
1938   **Sam Nunn** -- U.S. senator
1946   **Patrick Hombergen** -- Belgian tennis player
1946   **Ken Forsch** -- Professional baseball player
1946   **Ron "Pigpen" McKernan** -- American rock musician with the Grateful Dead

SEPTEMBER 8 -- EVENTS

1380   Dmitri Donskoi, the Prince of Moscow, defeated the Mongols in the Battle of Kulikovo.
1565   Spanish explorer Pedro Menendez de Aviles founded St. Augustine, Florida, the oldest city in the United States.
1664   Peter Stuyvesant surrendered New Amsterdam to the British fleet sent by the Duke of York. The British renamed the city New York.
1935   Senator Huey Long of Louisiana, the founder of the famous Long dynasty, was shot in the state capitol in Baton Rouge by Dr. Carl Weiss. He died two days later.
1941   Twenty-three German armies surrounded Leningrad and began a 17-month siege in World War II.
1943   Italy's unconditional surrender to the Allies in World War II, signed 5 days earlier by Marshal Badoglio, was announced by General Dwight D. Eisenhower.
1950   United Nations forces stopped the Communist advance at the Pusan Peninsula in southeastern Korea in the Korean War.
1968   Saundra Williams was chosen the first "Miss Black America."
1974   President Gerald Ford granted a "full, free, and absolute" pardon to former President Richard Nixon for all crimes he committed "or may have committed" while president.

SEPTEMBER 9 -- BIRTHDAYS

1585   **Cardinal Richelieu** -- One of the ablest of French statesmen, who as chief minister to King Louis XIII was the actual ruler of France from 1624 to 1642

1711   **Thomas Hutchinson** -- The last royal governor of the Massachusetts Bay colony, who precipitated the Boston Tea Party by refusing to let the tea ships leave Boston Harbor

1737   **Luigi Galvani** -- Italian pioneer in the study of electricity and its relation to living organisms

1754   **William Bligh** -- English captain of the HMS *Bounty* at the time of the famous mutiny in 1789

1828   **Leo Tolstoy** -- One of Russia's greatest writers, and the author of *War and Peace* (1865-1869) and *Anna Karenina* (1875-1877), two of the great books of world literature

1852   **John Henry Poynting** -- English physicist for whom the Poynting vector was named

1873   **Max Reinhardt** -- Austrian-American theatrical producer and director, noted for his spectacular productions

1877   **Frank Chance** -- Hall of Fame baseball player and member of the famed Tinker-to-Evers-to-Chance double play combination

1887   **Alfred M. Landon** -- U.S. presidential candidate in 1936

1890   **Colonel Harland Sanders** -- Founder of the Kentucky Fried Chicken restaurant chain

1894   **Arthur Freed** -- American lyricist and producer, noted for songs such as "You Were Meant for Me," "Singin' in the Rain," and "Temptation"

1898   **Frank Frisch** -- Hall of Fame baseball player and manager

1899   **Waite Hoyt** -- Hall of Fame baseball player

1900   **James Hilton** -- English novelist, noted for *Lost Horizon* (1933), in which the name Shangri-la was coined to denote a remote utopian land, and *Goodbye, Mr. Chips* (1934)

1905   **Joseph E. Levine** -- American motion-picture producer, noted for films such as *The Graduate* (1967) and *The Lion in Winter* (1968)

1924   **Jane Greer** -- American motion-picture actress

1925   **Cliff Robertson** -- American stage and motion-picture actor

1932   **Sylvia Miles** -- American stage and motion-picture actress

1941   **Otis Redding** -- American soul singer

1949   **John Curry** -- British-born ice skating virtuoso

1949   **Joseph Theismann** -- Professional football player

1952   **Jerry Mumphrey** -- Professional baseball player
1962   **Kristy McNichol** – American motion-picture and television actress

SEPTEMBER 9 -- EVENTS

1087   William the Conqueror died in Rouen at age 59 after an accident while riding his horse.

1492   Columbus and his men lost sight of land, 3 days after leaving the Canary Islands. They would not see land again until October 12, when the New World was discovered.

1499   Vasco da Gama, the great Portuguese navigator, returned to Lisbon after becoming the first man to reach India by sailing around the Cape of Good Hope.

1689   Peter the Great took power in Russia when he was 17 by deposing his sister Sophia, who had seized the regency when Peter was 10.

1776   The Continental Congress made the name *United States* official.

1850   California was admitted to the Union as the 31st state.

1901   Henri Toulouse-Lautrec, the great French painter, died at Chateau de Malrome at age 36.

1914   The Allies stopped the Germans, as the First Battle of the Marne ended in World War I.

1926   The National Broadcasting Company (NBC) was organized with 25 radio stations.

1934   The comic strip, *The Little King,* by Otto Soglow, first appeared.

1943   The U.S. Fifth Army under General Mark Clark invaded Italy at Salerno in World War II.

1965   Sandy Koufax pitched a perfect game (no runner reached base), as Los Angeles beat Chicago, 1-0. It was Koufax's fourth career no-hit game.

1965   Bert Campaneris of the Kansas City A's became the first major-league baseball player to play each of the nine field positions in a single game.

1971   The John F. Kennedy Center for the Performing Arts opened in Washington, D.C., with a performance of Leonard Bernstein's *Mass.*

1976   Chairman Mao Tse-tung of China died at 82.

SEPTEMBER 10 -- BIRTHDAYS

1487   **Julius III** -- Roman Catholic pope, 1550-1555

1624   **Thomas Sydenham** -- English physician and one of the best of his time

1638   **Marie-Therese** – Queen consort of Louis XIV, the great "Sun King" of France

1736   **Carter Braxton** -- American Revolutionary War statesman, member of the Continental Congress, and signer of the Declaration of Independence

1753   **Sir John Soane** -- English architect

1771   **Mungo Park** -- Scottish explorer of the Niger River in Africa

1839   **Isaac K. Funk** – Co-publisher of Funk and Wagnalls' dictionary

1873   **Charles Talbut Onions** -- British lexicographer

1885   **Carl Van Doren** -- American writer and winner of the 1939 Pulitzer Prize in biography for *Benjamin Franklin*

1886   **Hilda Doolittle** -- American poet, leader of the imagist movement, and author of "Sea Garden" (1916)

1890   **Franz Werfel** -- Austrian novelist, playwright, and poet, noted for works such as *The Song of Bernadette* (1941)

1890   **Elsa Schiaparelli** -- French clothing designer

1892   **Arthur H. Compton** -- American physicist who headed one of the groups that produced the atomic bomb, and shared the 1927 Nobel Prize for his discovery of the Compton effect

1898   **Bessie Love** – One of the greatest actresses of the D.W. Griffith era, whose career spanned 60 years

1900   **Francis Craig**–American composer and pianist, noted for songs such as "Near You" and "Beg Your Pardon"

1903   **Cyril Connolly** -- English novelist and editor of *Horizon*

1906   **Leonard Lyons** -- American newspaper columnist

1915   **Edmond O'Brien** – American motion-picture and television actor

1924   **Ted Kluszewski** -- Professional baseball player and coach

1927   **Yma Sumac** -- South American singer

1929   **Arnold Palmer** -- One of the world's greatest golfers, who dominated the game in the 1950s and 1960s, and became the first professional to win $1 million in tournament prize money

1934   **Roger Maris** – Professional baseball player who hit a record 61 home runs in 1961

1934   **Charles Kuralt** -- American broadcast journalist and host of the television shows, *On the Road with Charles Kuralt* and *Sunday Morning*

1944   **John Entwistle** -- British bassist for the Who musical group

1945   **Jose Feliciano** – Blind-from-birth Puerto Rican singer and guitarist

1945   **Marlin Briscoe** -- Professional football player
1951   **Gary Danielson** -- Professional football player
1953   **Amy Irving** -- American stage and motion-picture actress

SEPTEMBER 10 -- EVENTS

422 AD Saint Celestine I was elected Roman Catholic pope.
1419   John the Fearless of Burgundy was assassinated.
1533   Future Queen Elizabeth I of England was christened.
1608   John Smith was elected president of the colony council of Jamestown, Virginia.
1742   Faneuil Hall, the "Cradle of Liberty" in Boston, was completed.
1813   Commodore Oliver Hazard Perry defeated the British in the Battle of Lake Erie in the War of 1812, and sent the message: "We have met the enemy and they are ours."
1846   Elias Howe patented his sewing machine.
1938   The comic strip, *The Lone Ranger,* by Ed Kressy, first appeared.
1939   Canada declared war on Germany, the first time in history that Canada had declared war independently.
1944   The U.S. First Army fired the first American shells to reach German soil, near Aachen, in World War II.
1955   The television show, *Gunsmoke,* began its weekly run that lasted nearly 20 years.
1967   Gibraltar residents voted to remain British rather than join Spain.

SEPTEMBER 11 -- BIRTHDAYS

1524   **Pierre de Ronsard** -- French Renaissance poet, known as the "Prince of Poets," who led the influential group of poets called the Pleiade
1556   **St. Joseph Calasanzio** -- Spanish priest and teacher
1611   **Henri d'Auvergne Turenne** -- French marshal who led the Frondeurs in an unsuccessful uprising against Cardinal Mazarin
1700   **James Thomson** -- The most celebrated Scottish poet of the 1700s until Robert Burns
1743   **Nicolai Abraham Abildgaard** -- The most renowned Danish painter of the late 18th century
1744   **Sarah Bache** -- The only daughter of Benjamin Franklin
1854   **William Holabird** -- American architect
1862   **O. Henry (William Sidney Porter)** -- American master of the short story, noted for works such as "Cabbages and Kings" (1904) and "The Gentle Grafter" (1908)

1877   **Sir James Jeans** -- English physicist and mathematician, noted for his contributions to the kinetic theory of gases

1885   **D.H. Lawrence** -- Influential English novelist, noted for works such as *The Rainbow* (1915), *Women in Love* (1920), and *Lady Chatterley's Lover* (1928)

1885   **Herbert Stothart** -- American composer, conductor, and pianist, noted for songs such as "I Wanna Be Loved By You" and "The Donkey Serenade"

1911   **Ramez Idriss** -- American composer, author, and musician, noted for songs such as "The Woody Woodpecker Song"

1913   **Paul "Bear" Bryant** -- The winningest college football coach in history, with 323 career victories

1917   **Ferdinand Marcos** -- President of the Philippines

1917   **Jessica Mitford** -- English author and journalist

1922   **Charles Evers** -- American civil rights leader

1924   **Tom Landry** -- Highly successful professional football coach

1928   **Reuben Askew** -- Governor of Florida

1928   **Earl Holliman** -- American motion-picture and television actor

1932   **Bob Packwood** -- U.S. senator

1935   **Gherman Stepanovich Titov** -- Russian cosmonaut on the first manned space flight of more than a single orbit, in *Vostok 2* in 1961

1944   **Dave Roberts** -- Professional baseball player

1947   **Larry Cox** -- Professional baseball player

1958   **Don Slaught** -- Professional baseball player

1964   **Ellis Burks** -- Professional baseball player

SEPTEMBER 11 -- EVENTS

814 AD Louis I (the Pious) succeeded his father, the great French king Charlemagne, as King of the Franks and Emperor of the Romans.

1777   General Howe defeated George Washington at the Battle of Brandywine, enabling the British to occupy Philadelphia in the Revolutionary War.

1789   Alexander Hamilton was appointed America's first Secretary of the Treasury.

1814   American commander Thomas Macdonough defeated the British on Lake Champlain in the War of 1812, in one of the most decisive battles ever fought by the U.S. Navy.

1847   Stephen Foster's "Oh! Susanna" was first sung publicly, in Andrew's Eagle Ice Cream Saloon in Pittsburgh.

1850   Jenny Lind, "The Swedish Nightingale," opened her American concert series at Castle Garden in New York.

1941   President Franklin D. Roosevelt ordered the U.S. Navy to shoot on sight German U-boats threatening American ships.

1944   Prime Minister Churchill and President Roosevelt held their second Quebec Conference in World War II.

1945   Former Japanese premier Hideki Tojo attempted suicide in Tokyo. He was hospitalized and lived to be executed for war crimes.

1971   Nikita Khrushchev, the former Soviet premier, died at age 77.

1973   Chilean President Salvador Allende Gossens was deposed in a military coup, and, according to the new leaders, he committed suicide.

1985   Pete Rose broke Ty Cobb's long-standing record as he made his 4,192nd career base hit.

SEPTEMBER 12 -- BIRTHDAYS

1310   **Niccolo Acciaiuoli** -- Italian statesman and soldier

1494   **Francis I** -- King of France, 1515-1547, great patron of the Renaissance in France, and pleasure lover, whose self-proclaimed pastime was to "go a-whoring"

1575   **Henry Hudson** -- British sea captain who in his famous ship, the *Half Moon,* explored the Hudson River, the Hudson Bay, and Hudson Strait (date of birth uncertain)

1788   **Alexander Campbell** -- American religious leader, who was a co-founder in the early 1800s of the Christian Church (Disciples of Christ)

1812   **Richard March Hoe** -- American inventor and manufacturer, who in 1846 invented the rotary press used in modern newspaper printing

1818   **Richard Jordan Gatling** -- American inventor, best known for the invention of the Gatling gun, the first practical, quick-firing machine gun developed in the United States

1829   **Anselm Feuerbach** -- German painter

1852   **Herbert Henry Asquith** -- Prime minister of Great Britain, 1908-1916, during whose administration the Old Age Pension Act and the National Insurance Act were passed

1880   **H.L. Mencken** -- American journalist, author, and pungent critic, who greatly influenced American writing in the 1920s

1888   **Maurice Chevalier** -- French musical comedy actor, singer, and dancer, with a 60-year career

1892   **Alfred A. Knopf** -- American publisher and founder of Alfred A. Knopf, Inc.

1893   **Lewis B. Hershey** -- American army general who headed the national draft board in World War II and the Korean War

1898   **Ben Shahn** -- Lithuanian-born American artist, noted for his realistic paintings and drawings

1902   **Juscelino Kubitschek** -- President of Brazil who pushed through construction of the new capital of Brasilia

1907   **Spud Chandler** -- Professional baseball player

1913   **Jesse Owens** -- American athlete, who in one day set three world track records and tied another, and who was the hero of the 1936 Olympics in Berlin

1914   **Eddy Howard** -- American composer, conductor, and guitarist, noted for songs such as "Lonesome Tonight"

1916   **Charlie Keller** -- Professional baseball player

1938   **Tatiana Troyanos** -- American mezzo-soprano

1940   **Mickey Lolich** -- Professional baseball player

1942   **Linda Gray** -- American actress noted for her role as Sue Ellen in the long-running television series *Dallas*

SEPTEMBER 12 -- EVENTS

1185   Byzantine emperor Andronicus I was tortured and executed by the Greek nobility, led by Isaac Angelus, during a war between the Byzantines and Norman invaders of the empire.

1609   Henry Hudson, the famous British sea captain, discovered the Hudson River.

1687   John Alden, the last surviving member of the Pilgrims who came to America on the *Mayflower,* died at age 88.

1759   British troops scaled the heights below the Plains of Abraham before Quebec. The next morning they were there ready to face the startled French defenders of the city.

1846   Robert Browning and Elizabeth Barrett, the noted English poets, were married secretly because Elizabeth's father violently opposed the wedding.

1847   American general Winfield Scott attacked Chapultepec, a fortified hill guarding the gates to Mexico City in the Mexican War.

1848   The Swiss Confederation was formed with the adoption of a new constitution.

1908   Winston Churchill married Clementine Hozier.

1928   Katharine Hepburn, the great American actress, made her New York debut in the play *Night Hostess.*

1943   Benito Mussolini was rescued by German paratroopers from a hotel in Lake Bracciano, Italy, where he was held captive by the Italian government.

1944   General Hodge's First Army became the first American troops
        to enter Germany in World War II, as they smashed across the
        German border near Trier.
1953   John F. Kennedy married Jacqueline Lee Bouvier.
1959   Russia launched *Luna 2,* the first man-made object to reach
        the moon.
1960   Democratic presidential candidate John F. Kennedy told the
        Houston Ministerial Association: "I believe in an America where
        the separation of church and state is absolute."
1974   Emperor Haile Selassie I of Ethiopia was deposed by military
        leaders, after 58 years as absolute ruler.

SEPTEMBER 13 -- BIRTHDAYS

1813   **Daniel Macmillan** -- Co-founder of Macmillan and Company
        publishers
1819   **Clara Schumann** -- German pianist and wife of composer Robert
        Schumann
1826   **Anthony Joseph Drexel** – American financier and philanthro-
        pist, who in 1891 founded Drexel Institute of Technology
1851   **Walter Reed** -- U.S. Army pathologist who proved that yellow
        fever is transmitted by the bite of a mosquito
1857   **Milton Snavely Hershey** -- American industrialist who founded
        the Hershey Chocolate Corporation
1860   **John J. Pershing** – American general who commanded the
        American Expeditionary Forces in Europe during World War I
1863   **Cyrus Adler** -- American scholar, educator, and editor
1873   **Constantin Caratheodory** -- Noted Greek mathematician
1874   **Arnold Schoenberg** -- Austrian composer
1876   **Sherwood Anderson** -- American short-story writer and novel-
        ist, noted for works such as *Winesburg, Ohio* (1919)
1894   **John Boynton Priestley** -- English novelist, playwright, and jour-
        nalist, noted for such works as *The Good Companions* (1929) and
        Lost Empires (1965)
1905   **Claudette Colbert** -- French-born American stage and motion-
        picture actress, who won the 1934 Academy Award for best
        actress in *It Happened One Night*
1906   **Thornton Lee** -- Professional baseball player
1916   **Roald Dahl** -- English writer noted for works such as *The
        Gremlins* (1943) and *Charlie and the Chocolate Factory* (1964)
1916   **Dick Haymes** -- American singer and actor

1924	**Maurice Jarre** -- French composer who won Academy Awards for the scores of *Lawrence of Arabia* (1962) and *Dr. Zhivago* (1965)
1924	**Scott Brady** -- American motion-picture and television actor
1925	**Mel Torme** -- American composer, author, and singer, noted for songs such as "Stranger in Town," "The Christmas Song," and "Born to Be Blue"
1937	**Fred Silverman** -- American television broadcasting executive
1941	**Pierre Barthes** -- French tennis player
1944	**Jacqueline Bisset** -- English-born motion-picture actress
1945	**Rick Wise** -- Professional baseball player
1948	**Perry Curtis** -- Professional basketball player
1949	**Rick Dempsey** -- Professional baseball player
1949	**Jim Cleamons** -- Professional basketball player

SEPTEMBER 13 -- EVENTS

81 AD	Roman emperor Titus, who was on the throne when Pompeii was destroyed by the eruption of Mount Vesuvius, died in Rome at age 40.
604 AD	Sabinianus was elected Roman Catholic pope.
1592	Michel Eyquem de Montaigne, the great French writer, died at Chateau de Montaigne, near Bordeaux, at age 59.
1759	The British defeated the French in the Battle of Quebec, in which both generals Wolfe and Montcalm were killed, and as a result of which the French lost their American empire.
1788	The U.S. Constitutional Convention authorized the first national election in the United States.
1847	U.S. general Winfield Scott defeated the Mexicans in the Battle of Chapultepec, near Mexico City, one of the last engagements of the Mexican War.
1922	The temperature hit 136.4 degrees Fahrenheit in Al'azizyah, Libya, the highest recorded in history.
1931	The song, "Life is Just a Bowl of Cherries," was introduced by singer Rudy Vallee in a musical revue in New York.
1943	Chiang Kai-shek became president of China.

SEPTEMBER 14 -- BIRTHDAYS

1547	**Jan van Olden Barneveldt** -- Dutch prime minister and one of the foremost statesmen of his time

1618   Sir Peter Lely -- Dutch-English painter

1645   Jeremiah Dummer -- American silversmith

1742   James Wilson -- Pennsylvania signer of the Declaration of Independence and the United States Constitution

1760   Luigi Cherubini -- Italian-French composer of some 30 operas and 11 masses, best known for *Requiem in C minor* (1816), which commemorated King Louis XVI

1769   Alexander von Humboldt -- German scientist and geographer, who helped found modern geography and was a pioneer in climatology

1782   Christian Magnus Falsen -- Author of the Norwegian constitution

1859   Janis Cakste -- First president of the Republic of Latvia

1860   Hamlin Garland -- American author, noted for *Main-Travelled Roads* (1891)

1867   Charles Dana Gibson -- American illustrator who drew the famous *Gibson Girl* in the 1890s and early 1900s

1883   Margaret Sanger -- American nurse who led the birth-control movement in the United States and founded the Planned Parenthood Federation of America

1886   Jan Masaryk -- Czechoslovakian statesman and son of Tomas Masaryk, the co-founder of Czechoslovakia

1887   Karl Taylor Compton -- American physicist and specialist in the field of electrical discharge in gases, and chairman of the board that evaluated the Bikini atomic bomb tests in 1946

1891   John H. Striebel -- American cartoonist who, with J.P. McEvoy, created the comic strip *Dixie Dugan*

1896   John Robert Powers -- Founder of the famous Powers modeling agency

1899   Hal B. Wallis -- American motion-picture producer of over 400 films

1914   Clayton Moore -- American motion-picture and television actor, best known for his role as the Lone Ranger in the long-running television series

1921   Hughes Rudd -- American television news correspondent

1923   Bud Palmer -- American sports commentator

1924   Jerry Coleman -- Professional baseball player and manager

1934   Kate Millett -- American sculptor, feminist, and author of *Sexual Politics*

1944   Joey Heatherton -- American motion-picture and television actress

1958   Tim Wallach -- Professional baseball player

SEPTEMBER 14 -- EVENTS

1321	Dante Alighieri, the great Italian poet, died in Ravenna at age 56.
1638	Clergyman John Harvard died in Massachusetts and left half of his estate to the "seminary" that was to become Harvard University.
1741	George Frederick Handel finished his great *Messiah,* just 24 days after starting it.
1752	Great Britain and the American colonies formally made the switch to the Gregorian calendar by changing this day from September 3 to September 14, 1752.
1812	Napoleon occupied Moscow, and found himself in a deserted city. The next day he moved into the Kremlin and waited for Czar Alexander to sue for peace, which never happened.
1814	Francis Scott Key wrote "The Star Spangled Banner" while witnessing the bombardment of Fort McHenry in Baltimore harbor by the British in the War of 1812.
1847	General Winfield Scott's American army occupied Mexico City, marking the end of hostilities in the Mexican War.
1851	James Fenimore Cooper, America's first important novelist, died one day before his 62nd birthday.
1852	The Duke of Wellington, the English general who conquered Napoleon at Waterloo, died at age 83.
1901	Theodore Roosevelt became president upon the death of President William McKinley, eight days after McKinley had been shot by an assassin.
1923	Jack Dempsey defeated Luis Angel Firpo, the "Wild Bull of the Pampas," in the second round after being knocked clear out of the ring by Firpo in the first round.
1927	The great modern dance pioneer Isadora Duncan was killed in France when her scarf became entangled in the wheel of her sportscar.
1940	Congress passed the Selective Service Act, providing for the first peacetime draft in U.S. history.
1963	The first U.S. quintuplets, four girls and a boy, to survive early infancy were born to parents Andrew James and Mary Ann Fischer in Aberdeen, South Dakota.
1964	The third session of the ecumenical council Vatican II of the Roman Catholic Church opened in Rome.
1965	The fourth and final session of the ecumenical council Vatican II opened in Rome.
1975	Elizabeth Ann Seton was proclaimed the first U.S.-born saint of the Roman Catholic Church.

SEPTEMBER 15 -- BIRTHDAYS

53 AD   **Trajan** – Emperor of Rome, A.D. 98-117, who reigned during one of the empire's most prosperous periods

1613   **Francois de La Rochefoucauld** – French writer famous for his *Maxims* (1665), a collection of some 500 sayings that expose the vanity and hypocrisy in human behavior

1789   **James Fenimore Cooper** -- America's first important novelist, noted for *The Leatherstocking Tales*, which include, among others, *The Last of the Mohicans* (1826) and *The Deerslayer* (1841)

1795   **Zachariah Allen** -- Inventor of the first home hot-air furnace

1795   **Antoine Louis Barye** – French sculptor and painter noted for his portrayals of animals

1830   **Porfirio Diaz** – President of Mexico, 1877-1880 and 1884-1911, and a hero of the war against the French invaders from 1863 to 1867

1855   **Adam Geibel** -- German-American composer, organist, and conductor, noted for such songs as "Stand Up, Stand Up for Jesus"

1857   **William Howard Taft** -- 27th U.S. president, and the only man in history to serve first as president, then as Chief Justice of the Supreme Court

1876   **Bruno Walter** -- One of the leading symphony orchestra and opera conductors of the 1900s

1881   **Ettore Arco Isidoro Bugatti** -- Italian builder of the famous Bugatti automobile

1889   **Robert Benchley** -- American humorist, journalist, critic, writer, and actor, who won an Academy Award in 1936 for writing and starring in the picture *How to Sleep*

1890   **Dame Agatha Christie** -- English detective novelist, and author of over 60 popular works, such as *The Murder of Roger Ackroyd* (1926) and *Witness for the Prosecution* (1953)

1894   **Jean Renoir** -- Son of the famous French painter Auguste Renoir, and distinguished motion-picture director with a career of some fifty years

1899   **Milton Eisenhower** -- American statesman and brother of President Dwight D. Eisenhower

1903   **Roy Acuff** -- Noted American country music singer and musician

1904   **Humbert II** -- Son of Victor Emmanuel III and King of Italy for two months in 1946 before the Italians voted to abolish the monarchy

1907   **Fay Wray** -- Canadian-born actress who appeared in nearly 50 motion pictures including the original *King Kong*

1908   **Penny Singleton** -- American motion-picture actress noted for her portrayal of Blondie in the Blondie and Dagwood movies

1911   **Luther L. Terry** -- American physician who was the first U.S. Surgeon-General to warn that cigarette smoking causes cancer and who first promoted the idea of seatbelts in automobiles

1912   **Ray Gilbert** -- American composer noted for songs such as "The Three Caballeros," "You Belong to My Heart," "Zip-a-Dee-Doo-Dah," "Two Silhouettes" (lyrics), and "Casey at the Bat"

1914   **Creighton Adams** -- U.S. general and Army chief of staff

1916   **Margaret Lockwood** -- English stage and motion-picture actress

1920   **William Joseph Zellerbach** -- American paper industry executive

1921   **Jackie Cooper** -- American motion-picture actor, director, and executive, who began as a famous child star and successfully made the transition to adult roles

1928   **Julian "Cannonball" Adderly** -- American saxophonist and cool jazz musician

1938   **Gaylord Perry** -- Professional baseball pitcher who won the Cy Young Award in each of the two major leagues, and had over 300 career wins

1940   **Merlin Olsen** -- Professional football player and actor

1961   **Dan Marino** -- Professional football player

SEPTEMBER 15 -- EVENTS

1159   Alexander III was crowned Roman Catholic pope.

1776   The British occupied New York City in the Revolutionary War, forcing George Washington, who fought desperately, to retreat to Harlem Heights.

1789   Congress changed the name of the Department of Foreign Affairs to the Department of State.

1794   James Madison married Dolley Payne Todd.

1810   Miguel Hidalgo y Costilla, the "Father of Mexican Independence," rang the church bells in the village of Dolores and demanded Mexico's independence from Spain.

1812   On Napoleon's first full day of occupation of Moscow, the city mysteriously began to burn. In four days two-thirds of Moscow had been destroyed.

1882   The British army occupied Cairo and took control of Egypt, ending the bloody revolt of the Egyptians to free the government of non-Egyptian influence.

1916   The comic strip, *Mutt and Jeff,* by Bud Fisher, first appeared under that title.

1916	The British army introduced a new weapon, the tank, in the Battle of Flers-Courcelette in World War I.
1930	The comic strip, *Blondie,* by Chic Young, appeared for the first time.
1938	Prime Minister Neville Chamberlain of England met with Adolf Hitler at Berchtesgaden, and conceded the right of the Sudeten Germans in Czechoslovakia to self-determination.
1938	Thomas Wolfe, the great American novelist, died of tuberculosis of the brain in Baltimore at age 37.
1940	The RAF had their greatest day in the Battle of Britain in World War II, destroying 185 German planes.
1942	German armies attacked Stalingrad in World War II.
1949	Konrad Adenauer became the first chancellor of the German Federal Republic.
1950	In a surprise move that changed the course of the Korean War, U.S. troops made an amphibious landing behind enemy lines at Inchon.
1963	Four children were killed when a bomb exploded in a black Baptist church in Birmingham, Alabama, during the racial unrest of the 1960s.
1969	Pitcher Steve Carlton of the St. Louis Cardinals struck out a record 19 batters in a game with the New York Mets.
1978	Muhammad Ali won the heavyweight boxing title for an unprecedented third time, defeating Leon Spinks at the Superdome in New Orleans.

SEPTEMBER 16 -- BIRTHDAYS

1387	**Henry V** -- King of England, 1413-1422, who defeated the French in the Battle of Agincourt (1415), one of the most famous victories in English history
1462	**Pietro Pomponazzi** -- Italian Renaissance philosopher
1745	**Mikhail Kutuzov** -- Russian general who defended Moscow against Napoleon in the Battle of Borodino in 1812
1823	**Francis Parkman** -- One of America's greatest historians
1838	**James J. Hill** – American railroad operator and "Empire Builder," who constructed the Great Northern Railway from Lake Superior to Puget Sound, Washington
1875	**J.C. Penney** -- American merchant and founder of the J.C. Penney Company
1880	**Alfred Noyes** -- English poet noted for "The Highwayman"
1887	**Hans Arp** -- French sculptor and painter (known also as Jean Arp), who helped found the Dada movement in Zurich

1891	**Karl Doenitz** -- German World War II admiral who succeeded Adolf Hitler as German head of state
1911	**Jerry Wald** -- American motion-picture producer and screenwriter
1914	**Allen Funt** -- American television performer and star of the long-running show *Candid Camera*
1922	**Janis Paige** -- American singer and actress
1924	**Lauren Bacall** -- American stage and motion-picture actress and star for over 40 years
1925	**Charlie Byrd** -- American guitarist
1925	**Charles J. Haughey** -- Prime minister of Ireland
1925	**B.B. King** -- American blues singer and guitarist
1927	**Peter Falk** -- American motion-picture and television actor
1930	**Anne Francis** -- American motion-picture and television actress
1934	**George Chakiris** -- American motion-picture actor, singer, and dancer
1934	**Elgin Baylor** -- Professional basketball player and one of the game's superstars
1940	**Jim McManus** -- American tennis player
1940	**Earl Buchholz** -- American tennis player
1948	**Rosemary Casals** -- American tennis player
1949	**Ed Begley Jr.** -- American actor and son of the noted character actor Ed Begley
1953	**Bob Knapp** -- Professional baseball player
1953	**Jerry Pate** -- Professional golfer
1954	**Wilbert Montgomery** -- Professional football player
1955	**Robin Yount** -- Professional baseball player
1958	**Orel Hershiser** -- Professional baseball pitcher who won the Cy Young Award in 1988 and pitched a record 59 consecutive scoreless innings
1959	**Tim Raines** -- Professional baseball player and superstar

SEPTEMBER 16 -- EVENTS

335 BC	Alexander the Great destroyed every building in Thebes, Egypt, except the temples and the house of the poet Pindar.
1485	The Beefeaters, or Yeoman Warders, were established in London as the bodyguard of the king or queen by King Henry VII.
1492	Columbus and his men saw the first patches of seaweed in mid-ocean on the first voyage to America.

1620	The *Mayflower* left Plymouth, England, with 102 Pilgrims bound for America.

1620   The *Mayflower* left Plymouth, England, with 102 Pilgrims bound for America.

1630   The village of Shawmut, Massachusetts, changed its name to Boston.

1810   The Mexican revolution against Spain began, the day after Hidalgo y Costilla rang the church bells in Dolores, demanding Mexican independence.

1893   The Cherokee Strip was opened in Oklahoma to homesteaders. Over 100,000 homesteaders claimed 6 million acres from the U.S. government.

1908   The General Motors Company, which in 1916 became the General Motors Corporation of today, was incorporated in New Jersey.

1919   Congress granted a national charter to the American Legion.

1940   The Selective Service Act was signed into law by President Franklin D. Roosevelt.

1941   Mohammed Reza Pahlavi became Shah of Iran when the British and Russian occupiers of Iran forced his father Reza Khan to abdicate.

1942   German forces entered Stalingrad in World War II. They were never able to take the city, however.

1945   The British retook Hong Kong from the Japanese after World War II.

1966   The Metropolitan Opera opened in its new opera house at New York's Lincoln Center with the premiere of *Antony and Cleopatra,* by Samuel Barber.

SEPTEMBER 17 -- BIRTHDAYS

1271   **Wenceslas II** -- King of Poland, 1300-1305

1550   **Paul V** -- Roman Catholic pope, 1605-1621

1676   **Louis Juchereau de Saint Denis** -- French founder in 1714 of Natchitoches, Louisiana, the oldest city in the Louisiana Purchase

1730   **Baron von Steuben** -- German soldier who helped the Americans in the Revolutionary War

1743   **Marquis de Condorcet** -- French mathematician and philosopher, who was one of the leaders of the "Age of Reason" of the late 1700s

1826   **Georg Friedrich Riemann** -- German mathematician and one of the most creative of the 19th century

1855   **David Dunbar Buick** -- Pioneer American automobile manufacturer who in 1804 founded the Buick Manufacturing Company

1874   Ben Turpin – Slapstick American comedian of the silent screen

1883   **William Carlos Williams** -- American physician and poet, who won the 1963 Pulitzer Prize for *Pictures from Breughel*

1890   **Gabriel Heatter** – American radio news broadcaster, noted particularly for his optimistic newscasts during World War II

1900   **John Willard Marriott** -- American restaurant entrepreneur, who in 1927 founded the Hot Shoppe chain in Washington, D.C., which in 45 years grew into the Marriott Corporation

1905   **Dolores Costello** -- American motion-picture star of the 1920s, 1930s, and 1940s, and daughter of the famous actor Maurice Costello

1907   **Warren Burger** -- U.S. Supreme Court chief justice

1918   **Chaim Herzog** -- Israeli statesman and ambassador to the United States

1923   **Hank Williams** -- American country and western singer and composer, noted for songs such as "Your Cheating Heart," "Jambalaya," and "Cold, Cold Heart"

1927   **George Blanda** -- Professional football superstar who scored 2,002 points in a 26-year career

1928   **Roddy McDowall** -- English-born stage, screen, and television actor

1929   **Stirling Moss** -- English automobile racing driver, considered to be one of the world's best

1930   **Edgar D. Mitchell** -- U.S. astronaut and member of the *Apollo 14* mission which explored the moon in 1971

1930   **Thomas P. Stafford** -- U.S. astronaut and commander of the *Apollo 10* mission

1931   **Anne Bancroft** – American television and motion-picture actress

1933   **Dorothy Loudon** -- American singer and actress

1934   **Maureen Connolly** -- First woman to win the grand slam of tennis (1953), and one of the greatest women players of all time

1935   **Ken Kesey** -- American writer and author of *One Flew Over the Cuckoo's Nest*

1937   **Lamonte McLemore** -- Member of the 5th Dimension singing group

1940   **Roger Stewart Nichols** -- American composer noted for songs such as "We've Only Just Begun"

1944   **Reinhold Messner** – South Tyrolean alpinist and one of the world's greatest mountain climbers

1945   **Phil Jackson** -- Professional basketball player

1948   **John Ritter** -- American motion-picture and television actor, and son of cowboy actor and singer Tex Ritter

1951   **Kermit Washington** -- Professional basketball player
1952   **Harold Solomon** -- American tennis player
1957   **Earl Cooper** -- Professional football player

SEPTEMBER 17 -- EVENTS

1156   The Bavarian East Mark became the Duchy of Austria with a charter from the German emperor, Frederick I Barbarossa.
1771   Tobias Smollett, the noted English novelist, died near Leghorn at age 50.
1787   The Constitutional Convention delegates completed and signed the new Constitution of the United States.
1862   Northern troops under General McClellan defeated General Lee in the Battle of Antietam, one of the bloodiest of the Civil War.
1935   Manuel Quezon was elected as the first president of the Commonwealth of the Philippines.
1939   Russia invaded Poland in World War II, as had been secretly agreed on earlier in the Nazi-Soviet pact.
1940   Adolf Hitler indefinitely postponed Operation Sea Lion, the projected German invasion of the British Isles in World War II.
1946   The first postwar television sets went on sale in the United States.
1947   James V. Forrestal was sworn in as the first U.S. secretary of defense.
1948   Count Folke Bernadotte, U.N. mediator in the war between Israel and the Arab countries, was murdered near Jerusalem.
1978   Egyptian President Anwar Sadat and Israeli Prime Minister Menachem Begin concluded their summit meeting with President Carter by signing the Camp David agreement for peace.

SEPTEMBER 18 -- BIRTHDAYS

1596   **James Shirley** -- English playwright and poet
1709   **Samuel Johnson** -- One of the greatest English writers of his day and the subject of James Boswell's famous biography, one of the great works of world literature
1733   **George Read** -- Signer of the Declaration of Independence from Delaware, member of the Continental Congress, and member of the Constitutional Convention
1765   **Gregory XVI** -- Roman Catholic pope, 1831-1846
1819   **Jean Foucault** -- French physicist who measured the speed of light in different media, and discovered the existence of eddy currents in a conductor moving in a magnetic field

1895   John Diefenbaker -- Prime minister of Canada, 1957-1963

1897   Sam H. Stept -- Russian-born composer and conductor, noted for songs such as "That's My Weakness Now," "Don't Sit Under the Apple Tree," and "Please Don't Talk About Me When I'm Gone"

1901   Harold Clurman -- American theatrical director and drama critic

1905   Eddie Anderson -- American actor who played Rochester on the *Jack Benny Show*

1905   Greta Garbo -- Swedish film actress and one of the screen's greatest stars

1907   Edwin Mattison McMillan -- American physicist and co-discoverer in 1940 of the elements neptunium and plutonium

1912   Sarah Palfrey Danzig -- American Hall of Fame tennis player

1916   Rossano Brazzi -- Italian stage and motion-picture actor with a 40-year career

1916   John J. Rhodes -- U.S. congressman and minority leader

1920   Jack Warden -- American stage, screen, and television actor

1925   Harvey Haddix -- Professional baseball pitcher, who in 1959 pitched 12 perfect innings (no man reached base), only to lose the game in the 13th inning

1929   Phyllis Kirk -- American motion-picture and television actress

1933   Mark Di Suvero -- American sculptor

1934   Robert Blake -- American motion-picture and television actor

1939   Frankie Avalon -- American singer and actor

1944   Dick Crealy -- Australian tennis player

1950   Isabel Fernandez -- Colombian tennis player

1954   Dennis Johnson -- Professional basketball player and superstar

1955   Billy Sims -- Professional football player

1959   Ryne Sandberg -- Professional baseball player

SEPTEMBER 18 -- EVENTS

96 AD   Nerva became emperor of Rome after Emperor Domitian was stabbed to death with his wife's help.

1759   The British captured Quebec in the French and Indian War, five days after defeating the French on the Plains of Abraham before the city.

1793   President George Washington laid the cornerstone of the U.S. Capitol in Washington, D.C.

1810   Chile declared its independence from Spain.

1850   Congress passed a new Fugitive Slave Law imposing heavy penalties on persons who aided a slave's escape or interfered with his recovery.

1851   The New York *Times* began publication under the leadership of
        Henry J. Raymond and two associates.
1927   The Columbia Broadcasting System (CBS) first went on the air
        with a network of 16 radio stations.
1931   The Japanese invaded Manchuria, marking the beginning of the
        Sino-Japanese War.
1947   The United States Air Force was created as a separate department.
1949   The British devalued the pound from $4.03 to $2.80.
1961   Dag Hammarskjold, secretary-general of the United Nations,
        was killed in a plane crash in Africa.
1975   Patricia Hearst, the newspaper heiress, was rescued by the FBI
        19 months after being kidnapped by a terrorist organization, and
        arrested for collaborating with her captors.

SEPTEMBER 19 -- BIRTHDAYS

1551   **Henry III** -- King of France, 1574-1589, and the last of the
        Valois kings
1730   **Augustin Pajou** -- French sculptor and decorator
1739   **Andrew Pickens** -- American frontiersman and Revolutionary
        War soldier
1796   **David Hartley Coleridge** -- English poet and son of the famous
        poet Samuel Taylor Coleridge
1802   **Lajos Kossuth** -- Hungarian national hero of the rebellion of
        1848-1849 against Austria
1839   **George Cadbury** – Co-founder of the Cadbury Brothers choco-
        late manufacturing enterprise
1867   **Arthur Rackham** -- English artist and illustrator noted for his
        work for children's books such as *Peter Pan, Grimm's Fairy Tales,*
        and *Aesop's Fables*
1900   **Ferdinand Porsche** -- Austrian automotive engineer and son of
        Ferdinand Porsche, the designer of the German Volkswagen
1902   **James Van Alen** -- American Hall of Fame tennis player who
        developed the Van Alen Simplified Scoring System
1904   **Bergen Evans** – American language expert and televi-
        sion personality
1905   **Leon Jaworski** -- Second special prosecutor in the Watergate case
1907   **Lewis Powell** -- U.S. Supreme Court justice
1911   **William Golding** – English novelist noted for *Lord of the
        Flies* (1954)
1913   **Frances Farmer** -- American motion-picture and stage actress

1922   **Willie Pep** -- World featherweight champion, 1946-1948 and 1949-1950

1926   **Duke Snider** -- Hall of Fame baseball player who had 407 career home runs

1926   **Lurleen Wallace** -- Governor of Alabama, 1967-1970, and wife of Alabama governor George C. Wallace

1927   **Harold Brown** -- Secretary of defense under President Carter

1928   **Adam West** – American actor and star of television's *Batman* series

1930   **Bob Turley** -- Professional baseball player

1932   **Mike Royko** -- American newspaper columnist

1933   **David McCallum** -- Scottish motion-picture and television actor

1934   **Brian Epstein** -- Manager of the Beatles, 1962-1967

1937   **Orlando Cepeda** -- Professional baseball player

1940   **Paul Williams** -- American singer, composer, and actor, noted for songs such as "We've Only Just Begun," "An Old Fashioned Love Story," "Family of Man," and "Let Me Be the One"

1941   **Cass Elliot** -- American singer and member of the Mamas and the Papas

1943   **Joe Morgan** -- Professional baseball player

1945   **Jane Blalock** -- Professional golfer

1946   **Joe Ferguson** -- Professional baseball player

1947   **Larry Brown** -- Professional football player

1949   **Kerry Harris** -- Australian tennis player

1949   **Twiggy** -- English model and motion-picture actress

1949   **Sidney Wickes** -- Professional basketball player

1951   **Nathaniel Moore** -- Professional football player

SEPTEMBER 19 -- EVENTS

1356   Edward, the Black Prince of England, defeated the French in the Battle of Poitiers, and captured King John of France, in the Hundred Years' War.

1777   The First Battle of Freeman's Farm near Saratoga, New York, began, in the Revolutionary War. The series of battles ended a month later with the surrender of the British army.

1783   Etienne Montgolfier sent a sheep, a duck, and a rooster up a height of one mile in a balloon in Versailles, France, the first time animals had gone aloft in a man-made craft.

1796   President George Washington's Farewell Address first appeared in print, in the *American Daily Advertiser,* a Philadelphia newspaper.

1846   English poets Robert Browning and Elizabeth Barrett eloped to Pisa a week after their secret marriage, during which time they had seen each other only a few minutes.

1859   The Confederate war song, "Dixie," was sung for the first time, by its composer, actor Daniel Decatur Emmett, in a New York minstrel show.

1863   The Civil War Battle of Chickamauga began between Union general Rosecrans and Confederate general Bragg. It ended the following day in victory for the South.

1881   President James A. Garfield died of a gunshot wound inflicted by an assassin on July 2, 1881.

1928   Walt Disney's Mickey Mouse first appeared, in the animated cartoon, *Steamboat Willie,* at the Colony Theater in New York.

1934   Bruno Richard Hauptmann was arrested in New York and charged with kidnapping and killing the baby son of Charles A. Lindbergh in 1932.

1955   Juan Peron was deposed as president of Argentina.

SEPTEMBER 20 -- BIRTHDAYS

356 BC **Alexander the Great** -- King of Macedonia and one of the greatest generals in history

1762   **Pierre Leonard Fontaine** -- French architect

1819   **Theodore Chasseriau** -- French painter

1833   **Petroleum Nasby** -- American humorist (born David Ross Locke) of the Civil War era, whose humor was especially enjoyed by President Lincoln

1872   **Maurice Gamelin** -- French World War II general and chief of staff of the French army, whose endless delays in fighting contributed to the success of the Nazi blitzkrieg in France in 1940

1873   **Robert Duffield Wrenn** -- American Hall of Fame tennis player and four times National Singles Champion

1878   **Upton Sinclair** -- American writer and "muckraker," best known for his novel, *The Jungle* (1906), which exposed conditions in the meat-packing industry and resulted in the first pure food laws

1885   **Jelly Roll Morton** -- American jazz and blues pianist

1886   **Sister Elizabeth Kenny** -- Noted Australian nurse who developed a special method of treating poliomyelitis

1892   **Roy Turk** -- American lyricist noted for songs such as "Where the Blue of the Night Meets the Gold of the Day," "Gimme a Little Kiss, Will Ya Huh?" "Walkin' My Baby Back Home," and "I'll Get By"

1898   **Chuck Dressen** -- Professional baseball player and manager

1901   **Gus Edson** -- American cartoonist, creator of the comic strip *Dondi,* and continuer of the comic strip *The Gumps,* after the death of its creator, Sidney Smith

1908   **Zeke Bonura** -- Professional baseball player

1911   **Frank De Vol** – American composer, conductor, and arranger

1917   **Red Auerbach** -- Longtime coach of the Boston Celtics basketball team

1917   **Fernando Rey** -- Spanish motion-picture actor

1926   **Charles Bluhdorn** -- American corporation executive

1927   **Rachel Roberts** -- Welsh motion-picture actress

1934   **Sophia Loren** – Italian motion-picture actress who won the Academy Award for her performance in *Two Women* (1961)

1951   **Guy Lafleur** -- Professional hockey player

1953   **Randy Grossman** -- Professional football player

SEPTEMBER 20 -- EVENTS

451 AD   The Romans defeated Attila the Hun at Chalons-sur-Marne in France.

1378   The cardinals elected Clement VII pope shortly after they had elected Urban VI. This rivalry caused the "Great Schism of the West" in the Catholic Church that lasted 40 years.

1519   Ferdinand Magellan set sail from Sanlucar, Spain, with five ships and 240 men on his voyage that would become the first trip around the world.

1863   The Battle of Chickamauga ended in victory for the Confederate troops under General Bragg in the Civil War.

1870   Two German armies began a 135-day siege of Paris in the Franco-Prussian War.

1873   The New York Stock Exchange closed its doors as the Panic of 1873 reached its peak.

1881   Chester A. Arthur was sworn in as president, succeeding President James A. Garfield, who had died the previous day.

1906   Upton Sinclair published *The Jungle,* his famous novel that rocked the meat-packing industry and led to the nation's first pure food laws.

1920   The comic strip, *Winnie Winkle,* by Martin Branner, first appeared.

1973   Billie Jean King, the reigning women's tennis champion, defeated Bobby Riggs, the men's champion 30 years earlier, in a tennis match before 30,492 people in the Houston Astrodome.

1978   Russian cosmonauts Kovalyonok and Ivanchenko broke the space-flight endurance record after 96 days of a flight that would last 139 days.

SEPTEMBER 21 -- BIRTHDAYS

454 AD **Flavius Actius** -- Roman general and statesman
1411   **Richard, Duke of York** -- English statesman and father of Kings Richard III and Edward IV
1452   **Girolamo Savonarola** -- Florentine preacher and reformer, who was hanged and his body burned in 1498 for his fiery criticism of Pope Alexander VI
1737   **Francis Hopkinson** -- Signer of the Declaration of Independence who was a writer, musician, and artist, as well as a lawyer and a political leader
1756   **John Loudon McAdam** -- British engineer who originated the macadam type of road surface, and was the first to realize that pavement is useful only as a smooth surface and for keeping the soil dry
1788   **Margaret Mackall Smith Taylor** -- Wife of President Zachary Taylor
1855   **Sara Delano Roosevelt** -- Mother of President Franklin D. Roosevelt
1863   **John Bunny** -- The first comic star of the American screen
1866   **H.G. Wells** -- English novelist and historian, noted for works such as *The Time Machine* (1895) and *The War of the Worlds* (1898)
1867   **Henry L. Stimson** -- U.S. cabinet member for three presidents--William Howard Taft, Herbert Hoover, and Franklin D. Roosevelt
1876   **Julio Gonzales** -- Spanish sculptor
1885   **Harold Tucker Webster** -- American cartoonist and creator of Caspar Milquetoast, the titular hero of his comic strip, *The Timid Soul*
1893   **Frank Willard** -- American cartoonist and creator of *Moon Mullins*
1909   **Kwame Nkrumah** -- First president of Ghana, 1960-1966
1924   **Gail Russell** -- American motion-picture actress
1930   **Dawn Addams** -- English stage, screen, and television actress
1931   **Larry Hagman** -- American motion-picture and television actor and son of actress Mary Martin
1935   **Henry Gibson** -- American actor and comedian
1942   **Sam McDowell** -- Professional baseball player
1944   **Charles Harraway Jr.** -- Professional football player

1944   **Hamilton Jordan** – White House assistant to President Jimmy Carter
1947   **Reginald Rucker** -- Professional football player
1947   **Stephen King** -- American novelist noted for his horror stories, such as *The Stand, Carrie, The Shining,* and *Children of the Corn*
1949   **Artis Gilmore** -- Professional basketball player
1950   **Bill Murray** -- American actor and comedian

SEPTEMBER 21 -- EVENTS

19 BC   Virgil, the great Roman poet, died in Rome at age 50.
1327   King Edward II of England was cruelly murdered by two English knights, after being deposed and imprisoned by his wife Isabelle and her lover Mortimer.
1776   Nathan Hale, the famous American patriot of the Revolutionary War, was captured by the British.
1779   The Battle of Baton Rouge ended British hopes of controlling the Mississippi basin in the American Revolutionary War.
1780   Benedict Arnold, the American Revolutionary War traitor, met with British officer John Andre to arrange the surrender to the British of the American fort at West Point.
1792   The French National Convention voted to abolish France's monarchy.
1832   Sir Walter Scott, the great Scottish novelist, died at Abbotsford, his famous estate, at age 61.
1893   Frank Duryea drove the first successful gasoline-powered car in America, on the streets of Springfield, Mass. It was a one-cylinder model designed by him and his brother Charles.
1897   The famous editorial, "Yes, Virginia, there is a Santa Claus," first appeared, in the New York *Sun.*
1937   J.R.R. Tolkien first published *The Hobbit,* the famous forerunner of the epic volumes, *The Lord of the Rings*
1938   The Czechs, yielding to pressure from Britain and France, agreed to cede the Sudeten German area of their country to Hitler. The Czech cabinet then promptly resigned.
1949   The Chinese Communist victors in the Chinese Civil War proclaimed the formation of the People's Republic of China.
1949   West Germany came into existence with the formation of a national cabinet.
1955   Rocky Marciano retained his heavyweight boxing title, knocking out Archie Moore for his 49th professional victory.

SEPTEMBER 22 -- BIRTHDAYS

1515   **Anne of Cleves** -- Fourth wife of King Henry VIII of England, and one of the rare ones who was not executed

1694   **Lord Chesterfield** -- English statesman and writer (Philip Dormer Stanhope), noted for his 400 witty and sensible letters to his son, published in 1774, soon after Chesterfield's death

1725   **Joseph Siffred Duplessis** -- French painter noted for works such as *Benjamin Franklin* (1778)

1765   **Paolo Ruffini** -- Italian mathematician and physician

1791   **Michael Faraday** -- One of the greatest English chemists and physicists, who in 1831 discovered the principle of the electric motor and generator

1878   **Yoshida Shigeru** – Prime minister of Japan after World War II

1882   **Wilhelm Keitel** -- Chief of the German supreme command in World War II, who was tried and executed in Nuremberg

1884   **Erich Von Stroheim** -- Austrian-American motion-picture actor and director of both the silent and talking era, noted for his direction of the authentic classic, *Greed* (1923)

1891   **Edward Joseph Flynn** -- American political leader of the New Deal Era

1894   **Dave Dreyer** -- American composer noted for songs such as "Me and My Shadow" and "You Can't Be True, Dear"

1895   **Paul Muni** -- Austrian stage and motion-picture actor, who won the Academy Award in 1936 for *The Story of Louis Pasteur*

1902   **Howard Jarvis** – American social activist and principal author of California Proposition 13 to cut taxes

1902   **John Houseman** -- Romanian-born director, writer, and actor, who produced Orson Welles's *Citizen Kane* (1941), one of the greatest movies of all time

1903   **Fred Glickman** -- American composer and violinist, noted for songs such as "Mule Train"

1904   **Joe Valachi** -- American organized crime informant

1909   **David Riesman** -- American sociologist and co-author of *The Lonely Crowd*

1912   **Alfred Gwynne Vanderbilt** -- American horse breeder and president of the New York Racing Association

1914   **Martha Scott** -- American stage, screen, and television actress

1917   **Richard C. Hottelot** -- American broadcast journalist

1920   **Bob Lemon** -- Hall of Fame baseball player and manager

1927   **Tom Lasorda** -- Professional baseball player and manager

1932	**Ingemar Johansson** – Heavyweight boxing champion, 1959-1960
1946	**Larry Dierker** -- Professional baseball player
1948	**Mark Phillips** – Husband of England's Princess Anne
1949	**Harold Carmichael** -- Professional football player
1952	**Ken Schroy** -- Professional football player
1954	**Paul Kronk** -- Australian tennis player
1956	**Debbie Boone** -- American singer and daughter of singer Pat Boone
1959	**Wally Backman** -- Professional baseball player
1961	**Vince Coleman** -- Professional baseball player
1962	**Scott Baio** -- American motion-picture and television actor

SEPTEMBER 22 -- EVENTS

1503	Pius III was elected Roman Catholic pope.
1692	The last persons were hanged in the American colonies for witchcraft, in Salem, Massachusetts.
1776	The famous American patriot Nathan Hale was hanged as a spy by the British. His last words were, "I only regret that I have but one life to lose for my country."
1780	Charles Lynch gave the language the word *lynch* when he announced that he and his countrymen would properly punish the Tories who were plundering their Virginia land.
1792	The French National Convention met and declared France a republic.
1862	President Lincoln issued his preliminary Emancipation Proclamation, stating that if the South did not quit the Civil War by January 1, 1863, he would free the slaves.
1911	Cy Young, baseball's winningest pitcher, won his 511th and last game at age 44, as the Boston Braves beat the Pittsburgh Pirates, 1-0.
1927	Gene Tunney defeated Jack Dempsey in their second match, which was noted for the controversial "long count" in the 7th round.
1940	Japan invaded French Indochina.
1950	Omar Bradley was promoted to five-star general, joining Dwight Eisenhower, Douglas MacArthur, George Marshall and Hap Arnold as America's only five-star generals.
1960	The Sudan Republic became the Republic of Mali.
1964	*Fiddler on the Roof,* the long-running musical, opened on Broadway for the first of 3,242 performances.

1975   President Gerald Ford escaped a bullet fired at him in San Francisco by would-be assassin Sara Jane Moore.

1981   The U.S. Senate confirmed the nomination of Sandra Day O'Connor to become the first woman justice on the U.S. Supreme Court.

SEPTEMBER 23 -- BIRTHDAYS

63 BC   **Augustus (Octavian)** -- Roman emperor at the time of Christ, and the founder in 27 B.C. of the Roman Empire as it was known after the end of the Roman Republic of Julius Caesar's time

1745   **John Sevier** -- Governor of "The lost state of Franklin" and the first governor of Tennessee

1800   **William Holmes McGuffey** -- American educator and clergyman, noted for the McGuffey readers, published from 1836 to 1857

1838   **Victoria Claflin Woodhull** -- First woman presidential candidate (1872)

1859   **Thomas Mott Osborne** -- American prison reformer and writer, who organized the Mutual Welfare League to help prisoners rebuild their lives

1862   **James W. Blake** -- American composer, noted for "Sidewalks of New York"

1884   **Eugene Talmadge** -- Governor of Georgia who served three terms and was elected to a fourth but died before being inaugurated

1889   **Walter Lippmann** -- American political commentator, columnist, writer, and editor, who won the 1962 Pulitzer Prize

1890   **Friedrich Paulus** -- German World War II field marshal who surrendered to the Russians at Stalingrad

1898   **Walter Pidgeon** -- American stage and motion-picture actor and veteran of over 200 silents and 70 talkies

1899   **Tom Clark** -- U.S. Supreme Court justice, 1949-1967

1900   **Louise Nevelson** -- Russian-born American sculptor, best known for her large wooden constructions, or *assemblages*

1902   **Ayatollah Ruhollah Khomeini** -- Iranian religious leader and head of the revolutionary government that toppled the Shah

1910   **Elliott Roosevelt** -- Son of President Franklin D. Roosevelt

1913   **Stanley Kramer** -- American motion-picture producer and director, noted for films such as *High Noon* (1952) and *Judgment at Nuremberg* (1961)

1916   **Aldo Moro** -- Prime minister of Italy, 1963-1968

1920   **Mickey Rooney** -- American stage, screen, and television actor, with a career of over 50 years

1926   **John Coltrane** -- American saxophonist

1932   **Ray Charles** -- American pianist, singer, and composer

1938   **Romy Schneider** -- Austrian stage and motion-picture actress

1939   **Roy Buchanan** -- American guitarist

1943   **Julio Iglesias** -- Spanish popular singer and one of the best-selling musical artists in the history of recording, with over 100 million record sales

1949   **Bruce Springsteen** -- American singer, guitarist, and songwriter, noted for songs such as "Blinded by the Light"

1952   **Dennis Lamp** -- Professional baseball player

SEPTEMBER 23 -- EVENTS

480 BC   The Battle of Salamis, Greece, the greatest of ancient naval battles, was won by Greece over Persia. Over 1,000 Persian ships were sunk by fewer than 400 Greek vessels.

1492   The crew of Columbus sighted a dove, leading them to think land was near on the first voyage to America.

1588   The Duke of Medina Sidonia's flagship *San Martin* made port at Santander, Spain, with 43 other ships, survivors of the 130-ship Spanish Armada. Some 20 others arrived later.

1642   Harvard College held its first commencement exercises.

1779   John Paul Jones's *Bonhomme Richard* captured the British ship *Serapis.* During the battle when asked to surrender, Jones replied, "I have not yet begun to fight."

1780   British spy John Andre was captured by American militiamen, who found papers on him revealing Benedict Arnold's plot to surrender West Point to the British.

1806   The Lewis and Clark Expedition came to an end as the explorers completed their homeward trip to St. Louis.

1845   The Knickerbocker Baseball Club was organized in New York.

1846   The planet Neptune was discovered with a telescope by Johann Galle from the Urania Observatory in Berlin.

1912   The first Mack Sennett Keystone Kops Comedy film was released.

1926   Gene Tunney won the heavyweight championship title from Jack Dempsey in 10 rounds in Philadelphia.

1938   At a Godesburg meeting Adolf Hitler demanded of an astonished Neville Chamberlain that the Czechs cede much more of their country to Germany than had been agreed to earlier.

1939   Sigmund Freud, the great psychoanalyst, died of cancer in London at age 83.

1952   Vice presidential candidate Richard Nixon made his "Checkers speech," in which he referred to his dog Checkers in a television appeal to keep himself on the Eisenhower ticket.

1952   Rocky Marciano won the heavyweight championship title from Jersey Joe Walcott with a 13th-round knockout in Philadelphia.

SEPTEMBER 24 -- BIRTHDAYS

15 AD   **Aulus Vitellius** – Emperor of Rome who served less than one year in A.D. 69

1501   **Girolamo Cardano** -- Italian physician, mathematician, and astrologer

1583   **Albrecht Wenzel von Wallenstein** -- One of the most important figures of the Thirty Years' War and the most famous military commander of his age

1717   **Horace Walpole** – English letter writer, art lover, and author of *The Castle of Otranto* (1764), the first of the so-called Gothic novels

1739   **Grigori Aleksandrovich Potemkin** – Russian statesman and field marshal, and favorite of Catherine the Great

1755   **John Marshall** -- The "great chief justice" of the U.S. Supreme Court, and the fourth man to hold the position, 1801-1835

1837   **Mark Hanna** -- American industrialist and political kingmaker, who was the power behind President William McKinley's elections

1871   **Little Dod** -- British tennis player and five times Wimbledon singles champion

1884   **Ismet Inonu** -- President of Turkey who succeeded Kemal Ataturk in 1938

1890   **Allen J. Ellender** -- U.S. senator, 1935-1980

1896   **F. Scott Fitzgerald** -- The leading writer and glittering hero of America's "Roaring Twenties," noted for works such as *The Great Gatsby* (1925) and *Tender Is the Night* (1934)

1907   **Ben Oakland** -- American composer and pianist, noted for songs such as "I'll Dance at Your Wedding"

1910   **Dixie Walker** -- Professional baseball player

1912   **John Kluczko (Johnny Watson)** – American composer noted for songs such as "Racing With the Moon" (with bandleader-lyricist Vaughn Monroe, who adopted it as his theme song)

1921   **Larry Markes** -- American composer and author, noted for songs such as "Along the Navajo Trail" and "Mad About Him, Sad About Him, How Can I Be Glad Without Him Blues"

1924   **Sheila MacRae** -- American comedienne
1930   **John W. Young** -- American astronaut and copilot of *Gemini 3*
1931   **Anthony Newley** -- English singer and actor
1936   **Jim Henson** -- American puppeteer
1942   **Linda McCartney** -- Member of the rock band Wings and wife of Beatle musician Paul McCartney
1946   **Mean Joe Greene** -- Professional football player
1951   **Terry Metcalf** -- Professional football player
1952   **Joseph P. Kennedy III** -- U.S. Congressman and son of Robert F. Kennedy
1953   **Joe Washington** -- Professional football player
1955   **Christopher Wells** -- English tennis player
1956   **Hubie Brooks** -- Professional baseball player

SEPTEMBER 24 -- EVENTS

768 AD Pepin the Short, King of the Franks and father of the great Charlemagne, died at age 54.
1492   Columbus's fleet met variable winds and calm, and the sailors mistakenly believed they sighted land, on the first voyage to America.
1742   Faneuil Hall in Boston was opened to the public.
1789   Congress passed the First Judiciary Act, providing for an attorney general and a Supreme Court.
1846   Monterrey fell to U.S. general Zachary Taylor in the Mexican War.
1862   Otto von Bismarck became prime minister of Prussia.
1869   Black Friday occurred on Wall Street when Jim Fiske and Jay Gould tried to corner the market on gold. They made $11 million in the resulting crash.
1905   Sweden agreed to Norway's independence.
1906   Victor Herbert's operetta, *The Red Mill,* had its premiere at the Knickerbocker Theater in New York.
1934   Babe Ruth made his farewell as a New York Yankee player at Yankee Stadium.
1955   President Dwight D. Eisenhower suffered a heart attack while vacationing in Denver.
1956   Grace Metalious published her sensational sex novel *Peyton Place.*
1957   President Eisenhower dispatched U.S. troops to Little Rock, Arkansas, to enforce school integration at Central High.
1963   The U.S. Senate ratified the treaty with Great Britain and the Soviet Union limiting nuclear testing.

SEPTEMBER 25 -- BIRTHDAYS

1403   **Louis III** -- Duke of Anjou

1599   **Francesco Borromini** -- Italian architect, who, with Giovanni Lorenzo Bernini, led the baroque movement

1683   **Jean Philippe Rameau** -- French composer and theorist, whose *Treatise of Harmony* (1722) is a landmark in the development of modern theories of harmony

1807   **Alfred Lewis Vail** -- American inventor who perfected the code used with Samuel F.B. Morse's telegraph

1877   **Plutarco Elias Calles** -- Mexican reformer and president, 1924-1928

1887   **Mary Sutton Bundy** -- First American tennis player to win at Wimbledon (1905)

1897   **William Faulkner** -- One of the leading American novelists of the 20th century, noted for works such as *The Sound and the Fury* (1929) and *The Reivers* (1962)

1902   **Al Hoffman** -- Russian-born composer noted for songs such as "Heartaches," "Goodnight, Wherever You Are," "There's No Tomorrow," "Papa Loves Mambo," "I Apologize," and "Mairzy Doats"

1905   **Red Smith** -- American sports writer

1906   **Dmitri Shostakovich** -- One of the leading Russian composers of the 20th century

1917   **Johnny Sain** -- Professional baseball player and coach

1918   **Phil Rizzuto** -- Professional baseball player and sportscaster

1921   **Robert David Muldoon** -- Prime minister of New Zealand

1926   **John Ericson** -- American stage, screen, and television actor

1927   **Carl Braun** -- Professional basketball player who scored a career total of over 10,000 points

1931   **Barbara Walters** -- American television newscaster and interviewer

1932   **Adolfo Suarez Gonzalez** -- Prime minister of Spain

1932   **Glenn Gould** -- Canadian pianist, noted for his interpretations of the works of Bach

1933   **Erik Darling** -- American singer and musician with the Weavers musical group

1936   **Juliet Prowse** -- South African actress and dancer

1944   **Michael Douglas** -- American actor, producer, and son of actor Kirk Douglas

1947   **Cheryl Tiegs** -- American model and television personality

1949   **Jeff Borowiak** -- American tennis player

1951   **Bob McAdoo** -- Professional basketball player

1952	**Mark Hamill** -- American motion-picture and television actor
1952	**Christopher Reeve** -- American motion-picture actor
1957	**Glenn Hubbard** -- Professional baseball player

SEPTEMBER 25 -- EVENTS

1493	Christopher Columbus left Cadiz, Spain, on his second voyage to America with 17 ships and 1,000 men.
1513	Spanish explorer Vasco Nunez de Balboa discovered the Pacific Ocean from a mountaintop in what is now Panama.
1555	The Peace of Augsburg legalized the Lutheran-Roman Catholic split in Germany.
1690	America's first newspaper, *Publick Occurrences,* a 4-page "newespaper," was published in Boston by Benjamin Harris.
1775	American Revolutionary War hero Ethan Allen was captured by the British as he led an attack on Montreal.
1789	The U.S. Congress proposed 12 amendments to the Constitution and sent them to the states for ratification. Ten of them were ratified and became the Bill of Rights in 1791.
1804	The 12th Amendment to the Constitution went into effect, providing for separate electoral ballots for the offices of president and vice president.
1890	Congress established Yosemite National Park in California.
1890	Mormon Church President Wilford Woodruff issued a church statement formally renouncing polygamy.
1919	President Woodrow Wilson collapsed from fatigue and nervous tension in Pueblo, Colorado, while on a speaking tour of the West attempting to sell the League of Nations to the public.
1955	The comic strip, *Dondi,* by Gus Edson and Irwin Hasen, first appeared.
1957	Nine black students who had been forced to withdraw from Central High School in Little Rock, Arkansas, were escorted to classes with 300 U.S. Army troops standing guard.
1962	Sonny Liston won the heavyweight boxing title by knocking out Floyd Patterson in the first round in Chicago.

SEPTEMBER 26 -- BIRTHDAYS

| 1580 | **Francisco de Quevedo y Villegas** -- The leading Spanish humanist of the 1600s, and author of *Life of the Swindler* (1626) |
| 1651 | **Francis Daniel Pastorius** -- German lawyer and scholar, who founded Germantown, Pennsylvania, in 1683 |

1729   **Moses Mendelssohn** -- Jewish philosopher and grandfather of the great composer Felix Mendelssohn

1774   **Johnny Appleseed (John Chapman)** -- American pioneer who became a legendary figure because of the ardent way he distributed apple seeds and sprouts in central and northern Ohio in the early 1800s

1791   **Theodore Gericault** -- French artist noted for vivid pictures of horses and of events of his day

1849   **Ivan Petrovich Pavlov** -- Nobel Prize-winning Russian physiologist, noted for the concept of the conditioned reflex

1862   **Arthur Bowen Davies** -- American painter and illustrator and member of the group of realistic painters known as the Eight

1869   **Winsor McCay** -- American cartoonist noted for many comic creations, the most famous of which is *Gertie, the Trained Dinosaur*

1870   **Christian X** -- King of Denmark during the Nazi occupation in World War II

1875   **Edmund Gwenn** -- Veteran American stage and screen actor, who won an Academy Award for his part in *Miracle on 34th Street* (1947)

1888   **J. Frank Dobie** -- American author and educator, and a leading collector of Texas lore and folk tales

1888   **T.S. Eliot** -- One of the most important poets of the 20th century, and author of such works as *The Waste Land* (1922) and *Murder in the Cathedral* (1935)

1891   **Charles Munch** -- Conductor of the Boston Symphony Orchestra, 1949-1962

1895   **George Raft** -- American stage, screen, and television actor with a 50-year career

1897   **Paul VI** -- Roman Catholic pope, 1963-1978

1898   **George Gershwin** -- Popular American composer, noted for such works as *Rhapsody in Blue* (1924) and *Porgy and Bess* (1935), the most popular opera ever written by an American

1901   **Ted Weems** -- American bandleader of the Big Band Era and composer of songs such as "The Martins and the Coys"

1919   **Barbara Britton** -- American motion-picture actress

1925   **Marty Robbins** -- American country singer

1925   **Bobby Shantz** -- Professional baseball player

1926   **Julie London** -- American singer and actress

1927   **Patrick O'Neal** -- American stage, screen, and television actor

1934   **Greg Morris** -- American television actor

1947   **Lucius Allen** -- Professional basketball player

1947   **Lynn Anderson** -- American country music artist

1948	**Olivia Newton-John** -- Australian popular music singer and actress
1951	**David Casper** -- Professional football player
1962	**Melissa Sue Anderson** -- American television actress

SEPTEMBER 26 -- EVENTS

1580	Sir Francis Drake, the great English seaman, reached Plymouth, England, returning from his round-the-world voyage, the second such trip in history.
1777	The British occupied Philadelphia in the Revolutionary War.
1789	Thomas Jefferson was appointed first secretary of state, John Jay first chief justice, Samuel Osgood first postmaster general, and Edmund Randolph first attorney general.
1815	The Holy Alliance was signed in Paris, pledging most of the monarchs of Europe to act in accordance with Christian principles.
1820	The famous pioneer Daniel Boone died in Missouri at the age of 85.
1889	Emile Berliner, the noted German-American inventor, obtained the first U.S. patent on a flat disc Gramophone.
1892	John Philip Sousa, the great American composer and bandmaster, presented his first public concert, playing for the first time his "Liberty Bell March."
1914	The Federal Trade Commission was established by Congress.
1934	The Cunard liner, *Queen Mary,* was launched.
1937	Bessie Smith, "Empress of the Blues," died in a car crash in Coahama, Mississippi.
1938	Adolf Hitler, in a speech at the Sportpalast in Berlin, promised that if the "Czech problem" were solved, he would have no further territorial claims in Europe.
1950	United Nations troops captured Seoul, Korea, from the North Koreans in the Korean War.
1960	Presidential candidates John F. Kennedy and Richard M. Nixon met in Chicago for the first of their historic television "Great Debates."
1969	The Beatles released *Abbey Road*, the last album they recorded.
1971	Hirohito became the first Japanese emperor to set foot on U.S. soil, meeting President Nixon in Alaska.

SEPTEMBER 27 -- BIRTHDAYS

1601	**Louis XIII** -- King of France, 1610-1643

1627   **Jacques Benigne Bossuet** – French preacher, theologian, and historian, and one of the greatest masters of eloquence in sermons

1655   **Domenico Guglielmini** -- A founder of the Italian school of hydraulics

1722   **Samuel Adams** – American revolutionary patriot, one of the organizers of the Boston Tea Party, and the leading spokesman for American independence

1783   **Agustin de Iturbide** – Emperor of Mexico for 10 months, 1922-1923

1792   **George Cruikshank** – English artist and caricaturist, noted for his illustrations for the books of Charles Dickens, Oliver Goldsmith, Henry Fielding, and Miguel de Cervantes

1809   **Raphael Semmes** -- Rear admiral in the Confederate Navy who commanded the famous ship *Alabama* in the Civil War

1840   **Alfred Thayer Mahan** -- American admiral, one of the world's great authorities on sea power, and the author of the famous book, *The Influence of Sea Power upon History, 1660-1783* (1890)

1840   **Thomas Nast** -- One of the greatest American political cartoonists of all time, noted especially for popularizing the Democratic donkey and originating the Republican elephant symbols

1881   **William J. Clothier** – American Hall of Fame tennis player and 1900 Singles Champion of the United States

1885   **Joseph McCarthy** -- American lyricist noted for songs such as "You Made Me Love You," "I'm Always Chasing Rainbows," and "Alice Blue Gown"

1898   **Sam Ervin** -- U.S. senator and chairman of the Senate committee investigating the Watergate charges in 1973

1898   **Vincent Millie Youmans** -- American composer noted for songs such as "No, No, Nanette," "Tea for Two," "I Want to Be Happy," "More Than You Know," "Time on My Hands," and "The Carioca"

1901   **Beasley Smith** -- American composer, author, and pianist, noted for songs such as "That Lucky Old Sun," "Beg Your Pardon," "The Old Master Painter," and "Night Train to Memphis"

1907   **Whitlow Wyatt** -- Professional baseball player

1914   **Jim Lee Howell** -- Professional football player

1917   **Louis Auchincloss** -- American lawyer and novelist, and author of works such as *The Great World and Timothy Colt* (1956)

1919   **Charles H. Percy** -- U.S. senator

1920   **William Conrad** – American motion-picture and television actor and star of the long-running TV series *Cannon*

1922   **Arthur Penn** -- American writer and stage and motion-picture director, noted for films such as *The Miracle Worker* (1962)

1923   **Jayne Meadows** -- American television actress
1924   **Bud Powell** -- American pianist, composer, and modern jazz pioneer
1927   **Gardner Dickinson** -- Professional golfer
1930   **Dick Hall** -- Professional baseball player
1934   **Dick Schaap** -- American sportscaster
1938   **Don Farmer** -- American broadcast journalist
1939   **Kathy Whitworth** -- Professional golfer
1949   **Mike Schmidt** -- Professional baseball player and superstar with 548 career home runs
1959   **Shaun Cassidy** -- American singer and actor

SEPTEMBER 27 -- EVENTS

1066   William the Conqueror, with a Norman army of 5,000 men, set sail from France for England, to claim the English throne.
1825   George Stephenson, in England, operated the first locomotive to haul a passenger train.
1854   The first great Atlantic Ocean liner disaster occurred when the steamship *Arctic* sank with 300 people aboard.
1917   Edgar Degas, the famous French painter, died in Paris at age 83.
1938   The Cunard liner, *Queen Elizabeth,* was launched at Glasgow.
1939   Warsaw surrendered to the Nazis in World War II.
1940   Germany, Italy, and Japan signed the Pact of Berlin, a ten-year mutual military aid agreement.
1950   Ezzard Charles retained his heavyweight championship title by defeating Joe Louis, the former champion, who was trying to come back from retirement.
1954   A U.S. Senate select committee recommended a Senate vote of censure against Senator Joseph R. McCarthy for "contemptuous conduct" and abuse of the committee.
1954   NBC's *Tonight Show* made its television debut with Steve Allen as its host.
1959   A typhoon hit the main Japanese island of Honshu, killing some 5,000 people.
1964   The Warren Commission Report on the assassination of President Kennedy was released. It concluded that Lee Harvey Oswald had acted alone in the murder.

SEPTEMBER 28 -- BIRTHDAYS

1565   **Alessandro Tassoni** -- Italian writer, poet, and critic

1573   **Michelangelo Merisi da Caravaggio** -- The greatest naturalistic painter of the early 1600s

1612   **Michel Anguier** -- French sculptor

1803   **Prosper Merimee** -- French author best known for his novelettes, one of which, *Carmen* (1845), was the source for Georges Bizet's famous opera of the same name

1839   **Frances Elizabeth Willard** -- American women's rights pioneer and temperance leader

1841   **Georges Clemenceau** -- French premier during World War I

1856   **Kate Douglas Wiggin** -- American writer and author of *Rebecca of Sunnybrook Farm* (1903)

1856   **Edward Herbert Thompson** -- American archaeologist who explored the great Mayan city of Chichen Itza in the early 1900s

1863   **Carlos I** -- King of Portugal, 1889-1908

1871   **Pietro Badoglio** -- Italian World War II general, who succeeded Mussolini as head of state in 1943

1880   **Ralph Flanders** – U.S. senator who initiated the successful movement to censure Senator Joseph McCarthy for his senatorial behavior in 1954

1892   **Elmer Rice** -- American dramatist and champion of personal freedom, noted for plays such as *The Adding Machine* (1923)

1901   **William S. Paley** -- Founder and first president of CBS

1902   **Ed Sullivan** – American television's "King of Variety," 1947-1971 and host of the long-running show, *Toast of the Town*

1905   **Max Schmeling** -- World heavyweight champion, 1930-1932

1909   **Al Capp** -- American cartoonist and creator of the comic strip *Li'l Abner* (1934)

1911   **Henry Ellsworth Vines** – American Hall of Fame tennis player and 1932 Wimbledon singles champion

1913   **Alice Marble** – American Hall of Fame tennis player, who won four U.S. titles (1930-1940) and Wimbledon (1939)

1915   **Ethel Rosenberg** -- U.S. citizen who with her husband Julius was executed for espionage (1953)

1916   **Peter Finch** – British stage and motion-picture actor

1919   **Tom Harmon** -- Professional football superstar and sportscaster

1923   **Marcello Mastroianni** -- Italian stage and motion-picture actor

1923   **William Windom** -- American stage and television actor

1934   **Walter Blum** -- American jockey

1934   **Brigitte Bardot** -- French motion-picture actress and "sex kitten" of the 1950s and 1960s

1935	**Bruce Crampton** -- Professional golfer
1948	**Melvin Gray** -- Professional football player
1954	**Steve Largent** -- Professional football player
1955	**Gina Ponce** -- Mexican tennis player

SEPTEMBER 28 -- EVENTS

48 BC	Pompey the Great, the noted Roman general, was murdered in Egypt, one day before his 58th birthday.
1066	William the Conqueror and his Norman army arrived in England, landing at Pevensey.
1542	Juan Rodriguez Cabrillo, a Portuguese explorer employed by Spain, discovered California.
1781	American forces under George Washington began the siege of Yorktown, the last battle of the Revolutionary War.
1850	The flogging of sailors in the U.S. Navy was abolished.
1864	The First International, the first workers' organization, was formed in London.
1891	Herman Melville, one of America's greatest novelists, died in New York City at age 72.
1904	Police arrested a woman on Fifth Avenue in New York City for smoking a cigarette.
1920	Eight Chicago White Sox players were indicted for throwing the 1919 World Series to Cincinnati. This "Black Sox" scandal led to the appointment of a baseball commissioner.
1939	Germany and Russia partitioned Poland in World War II.
1951	Allie Reynolds pitched his second no-hitter of the season, as the New York Yankees beat the Boston Red Sox, 8-0.
1967	Walter Washington became the first mayor of Washington, D.C.
1978	Pope John Paul I died in the 34th day of his reign.

SEPTEMBER 29 -- BIRTHDAYS

106 BC	**Pompey the Great** -- Statesman and general of the Roman Empire, and chief rival of Julius Caesar
1518	**Tintoretto (Jacopo Robusti)** -- One of the last great Venetian painters of the Italian Renaissance
1547	**Miguel de Cervantes** -- The greatest Spanish writer in history, and author of *Don Quixote* (1605), one of the great works in world literature

1640   **Antoine Coysevox** -- The leading French sculptor during the latter part of the reign of Louis XIV

1703   **Francois Boucher** -- French painter noted for works such as *The Interrupted Sleep* (1750)

1725   **Robert Clive** -- British soldier and founder of British rule in India

1758   **Lord Horatio Nelson** -- Great Britain's greatest admiral and naval hero, whose great victory at Trafalgar over the French and Spanish fleets in 1805 established England's rule of the seas

1759   **William Beckford** -- English writer

1803   **Charles Francois Sturm** -- Noted French mathematician

1810   **Elizabeth Cleghorn Gaskell** -- English writer, best known for her novel *Cranford* (1853)

1831   **John McAllister Schofield** -- Commander of the Union forces in the Civil War that captured Wilmington, North Carolina, and successfully defended Franklin, Tennessee

1838   **Henry Hobson Richardson** -- First American architect to achieve international fame, and the dominant U.S. architect of the 1870s and 1880s

1864   **Miguel de Unamuno** -- Spanish essayist, poet, novelist, dramatist, and the leading humanist of modern Spain

1887   **Billy Bevan** -- Australian-born motion-picture actor, noted for his roles in some 70 Mack Sennett comedies and for his numerous character roles

1891   **Marquis James** -- American author noted for works such as *The Raven: A Biography of Sam Houston* (1930) and *Andrew Jackson: Portrait of a President* (1938)

1897   **Herbert Agar** -- American author and journalist

1901   **Enrico Fermi** -- Great Italian physicist who designed the first atomic piles and produced the first nuclear chain reaction in 1942

1901   **Richard B. Smith** -- American lyricist noted for songs such as "Winter Wonderland"

1902   **Miguel Aleman** -- President of Mexico, 1946-1952

1907   **Gene Autry** -- American singer, songwriter, and one of the most famous cowboy actors in motion-picture history

1908   **Greer Garson** -- Irish-American motion-picture actress and superstar of the 1940s

1910   **Virginia Bruce** -- Leading lady of Hollywood films of the 1930s and early 1940s

1912   **Michelangelo Antonioni** -- Italian motion-picture director, noted for films such as *Blow-Up* (1966) and *Zabriskie Point* (1970)

1916   **Trevor Howard** -- British stage, screen, and television actor with a career of over 40 years

1922   **Lizabeth Scott** -- American stage and motion-picture actress
1923   **Bum Phillips** -- Professional football coach
1925   **John Tower** -- U.S. senator
1927   **Paul McCloskey** -- U.S. congressman
1930   **Richard Bonynge** -- Australian conductor and musicologist
1931   **Anita Ekberg** -- Swedish motion-picture actress
1935   **Jerry Lee Lewis** -- American rock-and-roll singer and pianist
1942   **Madeline Kahn** -- American actress and comedienne
1948   **Bryant Gumbel** -- American sportscaster and television host on NBC's *Today* show
1953   **Warren Cromartie** -- Professional baseball player
1956   **Sebastian Coe** -- English runner who broke 3 world records--for the 800 meter, the 1500 meter, and the 1 mile distances--within 42 days in 1979
1960   **Wendy White** -- American tennis player

SEPTEMBER 29 -- EVENTS

440 AD Saint Leo I (the Great) was elected Roman Catholic pope.
1513   Spanish explorer Vasco Nunez de Balboa waded into the Pacific Ocean he had discovered 4 days earlier from a mountaintop, and claimed it for Spain.
1530   Andrea del Sarto, the great Italian painter, died in Florence at age 44.
1902   Emile Zola, the noted French novelist, died in Paris at age 62.
1910   Winslow Homer, the great American painter, died in Prout's Neck, Maine, at age 74.
1913   Rudolf Diesel, the inventor of the diesel engine, mysteriously disappeared from a German ship bound for England, and was never seen again.
1918   Bulgaria surrendered to the Allies in World War I.
1918   The Allies scored a decisive breakthrough of the Hindenburg Line in the Argonne Forest in World War I.
1930   Lowell Thomas, the great American traveler and commentator, began his nightly radio news program, which would be carried by NBC or CBS until 1976.
1938   Chamberlain, Daladier, Hitler, and Mussolini met at Munich to determine the fate of Czechoslovakia. In the first hour they agreed to dismember it.
1963   The second session of Vatican II opened in Rome.

1978   Pope John Paul I was found dead in his Vatican apartment after only 34 days in office.

SEPTEMBER 30 -- BIRTHDAYS

1594   **Sieur de Saint-Amant** -- One of the most original of French early 17th century poets

1802   **Antoine Jerome Alard** -- French chemist who in 1826 discovered the element bromine

1865   **William Jerome** -- American author, actor, and singer, noted for lyrics such as "Chinatown, My Chinatown," "Get Out and Get Under the Moon," and "And the Green Grass Grew All Around"

1875   **Fred Fisher** -- German-American composer noted for songs such as "Peg O' My Heart" and "Dardanella"

1882   **George Bancroft** -- American stage and motion-picture actor

1896   **Fred Howard Wright** -- American composer, author, and singer, noted for songs such as "The Strawberry Roan" and "My Pretty Quadroon"

1908   **David Oistrakh** -- The leading Russian violinist of the mid-twentieth century

1912   **Kenny Baker** -- American singer and actor

1915   **Lester Maddox** -- Governor of Georgia, 1967-1971

1921   **Deborah Kerr** -- English motion-picture actress and leading star of the 1950s and 1960s

1924   **Truman Capote** -- American novelist and playwright, noted for works such as *Breakfast at Tiffany's* (1958) and *In Cold Blood* (1966)

1926   **Robin Roberts** -- Hall of Fame baseball player

1928   **Elie Wiesel** -- American journalist and author

1932   **Angie Dickinson** -- American motion-picture and television actress

1932   **Johnny Podres** -- Professional baseball player

1934   **Freddie King** -- American blues singer and guitarist

1935   **Johnny Mathis** -- American singer

1943   **Jody Powell** -- White House press secretary under President Carter

1944   **Marilyn McCoo** -- Member of the 5th Dimension singing group

1951   **Catherine Ball** -- American swimmer who set the 100-meter breaststroke record of 1 minute 14.2 seconds in 1968

1954   **John Drew** -- Professional basketball player

SEPTEMBER 30 -- EVENTS

420 AD Saint Jerome, one of the great scholars of the early Christian church, died at age 80.

1492 Christopher Columbus completed three weeks with no sight of land on his first voyage to America. This was the longest voyage yet made out of sight of land.

1568 Sweden's King Eric XIV was deposed after years of insanity.

1630 The first execution took place in America as John Billington was hanged in Plymouth, Massachusetts, for fatally shooting John Newcomin.

1791 Mozart's great opera, *The Magic Flute,* had its premiere in Vienna.

1846 Dr. William Thomas Green Morton, a dentist in Charleston, Massachusetts, became the first to extract a tooth with the help of anesthesia.

1868 The Spanish Revolution of 1868 ended in the establishment of a provisional government under Generals Francisco Serrano and Juan Prim

1927 Babe Ruth hit his record-setting 60th home run of the season in New York's Yankee Stadium.

1935 George Gershwin's great opera *Porgy and Bess* had its world premiere at the Colonial Theater in Boston.

1938 The Munich agreement was signed by Hitler, Chamberlain, Daladier, and Mussolini, destroying Czechoslovakia. Chamberlain called it "peace for our time."

1939 The first football game was televised, between Fordham University and Waynesburg College.

1953 Earl Warren was named chief justice of the U.S. Supreme Court by President Eisenhower.

1954 The submarine *Nautilus*, the first atomic-powered vessel, was commissioned by the U.S. Navy at Groton, Connecticut.

1955 James Dean, American motion-picture actor, was killed in an automobile crash at age 24.

1984 Mike Witt pitched a perfect game (no batter reached base), as the California Angels beat the Texas Rangers, 1-0. It was only the 14th perfect game in baseball history.

10

October

October, the tenth month of the year, got its name from *Octobris*, the Latin word for *eighth*, because in the original Roman calendar it was the eighth month. When Romulus added October to his calendar he first gave it 30 days, but almost immediately he changed its length to 31 days. Caesar gave it 30 days in his Julian Calendar in 45 B.C., but in 8 B.C. Augustus restored it to its present length of 31 days. The Roman Senate tried to rename October *Antoninus* after a Roman emperor, *Faustinus* after his wife, and *Tacitus* after the great Roman historian, but all three attempts failed since the people continued to call it October.

Columbus Day is an October holiday commemorating Columbus's discovery of America on October 12, 1492. It is now celebrated on the second Monday of the month. Halloween is October 31, as is Reformation Day, celebrated by Protestants to mark the day in 1517 when Martin Luther nailed his 95 Theses of protest to the door of a church in Wittenberg, Germany. Six United States Presidents, John Adams, Rutherford B. Hayes, Chester A. Arthur, Theodore Roosevelt, Dwight D. Eisenhower and Jimmy Carter, were born in October.

The October birthstones are the opal and the tourmaline, and the special flowers are the calendula and the cosmos. Notable birthdays and events of October are as follows.

OCTOBER 1 -- BIRTHDAYS

1207   **Henry III** -- King of England, 1216-1264, whose 56-year reign was one of the longest in history, and who built the new Westminster Abbey as his most enduring monument

1507   **Giacomo da Vignola** -- Italian architect who succeeded Michelangelo as the architect in charge of building St. Peter's Basilica

1620   **Claes Berchem** -- Dutch landscape painter and etcher

1685   **Charles VI** -- Holy Roman Emperor, 1711-1740, and father of the great Austrian empress Maria Theresa

1730   **Richard Stockton** -- Member of the Continental Congress and New Jersey signer of the Declaration of Independence

1754   **Paul I** – Strange, and perhaps crazy, czar of Russia, 1796-1801, and son of Catherine the Great

1781   **James Lawrence** – U.S. naval commander of the *Chesapeake,* whose dying command, "Don't give up the ship," became a watchword of the U.S. Navy

1832   **Caroline Lavinia Scott Harrison** -- First wife of President Benjamin Harrison

1881   **William E. Boeing** – American industrialist and founder of the Boeing Airplane Company in 1916

1885   **Louis Untermeyer** -- American poet, critic, and editor who edited some 18 collections of poetry and wrote an autobiography, *From Another World* (1939)

1890   **Stanley Holloway** -- English stage and screen actor in over 100 films

1893   **Faith Baldwin** -- American novelist

1893   **Cliff Friend** – American composer, author, and pianist, noted for songs such as "When My Dreamboat Comes Home" and "The Merry-Go-Round Broke Down"

1899   **William Allan Patterson** -- American aviation pioneer

1902   **Joseph Rines** -- American composer and author, noted for songs such as "Halo, Everybody, Halo" and "Ajax, the Foaming Cleanser," two well-known commercials of his day

1904   **Vladimir Horowitz** -- Russian-born American piano virtuoso

1904   **Terry Shand** -- American composer, author, and conductor, noted for songs such as "I Double Dare You" and "Dance With a Dolly"

1907   **Hiram Fong** -- U.S. senator

1909   **Everett Sloane** -- American stage and motion-picture actor

1911   **Fletcher Knebel** -- American columnist and author

1920   **Walter Matthau** -- American stage, screen, and television actor
1921   **James Whitmore** -- American stage, screen, and television actor
1922   **Ernest Altschuler** -- American composer noted for songs such as "I Left My Heart in San Francisco" (with George Cory)
1924   **Jimmy Carter** -- 39th U.S. president
1924   **William Rehnquist** -- U.S. Supreme Court chief justice
1927   **Tom Bosley** -- American motion-picture and television actor
1928   **Laurence Harvey** -- English motion-picture actor
1933   **Richard Harris** -- Irish-born motion-picture and television actor
1933   **George Peppard** -- American motion-picture and television actor
1935   **Julie Andrews** -- English-born singer and stage and motion-picture actress
1936   **Stella Stevens** -- American motion-picture actress
1936   **Edward Villella** -- American ballet dancer and actor
1939   **George Archer** -- Professional golfer
1945   **Rod Carew** -- Professional baseball superstar and six-time batting champion
1950   **Conrad Dobler** -- Professional football player
1955   **Jeff Reardon** -- Professional baseball player
1963   **Mark McGwire** -- Professional baseball player and superstar

OCTOBER 1 -- EVENTS

331 BC   Alexander the Great defeated Persian emperor Darius III in the Battle of Arbela in Mesopotamia, in one of the fifteen decisive battles of history.
1422   King Charles VI of France died in Paris at age 53.
1553   Mary I ("Bloody Mary") of England was crowned in Westminster Abbey.
1800   Spain ceded Louisiana to France in a secret treaty.
1880   John Philip Sousa, the great bandleader and composer, became leader of the U.S. Marine Band, which under his guidance became one of the finest in the world.
1903   The first baseball World Series began in Boston between Boston and Pittsburgh. Pittsburgh won, 7-3, but Boston won the series, 5 games to 3.
1908   The famous Model T Ford, or "Tin Lizzie," was first put on sale by Henry Ford at a price of $850.
1931   New York's Waldorf-Astoria Hotel opened to the public.
1932   Babe Ruth allegedly called his home run off Chicago pitcher Charlie Root by pointing to the stands before lining a homer there in the third game of the 1932 World Series.

1933   The comic strip, *Smilin' Jack,* by Zack Mosley, first appeared.

1938   Adolf Hitler occupied the Sudetenland of Czechoslovakia in accordance with the infamous Munich Pact that he had concluded the previous day.

1943   The comic strip, *Kerry Drake,* by Alfred Andriola, first appeared.

1946   Nineteen top Nazis were found guilty in Nuremberg of war crimes. Rudolf Hess and 6 others were sentenced to prison, and 12, including Hermann Goering, were sentenced to death.

1949   Mao Tse-tung took over as Chairman of the People's Government Council in Peking, China.

1961   Roger Maris of the New York Yankees hit his record 61st home run of the season off Boston's Tracy Stallard at Yankee Stadium, breaking Babe Ruth's record of 60 set in 1927.

1962   Johnny Carson started his long tenure as host of NBC's *Tonight Show.*

1984   Peter Ueberroth became Commissioner of Baseball, succeeding Bowie Kuhn.

OCTOBER 2 -- BIRTHDAYS

1452   **Richard III** -- The last Yorkist king of England, 1483-1485, whose reign brought on the revolt that ended the Wars of the Roses

1800   **Nat Turner** -- Negro slave preacher who in 1831 led the largest slave revolt in American history

1831   **Edward L. Godkin** -- Irish-born American editor who in 1865 founded *The Nation,* a liberal weekly newspaper that soon established itself as one of the most influential periodicals in America

1832   **Sir Edward Burnett Tyler** -- Father of anthropology in the English-speaking world

1847   **Paul von Hindenburg** – World War I military leader and president of Germany, 1925-1934

1851   **Ferdinand Foch** -- French field marshal and supreme Allied commander in World War I, acclaimed by many to be the greatest Allied general of the war

1869   **Mohandas K. Gandhi** -- Indian nationalist and religious leader, honored by Indians as the *Mahatma* (Great Soul) and the father of their nation

1871   **Cordell Hull** -- U.S. secretary of state under President Franklin D. Roosevelt

1877   **Carl T. Hayden** -- American statesman who served Arizona for 56 years in both houses of Congress

1879   **Wallace Stevens** – American poet whose *Collected Poems* won
        the 1955 Pulitzer Prize

1890   **Groucho Marx** – American actor, member of the Marx Brothers
        comedy team, and one of America's greatest comedians

1895   **Bud Abbott** -- Straight man of the famous Abbott and Costello
        comedy team of the 1940s and 1950s

1904   **Graham Greene** -- English novelist, noted for works such as *This
        Gun for Hire* (1936) and *The Third Man* (1950)

1904   **Lal Bahadur Shastri** -- Prime minister of India, 1964-1966

1909   **Alex Raymond** -- American cartoonist and creator in 1934 of
        Flash Gordon

1926   **Frances Farenthold** -- American educator and political activist

1932   **Maury Wills** -- Professional baseball player who stole a record
        104 bases in 1962

1940   **Rex Reed** -- American film critic and actor

1945   **Don McLean** -- American singer and songwriter

1948   **Donna Karan** -- American fashion designer

OCTOBER 2 -- EVENTS

1187   The Moslems, led by their great warrior Saladin, captured
        Jerusalem, which brought about the Third Crusade.

1780   Major John Andre, the British officer who collaborated in
        Benedict Arnold's treachery, was hanged as a spy at Tappan,
        New York.

1835   The Texas Revolution began with a battle between U.S. settlers
        and Mexican cavalry near the Guadalupe River.

1889   The first Pan-American Conference, which included all the
        independent countries of the Western Hemisphere, was held in
        Washington, D.C.

1905   The keel was laid in secrecy in Portsmouth, England, for the
        construction of HMS *Dreadnaught,* which was to make existing
        battleships obsolete.

1938   Bob Feller, the Cleveland Indians' great pitcher, struck out a
        record 18 men in a game against the Detroit Tigers.

1939   Organized Polish resistance ceased as the Germans and Rus-
        sians completed the partition of Poland in World War II.

1950   The comic strip, *Peanuts,* by Charles Schulz, made its first
        appearance.

1967   Thurgood Marshall was sworn in as the first black member of the
        U.S. Supreme Court.

OCTOBER 3 -- BIRTHDAYS

1554   Sir Fulke Greville -- English poet and statesman

1800   George Bancroft -- U.S. historian and "Father of American History," who as secretary of the Navy in 1845 helped establish the U.S. Naval Academy at Annapolis

1818   Alexander Macmillan – Co-founder of Macmillan and Company publishers

1854   William Crawford Gorgas -- The world's leading sanitation expert of his time, who made possible the building of the Panama Canal by destroying mosquitoes that carried yellow fever and malaria

1859   Eleonora Duse -- Italian actress, who, with Sarah Bernhardt, ruled the stage in the late 19th and early 20th century

1867   Pierre Bonnard -- French painter noted for his rich textures and vivid colors, an example of which is *The Green Blouse* (1919)

1872   Cap Clarke -- Hall of Fame baseball player who hit .406 in 1897

1886   Alain-Fournier -- French novelist (Henri Alban Fournier)

1900   Thomas Wolfe -- American novelist, noted for *Look Homeward, Angel* (1929) and *You Can't Go Home Again* (1940), published after his death

1908   Johnny Burke -- Famous American lyricist, noted for songs such as "Moonlight Becomes You," "Personality," "Swinging on a Star," and "Pennies From Heaven"

1916   David A. Mann -- American composer and author, noted for songs such as "Somebody Bad Stole de Wedding Bell," "Dearie (You're Much Older Than I)," and "There, I've Said It Again"

1924   Harvey Kurtzman -- American cartoonist and creator of *Little Annie Fanny* in *Playboy* magazine

1925   Gore Vidal – American novelist, playwright, and pungent observer, noted for works such as *The Best Man* (1960), *Myra Breckenridge* (1968), and *Lincoln* (1984)

1933   Neale Fraser – Australian tennis player and Wimbledon singles champion in 1960

1938   Eddie Cochran -- Early American rock-and-roll musician

1941   Chubby Checker – American pop singer and recorder of "The Twist," which sold millions and led to the dance of the same name

1951   Dave Winfield -- Professional baseball player and superstar

1954   Dennis Eckersley -- Professional baseball player

OCTOBER 3 -- EVENTS

1226   Saint Francis of Assisi, the great Roman Catholic churchman and founder of the Franciscan order, died at his beloved Portiuncula chapel at age 44.

1656   Miles Standish, the great Pilgrim leader, died at age 72.

1863   President Lincoln proclaimed the last Thursday in November Thanksgiving Day.

1906   The great British battleship HMS *Dreadnaught* was completed in Portsmouth, England.

1913   President Woodrow Wilson signed the income tax bill into law, to be retroactive to March 1, 1913.

1919   President Wilson suffered a paralytic stroke that left him an invalid for the rest of his life.

1922   Rebecca L. Felton of Georgia became the first U.S. woman senator, having been appointed to serve the remainder of Thomas E. Watson's term.

1935   Italian troops invaded Ethiopia in one of the preludes to World War II.

1941   With German troops advancing toward Moscow, Adolf Hitler declared that Russia was defeated and "will never rise again."

1955   The television show *Captain Kangaroo,* with actor Bob Keeshan in the title role, made its debut. It was to run for nearly 30 years to December, 1984.

1962   U.S. astronaut Wally Schirra Jr. made six space orbits in *Sigma 7.*

1974   Frank Robinson was named manager of the Cleveland Indians, as the first black to manage a major league baseball team.

OCTOBER 4 -- BIRTHDAYS

1289   **Louis X** -- King of France, 1314-1316

1379   **Henry III** -- King of Castile before its merger with Aragon to form Spain

1472   **Lucas Cranach the Elder** -- One of the leading German painters of the Renaissance

1550   **Charles IX** -- King of Sweden, 1604-1611, who restored Lutheranism as Sweden's state religion

1720   **Giovanni Battista Piranesi** -- Italian etcher, architect, and archaeologist, who had a wide influence on etchers for 100 years

1814   **Jean Francois Millet** -- French painter famous for his rural life paintings, such as *The Gleaners* and *The Man with the Hoe*

1822   **Rutherford B. Hayes** -- 19th U.S. president
1858   **Michael Idvorsky Pupin** -- Hungarian-born American physicist who had 34 patents, and whose autobiography, *From Immigrant to Inventor* (1923), won the 1924 Pulitzer Prize
1861   **Frederic Remington** -- American painter and sculptor, best known for his action-filled paintings of the Western plains
1880   **Damon Runyon** -- American writer and author of *Guys and Dolls* (1932)
1895   **Buster Keaton** -- One of the great deadpan heros of the silent screen who made the transition to the talkies and had a career of nearly 50 years
1910   **Frank Crosetti** -- Professional baseball player and coach
1923   **Charlton Heston** -- American stage, screen, and television actor with a career of over 40 years
1928   **Alvin Toffler** -- American futurologist and author of *Future Shock*
1928   **Torben Ulrich** -- Danish tennis player
1941   **Robert Wilson** -- American playwright and producer
1943   **Owen Davidson** -- Australian tennis player
1944   **Tony LaRussa** -- Professional baseball player and manager
1946   **Susan Sarandon** -- American motion-picture actress

OCTOBER 4 -- EVENTS

1535   The first complete English translation of the Bible was published by Miles Coverdale, a bishop of Exeter, England.
1582   The Gregorian Calendar, introduced by Pope Gregory XIII, was announced to go into effect in most Catholic countries, with the following day, October 5, to become October 15, 1582.
1669   Rembrandt, the great Dutch painter, died in Amsterdam at age 63.
1769   Bangor, Maine, was settled.
1777   The British defeated the Americans under George Washington in the Battle of Germantown, near Philadelphia, in the Revolutionary War.
1853   Turkey declared war on Russia, starting a conflict which became the Crimean War when England and France joined the Turks the following March.
1905   Calvin Coolidge married Grace Anna Goodhue.
1931   The comic strip, *Dick Tracy,* by Chester Gould, first appeared.
1940   Adolf Hitler and Benito Mussolini met at the Brenner Pass in the Tyrol where Hitler bragged that "The war is won!"

1943   The plan for the "extermination of the Jews" is underway, an-
         nounced SS fuehrer Heinrich Himmler in a speech to his associates.
1957   Russia launched *Sputnik 1*, the first man-made satellite.
1970   American rock singer Janis Joplin died at age 27.

OCTOBER 5 -- BIRTHDAYS

1703   **Jonathan Edwards** -- Famous minister of Puritan New England
         and a leading intellectual figure in colonial America
1712   **Francesco Guardi** -- Italian painter
1713   **Denis Diderot** -- French satirist, encyclopedist, brilliant conver-
         sationalist, and one of the major philosophers of the Age of Reason
1752   **Nathan Bowen** -- American cabinetmaker
1830   **Chester A. Arthur** -- 21st U.S. president
1840   **John Addington Symonds** -- English poet, biographer, and historian
1848   **Edward Livingston Trudeau** -- Famous pioneer in the antituber-
         culosis movement in the U.S.
1864   **Louis Lumiere** -- French pioneer in photographic manufactur-
         ing, who with his brother Auguste invented the *cinematographe,*
         a combination motion-picture camera, printer, and projector
1895   **Walter Bedell Smith** -- American World War II general
1902   **Ray Kroc** -- American businessman who made McDonald's
         Hamburgers into an international chain
1902   **Larry Fine** -- American comedian and actor and one of the
         original Three Stooges
1904   **T. Murray Mencher** -- American composer noted for songs such
         as "Merrily We Roll Along"
1908   **Joshua Logan** -- American motion-picture director and play-
         wright, noted for the direction of films such as *Picnic* (1956) and
         Camelot (1967)
1908   **Robert Trout** -- American television newscaster
1914   **Eugene Fodor** -- American writer of travel guide books
1917   **Lew Worsham** -- Professional golfer
1919   **Donald Pleasence** -- English motion-picture actor
1923   **Philip Berrigan** -- American priest and social activist
1923   **Glynis Johns** -- South African motion-picture actress
1924   **Bill Dana** -- American comedian, actor, and author
1929   **Richard F. Gordon Jr.** -- American astronaut on *Gemini 11*
         (1966) and *Apollo 12* (1969), which landed on the moon
1930   **Skip Homeier** -- American stage, screen, and television actor

1933	**Diane Cilento** -- Australian stage, screen, and television actress
1936	**Odie Smith** -- Professional basketball player
1948	**Aurelio Lopez** -- Professional baseball player
1949	**Norman Holmes** -- American tennis player
1951	**Karen Allen** -- American motion-picture actress

OCTOBER 5 -- EVENTS

1795	Napoleon was appointed second in command of the Army of the Interior, paving the way for his assuming power in France.
1813	Tecumseh, the great Shawnee chief, was killed while aiding the British in the Battle of the Thames in Upper Canada in the War of 1812.
1823	Leo XII was crowned Roman Catholic pope.
1892	The Dalton brothers, a notorious Western gang of outlaws, tried their last holdup, in Coffeyville, Kansas. All the gang members except one were killed in the ensuing fight.
1918	The Allied armies broke the Hindenburg Line in World War I.
1921	The first World Series baseball game was broadcast on the radio, with sports writer Grantland Rice giving the play by play between the New York Yankees and the New York Giants.
1931	Clyde Pangborn and Hugh Herndon completed the first non-stop flight across the Pacific Ocean, arriving in the state of Washington 41 hours after leaving Japan.
1937	President Franklin D. Roosevelt called for a "quarantine" of the aggressor nations, Germany and Italy.
1947	President Truman made the first presidential telecast address from the White House.
1953	Earl Warren was sworn in as the 14th Chief Justice of the U.S. Supreme Court.
1962	The Beatles released their first hit single, "Love Me Do."
1969	The *Monty Python Show* made its debut in England.
1974	David Kunst returned to Waseca, Minnesota, completing a four-year walking trip around the world that began June 10, 1970.

OCTOBER 6 -- BIRTHDAYS

1289	**Wenceslas III** -- King of Hungary, 1301-1304
1510	**John Caius** -- English humanist and physician
1773	**Louis-Philippe** -- King of France, 1830-1848

1820   **Jenny Lind** -- Swedish operatic soprano known as the "Swedish Nightingale"

1831   **Richard Dedekind** -- German mathematician noted among other things for the "Dedekind cut"

1846   **George Westinghouse** -- American inventor responsible for the adoption of alternating current for use in the United States

1847   **Adolf von Hildebrand** -- German sculptor

1887   **Martin Luis Guzman** -- Mexican writer of the Mexican Revolutionary period

1887   **Le Corbusier** -- Swiss-born architect (Charles Edouard Jeanneret), considered by many to be the greatest of the 20th century

1893   **Milton Ager** -- American composer and pianist, noted for songs such as "Happy Days Are Here Again," "Ain't She Sweet," and "Auf Wiedersehen"

1896   **Joseph M. Davis** -- American composer noted for songs such as "Daddy's Little Boy" and "Basin Street Blues"

1902   **Jack Sharkey** -- World heavyweight champion, 1932-1933

1905   **Helen Wills** -- One of the greatest women tennis players of all time (known also as Helen Wills Moody), who won the Wimbledon title a record 8 times and the U.S. title 7 times

1906   **Janet Gaynor** -- American motion-picture actress and superstar, who won the first Academy Award ever given for best actress (1927-1928)

1908   **Carole Lombard** -- American motion-picture actress, and one of Hollywood's most talented and glamorous stars of the 1930s

1914   **Thor Heyerdahl** -- Norwegian adventurer and writer, and author of *Kon-Tiki* (1950) and *Aku-Aku* (1958)

1922   **Helen Roark** -- American tennis player

1923   **Lowell Thomas Jr.** -- American author, television producer, and son of the famous news commentator

1925   **Shana Alexander** -- American writer and journalist

1942   **Britt Eklund** -- Swedish-born motion-picture actress

1942   **Jerry Grote** -- Professional baseball player

OCTOBER 6 -- EVENTS

891 AD Formosus was elected Roman Catholic pope.

1536   William Tyndale, the great English Protestant leader and translator of the Bible, was burned at the stake as a heretic.

1683   The first permanent German settlement in America was made at Germantown, Pennsylvania.

1889   Thomas A. Edison first exhibited his kinetoscope, a device for producing moving pictures.

1890   The Mormon Church in Utah outlawed the practice of polygamy.

1892   Alfred, Lord Tennyson, the great English poet, died near Haslemere, Surrey, at age 83.

1915   Austro-German forces invaded Serbia in World War I.

1927   The first "talking" film, *The Jazz Singer,* starring Al Jolson, had its world premiere at New York's Warner Theater.

1938   Dr. Eduard Benes, under Nazi pressure, resigned the presidency of Czechoslovakia and left for Great Britain to fight for the freedom of his country.

1973   War erupted in the Middle East as Egyptian and Syrian forces attacked Israel.

1981   Egyptian President Anwar Sadat was murdered by Islamic extremists who opened fire on him in his reviewing stand during a parade on the anniversary of the 1973 war with Israel.

OCTOBER 7 -- BIRTHDAYS

1491   **Frederick I** -- King of Denmark

1573   **Archbishop William Laud** -- The dominant figure in the Church of England during the persecution of the Puritans in the time of King Charles I

1576   **John Marston** -- English dramatist and essayist of the Shakespearean age

1675   **Rosalba Carriera** -- Italian painter

1734   **Sir Ralph Abercromby** -- English army commander

1849   **James Whitcomb Riley** -- American poet who wrote his most popular works in the dialect of his home state, Indiana, and became famous as the Hoosier Poet

1866   **Martha McChesney Berry** -- Founder of the Berry Schools in Georgia for mountain boys and girls

1885   **Niels Bohr** -- Nobel Prize-winning Danish physicist, noted for the Bohr theory of the atom

1888   **Henry A. Wallace** -- Secretary of agriculture and vice president under President Franklin D. Roosevelt

1897   **Elijah Muhammad** -- Spiritual leader of the Black Muslim movement

1900   **Heinrich Himmler** -- Head of Adolf Hitler's Gestapo, and principal director of the systematic killings in World War II concentration camps

1900   **Ralph Rainger** -- American composer and pianist, noted for songs such as "Ebb Tide" and Bob Hope's theme song, "Thanks for the Memory"

1901   **Prince Souvanna Phouma** -- Laotian leader who helped negotiate Laos's independence from France in 1947-1949

1904   **Chuck Klein** -- Hall of Fame baseball player

1905   **Meyer Levin** -- American writer and novelist noted for works such as *Compulsion*

1905   **Andy Devine** -- American motion-picture and television actor

1907   **Helen MacInnes** -- Scottish-born American author

1911   **Vaughn Monroe** -- American singer and conductor of the Big Band Era, who wrote his own theme song, "Racing With the Moon" (with composer Johnny Watson)

1914   **Alfred Drake** -- American singer, actor, and director

1914   **Sarah Churchill** -- English actress and daughter of Sir Winston Churchill

1917   **June Allyson** -- American stage and motion-picture actress with a 40-year career

1926   **Diana Lynn** -- American motion-picture and television actress

1931   **Desmond Tutu** -- South African black clergyman, social activist, and 1984 Nobel Peace Prize winner

1934   **Willie Naulls** -- Professional basketball player with over 11,000 career points

1943   **Oliver North** -- Lt. Colonel in the U.S Marines and central figure in the 1986 Iran-Contra scandal of the Reagan administration

1951   **John "Cougar" Mellencamp** -- American rock musician

OCTOBER 7 -- EVENTS

1492   A second mistaken shout of "Land Ho!" created great disappointment among Columbus's crew on the first voyage to America.

1571   Spain and her allies defeated the Turks in the famous Battle of Lepanto, the last great battle of oar-driven ships, marking a turning point of Moslem power in Europe.

1765   The Stamp Act Congress met in New York to consider colonial grievances against England.

1777   The Americans repulsed the British in the Second Battle of Freeman's Farm in the Revolutionary War.

1780   The American frontiersmen defeated the British in the Battle of Kings Mountain (South Carolina).

1816   The *Washington,* the world's first double-decked steamboat, arrived in New Orleans.

1849   Edgar Allan Poe, the great American writer and poet, died in Baltimore at age 40.

1889   Barnard College was opened, six months after the death of its founder, Frederick Augustus Porter Barnard.

1916   Georgia Tech beat Cumberland University, 222-0, in the most staggering intercollegiate football defeat in history.

1940   German troops entered Romania "by invitation" to reorganize the Romanian army and take the Ploesti oil fields.

1949   Iva d'Aquino was sentenced to prison for her propaganda broadcasts for Japan as Tokyo Rose during World War II.

1960   John F. Kennedy and Richard M. Nixon held their second "Great Debate" in the 1960 presidential election.

1968   The Motion Picture Association of America adopted its film-rating system.

1984   Walter Payton of the Chicago Bears broke Jimmy Brown's National Football League career rushing record of 12,312 yards set in 1966.

OCTOBER 8 -- BIRTHDAYS

1585   **Heinrich Schutz** -- German composer noted for works such as the opera *Dafne* (1626) and *Musikalische Exequien,* the first German requiem (1636)

1609   **John Clarke** -- American colonist who helped found Portsmouth, Rhode Island, in 1638, and Newport, Rhode Island, in 1639

1697   **Cornelis Troost** -- Dutch painter

1838   **John M. Hay** -- U.S. secretary of state, 1898-1905, best known for his Open-Door Policy in China

1846   **Elbert Henry Gary** -- American industrialist and lawyer, who was the chief organizer of the United States Steel Corporation (1901), and for whom the city of Gary, Indiana, was named

1868   **Max Slevogt** -- German painter

1869   **J. Frank Duryea** -- Co-inventor with his brother Charles of the first successful gasoline-powered automobile in America

1876   **Hugh Doherty** -- Irish tennis superstar, who won the Wimbledon singles title 5 consecutive years (1902-1906), and who with his brother Reginald dominated the game in their day

1882   **Harry Kirby McClintock** -- American composer, author, and singer, noted for songs such as "The Big Rock Candy Mountain" and "Lonesome Trail"

1890   **Eddie Rickenbacker** -- America's flying hero and "Ace of Aces," who shot down 22 enemy planes and 4 balloons in World War I

1895   **Juan Peron** – President of Argentina, 1946-1955 and 1973-1974
1910   **Wally Moses** -- Professional baseball player
1910   **Gus Hall** – Leader of the American Communist Party in the 1940s and 1950s
1912   **John Gardner** -- Secretary of Health, Education, and Welfare under President Lyndon Johnson, and founder in 1970 of the citizens' group, Common Cause
1912   **Jorge Amado** -- Brazilian novelist
1916   **Spark Masayuki Matsunaga** -- U.S. senator
1938   **Fred Stolle** – Australian tennis star who won four Wimbledon titles
1940   **Keith Carradine** -- American actor and son of the great character actor John Carradine
1941   **Jesse Jackson** -- American civil rights leader and candidate for the Democratic Party's nomination for president in 1984 and 1988
1943   **Chevy Chase** -- American comedian and actor
1946   **Paul Splittorff** -- Professional baseball player
1949   **Enos Cabell** -- Professional baseball player
1949   **Sigourney Weaver** -- American stage and motion-picture actress and daughter of Pat Weaver, the president of NBC who launched *The Today Show* and *The Tonight Show*

OCTOBER 8 -- EVENTS

451 AD   The fourth Ecumenical Council of the Roman Catholic Church opened in Rome.
1769   Captain James Cook rediscovered New Zealand. (It had been discovered in 1642 by Abel Tasman, but he and his Dutch settlers tried to keep its discovery secret from the English.)
1869   Franklin Pierce died in Concord, New Hampshire, at age 64.
1871   The Great Fire of Chicago started when, according to legend, a cow kicked over a lantern in a barn owned by Mrs. O'Leary at 137 De Koven Street.
1882   "The public be damned," said industrialist William H. Vanderbilt, when questioned about running his railroad in the public interest.
1895   Engelbert Humperdinck's opera, *Hansel and Gretel,* had its American premiere at Daly's Theater in New York.
1904   George M. Cohan's immortal "Give My Regards to Broadway" was first sung publicly in his musical play, *Little Johnny Jones.*
1904   The first automobile race for the Vanderbilt Cup was won by George Heath, driving a Panhard.

1918 U.S. soldier Alvin York killed over 20 German soldiers and captured 132 others in World War I. He became famous as Sergeant York, but he was only a corporal at the time.

1923 Germany's post-war inflation made one United States penny worth 6,250,000 paper marks.

1934 Bruno Richard Hauptmann was indicted for murder in the death of Charles Lindbergh's infant son.

1956 Don Larsen pitched the only perfect game (no runner reached base) in World Series history, as the New York Yankees beat the Brooklyn Dodgers, 2-0.

1967 Che Guevara, the Cuban revolutionary, was captured and and killed by Bolivian troops in the Bolivian jungle.

1983 Carlos Buhler, Kim Momb, and Louis Reichardt, followed later by the rest of their American team, scaled the east face of Mount Everest, a sheer wall regarded before as unscalable.

OCTOBER 9 -- BIRTHDAYS

1757 **Charles X** -- King of France, 1824-1830

1782 **Lewis Cass** -- U.S. Army officer and Democratic presidential candidate in 1848

1835 **Camille Saint-Saens** -- French composer with a prodigious output of music, the best known of which is probably his opera, *Samson and Delilah* (1877)

1860 **Leonard Wood** – American commander of the "Rough Riders" in the Spanish-American War

1863 **Edward William Bok** -- American writer and journalist, who as editor of the *Ladies' Home Journal* was called "a lay preacher to the largest congregation in the United States"

1873 **Charles Rudolph Walgreen** – American druggist who founded the Walgreen drugstore chain in 1909

1884 **Martin Johnson** – American explorer and documentary filmmaker

1889 **Rube Marquard** – Hall of Fame baseball pitcher who won 19 consecutive games for the New York Giants in 1912

1890 **Aimee Semple McPherson** -- American evangelist and early radio preacher

1898 **Joe Sewell** -- Hall of Fame baseball player and the most difficult batter in history to strike out

1899 **Bruce Catton** -- American historian, journalist, and author of numerous Civil War books such as *A Stillness at Appomattox,* which won the 1954 Pulitzer Prize

1900   **Alistair Sim** -- Scottish stage, screen, and television actor with a career that spanned 45 years

1903   **Walter O'Malley** -- American baseball executive who moved the Brooklyn Dodgers to Los Angeles

1906   **Leopold Senghor** -- Poet, statesman, and president of Senegal

1908   **Jacques Tati** -- French motion-picture actor, master of pantomime, and director

1908   **Jim Folsom** -- Flamboyant populist governor of Alabama (1947-1951, 1955-1959), who refused to use racism as a campaign tool at a time when others were building careers on it

1914   **Edward Andrews** -- American stage, screen, and television actor

1918   **E. Howard Hunt** -- One of the better known participants in the Watergate break-in

1924   **Arnold Risen** -- Professional basketball player

1929   **Ernest Morial** -- First black mayor of New Orleans

1938   **Russell Myers** -- American cartoonist and creator of *Broom Hilda*

1940   **John Lennon** -- Member of the Beatles musical group and superstar on his own

1940   **Joe Pepitone** -- Professional baseball player

1940   **Gordon Humphrey** -- U.S. senator

1944   **Fred Patek** -- Professional baseball player

1949   **Jackson Browne** -- American rock singer

1950   **Brian Downing** -- Professional baseball player

1953   **Peanut Louie** -- American tennis player

1964   **Martin Jaite** -- Argentine tennis player

OCTOBER 9 -- EVENTS

1000   Leif Ericson, the great Norse explorer, became the first European to land in North America, which he called Vinland. (The date is celebrated as Leif Ericson Day in Norway.)

1469   Fra Filippo Lippi, the great Italian painter, died in Spoleto, Italy, at age 63.

1470   King Henry VI was restored to the English throne by the Earl of Warwick.

1701   Yale College was founded by 10 Connecticut clergymen. (It got its present name in 1718 when Elihu Yale contributed money and books to the school.)

1855   Joshua C. Stoddard of Worcester, Massachusetts, patented the first calliope.

1871	The Great Fire of Chicago burned itself out, after sweeping over 17,000 buildings, and leaving 98,000 people homeless.
1888	The Washington Monument in Washington, D.C., was opened to the public.
1905	The great French actress Sarah Bernhardt, in flinging herself off the castle parapet in *Tosca,* injured her leg so severely that it eventually had to be amputated.
1936	The first generator at Hoover Dam (originally Boulder Dam) was switched on.
1958	Pope Pius XII died in Rome at age 82.
1973	Elvis and Priscilla Presley were divorced in Santa Monica, California.

OCTOBER 10 -- BIRTHDAYS

1560	**Jacobus Arminius** -- Theologian and minister of the Dutch Reformed Church, who tried unsuccessfully to liberalize the severe Dutch Calvinistic views on predestination
1684	**Jean Antoine Watteau** -- French romantic painter, whose masterpiece, *Pilgrimage to the Island of Cythera,* currently hangs in the Louvre in Paris
1731	**Henry Cavendish** -- Famous English physicist and chemist who first showed that water was a compound of hydrogen and oxygen, and who discovered many fundamental laws of electricity
1738	**Benjamin West** -- American painter famous for his large pictures of historical subjects, which were scorned by his contemporary, the noted Gilbert Stuart, as West's "ten-acre" pictures
1813	**Giuseppe Verdi** -- Leading Italian opera composer of the 19th century, whose works are performed more often today than those of any other opera composer
1830	**Isabella II** -- Queen of Spain, 1833-1868
1833	**John Mohler Studebaker** -- American wagon and vehicle maker who with his brothers Henry and Clement formed the Studebaker company that eventually became one of the great U.S. automakers
1845	**George Saintsbury** -- English literary critic and historian
1861	**Fridtjof Nansen** -- Norwegian explorer and statesman who in 1888 crossed Greenland from east to west, a feat declared by experts as impossible
1882	**Jack Francis Mahoney** -- American lyricist noted for songs such as "When You Wore a Tulip and I Wore a Big Red Rose"
1890	**Richard Howard** -- American composer and author noted for songs such as "Somebody Else Is Taking My Place"

1900   **Helen Hayes** -- American actress and "First Lady of the American Theater"

1901   **Alberto Giacometti** -- Swiss sculptor and leader of the surrealism movement, noted for his long, thin human figures

1906   **Paul Creston** -- American composer, author, and conductor

1908   **Johnny Green** -- American bandleader and composer of hit songs such as "Body and Soul" and "I Cover the Waterfront"

1909   **Johnny Marks** -- American composer and author, noted for songs such as "Rudolph the Red-Nosed Reindeer," "A Holly Jolly Christmas," "Silver and Gold," and "Everything I've Always Wanted"

1911   **Leo Mannes (Zeke Manners)** -- American composer and singer, noted for songs such as "Pennsylvania Polka"

1913   **Claude Simon** -- French novelist

1917   **Jan Murray** -- American comedian

1918   **Thelonious Monk** -- American pianist and composer of jazz songs such as "Round Midnight" and "Blue Monk"

1926   **Richard Jaeckel** -- American motion-picture actor

1930   **Harold Pinter** -- English playwright and screenwriter, noted for works such as *The Dumb Waiter* (1957) and *Homecoming* (1965)

1930   **Adlai Stevenson III** -- U.S. senator in the 1970s and son of Adlai Stevenson, the Democratic candidate for president in 1952 and 1956

1937   **Bruce Devlin** -- Professional golfer

1946   **Gene Tenace** -- Professional baseball player

1946   **Ben Vereen** -- American actor, dancer, and singer

OCTOBER 10 -- EVENTS

1492   On the first voyage to America, Columbus's crew, after a near mutiny, agreed to sail on for three more days and then turn back if land were not found. It was--two days later.

1845   The United States Naval Academy opened at Annapolis, Maryland.

1858   The first Butterfield Overland Mail coach reached San Francisco from St. Louis.

1886   A tailless dress coat for men was introduced for the first time at the Tuxedo Park Club in New York. It shocked the guests but soon became commonplace as the "tuxedo."

1911   Chinese revolutionaries under Dr. Sun Yat-sen rebelled against the Manchu dynasty, which they overthrew by the end of the year.

1935	George Gershwin's opera, *Porgy and Bess,* opened on Broadway.
1938	Germany completed the occupation of the Sudetenland in Czechoslovakia in accordance with the Munich agreement.
1943	Generalissimo Chiang Kai-shek was sworn in as president of China.
1963	The limited nuclear test ban treaty went into effect between the United States and Russia.
1973	Vice President Spiro Agnew resigned, pleading "no contest" to a tax evasion charge. He was only the second American vice president to resign.

OCTOBER 11 -- BIRTHDAYS

1738	**Arthur Phillip** -- British admiral who settled Sydney, Australia, with convicts in 1788
1759	**Mason Locke Weems (Parson Weems)** — American clergyman who in about 1800 wrote the first popular biography of Washington, *The Life and Memorable Actions of George Washington*
1821	**Sir George Williams** -- A young English clerk who founded the YMCA
1835	**Theodore Thomas** -- Noted American conductor
1844	**Henry John Heinz** -- Founder of the H.J. Heinz company
1849	**William Knox D'Arcy** -- Founder of the Iranian oil industry
1872	**Harlan Fiske Stone** -- One of the great Supreme Court justices, who served as associate justice, 1925-1941, and as chief justice, 1941-1946
1884	**Eleanor Roosevelt** -- U.N. diplomat, humanitarian, and wife of President Franklin D. Roosevelt
1885	**Francois Mauriac** -- French novelist and 1952 Nobel Prize winner
1887	**Willie Hoppe** -- The greatest billiard player of all time and the winner of 51 world titles between 1906 and 1952
1897	**Nathan F. Twining** -- U.S. World War II Air Force general, and chairman of the Joint Chiefs of Staff, 1953-1960
1902	**Charles Revson** -- Co-founder of Revlon corporation
1902	**Leon Belasco** -- Russian-born motion-picture character comedian in some 60 pictures
1908	**Red Rolfe** -- Professional baseball player and manager
1910	**Joseph Alsop** -- American newspaper columnist
1918	**Jerome Robbins** -- One of the most popular choreographers of the 20th century, with credits such as *The King and I, West Side Story,* and *Fiddler on the Roof*

1939   **Maria Bueno** -- Brazilian tennis superstar and winner of three Wimbledon singles titles

OCTOBER 11 -- EVENTS

732 AD Charles Martel (Charles the Hammer), the great Frankish leader, defeated the Moors in the famous Battle of Tours, ending the Moorish advance into Europe.

1531   Huldreich Zwingli, Swiss Protestant leader, was killed in the Battle of Kappel, between the Catholic cantons and the Protestants.

1737   One of the greatest earthquakes in world history occurred in Calcutta, India, killing some 300,000 people.

1779   Polish general Casimir Pulaski died from wounds suffered two days earlier while fighting for American independence in the siege of Savannah, Georgia.

1811   The first steam-propelled ferry service began, as inventor John Stevens put his ferryboat, the *Juliana*, into operation between New York City and Hoboken, New Jersey.

1890   The Daughters of the American Revolution was founded in Washington, D.C.

1936   *Professor Quiz,* the first national quiz program on radio, started its long run on CBS.

1941   General Hideki Tojo, the leader of the extremist Japanese military group, became premier of Japan.

1962   The first session of Vatican II was opened in Rome by Pope John XXIII.

1968   *Apollo 7*, the first manned Apollo flight, was launched with astronauts Schirra, Eisele, and Cunningham aboard.

1973   Two Pascagoula, Mississippi, dockworkers, Charles Hickson and Calvin Parker, claimed to have been kidnapped by weird creatures and examined for 3 days in a UFO.

1975   NBC's comedy series *Saturday Night Live* made its debut with a cast known as "Not Ready for Prime Time Players."

1979   American physicist Allan McLeod Cormack and British engineer Godfrey Newbold Hounsfield won the Nobel Prize for medicine for their development of the CAT scan.

OCTOBER 12 -- BIRTHDAYS

1537   **Edward VI** -- Son of King Henry VIII by his third wife, Jane Seymour, and king of England, 1547-1553

1775 **Lyman Beecher** -- American Presbyterian minister and father of the noted writer, Harriet Beecher Stowe, and the famous preacher, Henry Ward Beecher

1803 **Alexander Turney Stewart** -- American merchant who founded the A.T. Stewart Department Store, the world's first true department store

1840 **Helena Modjeska** -- Noted Polish actress

1844 **George Washington Cable** -- American author and reformer, noted for his books about old French New Orleans

1860 **Elmer Ambrose Sperry** -- American inventor and manufacturer, noted for his development of the gyroscope

1866 **Ramsay MacDonald** -- Two times prime minister of Great Britain--in 1924 as the first Labour party prime minister, and in 1929-1935

1872 **Ralph Vaughan Williams** -- The dominant English composer of the first half of the 20th century

1891 **Perle Mesta** -- Prominent Washington, D.C., hostess and U.S. ambassador

1891 **Nelly Sachs** -- German-born Nobel Prize-winning poet and dramatist, noted for works such as *Eli: A Miracle Play of the Sufferings of Israel* (1950)

1905 **Rick Ferrell** -- Hall of Fame baseball player

1906 **Joe Cronin** -- Hall of Fame baseball player and president of the American League

1912 **Sol Marcus** -- American composer, author, and conductor, noted for songs such as "I Don't Want to Set the World on Fire" and "When the Lights Go On Again All Over the World"

1923 **Jean Nidetch** -- American businesswoman who in 1963 founded Weight Watchers International

1932 **Dick Gregory** -- American comedian and civil rights leader

1932 **Jake Garn** -- U.S. senator

1935 **Sam Moore** -- Soul singer of the Sam and Dave duo

1935 **Luciano Pavarotti** -- Noted Italian opera singer and one of the greatest tenors of the late 20th century

1936 **Tony Kubek** -- Professional baseball player and sports announcer

1944 **Jack Marin** -- Professional basketball player

1950 **Susan Anton** -- American motion-picture actress

1951 **Sally Little** -- Professional golfer

1957 **Jerry Butler** -- Professional football player

OCTOBER 12 -- EVENTS

1492   At 2 A.M. lookout Rodrigo de Triana shouted "Tierra!" as Columbus's fleet discovered America. The land sighted was San Salvador (now Watling Island or perhaps Samana Cay).

1492   Piero della Francesca, the great Italian painter, died in Borgo San Sepolcro at age 72.

1518   Martin Luther was interrogated on his Protestant views by Cardinal Cajetan at Augsburg.

1768   The first printed notice of the song, "Yankee Doodle," appeared in the New York *Journal.*

1870   Robert E. Lee, the great Confederate general, died in Lexington, Virginia, at age 63.

1895   Charles Blair MacDonald won the first amateur golf tournament played in the United States.

1899   President Kruger of the Transvaal issued an ultimatum to the Boers of the Orange Free State, which precipitated the Boer War that began two days later.

1920   Construction began on the Holland Tunnel linking New York City and Jersey City.

1950   Senator Estes Kefauver's Subcommittee to Investigate Interstate Crime opened its hearings.

1960   Soviet premier Nikita Khrushchev pounded his desk with a shoe during a dispute at a United Nations General Assembly session.

1973   President Nixon named Congressman Gerald Ford to become vice president, succeeding Spiro Agnew, who had resigned.

OCTOBER 13 -- BIRTHDAYS

1474   **Mariotto Albertinelli** -- Italian painter

1750   **Molly Pitcher (Mary Ludwig McCauley)** -- American Revolutionary War heroine who took the place of her fallen husband in the Battle of Monmouth

1769   **Horace H. Hayden** -- Founder of the first dental college

1821   **Rudolf Virchow** -- German pathologist, anthropologist, and statesman, considered to be the father of pathology

1852   **Lillie Langtry** -- British actress known as Jersey Lily, and a stage favorite in England and the United States in the late 19th century

1863   **Tod B. Galloway** -- American composer and singer, noted for songs such as "The Whiffenpoof Song" and "Little Boy Blue"

1876   **Rube Waddell** -- Hall of Fame baseball pitcher with a sensational career earned run average of 2.16

1877   **Theodore Bilbo** -- U.S. senator from Mississippi, 1935-1947

1885   **Harry Hershfield** -- One of the "grand old men" of the American comic strip, and creator of *Abie the Agent*

1889   **Ira Schuster** -- American composer, author, and pianist, noted for songs such as "A Shanty in Old Shanty Town" and "Did You Ever Get That Feeling in the Moonlight?"

1891   **Irene Rich** -- American stage and radio actress, and leading lady of the Hollywood silent screen

1900   **Gerald Marks** -- American composer noted for songs such as "Is It True What They Say About Dixie?"

1909   **Herblock (Herbert Lawrence Block)** -- One of the most famous 20th-century American political cartoonists

1910   **Art Tatum** -- Nearly blind American pianist and great jazz virtuoso

1910   **Ernest Kellogg Gann** -- American author

1915   **Cornel Wilde** -- American motion-picture actor

1917   **Laraine Day** -- American motion-picture actress

1921   **Yves Montand** -- Italian-French stage and motion-picture actor

1925   **Margaret Thatcher** -- Great Britain's first woman prime minister

1931   **Eddie Mathews** -- Hall of Fame baseball player with a career total of 512 home runs

1935   **Chi Chi Rodriguez** -- Professional golfer

1936   **Donald F. McHenry** -- U.S. ambassador to the United Nations under President Carter

1941   **Paul Simon** -- American singer and guitarist of the Simon and Garfunkel duo, and one of America's most successful songwriters

1942   **Pamela Tiffin** -- American motion-picture actress

1950   **Barbara Hawcroft** -- Australian tennis player

1959   **Marie Osmond** -- American singer and actor

OCTOBER 13 -- EVENTS

54 AD   Emperor Claudius died from poison given him by his physician Xenophon and his empress Agrippina, and Nero became emperor of Rome.

1399   Henry IV, the first English king of the House of Lancaster, was crowned.

1775   The American Navy was established by the Second Continental Congress.

1792   George Washington laid the cornerstone of the White House, known in the beginning as the President's House.

1860   The first aerial photograph in the United States was taken from a balloon over Boston.

1903   Boston defeated Pittsburgh to win the first World Series in history, 5 games to 3.

1924   Alfred Lunt and Lynn Fontanne began their famous joint stage careers in New York in the opening of *The Guardsman.*

1943   Italy declared war on her former World War II Axis partner, Nazi Germany.

1959   *Explorer 7* was launched from Cape Canaveral.

1960   John F. Kennedy and Richard M. Nixon held their third "Great Debate" in the 1960 presidential election.

1973   Gerald Ford was sworn in as vice president, succeeding Spiro Agnew, who had resigned.

1982   The International Olympic Committee announced that it would restore Jim Thorpe's two 1912 Olympic gold medals stripped from him for playing minor league baseball in 1911.

OCTOBER 14 -- BIRTHDAYS

1006   **Geoffrey Martel** -- Count of Anjou

1606   **Joan Maetsuyker** -- Governor general of the Dutch East Indies, 1653-1678

1633   **James II** -- King of England, 1685-1688

1644   **William Penn** -- Quaker leader and founder of Pennsylvania

1734   **Francis Lightfoot Lee** -- American Revolutionary War patriot and signer of the Declaration of Independence

1863   **Annie Laurie (Winifred Sweet)** -- Noted American newspaperwoman with the San Francisco *Examiner*

1872   **Sol Hess** -- American comic strip cartoonist and creator in 1923 of *The Nebbs*

1882   **Eamon De Valera** -- Leader in Ireland's fight for independence, and head of the government as prime minister, president of Ireland, and of the Irish Free State for most of the years 1937-1959

1888   **Katherine Mansfield** -- English short story writer, noted for collections such as *The Garden Party* (1927)

1890   **Dwight D. Eisenhower** -- 34th U.S. president and commander of the Allied European forces in World War II

1892   **Sumner Welles** -- Undersecretary of state and trusted aide to President Franklin D. Roosevelt

1893   **Lois Lenski** -- American author and illustrator of children's books, who received the Newbery Medal in 1946 for *Strawberry Girl*

1894   **E.E. Cummings** -- American poet and writer, noted for disregarding the rules of punctuation (he wrote his name e e cummings), and noted for works such as *The Enormous Room* and *Poems 1923-1954*

1896   **Lillian Gish** -- The greatest actress of the silent screen and one of the true giants of Hollywood, with a career of over 80 years

1901   **Harry A. Stuhldreher** -- One of the famed Four Horsemen of the Notre Dame football team

1906   **Hannah Arendt** -- German-born writer, newspaper correspondent, philosopher, and historian

1910   **John Wooden** -- Highly successful American basketball coach

1911   **Le Duc Tho** – North Vietnamese official who negotiated the Vietnam armistice with the United States

1914   **Harry Brecheen** – Professional baseball pitcher who won three games for the St. Louis Cardinals against the Boston Red Sox in the 1946 World Series

1928   **Roger Moore** -- English motion-picture and television actor

1930   **Joseph-Desire Mobutu** -- President of Zaire

1930   **Stella Castellucci** -- American composer, author, and harpist

1931   **Istvan Gulvas** -- Hungarian tennis player

1938   **John Dean** – Central Watergate figure in the implication of President Nixon

1938   **Farah Diba Pahlevi** – Shahbanou of Iran and wife of Iranian Shah Mohammed Reza Pahlevi

1939   **Ralph Lauren** – American fashion designer and nine-time winner of the Coty, the fashion industry's most prestigious honor

1941   **J.C. Snead** -- Professional golfer

1943   **Lance Rentzel** -- Professional football player

1946   **Al Oliver** -- Professional baseball player

1947   **Charles Joiner** -- Professional football player

1947   **Bob Kuechenberg** -- Professional football player

1948   **Ed Figueroa** -- Professional baseball player

1950   **Sheila Young** -- American speed skater, cyclist, and 1976 Olympic gold medal winner

1956   **Beth Daniel** -- Professional golfer

OCTOBER 14 -- EVENTS

996 AD Hugh Capet, the French king who founded the Capetian line, died in Paris at age 56.

1066   William the Conqueror defeated Harold Godwinson, heir to the English throne, in the famous Battle of Hastings, which resulted in the Norman conquest of England.

1586   Mary, Queen of Scots, went on trial in England for plotting to kill Queen Elizabeth I. She was later found guilty and beheaded.

1793   French queen Marie Antoinette was brought to trial on a charge of treason by the French revolutionists. She was executed two days later.

1806   Napoleon routed the armies of Prussia in the Battles of Jena and Auerstad.

1899   The Boer War began as the Orange Free State and the South African Republic declared war on Britain.

1912   Theodore Roosevelt was shot by a would-be assassin in Milwaukee, while campaigning for president. He made his speech anyway and was then rushed to a hospital to recuperate.

1930   Ethel Merman made her Broadway debut in the premiere of George Gershwin's musical comedy, *Girl Crazy*.

1944   Erwin Rommel, the famous German World War II field marshal, committed suicide after being implicated in the plot to kill Hitler.

1947   American pilot Charles Yeager became the first man to break the sound barrier, reaching a speed of 670 miles per hour--Mach 1.015--in a Bell X-1 rocket airplane.

1960   John F. Kennedy first suggested the idea of the Peace Corps, in a campaign speech at the University of Michigan.

1971   Iran held an elaborate celebration to mark the 2,500th anniversary of the founding of the Persian Empire by Cyrus the Great.

OCTOBER 15 -- BIRTHDAYS

70 BC   **Virgil** -- The greatest poet of the Roman Empire

1608   **Evangelista Torricelli** -- Italian mathematician and physicist, noted for his invention in 1643 of the barometer

1775   **John Vanderlyn** -- American artist

1785   **Jose Miguel Carrera** -- The first president of Chile

1814   **Mikhail Yuryevich Lermontov** -- Russian poet and novelist and outstanding leader of the late Romantic period

1830   **Helen Hunt Jackson** -- American poet, novelist, and author of *Ramona* (1884)

1844   **Friedrich Nietzsche** -- German classical scholar and philosopher, author of *Thus Spake Zarathustra* (1883-1885), and the originator of the "God is dead" religious philosophy

1847   **Ralph Blakelock** -- American landscape painter noted for works such as *Sunset* and *Moonrise*

1858   **John L. Sullivan** -- Famous American bare-knuckle fighter and world heavyweight boxing champion, 1882-1892, known as the "Great John L."

1871   **Frederick Knight Logan** -- American composer and conductor, noted for songs such as "Missouri Waltz," "Rose of My Heart," and "Moonlight Waltz"

1878   **Paul Reynaud** -- French prime minister in June 1940 when France fell in World War II

1879   **Jane Darwell** -- American actress who played Ma Joad in *The Grapes of Wrath* (1940), and appeared in over 200 films in a 50-year career

1881   **P.G. Wodehouse** -- Noted British-American humorist, novelist, and short-story writer

1882   **Ballard MacDonald** -- American composer and author, noted for songs such as "Back Home in Indiana," "Beautiful Ohio," and "Trail of the Lonesome Pine"

1897   **Ben L. Trace** -- American composer, author, and singer, noted for songs such as "You Call Everybody Darling" and "Sweet Dreams, Sweetheart"

1899   **William Claire Menninger** -- American psychiatrist and co-founder of the Menninger Clinic

1900   **Boris Aronson** -- Russian-born painter, sculptor, and designer

1900   **Mervyn LeRoy** -- American motion-picture producer and director, noted for films such as *Little Caesar* (1931) and *The Wizard of Oz* (1939)

1900   **Fritz Feld** -- German stage, screen, and television actor with a career of over 60 years

1905   **C.P. Snow** -- British novelist and scientist

1908   **John Kenneth Galbraith** -- Noted American economist and author of *The Affluent Society* (1958)

1909   **Mel Harder** -- Professional baseball player

1917   **Arthur Schlesinger Jr.** -- Noted American historian, and Pulitzer Prize winner in 1966 for the biography, *A Thousand Days: John F. Kennedy in the White House*

1917   **Alan Wendell Livingston** − American composer and author, noted for songs such as "I Taut I Taw a Puddy Tat" and "That's All Folks"

1920   **Claude Monteux** -- American flutist and conductor

1921   **Mario Puzo** -- American writer, and author of *The Godfather*

1924   **Lee Iacocca** -- American automobile executive with Ford and later Chrysler

1926   **Jean Peters** -- American motion-picture and television actress

1926   **Evan Hunter** -- American novelist noted for works such as *The Blackboard Jungle*

1937   **Linda Lavin** -- American actress noted for her starring role in the long-running television show *Alice*

1942   **Penny Marshall** -- American actress and comedienne

1945   **Jim Palmer** -- Professional baseball player and superstar

1946   **Richard Carpenter** -- American singer of the Carpenters duo

1951   **Roscoe Tanner** -- American tennis player noted for his powerful serve

1953   **Tito Jackson** -- American singer and guitarist with the Jackson 5 musical group

1955   **Victor Pecci** -- Paraguayan tennis player

OCTOBER 15 -- EVENTS

1582   The Gregorian Calendar of Pope Gregory XIII went into effect in most Catholic countries, with this day, which would have been October 5, becoming October 15, 1582.

1590   Urban VII was elected Roman Catholic pope.

1783   The brothers Jacques and Joseph Montgolfier sent up the first balloon carrying a man (J.F. Pilatre de Rozier), in Paris.

1846   Ether was used for the first time in a public demonstration, by Dr. William Thomas Green Morton in extracting a tooth in Boston, Massachusetts.

1858   The last Lincoln-Douglas debate was held in Alton, Illinois, before an audience of 6,000 people.

1894   Alfred Dreyfus, a French army officer, was arrested on the false charge of spying for Germany, in the famous Dreyfus case of political injustice.

1901   Geraldine Farrar, the brilliant American soprano, made her debut at the Berlin Opera House as Marguerite in *Faust*.

1905   The comic strip, *Little Nemo in Slumberland,* by Winsor McKay, first appeared.

1914   The Clayton Anti-Trust Act became law.

1917   Mata Hari, the most famous spy of World War I, was executed in Paris by a firing squad of Zouaves.

1928   The German dirigible *Graf Zeppelin* arrived in the United States on its first commercial flight.

1945	Pierre Laval, the French World War II traitor, swallowed poison in a suicide attempt, but was revived and shot by a firing squad.
1946	Hermann Goering, the Nazi World War II Reichsmarshal, committed suicide by taking poison a day before his scheduled execution.
1948	Gerald Ford married Elizabeth "Betty" Bloomer.
1951	The long-running television series *I Love Lucy,* starring Lucille Ball and Desi Arnaz, premiered on CBS.
1964	Nikita Khrushchev was ousted as premier and first secretary of the Russian Communist party.
1964	Cole Porter, the noted American popular music composer, died at age 72.

OCTOBER 16 -- BIRTHDAYS

1430	**James II** -- King of Scotland, 1437-1460
1483	**Gasparo Contarini** -- Venetian Humanist scholar and theologian
1620	**Pierre Puget** -- The most original of the French baroque sculptors
1708	**Albrecht von Haller** -- Swiss biologist and father of experimental physiology
1758	**Noah Webster** -- American educator famous for compiling *Webster's Dictionary,* the finest English dictionary of its time
1797	**James Thomas Brudenell Cardigan** -- English general who led the charge of the Light Brigade in 1854 in the Crimean War
1806	**William Pitt Fessenden** -- U.S. senator who helped found the Republican party in the 1850s
1815	**Francis Richard Lubbock** -- One of the early governors of Texas
1854	**Oscar Wilde** -- Irish wit, poet, and dramatist, noted for works such as *The Importance of Being Earnest* (1895)
1874	**Reginald Doherty** -- Irish tennis player and four times Wimbledon singles champion, 1897-1900
1881	**William Harridge** -- President of baseball's American League in the 1940s
1886	**David Ben-Gurion** -- Israel's first prime minister after it became independent in 1948
1888	**Eugene O'Neill** -- America's greatest playwright
1890	**Paul Strand** -- American photographer and documentary filmmaker
1898	**William O. Douglas** -- U.S. Supreme Court justice, 1939-1975
1900	**Goose Goslin** -- Hall of Fame baseball player

1905   **Rex Bell** -- American motion-picture actor
1906   **George Martin Lott** -- American Hall of Fame tennis player
1908   **Robert Ardney** -- American dramatist and scientist
1908   **Enver Hoxha** -- Albanian dictator, 1944-1985
1912   **Clifford Hansen** -- U.S. senator
1916   **Kathleen Winsor** -- American novelist noted for *Forever Amber* (1945)
1916   **Charles Everett Koop** -- American physician and U.S. Surgeon General under Presidents Reagan and Bush
1921   **Linda Darnell** -- American motion-picture actress
1925   **Angela Lansbury** -- English-born American stage, screen, and television actress, and star of the long-running TV series, *Murder, She Wrote*
1927   **Gunter Grass** -- German novelist and poet, noted for *The Tin Drum* (1959)
1929   **Nicholas von Hoffman** -- American journalist, writer, and television personality
1931   **Charles Colson** -- Aide to President Nixon who was convicted in the Watergate scandal
1940   **Dave De Busschere** -- Professional basketball player and super star
1941   **Mel Counts** -- Professional basketball player
1945   **Suzanne Somers** -- American television and motion-picture actress
1948   **Richard Caster** -- Professional football player
1949   **John Mengelt** -- Professional basketball player
1955   **Lynn Cain** -- Professional football player
1959   **Kevin McReynolds** -- Professional baseball player

OCTOBER 16 -- EVENTS

1553   Lucas Cranach the Elder, the great German painter, died in Weimar twelve days after his 81st birthday.

1793   French queen Marie Antoinette was executed on the guillotine by the revolutionists.

1813   The Battle of the Nations began at Leipzig between Napoleon and an allied force of five countries.

1815   Napoleon was exiled to St. Helena, where he remained for the rest of his life.

1845   Edgar Allan Poe read his new poem, "The Raven," to a Boston audience, but he did it in such a "singularly didactic" way that his listeners walked out on him.

1846	Boston dentist William T.G. Morton publicly demonstrated the use of ether as an anesthetic, as Dr. John Warren operated on a patient's jaw at Massachusetts General Hospital.
1859	John Brown, the noted abolitionist, made his famous raid on the U.S. arsenal at Harpers Ferry, Virginia.
1916	Margaret Sanger opened the world's first birth control clinic, in New York City.
1925	The Locarno (Switzerland) Conference ended, with the delegates having signed 7 treaties outlawing willful aggression in Europe and providing a neutral zone in the Rhineland.
1933	The comic strip, *Dan Dunn,* by Norman Marsh, appeared for the first time.
1934	The Chinese Communists began their "Long March" to the province of Shensi, where they planned to continue their struggle against Chiang Kai-shek.
1944	*The Robe,* the best-selling book by Lloyd Douglas, was first published.
1946	Ten top Nazis, including former foreign minister, Joachim von Ribbentrop, were hanged in Nuremburg for war crimes.
1962	President John F. Kennedy revealed to insiders in the United States government the existence of a Soviet missile buildup in Cuba.
1964	China joined the world's nuclear club, detonating its first atomic bomb.
1978	John Paul II was elected Roman Catholic pope.

OCTOBER 17 -- BIRTHDAYS

1582	**Johann Gerhard** -- Leading theologian of his era
1696	**Augustus III** -- King of Poland
1725	**John Wilkes** -- English journalist and politician
1780	**Richard Mentor Johnson** -- U.S. vice president, 1837-1841, who claimed to have killed the famous Indian chief Tecumseh
1813	**Georg Buchner** -- German writer, often considered a forerunner of the naturalism movement of the late 1800s
1859	**Buck Ewing** -- Hall of Fame baseball player
1859	**Childe Hassam** -- American painter noted for works such as *Union Square, New York* (1890)
1885	**Isak Dineson** -- Danish author who wrote most of her works in English, and who is known for novels such as *Out of Africa* (1937)
1893	**Spring Byington** -- American stage, screen, and television actress, who appeared in some 100 movies in a 40-year career

1895   **Doris Humphrey** -- Pioneer of the American modern dance
1900   **Yvor Winters** -- American poet and critic
1903   **Nathanael West** -- American novelist noted for works such as *The Day of the Locust* (1939)
1903   **Irene Ryan** -- American motion-picture and television actress noted for her role as Granny in the long-running series, *The Beverly Hillbillies*
1905   **Jean Arthur** -- American stage, screen, and television actress and comedienne
1906   **Paul Derringer** -- Professional baseball player
1912   **John Paul I** -- Roman Catholic pope who served only 34 days before his death in 1978
1912   **Jack Milton Owens** -- American composer, author, and singer, noted for songs such as "The Hut Sut Song"
1914   **Jerry Siegel** – American comic strip writer, and co-creator with Joe Shuster of *Superman*
1915   **Arthur Miller** -- A leading American playwright, and author of *Death of a Salesman* (1949)
1916   **Virgil Franklin Patch II** -- American cartoonist
1917   **Marsha Hunt** -- American motion-picture and television actress
1918   **Rita Hayworth** – Erotic queen of Hollywood films of the 1940s
1920   **Montgomery Clift** -- American stage and motion-picture actor and superstar of the 1950s and early 1960s
1927   **Johnny Klippstein** -- Professional baseball player
1927   **Tom Poston** -- American actor and comedian
1928   **Julie Adams** -- American motion-picture and television actress
1928   **Jim Gilliam** -- Professional baseball player
1930   **Jimmy Breslin** -- American newspaper columnist and writer
1933   **William A. Anders** -- American astronaut who participated in *Apollo 8*, the first manned flight to orbit the moon
1939   **Evel Knievel** -- American dare-devil performer
1947   **Ronald Johnson** -- Professional football player
1948   **Margot Kidder** -- Canadian motion-picture actress

OCTOBER 17 -- EVENTS

1529   Cardinal Wolsey was dismissed from office by King Henry VIII of England because of his disapproval of Henry's affair with Anne Boleyn.

1777	The Americans gained a decisive victory at Saratoga in the Revolutionary War, with British general Burgoyne surrendering his entire army of some 6,000 men.
1849	Frederic Chopin, the great Polish composer, died of tuberculosis in Paris at age 39.
1855	Henry Bessemer patented his Bessemer process for making steel.
1914	Babe Ruth married Helen Woodford in Ellicott City, Maryland.
1919	The Radio Corporation of America (RCA) was incorporated.
1931	Al Capone, the best-known racketeer in the United States, was convicted of income tax evasion and sentenced to eleven years in prison.
1933	The great German scientist Albert Einstein entered the U.S. as a refugee from Hitler's Germany.
1945	Juan Peron staged a coup in Buenos Aires, and seized power as absolute dictator of Argentina.
1974	The Oakland A's won their third straight World Series, beating the Los Angeles Dodgers 4 games to 1.
1989	An earthquake measuring 7.1 on the Richter scale hit the San Francisco-Oakland area, killing 67 people, injuring over 3700, and causing $6.5 billion in damage.

OCTOBER 18 -- BIRTHDAYS

1405	**Pius II** -- Roman Catholic pope, 1458-1464
1595	**Edward Winslow** -- A founder of the Plymouth colony in Massachusetts, whose marriage to Susanna White was the first wedding performed in the new colony
1631	**Michael Wigglesworth** -- Puritan pastor, doctor, and poet of colonial New England, best known for his poem, "The Day of Doom: or, A Poetical Description of the Great and Last Judgment" (1662)
1632	**Luca Giordano** -- Neapolitan painter
1697	**Canaletto** -- Italian painter (born Giovanni Antonio Canal)
1777	**Heinrich von Kleist** -- German writer and playwright, noted for works such as *The Broken Jug* (1808)
1785	**Thomas Love Peacock** -- English novelist and poet
1831	**Frederick III** -- King of Prussia and second emperor of modern Germany (for 3 months in 1888), and father of Wilhelm II, the German World War I kaiser
1839	**Thomas B. Reed** -- Speaker of the U.S. House of Representatives, 1889-1891 and 1895-1899, whose autocratic control of the House resulted in his nickname, "Czar Reed"

1859   Henri Louis Bergson -- Nobel Prize-winning French philosopher, noted for works such as *Time and Free Will* (1889)

1878   James Truslow Adams -- Pulitzer Prize-winning American historian, noted for works such as *The Epic of America* (1931)

1896   Nat Holman -- American basketball coach known as "Mr. Basketball"

1902   Miriam Hopkins -- American stage and motion-picture actress with a 45-year career

1905   Felix Houphouet-Boigny -- First president of the Ivory Coast

1906   Sidney Kingsley -- American dramatist who won a Pulitzer Prize for *Men in White* (1933)

1918   Robert William Troup Jr. -- American composer, author, and pianist, noted for songs such as "Route 66," "Daddy," and "The Girl Can't Help It"

1919   Pierre Elliott Trudeau -- Three times prime minister of Canada from 1968 to 1984

1921   Jesse A. Helms -- U.S. senator

1923   Melina Mercouri -- Greek motion-picture actress and politician

1926   Chuck Berry -- American rock and roll singer and songwriter

1926   John Morris -- American composer who wrote the music for Mel Brooks' films and for such musicals as *Bye Bye Birdie*

1927   George C. Scott -- American stage, screen, and television actor, who won the Academy Award for *Patton* (1970)

1929   Hilliard Elkins -- Broadway play producer

1930   Frank Carlucci -- Secretary of Defense under President Reagan

1939   Mike Ditka -- Professional football player and coach

1939   Lee Harvey Oswald -- Presumed assassin of President John F. Kennedy

1942   Willie Horton -- Professional baseball player

1947   Laura Nyro -- American popular song composer

1948   Ntozake Shange -- American poet and playwright

1949   George Hendrick -- Professional baseball player

1951   Pam Dawber -- American television actress

1956   Martina Navratilova -- Czechoslovakian-American tennis player and superstar

1958   Thomas Hearns -- American boxer who won titles in three classes

1961   Erin Moran -- American actress

1961   Wynton Marsalis -- American jazz trumpeter

OCTOBER 18 -- EVENTS

514 AD The great Mayan city of Chichen Itza was first occupied by the Itzas.

768 AD Charlemagne and his brother Carloman were crowned co-rulers of the Franks, after the death of their father, Pepin the Short.

1667 Brooklyn was chartered under the name Brueckelen by the governor of New Netherlands, Mathias Nicolls.

1685 The Edict of Nantes, which gave Protestants equal rights with Catholics in France, was revoked by Louis XIV, resulting in thousands of Huguenots leaving France.

1767 Charles Mason and Jeremiah Dixon completed their surveying of the Mason and Dixon Line between the Maryland and Pennsylvania colonies.

1813 Napoleon was defeated as the Battle of the Nations at Leipzig ended. Napoleon escaped but his rule of Europe was ended.

1859 U.S. troops under Colonel Robert E. Lee stormed the firehouse at Harpers Ferry, Virginia (now West Virginia), and arrested John Brown, who had raided the arsenal earlier.

1867 Alaska was formally transferred to the United States, as the American flag replaced the Russian flag at Sitka.

1873 Columbia, Princeton, Rutgers, and Yale officials drew up the first rules for intercollegiate football.

1898 The United States formally took over Puerto Rico from Spain.

1912 The Treaty of Lausanne was signed, giving Italy control of Libya.

1924 Grantland Rice coined the name, "The Four Horsemen," for Notre Dame football players, Stuhldreher, Miller, Crowley, and Layden, after their impressive win over Army.

1926 Bing Crosby, the great American popular singer, recorded his first record, "I've Got the Girl."

1931 Thomas A. Edison, the world's greatest inventor, died at age 84.

1944 Russian troops entered Czechoslovakia in World War II.

1950 Connie Mack, the Grand Old Man of Baseball, announced his retirement as manager of the Philadelphia Athletics after 67 years in the game.

1969 The U.S. government banned the use of the artificial sweeteners cyclamates because of evidence they caused cancer in rats. This claim was recanted in 1989.

OCTOBER 19 -- BIRTHDAYS

1433 **Marsilio Ficino** -- Italian philosopher and translator of Plato

1605 **Sir Thomas Browne** -- English physician and writer

1741   Choderlos de Laclos -- French writer

1784   **Leigh Hunt** -- English poet, journalist, and editor, noted for the poem, "Abou Ben Adhem"

1810   **Cassius Marcellus Clay** -- American politician and prominent abolitionist

1859   **Alfred Dreyfus** -- French army officer unjustly imprisoned in the famous Dreyfus affair

1861   **William J. Burns** -- Prominent American detective and founder of the William J. Burns International Detective Agency

1862   **Auguste Lumiere** -- French pioneer in photochemistry, who with his brother Louis Jean invented the *cinematographe,* a combination motion-picture camera, printer, and projector

1871   **Walter Bradford Cannon** -- First neurologist to use X-rays in physiological studies

1876   **Mordecai "Three Finger" Brown** -- Hall of Fame baseball pitcher with an amazing 2.03 career earned run average

1882   **Umberto Boccioni** -- The greatest Italian sculptor of the early 1900s, noted for works such as *Unique Forms of Continuity in Space*

1889   **Fannie Hurst** -- American novelist and short story writer, popular in the 1920s and 1930s

1895   **Lewis Mumford** -- American social critic and historian, and author of *The City in History,* which won the National Book Award for 1961

1901   **Arleigh A. Burke** -- American admiral and chief of naval operations, 1955-1961

1909   **Robert Beatty** -- Canadian motion-picture and television actor

1911   **George Cates** -- American composer noted for the music for "Auf Wiedersehen"

1918   **Russell Kirk** -- American writer and lecturer

1918   **Robert Strauss** -- Democratic Party leader and national chairman in 1980

1922   **Jack Anderson** -- American newspaper columnist and television commentator

1931   **Sandy Alomar** -- Professional baseball player

1931   **John le Carré** -- English novelist noted for *The Spy Who Came in from the Cold* (1963) and *The Looking Glass War* (1965)

1932   **Robert Reed** -- American television and motion-picture actor

1938   **Renata Adler** -- Italian-American novelist noted for works such as *A Year in the Dark* and *Pitch Dark*

1949   **Lynn Dickey** -- Professional football player

1955   **Martin Robinson** -- English tennis player

1967   **Amy Carter** -- Daughter of President Jimmy Carter

OCTOBER 19 -- EVENTS

202 BC   The Romans under Scipio Africanus defeated Hannibal's army of Carthaginians and Numidians in the Battle of Sama in the Second Punic War.

439 AD   Gaiseric, King of the Vandals, seized the Roman city of Carthage, and made it his capital.

1453   The English surrendered Bordeaux to France in the Hundred Years' War.

1469   Ferdinand V, King of Aragon, and Isabella I, Queen of Castile, were married in Valladolid, Spain.

1630   The first general court in New England was held, in Boston.

1745   Jonathan Swift, the great British writer, died in Dublin at age 77.

1765   The Stamp Act Congress, called by the colonies in New York, declared that the British stamp taxes could not be enforced without the people's consent.

1774   Outraged citizens of Annapolis, Maryland, destroyed the British brig *Peggy Stewart* and its cargo of tea in reprisal for the tea tax.

1781   British General Cornwallis surrendered to General Washington at Yorktown, Virginia, ending the last major battle of the Revolutionary War.

1807   Sir Humphry Davy, the great English chemist, announced his discovery of the element sodium.

1812   Napoleon evacuated Moscow with only 110,000 men left in his 600,000-man Grande Armee.

1879   Thomas A. Edison invented the electric light.

1944   Marlon Brando made his New York stage debut in the Broadway hit, *I Remember Mama.*

1950   United Nations forces captured the North Korean capital of Pyongyang in the Korean War.

1967   U.S. spacecraft *Mariner 5* passed within 2,500 miles of Venus.

1987   Stocks crashed on the New York Stock Exchange as the Dow-Jones Industrial Average dropped 508 points, or 22.6 %, with a volume of 604 million shares, all record numbers.

OCTOBER 20 -- BIRTHDAYS

1620   **Aelbert Cuyp** -- Dutch painter

1632   **Sir Christopher Wren** – The greatest English architect of his time

1677   **Stanislaw I** -- King of Poland

1784   **Viscount Palmerston** -- English statesman who served as foreign secretary and as prime minister during the Crimean War

1854   **Arthur Rimbaud** -- French poet and adventurer

1859   **John Dewey** -- American philosopher and educator

1874   **Charles Ives** -- American composer who won the 1947 Pulitzer Prize for his *Symphony No. 3,* composed in 1911 but not performed until 1946

1882   **Bela Lugosi** – Hungarian-American motion-picture actor, noted for his portrayal of Count Dracula

1891   **Jomo Kenyatta** -- First prime minister (1963) and first president, 1964-1978, of Kenya

1895   **Morrie Ryskind** -- American columnist and playwright noted for works such as *Let 'Em Eat Cake* (1933, with George S. Kaufman)

1900   **Wayne Morse** -- U.S. senator in the 1950s and 1960s

1901   **Frank E. Churchill** -- American composer noted for songs such as "Who's Afraid of the Big Bad Wolf?" and "Whistle While You Work"

1905   **Frederick Dannay** -- American writer, who, with Manfred B. Lee, published under the pen name Ellery Queen

1908   **Stuart Hamblen** -- American composer and singer, noted for songs such as "It Is No Secret," "This Ole House," and "Open Up Your Heart and Let the Sun Shine In"

1912   **Arlene Francis** -- American stage, screen, and television actress

1918   **Roy L. Ash** -- American industrialist and co-founder of Litton Corporation

1925   **Art Buchwald** -- American newspaper columnist and humorist

1928   **Joyce Brothers** – American psychologist and television personality

1930   **David Hall** -- U.S. senator

1931   **Mickey Mantle** -- The greatest switch-hitter in baseball history, with a career total of 536 home runs

1946   **Lewis Grizzard** -- American newspaper columnist

1952   **Melanie Mayron** – American television and motion-picture actress

1953   **Keith Hernandez** -- Professional baseball player

1954   **Lee Roy Selmon** -- Professional football player

OCTOBER 20 -- EVENTS

1740   Maria Theresa ascended the Austrian throne, causing the War of the Austrian Succession.

1803   The U.S. senate ratified the Louisiana Purchase.

1853   Benjamin Harrison married Caroline Lavinia Scott.

1873   P.T. Barnum, the great American showman, opened his Hippodrome in New York City.

1879   Thomas A. Edison's electric light bulb, which he had just invented the previous day, still burned all day. It lasted until he raised its voltage on the following day.

1903   A joint commission ruled in favor of the United States in settling the boundary dispute between Alaska and Canada.

1944   The U.S. Sixth Army landed on Leyte in the Philippines, as General Douglas MacArthur issued the proclamation: "I have returned."

1964   Herbert Hoover died in New York at age 90, the highest age attained by any former American president except John Adams.

1968   Former first lady Jacqueline Kennedy married Aristotle Onassis, the Greek shipping magnate.

1973   President Nixon fired special Watergate prosecutor Archibald Cox, setting off a nationwide storm of protest.

OCTOBER 21 -- BIRTHDAYS

1581   **Il Domenichino** -- Italian painter (born Domenico Zampieri)

1760   **Katsushika Hokusai** -- One of the best-known Japanese color-print artists

1772   **Samuel Taylor Coleridge** -- English poet of the romantic movement, and author of "The Rime of the Ancient Mariner," one of the greatest poems in English literature

1785   **Henry Miller Shreve** -- Pioneer American steamboat captain and founder of Shreveport, Louisiana

1790   **Alphonse de Lamartine** -- French poet, statesman, and man of letters

1808   **Samuel Francis Smith** -- American clergyman, editor, and poet, who wrote the words to the patriotic song "America" (1831)

1833   **Alfred Bernhard Nobel** -- Norwegian chemist who invented dynamite and founded the Nobel prizes

1876   **Jay Norwood "Ding" Darling** -- American political cartoonist

1909   **Bill Lee** -- Professional baseball player

1917   **Dizzy Gillespie** -- American trumpeter and composer

1928   **Vern Mikkelsen** -- Professional basketball player with over 10,000 career points

1928   **Whitey Ford** -- Hall of Fame pitcher who broke Babe Ruth's record by pitching 33 consecutive scoreless World Series innings in 1960-1962

1929   **Ursula K. LeGuin** -- American fantasy novelist noted for her *Earthsea* trilogy: *A Wizard of Earthsea, The Tombs of Atuan,* and *The Farthest Shore*

1939   **Boro Jovanovic** -- Yugoslavian tennis player

1943   **Brian Piccolo** -- Professional football player

1948   **Bill Russell** -- Professional baseball player

1956   **Carrie Fisher** -- American actress and daughter of singer Eddie Fisher and actress Debbie Reynolds

OCTOBER 21 -- EVENTS

1520   Ferdinand Magellan, on the first around-the-world voyage, entered the strait now called the Strait of Magellan.

1797   The United States frigate *Constitution* (Old Ironsides) was launched at the Boston Navy Yard.

1805   British admiral Horatio Nelson defeated the French and Spanish in the Battle of Trafalgar, one of the greatest naval battles in history. He was killed, however, in the action.

1907   Franz Lehar's operetta, *The Merry Widow,* had its New York premiere at the Amsterdam Theater.

1917   Soldiers of the First Division of the U.S. Army training in Luneville, France, became the first Americans to see action on the front lines of World War I.

1944   The U.S. First Army captured Aachen, the first German city to fall into Allied hands in World War II.

1959   The Solomon R. Guggenheim Museum in New York City was dedicated.

1960   John F. Kennedy and Richard M. Nixon held their fourth and last "Great Debate" in the 1960 presidential election.

1973   Oil-producing Arab states placed an embargo on oil for the United States.

1976   The Cincinnati Reds defeated the New York Yankees, becoming the first National League team since 1922 to win two consecutive World Series.

OCTOBER 22 -- BIRTHDAYS

1689   **John V** -- King of Portugal

1738   **James Manning** -- Baptist clergyman who founded Brown University in 1764

1811   **Franz Liszt** -- One of the greatest Hungarian composers and the most celebrated pianist of the 1800s

1818   **Charles M. Leconte de Lisle** -- French poet

1843 **Stephen Moulton Babcock** -- American agricultural chemist who devised in 1890 a test for measuring butterfat in milk

1885 **Giovanni Martinelli** -- Italian opera singer and actor, who was a leading tenor with the New York Metropolitan Opera Company in more than fifty operas

1887 **John Reed** -- American poet, adventurer, and journalist, who wrote the eyewitness account, *Ten Days That Shook the World* (1919), of the Bolsheviks' seizure of power in Russia

1899 **William Morris Jr.** -- American talent agent and founder of the William Morris agency

1900 **Edward R. Stettinius Jr.** -- Secretary of state under Presidents Franklin Roosevelt and Truman, who was a leader in organizing the United Nations

1903 **Curly Howard** -- American comedian and actor, and one of the original Three Stooges

1904 **Constance Bennett** -- American motion-picture actress and daughter of matinee idol Richard Bennett

1907 **Jimmie Foxx** -- First baseball player after Babe Ruth to hit 500 career home runs

1912 **Harry Callahan** -- American photographer

1917 **Joan Fontaine** -- One of Hollywood's leading actresses of the 1930s and 1940s, and sister of actress Olivia de Havilland

1918 **Harry Walker** -- Professional baseball player

1919 **Doris Lessing** -- English novelist noted for works such as *Canopus in Argos,* a sequence of fantastic novels set in space

1920 **Timothy Leary** -- American scientist, radical, and "visionary prophet"

1925 **Robert Rauschenberg** -- American artist and a founder of the pop art school

1925 **Dory Previn** -- American songwriter

1925 **Slater Martin** -- Professional basketball player

1937 **Bobby Seale** -- American black militant

1939 **Tony Roberts** -- American stage, screen, and television actor

1941 **Wilbur Wood** -- Professional baseball player

1942 **Annette Funicello** -- American actress and "Mouseketeer"

1943 **Catherine Deneuve** -- French motion-picture actress

1944 **Mike Wynn** -- Professional golfer

1954 **Jamie Quirk** -- Professional baseball player

1955 **Gary Green** -- Professional football player

1961 **Barbara Potter** -- American tennis player

OCTOBER 22 -- EVENTS

741 AD French king Charles Martel, the grandfather of the great emperor Charlemagne, died at age 53.

1303 Benedict XI was elected Roman Catholic pope.

1746 Princeton University received its charter from George II of England.

1797 Andre Jacques Garnerin became the first man to drop from a balloon in a parachute, over the Parc Monceau in Paris.

1836 Sam Houston was inaugurated as the first president of the Republic of Texas.

1883 The Metropolitan Opera House in New York celebrated its grand opening with a performance of Gounod's opera *Faust.*

1906 Paul Cezanne, the great French painter, died at age 67 in Aix-en-Provence.

1934 Pretty Boy Floyd, the notorious outlaw, was gunned down by the F.B.I. in a field in Ohio.

1934 The comic strip, *Terry and the Pirates,* by Milton Caniff, first appeared.

1954 West Germany was accepted as a member of NATO.

1962 President Kennedy announced the Soviet missile buildup in Cuba and ordered an American blockade of the island.

1973 Pablo Casals, the great Spanish cellist and conductor, died in Puerto Rico at age 96.

OCTOBER 23 -- BIRTHDAYS

1698 **Jacques Ange Gabriel** -- French architect

1715 **Peter II** -- Czar of Russia, 1727-1730

1734 **Nicolas E.R. De la Bretonne** -- French writer and printer

1750 **Thomas Pinckney** -- American soldier, diplomat, and vice presidential candidate in 1796

1817 **Pierre Larousse** -- Noted French encyclopedist

1835 **Adlai E. Stevenson** -- U.S. vice president, 1893-1897, and grandfather of 1952 and 1956 presidential candidate, Adlai E. Stevenson

1838 **Francis Hopkinson Smith** -- American novelist, painter, and engineer, who built the foundation for the Statue of Liberty

1844 **Sarah Bernhardt** -- One of the greatest actresses in the history of the stage

1844 **Robert Seymour Bridges** -- English poet and scholar, who became poet laureate of England in 1913

1844 **Wilhelm Leibl** -- German painter

1869 **John William Heisman** -- American football player and coach for whom the Heisman Trophy is named

1879 **Ernie Erdman** -- American composer noted for songs such as "Toot, Toot, Tootsie, Goodbye" and "Nobody's Sweetheart"

1883 **Hugo Wast** -- Argentina's most popular novelist

1901 **Moe Jaffe** -- American composer and author, noted for songs such as "Bell Bottom Trousers" and "The Gypsy in My Soul"

1906 **Gertrude Ederle** -- First woman to swim the English Channel (1926)

1913 **Bao Dai** -- Last emperor of Vietnam, 1925-1945

1918 **Paul Rudolph** -- American architect

1920 **Frank Rizzo** -- Mayor of Philadelphia in the 1970s

1920 **Vern Stephens** -- Professional baseball player

1920 **Bob Montana** -- American comic strip artist, and creator of *Archie*

1925 **Johnny Carson** -- American comedian and longtime host of NBC's *Tonight Show*

1931 **Jim Bunning** -- Professional baseball pitcher who pitched a perfect game (no batter reached base) in 1964

1931 **Diana Dors** -- English motion-picture actress

1938 **John Heinz** -- Heir to the H.J. Heinz fortune and U.S. senator

1940 **Pele (Edson Arantes do Nascimento)** -- Brazilian soccer player and possibly the most famous and highest paid athlete of his time

1943 **Milan Holecek** -- Czechoslovakian tennis player

OCTOBER 23 -- EVENTS

4004 BC The earth was created at 9 A.M., in the opinion of Bishop James Ussher, a 17th-century Irish clergyman.

42 BC Marcus Brutus, leader of the plot to murder Julius Caesar, committed suicide.

1386 The University of Heidelberg, the oldest in Germany, was founded.

1915 Twenty-five thousand women marched in New York City demanding the right to vote.

1917 The U.S. Army fired its first shots against the Germans in World War I, near Luneville, France.

1929 Stocks on the New York Stock Exchange lost an average 18.24 points, but stocks, experts said, had reached a "permanently high plateau." The market crashed 6 days later.

1940   Adolf Hitler conferred in France with Generalissimo Franco, seeking Franco's aid in World War II. Franco squirmed and hedged, but never committed himself.

1942   English general Bernard Montgomery began the Battle of El Alamein against German Field Marshal Erwin Rommel's Afrika Corps.

1944   The World War II Battle for Leyte Gulf began, the biggest naval battle in history. It ended 3 days later in a crushing defeat of the Japanese by the Americans.

1945   Vidkun Quisling, the Norwegian World War II traitor, was shot by the Norwegians.

1950   Al Jolson, Russian-born American singer, died at age 64.

1955   The South Vietnamese, in their first election, chose Ngo Dinh Diem as premier.

1956   The Hungarian Revolution against Russian rule began.

1970   Gary Gabelich, American racing car driver, drove an automobile a record 631 miles per hour at Bonneville Salt Flats, Utah.

OCTOBER 24 -- BIRTHDAYS

51 AD   **Domitian** -- Roman emperor, A.D. 81-96

1632   **Anton van Leeuwenhoek** -- Dutch scientist and microscopist, and first man to observe bacteria

1788   **Sarah Josepha Hale** -- American magazine editor and author of "Mary Had a Little Lamb"

1820   **Eugene Fromentin** -- French painter

1882   **Dame Sybil Thorndike** -- One of the great ladies of the British stage

1890   **Mainbocher** -- American fashion designer

1891   **Rafael Trujillo** -- Dictator of the Dominican Republic, 1930-1961

1899   **Ferhat Abbas** -- President of the Algerian Republic

1900   **Ossie Bluege** -- Professional baseball player and manager

1902   **Preston Foster** -- American stage and screen actor with a career of over 100 films

1904   **Moss Hart** -- American playwright and screenwriter, noted for works such as *Act One* (1959)

1911   **Clarence M. Kelley** -- Director of the F.B.I. under Presidents Nixon and Ford

1914   **Jackie Coogan** -- American motion-picture actor and noted child star

1915	**Tito Gobbi** -- Italian baritone

1915   **Tito Gobbi** -- Italian baritone

1916   **Bob Kane** -- American comic strip artist and creator of *Batman*

1925   **Bobby Brown** -- American physician, professional baseball player, and President of the American League

1926   **Y.A. Tittle** -- Professional football player and superstar

1936   **David Nelson** -- American motion-picture and television actor

1937   **Juan Marichal** -- Hall of Fame baseball player

1938   **Jack H. Watson Jr.** -- Presidential aide under President Carter

1940   **F. Murray Abraham** -- American motion-picture, stage, and television actor who won the Academy Award for best actor in *Amadeus* (1984)

1947   **Kevin Kline** -- American motion-picture actor

1948   **Bill Wyman** – British bassist with the Rolling Stones musical group

1950   **Rawley Eastwick** -- Professional baseball player

1950   **Tom Myers** -- Professional football player

1953   **Omar Moreno** -- Professional baseball player

OCTOBER 24 -- EVENTS

1537   Jane Seymour, third wife of King Henry VIII of England, died in childbirth, saving Henry the need for killing her.

1648   The Peace of Westphalia ended the Thirty Years' War between the Catholics and Protestants of various European countries, and effectively destroyed the Holy Roman Empire.

1861   The first transcontinental telegrams were sent, one from California to Washington, D.C., and one from New York to California.

1901   Anna Edson Taylor, a 43-year-old widow, became the first person to go over Niagara Falls in a barrel and live to tell about it.

1904   The first sections of the New York subway were opened to the public.

1922   Benito Mussolini issued his call for the "March on Rome," resulting in his becoming dictator of Italy a few days later.

1929   Prices on the New York Stock Exchange dropped sharply in "a little distress selling," as J.P. Morgan called it. The real collapse came five days later.

1931   The George Washington Bridge, between New York City and New Jersey, was opened to the public.

1940   The 40-hour work week went into effect under the Fair Labor Standards Act of 1938.

1945   The United Nations was formally established with the ratification of its charter by the 29th nation.

1952   General Dwight D. Eisenhower, candidate for president, said that if elected, he would go to Korea to try to end the war there.

1962   Six Soviet ships bound for Cuba "stopped dead in the water" at the edge of the quarantine line enforced by the U.S. Navy in the Cuban Missile Crisis.

1964   Zambia, formerly Northern Rhodesia, became independent.

OCTOBER 25 -- BIRTHDAYS

1767   **Benjamin Constant** de Rebecque-- Franco-Swiss novelist and political writer

1800   **Thomas Babington Macaulay** -- The most widely read English historian of the 1800s

1802   **Richard Parkes Bonington** -- English landscape painter

1811   **Evariste Galois** -- French mathematician noted for the development of group theory

1825   **Johann Strauss Jr.** -- Austrian composer and "Waltz King," whose most famous work is probably *On the Beautiful Blue Danube*

1837   **Anna M. Richardson Harkness** -- American philanthropist who established the Commonwealth Fund

1838   **Georges Bizet** -- French composer whose last and finest work was *Carmen* (1875), perhaps the most popular opera of all time

1864   **John Francis Dodge** -- Pioneer American automobile manufacturer, who with his brother Horace founded the Dodge Company and produced the Dodge automobile, one of the first with an all-steel body

1873   **John North Willys** -- American industrialist who founded the Willys-Overland motor car company in 1907

1881   **Pablo Picasso** -- The most famous painter of the 20th century

1885   **Samuel M. Lewis** -- American lyricist noted for songs such as "Rockabye Your Baby With a Dixie Melody," "Five Foot Two, Eyes of Blue," "I'm Sitting on Top of the World," and "In a Little Spanish Town"

1888   **Richard E. Byrd** – U.S. naval officer and polar explorer, who was the first to fly over the North Pole (1926), and who made three expeditions to the South Pole

1895   **Levi Eshkol** -- Prime minister of Israel, 1963-1969, who was in office at the time of the Six-Day War of 1967

1902   **Henry Steele Commager** -- American historian and educator, noted for his popular books on American history

1903   **Clay A. Boland** – American composer noted for songs such as "Stop Beatin' 'Round the Mulberry Bush" and "The Gypsy in My Soul"

1904   **Arshile Gorky** -- American artist and a leading member of the abstract expressionist movement

1912   **Minnie Pearl** -- American comedienne

1917   **Lee MacPhail** – Professional baseball executive and son of noted baseball owner Larry MacPhail

1921   **Michael** -- King of Romania, 1927-1930 and 1940-1947

1923   **Bobby Thomson** -- Professional baseball player who hit the dramatic home run that gave the New York Giants the pennant in the 1951 playoffs with the Brooklyn Dodgers

1935   **Russell Schweickart** -- U.S. astronaut who participated in the *Apollo 9* mission

1942   **Helen Reddy** -- Australian pop singer

1945   **Dan Gable** -- Professional wrestler

1948   **Dan Issel** -- Professional basketball player

1948   **Dave Cowens** -- Professional basketball player and superstar

1958   **David Woodley** -- Professional football player

OCTOBER 25 -- EVENTS

1400   Geoffrey Chaucer, the greatest English poet of the Middle Ages, died at approximately 57 years of age.

1415   King Henry V of England, with 13,000 troops, defeated the French army of 50,000 in the Battle of Agincourt (France) in the Hundred Years' War.

1529   Henry VIII of England appointed Sir Thomas More Lord Chancellor, succeeding Cardinal Wolsey, who had been dismissed for not approving Henry's affair with Anne Boleyn.

1555   Charles V, Holy Roman emperor and king of Spain, abdicated rule of the Netherlands.

1760   George III became king of England. He was to serve 60 years and preside over the loss of the American Colonies.

1764   John Adams married Abigail Smith.

1854   The Allies defeated the Russians in the Battle of Balaklava in the Crimean War. It was one of the most famous battles in history because of the charge of the Light Brigade.

1859   Chester A. Arthur married Ellen Lewis Herndon.

1924   The U.S. Navy's *Shenandoah* made the first transcontinental airship voyage.

1936   Germany and Italy formed the Rome-Berlin Axis.

1938   The Chinese Nationalist government fled to Chungking as the Japanese captured Hankow.

1950   Communist China entered the Korean War on the side of the
        North Koreans.

1971   The United Nations voted to seat the People's Republic of
        China and to unseat Nationalist China.

OCTOBER 26 -- BIRTHDAYS

1466   **Desiderius Erasmus** – The foremost Christian humanist of the
        Renaissance, noted for *Praise of Folly,* one of the great works of
        literature

1556   **Ahmad Baba** -- Jurist, writer, university chancellor, and cultural
        leader of the great black Songhay Empire in the late 16th century

1685   **Domenico Scarlatti** -- Italian composer, noted for some 550
        clavier sonatas, and son of Italian composer Alessandro Scarlatti

1757   **Charles Pinckney** -- American diplomat, governor, senator,
        congressman, and one of the American founding fathers

1759   **Georges Danton** -- One of the greatest leaders of the French
        Revolution

1800   **Helmuth Karl von Moltke** – Prussian military genius who ranked
        next to Bismarck as a builder of the German Empire

1842   **Vereshchagin** -- Russian painter

1849   **Ferdinand Georg Frobenius** -- German mathematician noted
        for the "method of Frobenius" of solving differential equations

1861   **Richard Dudley Sears** – American tennis player and the first
        U.S. Singles Champion

1863   **Ellsworth Milton Statler** -- American hotel proprietor who in
        1901 founded the Statler Hotel chain

1866   **Kid Gleason** -- Professional baseball player and manager

1910   **John Cardinal Krol** -- Archbishop of Philadelphia

1911   **Mahalia Jackson** -- American singer

1913   **Charlie Barnet** -- American bandleader of the Big Band Era of
        the 1930s and 1940s

1916   **Francois Mitterand** -- President of France

1918   **Snuffy Stirnweiss** -- Professional baseball player

1919   **Mohammed Reza Pahlavi** -- Shah of Iran, 1941-1979

1919   **Edward Brooke** -- First black U.S. senator since Reconstruction,
        1967-1979

1946   **Pat Sajak** -- American newscaster, disc jockey, and host of the
        TV shows, *Wheel of Fortune* and *The Pat Sajak Show*

1947   **Jaclyn Smith** -- American television actress

1948   **Toby Harrah** -- Professional baseball player
1949   **Steve Rogers** -- Professional baseball player
1950   **Chuck Foreman** -- Professional football player
1953   **Louis Breeden** -- Professional football player

OCTOBER 26 -- EVENTS

899 AD King Alfred the Great of England died in Wessex, England, at the approximate age of 50.

1676   Bacon's Rebellion in Virginia ended with the death of its leader, Nathaniel Bacon.

1774   The first Continental Congress adjourned in Philadelphia after nearly two months of meetings.

1825   The Erie Canal, the first important man-made waterway in the United States, was opened to traffic, connecting Lake Erie and the Hudson River.

1881   The Earps and Doc Holliday took on the Clantons and McLowrys in the Gunfight at the O.K. Corral in Tombstone, Arizona. Ike Clanton fled and his other cohorts were killed.

1905   Norway became independent of Sweden with a formal treaty dissolving their union.

1944   The Battle for Leyte Gulf ended with the U.S. Pacific Fleet crushing the Japanese fleet. The U.S. lost 6 ships and the Japanese lost 26 in the battle.

1951   The Conservative Party defeated the Labour Party in England to bring Winston Churchill back as prime minister.

1951   Rocky Marciano knocked out former champion Joe Louis in the eighth round at Madison Square Garden to retain his heavyweight championship.

1958   Pan American World Airways flew its first Boeing 707 jetliner from New York to Paris.

1962   The *Marucla,* sailing under the Russian flag, was stopped by the USS *Joseph P. Kennedy Jr.* and boarded, enforcing the Cuban Missile Crisis quarantine.

1970   The comic strip *Doonesbury,* by Garry Trudeau, first appeared.

OCTOBER 27 -- BIRTHDAYS

1401   **Catherine** -- Wife of King Henry V of England
1728   **Captain James Cook** -- British navigator and famous explorer of the Pacific Ocean

1736   **James Macpherson** -- Scottish poet whose alleged translations from a third century Gaelic poet were much admired but were later exposed as fraudulent by Samuel Johnson

1760   **August Gneisenau** -- Prussian field marshal and reformer

1782   **Niccolo Paganini** -- One of the greatest violinists of all time

1811   **Isaac Merrit Singer** -- American manufacturer who, more than any other man, made the sewing machine a universal household appliance

1858   **Theodore Roosevelt** -- 26th U.S. president

1870   **Roscoe Pound** -- American educator and authority on law, and the best known figure in American legal education in the early 20th century

1872   **Emily Post** – Well-known American authority on social behavior, whose faulty mathematics caused waiters' tips to be raised from 10 % to 15 % because, she said, of inflation during World War II

1877   **Walt Kuhn** -- American painter

1895   **Robert Paine Scripps** -- American journalist, publisher, and son of Edward Wyllis Scripps, the founder of the Scripps newspaper chain

1910   **Jack Carson** -- Canadian-born actor and comedian

1911   **Leif Erickson** -- American stage, screen, and television actor

1912   **C.L. Sulzberger** – American writer, novelist, and newspaper columnist

1914   **Dylan Thomas** – Welsh poet and writer, noted for works such as *Eighteen Poems* (1934) and *Portrait of the Artist as a Young Dog* (1940)

1918   **Teresa Wright** -- American stage and motion-picture actress

1920   **Nanette Fabray** -- American stage, screen, and television actress

1922   **Ralph Kiner** – Hall of Fame baseball player whose ratio of 7.1 home runs per 100 times at bat is second only to Babe Ruth's

1923   **Roy Lichtenstein** -- American cartoonist

1926   **H.R. Haldeman** -- Aide to President Nixon, imprisoned for his part in the Watergate scandal

1928   **Terry Horvitz Kovel** – American columnist and antique authority

1928   **Kyle Rote** -- Professional football player and sportscaster

1946   **Carrie Snodgress** – American stage, screen, and television actress

1946   **Peter Martens** -- Danish ballet dancer

1952   **Pete Vukovich** -- Professional baseball player

1958   **Simon Le Bon** – Lead vocalist of the Duran Duran musical group

OCTOBER 27 -- EVENTS

97 AD Roman emperor Nerva adopted Trajan as his successor.

1553 Michael Servetus, the great Spanish physician and theologian, was burned at the stake after being denounced as a heretic by John Calvin.

1787 The *Federalist* papers, a series of letters under the signature "Publius," but written by Hamilton, Madison, and Jay, began to appear in the New York *Independent Journal*.

1871 William Marcy "Boss" Tweed, corrupt political dictator of Tammany Hall, was arrested on charges of fraud.

1880 Theodore Roosevelt married his first wife, Alice Hathaway Lee.

1904 The first practical subway started operations, running from the Brooklyn Bridge to 145th Street in New York City.

1917 Jascha Heifetz, the great violinist, made his American debut in Carnegie Hall at age 16.

1920 The League of Nations moved its headquarters from London to Geneva.

1936 Wallis Warfield Simpson, later to be the wife of England's ex-king, Edward VIII, divorced her first husband.

1938 Du Pont announced the invention of nylon hosiery.

1961 The United States super aircraft carrier *Constellation* was commissioned.

OCTOBER 28 -- BIRTHDAYS

1017 **Henry III** -- King of Germany, 1039-1056, and Holy Roman emperor, 1046-1056

1435 **Andrea della Robbia** — Italian sculptor of the early Renaissance noted for the process of glazing terra cottas, passed down to him by his famous uncle, the sculptor Luca della Robbia

1793 **Eliphalet Remington** -- American inventor, noted for the flint-lock rifle

1847 **J. Walter Thompson** -- American advertising pioneer who in 1868 founded the J. Walter Thompson agency

1875 **Gilbert H. Grosvenor** — Editor of *The National Geographic Magazine* for more than 50 years

1896 **Howard Hanson** — American composer and educator, and winner of the Pulitzer music prize in 1944

1902 **Elsa Lanchester** -- English character actress with a 50-year career in Britain and Hollywood

1903   **Evelyn Waugh** -- The most brilliant satirical novelist of his day
1907   **Edith Head** -- Hollywood's best-known costume designer
1908   **James Edward Rogan** -- American composer, author, and violinist, noted for songs such as "You Started Something" and "Moonlight Mood"
1910   **Francis Bacon** -- One of the best-known British painters in the mid-1900s, noted for works such as *Study After Velazquez: Portrait of Pope Innocent X* (1953)
1914   **Jonas Salk** -- American physician who developed the Salk polio vaccine
1916   **Willard "Bill" Harris** -- American jazz musician
1917   **Joe Page** -- Professional baseball player
1924   **Edward George Kean** -- American composer, author, and pianist, noted for songs such as "It's Howdy Doody Time"
1925   **Leonard Starr** -- American comic strip artist, and creator of *On Stage*
1926   **Bowie Kuhn** -- Commissioner of Baseball, 1969-1984
1928   **Tony Franciosa** -- American stage, screen, and television actor
1933   **Suzy Parker** -- American model and actress
1937   **Len Wilkens** -- Professional basketball player
1939   **Jane Alexander** -- American stage and motion-picture actress
1949   **Bruce Jenner** -- American Olympic decathlon champion, 1976

OCTOBER 28 -- EVENTS

312 AD Roman emperor Constantine I, the Great, defeated Maxentius, his major rival in the west, at the Battle of the Milvian Bridge and became undisputed master of Rome.

1491   The last Moorish Emir of Granada consented to surrender the city to Ferdinand and Isabella of Spain within 60 days, removing the Moors from Spain.

1492   Columbus landed in Cuba, at what is now Bahia Bariay, after a few days on San Salvador on his first voyage to America.

1636   Harvard College was founded at Newtowne, Massachusetts, which was renamed Cambridge in 1638.

1646   John Eliot, the famous American missionary to the Indians of Massachusetts, preached his first sermon in America.

1726   Jonathan Swift published *Gulliver's Travels,* one of the greatest satires of world literature.

1886   The Statue of Liberty was dedicated in New York Harbor by President Grover Cleveland.

1918	The Czechoslovak National Committee in Prague proclaimed the establishment of the Republic of Czechoslovakia.
1919	Congress enacted the Volstead Act enforcing Prohibition over President Wilson's veto.
1922	Benito Mussolini's black-shirted Italian Fascists began their march on Rome, resulting in their taking power the following day.
1940	Italy invaded Greece in World War II.
1958	John XXIII was elected Roman Catholic pope.
1962	Russian premier Nikita Khrushchev agreed to remove the Soviet missiles from Cuba, ending the Cuban Missile Crisis.
1983	The United States invaded the island of Grenada for the stated purpose of rescuing the American students there from the Marxist government.

OCTOBER 29 -- BIRTHDAYS

1740	**James Boswell** -- English author, who in 1791 wrote *The Life of Samuel Johnson,* probably the most brilliant biography in the English language
1815	**Daniel Decatur Emmett** -- American minstrel performer, and composer of "Dixie" (1859), the war song of the South in the Civil War
1859	**Charles Ebbets** -- Baseball executive and long-time owner of the Brooklyn Dodgers baseball team
1879	**Franz von Papen** – German politician who helped Adolf Hitler come to power in 1933
1882	**Jean Giraudoux** -- The most prominent French playwright between the two world wars, especially noted for *The Madwoman of Chaillot*
1891	**Fanny Brice** -- American singer, dancer, and comedienne, who starred in the *Ziegfeld Follies* and for many years as radio's Baby Snooks
1897	**Joseph Goebbels** -- Adolf Hitler's minister of propaganda
1898	**Charles Garland** -- American Hall of Fame tennis player
1899	**Akim Tamiroff** -- Russian-born stage and motion-picture actor
1921	**Bill Mauldin** -- Noted American political cartoonist and author
1925	**Geraldine Brooks** -- American motion-picture actress
1927	**Frank Sedgman** -- Australian tennis player with six Wimbledon titles
1947	**Richard Dreyfuss** -- American stage and motion-picture actor
1948	**Kate Jackson** -- American television and motion-picture actress

1952   **Byron Bertram** -- South African tennis player
1959   **Jesse Barfield** -- Professional baseball player

OCTOBER 29 -- EVENTS

1618   Sir Walter Raleigh, English writer and adventurer, was be-
        headed on a trumped-up charge of conspiracy in the Old Palace
        Yard, Westminster, in London.
1682   William Penn arrived at what is now Chester, Pennsylvania, for
        the purpose of founding the colony of Pennsylvania.
1863   The International Red Cross flag was adopted.
1884   The Reverend Samuel Burchard, trying to help Republican
        candidate James G. Blaine, doomed Blaine with his speech
        blaming the Democrats for "Rum, Romanism, and Rebellion."
1901   Leon Czolgosz was electrocuted for the assassination of Presi-
        dent William McKinley.
1916   The comic strip, *Rosie's Beau*, by George McManus, first appeared.
1922   Benito Mussolini, with his Fascists, was invited to form an Italian
        government by King Victor Emanuel III.
1923   Turkey became a republic as its first president, Kemal Ataturk
        (Mustafa Kemal), took office.
1929   Pandemonium reigned on the New York Stock Exchange as
        stock prices collapsed, marking the start of the Great Depres-
        sion of the 1930s.
1940   The first peacetime military draft in United States history began
        as Secretary of State Henry L. Stimson drew the first num-
        ber, 158.
1945   Ballpoint pens first went on sale, at New York's Gimbel Brothers.
1956   Israel invaded Egypt to start the second Arab-Israeli War.

OCTOBER 30 -- BIRTHDAYS

1735   **John Adams** -- First vice president and second president of the
        United States
1751   **Richard Brinsley Sheridan** -- Irish dramatist, politician, author
        of *The School for Scandal* (1777), one of the great comedies of
        English drama, and creator of Mrs. Malaprop in *The Rivals* (1775)
1762   **Andre Marie de Chenier** -- French poet and satirist of the
        French Revolutionists, who condemned him to death without
        a trial
1829   **Roscoe Conkling** -- U.S. senator and Republican party leader of
        the "Gilded Age" of the late 1800s

1839   **Alfred Sisley** -- French impressionist painter best known for his landscape paintings

1840   **William Graham Sumner** -- American sociologist and prolific publicist for Social Darwinism

1867   **Ed Delahanty** -- Hall of Fame baseball player who hit over .400 three times in his career

1871   **Paul Valery** -- French poet noted for "La Jeune Parque" (1917) and "Le Cimetiere marin" (1920)

1873   **Francisco Madero** -- Mexican patriot who issued the call for the Revolution of 1910

1882   **William F. "Bull" Halsey Jr.** -- American naval officer and, according to General MacArthur, "the greatest fighting admiral" of World War II

1882   **Gunther von Kluge** -- German World War II general

1883   **Bob Jones** -- American religious leader for whom Bob Jones College is named

1885   **Ezra Pound** -- American poet and critic, and one of the most influential and controversial literary figures of his time

1893   **Charles Atlas** -- Ex-"97-pound weakling" who became famous for his male physique

1894   **Peter Warlock** -- English composer, critic, and editor

1895   **Dickinson Woodruff Richards Jr.** -- American Nobel Prize-winning physician, who developed a way to diagnose heart diseases by means of a catheter

1896   **Ruth Gordon** -- American stage and motion-picture actress with a career of some 70 years

1898   **Bill Terry** -- Hall of Fame baseball player who hit .401 in 1930

1914   **Ruth Hussey** -- American stage and motion-picture actress

1915   **Fred Friendly** -- American television producer and broadcaster

1917   **Bobby Bragan** -- Professional baseball player, manager, and executive

1923   **Herschel Bernardi** -- American stage and motion-picture actor

1927   **Joe Adcock** -- Professional baseball player who hit four home runs and a double in one game in 1954

1936   **Jim Perry** -- Professional baseball player

1943   **Henry Winkler** -- American motion-picture and television actor

1943   **Grace Slick** -- American singer with the Jefferson Airplane/Starship musical group

1948   **J.D. Hill** -- Professional football player

1950   **Phil Chenier** -- Professional basketball player

1954   **Jo Anne Russell** -- American tennis player

1962   **Danny Tartabull** -- Professional baseball player

OCTOBER 30 -- EVENTS

1340   The Battle of Rio Salado ended forever the Moorish threat to Spain.

1485   Henry Tudor was crowned Henry VII, King of England.

1768   Wesley Chapel in New York City, the first Methodist church in America, was dedicated.

1847   Henry Wadsworth Longfellow's poem, "Evangeline," was first published.

1912   Vice President James Sherman died in office during the presidential campaign of 1912, becoming the only vice president to die while running for reelection.

1914   Turkey joined the Central Powers, Germany and Austria-Hungary, in World War I.

1918   Turkey signed an armistice ending its part in World War I.

1922   Benito Mussolini became dictator of Italy.

1938   Orson Welles caused a national panic when he produced a radio dramatization of H.G. Wells's *The War of the Worlds.*

1953   U.S. General George C. Marshall received the 1953 Nobel Peace Prize and Dr. Albert Schweitzer received the 1952 Nobel Peace Prize (delayed until 1953).

1961   Russia exploded a 58-megaton hydrogen bomb in the Novaya Zemlya area of the U.S.S.R.

1974   Muhammad Ali regained the heavyweight boxing title by defeating champion George Foreman.

OCTOBER 31 -- BIRTHDAYS

1424   **Wladyslaw III** -- King of Poland, 1434-1444

1599   **Baron Denzil Holles** -- English statesman and churchman

1620   **John Evelyn** -- English writer, famous for his diary, which he kept from 1641 until his death in 1706

1632   **Jan Vermeer** -- One of the great masters of Dutch art in the 17th century, noted for paintings such as *The Milk Maid* and *View of Delft*

1638   **Meindert Hobbema** -- Dutch landscape painter, noted for the *Avenue of Middelharnis*

1795   **John Keats** -- One of the greatest English poets of all time, noted for works such as "Endymion" (1818) and "Ode on a Grecian Urn" (1819)

1815   **Karl Weierstrass** -- German mathematician and a founder of the theory of functions

1827   **Richard Morris Hunt** -- American architect noted for introducing the style of the French Gothic chateau to the United States and for designing the pedestal for the Statue of Liberty

1828   **Sir Joseph Wilson Swan** -- English physicist and inventor of the dry photographic plate

1860   **Juliette Gordon Low** -- Founder of the Girl Scouts of America (1912)

1863   **William Gibbs McAdoo** -- Secretary of the treasury during whose term the Federal Reserve System was created (1913-1918)

1883   **Sara Allgood** -- Irish stage and motion-picture actress with a 45-year career

1887   **Chiang Kai-shek** -- Ruler of China, 1928-1949

1888   **Sir Hubert Wilkins** -- Australian explorer, aviator, scientist, and photographer

1900   **Cal Hubbard** -- Professional baseball umpire

1900   **Ethel Waters** -- American blues singer and actress

1902   **Wilbur Shaw** -- American automobile racing driver who won the Indianapolis 500 three times and finished second three times

1912   **Dale Evans** -- American actress and wife of cowboy actor Roy Rogers

1915   **James Wechsler** -- Editor of the New York *Post* newspaper

1918   **Griffin Bell** -- Attorney general under President Carter

1922   **Barbara Bel Geddes** -- American motion-picture and television actress

1922   **Norodom Sihanouk** -- King of Cambodia

1929   **Lee Grant** -- American stage, screen, and television actress

1930   **Michael Collins** -- U.S. astronaut and command module pilot of *Apollo 11*, the first manned lunar landing mission in 1969

1931   **Dan Rather** -- American broadcast journalist and television anchor man

1936   **Michael Landon** -- American actor, producer, and director, noted for his roles in the TV shows *Bonanza* and *Little House on the Prairie*

1942   **Dave McNally** -- Professional baseball player

1942   **David Ogden Stiers** -- American television and motion-picture actor, noted for his role in the long-running TV show *M*A*S*H*

1948   **Mickey Rivers** -- Professional baseball player

1950   **Jane Pauley** -- Hostess of television's *Today Show*

1950   **John Candy** -- Canadian comedian and motion-picture actor

1960   **Reza Pahlavi** -- Crown prince of Iran and son of Shah Moham-
        med Reza Pahlavi

OCTOBER 31 -- EVENTS

1517   Martin Luther nailed his famous Ninety-Five Theses to the door
        of the Castle Church in Wittenburg, marking the beginning of
        the Protestant Reformation.

1754   King's College, which later became Columbia University, was
        chartered, the fifth college founded in the United States in colo-
        nial times.

1815   Sir Humphry Davy, the great English chemist, invented the
        miner's safety lamp.

1852   Michael Reagan and Catherine Mulcahy, great grandparents of
        President Ronald Reagan, were married in St. George's Catho-
        lic Church in London.

1864   Nevada was admitted to the Union as the 36th state.

1903   John Barrymore, the great American actor, made his first stage
        appearance, in *Magda* at the Cleveland Theater in Chicago.

1932   President Herbert Hoover, running for re-election, warned a
        New York audience that if Franklin D. Roosevelt was elected,
        "the grass will grow in the streets of a hundred cities."

1941   A German submarine torpedoed the destroyer *Reuben James,*
        making it the first American ship lost by enemy action in World
        War II.

1948   The Chinese Communists captured Mukden, Manchuria, in the
        Chinese Civil War.

1956   Great Britain and France joined the Israeli attack on Egypt,
        begun two days earlier.

1984   Indian Prime Minister Indira Gandhi was killed at age 66 in New
        Delhi by her Sikh bodyguards.

11

November

November, the eleventh month, gets its name from the Latin *Novembris*, meaning *ninth*, because in the ancient Roman calendar it was the ninth month. In the calendar of Romulus, November had 30 days, which Numa Pompilius reduced to 29 in his calendar. Caesar gave the month 31 days in the Julian Calendar, and Augustus reduced it to 30, its present number when he made his adjustments to the Roman calendar. The Roman Senate offered to name the month for the emperor Tiberius, the successor to Augustus, but he refused, asking, "What will you do if you have thirteen Caesars?"

Special days of November include election day in the United States, the first Tuesday after the first Monday of the month, and Thanksgiving Day, a legal holiday celebrated on the fourth Thursday. All Saints' Day is observed by the Roman Catholic Church on November 1, and Veterans Day, formerly Armistice Day, commemorating the end of World War I, is celebrated on November 11. Five American Presidents, James K. Polk, Zachary Taylor, Franklin Pierce, James A. Garfield and Warren G. Harding, were born in November.

The birthstone for November is the topaz, and the special flower is the chrysanthemum. Notable birthdays and events follow.

NOVEMBER 1 -- BIRTHDAYS

1500   **Benvenuto Cellini** -- Florentine goldsmith and sculptor, and author of *The Autobiography of Benvenuto Cellini,* one of the great works of world literature

1596   **Pietro da Cortona** -- Italian architect and painter

1636   **Nicolas Boileau-Despreaux** -- French poet and critic, and favorite of King Louis XIV

1757   **Antonio Canova** -- One of the most famous and influential European sculptors of the Napoleonic era, noted for works such as *Perseus* and *Cupid and Psyche*

1757   **George Rapp** -- German religious leader of the Harmonists who founded the village of Harmonie in Indiana, which later became New Harmony

1778   **Gustavus IV** -- King of Sweden, 1792-1809

1798   **Sir Benjamin Lee Guinness** -- Irish brewer

1815   **Crawford Williamson Long** -- First surgeon to use ether as an anesthetic (1842)

1861   **Joseph Sill Clark** -- American Hall of Fame tennis player

1871   **Stephen Crane** -- American novelist and poet, noted for *The Red Badge of Courage* (1895)

1880   **Sholem Asch** -- Polish novelist and playwright

1880   **Grantland Rice** -- One of the greatest sportswriters of all time

1890   **James Barton** -- American stage and motion-picture actor

1903   **Max Adrian** -- Irish stage and screen actor

1907   **Larry French** -- Professional baseball player

1911   **Sidney B. Wood** -- American Hall of Fame tennis player

1920   **James J. Kilpatrick** -- American journalist and author

1924   **Victoria de los Angeles** -- Spanish operatic soprano

1929   **Betsy Palmer** -- American stage, screen, and television actress

1936   **Gary Player** -- Professional golfer

1939   **Barbara Bosson** -- American television actress noted for her role in the long-running series *Hill Street Blues*

1941   **Robert Foxworth** -- American motion-picture and television actor

1942   **Larry Flynt** -- American magazine publisher

1949   **Jeff Kinney** -- Professional football player

1953   **Tim Fox** -- Professional football player

1960   **Fernando Valenzuela** -- Professional baseball player

NOVEMBER 1 -- EVENTS

1503 Julius II was elected Roman Catholic pope.

1512 Michelangelo's paintings on the ceiling of the Sistine Chapel in St. Peter's Cathedral were first exhibited to the Public.

1604 William Shakespeare's great play *Othello* was first presented, at Whitehall Palace in London.

1700 King Charles II of Spain died, leaving his crown in his will to French prince Philip of Anjou, which subsequently led to the War of the Spanish Succession.

1755 The Lisbon earthquake, the worst in Europe in 200 years, destroyed two-thirds of the city and killed more than 60,000 people.

1861 President Lincoln appointed General George B. McClellan to head the United States Army during the Civil War.

1913 Notre Dame defeated Army, 35 to 13, in a football game that featured a new play called the "forward pass." Notre Dame's star end, Knute Rockne, was the receiver a number of times.

1918 The empire of Austria-Hungary was destroyed as the Hapsburg monarchy was ended by a revolution in Hungary.

1923 The German mark fell to 130 billion to the American dollar, as Germany's unbelievable inflation continued.

1929 Former Secretary of the Interior Albert B. Fall was sentenced to one year in prison for his part in the scandals of the Harding Administration.

1950 Two Puerto Rican nationalists attempted to force their way into Blair House to assassinate President Harry Truman.

1952 American scientists detonated the first megaton-class hydrogen bomb.

1963 The first United States Christmas stamps went on sale.

1963 President Ngo Dinh Diem of South Vietnam was assassinated by a military junta which seized the government.

NOVEMBER 2 -- BIRTHDAYS

1470 **Edward V** -- King of England, 1482-1483

1699 **Jean Baptiste Simeon Chardin** -- One of the greatest French painters of the 18th century

1734   **Daniel Boone** -- The most famous American pioneer of colonial times

1755   **Marie Antoinette** -- Queen consort of King Louis XVI of France, who was beheaded by the French revolutionaries

1795   **James K. Polk** -- 11th U.S. president

1808   **Jules Amedee Barbey d'Aurevilly** -- French writer and critic

1815   **George Boole** -- Irish logician and mathematician, whose "Boolean algebra" of logic is basic to the design of digital computers

1865   **Warren G. Harding** -- 29th U.S. president

1894   **William "Little Bill" Johnston** -- American Hall of Fame tennis player and National Champion in 1915 and 1919

1897   **Richard B. Russell** -- U.S. senator, 1933-1971

1901   **Paul Ford** -- American character actor of stage, screen, and television

1913   **Burt Lancaster** -- American motion-picture actor who won an Academy Award in 1960 for the title role in *Elmer Gantry*

1914   **Johnny Vander Meer** -- Professional baseball pitcher who pitched two consecutive no-hit games in 1938

1917   **Ann Rutherford** -- American stage and motion-picture actress and leading lady of the 1930s and 1940s

1934   **Ken Rosewall** -- Australian tennis superstar and U.S. singles champion in 1956 and 1970

1938   **Patrick Buchanan** -- American columnist and television commentator, and speech writer for Presidents Richard Nixon and Ronald Reagan

1940   **James K. Bakken** -- Professional football player

1941   **Dave Stockton** -- Professional golfer

1942   **Stephanie Powers** -- American motion-picture and television actress

1942   **Shere Hite** -- American cultural researcher, historian, and author of the *Hite Reports* on sex and love

1946   **Tom Paciorek** -- Professional baseball player

1958   **Willie McGee** -- Professional baseball player

NOVEMBER 2 -- EVENTS

1769   Gaspar de Portola, Spanish governor of Baja California, discovered San Francisco Bay.

1783	General George Washington made his Farewell Address to the Continental Army near Princeton, New Jersey.
1889	North Dakota was admitted to the Union as the 39th state, and South Dakota was admitted to the Union as the 40th state.
1917	British Foreign Secretary Arthur Balfour proposed his Balfour Declaration pledging British support for Palestine as a national home for the Jews.
1920	The first regular radio broadcasts began, over station KDKA in Pittsburgh. A major news item was the reporting of the 1920 election returns showing Harding handily defeating Cox.
1930	Haile Selassie was crowned Emperor of Ethiopia at Addis Ababa.
1943	The comic strip, *Buz Sawyer,* by Roy Crane, first appeared.
1947	Howard Hughes' *Spruce Goose,* a 200-ton, eight-engine airplane, made its first and only flight, with Hughes at the controls, in Long Beach, California.
1948	Harry S Truman defeated Thomas E. Dewey in the biggest upset in the history of presidential elections.
1950	George Bernard Shaw, the great British playwright, died at Ayot St. Lawrence, England, at age 94.
1954	Strom Thurmond became the only write-in candidate ever elected to the U.S. Senate.
1976	Jimmy Carter was elected president, defeating incumbent president Gerald Ford.

NOVEMBER 3 -- BIRTHDAYS

1560	**Annibale Carracci** -- Italian painter
1718	**Earl of Sandwich (John Montagu)** -- English naval officer who ordered a servant to bring him two slices of bread with a piece of roast beef between them, and thus gave his name to the sandwich
1749	**Daniel Rutherford** -- Scottish physician who discovered the element nitrogen (in 1772)
1793	**Stephen F. Austin** – Colonizer of Texas for whom the city of Austin was named
1794	**William Cullen Bryant** -- The father of American poetry
1801	**Vincenzo Bellini** -- One of the foremost Italian opera composers of his day

1816   **Jubal Early** -- Confederate general in the Civil War

1834   **Charles Louis Fleischmann** -- Hungarian-American distiller who in 1868 developed Fleischmann's Yeast

1845   **Edward Douglass White** -- Ninth chief justice of the U.S. Supreme Court, 1910-1921

1879   **Vilhjalmur Stefansson** -- Canadian Arctic explorer and writer

1883   **Ford Sterling** -- American stage and motion-picture actor who helped Mack Sennett create the Keystone comedies of the silent era

1883   **Alfred Hart Miles** -- American lyricist noted for songs such as "Anchors Aweigh"

1893   **Robert Lindley Murray** -- American Hall of Fame tennis player and 1918 National Champion

1896   **William Raskin** -- American lyricist noted for songs such as "Wedding Bells Are Breaking Up That Old Gang of Mine"

1901   **Leopold III** -- King of the Belgians, 1934-1951

1901   **Andre Malraux** -- French novelist noted for works such as *The Royal Way* (1930) and *Man's Hope* (1937)

1909   **James Reston** -- American newspaper columnist

1918   **Bob Feller** -- Hall of Fame baseball pitcher who had a record 348 strikeouts in 1946

1918   **Russell B. Long** -- U.S. senator and son of Louisiana governor and senator Huey P. Long

1921   **Charles Bronson** -- American motion-picture actor and Golden Globe Award winner as the world's most popular actor in 1971

1930   **Philip M. Crane** -- U.S. congressman

1933   **Michael Dukakis** -- Governor of Massachusetts and Democratic candidate for president in 1988

1936   **Roy Emerson** -- Australian tennis player and Wimbledon singles champion in 1964 and 1965

1939   **Terrence McNally** -- American playwright

1945   **Ken Holtzman** -- Professional baseball player

1949   **Larry Holmes** -- World heavyweight champion

1951   **Dwight Evans** -- Professional baseball player

1952   **Roseanne Barr** -- American television actress and comedienne

1953   **Larry Herndon** -- Professional baseball player

1954   **Adam Ant (Stuart Goddard)** -- British singer and bassist

| 1955 | **Phil Simms** -- Professional football player |
| 1956 | **Bob Welch** -- Professional baseball player |

NOVEMBER 3 -- EVENTS

1003	Ethelred the Unready led the English in a massacre of the Danes.
1083	Queen Matilda, wife of William the Conqueror, died.
1493	Christopher Columbus landed in the West Indies, at an island he called Mariagalante after his flagship, on his second voyage to America.
1640	The Long Parliament met in London. It lasted without a break for 13 years.
1783	The Continental Army was disbanded by Congress.
1814	The Congress of Vienna opened to reshape Europe after the Napoleonic era.
1839	The Opium War began between China and Great Britain.
1848	The Prussian Revolution of 1848 ended with the king's forming a new ministry.
1903	Panama gained its independence from Colombia.
1918	Austria signed an armistice ending her part in World War I.
1936	President Franklin D. Roosevelt was reelected, defeating Alf Landon with a record landslide electoral vote of 523 to 8.
1942	The 1,523-mile-long Alaska Highway was completed, linking Dawson Creen, British Columbia, and Fairbanks, Alaska.
1954	Henri Matisse, the great French artist, died in Nice at age 84.
1957	The Russians launched their second satellite, *Sputnik 2*, carrying a dog named Laika, the first animal to be sent into space.
1964	In the first presidential election in which Washington, D.C., citizens were allowed to vote, Lyndon Johnson defeated Barry Goldwater in a landslide.

NOVEMBER 4 -- BIRTHDAYS

| 1575 | **Guido Reni** -- Italian Baroque painter and engraver |
| 1590 | **Gerrit van Honthorst** -- Dutch painter who influenced Rembrandt and Hals |

1840 **Auguste Rodin** – One of the world's greatest sculptors, and creator of the famous figure, *The Thinker*

1873 **Bobby Wallace** -- Hall of Fame baseball player with a 25-year major league career

1874 **Charles Despiau** -- French sculptor

1878 **Jean Schwartz** -- Hungarian-born composer and pianist, noted for songs such as "Chinatown, My Chinatown" and "Rockabye Your Baby With a Dixie Melody"

1879 **Will Rogers** -- American humorist, columnist, motion-picture actor, and folk hero

1889 **Charles Hackett** -- Noted American tenor

1896 **Harry MacGregor Woods** – American composer noted for songs such as "When the Red Red Robin Comes Bob-Bob-Bobbin' Along," "I'm Looking Over a Four Leaf Clover," and "When the Moon Comes Over the Mountain"

1906 **Bob Considine** – American newspaper correspondent and author

1907 **Paul Douglas** -- American motion-picture actor

1907 **Bennie Benjamin** – Canadian-born composer noted for songs such as "I Don't Want to Set the World on Fire," "Surrender," "Rumors Are Flying," and "Wheel of Fortune"

1911 **Dixie Lee** – American actress and first wife of singer Bing Crosby

1916 **Walter Cronkite** -- Noted American television news broadcaster and commentator

1917 **Gig Young** -- American stage and motion-picture actor

1918 **Art Carney** -- American motion-picture and television actor

1919 **Martin Balsam** – American motion-picture and television actor

1930 **Dick Groat** -- Professional baseball player

1933 **Tito Francona** -- Professional baseball player

1943 **Clark Graebner** -- American tennis player

1943 **Loretta Swit** -- American actress noted for her role as Hot Lips in the long-running television show *M*A*S*H*

1946 **John Cooper** -- Australian tennis player

1955 **Laurie Tenney** -- American tennis player

NOVEMBER 4 -- EVENTS

1677 William and Mary, the future co-rulers of England, were married.

1825   The Erie Canal was formally opened at New York City when the *Seneca Chief* arrived there. It had started from Buffalo on October 26.

1842   Abraham Lincoln married Mary Todd in Springfield, Illinois.

1847   Felix Mendelssohn, the great German composer, died in Leipzig at age 38.

1862   Richard Gatling patented his "Gatling gun," the first practical quick-firing machine gun developed in the U.S.

1880   James and John Ritty of Dayton, Ohio, patented the first cash register.

1884   Grover Cleveland, by a slim majority of 23,005 votes, was elected president over James G. Blaine.

1922   English archaeologist Howard Carter and his crew discovered the steps leading to the tomb of Tutankhamen, which Carter eventually entered on November 26.

1924   Calvin Coolidge defeated John W. Davis in the presidential election in a landslide.

1952   General Dwight D. Eisenhower was elected president over Adlai E. Stevenson.

1956   The Russian Army crushed the Hungarian Revolt.

1979   Iranian militants, with their government's approval, seized the U.S. embassy in Tehran, taking all the diplomats and personnel hostage.

1980   Ronald Reagan was elected president, unseating President Carter.

NOVEMBER 5 -- BIRTHDAYS

1494   **Hans Sachs** -- German poet and composer

1619   **Philips de Koninck** -- Dutch painter

1732   **John Glover** -- American revolutionary whose "amphibious" regiment took 2400 men of Washington's army across the Delaware in a blinding snowstorm on Christmas night, 1776, to capture Trenton

1779   **Washington Allston** -- The first American artist to paint in the romantic tradition of the 1800s, noted for works such as *Belshazzar's Feast* and *The Deluge*

1855   **Eugene V. Debs** -- American labor leader and five times Socialist Party presidential candidate

1857   **Ida M. Tarbell** -- American author and noted muckraker of the early 1900s

1876   **Raymond Duchamp-Villon** -- French sculptor

1879   **Will Hays** -- American political figure and czar of the motion-picture industry

1885   **Will Durant** -- American historian, philosopher, and author of *The Story of Philosophy* (1926), and co-author with his wife Ariel of *The Story of Civilization*

1891   **Earle "Greasy" Neale** -- Noted professional football player and coach

1894   **Beardsley Ruml** -- American congressman who proposed the withholding system of income tax payments, which was adopted by Congress in 1943

1895   **Walter Gieseking** -- German pianist

1905   **Joel McCrea** -- American motion-picture and television actor with a career of some 50 years

1905   **Annunzio Mantovani** -- Italian-born conductor

1912   **Roy Rogers** -- One of Hollywood's most popular singing cowboy stars

1913   **Vivien Leigh** -- English actress who achieved fame and worldwide popularity in her Academy Award-winning role of Scarlett O'Hara in the motion picture *Gone With the Wind* (1939)

1934   **Jeb Stuart Magruder** -- Convicted Watergate participant

1941   **Elke Sommer** -- German motion-picture and television actress

1941   **Art Garfunkel** -- American singer of the Simon and Garfunkel duo

1943   **Sam Shepard** -- American playwright

1947   **Peter Noone** -- Singer Herman with Herman's Hermits

1951   **Wendy Slaughter** -- English tennis player

1952   **Bill Walton** -- Professional basketball player

1957   **Kellen Winslow** -- Professional football player

1959   **Lloyd Moseby** -- Professional baseball player

1963   **Tatum O'Neal** -- American motion-picture actress and daughter of actor Ryan O'Neal

NOVEMBER 5 -- EVENTS

1605   Guy Fawkes was seized as he was about to blow up the English Houses of Parliament in the Gunpowder Plot.

1733 John Peter Zenger began publishing his newspaper, the New York *Weekly Journal.*

1757 Frederick the Great of Prussia, the outstanding commander of his age, decisively defeated the French in the Battle of Rossbach, the greatest battle of the Seven Years' War.

1862 President Lincoln relieved General George B. McClellan of the command of the Army of the Potomac and replaced him with General Ambrose E. Burnside.

1872 American suffragette Susan B. Anthony was arrested and later fined $100 (which she never paid) for trying to vote in the presidential election between U.S. Grant and Horace Greeley.

1895 George B. Selden, the noted American inventor, received the first U.S. patent for a gasoline-powered automobile.

1912 Woodrow Wilson was elected president of the United States over President William Howard Taft and ex-President Theodore Roosevelt.

1914 England and France declared war on Turkey in World War I.

1940 President Franklin D. Roosevelt was elected over Wendell Willkie to an unprecedented third term.

1942 General Bernard L. Montgomery announced that his British Eighth Army had won a complete victory over the Germans in Egypt in World War II.

NOVEMBER 6 -- BIRTHDAYS

1479 **Joanna the Mad** -- Queen of Castile

1771 **Aloys Senefelder** -- Inventor in 1798 of lithography

1814 **Adolphe Sax** – Belgian musical instrument maker and inventor in 1840 of the saxophone

1825 **Charles Garnier** -- French architect

1841 **Nelson W. Aldrich** -- U.S. senator and financier

1851 **Charles Henry Dow** -- A founder of Dow-Jones and Company

1854 **John Philip Sousa** -- Famous American bandmaster and "March King," who composed over 100 military marches, such as "Semper Fidelis," "The Washington Post," and "The Stars and Stripes Forever"

1861 **James A. Naismith** – Canadian-American teacher who in 1891 invented the game of basketball

1877   **William A. Dillon** -- American composer noted for songs such as "I Want a Girl Just Like the Girl That Married Dear Old Dad"

1880   **Robert Edler von Musil** -- Austrian novelist

1886   **Gus Kahn** – German-born lyricist noted for such songs as "Pretty Baby," "Charley My Boy," "Toot, Toot, Tootsie, Goodbye," "On the Alamo," and "The Waltz You Saved for Me"

1887   **Walter Johnson** -- Hardest throwing pitcher in baseball history and winner of 414 career games, second only to Cy Young

1892   **Ole Olsen** -- American comedian who with Chic Johnson formed the Olsen and Johnson comedy team

1893   **Edsel Ford** -- Only child of industrialist Henry Ford

1916   **Joseph Bushkin** -- American composer noted for such songs as "There'll Be a Hot Time in the Old Town Tonight"

1921   **James Jones** -- American novelist and author of *From Here to Eternity*

1923   **Robert Griffin** -- U.S. senator

1931   **Mike Nichols** -- American motion-picture director, noted for films such as *The Graduate* (1967)

1935   **Johnny Pott** -- Professional golfer

1939   **Pat Dye** -- College football coach

1941   **Ray Perkins** – Professional football player and college and professional football coach

1946   **Sally Field** -- American motion-picture and television actress who won best actress Academy Awards for *Norma Rae* (1979) and *Places in the Heart* (1984)

1953   **John Candelaria** -- Professional baseball player

1955   **Maria Shriver** -- American television personality and daughter of Sargent Shriver, first director of the Peace Corps

NOVEMBER 6 -- EVENTS

1492   Sonni Ali Ber, the founder of the great black African empire of Songhay, drowned in the River Koni.

1860   Abraham Lincoln was elected president over Stephen A. Douglas, John C. Breckinridge, and John Bell.

1861   Jefferson Davis was elected to a six-year term as president of the Confederacy.

1869   Rutgers defeated the College of New Jersey (now Princeton University), 6 to 4, in New Brunswick, New Jersey, in the first college football game.

1882   Lillie Langtry, the great English actress known as "The Jersey Lily," made her American debut in New York in the play, *An Unequal Match.*

1888   Benjamin Harrison defeated incumbent Grover Cleveland in the presidential election in spite of Cleveland's popular vote majority.

1893   Peter Ilich Tchaikovsky, the great Russian composer, died of cholera in St. Petersburg at age 53.

1900   The presidential ticket of William McKinley and Theodore Roosevelt defeated that of William Jennings Bryan and Adlai E. Stevenson.

1913   Mahatma Gandhi was arrested as he led a march of Indian miners in South Africa.

1917   The October Revolution (October 24 in the old Russian calendar) began in Petrograd, Russia, as the Bolsheviks under Lenin began taking over key points of the city.

1928   Herbert Hoover was elected president, defeating Al Smith.

1938   The comic strip, *Red Ryder,* by Fred Harmon, made its first appearance.

1968   The Vietnam peace talks began in Paris.

1984   Ronald Reagan was reelected president over Walter Mondale in a landslide in which he received all the electoral votes except those of Minnesota and the District of Columbia.

NOVEMBER 7 -- BIRTHDAYS

1598   **Francisco de Zurbaran** -- Spanish painter

1832   **Andrew D. White** -- First president of Cornell University and author of the monumental work, *A History of the Warfare of Science With Theology in Christendom* (1895)

1867   **Marie Curie** -- Polish-born French physicist and co-discoverer, with her husband Pierre Curie, of the elements radium and polonium

1878   **Lise Meitner** -- Austrian physicist who with physicists Otto Hahn and Fritz Strassmann succeeded in splitting the uranium atom in 1938

1879   **Leon Trotsky** -- One of the principal leaders of the Bolshevik Revolution and the second most powerful man in Russia while Lenin was alive

1890   **Phil Spitalny** -- Russian-born composer, conductor, and clarinetist, noted for his "All-Girl Orchestra" of the 1930s and 1940s

1903   **Dean Jagger** -- American stage, screen, and television actor with a career of over 50 years

1906   **Eugene Carson Blake** -- American church official

1909   **Norman Krasna** -- American playwright, screenwriter, producer, and director

1913   **Albert Camus** -- French novelist, journalist, and playwright, noted for *The Stranger* (1942) and *The Plague* (1947)

1918   **Billy Graham** -- Noted American evangelist and author

1922   **Al Hirt** -- American musician

1926   **Dame Joan Sutherland** -- Australian opera singer

1927   **Al Martino** -- American singer, pianist, and actor

1930   **Rudy Boschwitz** -- U.S. senator

1937   **Mary Travers** -- American singer with the Peter, Paul, and Mary musical group

1938   **Jim Kaat** -- Professional baseball player whose career spanned from the 1960s to the 1980s

1943   **Joni Mitchell** -- Canadian guitarist and singer

1944   **Joe Niekro** -- Professional baseball player and brother of baseball player Phil Niekro

1947   **Sue Mappin** -- English tennis player

1951   **Wallace Francis** -- Professional football player

1956   **Elvis Peacock** -- Professional football player

1964   **Dana Plato** -- American actress

NOVEMBER 7 -- EVENTS

1504   Christopher Columbus arrived in Sanlucar, Spain, ending his fourth and last voyage to America.

1811   General William Henry Harrison defeated Chief Tecumseh's Shawnee Indians in the Battle of Tippecanoe on the Wabash River.

1848   General Zachary Taylor defeated Lewis Cass in the presidential election.

1874   The Republican Party was first depicted as an elephant, in a cartoon by Thomas Nast in *Harper's Weekly.*

1876   The "stolen presidential election" took place between Samuel J. Tilden and Rutherford B. Hayes. A deal was finally worked out to give Hayes the victory the following March.

1885   The last spike was driven in the Canadian Pacific Railway, linking Canada's east and west coasts.

1910   Victor Herbert's operetta, *Naughty Marietta,* opened in New York. One of its biggest hits was "Ah, Sweet Mystery of Life."

1916   President Woodrow Wilson was re-elected, narrowly defeating Charles Evans Hughes.

1916   Jeannette Rankin became the first woman elected to the U.S. House of Representatives.

1917   The October Revolution ended in Russia (October 25 by the old calendar), as Lenin and his Bolsheviks seized Petrograd.

1940   "Galloping Gertie," the third largest suspension bridge in the world, at Tacoma, Washington, collapsed in a windstorm a few months after its completion.

1944   President Franklin D. Roosevelt won an unprecedented fourth term, defeating Republican Thomas E. Dewey.

1962   Mrs. Eleanor Roosevelt, the wife of President Franklin D. Roosevelt, died at age 78.

1962   Richard Nixon held his "last press conference," as he called it, telling reporters, "You won't have Nixon to kick around any more."

NOVEMBER 8 -- BIRTHDAYS

35 AD   **Marcus Nerva** -- Emperor of Rome, A.D. 96-98

1081   **Henry V** -- King of Germany and Holy Roman Emperor, 1106-1125, and the last of the Salian dynasty

1622   **Charles X** -- King of Sweden, 1654-1660, whose reign marked the height of Swedish power in Europe

1656   **Edmund Halley** -- English astronomer for whom Halley's Comet was named

1847   **Bram Stoker** -- British author, who wrote *Dracula* (1897), one of the most famous horror stories of all time

1867   Carl Sadakichi Hartmann -- American art critic

1883   Charles Demuth -- American painter known for works such as *My Egypt* (1927) and *I Saw a Figure 5 in Gold* (1928)

1896   Bucky Harris -- Professional baseball player and manager

1897   Dorothy Day -- Influential American lay Catholic

1900   Margaret Mitchell -- American author, noted for *Gone with the Wind,* one of the most popular novels of all time, and which was made into one of the greatest motion pictures of all time

1906   H.C. Hansen -- Danish prime minister

1907   Tony Cuccinello -- Professional baseball player

1907   Katharine Hepburn -- American stage and motion-picture superstar for over fifty years, and the only actress to win three Academy Awards for leading roles

1913   Robert Strauss -- American actor and comedian who played Animal in *Stalag 17* (1953)

1916   June Havoc -- American stage, screen, and television actress

1922   Christiaan Barnard -- South African surgeon who performed the first heart transplant (1967)

1922   Jack Fleck -- Professional golfer

1927   Patti Page -- Popular American singer of the 1950s and 1960s

1931   Morley Safer -- American broadcast journalist

1935   Alain Delon -- French motion-picture actor

1949   Bonnie Raitt -- American singer and musician

1952   John Denny -- Professional baseball player

1958   Terry de Miall Harron -- English musician with the Adam and the Ants musical group

NOVEMBER 8 -- EVENTS

1519   Hernando Cortes, the Spanish conqueror of Mexico, reached Tenochtitlan, the Aztec capital and site of present-day Mexico City.

1674   John Milton, the great English poet, died in London at age 65.

1793   The Louvre in Paris, originally built in stages as a palace, was first opened to the public as a museum.

1837   Mt. Holyoke Seminary for women in South Hadley, Mass., was opened with 80 students.

| 1864 | President Lincoln was re-elected, defeating General George B. McClellan. |

| 1880 | Sarah Bernhardt, the great French actress, made her American debut in New York in *Adrienne Lecouvreur*. |

| 1887 | Doc Holliday, the famous alcoholic Wild West gunslinger, died of tuberculosis in a Colorado sanitarium. |

| 1889 | Montana was admitted to the Union as the 41st state. |

| 1892 | Grover Cleveland defeated incumbent President Benjamin Harrison, becoming the only president to win two nonconsecutive terms. |

| 1895 | Wilhelm Konrad Roentgen, the great German physicist, discovered X-rays. |

| 1904 | President Theodore Roosevelt won a second term, defeating Democrat Alton B. Parker. |

| 1917 | The Second All-Russian Congress of Soviets opened and agreed to ask Germany for peace in World War I. |

| 1923 | Adolf Hitler and his Nazis staged the Beer Hall Putsch in Munich, a movement to seize the Bavarian government. The attempt failed and Hitler was subsequently jailed. |

| 1932 | Franklin D. Roosevelt was elected for his first term, defeating incumbent President Herbert Hoover. |

| 1942 | Operation Torch began, as Allied troops under General Eisenhower, landed at Casablanca, Oran, and Algiers in North Africa in World War II. |

| 1960 | John F. Kennedy defeated Richard M. Nixon in the presidential election, becoming at 43 the youngest president ever elected. |

| 1970 | Tom Dempsey of the New Orleans Saints kicked a record 63-yard field goal. |

NOVEMBER 9 -- BIRTHDAYS

| 1389 | **Isabella of France** -- Wife of King Richard II of England |

| 1801 | **Gail Borden** -- American inventor who developed the first successful milk-condensing process and who founded the Borden Company |

| 1818 | **Ivan Turgenev** -- One of the three greatest Russian novelists, noted for works such as *Fathers and Sons* (1862) and *Smoke* (1867) |

1841   **Edward VII** -- Oldest son of Queen Victoria and Prince Albert, and King of England, 1901-1910

1853   **Stanford White** – Prominent American architect who designed the Madison Square Garden in New York (1890)

1869   **Marie Dressler** -- Canadian-born stage and motion-picture actress and number one box office attraction in the 1930s

1881   **Herbert T. Kalmus** -- American inventor and motion-picture pioneer, noted for his invention of technicolor

1886   **Ed Wynn** – American stage, screen, and television actor and comedian, whose career spanned 40 years

1888   **Jean Monnet** -- French economist and architect of the European Common Market

1895   **Mae Marsh** – A leading lady of the silent screen who played "The Little Sister" in *The Birth of a Nation* (1915), and who made the transition to the talkies in a 50-year career

1913   **Hedy Lamarr** -- Austrian-born motion-picture actress and leading lady of the 1940s

1915   **Sargent Shriver** -- First U.S. Peace Corps director and vice presidential candidate with George McGovern in 1972

1918   **Florence Chadwick** -- American swimmer and first woman to swim the English Channel in both directions, in 1950 and 1951

1918   **Spiro T. Agnew** – U.S. vice president under President Nixon, and only the second vice president in history (after John C. Calhoun) to resign his office

1921   **Silvio Conte** -- U.S. congressman

1923   **Dorothy Dandridge** -- American actress, singer, and dancer

1931   **Whitey Herzog** -- Professional baseball player and manager

1932   **Frank Selvy** -- Professional basketball player

1934   **Carl Sagan** -- American astronomer, writer, and television personality

1935   **Bob Gibson** – Hall of Fame baseball pitcher with 3,117 career strikeouts

1941   **Bruce Gossett** -- Professional football player

1942   **Tom Weiskopf** -- Professional golfer

1958   **Ted Higuera** -- Professional baseball player

1962   **Dion James** -- Professional baseball player

NOVEMBER 9 -- EVENTS

1389   Boniface IX was crowned Roman Catholic pope.

1799   Napoleon Bonaparte, in the "Coup d'Etat of Eighteenth Brumaire," seized power in France.

1918   Kaiser Wilhelm, the German emperor, abdicated and fled to the Netherlands, as the German government was negotiating the surrender terms with the Allies in World War I.

1923   Adolf Hitler's Beer Hall Putsch was crushed and his followers were arrested in Munich. Hitler himself was arrested two days later.

1924   Nellie Tayloe Ross was elected governor of Wyoming, becoming the first woman governor in the United States.

1935   The Committee for Industrial Organization (CIO) was formed by John L. Lewis and other American labor leaders.

1938   Mary Martin, the great American actress, made her debut in the musical comedy, *Leave It to Me,* at the Imperial Theater in New York.

1938   Hitler and Goebbels set in motion Crystal Night--named for the smashed windows--in which Jewish shops and synagogues were burned and ransacked all over Germany by Nazi thugs.

1944   The first operation to save a "blue baby" was performed at Johns Hopkins Children's Hospital.

1953   Dylan Thomas, the noted Welsh poet, died in New York at age 39 while on an American tour.

1953   The Supreme Court upheld a 1922 ruling that the federal antitrust laws do not apply to major-league baseball.

1964   The comic strip, *The Wizard of Id,* by Johnny Hart and Brant Parker, first appeared.

1965   The great Northeastern United States power failure occurred, blacking out New York, Boston, Philadelphia, Baltimore, and two provinces of Canada.

1989   The Berlin Wall was opened by East Germany as the Communist regimes in Eastern Europe continued to topple.

NOVEMBER 10 -- BIRTHDAYS

1483   **Martin Luther** -- Founder of the Protestant Reformation, and called by some the most influential German who ever lived

1630   **Adriaen van de Velde** -- Dutch painter

1668   **Francois Couperin** -- French composer and musician greatly admired by Johann Sebastian Bach, his great contemporary

1683   **George II** -- King of England, 1727-1760, and the last British ruler to lead troops on the battlefield

1697   **William Hogarth** -- English painter and engraver, noted for such paintings as *The Rake's Progress* and *The Shrimp Girl*

1730   **Oliver Goldsmith** — Irish-born poet and playwright, noted for works such as the poem, "The Deserted Village" (1770), and the famous comedy, *She Stoops to Conquer* (1773)

1759   **Friedrich von Schiller** — The greatest German playwright of all time and with Goethe, one of the two greatest figures of German literature

1852   **Henry Van Dyke** -- American clergyman, short-story writer, poet, and essayist

1871   **Winston Churchill** -- American novelist, noted for works such as *Richard Carvel* (1899) and *The Crisis* (1901)

1874   **Donald Baxter Macmillan** -- American polar explorer who surveyed and charted Greenland and the Canadian Arctic

1879   **Vachel Lindsay** — American poet noted for works such as "Abraham Lincoln Walks at Midnight" (1914)

1880   **Sir Jacob Epstein** — American-born English sculptor whose subjects are noted for their strong and energetic appearance

1889   **Claude Rains** -- English stage and motion-picture actor with a career of over 50 years

1893   **John P. Marquand** -- American novelist who won the 1938 Pulitzer Prize for *The Late George Apley*

1895   **John Knudsen Northrup** — American aircraft designer and co-founder of Lockheed Aircraft Corporation

1896   **Jimmy Dykes** -- Professional baseball player and manager

1909   **Birdie Tebbetts** -- Professional baseball player

1913   **Karl Shapiro** -- American poet who won the 1945 Pulitzer Prize for *V-Letter and Other Poems*

1919   **Moise Tshombe** -- President of Katanga and premier of the Congo, now Zaire, 1964-1965

1919   **George Fenneman** — American radio and television announcer, who was Groucho Marx's straight man on the TV show, *You Bet Your Life*

1925   **Richard Burton** -- Welsh stage, screen, and television actor and superstar

1934   **Norm Cash** -- Professional baseball player

1935   **Roy Scheider** -- American stage and motion-picture actor

1939   **Russell Means** -- Native American leader of the 1960s and 1970s

1946   **David Stockman** -- U.S. budget director under President Reagan

1947   **David A. Loggins** -- American composer and singer, noted for songs such as "The Fool in Me," "Pieces of April," and "One Way Ticket to Paradise"

1949   **Donna Fargo** -- American singer

1953   **Larry Parrish** -- Professional baseball player

1954   **Bob Stanley** -- Professional baseball player

1955   **Jack Clark** -- Professional baseball player

1963   **Andres Thomas** -- Professional baseball player

NOVEMBER 10 -- EVENTS

1630   This was the famous "Day of Dupes" in France, a day when the enemies of Cardinal Richlieu thought he had fallen into disfavor, but when King Louis XIII restored him to power.

1775   The United States Marine Corps was authorized by the Continental Congress.

1798   Aloys Senefelder, German inventor, developed the lithographic printing process.

1834   Franklin Pierce married Jane Means Appleton.

1871   Henry M. Stanley, English explorer, discovered the missing missionary, David Livingstone, in Africa, and greeted him with: "Dr. Livingstone, I presume?"

1888   Fritz Kreisler, the great composer and violinist, made his American debut at age thirteen in Steinway Hall in New York.

1918   Kaiser Wilhelm II of Germany arrived in Belgium, asking for asylum, as World War I was ending.

1919   The American Legion held its first national convention, in Minneapolis.

1947   The comic strip, *Ferd'nand,* by Henning Dahl Mikkelsen, first appeared in American newspapers.

1961   Stalingrad, Russia, was renamed Volgograd.

1977   Louise Brown, the world's first test-tube baby, was conceived.

NOVEMBER 11 -- BIRTHDAYS

1050   **Henry IV** -- King of Germany, 1056-1106, who tried to depose Pope Gregory VII, and had to stand barefoot in the snow for 3 days before Gregory would pardon him (Henry got his revenge later)

1493   **Bernardo Tasso** -- Italian courtier, poet, and father of Torquato Tasso, one of the great masters of Italian poetry

1579   **Frans Snyders** -- Flemish painter

1679   **Firmin Abauzit** -- French theologian

1729   **Louis Antoine de Bougainville** -- French navigator who discovered the island of Bougainville in 1768

1781   **Cyrus Alger** -- American inventor who produced the first gun ever rifled in America

1821   **Fyodor Dostoevsky** -- One of the two or three greatest Russian novelists, whose *Crime and Punishment* (1866) and *The Brothers Karamazov* (1880) are among the world's greatest novels

1836   **Thomas Bailey Aldrich** -- American writer

1863   **Paul Signac** -- French painter

1868   **Edouard Vuillard** -- French painter and decorator

1869   **Victor Emmanuel III** – King of Italy, 1900-1946, during Mussolini's Fascist regime

1872   **Maude Adams** -- American stage actress, and one of the greatest of the 1890-1918 era

1882   **Gustaf VI** -- King of Sweden who succeeded his father, Gustaf V, in 1950

1885   **George S. Patton Jr.** -- One of the greatest and most colorful American generals of World War II

1891   **Rabbit Maranville** -- Hall of Fame baseball player who played 23 years and 2,670 games

1894   **Beverly Bayne** -- Popular leading lady of Hollywood silent films, who with Francis X. Bushman formed the first important love team of American movies

1898   **Rene Clair** -- French producer, director, and writer

1899	**Pie Traynor** -- Perhaps the greatest third baseman in baseball history

1899   **Pie Traynor** -- Perhaps the greatest third baseman in baseball history

1899   **Pat O'Brien** -- American stage and motion-picture actor, who appeared in 85 films in a career of over 60 years

1900   **Hugh Scott** -- U.S. senator and Minority Leader in the 1970s

1903   **Sam Spiegel** -- European-born motion-picture director

1904   **Alger Hiss** -- U.S. State Department official convicted of perjury in a famous case in 1949-1950

1909   **Robert Ryan** -- American stage and motion-picture actor

1914   **Howard Fast** -- American writer and novelist

1915   **George Case** -- Professional baseball player

1915   **William Proxmire** -- U.S. senator

1922   **Kurt Vonnegut Jr.** -- American novelist noted for works such as *Cat's Cradle* (1963) and *Slaughterhouse Five* (1969)

1925   **Jonathan Winters** -- American comedian and actor

1934   **Charles Manson** -- American convicted mass murderer and cult leader

1935   **Bibi Andersson** -- Swedish motion-picture actress

1937   **Rudy La Russo** -- Professional basketball player with 10,000 career points

1941   **Helga Masthoff** -- West German tennis player

1951   **Fuzzy Zoeller** -- Professional golfer

1956   **Ian Craig Marsh** -- English musician with the Heaven 17 musical group

NOVEMBER 11 -- EVENTS

1417   Martin V was elected Roman Catholic pope.

1534   The famous Act of Supremacy was passed at King Henry VIII's insistence, making the Church of England a separate institution with the king as its supreme head.

1647   King Charles I of England escaped from Parliament and fled to the Isle of Wight.

1675   Gottfried Wilhelm Leibniz, the great co-inventor with Isaac Newton of the calculus, first set down on paper an equation establishing the symbol for the integral sign.

1831	Nat Turner was hanged for his leadership of the largest slave revolt in American history.
1855	Soren Kierkegaard, the noted Danish theologian, died in Copenhagen at age 42.
1858	James A. Garfield married Lucretia Rudolph.
1889	Washington was admitted to the Union as the 42nd state.
1918	World War I ended at 11 A.M., following the signing of the armistice in a railway car in the Forest of Compiegne, in France.
1921	The Unknown Soldier of the United States was buried in Arlington National Cemetery.
1923	Adolf Hitler was arrested for his part in the Beer Hall Putsch in Munich, and was taken to prison.
1933	The first of the great dust storms of the 1930s, which lay waste thousands of acres of land, swept over North Dakota.
1939	Kate Smith sang Irving Berlin's "God Bless America" on her radio show, the first time it had been heard by the public.
1942	German troops occupied the previously unoccupied portion of France in World War II.
1954	Veterans Day was first celebrated in the United States. Previously the day was observed as Armistice Day, commemorating the end of World War I.
1975	Angola gained its independence from Portugal.
1985	The Colombian volcano Nevado del Ruiz erupted, burying the town of Armero and leaving some 15,000 dead, in the worst volcanic disaster in the Western Hemisphere in the 1900s

NOVEMBER 12 -- BIRTHDAYS

1493	**Baccio Bandinelli** -- Florentine sculptor and painter
1615	**Richard Baxter** -- One of the greatest English theologians
1770	**Joseph Hopkinson** -- American jurist and composer of "Hail Columbia" (1798)
1815	**Elizabeth Cady Stanton** -- Pioneer in the American women's rights movement and first president of the National Woman Suffrage Association
1833	**Alexander Borodin** -- Russian composer noted for the opera *Prince Igor,* and whose *Second Symphony* ranks among the best by any Russian composer

1842 **Lord John William Strutt Rayleigh** -- One of England's greatest physical scientists

1866 **Sun Yat-sen** -- Father of modern China and first president of the Republic of China, in 1912

1870 **Glen MacDonough** -- American lyricist noted for songs such as "Forgive and Forget" and "Toyland"

1889 **DeWitt Wallace** -- Founder of the *Reader's Digest* (1921)

1891 **Carl Mays** -- Professional baseball player

1891 **Richard A. Whiting** -- American composer noted for songs such as "Some Sunday Morning," "Sleepytime Gal," "Ain't We Got Fun?" "Beyond the Blue Horizon," "Guilty," and "Too Marvelous for Words"

1903 **Jack Oakie** -- American stage and motion-picture actor

1908 **Harry A. Blackmun** -- U.S. Supreme Court justice

1917 **Joseph Coors** -- American brewery executive

1918 **Jo Stafford** -- American singer

1922 **Kim Hunter** -- American motion-picture and television actress

1929 **Grace Kelly** -- American motion-picture superstar and Princess of Monaco

1945 **Neil Young** -- Canadian singer and guitarist with the Crosby, Stills, Nash, and Young musical group

1952 **Steve Bartkowski** -- Professional football superstar

1954 **Paul McNamee** -- Australian tennis player

1957 **Gerry Ellis** -- Professional football player

1958 **Dan Petry** -- Professional baseball player

1961 **Nadia Comaneci** -- Romanian gymnast and darling of the 1976 Olympic Games

NOVEMBER 12 -- EVENTS

1035 King Canute of England and Denmark died at Shaftesbury at an approximate age of 39.

1439 Plymouth, England, became the first English town incorporated by Parliament.

1875 The first Harvard-Yale football was played under the rules that permitted running with the ball and tackling.

1918   After its defeat in World War I, Austria proclaimed itself a separate state independent of Hungary.

1920   In the aftermath of the "Black Sox" scandal, Judge Kenesaw Mountain Landis was appointed the first commissioner of professional baseball.

1927   Joseph Stalin expelled Leon Trotsky from the Central Committee of the Communist party, paving the way for Stalin to become sole ruler of Russia.

1938   In the aftermath of Crystal Night, on which Nazi thugs destroyed Jewish shops all over Germany, Adolf Hitler ordered the Jews themselves to pay $400,000,000 for the damages.

1942   British troops captured Tobruk in World War II.

1944   The German battleship *Tirpitz* was destroyed by British bombers in World War II.

1948   The war crimes tribunal sentenced former World War II Japanese premier Hideki Tojo to death.

1954   The Ellis Island immigration station in New York Harbor was closed after processing more than 20 million immigrants beginning in 1892.

1965   The Cowboy Hall of Fame in Oklahoma City inducted its first five members: Theodore Roosevelt, Will Rogers, Charles Russell, Jake McClure, and Charles Goodnight.

1973   Egypt and Israel signed a cease-fire agreement, ending the Middle East War.

NOVEMBER 13 -- BIRTHDAYS

354 AD Saint Augustine – One of the earliest Christian theologians, and author of *The City of God* and *Confessions,* two of the best-known religious writings of all time

1312   Edward III -- King of England, 1327-1377, and father of Edward, the Black Prince, one of the greatest warriors in English history

1504   Philip of Hesse (the Magnanimous) -- Father of political Protestantism

1753   Ippolito Pindemonte -- Italian writer, poet, and translator of Homer's *Odyssey*

1809   John Adolphus Bernard Dahlgren -- American naval officer who invented the Dahlgren gun that became famous during the Civil War

1814   Joseph Hooker – U.S. Civil War general known as "Fighting Joe"

1831   **James Clerk Maxwell** -- Great English physicist noted, among other things, for "Maxwell's Laws," which form the basis for modern electromagnetic theory

1833   **Edwin Booth** -- Renowned American stage actor of the 19th century, and brother of John Wilkes Booth, the assassin of Abraham Lincoln

1850   **Robert Louis Stevenson** -- One of the world's most popular writers, and author of *Kidnapped* (1886), *Treasure Island* (1883), and *The Strange Case of Dr. Jekyll and Mr. Hyde* (1886)

1853   **John Drew** – Famous American stage actor who played over 100 leading roles in his 50-year career

1856   **Louis Brandeis** -- U.S. Supreme Court justice, 1916-1939, and one of the first men to advocate conservation

1875   **James Guilford Swinnerton** -- One of the "grand old men" of the American comic strip, and creator of *Little Bears and Tykes*

1890   **Conrad Richter** -- American Pulitzer Prize-winning novelist noted for works such as *The Town, The Waters of Kronos,* and *The Trees*

1900   **Alexander King** -- American writer, and author of *May This House Be Safe from Tigers*

1906   **Hermione Baddeley** – English stage, television, and motion-picture actress

1913   **Irving "Deacon" Crane** -- American pocket billiards superstar with a career of some 50 years

1915   **Nathaniel Benchley** – American humorist and son of humorist Robert Benchley

1922   **Oskar Werner** -- Austrian-born motion-picture actor

1923   **Linda Christian** -- Mexican-born motion-picture actress

1930   **Fred Harris** -- U.S. senator in the 1960s and 1970s

1938   **Jean Seberg** -- American motion-picture actress

1941   **Mel Stottlemyre** -- Professional baseball player and coach

1955   **Jenny Dimond** -- Australian tennis player

1956   **Bill Scanlon** -- American tennis player

NOVEMBER 13 -- EVENTS

1093   Malcolm III MacDuncan, King of Scots, was killed while laying
        siege to Alnwick in an invasion of England. He was succeeded
        by his brother Donald Bane.

1460   Prince Henry the Navigator, the great Portuguese promoter of
        exploration of the 1400s, died at age 66.

1775   American patriots occupied Montreal in the Revolutionary War.

1868   Gioacchino Antonio Rossini, the great Italian composer, died at
        Passy, France, at age 76.

1914   The elastic brassiere was patented by American heiress, Mary
        Phelps Jacob.

1921   The motion picture, *The Sheik,* starring Rudolph Valentino, was
        first released. Women fainted in the aisles during the performance.

1927   The Holland Tunnel, linking New York City to Jersey City, was
        opened to traffic.

1933   The first recorded "sit-down" strike in the United States was
        staged by workers in the Hormel Packing Company in Austin,
        Minnesota.

1940   Walt Disney's classic cartoon *Fantasia* was first released.

1941   The British aircraft carrier *Ark Royal* sank in the Mediterranean
        one day after it had been torpedoed by a German submarine in
        World War II.

1956   The U.S. Supreme Court struck down Alabama's laws calling for
        racial segregation on public buses.

1971   U.S. space probe *Mariner 9* went into orbit around Mars and
        began transmitting pictures of that planet's surface.

NOVEMBER 14 -- BIRTHDAYS

1650   **William III** – King of England, who with his wife ruled as William
        and Mary, 1689-1702

1668   **Johann Lucas von Hildebrandt** -- Austrian architect

1719   **Leopold Mozart** -- Austrian musician who wrote the first impor-
        tant book about violin playing and who was the father of the
        great composer Wolfgang Amadeus Mozart

1765   **Robert Fulton** -- American inventor and builder in 1807 of the
        Clermont, the first commercially successful steamboat

1803   Jacob Abbott -- American teacher and author of the Rollo series of books
1807   **Auguste Laurent** -- French chemist
1828   **James B. McPherson** -- U.S. Civil War general
1840   **Claude Monet** -- Noted French painter and one of the leaders of the Impressionist movement
1863   **Leo Hendrik Baekeland** -- American chemist noted for making the first Bakelite
1889   **Jawaharlal Nehru** -- First prime minister of India and father of India's first woman prime minister Indira Gandhi
1891   **Frederick Grant Banting** -- Canadian physician famous for discovering insulin
1896   **Mamie Doud Eisenhower** -- Wife of President Dwight D. Eisenhower
1897   **John Steuart Curry** -- American painter of the regionalism movement of the 1930s
1900   **Aaron Copland** -- American composer noted for works such as *Billy the Kid* (1938) and *Appalachian Spring* (1944)
1904   **Marya Mannes** -- American novelist and journalist
1904   **Dick Powell** -- American motion-picture actor and director
1906   **Louise Brooks** -- American motion-picture actress
1907   **William Steig** -- American cartoonist and author
1908   **Joseph R. McCarthy** -- U.S. senator who made sensational but unproved charges of Communist subversion in the government in the 1950s
1908   **Harrison Salisbury** -- American newspaper columnist
1912   **Barbara Hutton** -- Often-married heiress to the Woolworth fortune
1914   **Rosemary DeCamp** -- American motion-picture and television actress
1919   **Veronica Lake** -- Glamour star of Hollywood films of the 1940s, whose trademark was her long blond hair falling over one of her eyes
1921   **Brian Keith** -- American motion-picture and television actor
1923   **Johnny Desmond** -- American singer and actor
1924   **Jeri Kelli Sullivan** -- American composer, author, and singer, noted for songs such as "Rum and Coca-Cola"

1929   **Jim Piersall** -- Professional baseball player

1929   **McLean Stevenson** -- American television actor, noted for his role in the long-running series, *M*A*S*H*

1930   **Edward H. White** -- First U.S. astronaut to walk in space, in 1965

1933   **Fred W. Haise Jr.** -- American astronaut on the *Apollo 13* mission

1935   **Hussein I** -- King of Jordan who succeeded his father Talal in 1952

1945   **Mike Livingston** -- Professional football player

1948   **Prince Charles** -- Son of Queen Elizabeth II and heir to the English throne

1955   **Jack Sikma** -- Professional basketball player

NOVEMBER 14 -- EVENTS

1305   Clement V was crowned. He was the first Roman Catholic pope to reside at Avignon.

1784   Samuel Seabury was consecrated as the first American Episcopalian bishop.

1832   The world's first streetcar, the *John Mason,* made its appearance in New York. It was drawn by two horses on tracks on Fourth Avenue.

1851   Herman Melville's *Moby-Dick* was published by Harper and Brothers in New York. It was a failure during Melville's lifetime but is now one of the world's greatest books.

1881   The trial of Charles Guiteau, President Garfield's assassin, opened in Washington, D.C.

1889   Nellie Bly set out from Hoboken, New Jersey, to outdo the hero of *Around the World in Eighty Days.* She succeeded, completing the trip around the world 72 days later.

1896   England repealed the law banning motor vehicles on the highways.

1922   The British Broadcasting Corporation began domestic radio service.

1940   German planes dropped 225 tons of bombs on Coventry, England, in World War II, smashing the heart out of the old city through which Lady Godiva had ridden 900 years earlier.

1942   Captain Eddie Rickenbacker, American World War I ace, was rescued in the Pacific after floating 24 days on a raft, after his plane was forced down on a World War II mission.

1969   *Apollo 12* was launched with the second crew of astronauts, Richard Gordon, Alan Bean, and Charles Conrad, to make a lunar landing.

1972   The Dow-Jones Industrial Average closed at 1,003, the first time in its 76-year history that it had closed above 1,000.

1973   Princess Anne of England married Captain Mark Phillips.

NOVEMBER 15 -- BIRTHDAYS

1397   **Nicholas V** -- Roman Catholic pope, 1447-1455, who founded the Vatican Library

1666   **Robert Le Lorrain** -- French sculptor

1708   **William Pitt the Elder** -- British statesman known as the "Great Commoner," who transformed Britain into an imperial power

1738   **Sir William Herschel** -- British astronomer who in 1781 discovered the planet Uranus, the first planet discovered since prehistoric times

1797   **Thurlow Weed** -- American journalist and political leader who was largely responsible for the election of Presidents William Henry Harrison and Zachary Taylor

1862   **Gerhart Hauptmann** -- Nobel Prize-winning German dramatist, noted for works such as *The Weavers* (1892) and *Till Eulenspiegel* (1928)

1879   **Lewis Stone** -- American stage matinee idol and motion-picture actor in some 200 films

1882   **Felix Frankfurter** -- Influential adviser to Presidents Woodrow Wilson and Franklin D. Roosevelt, and U.S. Supreme Court justice, 1939-1962

1887   **Marianne Moore** – One of America's finest woman poets, ranking second perhaps to Emily Dickinson

1887   **Georgia O'Keeffe** -- American painter noted for her stark, simple paintings

1891   **W. Averell Harriman** – U.S. diplomat, statesman, governor of New York, 1955-1958, and son of industrialist Edward Henry Harriman

1891   **Erwin Rommel** -- One of the most brilliant German generals of
        World War II and famed leader of the Afrika Corps

1906   **Curtis LeMay** – U.S. Air Force general, commander of the
        Strategic Air Command, 1948-1957, and vice-presidential can-
        didate with third-party candidate George C. Wallace in 1968

1919   **Inez Eleanor James** – American composer, author, and pianist,
        noted for such songs as "Vaya Con Dios" and "Come to Baby Do"

1920   **Wayne Thiebaud** -- American painter

1925   **Howard Baker** -- U.S. senator and Majority Leader, 1981-1985

1928   **James Brady** -- American writer and television commentator

1928   **Gus Bell** -- Professional baseball player

1929   **Edward Asner** -- American stage, screen, and television actor

1932   **Petula Clark** -- English singer, songwriter, and actress

1940   **Sam Waterston** -- American stage, screen, and television actor

1942   **Daniel Barenboim** -- Israeli pianist and conductor

1946   **Janet Lennon** -- One of the singing Lennon Sisters

1947   **Bob Dandridge** -- Professional basketball player

1950   **Otis Armstrong** -- Professional football player

NOVEMBER 15 -- EVENTS

1315   The Swiss defeated the Austrians at Mortgarten, consolidating
        the Everlasting League of the Three Forest Cantons, the nucleus
        of modern Switzerland.

1777   The Articles of Confederation were adopted by the Continental
        Congress in York, Pennsylvania.

1806   American explorer Zebulon Pike first sighted Pike's Peak.

1837   Isaac Pitman published his shorthand manual *Stenographic Sound-
        hand.* Pitman's shorthand eventually became the most popular
        shorthand of all.

1864   Union general William Tecumseh Sherman burned Atlanta
        before completing his famous "March to the Sea" in the Civil War.

1881   The Federation of Organized Trades and Labor Unions was
        organized by Samuel Gompers and others. It was the forerunner
        of the American Federation of Labor.

1907   *Mr. A. Mutt,* by Bud Fisher, the first successful daily comic strip
        and the forerunner of *Mutt and Jeff,* made its first appearance, in
        the San Francisco *Chronicle.*

1917 The Bolsheviks took Moscow in the October Revolution. (It was October by the calendar in use at the time in Russia.)

1920 The first meeting of the League of Nations Assembly was held in Geneva.

1926 NBC made its debut with a four-hour radio broadcast from the Waldorf-Astoria Hotel in New York. It had a network of 24 stations.

1935 Manuel Quezon was inaugurated as the first president of the Philippines.

1959 Herbert Clutter, his wife, and his two children were killed in their home in Holcomb, Kansas, by two robbers, creating the basis for Truman Capote's novel, *In Cold Blood.*

1965 Craig Breedlove drove the jet-powered car, *Spirit of America,* 600.601 miles per hour at Bonneville Salt Flats, Utah, becoming the first to break the 600 mph barrier.

1969 A peaceful demonstration against the Vietnam War was staged in Washington, D.C., by 225,000 protesters.

NOVEMBER 16 -- BIRTHDAYS

42 BC **Tiberius** -- Roman emperor, A.D. 14-37, during the adult life of Christ

1766 **Rodolphe Kreutzer** – French composer and virtuoso violinist, to whom Beethoven dedicated his *Sonata in A Major* or *Kreutzer Sonata*

1793 **Francis Danby** -- English painter

1811 **John Bright** -- English orator, reformer, and statesman, who opposed slavery and England's recognition of the Confederacy in the American Civil War

1839 **Louis Honore Frechette** – Canadian poet of the School of Quebec

1873 **W.C. Handy** -- American composer, band leader, and father of the blues, who wrote "St. Louis Blues" and "Memphis Blues"

1886 **Arthur Krock** -- American newspaper columnist

1889 **George S. Kaufman** – American director and playwright, who co-authored the plays, *You Can't Take It With You* (1936) and *The Solid Gold Cadillac* (1952)

1894 **Mabel Normand** -- American actress and comedienne and superstar of the silent era

1895   Paul Hindemith -- One of the most important composers of the
        first half of the 20th century

1896   **Fibber McGee** -- American radio personality of the 1930s
        and 1940s

1896   **Sir Oswald Mosley** – British politician and member of Parliament

1908   **Burgess Meredith** -- American stage, screen, and television
        actor with a career of over 40 years

1919   **Anatoly Dobrynin** -- Russian diplomat and Ambassador to the
        United States

1921   **Ben Weisman** -- American composer and author, noted for
        songs such as "Let Me Go Lover" and "Love in the Afternoon"

1926   **Joan Gardner Janis** -- American composer, author, and actress

1935   **Elizabeth Drew** -- American journalist and author

1941   **Ann McLaughlin** – U.S. Secretary of Labor under President
        Reagan

1944   **Joanna Pettet** -- English-born stage and screen actress

1945   **Martine Van Hamel** -- Dutch ballerina

1946   **Jo Jo White** -- Professional basketball superstar

1953   **Mary Anne Butke** -- Professional golfer

1964   **Dwight Gooden** -- Professional baseball player

1966   **Lisa Bonet** -- American television and motion-picture actress

NOVEMBER 16 -- EVENTS

1272   King Henry III of England died at age 65, eight years after he had
        been deposed by reformers.

1532   Spanish conquistador Francisco Pizarro reached Cajamarca,
        capital of the Inca Empire, where he brought down the empire
        in a 30-minute fight and captured Emperor Atahualpa.

1864   Union general William Tecumseh Sherman started his "March
        to the Sea" from Atlanta in the Civil War.

1882   The Milwaukee *Journal* newspaper was founded.

1901   Three automobile racers in Brooklyn achieved a speed of more
        than a mile a minute, for the first time in history. The fastest,
        Henry Fournier, drove a mile in 51.8 seconds.

1907   Oklahoma was admitted to the Union as the 46th state.

1933   The United States recognized the Communist government of Russia.

1961   Speaker of the House Sam Rayburn died in Bonham, Texas, at age 79. He had served 49 years in Congress and a record 17 years as Speaker.

1969   A moon rock first went on display, at the Museum of Natural History in New York.

NOVEMBER 17 -- BIRTHDAYS

1503   **Il Bronzino** -- Italian Renaissance painter

1587   **Joost van den Vondel** -- Dutch poet and dramatist

1717   **Jean Le Rond d'Alembert** -- French mathematician and scientist, noted for d'Alembert's principle of motion

1755   **Louis XVIII** -- King of France, 1815-1824, known as "the Restoration King" because he ruled after the French Revolution and the execution of his brother, Louis XVI

1788   **Seth Boyden** -- American inventor who in 1819 developed patent leather

1790   **August Ferdinand Mobius** -- German mathematician noted for the Mobius strip and as one of the founders of topology

1793   **Sir Charles Eastlake** -- English painter

1878   **Grace Abbott** -- American pioneer in social work, noted for her part in child labor legislation and in the development of the Social Security Act

1887   **Bernard Law Montgomery** -- British World War II field marshal and hero of the Battle of El Alamein

1901   **Lee Strasberg** – Austrian-born motion-picture actor and director

1904   **Isamu Noguchi** -- American sculptor noted for works such as *The Seed, View Through Kouros,* and *Strange Bird*

1905   **Mischa Auer** -- Russian-born stage and motion-picture actor

1907   **Joe Day** -- Hall of Fame golfer

1912   **Bebe Rebozo** -- Close friend and associate of President Nixon

1923   **Mike Garcia** -- Professional baseball player

1925   **Rock Hudson** -- American motion-picture and television actor and leading man of the 1950s and 1960s

1930   **Bob Mathias** – American track athlete who won the decathlon at the 1948 and 1952 Olympic games

1937   **Peter Cook** -- English actor and irreverent comedian-writer of *Beyond the Fringe* fame

1938   **Gordon Lightfoot** -- Canadian singer and composer

1942   **Martin Scorsese** -- American motion-picture director, noted for films such as *Alice Doesn't Live Here Anymore* (1975)

1943   **Lauren Hutton** – American motion-picture actress and cover girl

1944   **Tom Seaver** -- Professional baseball star pitcher, with over 3,000 career strikeouts

1944   **Danny DeVito** -- American motion-picture and television actor

1945   **Elvin Hayes** -- Professional basketball superstar

1953   **Dino Martin** -- American actor and son of singer Dean Martin

NOVEMBER 17 -- EVENTS

1558   The glorious Elizabethan Age began as Queen Elizabeth I ascended the throne of England.

1603   Sir Walter Raleigh was imprisoned in the Tower of London where he stayed 12 years. The charge was conspiring to overthrow King James I.

1734   John Peter Zenger was arrested in New York and charged with libel in the famous case that gained the first victory for freedom of the press in the American colonies.

1800   The U.S. Congress convened in Washington, D.C., for the first time.

1805   The Lewis and Clark Expedition reached the Pacific Ocean at the mouth of the Columbia River in the Oregon Territory.

1869   The Suez Canal was opened to traffic.

1891   Ignace Paderewski, the great Polish pianist, made his American debut at New York's new Carnegie Hall.

1917   Auguste Rodin, the great French sculptor, died at Meudon at age 77.

1934   Lyndon B. Johnson married Claudia Alta "Lady Bird" Taylor.

1948   The House of Commons voted to nationalize the British steel industry.

1958   The comic strip, *Short Ribs,* by Frank O'Neal, made its first appearance.

NOVEMBER 18 -- BIRTHDAYS

1584   **Gaspar de Crayer** -- Flemish painter

1785   **Sir David Wilkie** -- Scottish painter

1786   **Carl Maria von Weber** -- The first important composer of German romantic opera, noted for works such as *The Freeshooter* (1821)

1787   **Louis Jacques Mande Daguerre** -- French inventor and painter, who perfected the daguerreotype process of making permanent pictures

1810   **Asa Gray** -- American botanist, who was the leading authority of his time on the plant life of the United States

1836   **William S. Gilbert** -- Collaborator with Sir Arthur Sullivan in the Gilbert and Sullivan operas

1860   **Ignace Jan Paderewski** -- Polish pianist, composer, and statesman

1870   **Dorothy Dix** -- Newspaper advice columnist (born Elizabeth Meriwether Gilmer) of the 1930s and 1940s

1871   **Amadeo Vives** -- Spanish composer of some 100 light operas

1874   **Clarence Day** -- American author, noted for *Life with Father* (1935), which was made into one of the most popular plays of the 1940s

1882   **D.B. Wyndham Lewis** -- British essayist, humorist, and biographer, noted for works such as "On Straw and Other Conceits" (1927) and *Emperor of the West, Charles V* (1932)

1899   **Eugene Ormandy** -- Conductor of the Philadelphia Orchestra, 1938-1980

1901   **George Gallup** -- Founder of the Gallup Poll

1908   **Imogene Coca** -- American actress and comedienne

1909   **Johnny Mercer** -- American composer, noted for songs such as "Moon River," "In the Cool, Cool, Cool of the Evening," "I'm an Old Cowhand," "On the Atcheson, Topeka, and Santa Fe," and "Autumn Leaves"

1910   **Francis X. Shields** -- American Hall of Fame tennis player

1918   **Cameron Mitchell** -- American stage, screen, and television actor

1923   **Alan B. Shepard Jr.** -- America's first man in space (May 5, 1961)

1923   **Ted Stevens** -- U.S. senator

1925   **Gene Mauch** -- Professional baseball player and manager

1926   **Dorothy Collins** -- American popular singer

1939   **Brenda Vaccaro** – American stage, screen, and television actress
1942   **Linda Evans** -- American television actress
1962   **Jamie Moyer** -- Professional baseball player

NOVEMBER 18 -- EVENTS

1302   Pope Boniface VIII issued the famous bull *Unam Sanctam,* asserting papal authority in Christian society and declaring everyone to be saved must "be subject to the Roman pontiff."

1820   U.S. sea captain Nathaniel Brown Palmer discovered the continent of Antarctica while searching for new seal-fishing grounds.

1852   The Duke of Wellington's funeral was held in London two months after his death. (The funeral was delayed to await the opening of Parliament.)

1865   Mark Twain's story "The Celebrated Jumping Frog of Calaveras County" first appeared, in the New York *Saturday Press.*

1883   Standard time with four time zones was adopted in the United States.

1886   Chester A. Arthur died in New York City at age 56.

1903   The United States and Panama signed a treaty providing for the Panama Canal.

1905   Haakon VII was elected king of Norway.

1922   Marcel Proust, the great French novelist, died in Paris at age 51 just after completing his monumental work, *Remembrance of Things Past.*

1928   Mickey Mouse, perhaps the most beloved cartoon character of all time, was created by Walt Disney.

1966   U.S. Roman Catholic bishops abolished the rule against eating meat on Fridays.

1978   Over 900 members of the People's Temple, a California-based cult, died in Guyana in a mass suicide-murder.

NOVEMBER 19 -- BIRTHDAYS

1503   **Pier Luigi Farnese** -- First duke of Parma
1600   **Charles I** -- King of England, 1625-1649, who was beheaded for treason in 1649

1616	**Eustache Le Sueur** -- French painter
1752	**George Rogers Clark** -- American frontier military leader who won the Northwest Territory from the British during the Revolutionary War
1770	**Bertel Thorvaldsen** – Denmark's greatest sculptor, whose best-known work is the *Lion of Lucerne,* carved in solid rock in Lucerne, Switzerland
1799	**Rene Auguste Caille** -- First European to survive a journey to Timbuktu
1805	**Ferdinand Marie De Lesseps** – French promoter of the Suez Canal
1831	**James A. Garfield** -- 20th U.S. president
1862	**Billy Sunday** -- Professional baseball player who became one of the most famous evangelists of his time
1891	**Clifton Webb** -- American stage and motion-picture actor
1897	**Bud Green** – Austrian-born lyricist noted for songs such as "Sentimental Journey," "Alabamy Bound," "That's My Weakness Now," and "Flat Foot Floogie"
1899	**Allen Tate** -- American poet, teacher, and novelist
1905	**Tommy Dorsey** -- One of the best-known bandleaders of the Big Band Era of the 1930s and 1940s
1908	**Alan Baxter** -- American motion-picture actor
1917	**Indira Gandhi** -- Prime minister of India for all but three of the years in the period 1966-1984, and daughter of the great Indian nationalist leader Jawaharlal Nehru
1921	**Roy Campanella** -- Hall of Fame baseball player and one of the three or four greatest catchers in the history of the game
1933	**Larry King** -- American broadcaster, newspaper columnist, and host of *The Larry King Show*
1935	**Jerry Gaylon Foster** -- American composer and singer noted for songs such as "Somebody Loves Me"
1936	**Dick Cavett** -- American television entertainer
1938	**Ted Turner** -- American television executive, sportsman, and founder of Cable News Network (CNN)
1942	**Calvin Klein** -- American fashion designer and founder of Calvin Klein Ltd., whose most famous design was his Calvin Klein jeans
1947	**Michael Phipps** -- Professional football player
1947	**Bob Boone** -- Professional baseball player

1947   **Scott Hunter** -- Professional football player
1949   **Ahmad Rashad** -- Professional football player
1951   **Wilbur Jackson** -- Professional football player
1953   **Richard Todd** -- Professional football player
1962   **Jodie Foster** -- American television and motion-picture actress who won the best actress Academy Award in 1989 for *The Accused*

NOVEMBER 19 -- EVENTS

1493   Columbus discovered Puerto Rico on his second voyage to America, and named it San Juan Bautista.
1828   Franz Schubert, the great Austrian composer, died in Vienna at age 31.
1850   Alfred, Lord Tennyson became poet laureate of England, succeeding William Wordsworth.
1863   Abraham Lincoln delivered his famous Gettysburg Address, and "Four score and seven years ago" became part of the American heritage.
1874   The Women's Christian Temperance Union was organized in Cleveland, Ohio.
1919   The Treaty of Versailles, ending World War I, was rejected by the United States Senate.
1942   The Russians counterattacked at Stalingrad, launching their winter offensive against the Russians along the Don River, in World War II.
1959   Ford Motor Company announced its would no longer produce the Edsel.
1969   The *Apollo 12* module, *Intrepid,* landed on the Ocean of Storms of the moon with astronauts Charles Conrad Jr. and Alan Bean, in the second moon landing in history.
1977   Egyptian President Anwar Sadat arrived in Israel on his historic mission to seek peace with the Israelis.

NOVEMBER 20 -- BIRTHDAYS

1602   **Otto von Guericke** -- Mayor of Magdeburg, Prussia, who in the 1640s invented the first air pump

1620   **Peregrine White** – The first English child born in New England, on the *Mayflower* in Cape Cod Bay

1726   **Oliver Wolcott** – Connecticut signer of the Declaration of Independence, army commander in the Revolutionary War, and governor of Connecticut, 1796-1797

1752   **Thomas Chatterton** -- English poet

1761   **Pius VIII** -- Roman Catholic pope, 1829-1830

1841   **Sir Wilfred Laurier** -- First French-Canadian to become prime minister of Canada, 1896-1911

1858   **Selma Lagerlof** – Nobel Prize-winning Swedish novelist, best known for *Gosta Berling's Saga* (1891)

1866   **Kenesaw Mountain Landis** – First commissioner of professional baseball, 1920-1944

1869   **Clark Griffith** – Professional baseball player and longtime owner of the Washington Senators baseball team

1884   **Norman Thomas** -- U.S. social reformer and six times Socialist Party candidate for president

1885   **Albert Kesselring** -- German World War II field marshal who led the German army in the final weeks before the collapse

1890   **Robert Armstrong** – American stage, screen, and television actor with a career of over 40 years

1891   **Jimmy Murphy** -- American cartoonist and creator of *Toots and Casper* (1919)

1891   **Reginald Denny** -- English stage and motion-picture actor who appeared in over 200 films

1900   **Chester Gould** -- American cartoonist and creator of *Dick Tracy* (1931)

1908   **Alistair Cooke** -- English-born American reporter and television narrator

1909   **Alan Bible** -- U.S. senator, 1954-1975

1916   **Judy Canova** -- American actress, singer, and comedienne

1917   **Bobby Locke** -- Professional golfer

1917   **Robert C. Byrd** -- U.S. senator and Majority Senator in the 1970s and 1980s

1920   **Gene Tierney** -- American stage, screen, and television actress

1921   **Phyllis Thaxter** -- American stage and motion-picture actress

1925   **Robert F. Kennedy** -- U.S. senator, attorney general, and brother of President John F. Kennedy

1926   **Kaye Ballard** -- American actress and comedienne

1927   **Estelle Parsons** -- American motion-picture and television actress

1929   **Don January** -- Professional golfer

1932   **Richard Dawson** -- English-born comedian and long-time host of the television game show *Family Feud*

1938   **Dick Smothers** -- One of the two Smothers Brothers, American comedians

1942   **Joseph Biden** -- U.S. senator

1944   **Louie Dampier** -- Professional basketball player

1945   **Jay Johnstone** -- Professional baseball player

1945   **Rick Monday** -- Professional baseball player

1946   **Duane Allman** -- Guitarist with the Allman Brothers musical group

1946   **Judy Woodruff** -- American broadcast journalist

1956   **Bo Derek** -- American motion-picture actress

NOVEMBER 20 -- EVENTS

1541   John Calvin reorganized the church in Geneva with the Presbyterian constitution.

1542   The first of the "New Laws" of Spain was passed to protect native laborers in America from unscrupulous settlers.

1866   The Grand Army of the Republic held its first national encampment at Indianapolis.

1910   Leo Tolstoy, the great Russian novelist, died at the railway station in Astapovo, Russia, at age 82.

1910   The Mexican Revolution of 1910 began, led by Francisco I. Madero.

1914   The United States Department of State first required photographs to be attached to passports.

1940   Hungary joined the Axis powers in World War II.

1943   U.S. marines landed on Tarawa, beginning one of the most savage battles of World War II.

1947   Elizabeth, the future queen of Great Britain, married Philip Mountbatten, formerly Prince Philip of Greece, in Westminster Abbey.

1947   The long-running television show *Meet the Press* first went on the air. It was moderated by Lawrence Spivak until November 1975.

1950   United Nations forces in Korea reached the Manchurian border.

1953   Texas millionaire Hugh Roy Cullen gave over $2 million to the University of Houston because of its 37-7 victory over Baylor.

1967   The United States population reached 200 million.

1975   Spain's Generalissimo Francisco Franco died two weeks before his 83rd birthday, after ruling as a dictator since 1936.

NOVEMBER 21 -- BIRTHDAYS

1495   **John Bale** -- English bishop and author of *Kynge Johan,* the first English history play

1659   **Henry Purcell** – English composer noted for *Dido and Aeneas* (1680), the first English opera, and which contains "Dido's Lament," one of the most beautiful songs of sorrow in opera

1694   **Voltaire (Francois Marie Arouet)** -- French philosopher and writer, who was one of the greatest 18th-century thinkers, and who wrote *Candide* (1759), one of the great works of world literature

1729   **Josiah Bartlett** -- A leading American patriot during the Revolutionary War and one of the New Hampshire signers of the Declaration of Independence

1787   **Sir Samuel Cunard** -- Founder of the Cunard steamship line

1834   **Hetty Green** -- American financier and "Witch of Wall Street," who at the time of her death was the richest woman in the world

1834   **Frederick Weyerhaeuser** -- American lumberman and founder of the Weyerhaeuser timber company in 1870

1889   **Leon Flatow** -- American composer noted for "Popeye the Sailor Man"

1898   **Rene Magritte** – Belgian surrealist painter noted for works such as *Golconda* (1953)

1904   **Coleman "Bean" Hawkins** -- American musician, who was the first important tenor saxophonist in jazz

1905   **Freddie Lindstrom** -- Professional baseball player

1907   **Jim Bishop** -- American newspaper columnist and author

1912   **Eleanor Powell** -- American motion-picture actress and dancer

1916   **Sid Luckman** -- Professional football superstar

1920   **Stan Musial** -- Hall of Fame baseball player and winner of seven batting championships

1920   **Ralph Meeker** -- American stage, screen, and television actor

1921   **Vivian Blaine** -- American actress and singer

1937   **Marlo Thomas** -- American television and motion-picture actress and daughter of actor and singer Danny Thomas

1940   **Natalia Makarova** -- Russian ballerina

1941   **David Hemmings** -- British motion-picture actor

1944   **Earl Monroe** -- Professional basketball superstar

1945   **Goldie Hawn** -- American motion-picture and television actress

NOVEMBER 21 -- EVENTS

235 AD St. Anterus became Roman Catholic pope.

1620   The *Mayflower* arrived at what is now Provincetown Harbor in Massachusetts, and the Mayflower Compact was signed by the Pilgrims on board the ship (November 11, Old Style).

1789   North Carolina ratified the Constitution, becoming the 12th state to do so.

1844   Charles Goodyear patented his rubber vulcanization process.

1864   President Lincoln wrote his famous letter of condolence to Mrs. Lydia Bixby, whose five sons had been killed in battle.

1874   Johann Strauss's operetta *Die Fledermaus* began its first American run, at the Thalia Theater in New York.

1877   Thomas A. Edison announced his invention of the phonograph, which he named a "talking machine."

1922   Rebecca L. Felton of Georgia was sworn in as the first U.S. woman senator. Her term, the unexpired term of the late Senator Thomas E. Watson, ended the next day.

1925   The great Red Grange played his last varsity football game with the University of Illinois before turning professional with the Chicago Bears.

1934   *Anything Goes,* one of Cole Porter's greatest musicals, opened at the Alvin Theater on Broadway.

1942   The Alaska Highway across Canada was formally opened.

1964   The Verrazano-Narrows Bridge between Staten Island and Brooklyn was opened to traffic.

1973 White House attorney Fred Buzhardt revealed the existence of an 18½ minute gap in one of the key Watergate tapes.

NOVEMBER 22 -- BIRTHDAYS

1515 **Mary of Guise** -- Wife of King James V of Scotland

1643 **Robert Cavelier, Sieur de La Salle** -- The greatest French explorer of North America, who claimed the entire Mississippi Valley for France

1744 **Abigail Smith Adams** -- Wife of President John Adams and first hostess of the White House

1808 **Thomas Cook** -- Innovator of conducted tours and founder of Thomas Cook and Son travel agency

1819 **George Eliot (Mary Ann Evans)** -- One of the greatest English novelists of the 19th century, and author of *Middlemarch: A Study of Provincial Life* (1871-1872) and *Silas Marner* (1861)

1842 **Jose Maria de Heredia** -- French poet

1857 **George Robert Gissing** -- English novelist, noted for *New Grub Street* (1891)

1868 **John Nance Garner** -- U.S. vice president under President Franklin D. Roosevelt, 1933-1941

1869 **Andre Gide** -- Nobel Prize-winning French author, noted for works such as *Strait Is the Gate* (1909)

1877 **Endre Ady** -- Greatest Hungarian lyric poet of the 20th century

1890 **Charles de Gaulle** -- The outstanding French patriot, soldier, and statesman of the 20th century

1891 **Edward L. Bernays** -- American publicist considered by many to be the father of public relations

1899 **Wiley Post** -- Pioneer American aviator who was the first man to fly around the world alone, and who piloted the plane in which he and humorist Will Rogers were killed in Alaska in 1935

1899 **Hoagy Carmichael** -- One of America's leading song writers, noted for such classics as "Stardust," "Lazy Bones," "Old Rockin' Chair," "Up the Lazy River," and "Georgia on My Mind"

1901 **Roy Crane** -- American cartoonist and creator of *Captain Easy, Wash Tubbs,* and *Buz Sawyer*

1902   Al J. Neiburg -- American composer and author, noted for songs such as "I'm Confessin' That I Love You" and "It's the Talk of the Town"

1907   **Dick Bartell** -- Professional baseball player

1912   **Doris Duke** – Often-married heiress to the Duke tobacco fortune

1913   Benjamin Britten -- British composer famous for his vocal music, especially his operas, such as *Peter Grimes, Billy Budd,* and *The Turn of the Screw*

1913   **Charles F. Berlitz** -- Language expert and author

1918   **Claiborne Pell** -- U.S. senator

1921   **Rodney Dangerfield** -- American comedian with the byword "I get no respect"

1924   Geraldine Page -- American stage, screen, and television actress

1926   **Lew Burdette** -- Professional baseball player

1935   Michael Callan -- American motion-picture and television actor, dancer, and singer

1938   **Charles Johnson** -- Professional football player

1943   **Billie Jean King** – American tennis superstar and six times women's singles champion at Wimbledon

1950   **Greg Luzinski** -- Professional baseball player

1958   **Jamie Lee Curtis** – American motion-picture actress and daughter of actor Tony Curtis and actress Janet Leigh

1961   **Mariel Hemingway** -- American motion-picture and television actress and granddaughter of writer Ernest Hemingway

1967   **Boris Becker** – German tennis player who by winning the 1985 Wimbledon championship became at 17 the youngest player to win a tennis Grand Slam tournament

NOVEMBER 22 -- EVENTS

1497   Vasco da Gama, the great Portuguese navigator, rounded the Cape of Good Hope on his historic trip to India.

1718   Blackbeard (Edward Teach), the famous British pirate, was caught by the British Navy off the North Carolina coast, and killed by 25 bullet wounds in his body.

1852   French citizens voted to establish the Second French Empire under Emperor Napoleon III.

1880	Lillian Russell, the great American actress, made her vaudeville debut at Tony Pastor's Theater in New York City.
1900	Sir Arthur Sullivan, the noted English operetta composer, died in London at age 58.
1906	The International Radio Telegraphic Convention, meeting in Berlin, adopted the SOS distress signal. SOS does not stand for anything; it was convenient to send by wireless.
1909	Helen Hayes, the great American stage actress, made her New York debut at age 9 in the play, *In Old Dutch,* at the Herald Square Theater.
1935	The first transpacific airmail flight began, as the *China Clipper* left San Francisco for Manila with 100,000 letters.
1942	The comic strip-within-a-strip, "Fearless Fosdick," by Al Capp, first appeared in *Li'l Abner.*
1943	President Roosevelt, Prime Minister Churchill, and Generalissimo Chiang Kai-shek opened the Cairo Conference in Egypt.
1963	President John F. Kennedy was shot at 12:30 P.M. in Dallas, Texas, while riding in a caravan in an open-top automobile. He died at 1 P.M.
1975	Juan Carlos I was installed King of Spain, two days after the death of dictator Francisco Franco.
1980	Mae West, one of the most famous American actresses, died at age 88.

NOVEMBER 23 -- BIRTHDAYS

912 AD	**Otto I (the Great)** -- King of Germany, A.D. 936-983, who was the first king to become Holy Roman Emperor (A.D. 961)
1608	**Francisco Manuel de Melo** -- Portuguese soldier, diplomat, and poet
1616	**John Wallis** -- English mathematician who contributed to the origins of calculus
1749	**Edward Rutledge** -- Member of the Continental Congress, governor of South Carolina (1798-1800), and signer of the Declaration of Independence
1804	**Franklin Pierce** -- 14th U.S. president
1834	**James Thomson** -- English Victorian poet

1859   **Billy the Kid (William H. Bonney)** -- Notorious outlaw of the American West

1862   **Sir Gilbert Parker** -- Canadian novelist

1876   **Manuel de Falla** -- Spanish composer, noted for works such as the ballet, *The Three Cornered Hat* (1919), one of the finest works of contemporary Spanish music

1878   **Holcombe Ward** -- American tennis player and U.S. Singles Champion in 1904

1878   **Ernest J. King** -- American fleet admiral, who, as commander-in-chief of the U.S. Navy in World War II, directed the greatest naval fleet in history

1883   **Jose Clemente Orozco** -- One of Mexico's greatest and best-known painters

1887   **Boris Karloff** -- English-born American actor with a 50-year career of some 140 films, the most notable of which was *Frankenstein,* in 1931

1888   **Harpo Marx** -- American comedian and the member of the Marx Brothers comedy group who always pretended to be mute

1896   **Ruth Etting** -- American singer, actress, and pioneer radio and recording star of the 1920s and 1930s

1902   **Victor Jory** -- American stage and motion-picture actor who typically played evil-eyed heavy roles in a career of over 40 years

1910   **Hal Schumacher** -- Professional baseball player

1915   **Ellen Drew** -- American motion-picture actress and leading lady of the 1940s and 1950s

1923   **Art Wall Jr.** -- Professional golfer with a record 41 career holes-in-one

1927   **Otis Chandler** -- Publisher of the Los Angeles *Times*

1930   **William E. Brock** -- U.S. senator and Secretary of Labor under President Reagan

1934   **Lew Hoad** -- Australian tennis superstar and Wimbledon singles champion, 1956-1957

1940   **Luis Tiant** -- Professional baseball player

1947   **Toshiro Sakai** -- Japanese tennis player

NOVEMBER 23 -- EVENTS

1644   John Milton, the great English poet, published his greatest prose work, "Areopagitica," a defense of freedom of the press.

1774   Massachusetts began organizing the Minutemen, so called because they were prepared to fight "at a minute's notice."

1863   The Battle of Chattanooga began and resulted two days later in Union control of Tennessee in the Civil War.

1876   Harvard, Yale, Princeton, and Columbia formed the American Intercollegiate Football Association, the first college football conference.

1903   Enrico Caruso, the great Italian tenor, made his American debut in *Rigoletto* at the Metropolitan Opera House in New York.

1940   The Greeks drove the last of the Italian invaders from their country in World War II.

1940   Romania joined the Axis powers in World War II.

1942   Congress established SPARS, the U.S. Coast Guard Women's Reserve. The name SPAR came from the first letters of the motto and its translation, Semper Paratus (Always Ready).

1943   U.S. marines captured Tarawa after one of the bloodiest battles of World War II.

1960   U.S. weather satellite *Tiros 2* was launched.

1971   The People's Republic of China was seated in the U.N. Security Council.

1980   President Jimmy Carter warned the Iranians of "extremely grave" consequences if any of the American hostages in the American embassy in Teheran were harmed.

NOVEMBER 24 -- BIRTHDAYS

1391   **Charles of Valois-Orleans** — Duke of Orleans and one of the greatest poets of France

1632   **Baruch Spinoza** -- One of the greatest Dutch philosophers of the 17th century (also known as Benedict Spinoza)

1655   **Charles XI** -- King of Sweden, 1660-1697

1713   **Laurence Sterne** -- English clergyman who became famous for the novel *The Life and Opinions of Tristram Shandy, Gentleman* (1760-1767)

1713   **Father Junipero Serra** -- Franciscan missionary who in 1769 founded the first mission in California (then called Upper California)

1784   Zachary Taylor -- American hero of the Mexican War and 12th U.S. president

1815   **Grace Darling** -- English heroine who saved nine survivors of a shipwreck off the English coast on September 7, 1838

1848   **Lilli Lehmann** -- German operatic soprano and leading member of the Berlin Royal Opera and the Metropolitan Opera Company of New York

1849   **Frances Eliza Hodgson Burnett** -- English-born American author noted for the novel, *Little Lord Fauntleroy* (1886)

1853   **Bat Masterson** -- Noted lawman of the American West

1864   **Henri de Toulouse-Lautrec** -- French painter noted for his lively pictures of Paris nightlife and for his lithographs and posters

1868   **Scott Joplin** – American composer and performer of ragtime music, credited with the first ragtime opera, *A Guest of Honor* (1903)

1875   **Ed Rose** -- American lyricist noted for songs such as "Baby Shoes" and "Oh Johnny, Oh Johnny, Oh"

1877   **Alben W. Barkley** – U.S. vice president under President Truman

1887   **Erich von Manstein** -- German World War II field marshal

1890   **George E. Stratemeyer** -- American World War II general

1896   **Corinne Griffith** – American motion-picture actress and "the world's most beautiful woman" in the silent screen era

1897   **"Lucky" Luciano** -- Notorious American racketeer

1905   **Harry Barris** -- American composer noted for songs such as "Mississippi Mud" and "Wrap Your Troubles in Dreams"

1911   **Joe "Ducky" Medwick** -- Hall of Fame baseball player with a .324 lifetime batting average

1914   **Geraldine Fitzgerald** – Irish-born stage and motion-picture actress with a career of some 50 years

1917   **Howard Duff** -- American motion-picture and television actor

1921   **John V. Lindsay** -- Mayor of New York City, 1966-1974

1923   **Scott Meredith** -- American literary agent

1925   **William F. Buckley Jr.** – American columnist, author, and television show host

1930   **Bob Friend** -- Professional baseball player

1938   **Oscar Robertson** -- One of professional basketball's greatest players, known as the "Big O"

1943	**Dave Bing** -- Professional basketball player
1948	**Steve Yeager** -- Professional baseball player
1948	**Rudy Tomjanovich** -- Professional basketball player

NOVEMBER 24 -- EVENTS

1564	Pope Pius IV published the *Index of Prohibited Books.*
1642	Abel Janszoon Tasman, the famous Dutch navigator, discovered the island of Tasmania.
1655	Use of the *Book of Common Prayer* was prohibited in England by Oliver Cromwell.
1832	South Carolina passed the Ordinance of Nullification, declaring the federal tariff statute null and void. (The ordinance was rescinded in March 1833.)
1859	Adelina Patti, the great operatic soprano, made her world debut in *Lucia di Lammermoor* at the Academy of Music in New York City.
1859	Charles Darwin, the famous evolutionist, published his book, *The Origin of Species.*
1874	Barbed wire was patented by its inventor, Joseph F. Glidden, of De Kalb, Illinois.
1918	The comic strip, *Gasoline Alley,* by Frank King, first appeared.
1944	U.S. Air Force B-29 superfortress bombers raided Tokyo from Saipan for the first time.
1947	The Hollywood 10, screenwriters and officials, were cited for contempt of Congress for refusing to say if they were Communists. They were later blacklisted and imprisoned.
1969	*Apollo 12* splashed down in the Pacific, returning from the second manned trip to the moon.
1971	A skyjacker calling himself D.B. Cooper leaped from a Boeing 727 with $200,000 and a parachute, in the most successful skyjacking of all time. Cooper was never found.

NOVEMBER 25 -- BIRTHDAYS

| 1562 | **Lope de Vega** -- The most important playwright of Spain's Golden Age, who wrote more plays (at least 400 with estimates up to 2200) than any other author in history |

1609   Henrietta Marie -- French wife of King Charles I of England

1835   **Andrew Carnegie** -- American steel industrialist and philanthropist, noted for founding the Carnegie Corporation of New York and Carnegie Technical Schools (now Carnegie-Mellon University)

1844   **Karl Benz** -- German automobile pioneer who designed and built the world's first practical automobile powered by an internal combustion engine and who founded Benz and Company

1846   **Carry Nation** – American temperance advocate famous for her hatchet attacks on barrooms

1870   **Maurice Denis** -- French painter

1874   **Joe Gans** -- World lightweight boxing champion, 1902-1908, known as the "Old Master"

1881   **John XXIII** -- Roman Catholic pope, 1958-1963, who called the Second Vatican Council (1962)

1890   **Isaac Rosenberg** -- English poet

1893   **Joseph Wood Krutch** – American writer, drama critic, and teacher

1895   **Anastas Ivanovich Mikoyan** -- First vice premier of Russia, and Russian president, 1964-1965

1895   **Ludvick Svoboda** -- Czech national hero of the two World Wars, and president of Czechoslovakia, 1968-1975, after the crushing by Russia of the 1968 Czech revolt

1896   **Virgil Thomson** -- American composer and critic, who won the 1949 Pulitzer Prize for the music for the movie *Louisiana Story*

1899   **W.R. Burnett** -- American novelist and screenwriter, noted for scripts such as *Little Caesar, High Sierra,* and *The Asphalt Jungle*

1900   **Helen Gahagan Douglas** -- Broadway leading lady and opera singer of the 1920s and 1930s, and U.S. congresswoman, 1945-1949

1900   **Arthur Schwartz** – American popular music composer and motion-picture producer

1914   **Joe DiMaggio** – One of the greatest outfielders in baseball history, with a record 56 game hitting streak in 1941

1919   **Steve Brodie** -- American motion-picture actor

1920   **Ricardo Montalban** -- Mexican-born motion-picture and television actor

1927	**Jeffrey Hunter** -- American motion-picture actor
1933	**Kathryn Grant** -- American motion-picture actress and wife of singer Bing Crosby
1945	**John McVie** -- English musician with the Fleetwood Mac musical group
1951	**Bucky Dent** -- Professional baseball player
1960	**John F. Kennedy Jr.** -- Son of President Kennedy

NOVEMBER 25 -- EVENTS

1277	Nicholas III was elected Roman Catholic pope.
1780	The British frigate *Hussar* sank in New York Harbor with 900,000 gold guineas aboard. (There is no record that it was ever recovered.)
1783	The last British redcoats in the United States left New York City after the Revolutionary War.
1795	William Henry Harrison married Anna Symmes.
1851	The first YMCA branches were organized in North America, at Montreal and Boston.
1899	The Baghdad Railway Commission was signed, giving a German company the right to build a railway from Constantinople to Baghdad to Basra.
1903	Bob Fitzsimmons became the first to win three different boxing championships, defeating George Gardner for the light heavyweight title.
1907	Mary Garden, the great American singing actress, made her American debut in *Thais* at the Manhattan Opera House in New York.
1920	Station WTAW, College Station, Texas, broadcast the first play-by-play radio account of a football game, between the University of Texas and Texas A & M.
1921	Hirohito became regent five years before becoming emperor of Japan.
1955	Bill Haley's "Rock Around the Clock" topped the United Kingdom's singles chart, the first rock and roll record to do so.
1963	President John F. Kennedy was buried at Arlington National Cemetery.

NOVEMBER 26 -- BIRTHDAYS

1607   John Harvard -- American minister and philanthropist for whom Harvard University was named

1731   **William Cowper** -- English poet, noted for works such as "The Olney Hymns" (1779) and "The Task" (1785)

1858   **Israel Abrahams** -- British Jewish scholar

1861   **Albert B. Fall** -- Secretary of the Interior under President Harding, who was sent to prison for accepting bribes in the notorious Teapot Dome Scandal

1866   Hugh Duffy -- Professional baseball player who hit .438 in 1894, the highest ever under the current rules

1879   **Charles W. Goddard** -- Author of *Perils of Pauline*

1894   **Norbert Wiener** -- American mathematician and logician, and founder of cybernetics

1895   **Bill W. (William Griffith Wilson)** -- Co-founder with Dr. Bob of Alcoholics Anonymous (1935)

1900   **Bruno Richard Hauptmann** -- Convicted kidnapper and murderer of Charles A. Lindbergh's infant son in 1932

1905   **Emlyn Williams** -- Welsh actor, playwright, screenwriter, and director

1909   **Lefty Gomez** -- Hall of Fame baseball pitcher who had a career won-lost percentage of .649

1911   **Samuel Herman Reshevsky** -- American chess master and one of the greatest players of the 20th century

1912   **Eugene Ionesco** -- Romanian-born French dramatist, noted for works such as *The Bald Soprano* (1948) and *The Pedestrian in the Air* (1962)

1912   Eric Severeid -- Influential American newscaster and commentator

1916   **Bob Elliott** -- Professional baseball player

1919   Frank Fletcher -- American cartoonist who continued the comic strip *Bringing Up Father* (Sunday page) when its creator, George McManus, died in 1954

1922   Charles Schulz -- American cartoonist and creator of *Peanuts,* one of the most successful of all American comic strips

1924   George Segal -- American sculptor noted for his realistic, life-size plaster figures

1925	**Eugene Istomin** -- American virtuoso pianist
1933	**Robert Goulet** -- American singer and actor
1938	**Tina Turner** -- American singer
1938	**Rich Little** -- Canadian-born impressionist and actor
1942	**Jan Stenerud** -- Professional football player
1947	**Larry Gura** -- Professional baseball player
1947	**Richie Hebner** -- Professional baseball player
1947	**Roger Wehrli** -- Professional football player
1952	**Wendy Turnbull** -- Australian tennis player

NOVEMBER 26 -- EVENTS

885 AD Danish Vikings attacked Paris and were paid by the Frankish emperor Charles the Fat not to destroy the city as they had in A.D. 845 and 856.

1789 The first national Thanksgiving Day was proclaimed by President Washington to observe the adoption of the U.S. Constitution. It was made an annual event in 1863.

1825 The first collegiate social fraternity, Kappa Alpha, was organized at Union College in Schenectady, New York.

1864 Edwin Booth, the great American actor, opened his run of Shakespeare's *Hamlet* at the Winter Garden Theater in New York.

1894 Nicholas II, the last czar of Russia, married Alexandra of Hesse.

1922 Howard Carter first saw inside the tomb of Tutankhamen at Luxor in Egypt's Valley of the Kings, making one of the greatest archaeological discoveries in history.

1928 The comic strip, *Jane Arden,* by Monte Barrett and Frank Ellis, first appeared.

1941 Secretary of State Cordell Hull submitted American proposals to the Japanese "peace" envoys in Washington, D.C., less than two weeks before the Japanese attacked Pearl Harbor.

1950 Communist China entered the Korean War, opening a great offensive against United Nations troops, forcing a general retreat.

1973 Rose Mary Woods, President Nixon's personal secretary, told a federal court she had mistakenly caused the 18½ minute gap in one of the key Watergate tapes.

NOVEMBER 27 -- BIRTHDAYS

1701   **Anders Celsius** – Swedish astronomer who in 1742 devised the Celsius, or centigrade, temperature scale

1746   **Robert Livingston** – American statesman who helped draw up the Declaration of Independence, administered the oath of office to George Washington, and negotiated the Louisiana Purchase

1865   **Jose Asuncion Silva** -- Colombian poet

1874   **Chaim Weizmann** -- First president of Israel, 1949-1952

1874   **Charles A. Beard** -- Noted American historian and author

1884   **Jose de Creeft** -- American sculptor

1901   **Ted Husing** -- American sports announcer

1909   **James Agee** -- American novelist and scriptwriter, noted for the Pulitzer Prize-winning novel, *A Death in the Family* (1957), and for movie scripts such as *The African Queen*

1912   **David Merrick** -- American Broadway producer of such hits as *Hello, Dolly!*

1921   **Alexander Dubcek** – Czech leader whose liberal reforms alarmed the Russians and led to the Russian occupation of Czechoslovakia in 1968

1925   **Marshall Thompson** -- American motion-picture and television actor

1937   **Gail Sheehy** -- American journalist and author, noted for the best-selling book *Passages*

1939   **Dave Giusti** -- Professional baseball player

1940   **Bruce Lee** -- American motion-picture and television actor

1942   **Jimi Hendrix** -- American guitarist and singer

1949   **Jim Price** -- Professional basketball player

1950   **Donald Strock** -- Professional football player

1952   **Ike Harris** -- Professional football player

1956   **Curtis Dickey** -- Professional football player

1957   **Caroline Kennedy** -- Daughter of President John F. Kennedy

1958   **Mike Scioscia** -- Professional baseball player

NOVEMBER 27 -- EVENTS

8 BC Horace (Quintus Horatius Flaccus), the great Roman lyric poet, died at Venusia, in Apulia, at age 56.

1095 Pope Urban II addressed the Council of Clermont, calling for the first Crusade to deliver the Holy Land from the Moslems.

1582 William Shakespeare and Anne Hathaway were issued a marriage license. He was eighteen and she was twenty-six.

1875 The Hoosac Tunnel, the first long railroad tunnel in America, was completed through the Berkshire Hills in western Massachusetts.

1889 Curtis P. Brady received the first permit to drive a car through New York's Central Park, contingent on his not "frightening horses" in the park.

1901 The Army War College, the highest educational institution of the U.S. Army, was founded in Washington, D.C. It was moved to Carlisle Barracks, Pennsylvania, in 1951.

1910 Pennsylvania Station, the largest railway terminal in the world at the time, opened in New York City.

1942 The French fleet at Toulon was scuttled by its crews to keep the Germans from taking it in World War II.

1945 General George C. Marshall was dispatched to China by President Truman to try to reconcile the Nationalists and the Communists.

1953 Eugene O'Neill, America's great playwright, died in Boston at age 65.

1970 Diego Velasquez's *Portrait of Juan de Pareja* sold at auction at Christie's in London for $5,544,000, a record price for a painting.

1973 The U.S. Senate voted 92-3 to confirm Gerald R. Ford to succeed Spiro Agnew as vice president.

NOVEMBER 28 -- BIRTHDAYS

1632 Jean Baptiste Lully -- Italian-born French composer, who wrote the first significant French operas, and influenced the work of Johann Sebastian Bach and George Frederick Handel

1757 **William Blake** -- Brilliant, unconventional English poet and painter, noted for such works as "Tyger! Tyger! burning bright"

1793 **Karl Jonas Ludvig Almqvist** -- One of the most prolific of all Swedish writers

1820   Friedrich Engels -- German social scientist, journalist, and pro-
       fessional revolutionary, noted for his close collaboration with
       communist Karl Marx

1829   **Anton Gregor Rubenstein** – Russian composer and one of the
       greatest pianists of the 19th century

1832   **Sir Leslie Stephen** – English essayist, biographer, critic, and editor

1866   **David Warfield** -- Noted American stage actor

1880   **Alexander Alexandrovich Blok** -- Russian poet and dramatist

1881   **Stefan Zweig**-- Austrian poet and novelist, noted for novels such
       as *Amok* (1922) and biographies such as *Marie Antoinette* (1932)

1887   **Ernst Rohm** -- Organizer of Adolf Hitler's SA (storm troops)

1894   **Brooks Atkinson** -- American journalist, author, and critic

1895   **Jose Iturbi** – Spanish-born American conductor and piano virtuoso

1904   **James O. Eastland** -- U.S. senator from the 1940s through
       the 1970s

1912   **Morris Louis** -- American painter

1925   **Gloria Grahame** – American stage, screen, and television ac-
       tress with a 40-year career

1929   **Berry Gordy** -- American songwriter and founder of Motown
       Records

1931   **Hope Lange** – American motion-picture and television actress

1936   **Gary Hart** – U.S. senator and candidate in 1984 and 1988 for the
       nomination of the Democratic Party for president

1942   **Paul Warfield** -- Professional football superstar

1948   **Romana Guerrant** -- American tennis player

1953   **Sixto Lezcano** -- Professional baseball player

1958   **Dave Righetti** -- Professional baseball player

NOVEMBER 28 -- EVENTS

1520   Ferdinand Magellan entered the Pacific Ocean after a month in
       the Strait of Magellan on his voyage around the world. He gave
       the new ocean the name Pacific because it was so calm.

1582   William Shakespeare married Anne Hathaway at Stratford-on-
       Avon.

1678   Catherine of Braganza, wife of England's King Charles II, was
       accused of treason for having no children.

1680 Gian Lorenzo Bernini, Italian sculptor who designed the great plaza of St. Peter's Church in Rome, died at age 82.

1780 Maria Theresa, Empress of Austria and Hungary, died at age 63.

1859 Washington Irving, one of America's greatest early writers, died in Sunnyside, New York, at age 76.

1863 The U.S. celebrated the first Thanksgiving Day set aside by President Lincoln's proclamation of October 3, 1863.

1895 J. Frank Duryea won the first gasoline-automobile race in America, between Chicago's Jackson Park and Evanston, Ind., averaging 7 mph in a car he and his brother Charles built.

1919 American-born Lady Astor was elected the first woman member of the British Parliament.

1929 Richard E. Byrd began his famous flight across the South Pole. On the next day he and his pilot would become the first men to fly over the pole.

1942 The Cocoanut Grove nightclub in Boston burned, with nearly 500 people losing their lives. Among them was the famous cowboy actor Buck Jones.

1943 The Tehran Conference of World War II began with President Roosevelt, Prime Minister Churchill, and Premier Stalin in attendance.

NOVEMBER 29 -- BIRTHDAYS

1781 **Andres Bello** -- South American poet and scholar

1797 **Gaetano Donizetti** -- Italian operatic composer, noted for works such as *Lucia di Lammermoor* (1835) and *Don Pasquale* (1843)

1803 **Christian Doppler** — German physicist who discovered the Doppler effect, which is the apparent change in the frequency of sound or light waves caused by motion

1811 **Wendell Phillips** -- American orator, reformer, and famous crusader for abolition in the pre-Civil War period

1816 **Morrison Remick Waite** -- Seventh chief justice of the U.S. Supreme Court, 1874-1888

1832 **Louisa May Alcott** -- American writer noted for *Little Women,* one of the best-loved stories in American literature

1849 **Sir Ambrose Fleming** -- British scientist noted for inventing the diode vacuum tube (1904)

1875   Stanley Murphy -- Irish-born lyricist noted for songs such as "Put On Your Old Gray Bonnet" and "Be My Little Baby Bumble Bee"

1895   **Busby Berkeley** -- American choreographer and director with a 50-year movie career

1895   **William V.S. Tubman** -- President of Liberia, 1943-1971

1895   **Yakima Canutt** -- American actor and stuntman, whose exploits became legendary

1897   **John Alexander** -- American stage and motion-picture actor

1898   **C.S. Lewis** -- British author of over 30 science fiction, religion, and fantasy literature books

1911   **Walter Kent** -- American composer and author, noted for songs such as "I'll Be Home for Christmas," "The White Cliffs of Dover," and "Come Rain Come Shine"

1917   **Merle Travis** -- American guitarist

1922   **Minnie Minoso** -- Professional baseball player who came back after many years of retirement when he was in his fifties, making him the oldest player in major league history

1923   **Frank Reynolds** -- American broadcast journalist

1928   **Paul Simon** -- U.S. senator and candidate for the Democratic nomination for president in 1988

1933   **John Mayall** -- British blues musician

1933   **David Reuben** -- American author, noted for *Everything You Always Wanted to Know About Sex*

1933   **James Rosenquist** -- American painter

1934   **Willie Morris** -- American writer and novelist

1940   **Chuck Mangione** -- American composer and rock and jazz musician

1947   **Joe Inman** -- Professional golfer

1950   **Mike Easler** -- Professional baseball player

1960   **Howard Johnson** -- Professional baseball player

NOVEMBER 29 -- EVENTS

1226   Louis IX (Saint Louis) assumed the throne of France.

1314   King Philip IV of France died at age 46 after a reign of 29 years.

1515   After a disastrous war for the Swiss, a pact of "perpetual peace" was signed between France and Switzerland.

1516   Giovanni Bellini, the noted Italian painter, died in Venice at age 66.

1643   Claudio Monteverdi, the great Italian composer, died in Venice at age 76.

1887   Josef Hoffmann, the noted Polish pianist, made his American debut at the Metropolitan Opera House in New York.

1890   The first Army-Navy football game was played at West Point, with Navy winning, 24-0.

1924   Giacomo Puccini, the great Italian opera composer, died in Brussels of throat cancer at age 65.

1929   Commander Richard E. Byrd completed the first flight over the South Pole.

1932   Cole Porter's song, "Night and Day," was first publicly sung at the Ethel Barrymore Theater in New York.

1945   Yugoslavia became a republic as Marshal Tito abolished the monarchy.

1947   The United Nations voted to end British control of Palestine and divide the country into an Israeli state and an Arab state.

1952   President-elect Dwight D. Eisenhower went to Korea to observe the war effort there, keeping a campaign promise he had made.

1963   President Lyndon B. Johnson appointed a commission headed by Supreme Court Chief Justice Earl Warren to investigate the assassination of President John F. Kennedy.

NOVEMBER 30 -- BIRTHDAYS

1466   **Andrea Doria** – Genoese statesman and foremost naval leader of his time

1508   **Andrea Palladio** – Italian Renaissance architect whose work inspired Thomas Jefferson in the design of Monticello

1554   **Sir Philip Sidney** – Author, courtier, and soldier during the reign of Queen Elizabeth I of England, whose greatest work is *Astrophel and Stella* (in the early 1580s)

1636   **Adriaen van de Velde** -- Dutch painter

1667   **Jonathan Swift** -- English author, churchman, and the greatest satirist in the English language, whose book, *Gulliver's Travels* (1726), is a masterpiece of world literature

1809   **Mark Lemon** – English publisher and founder of *Punch* Magazine

1810   **Oliver Fisher Winchester** -- Developer of the Winchester rifle

1817   **Theodor Mommsen** – Nobel Prize-winning German historian, noted for his monumental work, *History of Rome* (1854-1856)

1819   **Cyrus W. Field** -- American financier who promoted the first telegraph cable across the Atlantic Ocean, between Ireland and Newfoundland (1857-1866)

1825   **Adolphe William Bouguereau** -- French painter noted for works such as *The Proposal* (1872)

1835   **Mark Twain (born Samuel Langhorne Clemens)** -- The greatest humorist in American literature, and creator of *Tom Sawyer* and *Huckleberry Finn*

1874   **Sir Winston Churchill** -- British World War II prime minister and one of the greatest statesmen in world history

1889   **Edgar Douglas Adrian** -- British electrophysiologist noted for nerve cell discoveries

1898   **Firpo Marberry** -- Professional baseball player

1907   **Jacques Barzun** -- American teacher, historian, and author, noted for works such as *Teacher in America* (1945)

1920   **Virginia Mayo** – Glamorous beauty of Hollywood films of the 1940s and 1950s

1923   **Efrem Zimbalist Jr.** -- American motion-picture and television actor

1924   **Allan Sherman** -- American comedian

1924   **Shirley Chisholm** -- The first black woman to serve in the U.S. Congress (1969)

1926   **Richard Crenna** -- American motion-picture and television actor

1929   **Dick Clark** -- American television host, producer, and actor

1930   **G. Gordon Liddy** – American government official, writer, and Watergate figure

1932   **Robert Vaughn** – American motion-picture and television actor

1936   **Abbie Hoffman** – American revolutionary and leader of the Yippies in the 1960s

1937   **Richard Threlkeld** -- American broadcast journalist

1945   **Roger Glover** – Welsh singer with the Deep Purple musical group

1947   **David Mamet** -- American playwright

1949   **Jim Chones** -- Professional basketball player

1950   **Paul Westphal** -- Professional basketball player

1952   **Steve McCullum** -- Professional football player
1955   **Clarence Harmon** -- Professional football player
1955   **Billy Idle** -- British rock singer
1962   **Bo Jackson** -- Professional baseball and football player

NOVEMBER 30 -- EVENTS

70 AD   Saint Andrew, one of the Twelve Disciples of Christ, was mar-
        tyred on an X-shaped cross during the reign of Vespasian. The
        day is celebrated as St. Andrew's feast day.

1016   England's King Edmund Ironside was murdered at age 26,
        resulting in King Canute's ascending the throne of England and
        Denmark.

1290   John de Baliol was crowned King of Scotland, following the
        death of seven-year-old Queen Margaret, who had succeeded
        her grandfather, King Alexander III.

1628   John Bunyan, the future great English author of *The Pilgrim's
        Progress,* was baptized. He was probably born three days earlier.

1700   Charles XII, Sweden's great king, defeated the Russians at
        Narva in a half hour and took 6,000 prisoners.

1782   The Americans and British signed a preliminary peace treaty in
        Paris, ending the Revolutionary War.

1900   Oscar Wilde, the noted Irish writer, died in France at age 46,
        penniless and in debt, but with his wit intact. "I am dying beyond
        my means," he said on his deathbed.

1905   Japan took Port Arthur in northern China after winning the
        Russo-Japanese War.

1922   Sarah Bernhardt, the great French actress, made her last ap-
        pearance, playing in *Daniel* in Turin, Italy.

1939   Russian troops invaded Finland in violation of a nonaggression
        pact between the two countries.

1940   Lucille Ball and Desi Arnaz, the popular film entertainers,
        eloped to Greenwich, Connecticut.

1949   The Chinese Communists captured the Chinese Nationalists'
        World War II capital of Chungking in the Chinese Civil War.

1956   Floyd Patterson knocked out Archie Moore in the 5th round in
        Chicago to win the heavyweight boxing title.

1967   South Yemen gained its independence from Britain.

12

December

December is the twelfth month of the year, but its name comes from the Latin *Decembris*, meaning *tenth*. The name was appropriate when December was added to the Roman calendar by Romulus, since at the time it was the tenth and last month. Romulus gave the month 30 days, which was changed to 29 when Numa Pompilius issued his calendar. In the Julian Calendar, December had 30 days, and when Augustus adjusted the calendar he gave it its present 31 days. The emperor Commodus tried to change the name of the month to *Amazonius* in honor of his mistress, who he said had once been painted as an Amazon. This attempt, as well as a number of others, failed to catch on, and December, though mis-named, is still with us.

Christmas is doubtless the most famous holiday of December, and the important Jewish holiday of Hanukkah often also occurs in the month. Other special days are December 6, when many Europeans celebrate the Feast of Saint Nicholas and exchange gifts, Forefathers' Day on December 21, commemorating the landing of the Pilgrims at Plymouth Rock on that date in 1620, and, of course, New Year's Eve on December 31. Also, three American Presidents, Martin Van Buren, Andrew Johnson and Woodrow Wilson, were born in December.

The birthstones of December are the turquoise and the zircon, and the special flower is the poinsettia. Notable birthdays and events of December are as follows.

DECEMBER 1 -- BIRTHDAYS

1716   **Etienne Maurice Falconet** -- French sculptor

1761   **Marie Gresholtz Tussaud** -- Swiss modeler in wax, who in 1802 founded Madame Tussaud's Exhibition, the famous wax museum in London

1792   **Nikolai Lobachevsky** -- Russian mathematician who invented non-Euclidean geometry (simultaneously with, but independently of, Polish mathematician Janos Bolyai)

1844   **Princess Alexandra** -- Daughter of King Christian IX of Denmark and wife of King Edward VII of England

1876   **George Creel** -- American author and newspaperman

1877   **Rex Beach** -- Prominent American author of Western novels

1886   **Rex Stout** -- American detective-story writer, noted for the Nero Wolfe mysteries

1896   **Ray Henderson** -- American composer, author, and pianist, noted for songs such as "Alabamy Bound," "Button Up Your Overcoat," "Sonny Boy," "Bye Bye Blackbird," and "Life Is Just a Bowl of Cherries"

1899   **Robert Welch** -- Founder of the John Birch Society

1910   **Dame Alicia Markova** -- The first great English ballerina

1911   **Walter Alston** -- Manager of the Brooklyn and Los Angeles Dodgers baseball team for 22 years

1912   **Cookie Lavagetto** -- Professional baseball player

1913   **Mary Martin** -- One of the major talents of the American musical stage, motion-picture actress, and mother of actor Larry Hagman

1917   **Marty Marion** -- Professional baseball player

1923   **Stansfield Turner** -- Director of the CIA under President Carter

1923   **Dick Shawn** -- American comedian and comic actor noted for such roles as Adolf Hitler in Mel Brook's spoof, *The Producers*

1933   **Violette Verdy** -- French ballerina

1935   **Woody Allen** -- American motion-picture actor, director, screenwriter, playwright, and jazz clarinetist

1935   **Lou Rawls** -- American soul singer and motion-picture actor

1939   **Lee Trevino** -- Professional golfer

1939   **Dianne Lennon** -- One of the singing Lennon Sisters

1940   **Richard Pryor** -- American actor and comedian

1944   **John Densmore** – American drummer with the Doors musical group
1945   **Bette Midler** -- American singer and actress
1946   **Gilbert O'Sullivan** -- Irish pop singer and songwriter
1948   **Ian Fletcher** -- Australian tennis player
1948   **George Foster** -- Professional baseball player
1960   **Carol Alt** -- American model, noted cover girl, and actress

DECEMBER 1 -- EVENTS

1455   Lorenzo Ghiberti, noted Italian sculptor and goldsmith, died in Florence at age 77.
1648   The English army seized King Charles I and turned him over to Parliament for trial. He was executed the following year.
1822   Pedro I, son of King John VI of Portugal, became emperor of Brazil.
1824   The electoral college vote resulted in no presidential candidate receiving a majority in the 1824 election. The U.S. House of Representatives later chose John Quincy Adams.
1878   The first telephone was installed in the White House.
1909   The first Christmas Club saving plan was introduced by a bank, the Carlisle Trust Company, in Carlisle, Pennsylvania.
1913   The first drive-in automobile service station was opened, in Pittsburgh.
1917   Father Edward Joseph Flanagan founded Boys Town near Omaha, Nebraska.
1919   Lady Nancy Astor, American-wife of Waldorf Astor, became the first woman to serve in the British Parliament, succeeding her husband in the House of Commons.
1924   The first performance of George Gershwin's *Lady Be Good* was given at the Liberty Theater in New York, starring Fred and Adele Astaire.
1939   La Guardia Airport in New York was opened to the public.
1943   The Tehran Conference ended with a communique expressing Allied determination to destroy the German armies in World War II.
1955   Rosa Parks, a black woman, sat on a front bus seat usually reserved for whites in Montgomery, Ala., which started the civil rights movement led by Dr. Martin Luther King Jr.

DECEMBER 2 -- BIRTHDAYS

1694   **William Shirley** -- Colonial governor of Massachusetts, 1741-1756

1825   **Pedro II** -- Second and last emperor of Brazil, 1841-1889

1859   **Georges Seurat** -- Noted French artist who developed *pointillism,* a system of painting using uniform-sized dots side by side instead of brushstrokes

1863   **Charles Ringling** -- One of the Ringling brothers who built a small troupe of performers into the world's largest circus

1884   **Ruth Draper** -- American monologist and monodramatist

1885   **George Minot** -- American physician, who was one of the world's great authorities on blood diseases

1891   **Larry Gilbert** -- Professional baseball player and manager

1891   **Otto Dix** -- German painter

1896   **Georgi Konstantinovich Zhukov** -- Russian World War II marshal who organized the defense of Moscow and the victory at Stalingrad, and led the Russian forces that captured Berlin

1897   **Walter Hoving** – Chairman of the board of Tiffany's in New York

1899   **John Rhodes Cobb** -- American racing driver who drove a piston-powered automobile 394.196 miles per hour in 1947 for the world's record

1918   **Adolph Green** -- American playwright and lyricist

1923   **Maria Callas** -- American-born soprano and one of the best-known opera singers of the 1960s and 1970s

1924   **Alexander Haig Jr.** -- American general, aide to President Nixon, and secretary of state under President Reagan

1925   **Julie Harris** -- American stage, screen, and television actress

DECEMBER 2 -- EVENTS

1547   Hernando Cortes, Spanish conqueror of Mexico, died near Seville at age 62.

1804   Napoleon crowned himself Emperor of the French, when he snatched the crown from Pope Pius VII, who was in the act of crowning him, and placed it on his head himself.

1805   Napoleon crushed the Allied armies in the Battle of Austerlitz, in one of his most brilliant victories.

1816   The Philadelphia Savings Fund Society, the first savings bank in the United States, opened for business.

1823   President James Monroe, in a message to Congress, proclaimed the historic Monroe Doctrine.

1851   Louis Napoleon Bonaparte (Napoleon III) seized power in France in a coup d'etat.

1859   John Brown was hanged in Charles Town, Virginia (now West Virginia), on charges of treason for his famous raid on Harpers Ferry.

1886   Theodore Roosevelt married his second wife, Edith Kermit Carow.

1927   Henry Ford unveiled his Model A Ford, successor to the famed Model T.

1941   Advance units of General von Bock's German army penetrated to the suburbs of Moscow in World War II, the nearest the Germans came to taking the city.

1942   The world's first controlled, self-sustaining nuclear reaction was achieved at the University of Chicago by the Manhattan Engineering team led by Enrico Fermi.

1952   General Dwight D. Eisenhower, U.S. president-elect, arrived in Korea, keeping his campaign pledge to go there.

1954   The U.S. Senate voted to censure Senator Joseph R. McCarthy for "contemptuous" conduct and abuse of Senate members.

1970   The last anti-evolution teaching law in the U.S., that of Mississippi, was voided by the courts.

1982   The world's first permanent artificial heart was implanted, at the University of Utah Medical Center in the chest of retired dentist Barney Clark.

DECEMBER 3 -- BIRTHDAYS

1368   **Charles VI** -- King of France, 1380-1422

1596   **Nicolo Amati** -- Famous Italian violin maker, who also trained other great violin makers, including Antonio Stradivari and Andrea Guarneri

1753   **Samuel Crompton** -- English weaver, who invented the spinning mule, so called by him because it was a cross between the spinning jenny and the water frame

1755   **Gilbert Stuart** -- America's first great portrait painter, who became famous for his unfinished portrait of George Washington, probably the best-known portrait in America

1805   **Constantin Guys** -- French watercolorist and draftsman

1812   **Hendrik Conscience** -- Flemish romantic novelist

1826   **George B. McClellan** -- U.S. Civil War general and presidential candidate against President Lincoln in 1864

1833   **Carlos Juan Finlay** -- Chief sanitary officer of Cuba, 1902-1908, who was the first man to present evidence that yellow fever was transmitted by mosquitoes

1838   **Cleveland Abbe** -- American meteorologist prominent in the founding of the U.S. Weather Bureau

1857   **Joseph Conrad** – Polish-born English author, famous for his novels about the sea, such as *Lord Jim* (1900) and *The Nigger of the 'Narcissus'* (1897)

1883   **Anton von Webern** -- Austrian composer

1895   **Anna Freud** – Austrian psychoanalyst and daughter of the great psychoanalyst Sigmund Freud

1903   **John von Neumann** – Hungarian-born American mathematician and prominent contributor to the development of computers

1909   **Dana Suesse** -- American composer, author, and musician, noted for songs such as "Whistling in the Dark," "The Night Is Young and You're So Beautiful," and "You Ought to Be in Pictures"

1921   **John Doar** -- Special counsel to the House Judiciary Committee during the Nixon impeachment hearings

1927   **Phyllis Curtin** -- American operatic soprano

1930   **Jean-Luc Godard** -- One of the great French motion-picture directors of the 20th century

1930   **Andy Williams** -- American singer and television entertainer

1937   **Bobby Allison** -- Professional car racer

1947   **Jim Plunkett** -- Professional football player

1948   **Ozzy Osbourne** -- British rock singer

1955   **Brigitte Cuypers** -- South African tennis player

1957   **Kathy Jordan** -- American tennis player

1961   **Daryl Hannah** -- American motion-picture actress

DECEMBER 3 -- EVENTS

1639   Jonas Bronck purchased from the Indians the land that later became known as the Bronx, New York, because the Broncks lived there.

1818   Illinois was admitted to the Union as the 21st state.

1833   Oberlin College at Oberlin, Ohio, the first coeducational college in the United States, was opened.

1894   Robert Louis Stevenson, the great English novelist, died on the island of Samoa at age 44 of a stroke.

1910   Mary Baker Eddy, founder of the Church of Christ, Scientist, died at age 89.

1948   Whittaker Chambers claimed to have microfilm copies of secret government documents hidden in a pumpkin and given to him by Alger Hiss.

1967   South African surgeon Dr. Christiaan Barnard performed the first human heart transplant in history in Cape Town, South Africa, on 55-year-old Louis Washkansky.

1971   India launched a full-scale land, sea, and air attack on Pakistan, without a declaration of war.

1976   The 600-year-old monarchy in Laos was abolished as the Communists took control of the government.

1979   Iranian voters ratified a new constitution establishing the Islamic government and making Ayatollah Khomeini leader for life.

DECEMBER 4 -- BIRTHDAYS

1383   **Felix V** -- The last Roman Catholic antipope (one improperly elected, who sets himself up as pope in opposition to the regularly elected pope), 1439-1449

1584   **John Cotton** -- American Puritan minister who wrote the catechism, *Milk for Babes* (1646)

1795   **Thomas Carlyle** -- Scottish essayist and historian and one of the greatest social philosophers of Victorian England, who wrote the monumental work, *The French Revolution* (1837)

1835   **Samuel Butler** -- English author best known for the satirical novel *Erewhon* (1872) and for his other major work *The Way of All Flesh* (1903, after his death)

1860   **George Albert Hormel** -- Founder in 1892 of the George A. Hormel meat-packing company

1861   **Lillian Russell** -- American singer and actress, and "one of the most beautiful women of the American stage" during "The Gay Nineties"

1861   **James Thornton** -- English-born composer, author, and entertainer, noted for songs such as "When You Were Sweet Sixteen"

1866   **Wassily Kandinsky** -- Noted Russian artist, generally considered to be the first abstract painter

1868   **Jesse Burkett** -- Hall of Fame baseball player who hit .423 in 1895, .410 in 1896, and .402 in 1899

1875   **Rainer Maria Rilke** -- Czechoslovakian-born German poet regarded as one of the giants of modern literature

1880   **Gar Wood** -- Developer of the PT boats of the U.S. Navy in World War II

1885   **Grover Arnold Magnin** -- American chain store executive and son of the founder of I. Magnin and Company

1889   **Buck Jones** -- One of Hollywood's most popular cowboy stars of all time, who was a leading man in the 1920s and 1930s

1892   **Francisco Franco** -- Dictator of Spain, 1936-1975

1893   **Sir Herbert Read** -- English poet and critic

1896   **Lawrence Stock** -- American composer and author, noted for songs such as "Blueberry Hill," "You're Nobody 'Til Somebody Loves You," and "You Won't Be Satisfied Until You Break My Heart"

1897   **Robert Redfield** -- American cultural anthropologist

1921   **Deanna Durbin** -- Canadian-born actress and singer and internationally popular screen star of the late 1930s and early 1940s

1926   **Lee Dorsey** -- American soul singer

1930   **Harvey Kuenn** -- Professional baseball player

1932   **Horst Buchholz** -- German-born motion-picture actor

1932   **Thomas Morgan Edwards** -- American composer noted for the scores of such TV shows as *Gunsmoke, Twilight Zone,* and *Have Gun, Will Travel*

1941   **Marty Riessen** -- American tennis player

1944   **Dennis Wilson** -- American drummer with the Beach Boys musical group

1948   **Randel Vataha** -- Professional football player
1949   **Jeff Bridges** -- American motion-picture actor and son of actor
        Lloyd Bridges
1957   **Lee Smith** -- Professional baseball player

DECEMBER 4 -- EVENTS

771 AD Carloman, Charlemagne's brother and co-ruler of the Franks,
        died, leaving their empire to Charlemagne.
1154   Adrian IV became Roman Catholic pope, the only Englishman
        ever chosen.
1674   Father Marquette, the great French explorer and missionary,
        built the first house in what is now Chicago.
1679   Thomas Hobbes, the great English philosopher, died at Hard-
        wick, Derbyshire, at age 91.
1783   George Washington bade farewell to his officers of the Conti-
        nental Army at Fraunces Tavern in New York City: "With a
        heart full of love and gratitude, I now take leave of you."
1839   The Whig Party held its first national convention, nominating as
        its candidates in the 1840 election General William Henry
        Harrison and John Tyler, "Tippecanoe and Tyler, too."
1851   The "December 4 Massacre" occurred in Paris, as the govern-
        ment suppressed an uprising against Emperor Napoleon III.
1912   The comic strip, *Polly and Her Pals,* by Cliff Sterrett, first
        appeared.
1918   President Woodrow Wilson sailed for France to attend the
        Versailles peace conference, becoming the first president to visit
        a foreign country while in office.
1943   The Second Cairo Conference in World War II was held with
        President Roosevelt, Prime Minister Churchill, and President
        Inonu of Turkey attending.
1960   Alan Jay Lerner's *Camelot* opened on Broadway and became a
        favorite of President-elect Kennedy, whose term in office later
        became known as the "brief shining moment" of Camelot.
1963   The second session of Vatican II ended. One of its documents
        allowed the use of the local language in place of Latin in parts of
        the Mass.

DECEMBER 5 -- BIRTHDAYS

1443   **Julius II** -- Roman Catholic pope, 1503-1513, who began the construction of St. Peter's Basilica in 1506

1751   **Pierre Philippe Thomire** -- French sculptor

1782   **Martin Van Buren** -- 8th U.S. president, and the first who was a United States citizen at birth

1811   **David Van Nostrand** -- American publisher who founded the D. Van Nostrand publishing house

1830   **Christina Rossetti** -- English poet and sister of the famous poet, Dante Gabriel Rossetti

1839   **George Armstrong Custer** -- American army general who was killed and his unit wiped out by Indians in the Battle of the Little Bighorn ("Custer's last stand") on June 25, 1876

1859   **Sir John Jellicoe** -- British Grand Fleet commander at the Battle of Jutland in 1916, the only major engagement of World War I between the British and German fleets

1890   **Fritz Lang** -- Noted Austrian-born motion-picture director with a career of over 40 years

1897   **Nunnally Johnson** -- American motion-picture director and producer, and one of the screen's most prolific and highly respected writers, noted for scripts such as *The Grapes of Wrath* (1940)

1901   **Walt Disney** -- American producer of animated cartoons, movies, and television shows, and creator of Mickey Mouse and Donald Duck, two of the best-loved cartoon characters in American history

1901   **Werner Karl Heisenberg** -- German physicist, noted for the uncertainty principle of atomic theory

1902   **Strom Thurmond** -- U.S. senator and third-party presidential candidate in 1948

1903   **Arnold Gingrich** -- American publisher and founder of *Esquire* magazine

1905   **Gus Mancuso** -- Professional baseball player

1906   **Otto Preminger** -- Famous Austrian-born motion-picture director, noted for the controversial *The Moon Is Blue* (1953), and for such works as *Anatomy of a Murder* (1959)

1934   **Joan Didion** -- American novelist, journalist, and screenwriter

1936   **Chad Mitchell** -- American singer of the Chad Mitchell Trio
1946   **Jose Carreras** -- Spanish operatic tenor
1949   **Lanny Wadkins** -- Professional golfer
1954   **Gary Roenicke** -- Professional baseball player
1955   **Art Still** -- Professional football player
1957   **Art Monk** -- Professional football player
1963   **Carrie Hamilton** -- American stage, screen, and television actress, and daughter of comedienne Carol Burnett

DECEMBER 5 -- EVENTS

1484   Pope Innocent VIII issued the bull *Summis desiderantes,* initiating harsh measures against "witches" and "magicians."

1776   Phi Beta Kappa, the first scholastic fraternity in America, was founded at the College of William and Mary in Williamsburg, Virginia.

1791   Wolfgang Amadeus Mozart, the great Austrian composer, died in poverty at age 35. He was buried in an unmarked grave, the location of which is now unknown.

1812   Napoleon left the remnants of his Grande Armee in Smorgonie, Russia, to hasten back to Paris to put down the rumored revolts against him in France.

1831   Former president John Quincy Adams took his seat in the House of Representatives, the only ex-president to serve in that capacity.

1848   The California gold discovery, which led to the Gold Rush of 1849, was announced by President Polk in a message to Congress.

1870   Alexandre Dumas the Elder, the noted French novelist, died at Marly-le-Roi at age 68.

1929   The American League for Physical Culture, the first United States nudist group, was organized.

1933   Amendment 21 to the U.S. Constitution was proclaimed, repealing Prohibition.

1934   Sixty-two persons were executed in Russia for "plotting" against the Stalin regime.

1936   England's King Edward VIII announced his decision to abdicate to marry Wallis Warfield Simpson.

1955   The AFL and CIO, the two major American labor unions, merged to form the AFL-CIO. George Meany became its first president.

DECEMBER 6 -- BIRTHDAYS

1421   **Henry VI** -- The last king of England from the House of Lancaster, 1422-1461 and 1470-1471

1478   **Baldassare Castiglione** -- Italian Renaissance writer, best known for *The Book of the Courtier* (about 1518), which became a guide for social refinement in Spain, France, and England, as well as Italy

1732   **Warren Hastings** -- First British governor-general of India, 1774-1785

1778   **Joseph Louis Gay-Lussac** -- Noted French chemist and physicist, who discovered the law (now called Charles' Law) that deals with the effect of temperature on gases

1792   **William II** -- King of the Netherlands, 1840-1849

1822   **John Eberhard Faber** -- A founder of the Eberhard Faber Pencil Company

1833   **John Singleton Mosby** -- Famous Confederate ranger during the Civil War

1841   **Frederic Bazille** -- French painter

1859   **E.H. Sothern** -- One of the great dramatic actors of the American theater

1867   **Karl Bitter** -- American sculptor

1870   **William S. Hart** -- American stage and motion-picture actor, who was the first, and perhaps the most famous, cowboy actor of Hollywood Westerns

1876   **Frederick Duesenberg** -- Pioneer American automobile manufacturer

1886   **Joyce Kilmer** -- American author and poet, most famous for the short poem, "Trees" (1913)

1892   **Lynn Fontanne** -- English-born actress who with her husband Alfred Lunt formed one of the greatest acting teams in the history of the American theater

1893   **Lou Little** -- Professional football player

1896   **Ira Gershwin** – Noted American lyricist, who collaborated in much of his work with his famous brother, composer George Gershwin

1898   **Alfred Eisenstaedt** -- Noted American photographer

1898   **Gunnar Myrdal** -- Swedish sociologist and economist, who gained fame for the book, *An American Dilemma: The Negro Problem and Modern Democracy* (1944)

1899   **Jocko Conlan** -- Hall of Fame baseball umpire

1900   **George Eugene Uhlenbeck** -- Indonesian physicist who helped develop the concept of electron spin

1903   **Hardie Albright** -- American stage and motion-picture actor, and Hollywood leading man of the 1930s and 1940s

1903   **Tony Lazzeri** – Professional baseball player and member of the great New York Yankee teams of the Babe Ruth and Lou Gehrig era

1905   **James J. Braddock** -- World heavyweight champion, 1935-1937

1906   **Agnes Moorehead** -- American motion-picture and television actress

1909   **Stan Hack** -- Professional baseball player and manager

1913   **Eleanor Holm** – American swimmer who held 12 national titles and won the 100-meter backstroke race in the 1932 Olympics

1920   **Dave Brubeck** -- American pianist and composer

1921   **Otto Graham** -- Hall of Fame football player

1924   **Wally Cox** -- American comedian and actor

1927   **Patsy Mink** -- U.S. congresswoman

1943   **Ingrid Bentzer** -- Swedish tennis player

1945   **Larry Bowa** -- Professional baseball player and manager

1948   **Don Nickles** -- U.S. senator

DECEMBER 6 -- EVENTS

1362   Urban V was crowned Roman Catholic pope.

1492   Columbus discovered Hispaniola on his first voyage to America.

1506   Niccolo Machiavelli, the great Italian writer and statesman, created a Florentine militia, the first Italian national army.

1648   Colonel Thomas Pride's soldiers arrested and excluded 96 members of Parliament opposed to trying Charles I for treason. The remaining members formed the "Rump Parliament."

1847   Abraham Lincoln took his seat as a representative in the 30th U.S. Congress.

1864   Salmon P. Chase was appointed chief justice of the U.S. Supreme Court by President Lincoln.

1877   Thomas A. Edison shouted "Mary had a little lamb" into the horn of his newly invented phonograph, which, to the amazement of his shop foreman, repeated Edison's words.

1882   Anthony Trollope, the popular English novelist, died of a stroke brought on, it was said, by over-hearty laughter.

1884   Construction of the Washington Monument was completed after four years of work by Army engineers.

1889   Jefferson Davis, the former president of the Confederacy, died in New Orleans at age 81.

1917   Finland declared its independence from Russia, after the Russian Bolshevik Revolution.

1941   President Roosevelt sent a personal note to Emperor Hirohito of Japan seeking to dispel the "dark clouds" threatening war. (Japan attacked Pearl Harbor the next day.)

1973   Congressman Gerald Ford was sworn in as vice president of the United States, succeeding Spiro Agnew who had resigned in disgrace.

DECEMBER 7 -- BIRTHDAYS

1542   **Mary, Queen of Scots** -- The last Roman Catholic ruler of Scotland, who in 1587 was beheaded on orders of Queen Elizabeth I of England

1598   **Gian Lorenzo Bernini** -- Italian sculptor and architect, designer of the great plaza of St. Peter's Church, and one of the most famous artists of the 17th century

1784   **Allan Cunningham** -- Scottish poet

1823   **Leopold Kronecker** -- Polish mathematician, noted for his work in the theory of algebraic numbers and for the Kronecker delta, named in his honor

1863   **Pietro Mascagni** – Italian opera composer, noted for the verismo style that he made famous in *Cavalleria Rusticana* (1888), his greatest work

1863   **Richard Warren Sears** -- American merchant and co-founder with Alvin C. Roebuck of Sears, Roebuck and Company

1873   **Willa Cather** -- American novelist, noted for works such as *O Pioneers!* (1913), *My Antonia* (1918), and *Death Comes for the Archbishop* (1927)

1879   **Rudolf Friml** -- Austrian-born composer of operettas such as *The Firefly, Rose Marie,* and *The Vagabond King,* and for songs such as "Donkey Serenade" (1937)

1888   **Joyce Cary** -- One of the leading British novelists of the 1900s, noted for works such as *Herself Surprised* (1941) and *The Horse's Mouth* (1944)

1888   **Heywood Campbell Broun** -- One of America's most widely read newspaper columnists of the 1920s and 1930s

1894   **Stuart Davis** -- American painter and illustrator noted for works such as *Garage Lights* (1931) and *Seme* (1953)

1908   **John Hope Doeg** -- American Hall of Fame tennis player

1910   **Rod Cameron** -- Canadian-born motion-picture and television actor with a 40-year career

1911   **Denny Galehouse** -- Professional baseball player

1912   **Louis Prima** -- American musician

1915   **Eli Wallach** -- American stage and motion-picture actor

1923   **Ted Knight** -- American television actor

1924   **Mario Soares** -- Leader of Portugal's Socialist Party after the death of dictator Antonio Salazar in 1968

1925   **Max Zaslofsky** -- Professional basketball player

1928   **Noam Chomsky** – American linguistics expert and political theorist

1930   **Dan Sikes** -- Professional golfer

1932   **Ellen Burstyn** -- American stage, screen, and television actress

1942   **Alex Johnson** -- Professional baseball player

1947   **Johnny Bench** -- Hall of Fame baseball player, noted as one of the greatest catchers in the game's history

1956   **Larry Bird** -- Professional basketball superstar

DECEMBER 7 -- EVENTS

43 AD   Cicero, the great Roman orator and statesman, was assassinated by agents of Mark Antony.

1787   Delaware became the "First State" of the Union, when it ratified the U.S. Constitution.

1793   Madame du Barry, mistress of King Louis XV of France, was guillotined at age 47 by the French republicans.

1842   The New York Philharmonic gave its first concert, performing Beethoven's *Fifth Symphony,* the *Overture* from Weber's *Oberon,* and part of the score of Beethoven's *Fidelio.*

1917   The U.S. 42nd, or "Rainbow," Division arrived in France in World War I.

1941   Shortly before 8 A.M., Hawaiian time, Japanese naval and air forces suddenly attacked Pearl Harbor, plunging the United States into World War II.

1965   The Roman Catholic Church and the Eastern Orthodox Churches removed the sentences of excommunication they had imposed on each other in 1054.

1970   Rube Goldberg, the great American cartoonist, died at age 87.

DECEMBER 8 -- BIRTHDAYS

65 BC   **Horace (Quintus Horatius Flaccus)** -- One of the most familiar and admired of the Roman poets

1626   **Christina** -- Queen of Sweden, 1632-1654, whose court included Rene Descartes, the famous French mathematician and philosopher

1708   **Francis I** – Holy Roman Emperor, 1745-1765, and husband of Maria Theresa, the great queen of Austria

1765   **Eli Whitney** -- American inventor, noted for his invention of the cotton gin (1793) and for making guns by using machinery, which marked the beginning of mass production

1815   **Adolf von Menzel** -- German painter and printmaker

1816   **August Belmont** -- American financier, founder of the banking house of August Belmont and Company, and grandfather of the original owner of the famous racehorse Man O' War

1832   **Bjornstjerne Bjornson** -- Norwegian novelist and dramatist and the great national poet of Norway

1861   **Aristide Maillol** -- French sculptor noted for the serene, balanced style of his figures, which were almost exclusively female, such as *The Mediterranean* (1901)

1862   **Georges Feydeau** -- French writer

1865   **Jean Sibelius** – Finnish composer and musician, noted for *Finlandia* and his seven symphonies

1868   **Norman Douglas** -- British writer best known for his witty, satirical novel *South Wind* (1917)

1881   **Albert Gleizes** -- French painter

1885   **Kenneth Lewis Roberts** -- American novelist and essayist, noted for works such as *Northwest Passage* (1937) and *Lydia Bailey* (1947)

1886   **Diego Rivera** -- Mexican painter and outstanding leader in the birth of mural art in Mexico

1890   **Bohuslav Martinu** -- Czechoslovakian composer

1894   **E.C. Segar** -- American cartoonist and creator of *Popeye* (1929), one of the most successful comic strip characters in history

1894   **James Thurber** -- American writer, cartoonist, and perhaps America's finest humorist since Mark Twain

1902   **Oswald Jacoby** -- One of the greatest American bridge players of the 20th century

1904   **Wilmer Lawson Allison** – American Hall of Fame tennis player

1911   **Lee J. Cobb** -- Outstanding American character actor of the stage, screen, and television

1913   **Delmore Schwartz** -- American poet

1925   **Sammy Davis Jr.** -- American actor, singer, and dancer

1930   **Maximilian Schell** -- Austrian-born stage, screen, and television actor and director

1933   **Flip Wilson** -- American comedian and actor

1933   **John Green** -- Professional basketball player

1936   **David Carradine** -- American motion-picture and television actor, and son of actor John Carradine

1937   **James MacArthur** -- American motion-picture and television actor, and adopted son of playwright Charles MacArthur and actress Helen Hayes

1939   **James Galway** – Noted Irish flutist

1942   **Bob Love** -- Professional basketball player

1943   **Jim Morrison** -- American singer with the Doors musical group

1945   **Julie Heldman** -- American tennis player

1946   **John Rubinstein** -- American actor and son of pianist Arthur Rubinstein

1947   **Gregg Allman** – American singer with the Allman Brothers musical group

1953   **Kim Basinger** -- American motion-picture and television actress

1959   **Mark Dickson** -- American tennis player

DECEMBER 8 -- EVENTS

877 AD   Louis II, the Stammerer, was crowned King of France.

1854   Pope Pius IX defined the doctrine of the Immaculate Conception.

1863   President Lincoln announced his plans for Reconstruction of the South, one feature of which was to pardon Southerners who would take an oath of loyalty to the United States.

1864   Pope Pius IX issued the *Syllabus of Errors*, which, among other things, denied the equality of Catholicism and Protestantism.

1886   The American Federation of Labor (AFL) was created by the reorganization of the Federation of Organized Trades and Labor Unions.

1940   The House of Commons suffered heavy damage as 400 German planes raided London in World War II.

1941   President Roosevelt declared December 7, 1941, "a date which will live in infamy," and asked Congress to declare war on Japan. The declaration of war was signed at 4:10 P.M.

1949   Generalissimo Chiang Kai-shek fled with his Nationalist government to Formosa, surrendering mainland China to the Chinese Communists.

1953   President Eisenhower proposed his "atoms for peace" plan, providing for nations to pool their atomic information and materials for peaceful purposes.

1965   The fourth and final session of the ecumenical council Vatican II ended.

1978   Golda Meir, former prime minister of Israel, died at age 80.

1980   John Lennon, famous member of the Beatles musical group, was assassinated in New York City at the age of 40.

1987   President Ronald Reagan and Soviet leader Mikhail Gorbachev signed a landmark treaty banning intermediate-range nuclear missiles, in a meeting in Washington, D.C.

DECEMBER 9 -- BIRTHDAYS

1594   **Gustavus II** -- King of Sweden, 1611-1632 (known also as Gustavus Adolphus), who laid the foundations of the modern Swedish state

1608   **John Milton** -- One of the greatest poets of the English language, whose *Paradise Lost* (1667) is one of the world's greatest epics

1717   **Johann Winckelmann** -- German archaeologist and art historian

1842   **Peter Kropotkin** -- Russian prince and noted anarchist of the late 1800s

1848   **Joel Chandler Harris** -- American writer and creator of the famous character *Uncle Remus*

1897   **Hermione Gingold** -- English stage, screen, and television actress, with a career of over 70 years

1898   **Emmett Kelly** -- Noted American circus clown, famous for his sad-faced tramp

1902   **Margaret Hamilton** -- American actress in over 75 movies and as many stage plays, best remembered as the Wicked Witch of the West in *The Wizard of Oz* (1939)

1903   **Matty Malneck** -- Americn composer and violinist, noted for songs such as "Hey, Good Lookin'"

1909   **Douglas Fairbanks Jr.** -- American motion-picture and television actor, and son of the silent screen's most beloved hero

1911   **Broderick Crawford** -- American stage, screen, and television actor with a career of some 45 years

1912   **Thomas P. "Tip" O'Neill** -- Speaker of the U.S. House of Representatives

1915   **Elisabeth Schwarzkopf** -- Polish-born lyric soprano, who was highly successful in the 1940s and 1950s as a concert and opera singer

1916   **Kirk Douglas** -- American stage and motion-picture actor with a career of some 40 years

1922   **Redd Foxx** -- American motion-picture and television actor

1925   **Dina Merrill** -- American stage, screen, and television actress

1926   **Luis Miguel Dominguin** -- Professional bullfighter

1928   **Dick Van Patten** -- American stage, screen, and television actor

1929   **John Cassavetes** -- American motion-picture and television actor, director, and screenwriter

1930   **Buck Henry** -- American actor, author, and television comedy scriptwriter

1931   **Cliff Hagen** -- Professional basketball player with over 13,000 career points

1932   **Bill Hartack** -- American jockey with five Kentucky Derby winners

1941   **Beau Bridges** -- American motion-picture actor and son of actor Lloyd Bridges

1942   **Dick Butkus** -- Professional football superstar and actor

1944   **Del Unser** -- Professional baseball player

1947   **Steve Owens** -- Professional football player

1949   **Tom Kite** -- Professional golfer

1950   **Joan Armatrading** -- West Indian-born singer and guitarist

1954   **Renata Tomanova** -- Czechoslovakian tennis player

1955   **Otis Birdsong** -- Professional basketball player

1957   **Donny Osmond** -- American singer and actor

DECEMBER 9 -- EVENTS

1531   The Virgin of Guadelupe allegedly appeared to an Indian boy, Juan Diego, on Tepeyac Hill near Mexico City, and caused a picture of herself to appear on his cloak.

1641   Sir Anthony Van Dyck, the great Flemish painter, died in London at age 42.

1793   Noah Webster published *The American Minerva,* New York's first daily newspaper.

1824   The armies of Simon Bolivar and Antonio Jose de Sucre defeated the Spaniards at Ayacucho, ending the Latin-American wars of independence.

1854   Alfred Lord Tennyson published his famous poem, "The Charge of the Light Brigade."

1884   Levant M. Richardson of Chicago patented the ball-bearing roller skate.

1905   Church and state were separated by law in France, breaking the church-state connection established in 1801 by Napoleon and Pope Pius VII.

1917   British troops under General Viscount Allenby captured Jerusalem from the Turks in World War I.

1934   Ethiopian and Italian soldiers clashed at Wai Wai, providing the pretext for Italy's later invasion of Ethiopia.

1958   The John Birch Society was founded by Robert Welch, a retired business executive.

1965   Branch Rickey, the great baseball executive, died eleven days before his 84th birthday.

1984   Eric Dickerson of the Los Angeles Rams gained his 2,007th yard, breaking O.J. Simpson's single-season NFL record, as the Rams beat the Houston Oilers, 27-16.

DECEMBER 10 -- BIRTHDAYS

1538   **Battista Guarini** -- Italian Renaissance court poet

1610   **Adriaen van Ostade** – Dutch painter and printmaker of the Baroque period

1787   **Thomas Hopkins Gallaudet** -- Pioneer American teacher of deaf-mutes, and founder of the Hartford School for the Deaf (1817)

1804   **Karl Gustav Jacob Jacobi** -- Noted German mathematician who was famous for the development of elliptic functions

1805   **William Lloyd Garrison** -- American journalist and reformer who became famous in the 1830s for his denunciations of slavery

1822   **Cesar Franck** -- French composer best known for his *Symphony in D minor* (1888)

1830   **Emily Dickinson** – One of the greatest American poets, noted for works such as "I'm nobody! Who are You?" (published in 1891)

1851   **Melvil Dewey** -- American librarian who in 1876 developed the library classification method known today as the Dewey Decimal System

1870   **Pierre Louys** -- French novelist and poet

1870   **Adolph Loos** -- Austrian architect

1883   **Andrei Vishinsky** – Russian prosecutor in the Communist Party purge trials of the 1930s and chief delegate to the U.N. in the early 1950s

1886   **Victor McLaglen** – English character star in some 150 silent and sound movies

1891 **Harold Alexander** -- British World War II field marshal who commanded the evacuation of Dunkerque and was supreme Allied commander in the Mediterranean area

1902 **Vito Marcantonio** -- American Congressman noted in the 1940s and 1950s for his left-wing views

1903 **Una Merkel** -- American motion-picture actress in over 50 films

1911 **Chet Huntley** -- American television newscaster who teamed with newscaster David Brinkley in the Huntley-Brinkley Report of the 1950s and 1960s

1912 **Philip Hart** -- U.S. senator in the 1960s and 1970s

1913 **Morton Gould** -- American composer, conductor, and arranger, known for his clever use of American folk and popular music

1914 **Dorothy Lamour** -- American motion-picture actress and one of Hollywood's most popular stars of the 1930s and 1940s

1950 **Lloyd Neal** -- Professional basketball player

1952 **Susan Dey** -- American model and actress

DECEMBER 10 -- EVENTS

1520 Martin Luther burned the *Bull Exsurge* issued against him by Pope Leo X, demanding that he recant.

1607 Captain John Smith left Jamestown on the trip in which Pocahontas allegedly saved his life by intervening with her father, the Indian chief Powhatan.

1817 Mississippi was admitted to the Union as the 20th state.

1832 President Andrew Jackson proclaimed his nonrecognition of South Carolina's Ordinance of Nullification and ordered warships and troops concentrated near Charleston.

1848 Louis Napoleon, the nephew of Napoleon I, was elected president of France with 5.5 million votes out of 7.5 million cast.

1869 The Territory of Wyoming authorized women to vote and hold office, the first U.S. state or territory to do so.

1896 Alfred Nobel, the noted Swedish chemist, died at age 63. The Nobel Prizes, established by him, are awarded on this date in his honor.

1898 The Treaty of Paris ended the Spanish-American War, making Cuba independent and ceding Guam, Puerto Rico, and the Philippine Islands to the United States.

1901   The first Nobel Prizes were awarded.

1906   President Theodore Roosevelt was awarded the Nobel Prize for peace for his mediation in the Russo-Japanese War.

1910   Giacomo Puccini, the great Italian composer, attended the world premiere of his opera, *The Girl of the Golden West,* at the Metropolitan Opera House in New York.

1913   Leonardo da Vinci's masterpiece, the *Mona Lisa,* was recovered two years after it was stolen from the Louvre Museum in Paris.

1915   Henry Ford produced his one millionth Model T automobile.

1920   The Nobel Peace Prize for 1919 was awarded to President Wilson for his part in the World War I peace treaty and for establishing the League of Nations.

1931   Jane Addams, the noted American reformer, became the first American woman to win the Nobel Peace Prize, sharing the honor with Nicholas M. Butler.

1941   Japanese forces captured Guam and invaded the Philippine Islands, landing in northern Luzon in World War II.

1941   The British battleships *Prince of Wales* and *Repulse* were sunk by the Japanese in World War II.

1950   Ralph Bunche, American statesman, became the first black American to win the Nobel Peace Prize.

1958   The first domestic passenger jet flight took place in the United States, inaugurated by National Airlines from New York to Miami.

DECEMBER 11 -- BIRTHDAYS

1475   **Leo X** -- Roman Catholic pope who was in office when Martin Luther started the Protestant Reformation, and who was the second son of Lorenzo the Magnificent of the Medici family

1803   **Louis Hector Berlioz** -- French conductor and composer noted for such works as the *Fantastic Symphony* (1830) and *The Damnation of Faust* (1846)

1810   **Alfred de Musset** -- French poet, dramatist, and novelist, noted chiefly for his plays, *Comedies et Proverbes* (1840)

1822   **George David Cummins** -- Founder of the Reformed Episcopal Church

1843   **Robert Koch** -- German physician, noted for establishing bacteriology as a separate science

1882	**Max Born** -- German physicist who shared the 1954 Nobel Prize for physics for his contributions to quantum theory
1882	**Fiorello La Guardia** -- Famous mayor of New York City from 1934 to 1945
1890	**Mark Tobey** -- American painter
1892	**John Augustus Larson** -- American inventor who in 1921 made one of the first lie detectors, or polygraphs
1905	**Gilbert Roland** -- Mexican-born motion-picture actor with a career of over 50 years
1908	**Elliott Carter Jr.** -- American composer
1910	**Carlo Ponti** -- Italian motion-picture producer, noted for films such as *Two Women* (1960) (starring his wife, actress Sophia Loren) and *Dr. Zhivago* (1965)
1914	**Bill Nicholson** -- Professional baseball player
1918	**Alexander Solzhenitsyn** -- Nobel Prize-winning Russian novelist exiled from his country because of charges of slander by the Soviet government
1923	**Betsy Blair** -- American stage and motion-picture actress
1924	**Doc Blanchard** -- Noted football player, particularly with the great Army teams of the World War II years
1931	**Rita Moreno** -- Puerto Rican-born actress, singer, and dancer
1938	**Frederick Cox** -- Professional football player
1941	**Max Baucus** -- U.S. senator
1946	**Linda Day George** -- American actress
1950	**Christine Onassis Andreadis** -- Heiress and daughter of Greek shipping magnate Aristotle Onassis
1951	**Robert Cochran** -- American skiing champion
1953	**Bess Armstrong** -- American motion-picture and television actress
1954	**Jermaine Jackson** -- American singer and bassist with the Jackson 5 musical group

DECEMBER 11 -- EVENTS

1695	Captain William Kidd, the famous Scottish pirate, was commissioned a privateer (captain of an armed ship) by King William III of England to capture certain notorious pirates.

1718	Charles XII, the great king of Sweden, was killed in the siege of Fredrikstad, Norway, at the age of 36.
1719	The first recorded sighting of the aurora borealis occurred in New England.
1816	Indiana was admitted to the Union as the 19th state.
1844	An anesthetic (nitrous oxide, or laughing gas) was first used in dentistry, when American dentist Dr. Horace Wells used it on himself before having his tooth extracted.
1872	Pinckney Benton Stewart Pinchback became the first black governor in U.S. history, as he took office as acting governor of Louisiana.
1904	President Theodore Roosevelt stated that he would "not accept another nomination" for the presidency, an action he was later to regret.
1911	Great Britain under Prime Minister Herbert Asquith passed the first National Health Insurance act.
1936	King Edward VIII abdicated in order to marry Mrs. Wallis Simpson, and his brother George VI became King of England.
1941	Germany and Italy declared war on the United States, followed by a U.S. declaration of war on them.
1946	John D. Rockefeller Jr. announced his donation of a six-block parcel of land along the East River in New York City as a site for the United Nations headquarters.

DECEMBER 12 -- BIRTHDAYS

1745	**John Jay** -- First U.S. Supreme Court chief justice
1775	**William Henry** -- English chemist for whom Henry's law of gases was named
1786	**William L. Marcy** -- U.S. senator noted for the political slogan, "To the victor belong the spoils"
1791	**Marie Louise** -- Austrian princess and second wife of Napoleon Bonaparte
1805	**Henry Wells** -- Co-founder with William G. Fargo in 1852 of Wells, Fargo & Company
1821	**Gustave Flaubert** -- French writer whose first and greatest work, *Madame Bovary* (1857), is considered by many to be the world's "perfect novel"

1863' **Edvard Munch** -- Norwegian artist noted for his paintings and lithographs depicting man as helpless, isolated, and tormented by emotions

1864 **Arthur Brisbane** -- One of the first syndicated newspaper columnists in the United States, noted for his columns *Today* and *This Week,* which appeared in the 1920s and 1930s

1875 **Karl Rudolf Gerd von Rundstedt** – One of Hitler's ablest World War II field marshals, who directed the Battle of the Bulge in 1944

1879 **Laura Hope Crews** -- American stage and motion-picture actress, noted for her role as Miss Pittypat in *Gone With the Wind*

1881 **Arthur Garfield Hays** – American lawyer and civil liberties leader, who assisted Clarence Darrow in the famous Scopes trial of 1925

1881 **Harry Morris Warner** – One of the Warner Brothers who founded the motion-picture company of the same name

1883 **Cliff Sterrett** -- American comic strip cartoonist and creator of *Polly and Her Pals*

1893 **Edward G. Robinson** -- American stage and motion-picture actor with a brilliant 50-year career

1906 **Zack Mosley** – American comic strip cartoonist and creator of *Smilin' Jack*

1912 **Henry Armstrong** – The only boxer to hold three world championships at the same time--the welterweight, the lightweight, and the featherweight titles (1937)

1915 **Frank Sinatra** -- American singer, actor, and superstar performer for over 40 years

1923 **Bob Barker** -- American television game show host

1924 **Edward I. Koch** -- Mayor of New York City

1928 **Helen Frankenthaler** -- American abstract expressionist painter

1929 **John Osborne** -- English playwright and screenwriter, noted for his play, *Look Back in Anger,* which was made into a movie in 1959

1932 **Bob Pettit** -- Professional basketball superstar and the first to score 20,000 career points

1936 **Lucia Bassi** -- Italian tennis player

1938 **Connie Francis** -- American singer and actress

1940 **Tom Hayden** -- American social activist

1941	**Dionne Warwick** -- American soul singer
1945	**Ralph Garr** -- Professional baseball player
1948	**Randy Smith** -- Professional basketball player
1950	**Gorman Thomas** -- Professional baseball player
1952	**David Jaynes** -- Professional football player
1953	**Rafael Septien** -- Professional football player
1962	**Tracy Austin** -- American tennis player

DECEMBER 12 -- EVENTS

1398   Tamerlane, the feared Mongol conqueror, sacked Delhi, India, and massacred most of its 100,000 inhabitants.

1787   Pennsylvania ratified the Constitution, becoming the second state of the Union.

1850   *The Wide, Wide World,* by Susan Warner, was published. It is considered by many publishers to be the first U.S. "best-seller."

1870   Joseph H. Rainey of South Carolina became the first black U.S. Congressman.

1871   Wild Bill Hickok was fired as marshall of Abilene, Kansas, for mistakenly killing a law officer.

1889   Robert Browning, the great English poet, died in Venice at age 77.

1897   The comic strip, *The Katzenjammer Kids,* by Rudolph Dirks, first appeared.

1901   The message *S* was received from Cornwall, England, by Guglielmo Marconi in St. John's, Newfoundland, the first long-distance wireless message.

1937   Japanese planes sank the U.S. gunboat *Panay* in the Yangtze River in China. Their government apologized and paid a two million dollar indemnity.

1947   John L. Lewis withdrew his United Mine Workers from the AFL.

1953   U.S. Major Chuck Yeager flew a Bell X-1A jet plane at a record two-and-a-half times the speed of sound.

1963   Kenya became independent of Great Britain.

1968   Tallulah Bankhead, the noted American actress, died at age 65.

DECEMBER 13 -- BIRTHDAYS

1520 **Sixtus V** – Roman Catholic pope, 1585-1590, who established the Vatican Press, and urged King Philip of Spain to launch the Spanish Armada against England.

1553 **Henry IV** – The first Bourbon king of France, 1589-1610, noted for the famous Edict of Nantes

1560 **Maximilien de Bethune Sully** -- French minister of King Henry IV, and the first important person to hold the position of minister to a French king

1797 **Heinrich Heine** – One of the most popular writers in German literature, noted especially for his poem, "The Lorelei," published in his *Book of Songs* (1827)

1816 **Werner von Siemens** -- German engineer who developed an electroplating process and invented a dynamo, and for whom the electrical unit of capacitance is named

1818 **Mary Todd Lincoln** -- Wife of President Abraham Lincoln

1835 **Phillips Brooks** -- American clergyman best known as the composer of the famous Christmas carol, "O Little Town of Bethlehem," first sung in 1868

1887 **Alvin "Sergeant" York** -- American World War I hero who killed more than 20 Germans and forced 132 others to surrender on October 8, 1918

1890 **Marc Connelly** -- American playwright, journalist, and stage director, best known for *The Green Pastures* (1930), perhaps America's most popular religious drama

1897 **Drew Pearson** -- American muckraking newspaper columnist of the 1940s and 1950s

1903 **Carlos Montoya** -- Noted Spanish guitarist

1910 **Van Heflin** -- American stage and motion-picture actor in over 50 films

1912 **Curt Jurgens** – German stage and motion-picture actor in over 100 films

1913 **Archie Moore** -- World light-heavyweight champion, 1952-1962

1914 **Larry Parks** -- American motion-picture actor

1914 **Alan Bullock** -- English author best known for *Hitler: A Study in Tyranny* (1952), one of the earliest and best biographies of the Nazi dictator

1915   Balthazar Johannes Vorster -- Prime minister of the Republic of South Africa, 1966-1978

1915   **Ross Macdonald** -- American writer noted for works such as *The Dark Tunnel* (1944) and *Meet Me at the Morgue* (1953)

1918   **William Vukovich Sr.** -- American automobile racer

1920   **Don Taylor** -- American motion-picture actor and director

1920   **George P. Shultz** -- American cabinet member in the Nixon, Ford, and Reagan administrations

1923   **Larry Doby** -- Professional baseball player and first black player in the American League

1925   **Dick Van Dyke** -- American actor and comedian

1926   **Carl Erskine** -- Professional baseball player

1927   **Christopher Plummer** -- Canadian-born stage, screen, and television actor

1934   **Richard Darryl Zanuck** -- American motion-picture producer and executive, and son of the noted producer Darryl F. Zanuck

1935   **Lindy McDaniel** -- Professional baseball player

1941   **John Davidson** -- American singer and actor

1943   **Ferguson Jenkins** -- Professional baseball superstar

1947   **Lemar Parrish** -- Professional football player

DECEMBER 13 -- EVENTS

1250   Holy Roman Emperor Frederick II, the brilliant ruler of the Middle Ages, died in Ferentino 13 days short of his 56th birthday.

1294   Pope Celestine V abdicated under the persuasion of Cardinal Benedetto Gaetano, who succeeded him as Pope Boniface VIII.

1466   Donatello, the great Italian sculptor, died in Florence at an approximate age of 80.

1545   The first session of the Council of Trent met in Trent, a city in the Austrian Tyrol, to restate the doctrines of the Roman Catholic Church.

1577   Sir Francis Drake left Plymouth, England, beginning the second round-the-world voyage in history.

1642   Abel Tasman, the great Dutch navigator, discovered New Zealand.

1648   The "Rump Parliament" (96 members were arrested and excluded by the army) voted to try King Charles I of England for treason.

1784   Samuel Johnson, the great English man of letters, died in London at age 75.

1809   Dr. Ephraim McDowell performed America's first abdominal operation, removing a 22-pound ovarian tumor from Mrs. Jane Todd Crawford in Danville, Kentucky.

1862   The Confederates under General Robert E. Lee dealt the Union forces under General Ambrose Burnside a crushing defeat in the Battle of Fredericksburg in the Civil War.

1928   George Gershwin's *An American in Paris* was performed for the first time, by the New York Philharmonic Symphony Orchestra.

1937   Japanese soldiers captured Nanking, the former Chinese capital, in the Sino-Japanese War.

1975   Australians elected Malcolm Fraser's Liberal-National Country Party to office in a landslide victory over the Labour Party.

DECEMBER 14 -- BIRTHDAYS

1503   **Nostradamus (Michel de Notredame)** – French astrologer and physician, famous for his prophecies and for his book *Centuries* (1555), a series of prophecies in verse

1546   **Tycho Brahe** -- Noted Danish astronomer and associate of the great astronomer Johannes Kepler

1610   **David Teniers the Younger** – Flemish painter noted for works such as *Country Fair* (1641), *Tavern Scene* (1645), and *The Picture Gallery of Archduke Leopold Wilhelm* (1653)

1727   **Francois Hubert Drouais** -- French painter

1824   **Pierre Cecille Purvis de Chavannes** -- French artist and the most popular mural painter of the 1800s

1895   **Paul Eluard** -- French poet

1895   **George VI** -- King of England, 1936-1952

1896   **Jimmy Doolittle** -- Noted American flier who led the first bombing raid on Tokyo in World War II (1942)

1897   **Margaret Chase Smith** -- First woman to be elected to both houses of the United States Congress

1901   **Paul I** -- King of Greece, 1947-1964

1911   **Spike Jones** -- American composer, drummer, and leader of the band, Spike Jones and His City Slickers

1914   **Morey Amsterdam** -- American comedian, actor, and writer
1915   **Benjamin Wilfred Loewy** -- American composer, author, and leading tenor in musical comedy, plays, and on the radio
1917   **Dan Dailey** -- American actor and dancer
1918   **James Aubrey** -- American television executive
1919   **Shirley Jackson** -- American novelist and short-story writer, noted for works such as *The Lottery* (1949)
1922   **Charlie Trippi** -- Professional football player
1932   **Charlie Rich** -- American country singer
1935   **Lee Remick** -- American stage, screen, and television actress and attractive leading lady
1935   **Abbe Lane** -- Latin American singer
1946   **Stan Smith** -- American tennis player and 1972 Wimbledon singles champion
1946   **Patty Duke** -- American stage, screen, and television actress, billed also as Patty Duke Astin
1949   **Bill Buckner** -- Professional baseball player
1953   **Vijay Amritraj** -- Indian tennis player
1954   **Ib Andersen** -- Danish ballet dancer
1956   **Tony Nathan** -- Professional football player

DECEMBER 14 -- EVENTS

867 AD Adrian II was elected Roman Catholic pope.

872 AD John VIII was elected Roman Catholic pope.

1799   George Washington died at Mount Vernon at age 67. After he indicated to his secretary his burial instructions, he said "'Tis well," felt for his own pulse, and then died.

1812   Marshal Ney, Napoleon's second in command, crossed the Neman River after the Russian campaign with a tattered army of 30,000 men out of the original 600,000-man Grande Armee.

1819   Alabama was admitted to the Union as the 21st state.

1861   Prince Albert, husband of England's Queen Victoria, died of typhoid fever at age 42.

1910   The Carnegie Endowment for International Peace was established with a gift from Andrew Carnegie of $10 million, to "hasten the abolition of international war."

1911   Roald Amundsen, the great Norwegian explorer, discovered the South Pole.

1918   Women first voted in a British election. Complete woman suffrage was not granted in Great Britain, however, until 1928.

1962   U.S. space probe *Mariner 2* approached Venus, transmitting to Earth information about the planet's atmosphere and surface temperature.

1967   King Constantine II of Greece went into exile after unsuccessfully trying to overthrow the military junta that had ruled Greece since the preceding April.

DECEMBER 15 -- BIRTHDAYS

37 AD   Nero – Roman emperor who allegedly fiddled while Rome burned

1734   **George Romney** -- English portrait painter noted for works such as *Death of Wolfe* (1763) and *Lady Hamilton as a Bacchante* (1783)

1832   **Alexandre Gustave Eiffel** -- French engineer who designed the 984-foot Eiffel Tower in Paris (1889)

1852   **Antoine Henri Becquerel** -- French physicist who shared the 1903 Nobel Prize for physics with Pierre and Marie Curie for the discovery of natural radioactivity

1859   **Ludovic Lazarus Zamenhof** – Polish oculist who invented the universal language Esperanto

1861   **Charles Edgar Duryea** -- American automobile pioneer who with his brother Frank built the first successful gasoline-powered automobile in America (1893)

1861   **Pehr Evind Svinhufvud** -- First chief of state of an independent Finland

1888   **Maxwell Anderson** -- American playwright and screenwriter, noted for works such as *Elizabeth the Queen* (1930), *Key Largo* (1939), and *The Bad Seed* (1955)

1892   **John Paul Getty** -- American industrialist, founder of Getty Oil Company, and one of the richest men of his time

1892   **David Wendell Guion** -- American composer noted for songs such as "Home on the Range" and "Wild Geese"

1904   **Kermit Bloomgarden** -- American motion-picture producer

1907   **Oscar Niemeyer** – Brazilian architect noted for the design of the principal buildings of Brasilia, the new capital of Brazil

1911	Nicholas Dallis -- American cartoonist and co-creator of *Rex Morgan, M.D.*
1918	Jeff Chandler -- American motion-picture actor
1930	Edna O'Brien -- Irish writer
1933	Tim Conway -- American actor and comedian
1940	Nick Buoniconti -- Professional football player
1944	Stan Bahnson -- Professional baseball player
1948	Charles Scott -- Professional basketball player
1950	Jonathan Keyworth -- Professional football player
1950	Don Johnson -- American motion-picture and television actor, noted for his role in the long-running series *Miami Vice*
1965	Helen Slater -- American stage and motion-picture actress

DECEMBER 15 -- EVENTS

687 AD	Sergius I (Saint Sergius) was elected Roman Catholic pope.
1675	Jan Vermeer (Vermeer van Delft), the great Dutch painter, died at age 43.
1685	Izaak Walton, the noted English writer and fisherman, died in Winchester at age 90. He fished until he was 83.
1791	The U.S. Bill of Rights became law, having been ratified by the states.
1792	The Insurance Company of North America issued the first life insurance policy in America.
1864	The Battle of Nashville began in the Civil War. It ended the next day in a decisive Northern victory.
1890	Sioux Indian Chief Sitting Bull was shot and killed at the Standing Rock Reservation in South Dakota by federal troops.
1939	The great motion picture, *Gone with the Wind,* had its world premiere in Loew's Theater in Atlanta.
1945	Prince Fumimaro Konoye of Japan committed suicide to avoid facing trial as a war criminal.
1948	Alger Hiss, the former State Department official, was indicted on two perjury counts by a federal grand jury.
1961	Former Nazi Adolf Eichmann was sentenced to death in Jerusalem for World War II crimes committed against the Jews.

1971 The United States government announced the first devaluation of the dollar since the 1930s.

1978 President Carter announced that the United States would recognize China on January 1, 1979.

DECEMBER 16 -- BIRTHDAYS

1485 **Catherine of Aragon** – The first of the six wives of King Henry VIII of England, and the daughter of Ferdinand and Isabella of Spain

1716 **Thomas Gray** – English poet noted for "Elegy Written in a Country Churchyard" (1751), perhaps the best-known poem in the English language

1770 **Ludwig van Beethoven** -- Perhaps the greatest composer in musical history, and certainly one of the two or three greatest

1775 **Jane Austen** -- One of the greatest English novelists, noted for works such as *Pride and Prejudice* (1813), *Emma* (1816), and *Northanger Abbey* (1818)

1790 **Leopold I** -- First King of the Belgians, 1831-1865

1863 **George Santayana** -- Spanish-born American philosopher, poet, and critic, who also wrote the popular novel, *The Last Puritan* (1936)

1882 **Sir Jack Hobbs** -- English cricketer

1899 **Sir Noel Coward** -- English playwright and actor, noted for such works as the song, "Mad Dogs and Englishmen," and the play, *Blithe Spirit* (1941)

1901 **Margaret Mead** -- American anthropologist and writer, noted for her studies of the cultures of the Pacific Islands, the United States, and Russia

1917 **Arthur C. Clarke** -- English writer of science fiction and nonfiction, noted for works such as *Childhood's End* (1953)

1918 **Murray Kempton** -- American editor and writer

1939 **Liv Ullmann** -- Outstanding dramatic actress of Swedish and international motion-pictures, who gained fame in the 1960s and 1970s as the star of a number of Ingmar Bergman productions

1941 **Lesley Stahl** -- American broadcast journalist

1951 **Jean Fuget Jr.** -- Professional football player

1951 **Mike Flanagan** -- Professional baseball player

1962   **William "Refrigerator" Perry** -- Professional football player

DECEMBER 16 -- EVENTS

882 AD   Marinus I was elected Roman Catholic pope, replacing the murdered John VIII.

1653   Oliver Cromwell became Lord Protector of England.

1689   Parliament passed the English Bill of Rights.

1773   The "Boston Tea Party" took place in Boston Harbor, as 40 to 50 colonists disguised as Indians broke open 340 chests of tea in 3 British ships and dumped the tea into the harbor.

1809   Napoleon divorced Josephine in order to marry a younger woman to give him an heir for his empire.

1838   The Boers in South Africa crushed the Zulu king Dingaan.

1864   The Civil War Battle of Nashville ended with Union general Thomas smashing Confederate general Hood's army and ending Southern resistance in the West.

1893   Czech composer Antonin Dvorak attended the world premiere of his *New World Symphony* at Carnegie Hall in New York.

1905   *Variety,* a weekly show business periodical, was published for the first time.

1916   Grigori Rasputin, the Russian "mad Monk," was poisoned by a group of noblemen bent on ridding Russia of his corrupting influence. He lived until December 30 when he was shot.

1944   The Germans attacked the Americans in the Ardennes (Belgium), beginning the Battle of the Bulge in World War II.

1965   W. Somerset Maugham, the noted English author, died at Villa Mauresque in Switzerland at age 91.

DECEMBER 17 -- BIRTHDAYS

1632   **Anthony Wood** -- British antiquarian

1732   **John Townsend** -- American cabinetmaker

1734   **William Floyd** -- Leader in the struggle for American independence, and a New York signer of the Declaration of Independence

1734   **Maria I** -- Queen of Portugal, 1777-1816

1749   **Domenico Cimarosa** -- Italian composer, noted for such works as *The Secret Marriage* (1792)

1778   **Sir Humphry Davy** – English chemist noted for the invention of the Davy lamp, a miner's safety lamp, and for first isolating the elements sodium, potassium, barium, calcium, magnesium, and strontium

1797   **Joseph Henry** – American physicist and pioneer in electromagnetism, for whom the unit *henry* of electrical inductance is named

1807   **John Greenleaf Whittier** -- One of the best-known American poets, noted for such works as "Barefoot Boy" (1856) and "Snow-Bound" (1866)

1830   **Jules de Goncourt** -- French novelist, art critic, and diarist, who with his brother Edmond wrote *Germinie Lacerteux* (1864), one of the earliest examples of naturalism in fiction

1853   **Sir Herbert Beerbohm Tree** – One of the great figures of the English theater, and half brother of writer Max Beerbohm

1873   **Ford Madox Ford** -- English author of complex and symbolic novels, the best known of which form the series *Parade's End* of the 1920s

1874   **William Lyon Mackenzie King** -- Three times prime minister of Canada, 1921-1926, 1926-1930, and 1935-1948

1894   **Arthur Fiedler** – Conductor of the Boston Pops Orchestra, 1930-1980

1903   **Erskine Caldwell** -- American novelist noted for such works as *Tobacco Road* (1932) and *God's Little Acre* (1933)

1904   **Paul Cadmus** -- American painter and etcher

1906   **William McChesney Martin Jr.** -- American broker and chairman of the Federal Reserve System during the Eisenhower and Kennedy administrations

1908   **Willard Frank Libby** – Nobel Prize-winning American chemist who discovered carbon 14 (1947) and the process of carbon dating

1910   **Jimmy Caras** -- Hall of Fame pocket billiards player

1926   **Patrice Wymore** -- American stage and motion-picture actress

1926   **Allan V. Cox** – American geophysicist known for his study of the earth's magnetic poles

1929   **William Safire** -- American journalist and author

1930   **Bob Guccione** -- Publisher of *Penthouse* magazine

1942   **Paul Butterfield** -- American blues harmonica player

1957   **Bob Ojeda** -- Professional baseball player

DECEMBER 17 -- EVENTS

63 AD Lazarus died again (according to Biblical theory).

1187 Clement III was elected Roman Catholic pope.

1830 Simon Bolivar, the great South American liberator, died at age 47.

1843 The great novelist Charles Dickens published *A Christmas Carol,* one of the most famous stories ever written.

1892 Peter Ilich Tchaikovsky's famous ballet, *The Nutcracker,* was first presented, at the Maryinsky Theater in St. Petersburg.

1903 The Wright brothers, Wilbur and Orville, made the world's first airplane flight, at Kitty Hawk, N.C. Orville went first and Wilbur flew the longest of their four flights.

1919 Pierre Auguste Renoir, the great French painter, died in Provence at age 78.

1925 General Billy Mitchell was court-martialed for advocating a strong air force in defiance of his superiors. He later was given the Congressional Medal of Honor (1946).

1933 The Chicago Bears beat the New York Giants, 23-21, in the first world championship football game.

1936 Edgar Bergen, one of the most famous ventriloquists of all time, made his debut in New York with his dummy Charlie McCarthy.

1939 The German pocket battleship *Graf Spee* was scuttled in Montevideo Harbor on orders of Adolf Hitler to keep the British from taking her in World War II.

1971 Bangladesh became independent of Pakistan.

DECEMBER 18 -- BIRTHDAYS

1633 **Willem van de Velde the Younger --** Dutch painter

1707 **Charles Wesley --** The famous hymn writer of Methodism, who wrote some 6,000 hymns, and was the brother of Methodist Church founder John Wesley

1709 **Elizabeth --** Empress of Russia, 1741-1762, and daughter of Peter the Great

1835 **Lyman Abbott --** American Congregational preacher and editor, who popularized the reconciliation of evolution with the Biblical account of creation

1856   **Sir Joseph** John Thomson -- English physicist who in 1897 discovered the electron

1859   **Francis Thompson** -- British poet noted for "The Hound of Heaven" (1893)

1861   **Edward MacDowell** – American composer and pianist noted for such short piano pieces as "To a Wild Rose" and "To a Water Lily"

1863   **Francis Ferdinand** -- Austrian archduke whose assassination in 1914 triggered World War I

1870   **Hector Hugh** Munro -- British writer who wrote under the pen name Saki, noted for works such as *Beasts and Super-Beasts* and *The Square Egg*

1879   **Paul Klee** – Swiss-German artist and one of the greatest and most original masters of modern painting

1886   **Ty Cobb** -- One of the two greatest baseball players in history (with Babe Ruth), with a record .367 lifetime batting average

1886   **Chu Teh** -- Founder of the Chinese Communist army

1897   **Fletch Henderson** -- American bandleader

1904   **George Stevens** -- American motion-picture director who won Academy Awards for *A Place in the Sun* (1951) and *Giant* (1956), and who directed the famous Western, *Shane* (1953)

1907   **Christopher Fry** -- English dramatist who wrote in verse works such as *The Lady's Not for Burning* (1949)

1910   **Abe Burrows** -- Broadway play producer and dramatist

1911   **Jules Dassin** -- American motion-picture director, noted for works such as *The Naked City* (1948) and *Never on Sunday* (1960)

1913   **Willy Brandt** – Mayor of West Berlin after World War II and chancellor of West Germany in the 1970s

1916   **Douglas Fraser** – President of the United Automobile Workers in the 1970s and early 1980s

1916   **Betty Grable** -- American actress and "pin-up girl" of World War II GIs

1917   **Ossie Davis** – American actor, director, and playwright who wrote and starred in the play *Purlie Victorious* (1961) and the film version *Gone Are the Days!* (1963)

1927   **Ramsey Clark** -- Son of U.S. Supreme Court Justice Tom Clark, and U.S. Attorney General under President Lyndon Johnson

1931   **Gene Shue** -- Professional basketball superstar with over 10,000 career points

1932   **Roger Smith** -- American motion-picture and television actor
1943   **Keith Richards** -- British guitarist with the Rolling Stones musical group
1946   **Greg Landry** -- Professional football player
1947   **Steven Spielberg** -- American motion-picture director noted for films such as *Jaws*, *E.T.*, and *Raiders of the Lost Ark*
1952   **Stan Fritts** -- Professional football player
1953   **Johnny Gray** -- Professional football player
1956   **Jerry Robinson** -- Professional football player

DECEMBER 18 -- EVENTS

1534   The Act of Supremacy, making the Church of England a separate institution and establishing the king as its supreme head, was formally accepted by King Henry VIII.
1737   Antonio Stradivari, the greatest violin maker of all time, died at an approximate age of 93.
1787   New Jersey became the third state when it ratified the U.S. Constitution.
1812   Napoleon reached Paris after 13 days of traveling incognito from Russia after his disastrous invasion of that country.
1813   The British captured Fort Niagara in the War of 1812.
1865   The 13th Amendment to the Constitution was proclaimed, ending slavery in the United States.
1915   President Woodrow Wilson married his second wife, Edith Bolling Galt.
1931   Legs Diamond (John Thomas), the American gangland boss, was shot and killed by his enemies, contradicting his earlier remark that "the bullet hasn't been made that can kill me!"
1935   Dr. Eduard Benes was elected president of Czechoslovakia.
1956   Japan joined the United Nations.
1969   Great Britain abolished capital punishment.

DECEMBER 19 -- BIRTHDAYS

1683   **Philip V** -- King of Spain, 1700-1724, whose elevation to the Spanish throne caused the War of the Spanish Succession

1814   **Edwin M. Stanton** -- Secretary of war under President Lincoln

1849   **Henry Clay Frick** -- American industrialist and philanthropist

1852   **Albert A. Michelson** -- American physicist who established the speed of light as a constant, and who in 1907 became the first American to win the Nobel Prize in physics

1861   **Italo Svevo** -- Italian novelist and pioneer of the psychological novel in Italy

1865   **Minnie Maddern Fiske** -- One of America's leading stage actresses for more than 60 years

1879   **Beals Coleman Wright** -- American Hall of Fame tennis player and U.S. singles champion in 1905

1884   **Ernie Burnett** -- American composer noted for "My Melancholy Baby"

1888   **Fritz Reiner** -- One of the greatest symphony orchestra and operatic conductors of his time

1888   **Walter Donovan** -- American composer and pianist noted for songs such as "One Dozen Roses" and "Aba Daba Honeymoon"

1894   **Ford Frick** -- National League president, 1934-1951, and Commissioner of Baseball, 1951-1965

1902   **Sir Ralph Richardson** -- Eminent British character actor of stage and screen with a career of over 60 years

1906   **Leonid Brezhnev** -- Russian head of state who succeeded Khrushchev in 1964 and served until the early 1980s

1907   **H. Allen Smith** -- American humorist

1910   **Jean Genet** -- French novelist and playwright known for his violent, complex plays

1912   **Michel Andre** -- French actor and playwright and son of actor Marcel Andre

1915   **Carlton Franklin Stutz** -- American composer noted for songs such as "Little Things Mean a Lot" and "Jamestown Suite"

1920   **David Susskind** -- American television producer and talk show host

1923   **Gordon Jackson** -- Scottish motion-picture and television actor

1924   **Edmond Purdom** -- English stage and motion-picture actor

1926   **Bobby Layne** -- Professional football superstar

1933   **Cicely Tyson** -- American stage, screen, and television actress

1934   **Al Kaline** -- Hall of Fame baseball player

1943   **William C. DeVries** -- American surgeon who implanted the first artificial heart in a human being, in Barney Clark on December 2, 1982

1946   **Robert Urich** -- American actor

1947   **Janie Fricke** -- American country singer

1958   **Limahl** -- British singer with the Kajagoogoo musical group

1962   **Clay Parker** -- Professional baseball player

1963   **Jennifer Beals** -- American motion-picture actress

DECEMBER 19 -- EVENTS

1732   Benjamin Franklin began publishing *Poor Richard's Almanac.*

1776   Thomas Paine published the first installment of *The American Crisis* in the *Pennsylvania Journal.* The essay opened with the words: "These are the times that try men's souls."

1777   George Washington's army retired to Valley Forge for the "Winter of Despair" of 1777-1778 in the Revolutionary War.

1848   Emily Bronte, the great English novelist, died of tuberculosis at age 30.

1851   J.M.W. Turner, the noted English painter, died in Chelsea at age 76.

1871   Birmingham, Alabama, was incorporated.

1919   The comic strip, *Thimble Theater,* by E.C. Segar, first appeared. The fabled Popeye figure, however, was not added to its cast until January 17, 1929.

1924   William Green succeeded Samuel Gompers as president of the American Federation of Labor.

1941   Adolf Hitler dismissed his chief of staff, General von Brauchitsch, and assumed personal command of the German Army himself.

1946   Ho Chi Minh, Indochinese Nationalist leader, began his guerrilla war against the French.

1950   General Dwight D. Eisenhower was appointed commander of the NATO forces.

1959   Walter Williams, the last surviving veteran of the Civil War, died at age 117. He had fought in the Confederate Army.

1972   *Apollo 17* splashed down in the Pacific, completing the 9th trip to the moon.

1974   Nelson A. Rockefeller was sworn in as the 41st vice president of the United States.

DECEMBER 20 -- BIRTHDAYS

1629   **Pieter de Hooch** -- Dutch artist noted for works such as *The Mother* and *Interior with Figures*

1738   **Clodion** -- French sculptor

1838   **Edwin Abbott** -- English clergyman, writer, and author of *Flatland*

1867   **Pudge Heffelfinger** -- Professional football player

1868   **Harvey Firestone** -- Pioneer rubber manufacturer and founder of the Firestone Tire and Rubber Company

1871   **Henry Kimball Hadley** -- American conductor and composer

1875   **Charley Grapewin** -- American stage and motion-picture actor who played Jeeter Lester in *Tobacco Road,* and appeared in 100 movies and countless plays during a 60-year career.

1876   **Walter Sydney Adams** -- American astronomer

1881   **Branch Rickey** -- Professional baseball executive who devised the farm system, and broke the color line by bringing to the game the first black player, Jackie Robinson, in 1947

1886   **Hazel Hotchkiss Wightman** -- American tennis player for whom the Wightman Cup was named, four times U.S. champion, and one of the greatest women players in history

1888   **Abe Olman** -- American composer and pianist, noted for songs such as "Oh Johnny Oh," "Down Among the Sweltering Palms," "Down by the O-Hi-O," and "Come Back to Waikiki"

1894   **Sir Robert Gordon Menzies** -- Australian prime minister, 1939-1941 and 1949-1966

1895   **Suzanne K. Langer** -- American philosopher and educator, and author of *Philosophy in a New Key*

1898   **Irene Dunne** -- American stage, screen, and television actress, and one of Hollywood's top-ranking stars until her retirement in the 1950s

1899   **John J. Sparkman** -- U.S. senator and candidate for vice president on Adlai Stevenson's ticket in 1952

1900   **Gabby Hartnett** -- Hall of Fame baseball player and manager

1901   **Robert Jemison Van de Graaff** -- American physicist and inventor of the electrostatic generator, or Van de Graaff generator

1902   **Sidney Hook** -- American philosopher and writer

1902   **Max Lerner** -- Russian-born American writer and lecturer

1905   **Albert Dekker** -- American stage and motion-picture actor and director, with a 40-year career

1907   **Horace Coy Poe** -- American lyricist noted for songs such as "The Object of My Affection" and "What's the Reason I'm Not Pleasin' You?"

1907   **Paul Francis Webster** -- American lyricist noted for songs such as "Doctor, Lawyer, Indian Chief," "Secret Love," "Somewhere My Love," "Love Is a Many-Splendored Thing," and "The Shadow of Your Smile"

1914   **Harry F. Byrd Jr.** -- U.S. senator and son of the long-time senator from Virginia

1918   **Audrey Totter** -- American radio, motion-picture, and television actress

1922   **George Roy Hill** -- American motion-picture director who won the Academy Award for *The Sting* (1973)

1927   **Dean Burch** -- American political figure and FCC chairman under President Nixon

1941   **Dave Stallworth** -- Professional basketball player

1942   **Robert Hayes** -- Professional football player

1946   **Uri Geller** -- Israeli psychic noted for reading minds and moving watch hands without touching them

1949   **Cecil Cooper** -- Professional baseball player

1949   **Oscar Gamble** -- Professional baseball player

DECEMBER 20 -- EVENTS

44 BC   Cicero, the great Roman orator and statesman, delivered his third *Philippic* (one of 14 speeches against Mark Antony) in the Roman Senate.

1334   Benedict XII was elected Roman Catholic pope. He was the third of the Avignon popes.

1606   Captain John Smith and 120 colonists left London bound for America. They were to reach the Chesapeake Bay in April and found the Jamestown colony in May of 1607.

1690   Englishman Job Charnock of the East India Company founded Calcutta, India.

1790   The first successful U.S. cotton mill began operations, in Pawtucket, Rhode Island.

1803   Louisiana was officially transferred from French to United States control, following the Louisiana Purchase.

1860   South Carolina voted to secede from the Union, the first state to do so.

1880   Broadway became the "Great White Way," as it was illuminated by electricity for the first time.

1917   Communist dictator V.I. Lenin ordered the creation of the *Cheka,* a Russian secret police force designed to establish rule by terror.

1922   Fourteen republics of Russia were combined to form the Union of Soviet Socialist Republics.

1928   The Ethel Barrymore Theater, the first named for a living person, opened in New York City.

1941   Admiral Ernest J. King was appointed commander-in-chief of the United States Fleet in World War II.

1968   The noted American author, John Steinbeck, died at age 66.

DECEMBER 21 -- BIRTHDAYS

1401   **Masaccio (Tommaso Guidi)** -- The greatest painter in Florence during the early Renaissance, whose art was studied by both Michelangelo and Raphael

1639   **Jean Racine** -- One of the greatest French playwrights of all time

1804   **Benjamin Disraeli** -- One of Great Britain's greatest prime ministers, 1868 (ten months) and 1874-1880, who improved the common citizen's lot at home and extended the empire to its zenith abroad

1815   **Thomas Couture** -- French painter

1872   **Albert Payson Terhune** -- American author noted for his stories about dogs, especially collies

1879   **Joseph Stalin** -- Dictator of the U.S.S.R., 1929-1953

1891   **John W. McCormack** -- Speaker of the U.S. House of Representatives, 1962-1971

1892   **Walter Hagen** -- One of the superstars of professional golf, who won the U.S. Open in 1914 and the British Open four times in the 1920s

1905   **Harry Revel** – English-born composer and pianist, noted for songs such as "Did You Ever See a Dream Walking?" "With My Eyes Wide Open I'm Dreaming," and "Just the Way You Are"

1909   **George Ball** – American statesman and diplomat of the Kennedy and Johnson Administrations

1911   **Josh Gibson** -- Hall of Fame baseball player who was one of the greatest hitters in the so-called Negro leagues

1918   **Kurt Waldheim** -- Fourth secretary-general of the United Nations and President of Austria, who was accused of engaging in Nazi atrocities during World War II

1922   **Paul Winchell** -- American ventriloquist

1926   **Joe Paterno** -- Noted college football coach

1935   **Phil Donahue** -- American television talk show host

1937   **Jane Fonda** -- American motion-picture actress, daughter of actor Henry Fonda, and Academy Award winner as best actress for *Klute* (1971) and *Coming Home* (1978)

1940   **Frank Zappa** – American avant-garde rock guitarist and composer, chosen as Pop Musician of the Year in 1970, 1971, and 1972

1946   **Carl Wilson** -- American guitarist with the Beach Boys musical group

1948   **Dave Kingman** -- Professional baseball player who hit over 400 career home runs

1948   **Elliott Maddox** -- Professional baseball player

1949   **Patti Hogan** -- American tennis player

1952   **Joaquin Andujar** -- Professional baseball player

1954   **Chris Evert** -- American tennis superstar and one of the game's all time greatest women players, particularly on clay

1960   **Roger McDowell** -- Professional baseball player

1960   **Andy Van Slyke** -- Professional baseball player

DECEMBER 21 -- EVENTS

1124   Honorius II was elected Roman Catholic pope.

1620   After a month of exploring the Massachusetts coast, the Pilgrims in the *Mayflower* landed at Plymouth. The passengers disembarked 5 days later after further exploration.

1864	General William Tecumseh Sherman's Union troops occupied Savannah, Georgia, completing his famous "March to the Sea" in the Civil War.
1879	News of Thomas A. Edison's invention of the electric light was announced, astounding the world.
1881	Benjamin Disraeli, the famous English prime minister, died in London on his 77th birthday.
1898	The element radium was discovered by French scientists Marie and Pierre Curie.
1913	The first crossword puzzle was published, in the New York *World.* It was compiled by journalist Arthur Wynne and had 32 clues.
1914	The first feature-length silent film comedy, *Tillie's Punctured Romance,* was released, starring Charlie Chaplin and Marie Dressler, and directed by Mack Sennett.
1937	Walt Disney's animated motion picture, *Snow White and the Seven Dwarfs,* was shown for the first time.
1944	Horse racing was banned in the United States for the duration of World War II.
1945	General George S. Patton, the great American World War II general, died at age 60 of injuries suffered in an automobile accident.
1953	Ex-Premier Mohammed Mossadegh of Iran was convicted of trying to lead a revolt against the Shah.
1958	General Charles de Gaulle was elected first president of the French Fifth Republic.
1968	*Apollo 8* was launched with astronauts Borman, Anders, and Lovell aboard to orbit the moon.

DECEMBER 22 -- BIRTHDAYS

1696	**James Edward Oglethorpe** – English army officer who was the founder (1733) and first governor of Georgia
1723	**Karl Friedrich Abel** -- German symphonist
1727	**William Ellery** -- One of the Rhode Island signers of the Declaration of Independence and a member of the Continental Congress
1768	**John Crome** -- English painter noted for works such as *Boulevard des Italiens* (1815)

1802   **Sara Coleridge** – English author of children's verse, and daughter of the poet Samuel Taylor Coleridge

1831   **Charles Stuart Calverley** -- English poet and parodist

1856   **Frank B. Kellogg** -- U.S. secretary of state who won the 1929 Nobel Peace Prize for his work in framing the Kellogg-Briand Peace Treaty of 1928

1858   **Giacomo Puccini** – One of the five greatest opera composers of all time, noted for works such as *La Boheme* (1896), *Tosca* (1900), and *Madame Butterfly* (1904)

1862   **Connie Mack** -- Hall of Fame baseball player, manager, and owner, known as the "grand old man" of baseball

1869   **Edwin Arlington Robinson** – Pulitzer Prize-winning poet, noted for works such as "The Man Who Died Twice" (1925) and "Tristram" (1928)

1885   **Deems Taylor** -- American composer and music critic

1885   **Edgar Varese** -- Franco-American composer

1888   **J. Arthur Rank** -- British motion-picture magnate who for a quarter of a century owned more than half of the British studios and more than 1000 theaters

1901   **Andre Kostelanetz** -- American conductor of popular and classical music

1908   **Max Bill** -- Swiss artist

1908   **Giacomo Manzu** -- Italian sculptor

1912   **Lady Bird Johnson** -- Wife of President Lyndon B. Johnson

1917   **Gene Rayburn** -- American actor and television show host

1922   **Jim Wright** -- U.S. congressman and Speaker of the House, who because of ethics charges in 1989 became the only Speaker in history to resign in mid-term

1924   **Ruth Roman** -- American stage and motion-picture actress and short story writer

1938   **Matty Alou** -- Professional baseball player

1944   **Steve Carlton** – Professional baseball pitcher and superstar with a career total of over 3,500 strikeouts and 300 career wins

1945   **Diane Sawyer** -- American television reporter

1948   **Steve Garvey** -- Professional baseball player

1949   **Guy Ray** -- Professional football player

1951   **Jan Stephenson** -- Professional golfer

1954   **Ken Landreaux** -- Professional baseball player

1955   **Lonnie Smith** -- Professional baseball player

DECEMBER 22 -- EVENTS

69 AD   Roman Emperor Vitellius was killed in a street battle in Rome by soldiers of Vespasian, who succeeded Vitellius as emperor.

1775   The Continental Navy was established by the Continental Congress with Ezek Hopkins, a former New England sea captain, as the first commander-in-chief.

1807   Congress passed the Embargo Act, designed to cut off trade with Europe and bring the warring nations of Britain and France to reason.

1864   Union General William T. Sherman sent President Lincoln the message, "I beg to present you as a Christmas gift the city of Savannah."

1880   George Eliot (Mary Ann Evans), the noted English novelist, died at age 61.

1894   Alfred Dreyfus was found guilty of spying against France in the famous Dreyfus case. He was released in 1906 and pronounced innocent after an imprisonment on Devil's Island.

1894   The United States Golf Association was organized.

1944   "Nuts," said American General Anthony McAuliffe to German demands that he surrender at Bastogne in the Battle of the Bulge in World War II.

1962   "Telstar," by the Tornadoes, became the first record by a British musical group to top the U.S. charts.

1968   North Korea released 82 members of the U.S. intelligence ship *Pueblo*, eleven months after their seizure.

DECEMBER 23 -- BIRTHDAYS

1174   **Louis I** -- Duke of Bavaria

1682   **James Gibbs** -- British architect

1732   **Sir Richard Arkwright** -- British inventor and manufacturer, noted for a water-powered spinning machine

1777   **Alexander I** -- Czar of Russia, 1801-1825, who formed the coalition that defeated Napoleon

1804   Charles Augustin Saint-Beuve -- French critic, poet, and novelist

1805   **Joseph Smith** -- Founder and first president of the Mormon Church, officially called the Church of Jesus Christ of Latter-day Saints (in 1830)

1819   **George Barnard** -- American photographer

1856   **James Buchanan Duke** – American businessman and philanthropist, who organized the American Tobacco Company (1890) and established the Duke Endowment (1924)

1857   **Edward Reynolds Pease** -- Co-founder of the Fabian Society (1884), a group of British socialists

1860   Harriet Monroe -- American poet, editor, and founder of *Poetry: A Magazine of Verse* (1912)

1870   **John Marin** -- American painter, famous for his watercolor landscapes, such as *Off Stonington* (1921)

1885   **Vincent Sardi** -- Noted Italian-American restauranteur

1900   **Otto Soglow** -- American cartoonist and creator of the comic strip, *The Little King* (1934)

1907   **Don McNeill** – American radio show host on the *Don McNeill Breakfast Club*

1907   **Barney Ross** – World lightweight boxing champion, 1933-1935, and welterweight champion, 1934 and 1935-1938

1908   **Yousuf Karsh** -- Armenian-born Canadian photographer who made the famous picture of Winston Churchill used on commemorative stamps by six countries

1918   **Helmut Schmidt** -- Chancellor of West Germany in the 1970s

1918   **Jose Greco** -- One of the most famous Spanish dancers of his time

1929   **Dick Weber** -- Prominent American bowler

1935   **Paul Hornung** -- Professional football superstar

1943   **Jerry Koosman** -- Professional baseball player

1943   **Elizabeth Hartman** – American stage and motion-picture actress

1946   **Helen Gourlay** -- Australian tennis player

1948   **Susan Lucci** – American actress noted for her role in *All My Children* as Erica Kane, "the queen of soap-opera bitches"

1971   **Corey Haim** -- American television actor

DECEMBER 23 -- EVENTS

619 AD Boniface V became Roman Catholic pope.

1783 George Washington resigned his commission as commander-in-chief of the army and retired to Mount Vernon.

1823 The most popular Christmas poem in America, "A Visit from St. Nicholas," also known as "'Twas the Night Before Christmas," was published by the author, Clement Clarke Moore.

1834 George Hansom patented the Hansom cab, a horse-drawn one-seated vehicle that served as a big-city taxi in the 1800s

1863 William Makepeace Thackeray, the great English novelist, died in London at age 52.

1888 Vincent van Gogh, the great Dutch painter, cut off one of his own ears during an epileptic seizure. He also threatened to kill the painter Paul Gauguin who was visiting him.

1913 The United States Federal Reserve System was established, as President Wilson signed the Glass-Owen Currency Act.

1928 The National Broadcasting Company (NBC) established a permanent coast-to-coast radio network.

1938 A new kind of music, *boogie-woogie,* was introduced in Carnegie Hall by two pianists, Meade Lewis and Albert Ammons.

1941 Wake Island surrendered to the Japanese in World War II.

1948 Ex-Premier Hideki Tojo of Japan was hanged in Tokyo as a war criminal.

1953 Lavrenty P. Beria, head of the dreaded Soviet secret police, was executed in a purge of top Russian officials.

DECEMBER 24 -- BIRTHDAYS

3 BC **Servius Sulpicius Galba** -- Emperor of Rome, A.D. 68-69

1167 **John (Lackland)** -- King of England, 1199-1216, who was forced to approve the Magna Carta in 1215

1491 **Saint Ignatius Loyola** -- Spanish nobleman who in 1534 founded the Society of Jesus, better known as the Jesuits

1745 **Benjamin Rush** -- American physician, patriot, reformer, and Continental Army surgeon-general

1754 **George Crabbe** -- English poet

1791   **Augustine Eugene Scribe** -- French dramatist noted for the tragedy *Adrienne Lecouvreur* (1849) and for some 400 other dramatic pieces

1809   **Kit Carson** -- Famous American frontiersman, hunter, guide, and soldier

1818   **James P. Joule** -- English physicist who shared in the discovery of the law of conservation of energy, and for whom the unit of work, or energy, the joule, is named

1822   **Charles Hermite** – Noted French mathematician for whom the Hermite polynomials are named

1822   **Matthew Arnold** -- One of the greatest poets of Victorian England, noted for works such as "Dover Beach"

1845   **George I** -- King of Greece, 1863-1913, who succeeded Otto, the first king of Greece, and who was the ancestor of every later Greek king

1880   **Johnny Gruelle** -- Creator of *Raggedy Ann*

1881   **Juan Ramon Jimenez** -- Nobel Prize-winning Spanish poet (1956), whose masterpiece is "Platero and I" (1917)

1893   **Harry Warren** – American composer noted for songs such as "The Lullaby of Broadway," "Jeepers Creepers," "Chattanooga Choo Choo," and "I've Got a Gal in Kalamazoo"

1903   **Ad Reinhardt** -- American painter

1903   **Joseph Cornell** -- American sculptor

1905   **Howard Hughes** -- American financier, aviator, and one of the richest men of his time

1907   **I.F. Stone** -- American publisher

1907   **Adam Rapacki** -- Polish socialist and economist

1909   **Mike Mazurki** -- Austrian-American motion-picture actor

1910   **William Hayward Pickering** – American physicist and head of the team that developed *Explorer 1*, the first U.S. satellite

1930   **Robert Joffrey** -- American choreographer

1957   **Ian Burden** -- British musician with the Human League group

DECEMBER 24 -- EVENTS

640 AD John IV was elected Roman Catholic pope.

1492   Columbus lost his flagship, the *Santa Maria,* which was wrecked on a reef near the present Cap-Haitien in Haiti, on his first voyage to America.

1524 Vasco da Gama, the Portuguese explorer who first sailed to India around the Cape of Good Hope, died in Cochin, India, at age 55.

1814 The United States and Great Britain signed the Treaty of Ghent, ending the War of 1812.

1818 Joseph Mohr wrote the words to the famous Christmas carol "Silent Night," and Franz Gruber composed the music and presented it at the midnight mass.

1822 Dr. Clement Clarke Moore first read his newly written poem, "A Visit from St. Nicholas," to his children. He published it a year later.

1866 The Ku Klux Klan was founded at Pulaski, Tennessee, as a social group for war veterans.

1871 Giuseppe Verdi's great opera *Aida* had its world premiere in Cairo, Egypt.

1920 The comic strip, *Sappo,* by E.C. Segar, first appeared.

1920 Enrico Caruso, the great Italian operatic tenor, made his last appearance at the Metropolitan Opera House in New York in *La Juive.*

1942 French Admiral Jean Darlan, administrator of North Africa, was assassinated by a young anti-Vichy French patriot in World War II.

1943 General Dwight D. Eisenhower was appointed supreme commander of Operation Overlord (the invasion of Normandy) by President Roosevelt and Prime Minister Churchill.

1951 Libya was declared independent by the United Nations.

1968 U.S. spacecraft *Apollo* 8 flew around the moon, broadcasting a Christmas message to earth.

DECEMBER 25 -- BIRTHDAYS

4 BC **Jesus Christ** – Founder of the Christian religion (December 25 is traditional, and the year is scholars' best guess, since Christ was born in the age of Herod the Great, who died in 4 B.C.)

1564 **Abraham Bloemaert** -- Dutch painter

1717 **Pius VI** -- Roman Catholic pope, 1775-1799

1721 **William Collins** -- English poet

1801   **Wesley Harper** -- One of the four Harper brothers who founded the famous publishing house of Harper and Brothers

1821   **Clara Barton** -- American humanitarian "Angel of the Battlefield," and founder in 1881 of the American Red Cross

1847   **James D. Kelly** -- Composer of the U.S. Navy's anthem, "Anchor's Aweigh"

1855   **Pud Galvin** -- Hall of Fame baseball pitcher who was the first to win 300 career games and who won 46 games in the 1883 season

1863   **Charles Pathe** -- French industrialist and film pioneer, and cofounder with his brothers of the Pathe film company

1876   **Giuseppe De Luca** -- Italian baritone

1881   **Sir John Greer Dill** -- British World War II chief of staff

1883   **Maurice Utrillo** -- French artist known for his paintings of Paris street scenes

1885   **Paul Manship** -- American sculptor best known for his gilded bronze *Prometheus* fountain at Rockefeller Center in New York City

1886   **Kid Ory** -- American trombonist, composer, and jazz musician

1887   **Conrad Hilton** -- American businessman who in 1946 organized the Hilton Hotel Systems

1888   **David Lawrence** -- American journalist and publisher

1892   **Dame Rebecca West** -- English journalist, novelist, and critic, noted for works such as *Henry James* (1916) and *The Birds Fall Down* (1966)

1893   **Robert Leroy Ripley** -- American cartoonist who in 1918 created Ripley's *Believe It or Not*

1895   **Arthur H. Gibbs** -- American composer and pianist, noted for songs such as "Runnin' Wild"

1899   **Humphrey Bogart** -- American motion-picture actor who has become a Hollywood legend

1899   **John Bowers** -- American actor and handsome leading man of Hollywood silents

1902   **Barton MacLane** -- American motion-picture and television actor who appeared in over 200 films

1906   **Clark Clifford** -- Special counsel and speechwriter to President Truman and secretary of defense under President Lyndon Johnson

1907   **Cab Calloway** -- American singer and actor

1911   **Burne Hogarth** -- American artist who succeeded Harold Foster in drawing the comic strip *Tarzan*

1912   **Tony Martin** -- American singer and actor

1918   **Anwar Sadat** -- President of Egypt in the 1970s and early 1980s, who signed the historic Camp David peace agreement between Egypt and Israel

1924   **Moktar Ould Daddah** -- First president of Mauretania

1924   **Rod Serling** -- American writer and creator of television's *Twilight Zone*

1925   **Ned Garver** -- Professional baseball player

1927   **Nelly Fox** -- Professional baseball player

1935   **Little Richard (Richard Penniman)** -- American soul and rock singer

1937   **Kelly Isley** -- American singer with the Isley Brothers

1942   **Francoise Durr** -- French tennis player

1943   **Howard Twilley Jr.** -- Professional football player

1945   **Ken Stabler** -- Professional football superstar

1945   **Gary Sandy** -- American television actor

1946   **Norman Bulaich** -- Professional football player

1946   **Larry Csonka** -- Professional football superstar

1948   **Barbara Mandrell** -- American country singer and television entertainer

1949   **Sissy Spacek** -- American motion-picture actress

1950   **Manny Trillo** -- Professional baseball player

1954   **Annie Lennox** – British singer with the Eurythmics musical group

1955   **William Andrews** -- Professional football player

1956   **Billy Martin** -- American tennis player

1958   **Rickey Henderson** -- Professional baseball superstar

DECEMBER 25 -- EVENTS

336 AD The first recorded celebration of Christmas on December 25 took place in Rome.

800 AD Charlemagne was crowned the first Holy Roman Emperor by Pope Leo III in Rome.

1066   William the Conqueror was crowned King of England.

1170   Thomas a Becket, the archbishop of Canterbury, excommuni-
        cated all those who assisted at the coronation of English King
        Henry II. Becket was murdered 4 days later.

1356   Holy Roman Emperor Charles IV issued the famous *Golden
        Bull*, which regulated imperial elections.

1776   George Washington and his men made their famous crossing of
        the Delaware River to Trenton, New Jersey, where the next
        morning they wiped out the entire Hessian garrison.

1818   The famous Christmas carol, "Silent Night," written the previ-
        ous day by Joseph Mohr and Franz Gruber, was first publicly
        sung, by Gruber in the midnight mass in Oberndorff, Germany.

1868   President Andrew Johnson proclaimed an unconditional par-
        don and amnesty to all who "participated in the late rebellion."

1922   Russian Communist leader Lenin dictated the *Lenin Testament,*
        asking his comrades to remove Joseph Stalin as party general
        secretary, but he was too ill to carry it out.

1926   Hirohito became Emperor of Japan.

1936   Chiang Kai-shek was released 12 days after being kidnapped by
        mutinous war lords in China.

1941   British troops at Hong Kong surrendered to the Japanese in
        World War II.

1943   The British Navy sank the German battleship *Scharnhorst* off the
        coast of Norway in World War II.

1946   W.C. Fields, the great American motion-picture actor and
        comedian, died at age 67.

1977   Charlie Chaplin, the famous American comedian, died at age 88.

DECEMBER 26 -- BIRTHDAYS

1194   **Frederick II** -- Holy Roman Emperor, 1215-1250, known as
        "The Amazement of the World," and one of the most brilliant
        rulers of the Middle Ages

1792   **Charles Babbage** -- English mathematician who developed the
        idea of a digital computer in the 1830s, and whose principles are
        used in modern computers

1823   **John Elliott Cairnes** -- English economist

1837   **George Dewey** -- American admiral who won fame as the "hero
        of Manila" in the Spanish-American War

1838   Clemens Alexander Winkler -- German chemist who discovered the element germanium in 1886

1891   Henry Miller -- American novelist noted for works such as *Tropic of Cancer* (1934) and *Tropic of Capricorn* (1939)

1893   Mao Tse-tung -- Leader of the Chinese Communist revolution and first ruler of the People's Republic of China

1906   Elisha Cook -- American stage and motion-picture actor

1914   Richard Widmark -- American stage, screen, and television actor with a career of over 40 years

1917   Rose Mary Woods -- Personal secretary to President Nixon

1921   Steve Allen -- American comedian, writer, actor, and first star of NBC's *Tonight Show*

1926   Doris Lilly -- American writer

1927   Stu Miller -- Professional baseball pitcher who was once blown off the mound by the wind in an All Star game in San Francisco's Candlestick Park

1927   Alan King -- American comedian and actor

1940   Phil Spector -- American songwriter and record producer

1948   Carlton Fisk -- Professional baseball player and superstar

1948   Chris Chambliss -- Professional baseball player

1948   Dave Rader -- Professional baseball player

1954   Ozzie Smith -- Professional baseball player and superstar

1954   Jerry Eckwood -- Professional football player

DECEMBER 26 -- EVENTS

795 AD   Leo III was elected Roman Catholic pope.

1559   Pius IV was elected Roman Catholic pope.

1620   After spending five days in Cape Cod Bay, the *Mayflower* anchored at Plymouth harbor and the Pilgrims disembarked to found the Plymouth colony.

1776   After crossing the Delaware River, Washington and his men surprised the 1,000 Hessians at Trenton, New Jersey, taking all of them prisoner.

1799   Light-Horse Harry Lee eulogized George Washington as being "first in war, first in peace, and first in the hearts of his countrymen."

1825   The Decembrist Revolt in St. Petersburg, Russia's first modern
        revolution, was put down by government cannons.

1845   Marthasville, Georgia, changed its name to Atlanta.

1865   James Nason of Franklin, Massachusetts, was awarded a patent
        for his invention of the coffee percolator.

1908   Jack Johnson became the first black heavyweight boxing champion,
        defeating Tommy Burns in the 14th round in Sydney, Australia.

1944   The U.S. Third Army of General George S. Patton relieved the
        101st Airborne Division, which had been surrounded by the
        Germans at Bastogne, Belgium, in the Battle of the Bulge.

1972   Harry S Truman died in Independence, Missouri, at age 88.

DECEMBER 27 -- BIRTHDAYS

1571   **Johannes Kepler** — German astronomer who discovered three
        fundamental laws of planetary motion, one of which is that the
        earth and the other planets travel in orbits around the sun

1773   **Sir George Cayley** -- English scientist considered to be the father
        of modern aeronautics

1793   **Alexander Laing** — Scottish explorer who explored the Niger
        Basin in 1822

1806   **Ramon Cabrera** -- Spanish general who supported the Carlist,
        or Roman Catholic Church party position favoring Don Carlos
        to inherit the Spanish throne

1822   **Louis Pasteur** -- One of the world's greatest scientists and
        originator of the process of pasteurization

1879   **Sydney Greenstreet** -- English stage and motion-picture actor,
        noted for his urbane brand of villainy which made him one of the
        classic film heavies of all time

1883   **Cyrus** Eaton -- American industrialist known as the "last of
        the tycoons"

1895   **Robert H. Ellsworth** -- American composer noted for songs such
        as "Carmelita" and "Somebody Else Is Taking My Place"

1897   **Ivan Stepanovich Konev** -- Russian World War II field marshal
        whose troops were the first Russians to meet American forces in
        Germany, on the Elbe River

1901   **Marlene Dietrich** -- German-born stage and motion-picture
        actress and one of the screen's true immortals

1906　　**Oscar Levant** -- American pianist, composer, actor, and self-declared genius, who made over 100 recordings and wrote 3 autobiographical books

1910　　**Charles Olson** -- American avant-garde poet

1911　　**Anna Russell** -- English-born composer, author, singer, and comedienne, noted for works such as "Anna Russell Sings?"

1915　　**William H. Masters** -- American physician noted for human sexuality studies

1924　　**James A. McClure** -- U.S. senator

1927　　**Anne Armstrong** -- American ambassador to England under President Nixon

1933　　**Dave Marr** -- Professional golfer

1935　　**Bernard Lanvin** -- French fashion designer

1943　　**Roy White** -- Professional baseball player

1944　　**Tracy Nelson** -- American country singer

1952　　**Craig Reynolds** -- Professional baseball player

DECEMBER 27 -- EVENTS

537 AD　The third Cathedral of Santa Sophia at Constantinople was dedicated. The first two were destroyed, but this one is still in use, a masterpiece of Byzantine architecture.

1831　　Charles Darwin set out on the HMS *Beagle* on his exploratory trip to the Galapagos, where he formulated his theory of evolution.

1900　　Carry Nation, the famous temperance advocate, conducted her first big saloon raid, in Wichita, Kansas.

1903　　"Sweet Adeline," by Henry Armstrong and Richard Gerard, was sung for the first time, in New York City.

1904　　*Peter Pan,* the famous play of J.M. Barrie, was first performed, at the Duke of York's Theatre in London.

1927　　Jerome Kern's *Showboat* was performed for the first time, at the Zeigfield Theater in New York.

1932　　New York's Radio City Music Hall was opened to the public.

1937　　Maurice Ravel, the great French composer, died in Paris at age 62, following a brain operation.

1948　　Joseph Cardinal Mindszenty, Primate of Hungary, was arrested for espionage by the Communists.

1968 *Apollo 8* splashed down in the Pacific Ocean after orbiting the moon on Christmas Day.

1979 Russian troops invaded Afghanistan, executed its president, Hafizullah Amin, and replaced him by former Deputy Premier Babrak Karmal.

1981 Hoagy Carmichael, the noted American songwriter, died in Rancho Mirage, California, at age 82.

DECEMBER 28 -- BIRTHDAYS

1856 **Woodrow Wilson** -- 28th U.S. president

1860 **Harry Bache Smith** -- American lyricist noted for songs such as "The Sheik of Araby," "Yours Is My Heart Alone," and "Gypsy Love Song"

1865 **Felix Vallotton** -- Swiss painter

1894 **Alfred Sherwood Romer** – American evolutionist and paleontologist

1896 **Roger Sessions** – One of America's foremost composers, noted for works such as *The Trial of Lucullus* (1947)

1899 **Abner Silver** – American composer and author, noted for songs such as "How Green Was My Valley," "My Home Town Is a One Horse Town," and "On the Beach at Bali-Bali"

1900 **Ted Lyons** -- Hall of Fame baseball player

1905 **Cliff Arquette** – American entertainer known as "Charlie Weaver"

1905 **Earl "Fatha" Hines** -- American jazz musician

1906 **Tommy Bridges** -- Professional baseball player and superstar of the 1930s and 1940s

1908 **Lew Ayres** -- American motion-picture actor and leading man of the 1930s, with a 50-year career

1911 **Sam Levenson** -- American humorist and author

1914 **Lee Bowman** -- American stage, screen, and television actor

1920 **Steve Van Buren** -- Professional football superstar

1925 **Hildegarde Neff** – German stage and motion-picture actress, acclaimed by some as "the thinking man's Marlene Dietrich"

1927 **Simon Raven** -- English novelist, playwright, and journalist

1934 **Maggie Smith** -- English stage and screen actress and supremely gifted comedienne

1946	**Hubert Green** -- Professional golfer
1946	**William "Bill" Lee** -- Professional baseball player
1946	**Edgar Winter** -- American rock musician
1947	**Aurelio Rodriguez** -- Professional baseball player
1949	**John Milner** -- Professional baseball player
1952	**Ray Knight** -- Professional baseball player

DECEMBER 28 -- EVENTS

418 AD	Boniface I became Roman Catholic pope.
1688	The "Glorious Revolution" ended with the arrival in London of William and Mary to assume the throne of England.
1732	*Poor Richard's Almanack* was first advertised for sale by its author, Benjamin Franklin.
1832	Vice President John C. Calhoun resigned from his office, the first vice president to do so.
1846	Iowa was admitted to the Union as the 29th state.
1869	Chewing gum was patented by William F. Semple, a dentist from Mount Vernon, Ohio.
1895	The Lumiere brothers, Auguste and Louis, demonstrated their *cinematographe* in the Grand Cafe in Paris in the first commercial presentation of a movie.
1897	Edmond Rostand's play, *Cyrano de Bergerac,* opened in Paris.
1945	Theodore Dreiser, the great American novelist, died at age 74.
1958	Johnny Unitas led the Baltimore Colts to a 23-17 win over the New York Giants in the first sudden death in professional football history, to win the NFL championship.

DECEMBER 29 -- BIRTHDAYS

1695	**Jean Baptiste Pater** -- French painter noted for works such as *The Fair at Bezons* (1733)
1721	**Madame de Pompadour** -- Influential mistress of King Louis XIV of France
1729	**Benjamin Burt** -- American silversmith
1766	**Charles Macintosh** -- British chemist and inventor of waterproof fabrics, for whom the mackintosh jacket was named

1800   **Charles Goodyear** -- American inventor who discovered the process of vulcanizing rubber

1808   **Andrew Johnson** -- 17th U.S. president

1809   **William Ewart Gladstone** -- One of the most famous British political leaders of the 19th century, during which he served as prime minister four times

1816   **Carl Friedrich Wilhelm Ludwig** -- German physiologist

1859   **Venustiano Carranza** -- First president of the new Mexican Republic in 1915

1874   **Mark Charles Honeywell** -- American inventor, manufacturer, and founder of Honeywell Heating, one of the forerunners of the present Honeywell company

1876   **Pablo Casals** -- Spanish cellist and one of the outstanding string players of the 20th century

1877   **Bert Leighton** -- American composer, author, and singer, noted for songs such as "Frankie and Johnny" and "Ain't Dat a Shame"

1879   **Billy Mitchell** -- American army general and pioneer advocate of a separate U.S. Air Force, who was first court-martialed and later pardoned for his outspoken views

1881   **Jess Willard** -- World heavyweight boxing champion, 1915-1919

1898   **Jules Bledsoe** -- American actor, composer, and singer

1907   **Robert C. Weaver** -- First black U.S. cabinet member, under President Kennedy

1915   **Robert Ruark** -- American novelist

1917   **Tom Bradley** -- First black mayor of Los Angeles

1920   **Viveca Lindfors** -- Swedish stage and motion-picture actress with a 40-year career

1937   **Mary Tyler Moore** -- American motion-picture and television actress

1938   **Jon Voight** -- American stage, screen, and television actor and Academy Award winner for *Coming Home* (1978)

1947   **Dick Dell** -- American tennis player

1947   **Ted Danson** -- American motion-picture and television actor, noted for his role in the long-running TV show, *Cheers*

1950   **Joe Gilliam** -- Professional football player

DECEMBER 29 -- EVENTS

1170   Thomas a Becket, Archbishop of Canterbury, was murdered while at vespers in Canterbury Cathedral by four knights of King Henry II.

1775   The famous English actress Sarah Siddons made her debut in David Garrick's Drury Lane Theatre in London.

1825   Jacques Louis David, the great French painter, died in Brussels at age 77.

1845   Texas was annexed to the United States as the 29th state.

1848   The first gas lights were installed in the White House.

1851   The first Young Men's Christian Association (YMCA) in the United States opened its doors in Boston.

1890   The Wounded Knee massacre took place in South Dakota, as more than 200 Sioux men, women, and children were killed by U.S. troops.

1934   Japan renounced the Washington Naval Treaty of 1922 and the London Naval Treaty of 1930.

1940   President Franklin D. Roosevelt, in a "Fireside Chat," said that in aiding Britain the United States must "be the great arsenal of democracy."

DECEMBER 30 -- BIRTHDAYS

41 AD   **Titus** -- Roman emperor, A.D. 79-81, during whose reign the Colosseum was completed

1514   **Andreas Vesalius** -- Italian anatomist and the first person to describe the human body completely

1847   **John Peter Altgeld** -- Illinois reformist governor, 1893-1897

1851   **Asa Griggs Candler** -- American industrialist who bought the Coca-Cola company in 1891 for $2,300 and made it into the greatest soft drink company in the world

1865   **Rudyard Kipling** – English novelist and poet, noted for works such as the poem, "Recessional" (1897), and the novel, *Kim* (1905)

1867   **Simon Guggenheim** -- American philanthropist who established the John Simon Guggenheim Memorial Foundation in 1925

1872   **William A. Larned** -- American tennis player and seven times U.S. Singles Champion

1873   Alfred E. "Al" Smith -- Four times governor of New York and U.S. presidential candidate in 1928

1884   Hideki Tojo -- Japanese World War II premier who was later executed for war crimes

1895   Lin Yutang -- Chinese scholar and writer

1904   Dmitri Kabalevsky -- Russian composer

1906   Sir Carol Reed -- English motion-picture director, noted for films such as *The Third Man* (1949) and *Oliver!* (1968)

1910   Dennis Morgan -- American motion-picture actor in over 50 films

1911   Jeanette Nolan -- Noted American character actress of stage, screen, radio, and television, and wife of actor John McIntire

1914   Bert Parks -- American actor and television host

1914   Louis Oliveira -- Brazilian-born composer and author, noted for lyrics such as "Tico Tico"

1916   Marie Wilson -- American motion-picture and television actress

1919   Jo Van Fleet -- American stage and motion-picture actress

1928   Bo Diddley -- American blues guitarist

1928   Jack Lord -- American motion-picture and television actor and star of the long-running series *Hawaii 5-O*

1934   Russ Tamblyn -- American actor and dancer

1935   Sandy Koufax -- Hall of Fame baseball player and first pitcher to pitch four no-hit games

1937   Paul Stookey -- American singer and guitarist with the Peter, Paul, and Mary musical group

1942   Michael Nesmith -- American singer with the Monkees musical group

1947   Steve Mix -- Professional basketball player

1949   John Smith -- Professional football player

1959   Tracey Ullman -- English-born actress, singer, and comedienne

1961   Ben Johnson -- Canadian runner labeled "the fastest man on earth," who was disqualified in the 1988 Olympics 100 meter dash for using steroids

DECEMBER 30 -- EVENTS

1703   A Japanese earthquake and fire destroyed Edo (Tokyo) and killed 200,000 people.

1852   Rutherford B. Hayes married Lucy Ware Webb, later known as "Lemonade Lucy" because she served lemonade in the White House rather than the hard liquor of the U.S. Grant era.

1853   The Gadsden Purchase treaty was signed with Mexico, permitting the U.S. to annex a strip of land south of the Gila River.

1896   Jose Rizal, the Filipino hero, was shot by a Spanish firing squad.

1911   Dr. Sun Yat-sen was elected the first president of the Republic of China.

1916   Grigori Rasputin, the Russian "Mad Monk," was shot to death by Prince Felix Yusupov, two weeks after poisoning him had failed to work.

1948   Cole Porter's musical comedy, *Kiss Me Kate,* based on Shakespeare's play, *The Taming of the Shrew,* opened on Broadway, and became Porter's longest-running musical.

1963   The John F. Kennedy half dollar was authorized by Congress.

DECEMBER 31 -- BIRTHDAYS

1320   **John Wycliffe** -- A leading English philosopher in religion and politics during the Middle Ages, whose followers with his help translated the Bible into English about 1382

1491   **Jacques Cartier** -- French explorer whose daring explorations were the basis for French claims to Canada

1738   **Charles Cornwallis** -- British general defeated by George Washington at Yorktown, Virginia, in the last battle of the Revolutionary War

1815   **George G. Meade** -- U.S. Civil War general who commanded the victorious Union Army at the Battle of Gettysburg in 1863

1842   **Giovanni Boldini** -- Italian painter

1857   **King Kelly** -- Hall of Fame baseball player

1860   **John Taliaferro Thompson** -- U.S. brigadier general who invented the Thompson submachine gun, or Tommy gun

1869   **Henri Matisse** – French painter and one of the most influential artists of the 20th century

1870   **Tom Connolly** -- Noted major league umpire

1880   **George C. Marshall** -- American World War II chief of staff and secretary of state for whom the Marshall Plan was named

1885   **Edgar Leslie** -- American composer and author, noted for songs such as "For Me and My Gal," "Among My Souvenirs," "A Little Bit Independent," and "It Looks Like Rain in Cherry Blossom Lane"

1894   **Pola Negri** -- German-born motion-picture actress and one of the reigning queens of Hollywood in the 1920s and 1930s

1904   **Nathan Milstein** -- One of the greatest violinists of his time

1905   **Jule Styne** -- English-born composer, noted for songs such as "It's Magic," "Three Coins in the Fountain," "Diamonds Are a Girl's Best Friend," "I'll Walk Alone," and "Five Minutes More"

1919   **Tommy Byrne** -- Professional baseball player

1933   **Chryssa (Vardea)** -- Greek-born artist

1937   **Anthony Hopkins** -- British stage, screen, and television actor

1941   **Sarah Miles** -- English motion-picture actress

1942   **Andy Summers** -- English guitarist with the Police musical group

1943   **John Denver** -- American singer, songwriter, guitarist, and actor

1943   **Ben Kingsley** -- British motion-picture actor

1946   **Cliff Richey** -- American tennis player

1946   **Diane Von Furstenberg** -- Noted fashion designer

1948   **Donna Summer** -- American rock singer

1950   **Golden Richards** -- Professional football superstar

1961   **Rick Aguilera** -- Professional baseball player

DECEMBER 31 -- EVENTS

1375   Giovanni Boccaccio, the great Italian writer and humanist, died in Certaldo, Italy, at age 62.

1384   John Wycliffe, the noted English philosopher, died following a paralytic stroke at age 64.

1418   Rouen surrendered to King Henry V of England in the Hundred Years' War, after a two-month siege in which the English starved out the defending French.

1805   Napoleon abandoned the French Revolutionary Calendar.

1859   The comic weekly, *Vanity Fair,* began publication in New York.

1879   Thomas A. Edison gave his first public demonstration of his incandescent lamp to a New Year's Eve crowd in Menlo Park, New Jersey.

1923 The chimes of Big Ben, the great bell in the clock tower of the Houses of Parliament in London, were first broadcast on the radio.

1926 Harry Houdini, the great magician, died of a ruptured appendix at age 52.

1929 Big-band leader Guy Lombardo, with his Royal Canadians, began the tradition of broadcasting dance music on New Year's Eve in New York City.

1941 Admiral Chester W. Nimitz became commander of the U.S. Pacific Fleet in World War II.

1943 Frank Sinatra began a singing engagement at New York's Paramount Theater, which established him as the idol of the nation's "bobby soxers."

1946 President Harry S Truman officially proclaimed the end of World War II.

1972 Roberto Clemente, the great baseball player, was killed in an airplane crash at age 38, while aiding Nicaraguan earthquake survivors.

Index

Page numbers in italics refer to birthdays.

Aalto, Alvar, *82*
Aaron, Hank, *87*, 214
Aaron, Tommy, *123*
Aasen, Ivar, *436*
Abauzit, Firmin, *628*
Abbas I (the Great), shah of Persia, *65*
Abbas, Ferhat, *592*
Abbe, Cleveland, *675*
Abbe, Ernst, *57*
Abbott, Bud, *552*
Abbott, Edwin, *711*
Abbott, George, *357*
Abbott, Grace, *641*
Abbott, Jacob, *635*
Abbott, Lyman, *706*
Abbott, Sir John Joseph Caldwell, *161*
Abdul Jabbar, Kareem, 208, *227*
Abdul Rahman, Tuanku, *474*
Abel, Karl Friedrich, *715*
Abel, Niels Henrik, *436*
Abel, Sid, *123*
Abel, Sir Frederick Augustus, *400*
Abel, Walter, *321*
Abell, Kjeld, *475*
Abelson, Philip Hauge, *245*
Abercrombie, Lascelles, *27*
Abercromby, Sir Ralph, *559*
Aberdare, Henry Austin Bruce, *226*
Abernathy, Ralph, *160*
Abernethy, Tom, *264*
Abildgaard, Nicolai Abraham, *508*
Abney, Sir William de Wiveleslie, *412*
Abourezk, James, *127*
Abplanalp, Robert, *205*
Abraham, F. Murray, *593*
Abraham, Karl, *258*
Abrahams, Israel, *660*
Abrahams, Peter, *176*
Abramovitz, Max, *295*
Abzug, Bella, *413*
Academy Awards ceremony, 176
Academy of Motion Picture Arts and
    Sciences, 261
Acadians, 499
Acciaiuoli, Niccolo, *510*
Ace, Goodman, *40*

Achard, Franz, *247*
Acheson, Dean, *218*
Acheson, Edward Goodrich, *155*
Aconcio, Jacopo, *501*
Act of Habeas Corpus, 303
Act of Supremacy, 629
Actium, Battle of, 493
Actius, Flavius, *528*
Acton (John E.E.D. Acton), Lord, *30*
Acuff, Roy, *516*
Acushnet, 16
Adam Ant (Stuart Goddard), *612*
Adam, Adolphe Charles, *412*
Adam, Robert, *373*
Adamov, Arthur, *472*
Adams, Abigail Smith, 595, *651*
Adams, Alvan, *405*
Adams, Ansel, *118*
Adams, Brooke, *92*
Adams, Brooks, *355*
Adams, Charles Francis, *462*
Adams, Creighton, *517*
Adams, Don, *232*
Adams, Edie, 227
Adams, Edwin Plimpton, *57*
Adams, Henry, *109*
Adams, Herbert Baxter, 226
Adams, James Truslow, *582*
Adams, Joey, 22
Adams, John, 52, 85, 128, 376, 377, 448,
    587, 595, *602*
Adams, John Couch, *320*
Adams, John Quincy, 95, 121, 126, *389*,
    478, 502, 680
Adams, Julie, *580*
Adams, Larry, *335*
Adams, Louisa Catherine Johnson, *100*,
    478
Adams, Maud, *101*
Adams, Maude, *628*
Adams, Nick, *388*
Adams, Richard, *271*
Adams, Samuel, *540*
Adams, Sarah Flower, *122*
Adams, Walter Sydney, *711*
Adamson, Joy, *51*

736

Mormon Church, outlawing of polyg-
amy, *559*
Moro, Aldo, *532*
Morrall, Earl, *284*
Morrill, Justin S., *223*
Morris, Desmond, *59*
Morris, Eugene "Mercury," *20*
Morris, Garrett, *78*
Morris, Gouverneur, *73*
Morris, Greg, *538*
Morris, Jack, *282*
Morris, John, *582*
Morris, Lewis, *213*
Morris, Robert, *72*, 478
Morris, William, *184*
Morris, William, Jr., *589*
Morris, Willie, *666*
Morris, Wright, *22*
Morrison, Jim, *686*
Morrison, Robert, *19*
Morrison, Toni, *114*
Morrison, Van, *488*
Morrow, Anne (*see* Lindbergh, Anne
Morrow)
Morrow, Buddy, *92*
Morrow, Dwight Whitney, *32*
Morrow, Vic, *105*
Morse, Robert, *286*
Morse, Samuel F.B., *245*, 298
Morse, Theodora "Dolly," *389*
Morse, Theodore, *221*
Morse, Wayne, *586*
Morton, Craig, *87*
Morton, Jelly Roll, *526*
Morton, Sarah Wentworth
("Philenia"), 56
Morton, William Thomas Green, *445*,
547, 576, 579
Mosby, John Singleton, *681*
Mosconi, Willie, *349*
Moseby, Lloyd, *616*
Moseley, Mark, *162*
Moses, Grandma, *501*
Moses, Haven, *418*
Moses, Wally, *562*
Mosley, Sir Oswald, *640*
Mosley, Zack, 551, *695*
Moss, Geoffrey, *366*
Moss, Les, *278*
Moss, Stirling, *521*
Mossadegh, Mohammed, 466, 715
Mossman, Ted, *209*
Mostel, Zero, *136*
Mota, Manny, *115*

Mother's Day, 268, 270
Motley, John Lothrop, *224*
Motley, Willard Francis, *395*
Mott, Charles Stewart, *315*
Mott, Lucretia, *15*
Mottram, Christopher, *242*
Mottram, Linda, *284*
Moulton, Alycia, *115*
Mount Holyoke Seminary, 473, 622
Mount Saint Helens volcano, 287
Mount Vesuvius, eruption of, 474
Mountbatten, Lord Louis, *357*
Mountbatten, Prince Philip, *329*, 648
Mowbray, Alan, *462*
Moyer, Jamie, *644*
Moyers, Bill, *320*
Moyet, Allison "Alf," *344*
Moynihan, Daniel Patrick, *169*
Mozart, Leopold, *634*
Mozart, Wolfgang Amadeus, *65*, 255,
499, 547, 680
Mr. A. Mutt, 638
Mubarak, Hosni, *260*
Mudd, Roger, *95*
Mugabe, Robert, *120*
Muggeridge, Malcolm, *185*
Muhammad, Elijah, *559*
Muhlenberg, Frederick A. C., 200
Muir, Edwin, *254*
Muir, John, *235*
Muldoon, Robert David, *536*
Mulligan, Gerry, *209*
Mullins, Jeff, *174*
Mulroney, Brian, *178*
Mumford, Lewis, *584*
Mumphrey, Jerry, *506*
Munch, Charles, *538*
Munch, Edvard, *695*
Muncie, Chuck, *171*
Mungo, Van Lingle, *325*
Muni, Paul, *530*
Munich conference, 545, 547
Munoz-Marin, Luis, *114*
Munro, Hector Hugh, *707*
Munsel, Patrice, *278*
Munson, Thurman, *324*
Munson, William, *449*
Mura, Francesco de, *235*
Murat, Joachim, *186*
Murcer, Bobby, *290*
Murdoch, Iris, *397*
Murdock, Rupert, *160*
Murillo, Bartolome Esteban, *10*
Murkowski, Frank, *192*